MW00441723

Exploring the New Testament

JOHN CARMODY
University of Tulsa

DENISE LARDNER CARMODY
University of Tulsa

GREGORY A. ROBBINS
Wichita State University

PRENTICE-HALL
Englewood Cliffs, New Jersey 07632

Library of Congress Cataloging-in-Publication Data

CARMODY, JOHN.
   Exploring the New Testament.

   Bibliography: p. 434
   Includes index.
   1. Bible. N.T.—Textbooks.   I. Carmody, Denise
Lardner.   II. Robbins, Gregory A.
III. Title.
BS2535.2.C37 1986   225   85-19277
ISBN   0-13-297276-X

Editorial/production supervision and
   interior design: Patricia V. Amoroso
Cover design: Wanda Lubelska Design
Manufacturing buyer: Harry P. Baisley

© 1986 by Prentice-Hall
A Division of Simon & Schuster, Inc.
Englewood Cliffs, New Jersey 07632

*All rights reserved. No part of this book may be
reproduced, in any form or by any means,
without permission in writing from the publisher.*

Printed in the United States of America

10   9   8   7   6   5   4   3   2   1

The maps on pages 108, 119, and 232 were adapted from
The Westminster Historical Atlas to the Bible (revised
edition), edited by George Ernest Wright and Floyd
Vivian Filson. Copyright 1956, by W.L. Jenkins. Adapted
and used by permission of The Westminster Press.

ISBN 0-13-297276-X   01

PRENTICE-HALL INTERNATIONAL (UK) LIMITED, *London*
PRENTICE-HALL OF AUSTRALIA PTY. LIMITED, *Sydney*
PRENTICE-HALL OF CANADA INC., *Toronto*
PRENTICE-HALL HISPANOAMERICANA, S.A., *Mexico City*
PRENTICE-HALL OF INDIA PRIVATE LIMITED, *New Delhi*
PRENTICE-HALL OF JAPAN, INC., *Tokyo*
PRENTICE-HALL OF SOUTHEAST ASIA PTE. LTD., *Singapore*
EDITORA PRENTICE-HALL DO BRASIL, LTDA., *Rio de Janeiro*
WHITEHALL BOOKS LIMITED, *Wellington, New Zealand*

Contents

Preface   iv
1   Introduction   1
2   Historical Background   18
3   The Letters of Paul to Early Christians   28
4   The Letters of Paul's Followers   71
5   The Gospel for Mark's Church   105
6   The Gospel for Matthew's Church   143
7   The Gospel for Luke's Church   187
8   Acts: A History of Early Christianity   230
9   The Gospel for John's Church   265
10 The Book of Revelation: New Testament Apocalypse   310
11 Later "Letters" to the Church   336
12 Jesus   374
13 Conclusion   397
    Glossary   425
    Annotated Bibliography   433
    Demographic Chart   440
    Index   441

Preface

This book has rather modest aims. Assuming no special background, it seeks to lay out for college undergraduates (or perhaps good high school seniors) the main characteristics and ideas of the books of the New Testament. In part, it takes its origin from the fact that the majority of New Testament textbooks on the market are more sophisticated than the average freshman or sophomore can handle. These books are excellent in themselves, but their concentration on somewhat technical matters of history and textual analysis often loses the average introductory class.

Second, we have wanted to write a book that above all assists students in reading the New Testament literature itself. To this end we have worked out a recurring format, so that we approach each of the books in the same fashion, and we have spent most of our energy on explaining the ideas of the texts themselves. The recurring format, so far as we know, is unique. For each book we ask about the literary content, the likely purpose behind the writing, the background that the author presupposes in the reader, and the lasting significance of the work. This last question, which we also suspect is unique to our text, provides an opportunity to consider the New Testament in the horizon of the "great books" that have formed world culture.

In terms of the scholarly positions that we take, the book is rather centrist. Very radical historical critics will probably find us too traditional or conservative, following orthodox Christian interpretations. Very literalist or fundamentalist readers probably will find us too skeptical. But the 80 to 85 percent of New Testament readers who want to combine both an openness to the best current scholarship and some reverence for the special status of the Bible as sacred Scripture should find the book palatable.

In terms of how our collaboration has worked out, readers perhaps should know that John Carmody has been the principal writer, Denise Lardner Carmody has been a pedagogical control and kept an eye out for feminist issues, and Gregory A. Robbins has been the main scholarly control. Finally, we should like to thank Karla Kraft for typing the manuscript.

Introduction

SUNDAY MORNING

The man had a dark beard and wore a long black robe. Standing at a lectern to the side of the chancel choir, he greeted the congregation. After the children's choir had sung a peppy song based on an Israeli folk tune, the man opened a fat book and read a story. It told how Jesus called Simon and Andrew to become fishers of men (Mark 1:16–18). This was the day for **baptisms*** and **confirmations**, so the congregation was sensitive to the theme of building up its ranks. There was more singing, silent prayer, a long sermon, a collection of money gifts, two baptisms and five confirmations, time for the people to greet one another, a final blessing, and a rousing recessional. It was Sunday morning, when New Testament verses dominate the airwaves.

By most reckonings, in 1985 there were at least 50 million **evangelical** Christians in the United States. For all of them the New Testament was a privileged book, a privileged source of wisdom. Other Christians, not liking the connotation of **fundamentalism** that "evangelical" sometimes carries, did not designate themselves evangelicals. Nonetheless, many of them went to Sunday services or **masses** or **divine liturgies** in which the New Testament played a significant part. In fact, the logic of calling themselves "Christian" pressured more than half the 1985 population of the United States to make the New Testament a privileged book. Like many of their forebears in Western culture, these American Christians used the gospel stories about Jesus, the letters of the apostle Paul, and the other parts of the New Testament as their models of what God, the **Creator** of humankind, thought about the divine handiwork, about the natural world and all the different kinds of cultures.

*Terms in boldface are explained in the Glossary.

Standing apart from this Sunday morning American culture, disaffected Christians, unbelievers, and religious people of other traditions still found the New Testament making an impact on their lives. For example, disaffected Christians often retained warm feelings toward Jesus, wishing that the Christian churches were more like their simple Master. Unbelievers often considered the New Testament a major part of Western culture's problems. Sometimes they had studied the New Testament closely, often they had not, but unbelievers, both **atheists** and **agnostics**, regularly considered the New Testament or its God a source of emotional disturbance, or psychological immaturity, or sexism, or lethargy in the face of much-needed social changes. At the least, the New Testament was part of an old regime that many unbelievers were fleeing or struggling to overthrow.

In parallel ways, Jews, Muslims, and adherents of Asian religions found the New Testament making an impact on their lives. To Jews it was the book of a dissident Jewish **sect** that history had made dominant in the West, often to Jews' regret and suffering.[1] To Muslims the New Testament spoke of a **prophet** (Jesus) highly regarded by their own privileged book, the Qur'an. Although Jesus was a messenger superseded by Muhammad, he nonetheless deserved great esteem.[2] To adherents of Asian and other religions the New Testament seemed to have a centrality in Christians' lives unlike that which their own traditions accorded to any text. (The centrality of the Lotus Sutra to some Buddhists shows that there are important exceptions.[3] For if they asked what Christians believed, adherents of Asian religions usually found themselves directed to the New Testament. "Here," Christians seemed to say, "is the best place to begin to learn what we are all about."

So, in contrast to the work week, Sunday morning spotlighted a peculiar aspect of late twentieth-century American culture. There, for two hours or so, one found large numbers of Americans searching for their roots, their subculture and point of view, by use of the New (and Old) Testament. The Christian Bible gave the stories, the interpretive tales, through which millions of people were trying to discern the meaning of their joys and sorrows. Although most of American government ignored the New Testament on principle, most of American business ignored it by habit, and most American intellectuals considered it irrelevant, the New Testament continued to have a great effect on the American populace at large.

The first thesis we lay before you, then, is this: Whether embracing it or rejecting it, the American populace at large still feels the New Testament to be a very significant book. This is the first reason we offer you for taking the New Testament seriously. As a matter of fact, whether one likes it or not, the New Testament continues to play a significant role in American culture. No less than in the American past, it continues to lay out a very influential vision of what the world is like, what human beings may become, how good and evil are doing battle. If you want to understand late twentieth-century American culture, you must take a serious look at the New Testament.

JESUS

The dominant personality in the New Testament is Jesus of Nazareth. Although Jesus did not write the New Testament, he is never far from any page. Through the centuries, of course, people have composed quite different interpretations of Jesus. What the New Testament pages provide has been subject to quite diverse understandings. Thus the early Christians of the third century who went out to the desert for a life of strict disciplne stressed Jesus' trial in the desert by Satan (Mark 1:12–13) and his sufferings unto death.[4] For them Jesus was a warrior in combat with the forces of evil, a strange warrior who conquered death by dying.

When the Church councils of the fourth and fifth centuries had finished analyzing Jesus' significance, another interpretation came to the fore. Thenceforth Jesus was considered the Word of God Incarnate.[5] Coexisting eternally with God the Father, he had taken flesh through the Virgin Mary in order to save human beings from sin. Like the interpretation of Jesus as a warrior, this view also had a New Testament basis. Texts such as John 1:14 and Romans 5:8 seemed to sketch a great plan, conceived in heaven and executed on earth, by which God had intervened to save his people.

And so it went through the later Christian centuries. In both the Eastern and Western portions of **Christendom**, through medieval, Reformation, and modern times, people gathering for Sunday worship had different pictures of Jesus in their heads, but all of them drew upon the New Testament. Jesus existed yesterday, today, and tomorrow. He was past, present, and future. So the Book that spoke of Jesus referred as much to the present and the future as to the past. What God had done in Jesus broke any limits one might try to put on Jesus' significance. On Sunday mornings, and at other times of worship, Jesus and the New Testament impressed themselves upon Christians as limitless challenges and blessings. As Hebrews 3:15 told each generation of believers, "Today, when you hear his voice, do not harden your hearts as in the rebellion."

In this way, Jesus stayed contemporary with those who made him their religious guide. Over the centuries, most Christians emphasized Jesus' present relevance, not the details of his past history. So slowly such important factors as Jesus' Jewishness and the Greek milieu in which many of his early followers lived faded from popular awareness. In order to be a man for all seasons, Jesus had to stand somewhat apart from his own season, his original time and place. This parallels what happened to the Buddha, Moses, Confucius, and many other great religious figures. Most of their followers, too, have been less interested in original historical circumstances than in perennial example and wisdom. Relatedly, most of their followers have used the traditional writings about such leaders (the Buddhist sutras, the Hebrew Bible, the Confucian classics) as Christians have used the New Testament: in a devotional rather than a **critical** way. The traditional, sacred writings have been precious because they gave people access to a personality of earth-shaking significance. One read the books of Moses because they contained the words of God's greatest prophet. One

Hills of Judea seen from outside Jerusalem.   *(Photo by J.T. Carmody)*

read the Confucian classics because they were words of *the* Masterly Sage, and one read the New Testament because Jesus had the words of eternal life (John 6:68).

This remains more true than untrue for the majority of American Christians who consecrate Sunday morning today. For them, as for most of their ancestors in Christian faith, Jesus and the New Testament are objects of religious rather than scholarly interest. It is their power to change a personal life that makes Jesus and the New Testament absorbing. Scholars may say interesting things about the composition of the **Gospels** or the original circumstances of the Pauline letters. Scholars' labors can be very illuminating. But the bottom line remains the personal impact, the spiritual power, that believers find the Gospels and Epistles to carry. Otherwise, Jesus would have become just another curiosity, something of a dead letter. People do not consecrate Sunday mornings to dead letters. They consecrate Sunday mornings to images, writings, and ceremonies, to a person they feel tells them who they are and reminds them what they want to be.

Obviously, Jesus has another meaning for those who are not fervent Christians, but not necessarily a completely different meaning. Analogous to the way fervent Christians find Jesus and the New Testament full of life, anyone interested in striking ideas about the world and human nature can find Jesus an intriguing figure. In part, such intrigue attaches to any "classical" figure.[6] Plato is never out of date because Plato penetrated the human wellsprings. Shakespeare is always worth watching because Shakespeare penetrated the human wellsprings. So too with Jesus. When the New Testament has Jesus talk about God or faith or love, his philosophy and poetry go so deep, break forth so freshly, that Jesus is always relevant. If people still die, worry, hurt one another, or stand dazzled by the lilies of the field, Jesus is a man for their season. By studying the book that Jesus dominates, we can still taste Jesus' seasoning. With or without Sunday morning allegiance, we can still meet a figure who gave many centuries their savor.

SCRIPTURE

When a book becomes a privileged text by which people interpret the deepest meaning of their time we can call it a **Scripture**.[7] Thenceforth it is a writing that speaks for God or ultimate wisdom. The New Testament has had this status for Christians, and that gives today's students of the New Testament a number of special problems. When a text has become a Scripture, a writing that is sacred, it is hard to deal with that text dispassionately, as though it were not special. Believers coming to a Scripture bring a wealth of unusual emotions, some of them going back to early childhood. Unbelievers may come with similar baggage, curiosities or bad impressions implanted before the age of full reason. So a text that has been scriptural for a large portion of one's culture is seldom an indifferent writing. To study it unemotionally, letting the chips fall where they may, calls for a special discipline.

Byzantine Book Cover. Syrian, sixth–seventh century A.D. The decoration would be especially suitable for a Bible or book used at the divine liturgy. *(Nelson Gallery–Atkins Museum, Kansas City, Mo. [Nelson Fund])*

In the past century, biblical scholars have adopted tools of historical and literary analysis developed by scholars in other fields. The result has been a great increase in our knowledge of both Jesus' culture and the composition of the New Testament. Bracketing the question of whether or how the New Testament was inspired by God, recent biblical scholars have focused on the human features that the textual evidence discloses. For example, they have compared the **synoptic** Gospels (Matthew, Mark, and Luke, so called because one can take in their materials, which are quite similar, in a single glance across three columns) and have noted a peculiar combination of similarity and difference. By and large, the synoptic Gospels tell the same story of Jesus' preaching, healing, suffering, death, and resurrection. Yet, as they tell this common story, they place different emphases and so draw distinctive portraits of Jesus.

When biblical scholars ponder such distinctions, they draw upon whatever relevant knowledge other fields may offer. For example, linguistic studies of Hebrew, Aramaic, and Greek have helped sharpen scholars' sense of what the authors of the New Testament texts had in mind, where they came from, and what sorts of education they received. Historical studies of the New Testament period have provided further background, suggesting the impact that Roman law, Greek philosophy, or Jewish religious practices might have had. Finally, New Testament scholars recently have been drawing on sociological studies in an effort to penetrate the daily life, world-view, and psycho-social changes that came with entry into a given church.

Overall, today's biblical scholars try to operate like skillful surgeons or disciplined detectives. Patiently, clue by clue, they try to solve the puzzle of why a given Gospel has its particular structure, why the Jesus of **Matthew** is a little different from the Jesus of **Luke**. If we liken the New Testament to a body with several parts, we may liken the scholars who study it to specialist surgeons, expert in the tissues and nerves of the Johannine or Pauline parts. Layer by layer, they peel back the flesh and uncover the arteries. After years of practice, they know the anatomy of their texts very well. The result has been a great increase in our literary sophistication. Because intelligent people have given their lives to this patient research, we now know the New Testament to be a very diverse and complicated document, more like a miniature library than a single book.

However, what has this done to the scriptural status of the New Testament? After several generations of brilliant scholarly surgery, does it still make sense to accord the New Testament a privileged place? In some ways it does, and in some ways it doesn't. It does make sense to give the New Testament a privileged status if one finds the core message of the New Testament, its central statement, a thing of special depth and light. Scholarship never removes the need to situate ourselves in the world and find enough light and strength to live well. However, what light and strength we choose is a personal issue, a matter we each have to decide for ourselves. The most that a detached, unbiased scholar can say is that the New Testament has had a massive influence on Western culture and still says things worth pondering deeply. Minimally, we must place the New Testament with Plato's Laws, Aristotle's Metaphysics, the Muslim Qur'an, the Chinese Tao Te Ching, the Hindu Bhagavad-Gita, and the other great books that have formed humanity's soul.

On the other hand, it does not make sense to give the New Testament a privileged status if that means closing ourselves to the findings of modern biblical research. The recent linguistic, historical, and sociological studies of biblical scholars have shed great light on the New Testament writings. Not to make use of this light, not to follow the best findings of careful scholars wherever they lead, would be to violate our inmost conscience, our vocation to learn what is real and true. It is not always easy to follow our conscience, but it is always maturing to try. And with perseverance, by and by, we may glimpse both how to take the New Testament apart (with the tools of current scholarship) and how to deal with the New Testament as a wise whole (with the instincts of healthy religion, and a willingness to admit life's **mystery**).

CANONICITY[8]

A **canon** is a ruler or measuring rod. By the middle of the fourth century, Church leaders such as Athanasius, bishop of Alexandria, could say that certain Christian writings, such as Shepherd of Hermas, were not **canonical**. By this Athanasius meant that **Hermas** was not generally accepted as a presenting a normative, regulative expression of Christian faith. His writing might have many virtues, but it had not made the list of documents the Church as a whole had found completely trustworthy guides for Christian faith.

In his **Paschal Letter** of about 367 C.E. (Common Era), Athanasius listed the twenty-seven writings that compose our present New Testament. He was surer about some than others, but all finally won acceptance as Christian Scriptures. With the writings of the Hebrew Bible, some of which had been listed by the rabbis of Jamnia, a town on the Mediterranean west of Jerusalem, toward the end of the first century C.E., and all of which the rabbis eventually canonized around 300 C.E., the Christian writings composed a new Bible in two parts: the "Old" Testament of Jewish scriptures and the "New" Testament of writings generated by faith in Jesus Christ.

It is important to realize that this canonical status only came to the New Testament writings quite slowly and informally. For generations writings such as Shepherd of Hermas and the **Didache**, a short early manual on Christian morals and practice, exerted considerable influence. Only under the pressure of debates about Christian faith and practice did Church authorities reject some writings as less authoritative or even heretical. If we step back to gain a clarity that most of the early authorities never had, the criteria for canonicity included being thought to have had roots in a venerable Christian community, and being thought to conform to the **catholic** (universal) Church's understanding of correct faith. Under the sharp lens of today's historical scholarship these criteria prove loose indeed, but they indicate something of what early Church authorities were thinking when they formed their canonical expression of Jesus' teaching and the founding faith of Jesus' Church.

The practical significance of canonicity, for our purposes, is the way it sharpens what we said earlier about Scripture. The New Testament represents memories and wisdom that the early Church had sifted and found genuine. Because they had ties to Jesus, to Jesus' first disciples, to early communities revered for steadfast faith, and to the authentic, holy life of the most noteworthy early Christians, the books of the New Testament became one of the Church's main safeguards and reliances. As trusted expressions of the earliest sense of who Jesus was and what he had done, the New Testament books became a mirror in which later generations might see the state of their own faith and practice. Just as the Holy Spirit, the divine "advocate" that Jesus had left, was to rule Christians' hearts from within (John 14:26), so the New Testament could guide Christians' lives from without. Known intimately through prayerful reading, used extensively in worship, and revered in all the churches, the canonical writings soon became a major presence of God's power and grace.

Today's student of the New Testament has to try to gain a balanced perspective on this phenomenon. On the one hand, there is the question of the regulative nature of the New Testament. Without a doubt, the New Testament has been among the oldest and most important guides, expressions, and indexes of Christian faith. (Others have been the Christian liturgy and the Christian hierarchy or Church leadership.) On the other hand, Christian faith has included more than reading the New Testament. At worship Christians have used music, natural elements such as water and fire, and creeds and prayers not explicitly drawn from the New Testament. In their daily lives they have developed ethical guidelines and moral interpretations beyond those explicit in the New Testament. As the centuries have unfolded, Church leaders have met in councils to decide new theological questions that the New Testament writings did not have to treat. So, overall, historical changes have forced Christians to develop doctrines and practices that the New Testament at most had barely glimpsed. As a result, the basic issue has become the general orientation or world view and that faith in Jesus according to the Scriptures has produced.

One sees, then, that canonicity alone solves very few significant problems. Even after they had determined which writings were fully authoritative, Christians continued to have interpretational problems. This is all the more true today, when two thousand years separate us from Jesus and sophisticated scholarship reveals the New Testament to be a very complicated book. Because human beings change and "God" is always mysterious, even canonical writings turn out to be open ended. If they are to be books for all seasons, true classics, they must be susceptible of new interpretations. Consequently, the study of canonical Scriptures such as the New Testament can never be completed the way an experiment in physical science might be. There are no measurements, no critical experiments, by which one can establish the meaning of a religious text once and for all. At best there is a sensitive reading that lets rigorous studies clarify what a given text probably meant when it was first written.

Last, we should note that the canonical status of the New Testament has not allowed scholars to dispense with the arduous task of establishing a critical text. We have no autograph of the New Testament and the various manuscripts we possess differ significantly among themselves. Thus much work has gone into the comparison of manuscripts in order to evaluate which reading of passages that have variants is the most reliable. In some cases (e.g., Mark 16:9–20 and John 7:53–8:11), we still cannot be sure that we have what originally was part of a given Gospel. The critical studies necessary to obtain the text most likely to be authentic in historical terms therefore remind us that canonicity does not dispense with human authorship according to the ordinary psychological and literary patterns that obtain in other writings. For the New Testament to be Scripture does not mean that it wasn't composed by fully human processes. (These processes may, of course, have been inspired by God.)

The same sort of observation extends to the matter of biblical translations. All translations, even those from the best critical texts, are interpretations. Nuances and overtones vary from language to language, and translators vary in how they render original meanings into the contemporary idioms of different languages. We have chosen the Revised Standard Version because it is the translation most widely used and most widely approved across the ecumenical span of all the Christian churches. In general, it has won praise for its fidelity to the literal meaning of the original text. But other translations (for example, the Good News Bible) have considerable merit and sometimes are fresher or more intelligible. There is no perfect translation, and so there is no perfect English version of what the original New Testament authors were trying to say. We are always working with likelihoods, probabilities, and consensuses rather than certainties.

THE CHARACTER OF THE NEW TESTAMENT LITERATURE

Much of what we have said thus far boils down to a single thesis: The writings that were collected into the New Testament were expositions of Christian **faith**. The character of the Gospels, Epistles, and other New Testament writings is not that of detached or scholarly historical reports. Throughout, the New Testament is a collection of documents written by people who believed that Jesus was the most important human being who ever lived. Moreover, the authors of the New Testament writings composed their pieces for specific reasons. Either they were addressing particular churches' local problems, or they were gathering together the memories and traditions of particular communities so that these communities' understandings of Jesus and Christian life would be made explicit and not be lost.

If we take the traditional definition of theology, "faith seeking understanding," we can say that all the New Testament writings are theological. By making the principles of their religious lives express and articulate, the

New Testament authors raised their understanding of Jesus and Christian faith to a higher power. Under the pressure of trying to solve practical community problems, they reached back into the common store of memories about Jesus' words and deeds and reached forward into the realm of implication—of what the core tenets of faith were likely to imply for new missionary, **liturgical**, or ethical needs.[9] In some cases the writers were trying to provide converts with an understanding of Christian faith in terms of the converts' prior backgrounds. The Epistle to the Hebrews, for instance, works with themes of the Hebrew Bible, trying to show how Jesus fulfilled the religious expectations of his fellow Jews. The Epistles of Paul often address **Gentile** (non-Jewish) converts, trying to explain how Christian faith both is and is not like Judaism. In other cases the writers were expressing understandings of Jesus they thought would help people sorely pressed. **Revelation**, for example, reflects a desire to support the faith of believers who were undergoing political persecution.

Once again, these characteristics of the New Testament writings present today's student with special problems. On the one hand, as we have previously stressed in our discussions of Scripture and canonicity, the New Testament has been used by the Christian churches as a book for all seasons, a perennial classic. On the other hand, careful scholarly examination of the New Testament texts shows that they arose in response to quite particular needs or ambitions. Unless one takes such historical origins into account, one misreads the authors' original purposes. So, as we have already stressed, today's students of the New Testament must constantly perform a balancing act. Almost always they need an attitude of "both-and," rather than an attitude of "either-or." Both the nineteen-hundred-year practice of the Christian Church in using the New Testament as its constitutional or canonical Scripture and the original intent of the New Testament authors have to be taken into account. The first expressions of faith, from and for particular Christian communities, and the later interpretations all clamor to be heard.

We shall begin with the original intent of the New Testament authors. Regularly, however, we shall also look at classical or perennial aspects of the New Testament teachings and symbols in order to underscore their universal humanity, their more than original implications. Actually, in terms of what their full reality has been, the New Testament writings are both particular and universal. Prior to the rise of critical historical scholarship in the past century, the universal aspect was to the fore: Scripture as wisdom for all human beings. Today the particular aspect is to the fore: for example, how Matthew probably represents a compromise between right- and left-wing factions of the Church at Antioch.

In many Church circles today one must stress these particular aspects, because many Church circles remain resistant to critical scholarship. On the other hand, scholarly circles sometimes neglect the perennial or classical significance of the Gospels and Epistles. Having indicated what community **Mark** arose from and what problems it originally tried to solve, many scholars judge that their task is done. However, if Mark is not to be a dead letter, that is only part of the interpreter's job. The question of how true or profound Mark's teaching is, and what a person reading it today can make of it, remains on the agenda. Because many scholars do not tackle these questions does not mean they are not wholly valid.[10]

We aim for a middle road, stressing the original intents that are the major interest of today's New Testament scholars but not forgetting the perennial dimension. Throughout, we stress that the New Testament has been a document, an expression and solicitation, of faith. Scholars do not always handle faith well, since they frequently have not clarified the relation between textual judgments based on critical research and the general outlook or **horizon** that one brings to such research. (Since such a horizon is rooted in personal or **existential** decisions about good and evil, meaning and absurdity, a horizon is in good measure a matter of faith, one's overall response to life.) From time to time, we shall focus our concern for the perennial or classical character of the New Testament documents on this **methodological** question of the relation between one's research and one's general outlook or horizon.

FIRST GUIDELINES FOR STUDY

How, then, should beginning students approach the New Testament? Ideally, with a nice blend of openness and hardheadedness. The openness is warranted because the New Testament is part of humanity's classical literature, one of the writings that has formed humanity's soul. Today there are more Christians in the world than Muslims, Hindus, Buddhists, or programmatic unbelievers. For every Jew there are more than sixty Christians. If we should take the Qur'an seriously, and approach it with openness, because hundreds of millions of Muslims have tried to follow its teachings, so we should take the New Testament seriously and approach it with openness, because hundreds of millions of Christians have tried to follow its teachings. Indeed, not to approach the New Testament with the same openness that we would show the Qur'an or writings of Confucius would be simple bigotry. It would be saying, in the face of massive testimony to the contrary, that this book has nothing perennially worthwhile to say. There are people who take such a bigoted position—some Marxist-Leninists, for example—but the contradictions in which it involves them, the violations of conscience, take away their credibility.

Openness, however, is not the same as credulity. To let the New Testament present its message, to entertain its assumptions and follow its terms, is not the same as giving it a blank check. The New Testament does not contain the world's highest wisdom simply because some Christian preachers say it does. The large numbers we can enter in the column "Christian" do not assure that the New Testament is **inerrant**, or **infallible**, or something we must swallow whole. Actually, it distorts traditional Christian teaching to ask listeners to abandon their critical reason and give the New Testament a blank check. Certainly Jesus offered his hearers reasons for accepting his message, evidence that he was someone special. Certainly the great Christian "Fathers" and theologians exercised their minds mightily. So the virtue of docility or willingness to be taught does not mean abandoning our critical faculties. If the New Testament cannot illumine the dark questions of our human existence, it cannot be our canonical Scripture. In conscience, we have to deny it that status. We must try, then, in our study to combine both listening and questioning. We must try to hear the New Testament on its own terms, but also must press it to make sense on our terms and to speak meaningfully to our situation as late twentieth-century readers.

Under the first heading, hearing the New Testament on its own terms, we authors would stress trying to appreciate the distance between today's world and the world of the earliest Christians. In the world of the earliest Christians, there was no computer science, no molecular biology, no space shuttle. There was no ecological crisis, no United Nations, no threat of nuclear war. The human race was relatively small: The New Testament gives no consideration to North Americans or South Americans, shows no concern for Australians or Chinese. Most people were quite poor and most lives were quite short.

In such a world, "God" was an omnipresent agent. God made the sun to shine and the rain to fall on the just and unjust alike (Matthew 5:45). People knew little about the currents of the upper atmosphere, the influence of explosive sunspots. Their thinking about nature was more pictorial than scientific, more self-concerned than detached. The same was true of their thinking about society and the self. What we now call demographics, economics, and sociology were then merely slightly developed aspects of **common sense**. What we now call the unconscious and psychodynamics were only vague intuitions glimpsed by individuals who were especially inwardly oriented.

In the world of the New Testament authors, pictorial thinking increased the fear of Satan, a great agent of evil, and the fear of spiritual powers generally. It increased a suspicion that illness was the work of evil spiritual powers, and that "God" was a force that could cure illness. By filling the devout with Holy Spirit, God could make them whole and could "save" them from the evils at their left or their right. There were specifically Jewish forms of such pictorial thinking and specifically **Hellenistic** (late Greek) forms, which we shall study as the occasion arises. From the outset, however, students of the New Testament do well to realize the high demands that will be made on their imaginations. The only way to bridge the great distance from our late twentieth-century Western culture to the Palestinian or Greek culture of the end of the first century is to free our imaginations so that we entertain quite different ways of viewing the world and of conceiving the human situation.

These different ways are neither more nor less human than those our fellow twentieth-century Americans use. We have learned important things since Jesus' time, but our twentieth-century time is neither so peaceful nor so beautiful that it can legitimately spurn any classical wisdom. Indeed, it is hard to argue that the human condition has changed essentially since Jesus' time. For example, Albert Camus, the great twentieth-century French existentialist philosopher and novelist, wrote what may seem the bottom line in any time: People die and they are not happy. People died in Jesus' time, and people die today. People suffered and were unhappy in Jesus' time, and people suffer and are unhappy today. All human beings share a radical equality, whatever their time or place. After the Buddha as well as before, after Jesus as well as before, after Hiroshima as well as before, we all must grapple with a life that is greater than we are, a time we can never fully understand. So the world of the New Testament finally is quite like our own world of today. Ultimately, religiously, both worlds are looking for light and warmth, justice and peace.

THE FORMAT OF THIS BOOK

Very shortly you will plunge into the chapters in which we have tried to express our sense of how best to approach the New Testament literature. A word of orientation may ease your passage.

First, you will note that we begin the body of the text with the letters of the apostle Paul to various early Christian communities. We begin with these letters because they are the earliest of the New Testament writings. Our organizational principle, then, is chronological. By and large, we have placed the New Testament materials before you in the order in which it is likely that they were composed (or edited into their present form). The Pauline materials come first, then the Gospels and **Acts**, and third come Revelation and the miscellaneous Epistles. On the whole, this is the chronological pattern.

Prior to our exposition of the New Testament materials themselves, you will find a brief chapter that sketches the historical or cultural context in which the New Testament occurs. The dominant emphasis in most of our chapters is the New Testament text itself, so from the outset we want to make plain the overall Jewish, Greek, and Roman influences that the text assumes.

Following our exposition of the New Testament materials themselves, you will find two reflective or retrospective chapters. The first deals with Jesus, the dominant personality behind the New Testament; it attempts to indicate what a careful analysis of the New Testament suggests we can say about Christianity's originator and center. The second reflective chapter deals with the diversity and unity of the New Testament: how the different writings go their own ways and how they hang together. The aim of these two retrospective chapters is to help you synthesize the materials you have analyzed in the expository chapters.

The assumption behind our focusing first and mainly on the New Testament writings themselves (rather than on their historical background or theological interpretation) is that the best use of your study time is for you to read and reflect on the text itself. Front and center, then, will be the New Testament authors' own words. We begin with what Paul said to the **Thessalonians**, continue with the words of Mark and the other gospels, and end only when we have finished the last of the twenty-seven canonical writings.

Moreover, in our discussion of each New Testament writing we employ the same format, so as to offer you a consistent plan of attack. The assumption here is pedagogical: You learn best when you know what to expect and can settle into a steady rhythm. In addition, a consistent format can facilitate comparison of the New Testament writings. Both while you are moving through the materials of a given chapter, and when you go back over them in review, the consistent format should help you note how **Romans** is like and unlike **Ephesians**, how Matthew is like and unlike Luke.

The consistent format that we employ takes the shape of four questions. First we ask "What have we here?" In other words, what is the shape of the literary unit before us? Going right to the text, we scan its general character, provide a detailed outline and reading guide, and attend to key passages. The effort throughout this first exercise is to help you read the text intelligently. It is like a cultural excursion: You profit most when you see the general map first, then someone points out the peculiar twists and turns, and finally an informed commentary illumines the most famous sights.

Second we ask "Why was this written?" In other words, what was the occasion that gave rise to this piece of writing? To whom was it directed and what problems was it trying to solve? If you have read the text carefully, you should find these questions of literary intent quite interesting.

Third we ask "What background does this text presuppose?" In other words, what does today's reader need to know about the cultural milieu that the authors shared with the communities they were addressing? If we want to grasp the author's cast of mind and sense of reality, it is crucial to know their Jewish, Hellenistic, or other assumptions.

Fourth and last we ask "What lasting significance does this text have?" To answer we must involve ourselves with the "classical" or "perennial" dimensions of the New Testament. As well, we may have to compare the New Testament to such other religious classics as the Qur'an or the Bhagavad-Gita. Spatial limitations will keep our comparisons brief, but they and the other questions about lasting significance should assure that we do not neglect the New Testament's long use as a canonical Scripture.

Each chapter will conclude with a summary, which you should find a useful study aid. The questions at the end of the chapter are a second sort of summary, and the notes suggest further reading you may want to pursue.

WHAT YOU CAN GET FOR YOUR MONEY

To conclude this Introduction, let us sketch some of the benefits that we hope to help you derive from your study of the New Testament.

As we indicated at the outset, the New Testament is more than alive and influential in the United States today. On any given Sunday morning millions of people gather in churches and dozens of preachers fill the airwaves. Few sociologists would pretend to know exactly what all this Sunday morning activity means for American politics, or general culture.

Its rippling social effects are hard to measure, and its effects on people's inner souls usually lie beyond scientists' instruments. But when sizable portions of such disparate political phenomena as the New Right and the antinuclear movement both claim roots in biblical religion, it is hard to underestimate the significance of those Sunday morning gatherings. The New Right and the antinuclear movement both grabbed a fair share of the headlines in the early 1980s. Anyone who wanted to know what lay behind either the program of Reaganite militarists or the program of nuclear freeze advocates was well advised to look again at the New Testament.

We could offer analogous arguments concerning the foreign news. When the Polish labor union Solidarity stood up to its country's Communist regime, we heard hymns of a traditional Christian faith that had long hearkened to the New Testament. When Protestants and Catholics continued to make Northern Ireland a synonym for brotherly strife, we saw New Testament faith called into very deep question. When the white minority in South Africa continued to try to buttress its policy of racial segregation (apartheid) by appealing to Christian Scripture, many people the world over had to ask themselves whether the New Testament was more a blessing or a curse.

So, simply to understand the world in which we live, we do well to update our understanding of the New Testament. As these quite obvious examples suggest, the New Testament is a book subject to very different interpretations. Is the New Right more faithful in its **exegesis** of Jesus' sayings than the Christian portion of the antinuclear movement (including the American Catholic bishops)? Can either Protestant or Catholic Irishmen legitimately base their policy of an eye for an eye and a tooth for a tooth on the New Testament Jesus? Is apartheid in any way legitimated by Paul or John? These are not the sort of questions that news analysts usually handle. Indeed, no one can answer them adequately without considerable sophistication. If you are willing to grapple with them on the basis of a generous study of the New Testament, however, you can come away with a depth of "political" understanding few of your peers will be able to match.

Part of our sales pitch, then, is cultural: The New Testament is a key ingredient in many of the puzzles we must solve if we are to understand our contemporary world. Another part of our sales pitch is philosophical: Here is a book that millions have considered unequaled in wisdom, without peer in the things that matter most. Surely it would be a paltry education that took no hard look at such a book (or at the rest of the world's great wisdom literature). Surely not to know something about Plato, the Buddha, Confucius, Muhammad, the Hebrew prophets, Jesus, or humanity's other great seers would be to leave college half-baked.

We are quite aware that, by this criterion, many colleges are dumping on the market a lot of poor products. Liberal education (in which the world's wisdom literature figures prominently) is almost an endangered species. That does not mean, however, that either we as teachers or you as students have to accept such a bad state of affairs. Things are not yet so corrupt that any of us is forced to remain illiterate. The wisdom literature is still in our libraries. The tradition is not completely snuffed out. If any of us want to, we can still converse with the great minds of the past, still ponder the key questions of being human.

The New Testament ponders the key questions of being human and of finding "salvation" in the light of Jesus of Nazareth, a man whom it thinks was God's wisdom and power. In the light of Jesus, it describes where the world came from, where it is going, and what we should do until the climax comes. If we take these sayings at all seriously, they make us look hard at our money and banking, look long at our rush to arms. "You fool," Jesus said, "this night your soul is required of you" (Luke 12:20). In such a perspective, with time short and judgment near, what would you want to have done with your time? If you knew that God would judge you tomorrow, how would you want to have lived?

The problem with philosophy, the love of wisdom, is that it leads to such stark, uncomfortable questions. The unexamined life is easy enough: Just eat, drink, and make merry. But an easy, ordinary happening such as a car accident, a cancerous growth of cells, or the loss of a job can break the unexamined life. If we are at all realistic, only the examined life is worth living, the life in which "God," "salvation," "justice," "evil," and "love" cry out for constant study. When these propositions make sense, you're ready for the New Testament.

SUMMARY

Sunday morning in the contemporary United States shows that the New Testament remains a very influential book. As they have done for centuries, Christians continue to gather to ponder the sayings of Jesus and seek out the meaning of Jesus' life. In their pondering and seeking, they use the New Testament as "Scripture": writing that is sacred, privileged, canonical. The process by which the twenty-seven books of today's New Testament became the regulative expression of Christian faith was rather vague, but by the middle of the fourth century there was a rough consensus.

If one asks about the character of the New Testament writings, words such as "literature of faith" and "theological" come to mind. The New Testament books were not written to provide objective history but to express and elicit faith. The student of the New Testament therefore has to balance openness with hardheadedness, neither rejecting nor accepting such faith statements too quickly. Moreover, the world of the New Testament stands at some distance from our contemporary world, so it takes considerable imagination to travel the way back.

Our presentation of the New Testament materials will mainly follow the chronological order in which they were written. The format through which we hope to facilitate your travel back to the world of the New Testament is a recurring quartet of questions: What have we here? Why was this written? What background does this text presuppose? And what lasting significance does this text have? We hope this regular format will both ease your study and facilitate your comparisons. If it succeeds, you should emerge with not only a better sense of the New Testament literature but also a deeper understanding of contemporary culture and a sharpened view of your own life-options.

STUDY QUESTIONS

1. What does the function of Sunday morning in current American culture suggest about the present status of the New Testament?
2. In what sense is Jesus the dominant personality behind the New Testament?
3. What makes a set of writings into a "Scripture"?
4. Why does the process of canonization not mean an end to problems of textural interpretation?
5. What does the faith-character of the New Testament literature imply for New Testament studies?
6. Why does the student of the New Testament have to be hardheaded as well as open?
7. What is the function of our recurring question about the lasting significance of a given New Testament writing?
8. What do you personally hope to get for the money you are spending on this course?

NOTES

1. See Samuel Sandmel, *We Jews and Jesus* (New York: Oxford University Press, 1973).
2. See Geoffrey Parrinder, *Jesus in the Qur'an* (New York: Oxford University Press, 1977).
3. See Denise Lardner Carmody and John Tully Carmody, *Ways To the Center: An Introduction to World Religions*, 2nd ed. (Belmont, Calif.: Wadsworth, 1984), pp. 131–32.
4. See R.C. Gregg, trans., *Athanasius: The Life of Antony* (New York: Paulist, 1980).
5. See Frances M. Young, *From Nicaea to Chalcedon: A Guide to the Literature and its Background* (Philadelphia: Fortress, 1983).
6. See David Tracy, *The Analogical Imagination* (New York: Crossroad, 1981), pp. 99 ff.
7. See David H. Kelsey, *The Uses of Scripture in Recent Theology* (Philadelphia: Fortress, 1975); Brevard S. Childs, *Introduction to the Old Testament as Scripture* (Philadelphia: Fortress, 1979); David Bartlett, *The Shape of Scriptural Authority* (Philadelphia: Fortress, 1983); James Barr, *Holy Scripture: Canon, Authority, and Criticism* (Philadelphia: Westminster, 1983).
8. See James C. Turro and Raymond E. Brown, "Canonicity," in *The Jerome Biblical Commentary*, ed. Raymond E. Brown and others (Englewood Cliffs, N.J.: Prentice-Hall, 1968), vol. 2, pp. 515–34; A. C. Sundberg, Jr., "Canon of the New Testament," *The Interpreter's Dictionary of the Bible* (Nashville: Abingdon, 1976), suppl., pp. 136–40.
9. See N. A. Dahl, *Jesus in the Memory of the Early Church* (Minneapolis: Augsburg, 1976), especially pp. 11–29.
10. On the possibility of assigning these different questions to different specialists (e.g., exegetes, historians, philosophers) who would then coordinate their findings, see Bernard Lonergan, *Method in Theology* (New York: Herder & Herder 1972).

2

Historical Background

THE JEWISH CULTURAL BACKGROUND

Even when the authors of the New Testament are battling against Jewish opponents, trying to make the case that Jesus' fellow countrymen were wrong to reject him, they assume a Jewish framework of religious ideas. Judaism is usually said to have begun with Abraham about 1800 B.C.E. The Hebrews were in bondage to the Egyptians from about 1650 to 1250, and the usual dates given for Moses and the **Exodus** from Egypt are about 1200. One can see, therefore, that the memories preserved in the Old Testament go back much more than a thousand years before Jesus. Until about 1000 B.C.E. and the monarchy of David, who founded Jerusalem, the Israelites were a loose confederation of wandering tribes. The northern portion of David's kingdom fell to Assyria in 722, and the southern portion fell to Babylon in 586. This latter trauma, known as the Babylonian captivity, was a formative event for Jewish prophecy (Jeremiah, Isaiah 40–55). Alexander the Great conquered Palestine in 331 B.C.E. For a century or so after the successful Maccabean revolt of 167 (which had been occasioned by the effort of Antioches IV Epiphanes to paganize the Jews) there was autonomous rule, but from 31 B.C.E. to 306 C.E. the Romans held sway. Thus, for most of the six centuries preceding Jesus, and for the two centuries after him, Palestine was subject to strong foreign influence, if not outright rule.

The center of Jewish life, as it had stabilized in the centuries prior to Jesus, was **Torah**: teaching, guidance, law. All Jews felt that Torah was the result of God's having made a **covenant** with the people through Moses and given them commandments for living a holy, acceptable life. The writings that became collected in the Hebrew Bible were one form of Torah, but an oral tradition also expressed God's Law.

18

Terrain outside Jerusalem, looking toward Bethlemen. *(Photo by J.T. Carmody)*

Among the other major institutions of Jewish life that formed the people were the Temple and the synagogue. The first Temple was traditionally ascribed to King Solomon, the son of David, in the tenth century B.C.E. In 621 a reform of King Josiah eliminated all other shrines to Yahweh, the Jewish God, and made the Temple in Jerusalem the center of the people's cult. Solomon's Temple was destroyed by the Babylonians in 587, but after some of the Jews returned from exile a Second Temple was built in Jerusalem in 515. The Romans destroyed this Second Temple in 70 C.E. (A portion of it, known as the Western Wall, still stands in Jerusalem and is Judaism's most revered site.)

Joseph Tyson has described the sacrifices that went on in the Temple as follows:

> The primary function of the Temple was to serve as the place where the sacrificial rituals were performed. The sacrifices, of animals or grains, are required by the five books of Moses and are carefully described. Sacrifice involves the concept that the worshiper has certain obligations that can be fulfilled by presenting some possession to the divine. In Hebrew literature there are basically three forms of sacrifice. In the *thanksgiving* sacrifice, something is brought to the Temple and presented to God to express gratitude. For example, thanks for a good harvest of grain were expressed by presenting a portion of grain to God. The purpose of the *communion* sacrifice is to have fellowship with God in the form of a shared meal. In this sacrifice an animal is killed, and the blood and fat are drained and offered to God. The priests and communicants then eat the meat. The *atonement* sacrifice is per-

formed on the Day of Atonement (*Yom Kippur*) for the forgiveness of sins. The sacrifices were presided over by priests, who were required to be in a condition of purity—that is, they could have no physical defects and could not have had recent contact with a dead person or any other source of uncleanness. Contamination from such contact could, however, be removed by certain acts of ritual purification.[1]

The Temple was a lodestone, drawing the people not only to these sacrifices but also to the celebration there of the annual religious festivals, most of which commemorated important events of Israel's past. Thus Passover recalled the Exodus from Egypt. Pentecost was a Spring harvest festival and a commemoration of the forging of the covenant. Tabernacles was a Fall harvest festival and a commemoration of the Israelites' wandering in the wilderness before their entry into the promised land. At the time of feasts such as these, Jerusalem would swell with pilgrims from the outlying regions.

The synagogue perhaps arose during the Babylonian captivity, when Jews separated from their Temple center in Jerusalem fashioned another institution to preserve their community. Other scholarly opinion, however, holds that the synagogue was fashioned by the **Pharisees**, a lay religious group zealous for the study and application of Torah. At any rate, the synagogue became a place where Jews met to listen to Scripture and study the meaning of their religious teachings or Laws. Synagogues could be set up in all sorts of locations, and they generally served as the center of local Jewish life. In connection with the synagogue historians often mention the rise of academies to train Pharisaic scholars. Still another Jewish institution that was influential in Jesus' day was the **Sanhedrin**, a juridical body that dealt with both religious and political problems. After 70 C.E., when the Temple was destroyed, the Pharisaic leadership, focused in the synagogues, became crucial to Judaism's survival. Jews were deported from Jerusalem in 135 C.E., and thenceforth the Pharisaic sort of study of Torah and effort to lead a Torah-directed life became the main format of official Jewish piety.

In the century or so immediately prior to Jesus, **messianic** expectations had become strong and **apocalyptic** literature abounded. We deal with both of these matters, as they affect the New Testament, in the chapters that follow, but here it may be useful to note that messianism was a complicated phenomenon. (There were several sorts of figures, all "anointed" by God, on whom Jews close to Jesus' day could pin their hopes for an improved state of affairs. The **Messiah** could be a kingly, military, or prophetic sort of figure, and it was not usually clear just what he was going to do. Seldom, however, was he thought of as bringing an end to history. Usually he was anticipated as one who would bring the people a holistic prosperity: religious and political, spiritual and economic.)

The apocalyptic literature that flourished in the generations prior to Jesus and immediately after used messianic hopes but was distinctive for presenting visions of how God would restore his people's good fortunes and vindicate them against their oppressors. Apocalyptic writings did sometimes depict supernatural happenings and traffic in angels or cosmic powers. When the Romans destroyed the Temple in 70 C.E., and then crushed the revolt of Bar Kochba in 135 C.E., they consummated several centuries of pagan oppression (from the outrages of Antioches IV in 167 B.C.E. to the defeat of Bar Kochba in 135 C.E. is about three hundred years, only one hundred of which had the Jews in control of their land, and then only shakily).

The apocalyptic literature generated during this period (including the materials discovered at **Qumran**, near the Dead Sea, and thought representative of a separatist group called the **Essenes**) has been described as follows:

> In the intertestamental apocalyptic literature we find the expectation of a decisive culmination of history. The hope was widely shared. This world or this age was to come to a conclusion with the restoration of Israel's fortunes and the resurrection of her righteous dead, marking the inauguration of the messianic age. After a period of from several hundred to a thousand years, the general resurrection [that is, of all the dead] would take place as a prelude to the final judgment of God. Then God would usher in the "age to come," the consummation toward which all history was moving. It is too much to speak of a single plan or scheme, but the existence of similar ideas and expectations, if in less systematized form, in the New Testament shows that they were common currency in the Judaism of Jesus' day.[2]

After several generations, the followers of Jesus found themselves thoroughly at odds with the Jews who would not accept Jesus as the Messiah. By this time the Christian Church, which originally had been composed almost entirely of Jews (some Aramaic-speaking, some Greek-speaking), had begun to have more Gentiles than Jews in its membership. After the fall of the Temple in 70 C.E., the Pharisees became the predominant Jewish party, and they mounted a campaign against what they considered deviant understandings of Judaism (in the first century C.E. Judaism was remarkably diverse). Christianity was one such understanding, and around 85 C.E. the Pharisees were able in effect to have Christians excluded from worship in the synagogues. This troubled history stands in the background of Mark, Matthew, Luke, and **John** (which were all edited after the fall of the Temple, during the period of rising bitterness between Pharisees and Christians). Thus often what the Gospels are portraying in the interactions between Jesus and the Pharisees (or, for John, Jesus and "the Jews") refers as much to tensions of the authors' own day as to the actual historical disagreements between Jesus and his contemporaries. Within a religious context still largely set by the traditional Jewish sense of God, Torah, covenant, and the like, the Christians are trying to make their case that Jesus has made possible a definitive experience of **salvation**.

W. H. C. Frend has noted that the fall of Jerusalem in 70 C.E. was a surprise and something of a trauma for Christianity:

> The fall of Jerusalem left the Christians without a central point of reference. They were ill-prepared for this. Paul had established churches ruled by their

own officers, but had been less interested in any overall scheme of church authority for the interim period before the coming [the return of Christ], which he believed would be short. Apart from the shadowy figures of "the presbyter" Aristion and John of Ephesus, there is little evidence for authoritative leadership in this period. This lack showed itself in divergent and inconsistent attitudes towards society and differing interpretations of the faith even among communities that fell within the bounds of an emerging concept of *orthodoxy*. . . . [still] certain features emerge: First, the life, thought, and organization of the church can be understood only within the framework of Hellenistic Judaism. Were Christians the true Israel, bearers of the new covenant, the holy Remnant, or were they rebels and outsiders? Second, as a corollary to this controversy, the expansion of the church was accompanied by counterattacks by orthodox Jews and the pro-Jewish party within the church that have left their mark on the later books of the New Testament and on some of the sub-apostolic writings. Jews and Christians were rivals for proselytes in the Gentile world. . . . Finally, despite introspective tendencies among the Christian communities (very few references to secular events are to be found in the sub-apostolic writings), Christians began to impinge on the life of the empire and to come to the notice of the authorities independently of Judaism.[3]

THE GRECO-ROMAN CULTURAL CLIMATE

For the generation before Jesus, when "intertestamental" Judaism (between the Old and New Testaments) was flourishing, in Jesus' own lifetime, and during the formative first century of the Christian Church, Rome was the political power. The Roman empire was diverse, and so faced the problem of dealing with many different lands, languages, customs, and religions. The administrative style that Rome developed to deal with this diversity was to impose Roman rulers over local client kings. In other words, Rome allowed local, native powers but made them subject to resident representatives of the emperor in Rome. Thus each province had as its ultimate authority a governor appointed from Rome, Rome collected taxes from all its subject peoples, and garrisons of Roman soldiers were stationed in the provinces to ensure order and continued subjugation. If local peoples were not rebellious they could have considerable liberty to pursue their native cultural customs. Greek was the common language throughout most of the empire, Latin often functioned in legal documents, and local languages also functioned freely. In the provinces the Roman institution of slavery mixed with the officially marginal status of those who were not Roman citizens to create a majority population that had only minimal influence or control over its own fate.

The bond of the Roman empire was religion, in the sense of an agreement about the sacral order in which the authority and regularity of the state were thought to repose. Mircea Eliade has discussed the pragmatic and pietistic aspects of Roman religion that make it distinctive:

> The Roman religious genius is distinguished by pragmatism, the search for effectiveness, and, above all, the "sacralization" of organic collectives: family,

gens [race], fatherland. The famous Roman discipline, their honoring of obligations (**fides**), their devotion to the state, and the religious prestige they attributed to law are expressed by depreciation of the human person: the individual mattered only insofar as he belonged to his group.[4]

Devotion to the different Roman gods and respect for the prodigies of nature (Roman religion often has the appearance of being extraordinarily superstitious) therefore went hand in hand with an orderliness that propped up the impressive Roman civic structure. The army and the imperial administration were marvels of efficiency, and supporting them were a crisp Roman legal code and such physical helps as excellent engineering, sanitation, and road building. When Romans sought a word to summarize the admirable character that their religious rites were supposed to produce, *pietas* often came to mind. This means both a scrupulous observance of the religious rites that custom prescribed and a great respect for natural relationships among different groups of people. Family relationships, for example, were extremely important, so much so that the disobedience of a son to his father was considered a monstrous, grossly unnatural act. The individual was also supposed to display *pietas* toward the group, local or national, respecting its customs and showing it steadfast loyalty. The result of such "piety" was a profoundly conservative religiosity, and one that strove night and day to keep the traditional order well cemented.

For such a mentality, foreign religious customs were suspect from the beginning. Rome had such a diverse empire that simple practicality made it necessary to tolerate a variety of religious cults, but the Roman sense of the tie between religious cults and loyalty to the established order meant that the imperial forces were always on the lookout for religious zealots who might prove seditious. It is in this context that Jesus' opponents were able to daunt Pontius Pilate, the Roman governor, with the accusation that Jesus was preparing a political rebellion. Both the Roman and the Jewish conception of the intimate ties between religion and politics made it credible that a religious leader such as Jesus might well have political power as his objective.

Jews were despised by cultured Romans, who had taken in the humanistic ideals of Alexander the Great and later "Hellenists," because Jews seemed to hold themselves apart from other peoples. To the Greco-Roman mind that ruled the Mediterranean culturally in Jesus' day, Jewish customs such as **circumcision** and **kosher** dietary laws, as well as Jewish aversion to ordinary dealings with Gentiles (whom they considered unclean or polluting) stamped them as misanthropic: haughty despisers of other human beings.

John L. McKenzie has succinctly described both this low estimate that Gentiles (both Romans and Greeks) had for Jews and the scorn that Jews in turn had for Gentiles:

> The laws of ritual cleanliness made it impossible for Jews to live in Gentile neighborhoods or to do more than essential business with them; and ordinary

social intercourse between the two groups was extremely difficult. Gentiles thought Jews arrogant and supercilious. The Jewish law imposed a rigorous moral code in a world which was morally more tolerant even than our own. The Jews regarded the Gentiles as hopeless sinners devoid of even elementary human decency. They had no use for Gentile literature, which was a litany in praise of sin. Gentile wisdom was folly to the Jews; their sacred writings contained all the wisdom God had given to man, and these writings alone were worthy of serious study. Jews could not attend the theatre or the games, nor could they disport themselves in the public baths. The nudity which was so common and accepted in the Hellenistic world was appalling to the Jews. So was the common and socially quite acceptable prostitution and homosexuality. The Second Commandment made it impossible for them to admire, much less to imitate the art of the Hellenistic world. Art was idolatry.[5]

When the Christians first generated sufficient numbers to draw the attention of the Roman governors, they were categorized as a Jewish group. Thus, much of the stigma that attached to Jews was transferred to the early Christians. For their own part, Christians were ambivalent toward Gentiles (McKenzie may not give sufficient attention to the Jewish belief that individual Gentiles could be God-fearing and had a place in God's providential plan of salvation). Indeed, as more Gentiles entered the Church, and it became clear that the Christian community might have to work out an accommodation with the powers of the state, due to the delay of Jesus' return, the Roman government began to receive mixed reviews. On the one hand, passages such as Romans 13 indicate an early Christian sense that all political power ultimately comes from God. Biblical faith, both Jewish and Christian, thought that nothing truly good or holy existed apart from God (it had no conception of an indifferent or neutral "secular" realm that might operate on its own, apart from God). On the other hand, when Christians experienced (as Jews for some time had experienced) the animosity of the state and even persecution because they would not take part in the cult that seemed to divinize the emperor, their writings began to blacken the name of the Roman rule. For example, the book of Revelation equates Rome with the whore Babylon and speaks of it as a despicable beast soon to suffer God's avenging wrath.

The upshot, then, is considerable ambivalence about the prevailing state powers. In the New Testament era, both Christians and Jews had the feeling that their peace was a matter of sufferance by the government and thus was something quite fragile. They knew that by comparison with other pagan regimes Romans often seemed benevolent, yet they feared that the Roman immersion in **polytheism**, combined with what they considered the lax morals of the Greco-Roman culture at large, would ultimately make plain their own distance from pagan culture and so the sense in which they were indeed "enemies" of the status quo. Few Christians wanted to be military enemies or aspired to take over the Roman government. But many Christians, both Jewish and Gentile, knew in their bones that Christ and Caesar were very different Lords.

The last ingredient of the historical background to the New Testament literature that we want to elucidate is the Hellenistic religious synthesis that was extremely influential and furnished the surrounding pagan culture most of its sense of what human culture ought to provide. Alexander the Great, who probably died in 323 B.C.E., was the military genius who gave the ideal of a common humanity an empire on which to practice. Because of Alexander's conquests, the city-state, which had been the basic politico-religious unit, became passé. As well, the notion that there were irreconcilable differences between Greeks and "barbarians" (or among any groups of human beings) melted away. (One can see immediately how eccentric or antagonistic groups, such as Christians and Jews, who fought to preserve an ethnic and religious separateness, would be averse to this Hellenistic ideal.) The watchwords sent down from Alexander were "**ecumenical**," "cosmopolitan," and "universalistic." Despite much opposition, Alexander had spearheaded an increasing appreciation of the fundamental unity of the human race.

Eric Voegelin has written a difficult but masterful volume on what he calls "the ecumenic age" in which this fundamental unity of the human race became politically effective. The insights on which the ecumenic age rests go back to Israelite prophets and Greek philosophers who preexisted Alexander. They realized that the order—the proper outline of reality— given by God or grasped in human wisdom is universal. At the same time, they realized that no particular ethnic culture or political regime could contain this order or express it exhaustively. To the insight that all human beings share a fundamental unity they therefore added, at least in germ, the realization that this fundamental unity will also imply a cultural and political diversity. In other words, only a plurality of societies, religious rituals, and other factors will ever express the diversity to which the fundamental human unity (of spirit in the face of a transcendent God before whom all people are radically equal) will give rise. Voegelin's expression of this is demanding but well worth quoting:

> The men who had experienced the universality of transcendent order [the way that all human consciousness reaches out to the same mysterious divinity] were in search of social carriers of order other than the finite societies of their origin, because membership in the finite society seemed no longer to exhaust the meaning of human existence [i.e., being human was more than what being Jewish or being Greek could express]. The prophetic existence of the servant of God was separated from the collective existence of the Chosen People under the Torah [the classical biblical prophets realized that God has designs, ends, fulfillments for all human beings]; the philosopher's **bios theoretikos** [contemplative life dedicated to the pursuit of wisdom] from political life; universal humanity from parochial humanity. There began to differentiate a spectrum of order which required membership in a plurality of societies as its adequate form. In faint outlines there began to appear the fundamental division of temporal and spiritual order, of state and church.[6]

On a popular level, the most important effect of this Hellenistic effort to appreciate the ties between fundamental human unity and great diversity of cultural expression was the rich pluralism of the Hellenistic religions. Within the Roman empire and Greek range of cultural ideals many different religious groups offered fellowship, ritualistic experience, and ways to try to secure salvation or immortality. The sense was abroad that experiencing ecstasies, visions, the spiritual powers of the soul, or help by spiritualistic forces such as angels or divinities could give one relief from the physical or psychological pressures of the times. Jews and Christians tended to be very critical of these "pagan" rites, but they had to deal with potential converts, or even members of their own groups, who were greatly influenced by the atmosphere of secret knowledge, special wisdom, and salvation that the Hellenistic religions generated. Thus we find the Pauline Epistles greatly concerned with clarifying what is a proper Christian wisdom and attitude toward spiritual experiences. We find the **Epistle to the Hebrews** concerned with distancing Christ from the angels, whose prominence in contemporary Judaism was in good part due to Hellenistic influences. The Platonic, Stoic, and Epicurean philosophies that shaped the intelligentsia all were religions more than academic ventures. There was a sense that Dionysius, Isis, Mithra, Demeter, and the other divinities that focused the Hellenistic cults all ran together, and so there was a danger that Jesus would become swept up into the crowd and lose his special identity. The more Christianity penetrated the Gentile world and moved into Asia Minor, the more it had to deal with these matters. By the end of the New Testament period, therefore, not just the Jewish religious culture but also the Hellenistic **mystery religions** and concerns for salvation were molding Christian theology.

SUMMARY

We have sketched a bare outline of the Jewish and Greco-Roman historical context of the New Testament. The New Testament assumes Jewish religious history as its basic framework, a history that went back as far as Abraham, around 1800 B.C.E. Key moments were the Exodus from Egypt and giving of the Law under Moses, the Kingship of David, the Babylonian Captivity, the Conquest of Alexander, and the Maccabean Revolt.

The center of Jewish life was the Torah and the Temple was the physical hub. In later times the synagogue, Pharisaic leadership, and apocalyptic literature played large roles. Jews and Christians held much of their debate over the significance of Jesus in terms of messianism, and often the gospel portraits of Jesus' Jewish opponents reflect bitter Christian-Jewish disputes of the evangelists' own day. To outside, Gentile eyes, the first Christians were merely a Jewish sect.

The Greco-Roman world furnished Christianity the other half of its historical context. Rome was the current political power, rather tolerant of the great ethnic diversity of the peoples in its empire, and the bond of the Roman system was religion. To Roman religious pragmatism and piety, non-Roman religious cults always seemed potentially seditious. Jews considered Romans and other Gentiles religiously unclean and morally inferior, while Romans and Greeks thought Jews misanthropic (or at least unwilling to subscribe to the Hellenistic ideal of a universal humanity and fellow feeling), so there was considerable friction between the two groups. One sees in the ambivalent early Christians' attitude toward the state a reflection of these tensions.

The Hellenistic cultural ideals of ecumenism and universality that were passed down from Alexander the Great set the tone of the surrounding Mediterranean world and to some extent made both Christians and Jews outsiders. On the other hand, they gave both Christians and Jews wide horizons upon which to reflect. The Hellenistic religious synthesis of many different cults, Greek, Roman, and Eastern, provided an atmosphere of salvation and special knowledge with which the New Testament writers had to contend, and they finally ensured that the meaning of Jesus would be translated into Hellenistic as well as Jewish terms.

STUDY QUESTIONS

1. What was the significance of the Jerusalem Temple?
2. What expectation of a decisive culmination of history had shaped the generations prior to Jesus?
3. How are the tensions of the gospel writers' day likely to color their portrait of the Pharisees?
4. What was the significance of Roman *pietas*?
5. Why did many Gentiles consider Jews misanthropic?
6. How did the Hellenistic religions suggest that salvation was an ecumenical concern and thus threaten the uniqueness of Jesus?

NOTES

1. Joseph B. Tyson, *The New Testament and Early Christianity* (New York: Macmillan, 1984), p. 91.
2. Robert A. Spivey and D. Moody Smith, *Anatomy of the New Testament*, 3rd ed. (New York: Macmillan, 1982), pp. 32–33.
3. W.H.C. Frend, *The Rise of Christianity* (Philadelphia: Fortress, 1984), pp. 120–21.
4. Mircea Eliade, *A History of Religious Ideas* (Chicago: University of Chicago Press, 1982), vol. 2, p. 115.
5. John L. McKenzie, *The New Testament Without Illusion* (Chicago: Thomas More, 1980), pp. 14–15.
6. Eric Voegelin, *Order and History* (Baton Rouge: Lousiana State University Press, 1974), vol. 4, p. 116.

3

The Letters of Paul
To Early Christians

1 THESSALONIANS

What Have We Here?

In 1 Thessalonians we have the earliest writing of the New Testament. Currently scholarly consensus is that Paul himself wrote this letter from Athens or Corinth about the year 51c.e. He had founded a Christian church in Thessalonica, a port city of what then was known as Macedonia. Today the same area is thought of as northern Greece, and the name of the city has only changed slightly: Thessaloniki. Now, as in Paul's day, the city is on a bay or inlet of the Aegean Sea. In ancient times, however, it also lay along one of the main roads of the Roman empire, the Via Egnatia. Paul, probably using the Via Egnatia, had stopped in Thessalonica. His preaching about Jesus had met with success, but then he had felt bound to move on. Later he sent back to Thessalonica two companions, Silvanus and **Timothy**, who probably had helped him found the Thessalonian church. When Silvanus and Timothy rejoined Paul and gave him a very favorable report about the welfare of the Thessalonians, Paul determined to write them a letter.[1]

1 Thessalonians is not a typical letter for Paul. It spends much more time thanking God than is his usual practice. Paul reviews the good job that the Thessalonians are doing, goes back in memory to the time that he spent with them, and then describes his own current situation, thanking God at each juncture. Then, shifting gears, he gives the Thessalonians instruction on ethical and doctrinal points, before concluding with a prayer and a blessing. A brief outline of the letter looks like this:

Introduction 1:1
Thanksgiving 1:2–3:13

The Arrival of the Gospel in Thessalonica 1:2–10

Paul's Stay in Thessalonica 2:1–12*

Paul's Current Situation 2:17–3:13

Instructions to the Thessalonians 4:1–5:22

Admonitions concerning Chastity 4:1–12

Instructions on the Day of the Lord 4:13–5:11

General Directives on Christian Conduct 5:12–22

Concluding Prayer and Blessing 5:23–28[2]

The Introduction is remarkable only for (1) associating Silvanus and Timothy with Paul in greeting the Thessalonians, and (2) expressing Paul's passionate conviction that a church like the group at Thessalonica belongs to God the Father and the Lord Jesus Christ.

The Thanksgiving first stresses Paul's gratitude to God for the strong faith that the Thessalonians are showing—so strong that they are a model to other believers in their area. Then it recalls Paul's original warm reception in Thessalonica. Unlike the reception he has experienced in other places (Philippi, for example), in Thessalonica all went well. True, Paul's own conduct had been spotless. He had gone out of his way to distance himself from the charlatans and hawkers of religion who give public preaching a bad name. He had supported himself by manual labor and treated his Thessalonian converts like a gentle parent. Still, those were unusually good times, times of God's manifest grace, for which his heart overflows in gratitude.

Currently, however, Paul feels like an alien, cut off from his Thessalonian family. Out of concern for them he sent Timothy back to strengthen their faith, and Timothy's good report has greatly consoled him. So Paul prays that the Thessalonians' faith will only grow richer: "And may the Lord make you increase and abound in love to one another and to all men, as we do to you, so that he may establish your hearts unblamable in holiness before our God and Father, at the coming of our Lord Jesus with all his saints" (3:12–13).

After this long outpouring of thanksgiving and hope, Paul offers his religious family some moral and doctrinal guidance. It is important that the Thessalonians keep a high level of sexual conduct, not falling into the lusts so prevalent among the pagans. They should love one another chastely, keep the peace, and work with their hands. Doctrinally, Paul stresses that those who die believing in Christ will share in Christ's resurrection. Indeed, when the Lord returns all the faithful, both the living and dead, will celebrate his triumph. None of us knows when this return will be, so all of us should stay watchful.

Returning to general advice, Paul urges the community to prize good order: peace, mutual encouragement, joy, and openness to the different gifts of the Spirit. In conclusion he prays that God will keep the Thessalo-

*1 Thessalonians 2:13-16 is often considered an addition by someone other than Paul.

nians whole and entire, perfecting them in holiness, so that they may be without reproach when the Lord returns. Paul would greet all members of the community, and all are to hear this letter read. God, who is trustworthy, is calling the Thessalonians, so they can expect to succeed on the Day of the Lord.

Why Was This Written?

There is little mystery about the reason Paul wrote the Thessalonians this letter. The good report he had heard about their faith had fired his spirit. As well, Paul always kept the communities he had started in mind. His other letters show that he constantly wished that he could commune with his spiritual offspring and continue to build up their faith. Only a fool would be unaware of the many dangers to which a young faith like that of the Thessalonians was liable. The loose morals of the neighboring pagans, and such perplexing experiences as members of the community dying before the Day of the Lord, were always a threat to cause upset or confusion. Indeed, Paul had grounds for thinking the Thessalonians had placed too much emphasis on his promise that the resurrection of Christ meant that the end of history was very near. Moreover, the Christian community's ideal of love was so high that any strife or misunderstanding was a serious blow to Paul's hopes for his children. So, as the father of this community, the one who had brought them the surpassing good news of Christ, Paul naturally would write to them whenever the opportunity arose. Naturally he would make use of this way to return to them in spirit whenever he could.

What Background Does This Text Presuppose?

To understand Thessalonians, one must know a little about Paul and his mission, and also something about the conventions of letter writing in antiquity. Born a Jew, Paul (originally Saul) had been very zealous in his religious observance. In fact, he had been most offended by the claims of Christians that Jesus was the **Christ** (Messiah) and that Judaism had entered a new phase. But in the very process of trying to defeat the Christians and such claims Paul had an astounding experience. As reported by the author of Acts,

> But Saul, still breathing threats and murder against the disciples of the Lord [the Christians], went to the high priest and asked him for letters to the synagogues at Damascus, so that if he found any belonging to the Way [Christianity], men or women, he might bring them bound to Jerusalem. Now as he journeyed he approached Damascus, and suddenly a light from heaven flashed about him. And he fell to the ground and heard a voice saying to him, "Saul, Saul, why do you persecute me?" And he said, "Who are you, Lord?" And he said, "I am Jesus, whom you are persecuting; but rise and enter the city, and you will be told what you are to do." [9:1–6]

When Paul had had a chance to digest what this experience implied, the living reality of Jesus took over his life. He became convinced that the claims Christians were making for Jesus were true and, consequently, that the death and resurrection of Jesus was the most important thing in the world. In the death and resurrection of Jesus, he felt, the God of the Jews had opened salvation to all people. No longer was the covenant or special relationship with God limited to descendents of Abraham, the father of the Jews. Moreover, what Jews had been trying to accomplish by keeping the **covenant Law**, and pagans had been trying to accomplish by idol worship or secret rites, God personally had brought about: salvation and healing of the wounds that make human life so painful. By faith in Jesus, Paul believed, one could become free of anxiety and hopelessness, charged with energy, life, and purpose.

We shall see other aspects of Paul's Christian faith when we deal with his other letters. For the moment it is enough to underscore his great gratitude to God for the gift of life in Christ and his sense that God had called him personally to dedicate all his energy to preaching the good news about Jesus. From shortly after his conversion experience, Paul felt that his mission was to bring as many people as possible into the orbit or power of the astounding **grace** or favor that Jesus signified. So, in the background of Thessalonians is Paul's previous Jewish faith. In the foreground is the pagan atmosphere of the Mediterranean area in which Paul did most of his work. And pressuring Paul himself at this time, when his understanding of the Christ-event was still developing, was the notion of the Day of the Lord, the time of fulfillment when Christ would return. Sometimes this preoccupation with the return of the Messiah is called **eschatology**.[3] To understand early Christianity we must appreciate how urgently Paul and some of the other New Testament authors waited for the **eschaton** or last thing (Day of the Lord). That would be a wonderful day of judgment, justice, and complete fulfillment. It could come at any moment, so Christian life was expectant, faith was on the alert.

In addition to knowing something about Paul's conversion, we also will appreciate the Pauline Epistles better if we know something about the conventions of letter writing in the ancient Greco-Roman world. Scholars occasionally have distinguished between "letters" (person-to-person communications) and "epistles" (treatises addressed to the general public), but this distinction cannot be applied to the New Testament without nuance. On the one hand, most of Paul's writings require some knowledge of his personality and career, and so they have characteristics of the interpersonal "letter." On the other hand, his letters probably were written with the intention that they be read to whole churches or networks of communities, and often they deal with matters of faith in the manner of a treatise.

It is also useful to know that most ancient letters were dictated to a scribe, who frequently had considerable liberty to express the dictator's main ideas as he thought best. Letters generally followed a fairly set format, at least so far as the introduction and conclusion went. Thus the formulaic character of the opening and closing in the Pauline letters conformed to the custom of the Greco-Roman world. As an opening, one usually gave the sender's name, the name of the recipient, and wishes for the recipient's health. To close, one repeated the wishes for the recipient's health, and usually the actual sender (rather than the scribe) wrote this word, as a sort of authentication. The ancient letter writers did not have the modern convention of signing the sender's name. Both the introduction and the conclusion might be expanded if the sender wished to elaborate on his desires or hopes for the well-being of the recipient. By noting the variations on this general scheme that the New Testament Epistles introduce, we get a good sense of the fresh ideas that were uppermost in their minds. Above all, we appreciate better the **doxologies** or expressions of praise to God for salvation that pepper the New Testament letters.

What Lasting Significance Does This Have?

1 Thessalonians is not a masterpiece of Christian reflection. Its importance lies not in its depth or novelty of teaching but in the warm affections it reveals and the light it sheds on what Christian faith was like in a typical little community about twenty years after Jesus' death. Paul's letter suggests a group whose community life pivoted on what Jesus had been, said, and done. Above all, it suggests a community life pivoted on the death, resurrection, and return of Jesus the Lord. What had happened in and through Jesus was a new moment in human history, a new phase of revelation. 1 Thessalonians lets us glimpse a group of people joyously defining themselves through this Pauline faith. Paul had gathered them together by preaching the significance of Christ; living in the glow of Paul's message was giving the Thessalonians great joy, although they were becoming anxious at the delay of the eschaton.

Beyond this lasting significance for Christians, 1 Thessalonians invites any reader to reflect about life's deepest meaning. Paul's conversion had brought a sharp new focus to his life. The Thessalonians accepted his message and were trying to focus their lives on his Christ. All the religions (Buddhism, Islam, Hinduism, and so on) that have shaped world history have had their greatest influence this way: by giving people a sharp focus, something challenging and fulfilling on which to center their lives. Whether or not what Paul offered the Thessalonians appeals to a given person reading about it nineteen centuries later, this more basic issue of a life-center remains. What is the center of our lives, our culture? How satisfying is our world view or set of values? Does it produce burning passion, deep loyalty, rich love and joy? Do we too hunger for something like a "Day of the Lord," a time of complete fulfillment? Or is the faith of Paul and the Thessalonians impossibly naïve, sheer fantasy and wish fulfillment? If these are valid questions, 1 Thessalonians remains quite significant.

GALATIANS

What Have We Here?

New Testament scholars generally consider the letter to the **Galatians**, like 1 Thessalonians, to be from the hand of Paul himself at a time rather early in his career. Beyond that, opinions about where the Galatians lived and precisely when Paul wrote this letter to them vary quite widely. So, for example, one highly respected scholar has recently written:

> The location of "the churches of Galatia," to which Paul wrote a letter and which he mentioned to the **Corinthian** Christians (Gal. 1:2; 1 Cor. 16:1), cannot be determined with any certainty. In other cases, although Paul speaks of "believers in Macedonia and Achaia" (1 Thess. 1:7; cf. Rom. 16:26; 1 Cor. 16:15; 2 Cor. 9:2; 11:9f.) or in the province of Asia (Rom. 16:5; 1 Cor. 16:19), his letters are addressed to Christians in specific cities. Yet nowhere in Paul's letters is a city mentioned which lay within the Galatian province. The account in Acts only complicates the puzzle further. Acts does describe evangelization by Paul and his companions in Pisidian Antioch, Iconium, Lystra, and Derbe—four of the Roman colonies established as part of the romanization program undertaken by the province's first governor, Marcus Lollius, under Augustus. The author of Acts, however, does not use the name Galatia to refer to these places, but the ethnic regional terms Pisidia and Lycaonia. Further, Acts reports a journey through "the Phrygian and Galatian country" (16:6) and, although it records no missionary activity and names no specific locations, later tells of a return trip "strengthening all the disciples" in the same areas (18:23).[4]

Precisely where the Galatian Christians lived, then, is disputed. Disputed too are the date when Paul wrote this letter (between 49 and 55) and the place from which he wrote (Ephesus is most favored). Not disputed is the general identity of the Galatians: "The inhabitants after whom Galatia was called, the *Galatai*, were a branch of the Indo-European tribe of the Celts or Galli (Gauls). The group which settled in Asia Minor came to be referred to as Galatians rather than Celts, although etymologically the names are identical."[5]

In simple outline the letter breaks down into five sections:

Greetings and Introduction 1:1–10

Paul, Paul's Gospel, and Peter 1:11–2:21

How to Please God 3:1–4:31

Practical Exhortations 5:1–6:10

Conclusion 6:11–18[6]

Paul's Greetings and wish that the Galatians receive the grace and peace of God the Father and the Lord Jesus Christ are warm enough, but his Introduction is blistering:

> I am astonished that you are so quickly deserting him who called you in the grace of Christ and turning to a differing gospel—not that there is another gospel, but there are some who trouble you and want to pervert the gospel of Christ. But even if we, or an angel from heaven, should preach to you a gospel contrary to that which we preached to you, let him be accursed. As we have said before, so now I say again, if any one is preaching to you a gospel contrary to that which you received, let him be accursed. Am I now seeking

the favor of men, or of God? Or am I still trying to please men? If I were still pleasing men, I should not be a servant of Christ. [1:6–10]

What is the trouble? How have the Galatians fallen away from what Paul first taught them? Who is perverting their faith? Why does Paul feel that he has to rebuke them so fiercely and defend himself against charges of watering down the gospel?

Apparently some people had been questioning Paul's message and credentials, even charging him with leading the Galatians astray. So Paul reviews his conversion experience, interpreting what happened to him on the road to Damascus as a direct revelation from God, the Father of Jesus, that he Paul should preach Jesus Christ among the Gentiles. Early on Paul had had this mission confirmed or accepted by the Christian leaders in Jerusalem (he mentions Cephas or **Peter** and **James** by name). Then, fourteen years later, he had again laid his interpretation of the gospel before the Jerusalem leaders. The key point in this interpretation was Paul's conviction that Gentiles did not have to be circumcised when they joined the Church. This rite, which had been mandatory for entry into the Jewish community, was not necessary for Church membership. Peter and the other leaders had accepted this interpretation, because it was manifest that God had given Paul the grace or gift of dealing with the Gentiles in this way. Moreover, when Peter later waffled, seeming to retract the Gentile's freedom, Paul met him at Antioch and rebuked him to his face.

Why is this matter of circumcision so important in Paul's eyes? Because on it depends Paul's whole understanding of the new thing that God did in Jesus Christ. In the death of Christ the entire Jewish system of gaining **righteousness** (acceptability) before God was overturned. Christ on the cross meant the end or death of the covenant Law as a means of pleasing God. Thus those who believe in Christ are also dead to the Law: "For I through the Law died to the Law, that I might live to God. I have been crucified with Christ; it is no longer I who live, but Christ who lives in me; and the life I now live in the flesh I live by faith in the Son of God, who loved me and gave himself for me. I did not nullify the grace of God; for if justification were through the Law, then Christ died to no purpose" (2:19–21).

After this passionate outburst, Paul only moves deeper into his exposition of the newness of Christianity. The Galatians had received the Spirit of God by faith, not by doing the things (such as circumcision) commanded by the covenant Law. It was their faith in Jesus, crucified and raised, that had brought them divine life, not any legalistic obedience. Indeed, from the time of Abraham faith had always been the key matter. No one can fulfill all the precepts of the covenant Law. Christ himself came under the curse of the Law, because under the Law crucifixion was an abomination. God allowed Jesus to be crucified so that the Gentiles might gain the blessing previously reserved for the children of Abraham. The covenant Law, which was given to Moses, came after the promise made to Abraham. So the relation to God by faith (rather than by doing the commands of the Law) was older and more venerable. The Law, then, was a temporary thing, a sort of tutor, until the coming of Christ, who fulfilled what had been promised in the beginning to Abraham. Faith in Christ brings about a new situation, in which all people have a fresh start: "There is neither Jew nor Greek, there is neither slave nor free, there is neither male nor female; for you are all one in Christ Jesus. And if you are Christ's, then you are Abraham's offspring, heirs according to promise" (3:28–29).

Previously, before Christ and the outpouring of the divine Spirit, people like the Galatians had been slaves. They did not know the true God. But the Father has put the Spirit of the Son into the Galatians' hearts, to make them children and heirs of Abraham. They are free—and yet they are acting as though they are still in bondage to the Law. Paul is beside himself with frustration. When he was with the Galatians they would have done anything for him. Now he would have them realize what they forfeit by taking up the obligations of the Law, the slavery they fall back into.

After this rather convoluted argument (and use of Hebrew Scripture) to try to get the Galatians to see correctly the difference between faith in Christ and doing the works of the covenant Law, Paul turns to some practical matters. Faith should give the Galatians freedom. Accepting circumcision means having to carry out a burdensome Law. On the other hand, freedom does not mean license. Unless the Galatians love one another, they will not use their freedom well (and so they will not fulfill the basic intent of the covenant Law). Using freedom well means living according to what Paul calls the Spirit, the divine impulse, rather than according to the flesh, the ungodly or worldly impulse. It is not hard to distinguish these two different orientations. The fruit of the Spirit is such good things as love, joy, peace, and patience. The effects of the flesh are such bad things as fornication, impurity, licentiousness, and idolatry. Faith in Christ demands that one crucify the flesh and live by the Spirit of brotherly and sisterly love. Faith leads to humility and mutual help. Dissension and boasting are signs of the flesh.[7]

In conclusion, Paul returns to his theme of freedom from circumcision (which by now has become a key symbol of "fleshly" living): "It is those who want to make a good showing in the flesh that would compel you to be circumcised, and only in order that they may not be persecuted for the cross of Christ" (6:12). By contrast, the cross of Christ is the only thing in which Paul himself will glory. For the cross of Christ leads to a new creation, in terms of which neither being circumcised nor being uncircumcised matters. That is what the Galatians should keep in mind: the new creation that comes with faith in Christ.

Why Was This Written?

Although we do not know the names of Paul's specific opponents, it is clear that they were Christians with a different view of the Christ-event. They had come to the Galatians and had been countermanding Paul's original preaching. Paul wrote this letter to rebut such meddlers as strongly as he knew how. In his view, great damage would befall both the Galatian church and the whole Gentile mission unless his original interpretation of the Gentiles' freedom were allowed to stand. Paul could no more doubt his own interpretation than he could doubt the revelation God had made to him on the road to Damascus. They stood together as part and parcel of the same event. To insist that new converts to the Body of Christ, the Church, had to take on circumcision and the other obligations of the Jewish Law (dietary regulations, Sabbath rules, and the like) was tantamount to denying the value of Christ's death. In terms of the Law, Christ died as a criminal, one accursed. So it boiled down to an either-or: either Christ (and freedom) or the Law (and the old slavery). Paul wrote to keep his spiritual children free and to vindicate his whole life's mission as an apostle to the Gentiles, to all the non-Jews to whom God was offering salvation.

What Background Does This Text Presuppose?

As no doubt is clear, this text presupposes some understanding of the Jewish Law. In all likelihood the people who were troubling the Galatians and defaming Paul were Jewish Christians. Most likely they had accepted Jesus as the Messiah and thought that Jesus had changed Jewish religion, but they did not appreciate how radical this change really was. In their view, such old obligations as circumcision and keeping the kosher laws remained in force. In Paul's view they misunderstood the whole significance of both Christ's death on the cross and the power of the Spirit now active in so many Gentile communities. The Law had become a complicated matter of keeping at least 613 regulations. Paul suspected that it filled the typical Jew's religious horizon, blotting out the primacy of faith. Retaining the Law after Christ was thoroughly wrong-headed. The Spirit that poured forth after the death of Jesus made human existence like a new creation. It was a completely fresh start. So forcing Christian converts to obey the Jewish Law was like herding people who had been liberated back into prison. Only a fool would command it.

We know from other writings of Paul (Romans, for example), and from other books of the New Testament (Matthew, for example), that the view of the Law presented in Galatians is extreme. Perhaps it says as much about Paul's own early journey in faith as it does about the general convictions of the early Christians. For in many early Christian communities it was not so clear that belief in Christ meant the end of trying to keep the covenant Law. For example, the leaders of the Church at Jerusalem, James and Peter, seem to have been more conservative in their attitudes toward the Law. True, they had agreed with Paul that Gentiles need not be circumcised, but they seemed to assume that Jews who accepted Jesus would continue to go to the synagogue and keep many of the covenant laws.

Indeed, in the first generation after Jesus it was still unclear how things would turn out between Jews who accepted Jesus as the Messiah and Jews who rejected him. To an outsider the whole business probably seemed like a family squabble, something quite intramural. As scholars have become more sophisticated at sifting out the implications of the New Testament documents, they have been teaching us that early Christianity was really quite a diverse movement. Although all the churches felt a common kinship, different areas developed different local customs and traditions. In one place, where Gentiles were in the majority, freedom from the Law (such as the changes Paul advocated) might be the dominant mood. In other places, where either Greek-speaking Jews or Aramaic-speaking Jews were the majority, the dominant mood might be more conservative. So we have to take Paul's strong statements here with a grain of salt. They have been profoundly important in the overall Christian understanding of Christ, but at the time Paul wrote they were by no means the only option. And nowadays, when we better realize how the whole history of Western anti-Semitism frequently appealed to strong statements in the New Testament, we have to sympathize with Paul's Jewish opponents.

What Lasting Significance Does This Have?

Through the Christian centuries, the main themes of Galatians, especially that of freedom from the Law and that of the difference between flesh and Spirit, have been extremely significant. As more and more Gentiles entered the Christian Church, Paul's theology more and more shaped the Christian understanding of the newness that Christ meant. So Paul became in fact as well as claim the apostle to the Gentiles: the one who spearheaded the development of Christianity as a faith somewhat independent of its Jewish parentage. Whenever Christianity ran the danger of becoming legalistic, of seeming to teach people that they could please God by obeying a lot of rules, Pauline writings such as Galatians seemed to rise up as a rebuke.

Similarly, passages such as Galatians 5, on the differences between life in the Spirit and life in the flesh, entered into the permanent treasury of Christian wisdom. Paul was by no means a lawless person. To his mind the inner guidance of Christ's Spirit was a more demanding regime than the Law, not a less demanding one. But it was also a regime of greater freedom because it was a discipline of love. The Spirit of Christ prompting Christians to cry out "Abba, Father" was a breath and flame of love. Just as the Father had given Christ the power to love even through his death on the cross, so the Spirit could empower Christ's followers to bear one another's burdens and form a wonderful community. True, this power was paradoxical, like the strength of Jesus himself. Yet there it stood: The cross of Jesus had been the gateway to his resurrection. For Paul it was the very power and wisdom of God.[8]

Backing away from Christian tradition proper, we may note several other lasting significances of Galatians. For instance, it raises, as the Protestant Reformers of the sixteenth century especially realized, the perennially central religious question of the relation between faith and works. This is a question that no religion or philosophy can long avoid without becoming trivial. How do we human beings gain a sense of rightness or at-homeness in the world? What is our path to joy and peace? In ancient China Confucians and Taoists engaged in a debate analogous to that between traditional Jews and Pauline Christians. The Confucians gave great importance to the customs of the Chinese ancients—rules, protocol, ritual. They did not think of these customs as the Law of a covenant between the Chinese people and a personal God, but they did think of them as the wisdom that could make social life good.[9] The Taoists were freer spirits. To their mind a "Way" (Tao) moved through the world and if one could move as it did, go along with it harmoniously, life would turn out fine. Human customs and conventions obstructed union with this Tao as often as they helped. It was not outer formalism but inner listening that mattered.

The terms of the debate between those who wanted to retain adherence to Torah or covenant Law and those who stressed listening to the Spirit of Christ obviously were somewhat different, yet a certain parallelism obtains. Probably human beings have always struggled after a balance between an inner reliance on faith and love and an outer concern with social proprieties. Probably wisdom has always lain in striking some compromise or balance. For Paul the overwhelming reality of the Spirit of Christ put everything else in the shade. Other personalities, with different formative experiences, naturally have seen things differently.

On one point, however, Christian theology as a whole has completely sided with Paul. In the ultimate analysis, as all orthodox Christian theologians have said, all human beings are only saved or made right with God by grace, God's free gift. Yet it is doubtful that Jews of any depth have ever felt differently. Like Muslims overwhelmed by the sovereignty of Allah, or humanists impressed by the irreducible mystery of life, traditional Jews have always given God all the priority. So Galatians, in this perspective, is but one especially passionate human document of the many that have cried out that human beings are not the final measure. For Paul the final measure was Christ on the cross. For other great geniuses it has been other symbols of God's more than human wisdom. Consistently, though, the greatest human minds have grown still and humble before the mysteries of creation and the Creator. Consistently, they have all said that human laws and human conceptions are far from the final verdict.

1 CORINTHIANS

What Have We Here?

Paul's two Epistles to the Christians of Corinth comprise one of our best sources of information about the tensions and self-conceptions of the early Christian Church. By general agreement they are authentic letters of Paul himself, two of a series that he wrote to this church that he had formed (the others have been lost). In Robert Jewett's chronology of Paul's life, they (with **Philippians** and **Philemon**) probably were written in 55 or 56. Other scholars place them earlier, perhaps 52 to 54. For Jewett, Paul was probably converted in 34 and wrote Thessalonians in 50. Galatians probably came in 53 and Romans in 57.[10] Other scholars suggest slightly different dates, but most agree that the Corinthian correspondence is later than Galatians, earlier than Romans, and about the same time as Philippians.

The most likely location of Paul at the time of his writing to the Corinthians was Ephesus. Acts 18:11 says that Paul had spent eighteen months working in Corinth, and both letters assume a deep familiarity with the Corinthian situation. Jewish, Roman, and Greek cultural influences were all strong, along with several oriental religions. The city was a thriving seaport and had gained considerable notoriety as a place where all sorts of pagan rituals and sexual vices flourished. In fact, Corinth was a center for the worship of the Greek goddess of love, Aphrodite, whose cult involved ritual prostitution.[11] It is no wonder, therefore, that much of 1 Corinthians deals with sexual morality and sacrifices to idols.

For Hans Conzelmann, who has written a large commentary on 1 Corinthians, the Epistle breaks down as follows:

Opening and Thanksgiving 1:1–9

Divisions in the Community 1:10–4:21

Crisis about "Life" 5:1–6:20

Answers to Various Questions 7:1–15:58

    Celibacy and Marriage 7:1–40

    Freedom and Idol Sacrifices 8:1–11:1

    Divine Worship 11:2–14:40

    The Resurrection of the Dead 15:1–58

Information and Greetings 16:1–14[12]

Paul begins 1 Corinthians by joining himself to his "brother" Sosthenes (a Corinthian?) and sending to the church at Corinth, to those who are called to be "saints," grace and peace from God the Father and the Lord Jesus Christ. God's grace has already been poured out at Corinth abundantly, as the profusion of the Corinthians' spiritual gifts testifies. These gifts will sustain the community until the "revealing" of Jesus: the Day of the Lord.

Moving into the body of his communication, Paul first takes up some reports of divisions in the Corinthian community. He has been told by members of the household of Chloe (perhaps a wealthy Christian woman of Corinth) that some Corinthians identify themselves as belonging to him, others identify themselves as belonging to Apollos, still a third group say they belong to Cephas (Peter), and a fourth group says it belongs to Christ. This factionalism and rivalry mocks the unity of the Church. It is a species of worldly wisdom far removed from the Christian wisdom that centers in Christ's cross: "For the word of the cross is folly to those who are perishing, but to us who are being saved it is the power of God. For it is written [Isaiah 29:14], 'I will destroy the wisdom of the wise, and the cleverness of the clever I will thwart'"(1:18–19).

Both the Jews who ask for signs other than Christ's cross and the Gentiles who find Christ's cross folly miss the wisdom of God. The wisdom of God is foolishness to worldly people. They see the divine way of pro-

St. Tecla and the Beasts.
Rondelle with scene of St.
Tecla in the lions' den.
Sculpture, Coptic, fifth
century A.D. This rondelle
probably served as a graphic
symbol of fortitude for the
faithful of upper Egypt.
According to tradition,
Tecla was converted by Paul
and suffered many torments
for her faith, including
flames of fire and wild
beasts in the arena (as
shown in the rondelle).
*(Nelson Gallery–Atkins Museum, Kansas
City, Mo. [Nelson Fund])*

ceeding as weakness and scandal. But God has called into the Church weak,
lowly people to confound the worldly wise. Paul himself did not make an
impressive appearance in Corinth, lest he detract from Christ crucified and
the power of the Spirit. On the other hand, people of mature faith recognize in God's paradoxical ways of proceeding a profound wisdom. The
Spirit and the death-resurrection of Christ are like a secret that God had
been keeping from all eternity. Those who have the Spirit grasp this secret.
Those who do not have the Spirit miss it. In itself this secret is the fulfillment anticipated by Isaiah 64:4: "What no eye has seen, nor ear heard, nor
the heart of man conceived, what God has prepared for those who love
him" (2:9).

Paul could not discourse on these things of the Spirit when he first
instructed the Corinthians, because then they were mere beginners. Their
current strife shows they are beginners still. It is immaterial who baptized
them. Paul, Apollos, or any other minister pales in comparison to the
master worker God. Paul wanted to build their community on Christ, the
only sure foundation. He wanted them to appreciate both that they are a
holy temple and that they are a people free to enjoy all of God's gifts. But
where they should be good stewards of all God's gifts, in all humility,
instead they have become vain and boasting. What an ironic contrast to
Paul's own lowly circumstances, or to any real apostle's failures and sufferings. As their spiritual father Paul would like to come to them in gentleness,
but if need be he will come with a rod to chastise them.

In chapters 5 and 6 Paul focuses on the concrete aberrations to which
the Corinthians' folly has taken them. The outstanding instance is a member of the community living incestuously with his father's wife. This trans-
gressed human law, but more, it was an unthinkable violation of Christian
purity, as was the community's general tolerance of the strife and immor-

ality of its members. God made the human body to be a temple of the Spirit. Sexual immorality pollutes this temple, just as community strife and running off to the civil courts mock the unity a local church should have. Any absolutism in Paul's tone should be qualified by a realization that pagan sexual ethics were rather loose and that Paul thought the Day of the Lord was soon to arrive.

With chapter 7 we enter upon the long list of questions about practical aspects of Christian life that has made 1 Corinthians famous. Paul first gives advice about Christian marriage: The single life is preferable to marriage, but marriage is quite legitimate. Husband and wife have mutual sexual rights, and divorce is not allowed. Christians married to non-Christians sanctify them. To Paul's mind, all people should remain in the state—single or married, circumcised or uncircumcised, as a slave or a free person—that they were in when they became believers. In view of the short time left before the Day of the Lord, all Christians have better things to preoccupy them than such worldly matters as changing their marital status. Widows and widowers should not remarry. Spiritual things should be uppermost in the minds of all.

Chapters 8–10 are a complicated response to a nest of problems concerning how the Corinthian Christians should deal with external, pagan society (and also how they should bridge social distinctions among themselves)[13]. First there is the matter, troubling to some, of whether it is licit to eat food that has been set aside for pagan gods ("idols"). Paul's position entails some nuance. Nothing in itself is unclean, so objectively there is no problem with eating such food. However, if some members of the community fear to do this, thinking it might ensnare them in pagan worship, the other members should respect the consciences of those who are afraid. The peace of the community is more important than exercising such an insignificant right as eating pagan meat.

This focus on prudence and considerateness seems to shunt Paul over to another matter of conscience. It had generally been admitted in the Church that missionaries or ministers had the right to be supported by the communities they were serving. But Paul did not avail himself of this right. In order to place no obstacles to the Corinthians' reception of the gospel, he supported himself. In fact he generally tried to make himself all things to all people, so that the gospel might thrive. The implication seems to be twofold: (1) The Corinthians should show one another a similar sensitivity, and (2) any charges that Paul has not been a whole-hearted, self-spending missionary are patently false.

Chapter 10 extends the theme of idols in another direction. Recalling the biblical story of the idolatry of the Israelites when they were with Moses wandering in the desert, Paul argues that those who partake of the body and blood of Christ (the Christian **eucharist**) should beware of similarly succumbing to idolatry. Christian faith, the peak of which is participating in the sacrament of table fellowship with Christ and one another, demands a severe break with idols, demons, and anything else competing with the one true God. The main point to the eucharistic reform that Paul demands, however, is the common good. Repeating himself, he drives home the point that what I am permitted to do (e.g., eat pagan meat) may not be what is best for me to do in view of the common good and the consciences of other people.

Chapter 11 turns the discussion to specifically Christian worship. Paul first reviews the dress and roles that have become customary for men and women. The key point to the convoluted discussion of the need for men to pray with their heads uncovered, and the complementary need for women to pray with their heads covered, seems to be the contemporary Jewish-Christian notions of what was seemly and what unseemly, in view of the worshipper's presence before God, Christ, and the angels. Verses 8–12 have had a significant part in both traditional and recent discussions of women's place in the Christian scheme of things. On the one hand Paul seems to express the assumptions of his patriarchal culture that woman was created for man. On the other hand, verses 11 and 12 suggest the equality of woman and man. The overall significance of this passage for today's issue of Christian women's liberation therefore is moot. Either one can read it as part of a tradition that subordinated women, or one can find in it seeds of women's strict equality in Christian dignity. As a result, the views that people bring to the passage often are the determining factor in their interpretations.

Next, Paul berates the Corinthians for their strife. At so holy a moment as the **Lord's Supper** (eucharist) they pull rank and humiliate one another. This violates the inmost meaning of Christian table fellowship, tainting one of the Church's holiest traditions. As Paul gives this tradition in one of the most important passages of 1 Corinthians:

> For I received from the Lord what I also delivered to you, that the Lord Jesus on the night when he was betrayed took bread, and when he had given thanks, he broke it, and said, "This is my body which is for you. Do this in remembrance of me." In the same way also the cup, after supper, saying, "This cup is the new covenant in my blood. Do this, as often as you drink it, in remembrance of me." For as often as you eat this bread and drink the cup, you proclaim the Lord's death until he comes. [11:23–26]

Since they are dealing with something of Christ's own institution, the holy way Christ wanted to remain with his followers as their bond, the Corinthians' careless and divisive behavior at the eucharist borders on sacrilege.

Chapter 12 is also famous and especially important, because here Paul discusses the different gifts or **charisms** of Church life. The Spirit gives some people the power to speak in tongues, others the power to prophesy, others the power to heal or work miracles. Similarly, wisdom and knowledge are gifts of the Spirit. The point is that all these gifts ought to build up the whole community. People with different gifts ought not to compete but to complement one another. The best gifts are those that help the whole local church. So, in chapter 13, Paul sings the praises of what to his mind is the very best Christian charism: love. Without love, any of the gifts is useless. With love, as chapter 14 suggests, other gifts such as prophecy become very helpful. (Prophecy is better than speaking in tongues because prophecy helps all the church members, while speaking in a strange tongue only helps the individual speaker.)[14]

Chapter 15 moves to a final matter the Corinthians have been agitating: the resurrection. The resurrection of Christ was front and center in the gospel Paul preached to them. How, then, can some claim there is no resurrection? Christ is but the first fruits of the resurrecting power of God that will raise all who die in faith. As the sin of Adam made all mortal, so the resurrection of Christ can give all eternal life. Paul then struggles to imagine what the resurrected body will look like, but he confesses that this is mysterious. He has no doubt, though, that those united to Christ in faith come to share in Christ's immortality. The resurrection of Jesus was the radical conquest of death: "When the perishable puts on the imperishable, and the mortal puts on immortality, then shall come to pass the saying that is written: 'Death is swallowed up in victory.' 'O death, where is thy victory?' 'O death, where is thy sting'" (15:54–55). 1 Corinthians 15 stands out as the most extensive New Testament treatment of the Christian afterlife. Indeed, it is the fullest scriptural basis for Christian hopes that God will take the whole faithful personality up into the divine sphere of deathlessness. Because of Christ's Easter experience, Paul fashions something remarkable in the history of religious ideas. To be sure, he uses previous biblical notions, and the centuries immediately preceding Jesus had seen the rise of the notion of resurrection as a solution to the problem of how God will redress the evils that the just have suffered for their faith. But it is Paul's reflections on the resurrection of Jesus that introduce the full force that resurrection has come to have in Western religious history.

Nothing quite like this notion developed in Eastern religions, nor did the Greek notion of the immortality of the soul connote what Paul has in mind. Indian thought, for example, focused on the imperishability of the **atman** or spiritual self, while Greek thought spoke of an immaterial soul that could survive the destruction of the body. Paul's notion is more holistic. Salvation, as the resurrection of Christ shows its full term, is God's healing embrace of the whole human entity, matter and spirit, body and soul. These may not be divided, and when the divine fullness of life comes to a creature it takes the whole personality out of death's downward gravity, up into the heavenly light. The Corinthians err in thinking that baptism has completed their rise into a share in Christ's relationship with God. The resurrection of Christ says there will be considerably more.

To conclude, Paul gives some directives concerning monetary contributions that he is collecting for the church at Jerusalem. Then he tells the Corinthians about his hopes to visit them after passing through Macedonia and mentions various individuals who may visit them or whose importance at Corinth deserves mention. At the end he utters the famous early Christian outcry of longing for the Day of the Lord: "Our Lord, come!"

Why Was This Written?

1 Corinthians was written because Paul had received troubling reports about his religious offspring at Corinth and wanted to get their

faith back on the right track. It was not, as had been the case with the Galatians, that the Corinthians were in danger of taking up the Jewish covenant Law. Instead, they were tearing their community apart with petty conflicts, becoming morally lax, and generally not appreciating the deeper realities of the life of faith they had embraced. Where they ought to have been growing more mature in faith, they were becoming superficial, arrogant, and vain. Where they ought to have been deepening their appreciation of being members of one another, parts of one whole organic union with Christ, they were riding roughshod over one another's consciences, bickering about their different spiritual gifts, and letting the eucharistic assembly get so far out of hand that it was scandalous. The wisdom of God, the inspiration of Christ's Spirit, that ought to have been riveting them to the cross of Christ was proving too deep for them. They were botching such basic matters as love and faith, sexual purity, and attention to the coming Day of the Lord. They were developing some attitudes that later became a full-blown problem in **Gnosticism.** Even so central a notion as the resurrection, the keystone of Paul's preaching about Christ, the centerpiece of the Christian understanding of God's victory over sin and death, had eluded them (probably because Greek culture tended to think that only the immaterial part of a human being could be immortal). Paul wrote as a parent sick at heart, a teacher close to despair. His children and students were missing the whole point and were on the verge of ruining the holy church he had founded.

What Background Does This Text Presuppose?

We have already explained some general aspects of Paul's thought that are necessary to understand 1 Corinthians. For example, without an appreciation of the Day of the Lord, or the centrality of the death and resurrection of Jesus, neither Paul's views of marriage nor his discussion of wisdom will make sense. However, 1 Corinthians brings several other Pauline convictions to the fore. For instance, there is the dynamic power Paul attributes to the Spirit of Christ. One must have the Spirit of Christ (God in the aspect of inspiring faith, hope, and love) to grasp anything of the mystery of salvation, the paradoxical way the God of Israel chose to free believers from sin and death. It is the Spirit of Christ who moves in the different charisms of the local church, making it plain that they should knit together into something orderly, edifying, and helpful to the common weal.

Relatedly, for Paul the Spirit of Christ makes the individual Christian a holy temple. That is why sexual immorality, or any other abuse of the body, is so wrong. That is why getting involved with pagan idols, and being insensitive to other Christians' consciences, shows a grievous lack of understanding: Only the Spirit should rule the Christian's heart, the Christian's self. The eucharistic gatherings of the Corinthians that degenerate into strife abuse the Spirit as well as the Lord's own tradition and gift. The denial of the resurrection shows Paul that many do not appreciate the power of God and perhaps do not really believe the good news of Christ's victory. Unless we can imagine how vivid Christian life was for Paul, how realistically he regarded the Spirit's work to sanctify individuals and knit the whole Church into the risen Christ, we cannot appreciate why he is upset with the Corinthians. To his strong Jewish tradition of a living divine Spirit Paul had joined his own experience of the living, suffering Christ. Thus he saw the deficiencies of the Corinthians as slashes at a beautiful Body, wounds to a presence of Christ as real as the sunrise outside his window or the food on his table.

What Lasting Significance Does This Have?

Perhaps the greatest lasting significance of 1 Corinthians is the Spiritualism we have been stressing. 1 Corinthians shows beyond a doubt that early Christianity was a thoroughly charismatic or **pneumatic** religion. Not doctrines but experiences of God were the moving force in the early Church. More broadly, these Pauline reflections on wisdom and the Spirit place high on the agenda of any serious discussion of human nature the dimension of interiority or depth, where many religious **seers** have claimed to find the human spirit intersecting with the divine. This claim came out of the experiences of the Hebrew prophets, and out of the experiences of the classical Greek philosophers as well.[15] It came out of the Hindu experience of the union of atman and Brahman, out of the Chinese Taoist experience of soaring in the Way.[16] The cautions that Paul puts forward about such **enthusiasm** have become classical axioms in Christian spiritual direction. After reading 1 Corinthians, it is hard not to want reason to remain very important, emotion to remain carefully controlled. On the other hand, after reading 1 Corinthians it is also hard not to want a view of human nature, an understanding of religion, that is **ecstatic**, taking us out of our workaday ruts and showing us something of God's dazzling beauty and power.

2 CORINTHIANS

What Have We Here?

2 Corinthians is a passionate letter, somewhat in the style of Galatians. Evidently there had been misunderstandings between Paul and the Corinthians subsequent to 1 Corinthians. These had been patched up, but Paul still feels obliged to defend himself and his ministry. Changes in mood and logic suggest that either Paul composed the letter in several sittings or parts of what we now have were interpolated by other hands.[17] Once again, however, we have a letter that shows us the strong personal emotions and bonds that characterized the early Christian communities. Even when Paul is angry or sarcastic, no one can doubt his concern for the people to whom he writes.

In outline we may distinguish six main parts of 2 Corinthians.[18]

Introduction 1:1–11
Paul's Past Plans for Corinth 1:12–2:13
Paul's Mission and Ministry 2:14–7:4
Paul's Future Plans for Corinth 7:5–9:15
Threats to the Future 10:1–13:10
Conclusion 13:11–13

The Introduction to 2 Corinthians has the usual wishes for grace and peace, and an unusual reference to Paul's sufferings. The afflictions he undergoes in his work unite him to the sufferings of Christ, and the Corinthians too are bound up with his trials.

In reviewing what he had in mind when he came as a missionary to Corinth, Paul makes the boast that from the outset his conduct was irreproachable: holy and godly. (This leads us to suspect that some enemies had been criticizing his motives, doctrine, or personal bearing.) He has always wanted to return to Corinth (perhaps the enemies were questioning the sincerity of his ties). He has always shown himself toward the Corinthians the way God has in Christ shown himself toward us: utterly affirmative, completely a "yes!" The actual reason Paul did not visit in the recent past was to spare the Corinthians the pain of his rebukes. But let past things be past. The painful disagreement between Paul and his religious children has hurt everyone. It is time to forgive those who caused the pain and reaffirm the bonds of love.

The long section from chapter 2 to chapter 7 deals mainly with the Christian ministry. This has been moving along like a triumphal procession. Yet Paul rejects the charge that such a positive view of his own and others' **evangelization** is boasting. God is the one who brings about good effects such as the faith of the Corinthians. The Spirit is the one who gives life to any good work or faith. The Spirit, in fact, presides over a whole new dispensation. To Paul's mind, this new dispensation or state of affairs is more splendid, free, and glorious than the dispensation God gave under Moses (the covenant bond with Israel). Since Paul's ministry serves this glorious new dispensation, this powerful reality of the freeing Spirit, he can try to carry it out confidently, hopefully, with entirely upright means. Indeed, his ministry is quite simple; he need only preach the lordship (resurrection) of Christ: "For what we preach is not ourselves, but Jesus Christ as Lord, with ourselves as your servants for Jesus' sake. For it is the God who said, Let light shine out of darkness,' who has shone in our hearts to give the light of the knowledge of the glory of God in the face of Christ" (4:5–6).

In referring to light shining from darkness, Paul calls to mind the account of creation in Genesis (1:3). Christ is like a new creation. The Spirit is, as it were, again moving over the waters. The wealth of what shines forth from the face of Christ leads Paul to a cluster of Greek terms: *photismon tes gnoseos tes doxes tou Theou* (the radiancy of the knowledge of the glory of God). Still, this richness does not take away the minister's frailty. It is a treasure housed in an earthen vessel. But the glory to come (at the Day of the Lord or in the resurrection) gives Paul courage to persevere. Although present life is like living in a tent, future, fulfilled life will be like living in a heavenly dwelling. Either way, whether in earthly toil or heavenly fulfillment, the important thing is to please Christ. Either way, the love of Christ is the key. In the love of Christ, the new creation stands clear. For in Christ God reconciled himself to the whole world. Christ the sinless became sin so that people like themselves might know God's righteousness. The Corinthians must not let this grace slip away. Paul has done everything he could, suffered everything he had to, for their sake. Let them therefore stay away from wicked and idolatrous people. Let them act like what they are: the temple of God. Let them, finally, admit that Paul has not wronged them and reopen their hearts to him.

In fact, the Corinthians' repentance, their grief over their past bad behavior, has heartened Paul. The good things he told **Titus** about them have been proven true. This leads Paul to ask the Corinthians to imitate the Macedonians in contributing generously to the collection that Titus is taking up for the church in Jerusalem. Their generosity will please Paul, who has boasted about their goodness. It will please God, who loves a generous response. And it will show the mother church at Jerusalem how greatly the Corinthians appreciate Christian unity and sharing.

With chapter 10 we get an abrupt change of topic and mood. Paul is testy, defending himself, his appearance, and his power. Apparently some people have been belittling his accomplishments. So he speaks up for his status and gospel. He has a solid commission from God, and he never burdened the Corinthians with his financial support. Indeed, if it is a matter of comparing religious pedigrees and spiritual accomplishments (with his accusers), he has all sorts of impressive things to trot out: a Jewish lineage, great sufferings for Christ, high mystical revelations. Yet this is a foolish way to talk. It is rather his weakness he should exhibit, since his weakness most shows the power of Christ.

All this attack on his reputation clearly has upset Paul and made him wonder what he will find in Corinth on his next visit. He would like to come and be pleased with the Corinthians, but perhaps he and they will find one another wanting. So Paul exhorts the Corinthians to mend their ways, lest he have to show them the Christ's (chastising) power: "He is not weak in dealing with you, but is powerful in you. For he was crucified in weakness, but lives by the power of God. For we are weak in him, but in dealing with you we shall live with him by the power of God" (13:3–4).

In concluding, Paul again asks the Corinthians to mend their ways. If they will get along with one another and live in peace, the God of love and peace will be with them. The closing mood is warm: "Greet one another with a holy kiss. All the saints greet you" (13:12–13). The signoff is a blessing rich in **Trinitarian** overtones: "The grace of the Lord Jesus Christ and the love of God and the fellowship of the Holy Spirit be with you all" (13:14).

Why Was This Written?

Clearly 2 Corinthians was written because relations had deteriorated between Paul and the church he had founded in Corinth. Probably much of the cause was the influence of other missionaries (perhaps with credentials from the church in Jerusalem) who had attacked Paul. C. K. Barrett has suggested, in fact, that these troublemakers

> were representatives of the church of Jerusalem, charged with the task of bringing into connection (perhaps even, into obedience) to Jerusalem the churches that were springing up in the Gentile world. In this sense at least they were Judaizers; whether, like the Judaizers of Galatia, they demanded circumcision as well as a general respect for the law we cannot be sure; probably, since Paul does not mention the matter, they did not. It is more likely that they took their stand on some such summary of the law as the so-called Decree of Acts xv.20, 29, or possibly on the Noachian precepts. They did not accept Paul's apostolic status; he carried no letter of recommendation, and his Gospel of justification by faith only apart from works of the law was suspect. Perhaps not at first, but probably later, they described him as a false apostle (his own use of this term, in xi. 13, would then be a counterblast), lacking in qualification and authority. In contrast with him, they left the authority they claimed in no doubt and behaved in an aggressive and authoritarian manner.[19]

Thus 2 Corinthians is an **apologia** of Paul for his mission, a self-defense that he hoped would reestablish good relations between him and the Corinthians.

What Background Does This Text Presuppose?

Certainly 2 Corinthians presupposes a general knowledge of the tension in the early Church between the liberal wing that downplayed the importance of the covenant Law and the conservative wing that felt the Law was still important. It also helps if the reader is used to Paul's **dialectical** or back-and-forth way of dealing with concepts such as "weakness" and "power." The sense of identification with Christ, living one's life "in Christ," that we have seen before is important in 2 Corinthians. The theme of the community being a holy site, a temple of God, becomes more pronounced. However, here Paul also develops a new figure for the superiority of the role of Christ's Spirit to the old covenant: the unveiled glory shining from the face of Christ. Nonetheless, this figure presupposes the old ties to God established through Moses. Most of the other background matters are available if one grants the reasonableness of spending life as Paul had chosen: voyaging, suffering, laboring as a preacher of Christ.

What Lasting Significance Does This Have?

Strangely enough, the most significant feature of 2 Corinthians may be the unattractive aspects of Paul's personality that it highlights. All Paul's boasting, self-defense, complaining, sarcasm, and threatening makes the reader face squarely the theme of human weakness (Paul's own figure of "earthen vessels"). One of the greatest of the Christian apostles clearly was a quite flawed human being. All his gifts and graces did not remove his sensitivity to his own status, his irritability. Along with its unattractive portrait of a contentious, bickering early Church, this portrait of Paul in 2 Corinthians argues for a solid humility on the part of Christians, or any other people, who would presume to lecture the world. The best religious figures (for example, Jesus), have tended to point away from themselves, stressing not their personal concerns but the ultimate or divine mystery at the beginning, foundation, and end of the world. That has been a large part of their godliness. On the other hand, biblical religion finally accepts human weakness. Human folly, both the Hebrew Bible and the New Testament say, is not a sufficient reason to reject God or a good creation. 2 Corinthians is an effective if somewhat negative stimulus to meditate on the comedy of silly human beings trying (being called by God!) to deal with holy, heavenly powers and wisdoms.

PHILIPPIANS

What Have We Here?

Philippians is another letter that New Testament scholars tend to agree probably was written by Paul himself to a church that he had personally founded. Philippi was a prominent town of the Roman province of Macedonia, lying east of Mount Pangaeus on the Via Egnatia. Around 50 c.e. Paul had founded a church there. According to Acts 16:16–24 Paul and Silas had made a dramatic impression in Philippi by **exorcising** a slave girl. This upset the girl's masters, who feared they would lose their source of income. So Paul and Silas were arrested, flogged, and imprisoned. They escaped in the confusion of an earthquake, but Paul gained an apology for the way they had been treated by appealing to his rights as a Roman citizen.

The Philippian Christians had a history of generously sending Paul money, and the occasion for Paul's writing this warm letter to them is his receipt of a recent gift. He is in prison (probably in Ephesus, although some scholars think in Caesarea or in Rome), and he wants both to thank the Philippians for their most recent gift and to send back to them Epaphroditus. Epaphroditus had brought the money gift and then become ill, causing the Philippians some concern. Also, Paul has heard that Judaizers have come into the area of Philippi so he wants to warn the Philippian Christians against those mischief makers. A likely date for Philippians is 56 c.e., perhaps just before 2 Corinthians.

We may outline Philippians in five parts:

Introduction 1:1–11

News and Instructions 1:12–3:1

Paul Himself as an Example of Faith 3:2–4:9

Paul's Gratitude for the Philippians' Gift 4:10–20

Conclusion 4:21–23[20]

The Introduction is especially warm and interesting. Paul allies himself with Timothy, and he directs this letter not only to the "saints" at Philippi but also to their "bishops" and "deacons" (an indication that some early churches had a rudimentary power structure or **hierarchy**). Paul constantly thanks God for the Philippians in his prayers, and he feels supported by them in his imprisonment. The ending of his Introduction is famous and beautiful: "And it is my prayer that your love may abound more and more, with knowledge and all discernment, so that you may approve what is excellent, and may be pure and blameless for the day of Christ, filled with the fruits of righteousness which come through Jesus Christ, to the glory and praise of God" (1:9–11).

As he starts to give the Philippians news of his current situation, Paul strikes an upbeat note. Actually his imprisonment has turned out to be a blessing, for he has been able to make the gospel known to the whole Praetorian Guard, and other missionaries have learned not to fear imprisonment (and so are preaching the gospel all the more boldly). Sad to say, though, there are rivalries among the preachers of Christ, and some seem to mock Paul's imprisonment. That doesn't finally matter, however. The only important thing is that, from whatever motive, Christ is proclaimed. Thus Paul finds grounds for rejoicing.

He also finds grounds for facing his imprisonment and possible execution peacefully. It doesn't matter whether he lives or dies, so long as Christ be honored. Therefore he hopes not to be shamed by his imprisonment and future fate, "but that with full courage now as always Christ will be honored in my body, whether by life or by death. For to me to live is Christ and to die is gain" (1:20–21). If he dies he gains closer union with Christ. If he lives he may continue to be helpful to people like the Philippians.

Indeed, Paul thinks gladly of coming to visit Philippi again, and he wants the Philippians to live uprightly so that if he can visit them he will find them standing firm in their faith. They should not let their opponents frighten them. They should consider their sufferings things they undergo for the sake of Christ. They will do this best if they share a common mind, keeping their community united in Christ. When Paul reflects on the common mind that he would have the Philippians maintain, he thinks of Christ's own mind. So, in what is probably the most famous passage of Philippians (perhaps quoting an early Christian hymn), Paul describes the "emptying" (**kenosis**) involved in Christ's coming to earth and dying on the cross:

> Have this mind among yourselves, which is yours in Christ Jesus, who, though he was in the form of God, did not count equality with God a thing to be grasped, but emptied himself, taking the form of a servant, being born in the likeness of men. And being found in human form he humbled himself and became obedient unto death, even death on a cross. Therefore God has highly exalted him and bestowed on him the name which is above every name, that at the name of Jesus every knee should bow, in heaven and on earth and under the earth, and every tongue confess that Jesus Christ is Lord, to the glory of God the Father. [2:5–11]

Remarkable in this passage are the seeds of the later Christian doctrine that Christ (as the Son or Word of God) existed in heaven before his earthly birth or **incarnation**. As always Christ's death on the cross strikes Paul in Jewish terms, as a thing of apparent disgrace (but real glory before God). The exaltation of Christ is his resurrection by the Father. This gives Christ the name (living symbol) that all creation praises—a suggestion that Christ's lordship is cosmic or ecological. The last image, of all tongues confessing Jesus, recalls the notion of the Hebrew Bible (for example, of the Psalms) that praising God is the highest human activity, the ultimate reason that creatures exist.[21]

Paul would have the Philippians take Christ's obedience (to the Father) to heart and themselves obey the requirements of good Christian living. He would have them work out their salvation "in fear and trembling"—a phrase the Danish existentialist Søren Kierkegaard used as the title of one of his most famous books.[22] They should not grumble but bear up under their troubles cheerfully. Paul hopes to send Timothy to them and to follow shortly after himself. He also has sent Epaphroditus, whose recovery from near death should give them great joy.

In chapter 3 Paul takes on his old enemies, the advocates of circumcision. A single sentence conveys his estimate of these people: "Look out for the dogs, look out for the evil-workers, look out for those who mutilate the

Crucifix. Sculpture, South Scandinavian. Romanesque, mid-twelfth century. The later tradition often used the Pauline and Johannine notions of exaltation to depict Christ as ruling from the cross.   *(Nelson Gallery–Atkins Museum, Kansas City, Mo. [Nelson Fund])*

flesh" (3:2). If he wished, Paul himself could boast of circumcision and rigorous adherence to the Law. Prior to his conversion he had been a zealous Pharisee (member of a strictly observant religious party). But he has thrown all this over for the incomparable value of Christ, who makes old, fleshly things insignificant. Now the only righteousness that Paul wants comes through faith in Christ: "that I may know him and the power of his resurrection, and may share his sufferings, becoming like him in his death, that if possible I may attain the resurrection from the dead" (3:10–11).

Not that Paul thinks he has completed his work or spiritual journey. No, he still presses on. The Philippians likewise should press on, imitating him. Not for them the ways of those who are "enemies of the cross of Christ," selfish people concerned with their own pleasures. They should keep their minds fixed on heaven, whence will come their Savior, the Lord Jesus Christ. Thus Euodia and Syntyche, who apparently have had some disagreement, should make up their quarrel. All the Philippians should rejoice in their faith and have no anxiety. If they place all their needs before God in prayer, "the peace of God, which passes all understanding, will keep your hearts and your minds in Christ Jesus" (4:7). In a lovely extension of this thought, Paul expresses how faith can make the Philippians free to enjoy the world. They need only focus on the good things of creation: "Finally, brethren, whatever is true, whatever is honorable, whatever is just, whatever is pure, whatever is lovely, whatever is gracious, if there is any excellence, if there is anything worthy of praise, think about these things" (4:8–9).

This seems to remind Paul again of the Philippians' generous gift, and he thanks them once more for the concern it expresses. He has learned to be content, whatever his circumstances, but he appreciates their kindness. Yet this most recent kindness is only in keeping with the special generosity they have always shown him. (Clearly they are one of his favorite churches.) As they have been so generous, he is sure that "my God will supply every need of yours according to his riches in glory in Christ Jesus. To our God and Father be glory for ever and ever. Amen" (4:19–20). In concluding Paul wants greetings given to each of the Philippian saints and wishes them the grace of the Lord Jesus Christ.

Why Was This Written?

We have indicated Paul's main reasons for writing to the Philippians. They were one of his most cherished churches and had always been generous to him. Their most recent gift and expression of concern had only rekindled his love for them. In addition, he wanted to assure them that he was enduring prison well, warn them against the proponents of circumcision, and lay before them more of the treasures of faith.

This last point bears reflection. It becomes clear as one reads through Paul's letters that thinking about the treasures of faith, probing once again the rich implications of the Christ-event, is one of Paul's chief delights. This was partly a matter of his zeal to preach the gospel and communicate its power. It was partly a matter of serving Christ his Lord. But it was also partly a matter of the pleasure that a keen mind and a warm heart took in reflecting on the poetry of faith, the beauty of God's saving love. Beyond all the practical reasons Paul had for writing his letters, all the instructions and advice he wanted to convey, lies the pure joy of proclaiming his faith, singing his praise of the God who had done such (nearly incredible) good things in Christ Jesus.

What Background Does This Text Presuppose?

This text perhaps presupposes the general situation in the Roman provinces, where troublemakers could expect to end up in prison. By and large the Romans granted their subject peoples considerable religious liberty, and the Jews had long had the privilege of worshiping and congregating according to their own singular religious customs. But the Romans always had the tendency to think that acknowledging the gods of the empire was an important civic duty and civil bond. And they also had the administrator's mentality that believes that any commotion is trouble. Thus commotion caused by non-Roman religious preachers or agitators was doubly suspicious. Still, Paul clearly had some freedom in prison to continue his work, and for a man detached from worldly comforts prison conditions probably were not especially difficult.

In terms of ideas, Philippians plays variations on the theme of identity with Christ, the idea of new life in Christ's Spirit, that we have seen before. When Paul says that for him to live is Christ and to die is gain he verges on the almost mystical identification he had made in Galatians 2:20: "It is no longer I who live, but Christ who lives in me; and the life I now live in the flesh I live by faith in the Son of God, who loved me and gave himself up for me." Until we sense how Paul had come to define his own deepest identity in terms of his bond to Christ, we will miss much of the passion that drives him. Christ finally is the great love of Paul's life, his grand romance.[23]

What Lasting Significance Does This Have?

The picture of the resurrection that Paul painted in 1 Corinthians 15 had considerable influence on how Christians, indeed all Westerners, thought about their lives, only ceasing to shape the general culture when "modernity" placed large brackets around the notion of an afterlife.[24] Equally, the picture of the Son's "emptying" that Paul paints in Philippians 2:5–11 contributed to the general Christian conviction that the Son or Word preexisted the world in "heaven" and condescended to become human out of love for humankind. This "humiliation" came to climax in the crucifixion, where Jesus' love of his Father and fellow human beings reached the extreme of an agonizing death. No doubt the **Passion narratives** of the synoptic Gospels, which tell the story of Jesus' suffering and death on the cross, were the main sources of influence, the most vivid shapers of the Western imagination. But in the background Paul (and John 1) suggested the notion that the one who suffered on the cross had enjoyed all the privileges of heaven—indeed, had been equal to God, co-godly. When it came time, in the **conciliar** debates of the fourth and fifth centuries, for the Church leaders to debate the question of whether Christ was strictly divine, such texts as Philippians 2:5–11 were used as a basis for the affirmative answer that became orthodox Christian faith. The one who was born of Mary, and who died on Calvary, was strictly divine, of the same substance as the Father.

This is a later Christian theology, of course, at most latent in the New Testament texts. But the Church fathers who proclaimed it thought they were making explicit and germane to their own times what had been in the mind (or faith) of a Paul or John. Paul is so preoccupied with his experience of Christ, the risen Jesus whom he calls his Lord (the one holding all his allegiance), that he does not focus very steadily on the preexistence motif. Still, he is quite willing to allude to Christ, like Adam, being in the form of God, along with the emptying theme, as an apt illustration of the mentality he wants to encourage in the Philippians. At the least, they should imitate Christ's version of being in the form of God, rather than Adam's version. At the least, they should be humble and not transgress their creaturely boundaries.

Apart from its importance to Christian faith, and so to Western culture, the notion of Christ's divinity has lasting significance for human reflection generally. It raises in acute form the ultimate question of what we mean by "divinity" and "humanity," terms we tend to toss about all too casually. In the view of the writers of the Hebrew Bible, there could be only one God. All the natural forces or gods and goddesses that the tribes surrounding Israel worshiped were false and dangerous. However, Israel experienced the one God, the sole maker of heaven and earth, as a partner to its time, a personal holiness who had made a compact with it. The one God was active, involved, concerned with what happened in space and time. How this could be, what part an utterly **transcendent** (beyond) divinity could have with earthly things, never was made clear. Perhaps it could not be made clear and was something strictly mysterious. Whatever the logic, Israel clung stubbornly to both ends of this faith: God was only one (sovereignly free), yet God was completely engaged with human events.

To say that Jesus was the Messiah, the anointed king whom Israel awaited (and pious Jews today still await) to usher in God's reign of justice, was hard enough. We have already seen that this claim divided Jews who accepted Jesus from Jews who felt they could not accept Jesus, eventually creating two separate religious groups. To say that Jesus was divine, somehow either identified with the One God or his unique manifestation, was worse than to claim he was the Messiah. To pious Jewish ears, it was blasphemous. Throughout the centuries, it has remained blasphemous (or incomprehensible) to both Jews and Muslims. Indeed, along with the Christian doctrine of the Trinity (God as Father-Son-Spirit) to which the doctrine of Jesus' divinity led, it has brought both Jews and Muslims to charge that Christians are not **monotheists**, that they violate the central claim of the Bible and the Qur'an. The biblical claim, made clear in such texts as Deuteronomy 6:4 ("Hear, O Israel: The Lord our God is one Lord"), and the Qur'anic claim, made clear in the core expression of Muslim faith ("There is no God but God"), have no place for an Incarnation. They cannot admit a divine Son existing in eternity and then condescending to enter into time and take a human form. Even less can they imagine such a God-man suffering on a cross, dying a criminal's death. (For that reason, the Qur'an [4:156–57] says that Jesus only seemed to die.) Many Greek and Indian philosophers have tended to agree: The divine is impassible (cannot suffer); it is a contradiction in terms to speak of the divine as taking on the limitations of a creature, feeling pain, or embracing death.

So the New Testament portrait of the Christ, especially when we view it as the stimulus to the fully developed Christian doctrine of God, can be very provocative. How does the source of the world relate to the world's sufferings and evils? What sort of a community life, set of relationships with creatures, stance toward death (and resurrection) should we picture life's mystery (the way the divine may appear to any person) as having? Is the divine or ultimate reality best symbolized by the lifeless wastes of outer space, the dancing destructiveness of the Hindu god Shiva, or the suffering love Paul saw revealed on the cross? The mind stretches, the heart probes, and neither ever knows for sure, at least on its own. The only ones who claim to know for sure are mystics like Paul who have experienced God—people whose lives have been changed by a personal **revelation**. The rest of us have to walk a fine line between openness and gullibility, skepticism and blindness.

PHILEMON

What Have We Here?

In the short letter of Paul to Philemon we have a brief but touching little glimpse into ancient Christian life. Some New Testament scholars think it probably was written about the same time (56 C.E.) and in the same circumstances (prison in Ephesus) as Philippians. (Other scholars believe it originated from Caesaria or Rome.) In outline it breaks down into four main parts:

Introduction and Greeting 1:1–3

Thanksgiving and Prayer 1:4–7

Request 1:8–21

Conclusion 1:22–25[25]

Paul and Timothy address themselves to Philemon, their beloved fellow worker. Paul describes himself as a prisoner for Christ and describes Timothy as his brother. Along with Philemon he addresses Apphia and Archippus, the one his sister in faith and the other his fellow soldier. He also addresses the "church in your house," reminding us that the early Christian "church" was not a building but the group that usually congregated in members' homes. Paul's wish for Philemon and the others is his standard: "Grace to you and peace from God our Father and the Lord Jesus Christ" (1:3).

In his Thanksgiving and Prayer, Paul praises Philemon's love and faith, asking that this love and faith forward the knowledge of the good things God has done in Christ. In other words, Paul prays for the progress of the gospel. Philemon's love has comforted Paul and refreshed the other saints.

Because of the bond they share, Paul feels bold enough to issue Philemon a command. However, he prefers to change his command into a request. He asks that Philemon accept back Onesimus, a slave of Philemon's who had run away. Onesimus had come to Paul in prison and Paul took him to heart like a son. Paul was minded to keep Onesimus with him in prison but prefers to send him back to Philemon and win Philemon's free consent. Since Onesimus has become a Christian, Paul hopes Philemon will now see in him not a slave but a beloved brother. Paul asks that Philemon receive Onesimus as he would receive Paul himself, charging any debt that Onesimus owes to Paul's account. Paul gave Philemon his very self (his new Christian identity), and he now asks recompense in the form of Philemon's discharging Onesimus' debt. Paul will take this favor as a support to his own faith. He has every confidence that Philemon will do as he asks.

In concluding Paul asks Philemon to prepare a guest room for him, since he hopes to make a visit soon. Epaphras, a fellow prisoner for Christ, and several of Paul's fellow workers (including a Luke) send their greetings. In signing off Paul wishes Philemon's spirit the grace of the Lord Jesus Christ.

Why Was This Written?

Philemon was written because a slave wanted to be reconciled to his master (and perhaps set free for Christian ministry). Alternatively it was written because Paul perceived Christian faith as resetting all social relationships. As the father of Philemon's faith, he could ask a favor like this. As a fellow Christian, Onesimus had become Philemon's brother. Paul has been won over by Onesimus and he asks Philemon to honor his affection. So we might say that Philemon was written because small, personal problems were not beyond the interest of the apostle to the Gentiles. His faith pertained to all aspects of daily life and left no social relationship unchanged.

What Background Does This Text Presuppose?

Philemon presupposes the institution of slavery. Onesimus was legally the property of Philemon, and his having run away constituted a theft. In terms of the civil law Onesimus was a criminal, and Paul risked the charge of abetting his desertion. Perhaps for this reason Paul is careful to show that he respects Philemon's rights (all the while, on the spiritual level, he is in effect dismissing those rights). By making the matter something personal between himself and Philemon, he places it on a completely new level. We therefore should remind ourselves of Paul's theme of the new creation. In Christ there is no Jew or Greek, male or female, slave or free (Galatians 3:28). There is, however, spiritual parenthood and spiritual childhood. There is the sort of debt offspring owe those who give them life. If Philemon really treasures his faith, his new life in Christ (what Paul calls "your own self"), he will be helpless but to honor Paul's request. Paul seems to have sufficient knowledge of Philemon's character to be sure that he will.

What Lasting Significance Does This Have?

The lasting significance of Philemon is the light it sheds on Christianity's relations to such historical phenomena as slavery, and the general questions it prompts about the relation between religious ideals and imperfect worldly realities. Paul may provide grounds for resetting the relationship between Philemon and Onesimus in terms of equality or brotherhood, but he does not attack the institution of slavery. In his (and Jesus') day, slavery was part of the landscape. Indeed, one could say that the Old Testament had sanctified slavery (see, for instance, Exodus 21). On the other hand, the teachings of Paul, Jesus, and other great religious figures have been one of the major forces that eventually led to the abolition of slavery (and other noxious institutions) in many parts of the world. At the time of the American Civil War Philemon could be cited in defense of holding black slaves, but in the long run this argument did not win the theological day.

The still broader question of how religious ideals relate to harsh worldly realities bedevils all cultures, Christian, Eastern, and contemporary American. Slavery, war, and crime mock Hindus and Buddhists, Jews and Muslims, Christians and humanists equally. Philemon obliquely points to a certain tolerance of evil, a certain limited, dangerous, but perhaps ultimately necessary acceptance of a human society bound to be imperfect.

ROMANS

What Have We Here?

In **Romans** we have Paul's most influential letter. Of the Epistles considered to have come from his own hand, Romans is the longest, the most mature, the most carefully wrought, and the most profound. Because it played such an important role in the thought of Martin Luther, and so in the Protestant Reformation, it has become practically synonymous with "evangelical" theology: Christian reflection that takes its stand on the New Testament as a document of justification by faith (and freedom from the Law). The mainstream scholarly opinion is that Paul wrote to the church at Rome from Corinth in the winter of 56–57 or early in 58.[26] In outline we may distinguish eight parts:

Prelude 1:1–17

God's Wrath 1:18–3:20

God's Righteousness 3:21–4:24

Righteousness and Conformity to Christ 5:1–8:39

God's Righteousness to Israel 9:1–11:36

The Shape of Righteousness 12:1–15:13

The Reason for this Letter 15:14–33

Appendix 16:1–27[27]

In the Prelude Paul describes himself as a servant and apostle of Jesus Christ, one set apart to serve the gospel. He then summarizes this gospel: It was promised by God through the (Israelite) prophets in the (Hebrew) scriptures; it concerns God's Son, "who was descended from David according to the flesh and designated Son of God in power according to the Spirit of holiness by his resurrection from the dead" (1:3–4). This same is Jesus Christ, Paul's Lord, through whom Paul received his apostolic commission. It is a commission to bring about "the obedience of faith for the sake of his name among all the nations, including yourselves who are called to belong to Jesus Christ" (1:5–6). From the outset, then, Paul's tone is authoritative and lofty. He is speaking as one peculiarly singled out by God, and he is speaking about the gospel of Christ that fulfills what God began centuries previously with Israel and the prophets. The fulfillment is the outreach of God's grace, through Jesus Christ, beyond Israel to all the nations (including the vast nation centered in Rome, the capital of Paul's world).

Paul offers the Romans his usual salutation of grace and peace. Then he notes the fame of the Roman church, whose faith is proclaimed in all the world, and assures it that he has long been praying for it and wanting to visit. If he could see the Romans he and they might encourage one another mutually. He has long wanted to visit them because they fall in his province, which includes all Gentiles, both Greeks and barbarians. He is not ashamed of the gospel he preaches to the Gentiles: "It is the power of God for salvation to everyone who has faith, to the Jew first and also to the Greek. For in it the righteousness of God is revealed through faith for faith; as it is written, 'He who through faith is righteous shall live'" (1:16–17). (This "righteousness" [or "justice"] of God [*dikaiosyne*] is a famous Pauline notion. According to the New Oxford Annotated Bible it is "a state of pardon, or acceptance with God, which is not man's achievement but God's gift, originating in God's own righteous nature."[28] According to Leander Keck, Paul's main point is achieving a right relationship to God.[29] Paul's quotation is from the prophet Habakkuk [Habakkuk 2:4]. Paul himself had expressed similar sentiments in Galatians 3:11 and Philippians 3:9.

Having struck a sort of overture to the main theme of righteousness that he will play out at length, Paul enters into a negative movement, meditating on God's wrath. This is the divine anger caused by human ungodliness and wickedness, which suppress the truth. In a very influential passage, Paul claims that ever since the creation of the world his invisible nature, namely, his eternal power and deity, has been clearly perceived in the things that have been made. So they are without excuse; for although they knew God they did not honor him as God or give thanks to him, but they became futile in their thinking and their senseless minds were darkened. Claiming to be wise, they became fools, and exchanged the glory of the immortal God for images resembling mortal man or birds or animals or reptiles. [1:20–23]

From Paul's perspective, the world obviously bespeaks a divine Creator. God has in creation shown all rational beings something of the divine nature, much the way an artist shows anyone who beholds her work something of herself. For Paul the things of the world tell of God's eternal power. No one can live in the world with a reflective, human consciousness and not know something about this power. The tendency of human beings to construct idols is a deflection or foolish neglect of this knowledge.

Similarly, the lusts and creature-worshiping revealed in pagan immorality stem from a failure to act upon a natural, in-given awareness of the divine Creator. Here we sense the imprint of Jewish monotheism on Paul, his deeply ingrained passion for God's oneness and purity. Pagan polytheism affronts him deeply. To his mind it, along with human vice, shows God's wrath, God's letting people go their own self-destructive way. Paul particularly singles out homosexuality (abhorrent to a Jew brought up on a central command to "be fruitful and multiply" [Genesis 1:28], and then lists a catalog of the evils that befall a humanity closed to God and denying God's creatorship: "Full of envy, murder, strife, deceit, malignity, they are gossips, slanderers, haters of God, insolent, haughty, boastful, inventors of evil, disobedient to parents, foolish, faithless, heartless, ruthless" (1:29–31). In Romans Paul uses no rose-tinted glasses. The problem of human evil rivets his gaze. There is more to be said about such complicated questions as homosexuality, of course, and the Paul who teaches that grace has abounded over sin must never be forgotten. But Romans 1 remains a sobering chapter.

Nonetheless, in these matters we judge others at our own peril. If we err like pagans we will be as subject as pagans to God's judgment. God's kindness is not an indulgence. It is meant to bring our repentance. On Judgment Day God will show no partiality. He will render all people honor or fury according to their works. Those who have lived under the covenant Law will be judged by that Law. Those who have lived outside the covenant Law will be judged outside it. Gentiles have an inner law of conscience to which they are bound. Jews who boast of the Law, thinking that knowing it makes them a guide to the blind, deceive themselves. It is only by following the Law that they can be justified. True Jewishness is something inward, a matter of the heart. It is not outward circumcision. An uncircumcised person who keeps the precepts of the Law is better off than a circumcised person who violates them. On the other hand, circumcision and the Law have had considerable value. To the Jews God gave his oracles (the Scriptures). It is not God's fault that these treasures have been neglected or that those who should have been faithful often were not.

However, there is a fundamental level at which Jews, despite having the Scriptures, are no better off than Gentiles. Both Jews and Gentiles remain under the fury of sin. Quoting from the Psalms (14, 53, 140, and 10), Paul proclaims: "None is righteous, no, not one; no one understands, no one seeks for God. All have turned aside . . ." (3:10–11). Whenever law provides a measure for human behavior, people are found wanting. Therefore Paul concludes: "For no human beings will be justified in his sight by works of the law, since through the law comes knowledge of sin" (3:20).

With Jesus, however, things have changed. (At least, Paul has had to expand his horizons and see that God is righteousness not as judgment but as grace.) God has made the divine righteousness manifest apart from the Law. Those who believe in Jesus Christ have access to this righteousness. Because all people have sinned and fallen short of God's glory, the righteousness of any person is a gift, a boon due only to the redemption worked by God in Christ's blood. Thus has God shown his forbearance and passed over human sins. Consequently, no human being can boast. No human works bring justification. The basis of any human success, Jewish or Gentile, is faith.

This, however, does not overthrow the Law but upholds it. (Throughout Romans, as the observant reader will already have noted, Paul is more positive toward the Law than he was in earlier letters, and he makes more careful distinctions.) Beginning with Abraham, the father (with Moses) of the dispensation that became focused through the Law, faith was the real issue. Abraham was considered righteous before he was circumcised, and David (the ideal king and reputed author of the Psalms) blessed the person whom God considers righteous apart from works. Abraham therefore is more the father of the faithful than the father of the circumcised. The promises made to Abraham depend far more on faith than on works of the Law. Paul sees these promises fulfilled in Jesus. "It [righteousness] will be reckoned to us who believe in him that raised from the dead Jesus our Lord, who was put to death for our trespasses and raised for our justification" (4:24–25).

In what we are calling the fourth part of Romans, Paul builds on this fulfillment in Christ. Through Christ Christians have the grace or favor of God and a hope of sharing in God's glory. Even in the midst of suffering this hope does not disappoint them, "because God's love has been poured into our hearts through the Holy Spirit which has been given to us" (5:5). Indeed, God showed the divine love most fully by having Christ die for us while we were sinners. It is his blood that will save us from God's wrath and give us reconciliation. Just as Adam fathered a race of sinners, so Christ is the head of a new race that is graced. Yet there is no equality between the two: "Where sin increased, grace abounded all the more, so that, as sin reigned in death, grace also might reign through righteousness to eternal life through Jesus Christ our Lord" (5:20–21). In later Christian theology, under the influence of Augustine's interpretation of Adam's sin and the reign of death, "original sin" became an important notion. Apart from faith in Christ, people were considered unrighteous and alienated from God. Indeed, they were considered born into sin.

This does not mean Christians should not struggle against sin. When they were baptized they were buried with Christ (died to sin). They should now live with Christ in grace. This means giving themselves over to God, no longer obeying the urgings of sin but obeying the promptings of grace. The old situation—living under a law that pointed out the rule of sin—is no more. It is as though the Christian has been widowed: The old obligations no longer hold. Not that the Law itself is sin. But the Law pointed out human sinfulness, as it were to show human beings their need of a new situation or solution. Portraying the struggle the legalistic way of dealing with sin had produced inside the person who wanted to be good, Paul concludes that only God through Jesus Christ can liberate such a one.[30]

This brings us to chapter 8, by many accounts the high point of Romans. Paul begins it by boldly announcing, "There is therefore now no condemnation for those who are in Christ Jesus. For the law of the Spirit of life in Christ Jesus has set me free from the law of sin and death" (8:1–2). In the flesh of Jesus, God condemned sin. Those who set their minds on the flesh are hostile to God. Those who have the Spirit of Christ belong to Christ. Christians are those who have the Spirit. And the Spirit will give them (resurrected) life, just as the Father gave Jesus resurrected life: "If the Spirit of him who raised Jesus from the dead dwells in you, he who raised Christ Jesus from the dead will give life to your mortal bodies also through his Spirit which dwells in you." (Note that here the Spirit is pictured as belonging to the Father.) This is the Spirit by which the Christian ought to live. It makes Christians children of God, people who cry out, "Abba! Father!" It places them with Christ as fellow heirs, children who also will be glorified.

Then Paul contemplates the way in which glory (participating in the splendor of God) will overbalance the sufferings of present days. Indeed, all creation groans for fulfillment, like a woman in labor. Believers await the redemption of their bodies, and while they wait the Spirit helps them in their weakness. Romans 8:26–27 is one of the most profound Christian depictions of the work of the Spirit: "Likewise the Spirit helps us in our weakness; for we do not know how to pray as we ought, but the Spirit himself intercedes for us with sighs too deep for words. And he who searches the hearts of men [the Father] knows what is the mind of the Spirit, because the Spirit intercedes for the saints according to the will of God." Moreover, it is Paul's faith that God works for good with those who love him, in everything that befalls them. For God has foreknown and predestined his children. Everything therefore is on the believer's side. If God is for us, who can be against us? Neither angels nor principalities (other supernatural beings) "nor anything else in all creation will be able to separate us from the love of God in Christ Jesus our Lord" (8:39). It is hard to find a more radically hopeful Christianity than that of Romans 8.

In chapters 9 through 11 Paul reflects on God's relations with Israel, on the history of the first phase of the divine righteousness. His first mood is sorrow that his fellow Jews have largely rejected the good news offered in Christ. Still, there is another way of looking at the promises made to Israel. Reflecting back over key moments in biblical history, Paul sees God as always having acted freely to choose whom he would. There are precedents, then, for the current situation, in which Gentiles have attained right-eousness outside the Law and Jews have missed righteousness inside the Law. The key is faith, not works. By the touchstone of faith, Christ has become a stumbling block, in line with the theme of the prophet Isaiah: "Behold, I am laying in Zion a stone that will make men stumble, a rock that will make them fall; and he who believes in him will not be put to shame" (Isaiah 28:16, 8:14–15).

It is not that many Jews are not zealous for God. It is that they have not seen that righteousness comes only from God (not human works) and that Christ is the end of the Law. In Paul's view, the confession of Christ, which is open to everyone regardless of ethnic origin, is the main formula of this righteousness: "If you confess with your lips that Jesus is Lord and believe in your heart that God raised him from the dead, you will be saved" (10:9). This means that preachers must make known the Jesus upon whom people can call and be saved. It also raises the question of why many Jews reject such preaching. Using a theme of Deuteronomy 32 and Isaiah 65, Paul speculates that in gifting the Gentiles God is trying to raise a holy jealousy among the Jews, in order to bring them around to Christ.

For Paul is convinced that God has not rejected Israel. At least he has kept a remnant, and he has providential plans for the rest. One part of this providential plan has been the opening of salvation to the Gentiles. Paul hopes that another part will be the Jews' acceptance of the gospel. Either way, Gentiles ought to be humble, acknowledging the simple truth that they owe their faith to Israel. For clearly, the Jews are the parent stock of the Christian tree. Paul believes that the current hardening of Israel is only temporary. When the full number of Gentiles has come in, all Israel will be saved (11:26). The gifts God has lavished upon Israel, the calls God has made, are irrevocable. Yet this is all a mighty mystery: "O the depth of the riches and wisdom and knowledge of God! How unsearchable are his judgments and how inscrutable are his ways!" (11:33). This passage counter-balances some of Paul's attacks on Judaism and suggests how Christians might regard Judaism very positively and see in it God's continuing providence.

Chapters 12 through 15 are somewhat more practical, dealing with the obedient living out of Christian righteousness.[31] Christians should think of themselves as a living sacrifice to God and so not live by worldly standards. They should be humble and realize that the Body of Christ (the Church) has many different members and gifts. They should try to be zealous and hospitable, even blessing those who persecute them. They should leave vengeance to God and treat their enemies well. In chapter 13 Paul urges obedience to the state authorities, seeing them as agents of God. So Christians should avoid getting into trouble with the law and should pay their taxes. By loving their neighbors Christians can fulfill all the commandments. Salvation (the Day of the Lord) is near so all should stand ready.

Brotherly and sisterly love means respecting other people's scruples about such things as diet and holy days. Christians should not pass judgment on one another but keep their eyes on the only important thing, their allegiance to Christ the Lord. Community peace is more important than diets or peculiar practices. The strong ought to bear with the weak. All ought to consider the example of Christ, who did not please himself but "became a servant to the circumcised to show God's truthfulness, in order to confirm the promises given to the patriarchs, and in order that the Gentiles might glorify God for his mercy" (15:8–9). In urging these practical or ethical standards, Paul shows what concrete behavior the lofty life of grace should produce.

Paul has written to the Romans out of his responsibility to be a minister of Christ Jesus to the Gentiles. He hopes to see them in person as he passes on to Spain, after going to Jerusalem with the collection for the Jerusalem church. He asks the prayers of the Romans for the success of this trip to Jerusalem.

Chapter 16, once considered an appendix, now is accepted as an integral part of Paul's letter.[32] It was written mainly to commend the deaconess Phoebe and convey Paul's greetings to some of the Roman Christians he personally knows. He would have the Romans cling to sound doctrine and avoid people who cause dissension. The ending is a glorification of God for the revelation of the long-held mystery of salvation.

Why Was This Written?

Unlike Paul's other letters, Romans was written to a community he had not himself founded, a church he did not personally know. Probably the main influence behind the founding of the Roman church had been the Jewish Christianity of the Jerusalem church led by Peter and James. Raymond E. Brown, for example, has argued that most of the records depict early Roman Christianity as more Jewish and moderate (on questions of the Law) than Paul's views.[33] In later times, when the Roman church had come to consider Paul one of its own heroes (because of his imprisonment and martyrdom there), Peter and Paul together served as founding apostles. At the time Paul wrote this letter, however, the Roman Christians probably had more reasons to be leery of him than to welcome his overtures wholeheartedly. Thus Paul went out of his way to explain his gospel in depth and length, rejecting the misinformation that his detractors had been spreading about him and trying to show the Roman church that his mission to the Gentiles deserved their support.

But why did Paul especially need this Roman support? Lucas Grollenberg, whose little books on Paul and Jesus explain the human side of these prime New Testament personalities exceedingly well, thinks Paul had gotten sick of battling with the Judaizers and wanted to strike out for completely virgin territory west of Rome (thus Paul's ambition to reach Spain). In that case Rome would become his base-church:

> Paul's preaching in the Gentile world sometimes led to the formation of a new community "in Christ," but no sooner had he left them than Jewish Christians came along to trouble the young believers, often deliberately acting against Paul. It was perhaps because of all this that he arrived at the remarkable and,

one might also say, contradictory plan which finally led to his death. He probably decided on it during the three months when he stayed in Corinth after being in Macedonia (probably in AD 56). Relationships with the Christians there had been improved by the letter which Titus and his companions had taken and perhaps also through other contacts. . . . He had made his plans: he wanted to take the gospel to the western part of the Roman empire, beginning in Spain. He wanted to work a long way away, among people who had not yet heard the name of Christ, and where Jewish sympathizers would not keep interfering. He would go there via Rome. The Christian community in Rome was to be the base for his new enterprise.[34]

Other commentators think that Paul wanted to enlist the prestige of the Roman church to bolster his standing with the Jerusalem church and make the collection he was gathering (to take to Jerusalem) more acceptable (and so more effective as a sign of Gentile-Jewish Christian unity). Acts 20 and following tell the story of how Paul's ambitions were thwarted: the visit to Jerusalem (to deliver the collection), the arrest, the imprisonment, and the shipping to Rome.

What Background Does This Text Presuppose?

Romans presupposes enough background in the Jewish thought of Paul's day to understand the main twists and turns of Paul's arguments. He is trying to refute the charges of those who think he has vilified the Jews and their covenant. Yet he is also trying to make sense of the huge reality shaping his own ministry: God has opened the covenant to the Gentiles. In his ruminations over this astonishing reality, Paul works with Jewish legal categories.

Here again we come up against a way of thinking which is alien to us. For us, legal terms are indeed impersonal. There is a body of law which all of us have to observe, including the judge who condemns infringements of it. Sometimes Paul thinks in the same way. But in addition (and occasionally at the same time), we find a different way of looking at the law which he has inherited from the Old Testament. In the Old Testament world, justice was administered by the king. He was not bound to an impersonal body of law, so that he could act "outside the law" and be influenced by his personal feelings towards his subjects. The best thing I can do here is to point to chapters 40–55 of the book of Isaiah. Here we can see the connection between the proclamation of the good news (the gospel) that God is going to demonstrate his justice and the way in which it is understood as salvation, as deliverance for his people. In this text, the good news is for the remnants of God's defeated people. The new element in Paul's gospel is that God means to give his righteousness, i.e. his salvation, his deliverance, to *all* men.[35]

In addition to this general view of law, Romans presupposes knowledge of such particular things as Jewish views of blood and sacrifice. So, for instance, the mention in Romans 3:25 of **expiation** (for sins) by Christ's blood probably called to readers' minds the description in Leviticus 16:15–16 of the ritual for the Day of Atonement (Yom Kippur):

Then he [Aaron, the priest] shall kill the goat of the sin offering which is for the people, and bring its blood within the veil, and so with the blood as he did with the blood of the bull, sprinkling it upon the mercy seat and before the mercy seat; thus he will make atonement for the holy place, because of the uncleanlinesses of the people of Israel, and because of their transgressions, all their sins.

Exodus 24 might be another text Paul had in mind. The point is that blood represented the life-force. In the transaction depicted in Leviticus 16 the people were acting out their contrition for their offenses against God and their conviction that God would forgive them. Paul transfers this sort of transaction to the death of Christ, in which he sees the action of God to remove all human beings' sinfulness and repair the alienation between all people (including, in principle, all the wicked people he has described in chapter 1) and the holy God.

What Lasting Significance Does This Have?

Romans will continue to be influential as long as Christians, or any people, meditate on the relations between human sinfulness and divine grace, the evils of the world and the forces of repair and new beginnings. It offers some very provocative reflections on the relations between outward observance and inner faith, human effort and divine grace. To the ears of most Christians, Paul's overall message sounds very liberating. It stresses the priority of inner dispositions (faith, love) over outer works, the priority of divine grace over human sinfulness. If "Adam," the **corporate personality** who stands for humankind in Genesis, was for Paul's readers a sorry figure, a symbol of humanity suffering because of its disobedience to God's will, Christ was a new corporate personality, a new collective real-symbol for the victory of God's grace. Had Christ only died, Paul might have been able to sing the praises of God's love, but he would not have been able to speak of a new creation, a completely fresh beginning. Because the Father had raised Jesus, Genesis was redone. A new Adam placed all human beings in a right relationship with God. Any person who identified with Christ and made the commitment of faith could share in this right relationship and be a child of God, an intimate of the divine Spirit.

In Christian terms, then, Romans is an eloquent statement of the power of God's grace: Nothing can separate the believer from God's love. In more general terms, it can seem a quite modern work, very psychological or sensitive to the confusion of human motivation, the turmoil of human attraction toward both the holy and the corrupt. We must be careful not to read too much modern psychology into Paul. On his own terms, he probably was not agonizing the way that Luther, or others who have found profound psychological drama in Romans, imagined. On the other hand, any text has a certain independence of its author. What later generations find in it, due to their own interests, has a certain legitimacy.[36] The more profound the text, the greater the diversity of things later generations of readers are likely to find. So Shakespeare has different overtones in the twentieth century than he had in the sixteenth. Romans could spark

Adam. Auguste Rodin. Both theologians and artists have taken Adam as the epitome of humanity—not just the first man but the one in whom the whole race subsisted. *(Nelson Gallery–Atkins Museum, Kansas City, Mo. [Nelson Fund])*

such different figures as Luther and the great twentieth-century Swiss theologian Karl Barth.

For the modern reader, Christian or non-Christian, Paul can present many problems. We shall deal with some of these (women's rights, homosexuality, Jewish-Christian relations) in the next chapter, when we make an overall estimate of Pauline thought. Here the best reflection might be a followup on what we have already said about law. Paul seems mesmerized by the place the covenant Law had in his formation as a Jew. Even when he thinks that Christ has meant the end of the Law, he continues to work in Jewish legal categories. He wants to say that Christ has put things between God and human beings on a completely new footing. But he lacks the new terminology he would need to spell out this new footing, so he has to make many of his points by negating the old, legalistic footing.

The heart of the Pauline conviction is that God raised Jesus from the dead. This means that the death of Jesus as a criminal on the cross was not the curse the covenant Law (at least in Paul's reading) thought it to be. Indeed, it means that God can do crucially important things apart from the Torah or covenant Law. He can bring about reconciliation. He can distribute the gifts of the divine Spirit (for example, to the Gentiles). And God chooses to do all of this by linking the Spirit to the death and resurrection of Christ.

Thus Ernst Käsemann, a leading New Testament scholar, has written of Paul's views of the Spirit:

The Pauline doctrine of the Spirit is constitutively shaped by the fact that the apostle, so far as we can see, is the first to relate it indissolubly to **christology** [the doctrine of Jesus' lordship]. In the Spirit the risen Lord manifests his presence and lordship on earth. Conversely, the absolute criterion of the divine Spirit is that he sets the community and its members in the discipleship of the Crucified, in the mutual service established thereby, and in the assault of grace on the world and the sphere of corporeality. The difference from enthusiasm [an uncritical reliance on spiritual ecstasy] is that the Spirit is to be tested in terms of christology, and christology is not set under the shadow of **ecclesiology** [the doctrine of the Church]. In this way the history of primitive Christianity enters a new phase.[37]

As we emphasized in dealing with Romans 8, this letter has some of the most profound Christian reflections on the way the Spirit moves in the believer's heart and shapes the believer's prayer. As the famous fourth- to fifth-century Christian church father Augustine put it, the Pauline spirit is "more intimate to me than I am to myself." Apart from Christian assumptions, Romans asks any readers to think about the prime experiences of their lives. What have been the peak moments, when things fell into place, when one could say in utter fervor that it is good to be alive? What, by contrast, have been the times of desolation, when anything like a supportive Spirit seemed lacking?

In the tracks of Paul Christian ascetics and mystics have developed a rich storehouse of wisdom about these different sorts of experiences. Under the name of "the discernment of spirits," they have spoken about life in the grasp, even the amorous embrace of God, in contrast to life bereft of God. Life (apparently) bereft of God, for these post-Pauline Christian writers, has reached such low points as the dark night of the soul. Life in the amorous embrace of God has been more fulfilling than anything they ever expected. The widespread presence of these two sorts of experiences outside organized Christianity (for example, among Sufi Muslims, Hasidic Jews, and Hindu saints) raises the question of whether the Spirit isn't active even more broadly than Paul suspected, making people cry "Abba! Father!" even when they don't know the name of Jesus and cannot explicitly call upon the Christ.

SUMMARY

We have considered seven letters most likely written by the apostle Paul himself: 1 Thessalonians, Galatians, 1 and 2 Corinthians, Philippians, Philemon, and Romans. They all probably fall in the seven-year period 51–58 C.E. Although we cannot be sure in several cases where the letters originated, Ephesus and Corinth probably accounted for most.

1 Thessalonians, the earliest Pauline letter and writing of our current New Testament, is remarkable for its full expression of thanksgiving to God for both the Thessalonians' faith and Paul's own perseverance. Against the horizon of the soon-coming Day of the Lord, Paul urges his religious children to live upright, diligent lives.

Galatians is heavier, more choleric fare. The work of Paul's enemies, who are trying to undermine the freedom he offers the Gentiles and make the Gentiles come under the covenant Law, has upset Paul terribly. So he lashes out at those who disparage his apostolic authority and repeats even more vigorously his view that the death of Christ was the end of the Law. Galatians is our fiercest glimpse of Pauline freedom.

1 and 2 Corinthians give us invaluable insights into the church life of one of Paul's most important early communities. The very troubles Paul had with this church became the occasion for a fascinating correspondence. 1 Corinthians is an effort to bring down to earth those who have become overly impressed by their spiritual gifts. What most matters is the good of the whole Church, the coordination of all the members of Christ's Body. Practical questions about meat offered to idols, whether betrothed should marry, how women ought to comport themselves in church, and the like give us the sense that Paul is still awaiting the Day of the Lord. Chapters 12 and 13 show the tensions the early Christians' diverse spiritual gifts raised, while chapter 15 is a colorful account of the early Christian insistence on the resurrection. 2 Corinthians is another passionate letter, like Galatians, in which Paul defends his apostolic authority and view of the gospel. Against the Judaizers, Paul insists that the Gentile converts are free of the law.

Philippians is a warm, deep letter, written to Paul's favorite, most generous church. Paul writes from prison, but tells his friends not to lament his circumstances. Chapter 2 includes a profound hymn that suggests the preexistence of Christ and shows the utter abasement God's love was willing to endure. The Philippians' monetary gifts serve Paul as a symbol for all the churches' mutual concern.

Philemon shows something of the personal relations that wove the early Christian communities together. It also shows how Christians both did and did not change the social institutions, such as slavery, that they inherited.

Romans is Paul's greatest letter, carefully written to the great church he hoped would sponsor his western mission. In Romans we find such important Pauline themes as the wrath of God, the old and new Adam, the inner gift of the Spirit, the function of the law in revealing sin, the continuing role of Israel and the old covenant, and the relation of Christians to civil authorities. It is prime evidence for both Paul's mature understanding of the Law and his overwhelming conviction that Christ is a new creation.

STUDY QUESTIONS

1. What are the four main sections of 1 Thessalonians?
2. What is the significance of the Day of the Lord?
3. What are the five main sections of Galatians?
4. What is the relation between faith and circumcision?
5. In what sort of a surrounding society did the Corinthian Christians live?

6. What is the relation of 1 Corinthians 13 to 1 Corinthians 12?

7. How is the light shining from the face of Christ (2 Corinthians 4:5–6) a new creation?

8. What were the bonds between Paul and the Philippians?

9. What is the significance of the Philippian *kenosis*?

10. How is Philemon a window into the social world of early Christianity?

11. Evaluate Paul's argument in Romans 1:20 that creation reveals the Creator.

12. How does the Spirit function in Christian salvation?

13. What does Romans 9–11 suggest about the permanent relations between Christians and Jews?

14. Give a balanced view of Paul's appreciation of Torah (covenant Law).

NOTES

1. On ancient letter writing, see John L. White, ed., *Studies in Ancient Letter Writing*, Semeia 22 (Chico, Calif.: Scholars Press, 1981); William G. Doty, *Letters in Primitive Christianity* (Philadelphia: Fortress, 1973).

2. See Ivan Havener, *Collegeville Bible Commentary* 8 (Collegeville, Minn.: Liturgical Press, 1983), pp. 10 ff.

3. See Xavier Leon-Dufour, *Dictionary of the New Testament* (San Francisco: Harper & Row, 1980), p. 180.

4. Wayne Meeks, *The First Urban Christians* (New Haven: Yale University Press, 1983), p. 42. For general background, see Barbara M. Levick, *Roman Colonies in Southern Asia Minor* (Oxford: Clarendon Press, 1967). For maps see Herbert G. May, ed., *Oxford Bible Atlas*, 2nd ed. (New York: Oxford University Press, 1974).

5. M. J. Mellink, "Galatia," *The Interpreter's Dictionary of the Bible* (Nashville: Abingdon, 1962), vol. 2, p. 336.

6. See John J. Pilch, *Collegeville Bible Commentary* 6 (Collegeville, Minn.: Liturgical Press, 1983), p. 6.

7. See Hans Dieter Betz, *Galatians* (Philadelphia: Fortress, 1979).

8. For a good evangelical treatment, see F. F. Bruce, *The Epistle to the Galatians* (Grand Rapids, Mich.: Eerdmans, 1982).

9. Herbert Fingarette, *Confucius: The Secular as Sacred* (New York: Harper Torchbooks, 1972).

10. See Robert Jewett, *A Chronology of Paul's Life* (Philadelphia: Fortress, 1979), p. 161.

11. See Christine Downing, *The Goddess* (New York: Crossroad, 1981), p. 206.

12. See Hans Conzelmann, *I Corinthians* (Philadelphia: Fortress, 1975), pp. vii–viii.

13. See Gerd Theissen, *The Social Setting of Pauline Christianity: Essays on Corinth* (Philadelphia: Fortress, 1982).

14. See David Aune, *Prophecy in Early Christianity and the Ancient Mediterranean World* (Grand Rapids, Mich.: Eerdmans, 1983).

15. See Eric Voegelin, *Order and History*, vol. 4 (Baton Rouge: Louisiana State University Press, 1974), pp. 239 ff.

16. See Denise Lardner Carmody and John Tully Carmody, *Eastern Ways to the Center* (Belmont, Calif.: Wadsworth, 1983), pp. 54–58, 149–55.

17. See Dieter Georgi, "Corinthians, Second," *The Interpreter's Dictionary of the Bible, Supplementary Volume* (Nashville: Abingdon, 1976), pp. 183–86.

18. See C. K. Barrett, *A Commentary on the Second Epistle to the Corinthians* (New York: Harper & Row, 1973), pp. 51–52.

19. Ibid., pp. 6–7. For the precepts given to Noah see Genesis 9:1–7. Note the prohibition against eating foods with blood. The "Judaizers" or early Christians who wanted to keep some of the covenant Laws asked that the Gentiles obey this precept. See Acts 15:29.

20. See Joseph A. Fitzmyer, "The Letter to the Philippians," *The Jerome Biblical Commentary*, ed. Raymond E. Brown and others (Englewood Cliffs, N.J.: Prentice-Hall, 1968), vol. 2, p. 248.

21. See Claus Westermann, *The Psalms* (Minneapolis: Augsburg, 1980).

22. See Søren Kierkegaard, *Fear and Trembling* (Princeton, N.J.: Princeton University Press, 1941).

23. For a stunning interpretation of Christian faith in terms of romantic love, see Rosemary Haughton, *The Passionate God* (New York: Paulist, 1981).

24. See Hans Küng, *Eternal Life?* (Garden City, N.Y.: Doubleday, 1984).

25. See Ivan Havener, *Collegeville Bible Commentary* 8, pp. 46–50.

26. See Robert Jewett, *A Chronology of Paul's Life*, p. 161; John J. Pilch, *Collegeville Bible Commentary* 6, p. 28.

27. See Ray A. Harrisville, *Romans* (Minneapolis: Augsburg, 1980), pp. 3–5.

28. *The New Oxford Annotated Bible*, Revised Standard Version, ed. Herbert G. May and Bruce M. Metzger (New York: Oxford University Press, 1977), p. 1362.

29. See Leander E. Keck, *Paul and His Letters* (Philadelphia: Fortress, 1979), pp. 118–23.

30. See Krister Stendahl, "The Apostle Paul and the Introspective Conscience of the West," in his *Paul among Jews and Gentiles* (Philadelphia: Fortress, 1976), pp. 78–96.

31. See Paul Minear, *The Obedience of Faith* (London: SCM Press, 1971).

32. See Harry Gamble, Jr., *The Textual History of the Letter to the Romans* (Grand Rapids, Mich.: Eerdmans, 1977).

33. See Raymond E. Brown and John P. Meier, *Antioch and Rome* (Ramsey, N.J.: Paulist, 1983).

34. Lucas Grollenberg, *Paul* (Philadelphia: Westminster, 1978), pp. 155–56. See also his *Jesus* (Philadelphia: Westminster, 1978).

35. Grollenberg, *Paul*, p. 160.

36. See Paul Ricoeur, *Essays on Biblical Interpretation* (Philadelphia: Fortress, 1980). .

37. Ernst Käsemann, *Commentary on Romans* (Grand Rapids, Mich.: Eerdmans, 1980), p. 213.

4

The Letters of Paul's Followers

2 THESSALONIANS

What Have We Here?

2 Thessalonians is a letter that has caused considerable controversy among New Testament scholars. Presently the majority opinion seems to be that it was not written by Paul himself. Gerhard Krodel recently has summarized the main arguments for this opinion.[1] First, there is the fact that the eschatological argument of 2 Thessalonians 2:1–10 points the reader in a direction opposite to the argument found in 1 Thessalonians 4:13–5:11. Whereas in 1 Thessalonians the author spoke of the Day of the Lord as imminent, in 2 Thessalonians the author lists various things that must occur before the Day of the Lord arrives, implying that it is not imminent.

Second, there are literary discrepancies. In terms of structure, verbal parallels, style, and concrete personal data, 2 Thessalonians suggests a hand different from that which drafted 1 Thessalonians. Third, there are theological differences. For example, the phrase "Beloved of God" of 1 Thessalonians 1:4 is replaced by the phrase "beloved by the Lord" in 2 Thessalonians 2:13. 2 Thessalonians lacks the stress on joy that characterizes most Pauline writings, and it lays little stress on the central Pauline symbol of Christ's death-resurrection. It also little discusses the Spirit. So if the apostle Paul wrote 1 Thessalonians, 2 Thessalonians probably was not his own work.

The apocalyptic tone of 2 Thessalonians further suggests that it was written in a time of trouble, when Christians were either suffering or fearing persecution.

The intensity of such a persecution as well as its widespread nature may have been interpreted by some Christians as a sure sign that the world was coming to an end and that judgment day had fallen upon them. The dating of the letter could fall anywhere then between A.D. 70 (the fall of Jerusalem) and the early years of the second century. Two eras of intermittent persecution fell in this period: A.D. 81–96 under Domitian and A.D. 98–117 under Trajan. Since the effectiveness of a writing written under Paul's name would be questionable in areas where Paul's genuine letters were well known, the author's community is probably to be found in Asia Minor instead of Macedonia or Achaia and almost certainly not in Thessalonica itself.[2]

In outline we may sketch 2 Thessalonians as follows:

Introduction and Greeting 1:1–2
Thanksgiving A 1:3–12
Eschatological Doctrine 2:1–12
Thanksgiving B, Admonition, Blessing 2:13–3:5
More Admonitions 3:6–16
Closing 3:16–18

The Introduction parallels that of 1 Thessalonians: Paul, Silvanus, and Timothy address the church of the Thessalonians in God the Father and the Lord Jesus Christ. But whereas in 1 Thessalonians the authors sent grace and peace, in 2 Thessalonians they send "Grace to you and peace from God the Father and the Lord Jesus Christ" (1:2).

The parallel continues in the first section of the Thanksgiving. Both letters begin with a thanks to God for the Thessalonians. In 2 Thessalonians, however, the notion of persecution quickly joins the notions of faith, love, and steadfastness: "Therefore we ourselves boast of you in the churches of God for your steadfastness and faith in all your persecutions and in all the afflictions which you are enduring" (1:4). Then 2 Thessalonians begins to elaborate on the theme of endurance. What the Thessalonians (or whoever were the actual intended recipients) are suffering shows God's righteous judgment. It is God's way of making his people worthy of his kingdom. Moreover, God calls it just to afflict those who are afflicting the Thessalonians, and God will grant rest to those presently suffering. God will do this when the Lord Jesus is revealed from heaven. The author paints the scene of that Day of the Lord dramatically: mighty angels, flaming fire, vengeance upon those who do not know God or will not obey the gospel of Christ. Such wicked people will suffer the punishments of eternal destruction. They shall have no part in the presence and glory of the Lord when he comes to be glorified in his saints. The author prays that the Thessalonians always live to the glory of the Lord's name.

After this somewhat grisly thanksgiving, the author reflects further on eschatological matters, elaborating more fully his or her sense of the final days. First, a letter that the Thessalonians had received (purporting to be from Paul and saying that the Day of the Lord had come) was false. Prior to the Day of the Lord there must be a rebellion and the revelation of a man of lawlessness. This son of perdition takes his seat in God's temple and claims divinity. The author had told the Thessalonians about this person (whose identity commentators debate, some suggesting the Roman emperor and others Satan), and about the mystery of his present "restraint" and future revelation. The revelation of the lawless, evil power will lead to Jesus' slaying it or him. Jesus will conquer him on the Day of the Lord, but prior to that day signs and wonders will help the cause of evil, leading those who refuse to love the truth to perish.

In 2:13 the theme swings back from this mystery of evil, restraint, and conquest to thanksgiving. The author praises the choice of God that from the beginning singled the Thessalonians out to be saved. May the Lord Jesus and God the Father comfort this people. They should pray hard for the triumph of the Word of the Lord, realizing that although not all human beings have faith God remains faithful.

2 Thessalonians 3:6–16 details more moral imperatives. The Thessalonians should separate themselves from idlers and those who do not keep the Christian traditions. The example of Paul supporting himself by his own work (the author quotes 1 Thessalonians 2:9) should be their model. Let all community members be good workers. Let all remain strong in doing good and obey the precepts of this letter. Finally, have nothing to do with those who won't work or take this letter to heart.

The letter closes with a prayer for the Thessalonians' peace and a note that Paul marks it with his own hand. (The claim that Paul does this in all his authentic letters is exaggerated.)

Why Was This Written?

For Krodel 2 Thessalonians had four purposes. The author wanted to oppose an interpretation of the Day of the Lord that made it so near that people were neglecting their everyday responsibilities. Relatedly, he wanted to stop the idle from living off the diligent. He wanted to strengthen what he took to be the authentic Pauline traditions. And he wanted to warn against a previous letter attributed to Paul that he found harmful.[3] Apparently there was some confusion in this Christian community (the "Thessalonians") about the meaning of the current hard times. Some people took the persecution to be the penultimate act of history, the last events prior to the Lord's return. Drawing on rather obscure apocalyptic traditions, including imagery we can find in the book of Daniel, the author tried to make the case that the end was not yet at hand. Certain signs, such as a widespread rebellion (against God?), the appearance of a great wicked leader, and the demise of a force (quite obscure) that presently was restraining the powers of evil, had first to appear. So it was wrong to live in idleness or as though present days did not matter. As Paul himself had worked hard at manual labor, so should all Christians, not letting themselves be distracted by false announcements that the end was nigh. Generally, then, the author wanted to restore good order to a confused congregation, both buttressing their faith and teaching them a more hardheaded realism.

What Background Does This Text Presuppose?

2 Thessalonians presupposes some knowledge unavailable to us and a general appreciation of apocalyptic. The knowledge unavailable to us includes the content of the prior letter that the author denounces as misleading and the

reasons for the signs that will precede the Lord's return, especially the signs of the evil power and that power's restraint. Apparently the group to whom the author was writing understood these matters and had some local traditions. Other New Testament texts such as 2 Peter 3:10 ("But the day of the Lord will come like a thief, and then the heavens will pass away with a loud noise, and the elements will be dissolved with fire, and the earth and the works that are upon it will be burned up") suggests that apocalyptic notions were widespread, but the particular teaching of 2 Thessalonians about restraint (*to katechon*) is puzzling.[4]

Apocalyptic in general is the peculiar literature of the biblical period, usually produced in times of persecution, that purports (on the basis of a revelation [*apocalypsis*]) to describe how God will bring an end to the present evil age, rendering justice to both the wicked persecutors and the good people who are suffering in faith. It takes what we moderns would consider great liberties with imagination, letting its trust in God paint scenes of vivid rescue (and somewhat bloodthirsty vengeance) and then calling these scenes "prophecy" or "revelation." We today best make sense out of apocalyptic by stressing its symbolic character, its dramatic way of imagining God's justice and help. If we take it literally we run into hopeless tangles.

A last bit of background that 2 Thessalonians presupposes is the ancient practice of **pseudepigraphy**—writing in another (famous or authoritative) person's name. Pseudepigraphy was a fairly commonplace way of trying to gain authority for one's work, or of honoring a great figure of the past, and it did not carry the overtones of dishonesty that we tend to find in it today. Indeed, ancient writers felt free to compose a pseudepigraphal letter to counter a previous pseudepigraphal letter, so that all the venerable past authorities might have a say in a debate.[5]

What Lasting Significance Does This Have?

2 Thessalonians shows us the early Christian struggle to come to grips both with a delay of the Day of the Lord and with persecution. As it became clear that Jesus would not return immediately, such responsibilities as hard daily work regained their importance. When the early Christians tried to comfort themselves against persecution and stir up their faith in God's rescue, they drew upon apocalyptic symbolism to probe the mystery of evil, of the puzzles inherent in God's giving malicious people and forces leeway to operate. Both of these issues remain with us today. We too must struggle with the problem of evil, gaining some way of believing that grace or goodness is stronger than sin.

COLOSSIANS

What Have We Here?

Colossians is another letter that sometimes is called "deutero-Pauline." By this phrase commentators mean that it more likely was written by disciples of Paul than by the apostle himself. (Thus it is not "primary"

Paul but "secondary" or "deutero" Paul.) The arguments for an authorship other than Paul's (another case of pseudepigraphy) are similar to those used to call 2 Thessalonians the work of a disciple: differences in theology and literary style. In addition, however, the claim within the letter (e.g., 4:3, 10) that Colossians was written from circumstances similar to those of Philemon (when Paul was in prison, probably in Ephesus) doesn't square well with the fact that it seems more sophisticated than Romans (which, if written about the time of Philemon, it would predate). Presumably a more developed or sophisticated outlook than Romans suggests a later, more mature phase of the Pauline theology.

We shall see the distinctive theology of Colossians in the following paragraphs. Here the first consequence of attributing the letter to someone other than Paul is that we can only estimate its date quite roughly (perhaps between 63 and 90 C.E.). Equally, we can only guess who the "Colossians" might have been, since both the loose date and the omission of any reference to Philemon (a key figure in the Colossian community) make it quite possible that the actual recipients were not the Christian community in the town of Colossae in Phrygia (present-day Turkey).

In outline we may break Colossians down as follows:

Introduction 1:1–2

Thanksgiving and Prayer 1:3–20

Apostolic Ministry 1:21–2:5

False Teaching 2:6–23

Instructions on the Ideal Christian Life 3:1–4:6

Conclusion 4:7–18[6]

The Introduction links "Paul" with Timothy and underscores his call to be an apostle. It wishes "the saints and faithful brethren in Christ at Colossae" grace and peace from God the Father.

In making thanksgiving, the author addresses the Father and is moved by the good report he has heard about both the faith of the people to whom he is writing and the love they bear all the saints. The author also mentions (most likely as his understanding of the "Colossians'" religious motivation) the hope laid up for them in heaven. They got their faith, the gospel truth, from Epaphras, whom the author calls "a faithful minister of Christ on our behalf" and whom he cites as the source of his information about the community.

In praying for this community the author asks "that you may be filled with the knowledge of his will in all spiritual wisdom and understanding" (1:9). Since the letter to the Colossians is perhaps best known for the depth of its spiritual vision, in retrospect this verse seems a sort of announcement: Wisdom will be the theme. The author also prays that the community grow strong with God's might, able to endure in patience and joy, giving thanks to God for the divine gifts. These gifts preeminently consist of the share

God has given believers in the inheritance of the saints in light, in the divine truth. God, in fact, has carried believers out of Satan's dominion of darkness into the kingdom of his beloved Son. In the Son believers have redemption, the forgiveness of their sins.

Colossians 1:15–20 is probably the most famous section of the letter, and the general consensus nowadays is that it comes from a hymn that the author is quoting:

> It is no longer a matter for dispute that we have in these verses a hymn which has been taken over by the author. The prerequisites for this are present, as far as form is concerned; there is a certain rhythm in the construction both as a whole and in detail. There is also a portrayal of Christ, self-contained and surpassing anything that might be expected in the context; and again, there is the customary opening by means of the relative pronoun.[7]

Scholars have debated the origin of this hymn, some suggesting that most of it came from pre-Christian Gnostic (secret wisdom) sources and others suggesting that it bears overtones of the Jewish Day of Atonement. In Eduard Lohse's view, however, it comes from Hellenistic (Greek speaking and thinking) Jewish reflections on wisdom:

> The exalted Christ is called "the image of God, the first-born of all creation" . . . and he is also called "the beginning." . . . With these designations the hymn relates to the characterizations which Hellenistic synagogues gave to Wisdom. They praised Wisdom (*sophia*) as created before all creatures, as the first-born of God, the primordial beginning—in view of creation as well as the redemption she grants as the mediatrix of salvation. In the Jewish **Diaspora** [dispersion outside of Palestine], moreover, there was much borrowing from the concepts of popular Hellenistic philosophy. . . . [8]

The verses themselves deserve quotation in full:

> He is the image of the invisible God, the first-born of all creation; for in him all things were created, in heaven and on earth, visible and invisible, whether thrones or dominions or principalities or authorities—all things were created through him and for him. He is before all things, and in him all things hold together. He is the head of the body, the church; he is the beginning, the first-born from the dead, that in everything he might be preeminent. For in him all the fullness of God was pleased to dwell, and through him to reconcile to himself all things, whether on earth or in heaven, making peace by the blood of his cross. [1:15–20]

It's hard to know precisely what the original author of a hymn like this (or the author of Colossians who took it over) had in mind. Depending upon what background one thinks best explains the hymn (e.g., Lohse's hypothesis about Hellenistic Jewish reflections on wisdom), one may conjecture in several different directions. But for the hymn to have entered the Christian liturgy, and then entered a document that became a part of Christian Scripture, it must at some point have become pregnant with interpretations that made it illumine deeper significances of Jesus Christ

Crucifixion. El Greco. About 1610–14. The mystical style of El Greco is reminiscent of the tendency of Colossians and Ephesians to ponder the cosmic significance of Jesus the Word. *(Nelson Gallery–Atkins Museum, Kansas City, Mo. [Nelson Fund])*

that the general Church found pleasing. Certainly traditional Christian theology, since the time of the Church fathers (fourth century and following) has regarded Colossians 1:15–20 as a profound meditation on the Incarnate Word. Along with Philippians 2:5–11, John 1:1–18, and a few other key passages, it has been a main anchor for Christian faith in the preexistent divinity of Jesus Christ, a prime stimulus to wide-ranging reflections on the Word made flesh.

If we briefly take the hymn along this traditional path of interpretation, we note first the motif of image (*eikon*). The one being hymned is the picture or representation of the invisible God. Here is a basic foundation or justification for the iconography that has been especially important in Eastern Christianity. In the East, the representational character of Jesus Christ has justified an especially rich liturgical art. Second, in calling Jesus the first-born of all creation, the text sowed seeds of a later controversy (**Arianism**) about the exact status of the Word Incarnate: Was he a creature, or does "first-born" mean a kind of generation by God different from both human birth and the creation described in the early chapters of Genesis? In saying that Jesus was the one in whom all things were created, the text tilted toward a special, perhaps mediating relationship between the Word and the rest of creation. Certainly later Christian theology spoke of creation as occurring within the relationship between the Father who spoke the eternal Word and the Son who was spoken. In other words, later Christian theology made creation a subset or insert of the eternal relations of the Trinity, God as an active community of Father-Son-Spirit. Recently the idea that all things hold together in Christ has given Christian evolutionists such as Pierre Teilhard de Chardin a basis for speaking of "Christogenesis": the development, becoming, or growth of a Word-centered creation as something organic.

The notion that the Church is the Body of Christ is familiar from Paul's authentic writings, and it too strikes an organic note: Between believers and their Lord something whole is fashioned, a community of life like that which exists among the members of a single human body. In saying that Christ is the beginning, the first-born from the dead, the hymn suggests Paul's notion of a new creation: With the resurrection of Jesus God has started all over and launched a new enterprise based on a new Adam. If the fullness of God dwells in Christ, he is both *the* place where the world may see and be connected with divinity and probably something strictly divine. As for Jews the **Shekinah** or glory of the Israelite God "contained" the divine fullness (so did the ark of the covenant and the Torah, from other points of view), so for Christians given to metaphysical broodings on the Christ-event Jesus has "contained," embodied, or made manifest the divine fullness (pleroma). In addition, it was right there in the Word Incarnate that God reconciled all things, in earth or heaven, to himself. It was when Christ died on the cross and rose from the dead that an old order died and a new kingdom of peace was born.

So one can see how freighted with heavy conceptions these verses of Colossians later became. What is fascinating when one takes them more lightly, trying to see them afresh, naked of the later centuries of theology, is their richness and ambiguity. As poetry is both richer and more ambiguous than ordinary prose speech, so this liturgical hymn is both richer and more ambiguous than a theological doctrine. In it we most likely have a believing poet letting imagination fly away to the origin of Jesus, the reality Jesus had and has with God apart from the world or at the world's foundations. For this poet Jesus Christ has become the point of juncture, fusion, connection between the heavenly sphere of the biblical God and the worldly sphere of space and time that that same God chooses to deal with by grace, in kindness and love. *There*, in Christ, is the axis of all the action. There is what the French call the *carrefour*: the crossroads where all the main traffic (creation, Incarnation, redemption) is intersecting. Colossians 1:15–20 is a blockbuster passage, one of the truly major New Testament theological lodes, at least in terms of what the later centuries made of it. Even today it is a major conceptual resource for theologians trying to work out a more ecological Christianity.[9]

After this hymn, the author begins to return to earth. People like those in the community he is addressing are the beneficiaries of Jesus' redemptive suffering, because although they were once alienated from God now they may approach God as blameless and irreproachable. If they continue in faith they continue to stand with the crucified and risen Christ and so to be pleasing to the Father. The section 1:21–2:5 makes a faith-tie to the Christ hymned in 1:15–20, to lay a foundation for Church ministry. Thus the author correlates the sufferings of a Church servant like himself with the suffering of Christ, seeing his own labors as a certain completion of Christ's afflictions for the sake of the Body of the Church. The characteristic note of this apostolic service is quite Pauline: to publish or preach the mystery of God's revelations to the Gentiles. The preaching boils down to Christ, who lives in the community of the "Colossians" and is their hope of glory.

The author stresses the toil of the ministry and the energy that it requires, suggesting that God has to be the source of this energy. He (the author) has striven for this community and the people at Laodicea, that they might be encouraged, be knit together in love, and know God's mystery, the Christ in whom are all the treasures of wisdom and knowledge. Once again there is a great stress on wisdom, a strong suggestion of deep things not accessible to people who lack faith. For the author to make this wisdom the goal of the Church's ministry establishes Christianity as a powerful contender in the battles that were raging among the many different philosophies and mystery religions that were offering a saving wisdom (**gnosis**).

This context helps us to appreciate the warnings in 2:6–23 against false teachings. It is important that the "Colossians" keep to the gospel about Christ, the original faith, that they were taught, not letting themselves be misled by false philosophies. Christ must be their foundation, "for in him the whole fulness of deity dwells bodily" (2:9). He is the head ruler, the prime authority, the one into whom, as it were, the members of the community were all circumcised. They were buried with him when they were baptized, rose with him in resurrection. God canceled the debt of their sins, as if nailing their legal penalty to the cross, and triumphed over all the principalities and powers (spiritual forces). The community therefore should feel free in matters of food, stand free of any worship of angels, keep free of prideful visions. Their concern should be to hold fast to Christ their head, living as if dead to worldly regulations (covenant Law). These things may have an appearance of wisdom but "they are of no value in checking the indulgence of the flesh" (2:23).

Beginning with chapter 3, the author paints a more positive picture of how Christians ought to live. They should seek heavenly things, aiming to be mentally where Christ is: seated at the right hand of God. They should live as though they had died (to the world) and their life were hidden in Christ. He is their true life. When he appears they will appear with him full of glory. So let them put all earthly, sinful things aside as incompatible with their new life in Christ. Fornication, impurity, anger, malice, and the like belong to their old nature, which they have put aside. Their new nature "is being renewed in knowledge after the image of its creator" (3:10). In their new nature there is no place for distinctions between Greek and Jew, circumcised and uncircumcised, slave and free. Rather Christ is all and in all.

What becomes a person identified with Christ? Such virtues as compassion, kindness, lowliness, meekness, patience, and mutual forgiveness. Above all, "love, which binds everything together in perfect harmony" (3:14). There should be peace, focusing on the word of Christ, teaching, singing spiritual songs, doing everything in the name of the Lord Jesus, giving thanks to God the Father through him. The author asks wives to be subject to their husbands, husbands to love their wives. Children should obey their parents, fathers should not provoke their children. Slaves should obey their masters wholeheartedly. In this orderliness the author points to the deep significance that work or family relations can have: "Whatever your task, work heartily, as serving the Lord and not men, knowing that from the Lord you will receive the inheritance as your reward; you are serving the Lord Christ" (3:23–24). Masters should know that they have a Master in heaven, and so should treat their slaves justly. Let all continue steadfastly in prayer, "and pray for us also, that God may open to us a door for the word, to declare the mystery of Christ, on account of which I am in prison, that I may make it clear, as I ought to speak" (4:3–4).

In conclusion the author mentions such companions of the apostle Paul as Tychicus, Onesimus, Aristarchus, Mark, and Barnabas. This knowledge, along with his familiarity with Pauline theology, suggests that he was an intimate member of a Pauline community. He sends the greetings of these Pauline companions and other Christians laboring in the ministry, and asks that this letter also be read by the Laodiceans. He claims to be signing as Paul and asks that his readers remember his chains.

Why Was This Written?

Colossians probably was written for the general reasons we have discussed in the case of other Epistles (for example, to comfort and reinvigorate a needy community), but it is also likely that it was written to combat some specific dangers. The internal arguments of the letter suggest that false teachers were troubling the "Colossian" community. These troublers were in part teaching the covenant Law, with its prescriptions for diet and days of religious observance. To help with that part of the danger, the author makes the familiar Pauline case that since the coming of Christ such matters as kosher laws have no significance. However, the false teachers must also have been offering what the author considered a new, twisted kind of "wisdom" that detracted from the centrality of Christ. By referring to principalities and powers (cosmic spirits), asceticism, and visions, the author conjures up a species of Gnosticism.[10]

Gnosticism as a general movement perhaps predated Christianity, and after the rise of Christianity it tried to absorb some of the Christian teachings. Basically, however, Gnostics all claimed a secret knowledge, not open to the masses, about God's way of saving the fallen human race. The typically Gnostic position was that the world of matter and flesh was evil, the result of a mistake in creation. Salvation came from disciplining the flesh and liberating the sparks of divinity present in human immateriality or spirit. Gnosticism could use a terminology like that of biblical religion, speaking of "revelation," "salvation," "heavenly life," "light," and the like. From early on, however, the Christian churches sensed that Gnosticism denied their most fundamental tenet: the unique presence of God's grace, kingdom, will, love, word, and the rest in the concrete, completely flesh-and-blood Jesus of Nazareth.

In his own peculiar way, the author of Colossians is as insistent on the centrality of this historical Christ as are any of the writers of the Gospels that depict how the historical Christ spoke, healed, and died. The author of Colossians wants to cast his message, his interpretation of the gospel, in terms of a wisdom or philosophy, however, so as to compete with the (probably Gnostic) seductions of the false teachers who were endangering the community to which he wrote. Everything such false teachers might want to say about the core of things, the depth of reality, or the processes of salvation had a correlative in Christianity. But the special mark of Christianity, the distinguishing characteristic, was the centrality of Jesus Christ. It was in the completely real life, death, and resurrection of Jesus that revelation and salvation had actually occurred. No wisdom that wandered away from him to discourse about angels or principalities, dietary regulations or circumcision, was the true, traditionally Christian wisdom or salvation.

What Background Does This Text Presuppose?

In explaining why Colossians may have been written we have touched on the Jewish and Gnostic backgrounds that it probably presupposed. The Jewish background was simply the reverence for covenant Law with which we have regularly seen Paul contending. The minimal Gnostic notions necessary to catch the author's nuances regarding "wisdom" are probably those we have just described.[11] Broader even than the Gnostic movement, however, was the reverence for wisdom that pervaded the Mediterranean world of the first century C.E. For example, in the last spate of writing that (eventually) was included within the Hebrew Bible, wisdom concerns played a prominent part. Drawing on the proverbs and prudential maxims of countries such as Egypt, and on the speculations of Hellenistic philosophy, Jewish thinkers had written about wisdom as a heavenly being, a feminine figure pleasing to God who joyfully had observed the creation of the world. One of the texts, for instance, that Lohse has in mind when he speaks of the wisdom tradition in the background of Colossians 1:15–20 is Proverbs 8:22–31:

> The Lord created me at the beginning of his work, the first of his acts of old. Ages ago I was set up, at the first, before the beginning of the earth. When there were no depths I was brought forth, when there were no springs abounding with water. Before the mountains had been shaped, before the hills, I was brought forth; before he had made the earth with its fields, or the first of the dust of the world. When he established the heavens, I was there, when he drew a circle on the face of the deep, when he made firm the skies above, when he established the fountains of the deep, when he assigned to the sea its limit, so that the waters might not transgress his command, when he marked out the foundations of the earth, then I was beside him, like a master workman, and I was daily in his delight, rejoicing before him always, rejoicing in his inhabited world and delighting in the sons of men.

The mystery religions that had come into the Mediterranean world from Egypt and the Orient were another pressure on both Christians and Jews to develop doctrines and rituals that palpably gave a knowledge of salvation. In the context of the **syncretism** that prevailed in the ancient Mediterranean world, many people felt free to add doctrinal or ritualistic elements from several traditions and make a composite religion. Everywhere, however, people were asking how they could be made whole in this life and could gain immortality in a spiritual life to come. Since the time of the classical Greek philosophers Socrates, Plato, and Aristotle (fifth century B.C.E.), the idea of an immortal soul had been a powerful force in the Hellenistic world. The Greek mystery religions centered at Eleusis or focused upon the myth of Orpheus promised to bring the devotee to a vision of the light of immortality. Not surprisingly, therefore, Christians sometimes described their sacraments of baptism and the eucharist as rites of initiation, enlightenment, and saving wisdom. The difference, Christians thought, was that their sacred actions brought people into contact with the gospel, wisdom, and personal love of the true God, while the other rites dealt with false gods or mere "principalities and powers." Thus in the background of early Christian wisdom writings such as Colossians there existed a great deal of "philosophical" competition. Colossians was an effort to show that Christians, too, had a powerful gnosis.

What Lasting Significance Does This Have?

As we mentioned, Colossians 1:15–20 exerted a great influence on Christian speculation about the Incarnate Word, and it continues to be a text that Christians interested in **cosmology**, an understanding of the physical world, quote and reflect upon. Apart from Christian faith, however, Colossians raises questions about the nature of God, the source of the world, and also about the kind of knowledge or wisdom that human beings most need. Indeed, whether or not one finds this New Testament writing persuasive, the questions it raises are profoundly germane to liberal education. If only for that reason it deserves a place in a humanities curriculum.

For example, consider the whole matter of gnosis, or saving knowledge. In germ it is the crux of all education. What is it we are trying to learn, if we are wise? What information, or vision, or redoing of our sense of reality is most likely to make us whole, make our society just, remove the evils that slash human life, and fulfill our best hopes and our richest aspirations? In asking this sort of question we stumble into the quest for salvation. Whether we realize it or not, we raise our sights toward the sort of health (*salus*) that Judaism, Christianity, Gnosticism, the mystery religions, and all the rest of the cultural forces of Colossians' day were riveted upon. We also challenge any notion that education can be only professional or vocational, that it can only be interested in training people for specific jobs. When an education is not interested in saving wisdom, it loses most of its claim to respect. Human beings are the only animals who can keep asking "Why?"

and searching for saving wisdom. Not to make this unique capacity the center of our efforts to draw out the best in students is to warp them with an inhumane education.

Colossians asserts that Christ is the most saving wisdom. For instance in 2:2–3 the author hopes that even disciples whom he does not know will be encouraged "as they are knit together in love, to have all the riches of assured understanding and the knowledge of God's mystery, of Christ, in whom are hid all the treasures of wisdom and knowledge." This sort of assertion comes from a thought-world different from our contemporary own. In that thought-world things like "mystery" and "wisdom" were not just vague names. They stood for spiritual realities and for somewhat objective experiences that people considered most precious. For good reasons and bad, we in the contemporary West tend to be chary of such spiritual realities and to doubt the worth of such (religious) experiences. We have seen ignorance and hysteria run riot in the name of religious experience and have suffered everything from simple foolishness to diabolical bloodletting. Scientific and technological training have made it habitual for us to look for empirical evidence, to seek out hard data. So we have a healthy bias against mystification and tend to shy away from woolly talk about great entities like "Truth" or "Justice" or "the Lord."

On the other hand, we also run the danger of closing ourselves off from the profound spiritual heritage of humankind, which has always painted "reality" as something larger and deeper than the senses alone can report or test, and which has always honored the productions of the mind and the imagination, the unconscious and the holistic depths of the spirit.[12] When our culture, education, ways of interacting with nature, and the rest make little provision for mystery or don't do justice to the surplus or excess of intelligibility that such frontier works as theoretical physics and poetry constantly run into, we court the risk of selling our birthright for a tunafish sandwich, concentrating so heavily on noise and money that we ignore the great things necessary for our peace. A text such as Colossians, like a Hindu Upanishad (or a Buddhist sutra, or the discourse of a Sufi or Hasidic saint), does us the service of pointing out our amnesia, asking us how we can possibly pay such homage to plastic.

Regardless of one's position on Christian gnosis, then, one needs to come to grips with the perennial biblical or religious challenge to lay out a wise path and train the people for true prosperity. We might pose the issue that divided Judaism and Christianity nearly two thousand years ago in these terms: Which is the better path to wisdom and knowledge of God, the Law or the Gospel, the Torah of Moses or the Spirit of Christ? We might pose in similar terms the issue that divides Christianity, and most of the other traditional religions, from the (largely tacit) **empiricism** (focus on data) that rules American academic and business life today: Which is the better path to wisdom, wholeness, justice, creativity? Biblical religion, from the time of the Psalmist, believes that only fools say in their hearts that there is no God. A great deal of contemporary American culture says on its lips, if not in its heart, that there is no God. Is the biblical tradition right in believing that this makes a great deal of American culture foolish (trivial, warped, vicious)?

The other question that we found Colossians to raise, about the nature of God, brings to mind the image of Hebrews 4:12: a two-edged sword. The Word of God slashes at many in the churches, as well as at foolish atheists. For the Christ depicted in Colossians is not the tame figure dealt with in many American Christian churches each Sunday morning. He is not the gentle Jesus meek and mild. In 1:15–20, but also in other passages, the Colossian Christ is a force that goes back to the very act that originated the world. Think in terms of the big bang, or however else respectable physical science now suggests we should picture the beginnings of the physical universe. The Christ of Colossians has a part in this; he is the one in whom such creation occurred. Indeed, he is the one in whom all creation holds together. So, for instance, as the **exegete** (interpreter) William Barclay has written, Colossians

> uses the strange phrase: "In him all things hold together." This means that not only is the Son the agent of creation in the beginning and the goal of creation in the end, but between the beginning and the end, during time as we know it, it is he who holds the world together. That is to say, all the laws by which this world is order and not chaos are an expression of the mind of the Son. The law of gravity and the rest, the laws by which the universe hangs together, are not only scientific laws but also divine.[13]

Simply because Colossians says this, of course, does not make it so, let alone make it something scientists have to contend with in their laboratories. Science and faith have a proper separation, as well as a proper correlation. But simply because Colossians says this we cannot honestly restrict Christian faith to a diluted ethics, cannot fail to see that the Christian churches that give the Christ no physical part in creation ignore their own Scripture.

Colossians says that the world holds together in the Christ of God.[14] For Christian faith, the world is not something casual, accidental, haphazard, or absurd. The world reposes in the greater mystery of the source of all creativity, physical and mental, of molecules and beautiful children like Jesus. Nothing simply exists, two-dimensionally, as a brute, flat, or uninteresting fact. That anything exists at all leads us into mystery, the light-power-meaning that is too much for our little minds to grasp, too rich for our intellectual poverty. The lasting significance of Colossians is its testimony to this ultimate mystery, its insistence that the world reposes in God's self-communication, God's speaking-loving-making-saving. We may not like this testimony or insistence, but if we reject them the judge at the center of our consciences will ask us for reasons why, pointing out that rejection may well mean incurring the responsibility ourselves to generate a deeper, richer, or more helpful ultimate wisdom.

EPHESIANS

What Have We Here?

In Ephesians we have a letter quite reminiscent of Colossians, upon which it frequently draws. The **sapiential** interests are similar, although Ephesians gives a more extended discussion of the Church. Both style and doctrine separate the letter from Paul's own writings, and the dependencies on Colossians suggest a date toward the end of the first century. The lack of any mention of Ephesus in some manuscripts of this letter argues that it may not originally have been written for the Christian community that had grown up in the seaport town of Ephesus on the southwestern coast of Asia Minor (present-day Turkey). Finally, we do not know where the letter was written. In terms of all the concrete details that would anchor Ephesians in space and time, therefore, we are quite ignorant.

Indeed, as J. Paul Sampley has pointed out, we do not even know why this letter was written:

> Not only do we not know who were the intended recipients of the letter, we also cannot be sure exactly why it was written. Paul's letters usually respond to a discernible and very specific historical situation. A crisis or problem brought most Pauline letters into existence. Even Romans, written to a church that Paul's preaching did not establish, is a "bread-and-butter" letter written in advance of his journey, seeking support for his mission to Spain. . . . Ephesians, however, lacks clues concerning a concrete crisis or occasion. There are urgings for unity scattered through the letter (cf. esp. 4:1–16); perhaps there was some threat to unity. But if there were such a threat, the clues are so general that we cannot reconstruct the specifics.[15]

In outline we may divide Ephesians as follows:

Greeting and Blessing 1:1–14

Thanksgiving 1:15–23

God's Plan for Gentile Christians 2:1–22

Apostolic Role and Prayer 3:1–21

The Unity of the Church Body 4:1–16

Vices, Virtues, and Duties 4:17–6:9

Cosmic Forces 6:10–17

Concluding Prayers and Notices 6:18–24

The Greeting notes that "Paul" has been called to be an apostle of Jesus Christ by the will of God and wishes the saints who are faithful grace and peace from God the Father and the Lord Jesus Christ. The blessing ascends toward the Father, who has given believers all blessings in Christ, just as he chose believers in Christ before the foundation of the world to be holy and blameless in him. These echoes of Colossians ripen distinctively with the lines,

He destined us in love to be his sons [children] through Jesus Christ, according to the purpose of his will, to the praise of his glorious grace which he freely bestowed on us in the Beloved. In him we have redemption through his blood, the forgiveness of our trespasses, according to the riches of his grace, which he has lavished upon us. For he has made known to us in all wisdom and insight the mystery of his will, according to his purpose which he set forth in Christ as a plan for the fullness of time, to unite all things in him, things in heaven and things on earth. [1:5–10]

To Colossians' interest in God's mystery Ephesians therefore adds a stress on predestination: The saving life of Christ and the Church are part of a plan that God has had from before the beginning of time.

The Blessing, which somewhat parallels the hymn of Colossians 1:15–20, concludes by saying of God's plan and purpose, centered in Christ: "In him you also, who have heard the word of truth, the gospel of your salvation, and have believed in him, were sealed with the promised Holy Spirit, which is the guarantee of our inheritance until we acquire possession of it, to the praise of his glory" (1:13–14). For Ephesians, therefore, the mystery of salvation has a specific structure. It passes through Christ and aims at the believer's entry into divine life. And all of it rebounds to God's glory. All of it glows with the holy love that makes God God.

Blessing God for this splendid plan leads the author to thanksgiving. He thanks God for the faith of the "Ephesians" and asks that the Father of glory give them a spirit of wisdom and knowledge. This spirit will enlighten the eyes of their heart (biblical authors tend to make wisdom a combination of warmth and light that lodges in the center of the personality, the "heart"). It will clarify their hope, the rich inheritance to which God calls them as saints. It shows the immeasurable greatness of the divine power, which is the source of the saints' faith. This same power accomplished the great deed of raising Christ from the dead and enthroning him in the heavenly places. There he sits at the right hand of God, far above every lesser power and dominion, either of this age or of the age to come. God has put all things under the feet of Christ and has made Christ head of all things for the Church. The Church is the body of Christ, "the fulness of him who fills all in all" (1:23).

This language is like that of Colossians but if anything more grandiose and spiritualistic. Clearly the author has a great vision of Christ as the ascended Lord presiding over both the Church and the rest of physical creation. The Church, all the faithful, stand in organic unity with Christ and in some ways constitute his fullness. Yet he fills everything; he is what the Eastern Orthodox Church has called the **Pantokrator** or ruler of all. So the author must think of Christ as released, through the resurrection, from earthly boundaries. As in many other Pauline writings, it is not clear how the ascended Lord differs from the Holy Spirit. It is very clear, though, that he is a pneumatic Lord, a ruler active like the breath that fills a living body.

With chapter 2 the author begins a deep meditation on the effects of God's gracious activity in Christ. Although the Ephesians were spiritually dead because of their sins, God made them alive. Thus they no longer walk like worldlings, followers of "the prince of the power of the air, the spirit that is now at work in the sons of disobedience" (2:2). This strange princely being is usually understood to be Satan, the personification of evil and rebellion against God. Concerning Ephesians' peculiar connection of the satanic spirit with the air Markus Barth has written:

> . . . if "spirit" is understood as an apposition to the preceding noun only ("atmosphere," lit. "dominion of air"), it may qualify the air as a substance that is breathed by man and poisons his thoughts and actions. In this case the devil would be denoted as the ruler who poisons the atmosphere, producing a devastating stench or killing in the manner of the aftereffect of atomic explosions or industrial air pollution.[16]

The author describes himself along with the community to which he is writing as people who once, prior to conversion, lived among the children of disobedience, following a life of bodily passions that put them at odds with God—indeed, that made them children of wrath. "But God, who is rich in mercy, out of the great love with which he loved us, even when we were dead through our trespasses, made us alive together with Christ (by grace you have been saved)" (2:4–5). Those are lines worthy of the author of Romans 8, so deeply do they penetrate the sheer goodness behind the divine work of salvation. For the Hebrew Bible God's loving-kindness or mercy (*hesed*) was his main attribute. By sheer goodness he has multiplied this kindness in Christ, snatching people who were dead in sin back to "life" (openness to the divine source that alone can make them prosper). Now, therefore, Christians sit with Christ at the right hand of God. They are (in their most ultimate identity) where he is, in the heavenly sphere of God, the realm where the powerful goodness that worked Christ's resurrection is fully operative. And all of this, the author emphasizes in good Pauline fashion, is the doing of God's grace. Human beings can boast none of it.

With verse 11 the distinctively Gentile dimensions of God's gracious plan come into focus. The Ephesians should remember that they used to be strangers to the promises made to Israel, people standing outside the covenant and having no hope, no real God. Now they have in Christ been brought near to God. Christ indeed is the force uniting all God's people. He has in his flesh abolished the wall of hostility that used to separate Jews and Gentiles, abolishing the force of the Jewish commandments. The operative word for the author of Ephesians in this regard is *peace* (perhaps because he had inherited several generations worth of disputes between the Jewish and Gentile wings of the Church). Christ is "our peace." At any rate, both Jews and Gentiles now have through Christ the one essential thing: "for through him we both have access in one Spirit to the Father" (2:18). Jews and Gentiles in the Church should therefore consider themselves fellow citizens. They share the same human community structure, built on the same foundation of the apostles and prophets, finally based on the same cornerstone, Christ himself. Together they make a holy temple, a dwelling place of God in the Spirit. (Here the author seems deliberately to make the community of Jesus' followers what the Jerusalem Temple was for Judaism: the special place where God had residence.)

With chapter 3, "Paul" (who calls himself a prisoner for Christ Jesus on behalf of the Gentiles) reflects on the mystery of God's opening the covenant to the Gentiles—the mystery that has defined his life's work as an apostle. He alludes to the revelation that he received from God (probably the author could assume that the story of what happened to Paul on the way to Damascus, as now recorded in Acts 9:3–4, 22:6–16, and 26:12–23, was known to his readers). He summarizes this divine revelation as "how the Gentiles are fellow heirs, members of the same body, and partakers of the promise in Christ Jesus through the gospel" (3:6). This is precisely the good news that Paul was called to serve, even though he was the least of the saints. It might be called the unsearchable riches of Christ, or the plan hidden for all ages in the Creator, or the manifold wisdom of God that is now manifest in the Church. For this author, indeed, it is in the Church, the human community of Jesus' followers, that even the principalities and powers in heavenly places get their knowledge of God's great plan. Against any Gnostic tendencies to minimize the work of mere human beings, Ephesians gives the Church a cosmic role, implying that when God decided to have the divine saving plan pass through flesh and blood he accepted all the consequences of this decision: not only a full human being like Jesus of Nazareth but also an "extended" body of fully human followers, a Church of flesh and blood. One more time the author stresses the eternal purpose behind the events that have transpired in Christ, how *the* great design of God to bring people to him in grace was realized in the death, resurrection, and now **ecclesial** (churchly) reality of Jesus.

Verses 14–19 are a famous prayer well worth quoting:

> For this reason I bow my knees before the Father, from whom every family in heaven and on earth is named, that according to the riches of his glory he may grant you to be strengthened with might through his Spirit in the inner man, and that Christ may dwell in your hearts through faith; that you, being rooted and grounded in love, may have power to comprehend with all the saints what is the breadth and length and height and depth, and to know the love of Christ which surpasses knowledge, that you may be filled with all the fulness of God.

Reference to the breadth, length, height, and depth shows how the author is drawn to the fullness (pleroma) of God, the divinity as filling every nook and cranny of reality, as being a richness or vastness or density that is for the believer as pervasive as the atmosphere. One thinks here of the lines from Paul's speech in the Aeropagus in Athens (Acts 17:27–28): " . . . that they should seek God, in the hope that they might feel after him and find him. Yet he is not far from each one of us, for 'in him we live and move and have our being. . . .'" The last lines of the author's prayer here in Ephesians link the fullness of God to the love of Christ. If believers come to know the love of Christ (which surpasses knowledge in any purely intellectual sense, which is an understanding that is bedrock and holistic), they will be filled with all the pleroma of God. The prayer concludes with a wish for God's glorification in the Church and in Christ Jesus forever.

Chapter 4 examines the unity of the Church. The author asks his readers to be patient, meek, and forbearing with one another, maintaining the "unity of the Spirit in the bond of peace" (4:3). The followers of Christ have many bonds of unity: "There is one body and one spirit, just as you were called to the one hope that belongs to your call, one Lord, one faith, one baptism, one God and Father of us all, who is above all and through all and in all" (4:4–6). However, members of the Church have different (complementary) gifts. When the Christ who has plumbed the depths and risen to the heights distributed his gifts some members became apostles, others prophets, others teachers, and so on—whatever was needed to build up the Body of Christ, the Church. A certain evolutionary or organic note enters in: The Church is growing toward "the measure of the stature of the fulness of Christ" (4:13). So members should not be children or weaklings tossed about by vicious human wiles. They should through truth and love contribute to the knitting together and growth of the Christian Body.

From 4:17 to 6:9 the author discusses ethical questions, describing what is and what is not in keeping with a holy life in the Christian Body. Certainly the (unconverted) Gentiles are a bad example, with all their ignorance and lust, their hardness of heart and uncleanness. When believers "learn Christ" they put away this old nature and put on a new nature of righteousness and holiness. (This is another place where Ephesians parallels Colossians. See Colossians 3:5–10.) Falsehood, anger, stealing, evil talk, and the rest have no place in a faithful Christian. Rather hard work, edifying talk, tenderheartedness, and forgiveness are the hallmarks of good faith. Exhibiting these, Christians do not grieve the Holy Spirit in whom they have been sealed but positively imitate the way that God has treated them: graciously, mercifully.

Chapter 5 specifies model Christian behavior as a "walk" in love that is an imitation of God and Christ: "Therefore be imitators of God, as beloved children. And walk in love, as Christ loved us and gave himself up for us, a fragrant offering and sacrifice to God" (5:1–2). (In the last phrase the author conjures up the Temple sacrifice.) Imitating God means avoiding fornication, impurity, covetousness, and the other pagan vices. (The author seems to have standardized lists of vices and virtues from which to draw.) Verse 8 introduces the symbol of light: "For once you were darkness, but now you are light in the Lord; walk as children of light (for the fruit of light is found in all that is good and right and true)" (5:8–9). The walk of love is therefore a walk of light as well. For the author of Ephesians, as for the Johannine literature of the New Testament, light and love flow together, and light-love represents something close to the core of the divine nature. Therefore light-love can specify or animate the distinctive behavior of the children of God, those whom God has called to share in the divine life. Where life apart from God is a shameful matter of dark secrets, life in Christ is open and full of light. Believers should be wise, letting the Spirit be their intoxication, not worldly wine. They should constantly be singing the praises of God.

Verses 21–33 develop a famous symbolism in which the relationship between husband and wife and the relationship between Christ and the

Church are set side by side to illumine one another. All Christians should be subject to one another, out of reverence for Christ. Wives should be subject to husbands as the Church is subject to Christ. (In first-century social codes this generally was thought to represent good order.) Husbands should love their wives as Christ loved the Church, giving himself up for her. The Church, indeed, is the Bride of Christ, called to be spotless and splendid. Husbands should love their wives as they love their own flesh. Christ cherishes the Church as his own flesh. In marrying husbands and wives become one flesh. The mystery of such a union sheds light on the mysterious oneness of Christ and the Church. They too share a common life.

Continuing his concern for good order, the author tells children to obey their parents and fathers not to provoke their children to anger (again echoing Colossians). Slaves should obey their masters as though they were obeying Christ. Masters should not threaten their slaves but remember that God is the master of us all.

The author then urges the Ephesians to stand strong against the devil, realizing that the Christian fight is against more than flesh and blood. Believers should take on the armor of God, which is made up of such virtues as truth, righteousness, and peace. They should pray constantly, not forgetting (as the author of Colossians also asked) the apostle who is in prison, that he may proclaim the gospel boldly. Tychicus will give them news of how the author is doing. The conclusion is a sending of peace, love, faith, and grace.

Why Was This Written?

We have already quoted one New Testament authority to the effect that there is no consensus on why Ephesians was written. Another quotation can amplify this opinion and show some of the very many motives that scholars have seen in the letter:

> K. H. von Weizsacker understood Ephesians and Colossians as writings composed for countering competition offered in Asia Minor by the Johannine literature, and for defending Paul against a theology promoted under Peter's name. A similar historical purpose is ascribed to Ephesians by H. Chadwick: a spiritual crisis of post-Pauline Gentile Christianity was to be met by the emphasis placed upon the unity of the church—a unity founded upon the communion of Judaeo-Christian and Gentile-Christian congregations. Another recent thesis . . . holds that the crisis was caused by the influx of Gnosticism, and Ephesians intended to meet Gnosticism with Gnosticizing arguments.

> Still more definitions of the purpose can be found. Whether or not the Gnostic background and Pauline authorship are endorsed, Ephesians is often treated as an attempt to sum up and to recommend to a later generation the apostle Paul's teaching. . . . Schiler understands Ephesians as a Wisdom speech, a meditation upon Christ's wisdom which can be ascribed to Paul himself. . . . Different again is the description of the purpose of Ephesians given by those who see in it a discourse on baptism written for the benefit of

newly baptized Gentiles. Some believe that the purpose of Ephesians was to ward off an enthusiastic or mystery-religion-like misunderstanding of baptism.[17]

These are only a fraction of the different interpretational opinions. Clearly the author of Ephesians had a certain genius for seducing people to find in his writing what emphases they would. At times Ephesians seems like the New Testament's Rorschach blot.

Perhaps the least misleading view is that Ephesians, like 1 Peter, was a universal letter, a sort of **encyclical** to the whole Church (or at least to that Pauline part of the Church which the author felt free to instruct). As such it contrasts with the letters that are certainly from Paul's hand, all of which address specific churches and problems.[18] Particular troubles may have played some role, but the more general purpose probably was to lay out the profound view of the mystery of salvation, with special emphasis on the Church (understood as embodying the resurrected, cosmic Lord) that several decades of Pauline reflection had matured.

What Background Does This Text Presuppose?

Ephesians presupposes the apostle Paul's revealed mission to preach the gospel to the Gentiles. It presupposes the division between Jews and Gentiles that preceded Christ, and the continuance of tensions between these two groups within the Church. Like the Pauline literature as a whole, it presupposes the earthly career of Jesus (although, in equally characteristically Pauline fashion, it makes no reference to Jesus' preaching, healings, and the like). It especially presupposes Jesus' death and resurrection. Finally, like Colossians, it presupposes a view of reality in which spiritual entities are considered completely real.

Ethically, the letter largely accepts the hierarchical order of relations between men and women, parents (especially fathers) and children, and masters and slaves that structured Hellenistic society. It assumes that pagans will have troubled passions, lustful hearts, and dark minds, because they will not know the true God. By contrast, vital Christians will manifest the grace of God in their hearts by sober, chaste, loving behavior toward one another.

Religiously, Ephesians, perhaps more than any other work in the Pauline corpus, assumes the language and experience of deep prayer. In his thanksgivings to God the author rides certain core images like winged horses, letting them take him up to the heavenly realm, where the glory of God the Father and the exalted lordship of the Christ who sits at the Father's right hand are the central panels in a dazzling layout of divine light and love. His prayer is imaginative and contemplative, full of petition, yes, but more basically an outcry of gratitude and praise for the power and beauty of the God who has unveiled such a wonderful plan of salvation. Unless we can generate some sympathy for such a prayer, such an enraptured, loving acclamation of an unlimitedly powerful and lightsome God, we will not follow Ephesians' religious logic. To its author the heavenly realm was more real than the earthly realm, probably because in his Hellenistic world lower things generally were thought to participate in higher things; what was below was real only in the measure that it drew its form from what was above.

What Lasting Significance Does This Have?

Within the storehouse of Christian basic symbols or originating ideas, several that bear on the Church, the pervasive presence of God, and the reconciling character of Christ owe a great deal to Ephesians. For instance, Ephesians presents one of the most profound, mystical views of the Church, taking it as both the fullness of Christ and Christ's Bride. Both figures complement the Johannine image of branches joined to a vine. Both are more personal. The figure of fullness dovetails with the stress throughout Ephesians on pleroma, with the general sense of fulfillment the letter conveys. The image of a marriage between Christ and the Church adds overtones of intimacy, tenderness, and a completely shared fortune and fate.

When Ephesians speaks of the principalities and powers of this age, it works with the notion, common in Hellenistic culture, that angels, demons, and other spiritual beings populate the "zones" between human beings and God. When it makes the risen Christ the Lord of these zones, as well as of space and time, it conveys the sense that the saving God is at work everywhere. Many of the principalities may oppose him, but he is by far the stronger power.

The God of Ephesians is a pervasive presence, not so much a being who stands over or against the world as a foundation or inflowing cause that neglects no part of creation. This is not a philosophical point of view, however, so much as a religious point of view. Philosophically, any system that makes a "God" the creator or foundation of the world can quickly reason to a certain presence of that God in or to anything that depends upon him, her, or it. For example, medieval Christian philosophy said that all **contingent** beings, all creatures, would cease to exist if God did not grant them existence and allow them to participate in the divine font of being moment by moment. With different overtones, Hindu Vedanta philosophy said many of the same things: the Brahman or atman that is the ultimate reality of the world is present in each being (indeed, is the realest part of each being).

The viewpoint of Ephesians diverges from these philosophical viewpoints in that it appears to be speaking on the basis of a religious experience or sense of a personal divine power, either that of Christ the risen Lord or that of God the Father (the Spirit is less prominent in Ephesians than in the letters more certainly written by Paul). The author describes the permeation of the world by God on the basis of his experience of and conviction about salvation, on the basis of his interpretation of specific historical events such as the death and resurrection of Jesus. Further, the cultic activity of the Church, especially its baptismal ritual and eucharist, certainly formed the author's convictions. So the pervasive God that he describes is more an object of worship than an object of detached speculation. The author's diction is more that of prayer than of detached metaphysical analysis.

Concerning the reconciling character of Christ, the grace note of Ephesians is peace. Perhaps the **shalom** of the Israelite God, the holistic peace and rightness of that God's reign and benevolence, shaped the author at this point. Whatever the source, his peace is a lovely concept, but one that the long history of Church divisions now makes somewhat rueful. Apparently Ephesians did not have within the Christian community a lasting significance sufficiently deep to prevent the numerous **schisms** that fractured Christ's peace. Apparently it did not communicate its organic view of the Church as a body of reconciled members sufficiently cogently to make Church division unthinkable. The oneness of faith that the author hymns contrasts awkwardly with the plurality of Christian ecclesial bodies and the hatred that generated "Christian" warfare. So in an age seeking ecumenical reunion, Ephesians is apt to taste bittersweet. Today its most lasting ecclesial significance might be the suggestion that one only sees unity to the intense degree that the author of Ephesians did when one has meditated as profoundly as he did on the way only one Lord fills the Church, only one treasure (the grace of Christ) is paramount.[19]

Moving the question of lasting significance outside the borders of Christianity, among the several characteristics of Ephesians that come to mind are the spiritualism it shares with Colossians (the significance of which we discussed sufficiently above) and its dynamic moralism. By this last phrase we mean its notion that faith (or any real set of personal values) is a walk (2:2, 2:10, 5:2, 5:8, 5:15) or a "way," in the case of Christianity a way of love and light pioneered by Christ. (It is the Epistle to the Hebrews that proposes this image of Christ as the pioneer of faith, but the image is not contrary to the spirit of Ephesians.) We know that in the Acts of the Apostles "the Way" is a synonym for the Christian faith or lifestyle (see, for instance, Acts 9:2; 18:25 f; 19:9, 23; 22:4, 14, 22). Other religions, too, have used the image of the way, and almost always with the same dynamic impact upon their ethical teachings.

In the case of Ephesians, while the author may draw upon rather trite catalogues of virtues and vices when he wants to exhort his readers to stay away from sinful behavior and manifest gracious behavior, the more powerful insight at work in his ethical exhortation is his appreciation of the play of light and darkness in his readers' souls. For him Christian faith is a wholesale movement toward the light, producing such a clear conscience that one can stand by one's deeds, with no ugly vices or secrets in the closet. Christian morality is not a matter of obeying a list of dos and don'ts but a matter of moving forward toward the light, growing more gracious and lovely because one is coming closer to, becoming more filled with, the gracious and loving God.

The analogies to classical Greek philosophy are quite striking at this point, and they can be terribly significant for the proper analysis of the spiritual diseases of our own or any age. So, for example, Eric Voegelin, a profound interpreter of Plato, has made the Platonic symbol of the pulls towards life and death (which seem quite equivalent to Ephesians' symbol of light and darkness) penetrate the heart of the condition that all humans share as mortal beings, people who know in our bones we soon must die:

> In the *Laws*, Plato has developed the myth of the puppetplayer who pulls the human puppets by the various metal cords, by the golden cord of reason and by the lesser cords of the passions. One could, and still can, refer to this myth for understanding the interplay of the pulls in man's existence, but one must not forget the cosmic drama in which it has its place. The pull (*helkein*) of reason and the counterpull (*anthelkein*) of the passions are real enough but they are countermovements experienced by the *psyche* in its state of entombment in a mortal body. The reason why man should follow one pull rather than the other is not to be found in the "psychodynamics" of the puppetplay, nor in some standards of "morality," but in the potential immortality offered by the divine presence in the *metaxy* [state between divinity and prime matter that characterizes human existence]. In the classic experience of noetic [rational, reason-stressing] existence man is free either to engage in the action of "immortalizing" by following the pull of the divine *nous* [mind], or to choose death by following the counterpull of the passions. The psyche of man is the battleground between the forces of life and death. Life is not given; the God of the *Laws* can only suffer it through the revelation of his presence; life to be gained requires the cooperation of man.[20]

The author of Ephesians would want to say further things about the resurrection of Christ as the prime revelation of the true God's presence and immortalizing power, but the basic thrust of this analysis would be very congenial to him and would fit quite well his symbolism of a walk in love and light.

CONCLUSION: THE PAULINE VISION

Leading Pauline Convictions

When we look back over the messages we have seen Paul or his disciples (in his name) sending to some of the early Christian communities, what are the things that stand out as most important?

First, there is Paul's own sense of the gospel: what he preaches, the vision that took over his life. Paul preaches Christ crucified and resurrected. He understood the revelation that took over his life to be God's telling him that Jesus, who had hung from a cross accursed, had been resurrected to make a new phase in the history of God's dealings with humanity, a new plot line for the story that had begun back with Abraham (or Adam) and hitherto had been thought to have its major shape or interpretation from Moses and the covenant Law. In experiencing Christ as alive, as raised by God, Paul experienced the crumbling of his prior world view. Something inconceivable had happened. God had acted apart from or beyond Torah. Faith in the power of Jesus' sacrifice had replaced the works of the Mosaic Law as the way to salvation.

Moreover, in acting apart from or beyond Torah God had made clearer both the divine nature and the human vocation. The human vocation, the call sent out to all people, Gentiles as well as Jews, now was that they come to intimacy and peace with God on the basis of the forgiveness God had powerfully worked through the death and resurrection of Jesus. People should accept the Spirit and enter the Church, the fullness of Christ. High and low, far and wide, Paul would preach this astounding good news, this nearly unthinkable mystery and eternal plan that had so recently been revealed. It was the mystery and plan set forth to reorient all people's lives, to redefine what any human being was made for.

This gospel also brought forward a new picture of divinity, with the accent on God's justifying, and making whole or right, even the ungodly, those who had no basis for expecting God's favor. Leander Keck has explained this righteousness of God as follows:

> Paul's understanding of the righteousness of God who rectifies the ungodly is grounded in Jesus' cross/resurrection, as Rom. 4:25 makes clear: Jesus "was put to death for our trespasses and raised from our justification" (rectification). The discontinuity between the God who justifies his godly clients and the God who rectifies the ungodly is grounded in the fact that God resurrected a Jesus who died under a curse. In Gal. 3:13 Paul quotes Deut. 21:23, "cursed be everyone who hangs on a tree," which he interprets as a reference to the crucifixion. Therefore Christ became "a curse for us"—that is, he died as a cursed man. . . . Because Jesus was executed as one accursed by the law, the resurrection of precisely this Jesus reveals that God's verdict on him cannot be inferred from the cross. Were that the case, God would indeed rectify the godly who put him there in the name of the law, and in the name of law and order. But Jesus' resurrection reveals God's freedom and otherness. Moreover, unless God's resurrecting Jesus was arbitrary (unthinkable to Paul), the resurrection must reveal God's fidelity to Jesus and to himself; that is, it revealed God's integrity over against what was presumed to be his integrity. The fact that the Christ-event occurred in a sinful world shows Paul that God is free to rectify the world and persons in it, and that this rectification does not depend on human readiness, achieved goodness, or self-wrought rectitude but solely on God's grace. Whoever trusts this God is therefore not only rightly related to God (rectified), but must realign every conception of God and of the human condition according to this event.[21]

Second, the Pauline view of the Church is as much determined by the central event of the resurrection of Jesus as are the Pauline revisions of the nature of God and of human beings. The Church is the people who open themselves to the rectification that God has offered and manifested in Jesus Christ. It is the living Body of Christ, formed by the Spirit of the resurrected Christ and enjoying the grace of favor with God now, the hope for heavenly union with God in a resurrection of its own.

A predominant problem that we saw stalking Paul in all the letters certainly from his own hand was the relation of this Church to Israel, the people of the Mosaic covenant. Taken overall, Paul's resolution of this problem carries considerable nuance. Clearly the dramatic new situation that had come about through the death and resurrection of Jesus had the

Mosaic covenant Law as its background. But Paul increasingly came to judge that circumcision, kosher regulations, and the rest of the Mosaic Law ought not to be binding on Gentile Christians. He thought he had worked out a compromise with the leaders of the Jerusalem church, who were sensitive to the values of the covenant Law, but he found himself dogged by troublemakers who would not let the Gentiles be. So he had to think longer and deeper about the function of Torah in God's plan of salvation, and eventually it took on the status of something both provisional and revelatory of human sin.

If God had overcome human sinfulness in the death and resurrection of Christ, then for both Jews and Gentiles the covenant Law stood in a new context. In Christ God had fashioned for himself an acceptable sacrifice. The point now was to live in the faith, hope, and love of the new rectified relationship opened up by that sacrifice. Covenant regulations and all the rest were beside the point. Paul could agree (according to Acts 15:30–32) to compromises such as asking the Gentiles not to eat things strangled or bloody, and he could say that in its time the Law had been good (and had fashioned a people for whom God still had holy purposes). But at bottom the newness of the Christian situation made Paul impatient with the faith he had grown up in. At bottom he was eager to bring all the world into the largess of the divine offer of salvation that had erupted on the cross.

We shall take up the ethical and sociological dimensions of this Pauline vision momentarily. Here, however, let us pause to assess Paul's Gospel. Certainly it has been a major factor in Christians' self-understanding, and certainly it was a powerful force in the spread of Christian faith throughout the inhabited world. But, along with other books of the New Testament that we shall soon take up, it also contributed to the puzzling (and at times bloody) question, "How could anyone refuse the offer that God made in the death and resurrection of Christ? How could the Jews not embrace Jesus; how could so many Gentiles prefer their idols and lusts?"

Paul's very ardor for the gospel understandably makes him impatient with those who do not welcome it and inclines him even to attribute their rejections to sin and willful blindness. They then come to stand under the wrath of God, condemned as depraved and ungrateful. In the history of Christianity this kind of thinking has walked hand in hand with persecutions of Jews, crusades against Muslims and other "infidels," and cruel treatments of groups (for example, homosexuals and uppity women) who did not hew to the Christian main line. What is one to make of such ardor gone awry? Is there no golden mean between a tolerance that expresses tepidity and a passion that creates bigotry? Are there no resources in the Pauline vision, no places where the apostle himself shows he knew better, that would help us not reject any person of goodwill?

Without a doubt there are, although of course in spotlighting these places or especially praising them we make a choice, a judgment, with which not all readers of Paul will agree. For example, in saying that Romans 9–11 represents a more mature view of Judaism than the view set forth in Galatians we judge that the Paul of Romans was fairer to the faith in which he had been brought up, the faith which he had practiced with

Pharisaic learning and rigor. As a number of recent studies of the Pharisaic Judaism that was contemporary with Paul have suggested, that Judaism was by no means a simple legalism; it did not at all assume that people could bootstrap themselves up to righteousness before God. Deep in the religious understanding of the leading rabbis of Paul's day lay a strong appreciation of the priority of grace, a rich awareness that Israel's prosperity in faith mainly depended on the sheer loving-kindness of its Lord. Indeed, one can interpret the zeal of many Pharisees to keep the Law minutely and exactly as an effort to praise and glorify this great Lord.

In fact, Paul took over his conviction about grace, and several other key convictions, from his years of Jewish faith:

> For the reader of Paul's letters one thing is striking: the Pharisaic faith involved an amazing number of convictions which we also find in Paul's teaching. We might have wondered, how can one convert from such a beautiful faith? And we can begin to appreciate why the majority of the Jewish people did not convert to the Gospel, a painful fact for Paul (cf. Romans 9–11). Their faith did involve a total devotion to the true God and made out of them his zealous servants, but Paul converted and considered all this zealous service to God as a loss.[22]

Paul converted and felt this way because he experienced Christ to be alive. Thus he thought he had irrefutable proof that God had established a new order of salvation. Nonetheless, Paul's own gospel of grace allows us to esteem the Jewish order of salvation as a rich mercy of God whose implications none of us has ever fully fathomed or exhausted.

Somewhat relatedly, we may turn the Pauline stress on God's gracious mystery of salvation, which comes to sweetest fruition in Colossians and Ephesians, against the grim surface of such passages as Romans 1. Paul surely had the right, perhaps even the duty, to describe the wrath of God and the depths of human depravity that the blinding light of the cross and resurrection revealed. The human sufferings that human depravities cause, to say nothing of the way they mock the generosity of a good Creator, are reason enough to excoriate them as Paul does. But the correlations that Paul makes between outward behavior and inner motivation, "immorality" and a godless heart, deserve far more nuance, especially in a psychologically sophisticated time like our own. Certainly one can suspect that people should know, from observing nature, that there is a great mystery to creation, and that they should know that for creation to make sense or exist there probably has to stand behind it a Being of a quite different order. But this is neither an easy inference to make, so complicated is creation (especially after the rise of modern science), nor an inference so absent from the hearts of the majority of human beings that we must speak of a wholesale human depravity. Probably more people than not do sense something holy at the depths of creation. And probably more people than not do honor that mystery, do pay it the respect befitting a Creator, by living more toward the light than toward the darkness, more toward love and goodness than toward hatred and evil.

The crux of such an estimate, by Paul's own standards, would be the way people actually lived. If "idol worshipers" proved honest in business, loving in parenting, self-spending in friendship, and the like, would Paul not have to grant them a knowledge and service of God? If homosexuals proved decent neighbors, honest craftspeople, and faithful lovers and worshipers, would Paul not have to take his analysis of their "shameless acts" to a deeper, more interior and adequate level? We think Paul would and could, so rich do we find the treasure of grace that dominates his apostolic vision. The alternative would be a state of affairs in which sin had abounded over grace, and that certainly would not be Pauline.

Ethical and Sociological Dimensions

For many centuries after the letters of Paul and his school had become part of the Christian religious treasury, people read them with little sense of history, little awareness of how conditioned the letters were (as any writings are) by the cultural milieu in which their writers had been immersed. The rise of modern critical history made scholars dig into the background of Paul's times and recover many of the practices (e.g., sacrifice) and ideas (e.g., Gnostic wisdom) that probably shaped him. Similarly, the rise of modern literary methods showed the Epistles to be complicated works that on occasion wove in bits of hymns, stock ethical advice, and the like.

Today New Testament scholars seem particularly impressed by the light that social science may shed on early Christianity. Adapting techniques of sociologists, cultural anthropologists, economic historians, and others, they have developed a number of interesting conjectures about the social world of Paul and his followers. While some of their results await thorough verification, we can indicate how social science now suggests we may fill out the picture of Paul and early Christianity by reading beneath the surface of the Epistles.

One of the most praised studies of Paul from a sociological perspective is Wayne A. Meeks' recent *The First Urban Christians: The Social World of the Apostle Paul*. Among Meeks' findings is the likelihood that the people in Paul's congregations both represented a fair cross section of the urban society of his time and probably averaged a middle-class degree of wealth and status:

> The extreme top and bottom of the Greco-Roman social scale are missing from the picture. It is hardly surprising that we meet no landed aristocrats, no senators, *equites* [knights], nor (unless Erastus might qualify) *decurions* [councilors]. But there is also no specific evidence of people who are destitute— such as hired menials and dependent handworkers; the poorest of the poor, peasants, agricultural slaves, and hired agricultural day laborers, are absent because of the urban setting of the Pauline groups. There may well have been members of the Pauline communities who lived at the subsistence level, but we hear nothing of them. The levels in between, however, are well represented. There are slaves, although we cannot tell how many. The "typical" Christian, however, the one who most often signals his presence in the letters

by one or another small clue, is a free artisan or small trader. Some even in those occupational categories had houses, slaves, the ability to travel, and other signs of wealth. Some of the wealthy provided housing, meeting places, and other services for individual Christians and whole groups. In effect, they filled the roles of patrons.[23]

Meeks takes interesting leads from studies of cemetery markings and the like that suggest how the early Christians might have perceived their churches as similar to the burial societies and religious clubs that flourished in contemporary Hellenistic society. Drawing on studies of social status in Paul's time, he suggests ways that Christian church membership might have appealed to upwardly mobile people, or to women and slaves who found that it enhanced their status. The baptismal and eucharistic doctrines of the Pauline writings take on more vivid coloring when we see their probable social setting. Concerning baptism, for instance, Meeks reasons:

> Descent into the water obviously did not mime Jesus' death, but it could be construed as being "buried with Christ" (Rom. 6:4; Col. 2:12), and rising from the water could very well signify "being raised with Christ" (Col. 2:12; 3:1; Eph. 2:6). For death itself, some other action would have to be found; the Pauline Christians found it in the removal of clothing before entering the water. That became "taking off the body" or "the old human." Reclothing afterward could then represent the new life of resurrection. The clothing imagery comprises an elaborate complex of metaphors. What is "taken off" is variously construed as "the old human," "the body of flesh," and the vices associated therewith. This "removal of the body of flesh" is "the circumcision of Christ," that is, the Christian equivalent of Jewish circumcision of proselytes (Col. 2:11). What is "put on" is Christ himself, as "the new human," who is "being renewed . . . according to the image of his creator" (Col. 3:10). Characteristic of the "new human" is unity, the end of the opposed sets of roles that typified the "old human": Jew/Greek, slave/free, male/female (Gal. 3:28; I Cor. 12:13; Col. 3:10f.).[24]

One of the most provocative suggestions from sociological analyses of early Christian literature has been that the social existence that came in the wake of conversion, baptism, and Church membership was quite ambivalent. This is clear even from the slight evidence we have considered in the past few pages. On the one hand, many members of the early Christian communities probably were middle-class, small-artisan types, trying to make a living in ordinary society. That society was carefully stratified and such working people had to know their place. On the other hand, the Christian community that one joined through baptism downplayed social gradations, speaking of a unity in faith that put master-slave and other relations of superior to inferior aside. Clearly Paul and the other early Christians struggled to reconcile these two sides of their lives, the workaday-realistic side and the Sunday-idealistic side. When it became clear that the Day of the Lord was not imminent, the idealistic side became a serious challenge to develop a specifically Christian social ethic.

One can see this challenge in the expectations of such early Christian groups as slaves and women. For instance, Elisabeth Schüssler-Fiorenza has argued that slaves who joined the Christian community expected their freedom to be bought by the Church:

> A letter of Pliny to the Emperor Trajan confirms that at the beginning of the second century women "servants" (slaves?) were ministers in the church of Bithynia. Around the same time, Ignatius writes to the bishop Polycarp of Smyrna, telling him not to set free either male or female slaves at the expense of the church (4:3). This exhortation presupposes that slaves who joined the Christian community expected their freedom to be bought by the church.

> Such expectations were supported by the Christians' belief that they were truly set free by Christ. Such formulas occur again and again in the Pauline letters: "You were bought with a price, do not become human slaves" (I Cor 6:20, 7:23). Or "For freedom Christ has set us free . . . do not submit again to a yoke of slavery" (Gal 5:1). The goal of Christian calling is freedom: "You were called to freedom" (Gal 5:13), because "where the Spirit of the Lord is there is freedom" (2 Cor 3:17). To argue that Christian slaves who understood their call to freedom had only a "superficial understanding of the gospel" is to minimize the impact of this language in a world where slavery was a commonly accepted institution. Liberation from the slavery of sin, law, and death, from the conditions of the "present evil age" (Gal 1:4), has "freedom" as its purpose and destiny. "As a result, *eleutheria* (freedom) is the central theological concept which sums up the Christian's situation before God as well as in this world." Therefore, a slave woman who became a Christian in the first century heard this baptismal pronunciation as a ritual, "performative utterance," which not only had the power to shape the "symbolic universe of the Christian community" but also determined the social interrelationships and structures of the church.[25]

Freedom, though, came to have definite limitations, even within the Christian community itself. In part because most of the early Christian communities were house-churches, assemblies that came together like an extended family, many of the customs or assumptions of Hellenistic society regarding proper order in a family circle found their way into the Christian ethicomoral codes. So, for example, chapter 3 of Colossians uses almost the same view of freedom that we find in Galatians 3:28, where Paul says there is no Jew or Gentile, slave or free, male or female, but it drops the dissolution of the male-female difference and goes on to tell both women and slaves to be submissive: "Here [in the new nature] there cannot be Greek and Jew, circumcised and uncircumcised, barbarian, Scythian, slave, free man, but Christ is all, and in all. . . . Wives, be subject to your husbands, as is fitting in the Lord. . . . Slaves, obey in everything those who are your earthly masters . . ." (Col. 3:11, 18, 22). One sees that despite the equality and newness promised in the baptismal formula of Galatians 3:28, the social customs of the time, with its dominant view of male-female and master-slave relations, came to structure the author's behavioral counsel:

> In taking over the Greco-Roman ethic of the patriarchal household code, Colossians not only "spiritualizes" and moralizes the baptismal community understanding expressed in Gal 3:28 but also makes this Greco-Roman household ethic a part of a "Christian" social ethic. However, it is important to

keep in mind that such a reinterpretation of the Christian baptismal vision is late—it did not happen before the last third of the first century. Moreover, it is found in only one segment of early Christianity, the post-Pauline tradition, and had no impact on the Jesus traditions.[26]

We shall see more of the Jesus traditions in the next chapters, when we deal with the synoptic Gospels. Here we need to summarize the socioethical legacy of the apostle to the Gentiles and his disciples. It turns out to be mixed. At a radical level, Paul and the authors of Colossians and Ephesians discern a new creation or new nature. The Christ-event has been so deep a redoing of the order of things that it calls to mind the original creation from formless waste described in Genesis. One can say that all social relations have been recast, old notions of superiority and inferiority have been overthrown. If Christ is a blazing new creation, and all sorts of people can be incorporated into Christ, then all sorts of people can be equal in the one new thing that is really necessary: adherence to the resurrected Savior.

However, it is possible to draw two different sets of conclusions from this radical equality and newness in Christ. One set says that people should work out a new social-economic-political order in terms of their radical equality. They should strive, in the ways in which they communicate with one another, do business, and establish their organizations, to express their bedrock equality and do justice to the primacy of their common adherence to Christ. The other set says that the radical equality created by faith means that social-economic-political differences are insignificant. There is no need to reset the relations one sees in one's unconverted (surrounding) milieu. Wives and husbands, children and parents, slaves and masters can continue to relate to one another as inferior and superior, because their common faith and mutual love remove any sting from these designations of "inferior" and "superior" and make such designations only social conveniences approved by God to facilitate good order. Not changing the codes of the surrounding society also will make it easier for Christianity to appeal to the citizenry of that society, to seem quite sane and reasonable. It will mean that potential converts have to change few of their workaday ways of regarding the opposite sex, underlings, or bosses.

To this day Christians continue to quote different Pauline texts (usually with little awareness that Paul's own letters, those of his first generation of disciples, and the later "pastorals" probably arose in quite different social contexts), depending on the sociopolitical orientation they favor. To this day the vision of Paul and his disciples continues to be complicated and volatile. So, in this day, readers have to choose which values they shall make central and which peripheral, where the whole Pauline vision or world view finds its best point of balance.

SUMMARY

In this chapter we have mainly considered Epistles shaped by Paul's ideas and values but most likely not written by the apostle himself. Such criteria as literary style and theological emphasis have led a large number of scholars to consider 2 Thessalonians, Colossians, and Ephesians the work of disciples of Paul. Since the phenomenon of pseudepigraphy or writing in the name of an authoritative figure was widespread in antiquity, the fact that the letters claim to be written by Paul does not itself prove that they were.

2 Thessalonians probably was written in a time of persecution, after 70 C.E., to support Christians who were feeling hard pressed. It arranges many of its materials parallel to the arrangements of 1 Thessalonians, but it lacks the joy, stress on Christ's death and resurrection, and stress on the Spirit that characterize 1 Thessalonians. Rather the distinctive note of 2 Thessalonians is apocalyptic. The Day of the Lord is on the horizon, not imminent but sure eventually to recompense those who suffer for their faith. Before the Day of the Lord there must occur a rebellion and the revelation of a man of lawlessness. The power presently restraining the forces of evil must wane, so that evil can flare up, and then the Lord Jesus will come to slay the evil powers. 2 Thessalonians wants Christians to live responsibly (for example, working hard) in the interval between the present and the Day of the Lord. To understand this writing we must especially appreciate the general style and themes of apocalyptic literature. Its lasting significance is probably the sharp focus it places on the problem of evil.

Colossians seems to have been written between 63 and 90 and to represent a mature form of Pauline reflection, perhaps one shaped by Gnostic challenges. It is interested in Christian wisdom, uses a lyric hymn to talk about Christ's centrality in creation, and depicts the ethical behavior of good and wise Christians in contrast to the wicked, vice-ridden ways of the world. It accepts much of the patriarchal house-code that ruled Hellenistic family life, and it makes its greatest impact as an expression of the cosmic outreach of Paul's thought. Whether or not it was a response to particular Gnostic challenges, it helped make Christianity competitive with the wisdom literature of the other religious movements of the time. Today it may be most significant for making us ask what sort of knowledge really is wise.

We do not know the occasion or the date of Ephesians, and probably the best suggestion as to its nature is that it was an encyclical or universal letter, rather than an address to one particular church. It quotes Colossians at many points and falls in the same category as Colossians: Christian wisdom literature. While Ephesians has no stunning textual gem such as Colossians 1:15–20 or Philippians 2:5–11, the prayer in 3:14–19 is famous, lyrical, and profound. Chapter 5 is famous for its description of Christian life as a walk in love and light, and also for its paralleling Christ's relation to the Church to a marriage between a husband and wife. The ethical sections of the letter ask for orderly social relations and decent control of one's passions. Probably the best way to view the letter overall is as a meditation on the splendid plan of God, a prayerful appreciation of the divine mystery. As such it can continue to provoke useful questions about the depth of creation and the correct ethical path through life today.

In concluding our study of Paul and the Pauline world view, we stressed Paul's gospel of Christ crucified and resurrected, Paul's view of the Church and the relations between Jews and Gentiles, and Paul's ethical judgments (criticizing them in the light of his own gospel of grace). Turning then to the ethical and sociological dimensions of Pauline Christianity, we reported on the new look at the (rather middle-class) population of the Pauline churches that social scientific methods have recently been offering, and also at the tensions they have revealed in a Christianity that spoke on the one hand of a new creation and on the other hand of obeying with docility the prevailing hierarchical patterns of Hellenistic society.

STUDY QUESTIONS

1. What are the main reasons for considering that 2 Thessalonians was not written by Paul himself?

2. How does 2 Thessalonians describe what will precede the Day of the Lord?

3. Summarize the faith expressed in Colossians 1:15–20.

4. How does Colossians anchor wisdom to Christ?

5. In what way are Colossians' views of Christian social relations conservative?

6. What is the mystery or providential plan that Ephesians finds so dazzling?

7. In what sense is Ephesians shaped by an attitude of prayer or worship?

8. Evaluate the effort in Ephesians 5 to compare the relation of Christ and the Church to a human marriage.

9. Evaluate the demonology of Ephesians.

10. Evaluate the judgments Paul passes on Jews and pagans who reject Christ or the biblical God.

11. How adequate is Pauline Christianity for women?

NOTES

1. See Gerhard Krodel, "2 Thessalonians," in Gerhard Krodel, ed., *Proclamation Commentaries: Ephesians, Colossians, 2 Thessalonians, the Pastoral Epistles* (Philadelphia: Fortress, 1978), pp. 73–84; also Daryl Schmidt, "The Authenticity of 2 Thessalonians," *SBL Seminar Papers 1983*, ed. K. H. Richards (Chico, Calif.: Scholars Press, 1983), pp. 289–96.

2. Ivan Havener, *Collegeville Bible Commentary* 8 (Collegeville, Minn.: Liturgical Press, 1983), pp. 52–53.

3. See Gerhard Krodel, "2 Thessalonians," p. 96.

4. See Jouette H. Bassler, "The Enigmatic Sign: 2 Thessalonians 1:5," *Catholic Biblical Quarterly* 46 (1984), 496–510.

5. See James H. Charlesworth, ed. *The Old Testament Pseudepigrapha* (Philadelphia: Fortress, 1983), vol. 1.

6. See Ivan Havener, *Collegeville Bible Commentary* 8, p. 67.

7. Eduard Schweizer, *The Letter to the Colossians* (Minneapolis: Augsburg, 1982), p. 56.

8. Eduard Lohse, *Colossians and Philemon* (Philadelphia: Fortress, 1971), p. 46.

9. See John Carmody, *Ecology and Religion* (Ramsey, N.J.: Paulist, 1983), pp. 84 ff.

10. See Fred O. Francis and Wayne A. Meeks, *Conflict at Colossae* (Missoula, Mont.: Scholars Press, 1975).

11. See Pheme Perkins, *The Gnostic Dialogue* (New York: Paulist, 1980).

12. See two works of Huston Smith, *Forgotten Truth: The Primordial Tradition* (New York: Harper & Row, 1976); *Beyond the Post-Modern Mind* (New York: Crossroad, 1982).

13. William Barclay, *The Letters to the Philippians, Colossians, and Thessalonians*, rev. ed. (Philadelphia: Westminster, 1975), p. 120.

14. On the connections between this cosmic Christ and Hindu views of creation, see Raimundo Panikkar, *The Unknown Christ of Hinduism*, rev. ed. (Maryknoll, N.Y.: Orbis, 1981).

15. J. Paul Sampley, "The Letter to the Ephesians," in Krodel, ed. *Proclamation Commentaries*, p. 9.

16. Markus Barth, *Ephesians 1–3* (Garden City, N.Y.: Doubleday Anchor, 1974), p. 215.

17. Ibid., p. 57.

18. See Nils A. Dahl, "The Particularity of the Pauline Epistles as a Problem in the Ancient Church," *New Testamentica et Patristica* (Leiden: E. J. Brill, 1962), pp. 261–71.

19. See John Carmody, *The Heart of the Christian Matter: An Ecumenical Approach* (Nashville: Abingdon, 1983).

20. Eric Voegelin, *Anamnesis* (Notre Dame, Ind.: University of Notre Dame Press, 1978), p. 105.

21. Leander E. Keck, *Proclamation Commentaries: Paul and His Letters* (Philadelphia: Fortress, 1979), p. 73.

22. Daniel Patte, *Paul's Faith and the Power of the Gospel* (Philadelphia: Fortress, 1983), p. 117.

23. Wayne A. Meeks, *The First Urban Christians: The Social World of the Apostle Paul* (New Haven: Yale University Press, 1983), p. 73.

24. Ibid., p. 155.

25. Elisabeth Schüssler-Fiorenza, *In Memory of Her: A Feminist Theological Reconstruction of Christian Origins* (New York: Crossroad, 1983), pp. 209–10. The phrase about a superficial understanding of the gospel comes from J. E. Crouch, *The Origin and Intention of the Colossian Haustafel* (Göttingen: Vanderhoeck & Ruprecht, 1972), p. 127. The claim that freedom was the central theological concept summing up the Christian's situation comes from H. D. Betz, *Galatians* (Philadelphia: Fortress, 1979), p. 255.

26. Ibid., pp. 253–54. See also Wayne A. Meeks, "The Image of the Androgyne," *History of Religions* 13 (1974), pp. 165–208.

The Gospel for Mark's Church

WHAT HAVE WE HERE?

In Mark we most likely have the oldest or earliest collection of traditions about Jesus into the literary form called a "Gospel." Whereas in connection with Paul the word "Gospel" mainly means the good news of Christ's death and resurrection that Paul was commissioned to preach, in connection with Mark, Matthew, Luke, and John "Gospel" designates not only their versions of this good news but also the form in which they cast their versions. It will make our task in this middle portion of the textbook clearer if we take the time now to clarify quite thoroughly the main implications of this literary form in which the most vivid materials of the New Testament have been cast.

To speak of the Gospel as a literary form is to speak somewhat contrary to the New Testament itself—to use a somewhat academic designation that scholars have found highly useful. As Josef Schmid has put it:

> Throughout the New Testament, "gospel" means the *living, spoken word of Christ's saving message*, and is thus never a literary concept. Also, since there is only *one* saving message, the word is consistently used only in the singular. Even in the second century, this primary meaning predominates. . . . The individual gospels, too, are referred to as *to euangelion kata Matthaion, kata Markon,* etc. ("the gospel according to Matthew, according to Mark," etc.).[1]

With time, however, Christians came to refer to Mark or Matthew as "Gospels," largely because these writings were recognized as having the same value as oral preaching. They too could awaken or confirm Christian faith. Through them, too, people had access to the words and acts of Jesus Christ, just as people had such access through the preaching of a Peter or Paul.[2] Thus these writings became treasured for demonstrating the messiahship of Jesus. That was what they were communicating, not a detached account of Jesus' biography. Mark, Matthew, and the rest grew out of the oral preaching of the apostles who had been eyewitnesses of Jesus.[3] As the preaching of the apostles, their proclamation of the good news, was selective and aimed at rousing faith, so were the written Gospels selective and concerned with rousing faith. While they collected various sayings and **parables** (teaching stories) of Jesus, the written Gospels stressed above all Jesus' death and resurrection. Thus their emphasis was quite parallel to that which we have seen in Paul.

So, the literary units that we now call Gospels were a new form of writing, determined by the new occasion of proclaiming the religious significance of the life, works, teachings, death, and resurrection of the man Jesus of Nazareth, whom many first-century people had come to consider the Christ or Jewish Messiah. This explains the principles of selection and arrangement that we find in the Gospels. For while each of the New Testament four has its own design, all mold their materials for **kerygmatic** or proclamational ends. All four, in other words, group their stories and describe Jesus' death and resurrection so as to announce the achievement of God's purposes in Jesus, the arrival of the Kingdom of God, or the triumph of the saving Messiah. This is especially true in their accounts of Jesus' Passion (suffering and death). For the writers of the Gospels the point is not the maneuvers of Jesus' human opponents but the working out of God the Father's will to save sinful humankind. In addition, the writers have **apologetic** ends, in that they are trying to make the case that Jesus was the Messiah to an increasingly hostile Jewish community.

Since the purpose of a Gospel such as Mark is so different from what a twentieth-century author would have in mind were he or she to set out to write a life of Jesus, and since the four New Testament Gospels are virtually our only accredited sources of historical information about Jesus of Nazareth,[4] it follows that we shall never have, either from the New Testament or from anywhere else, a biography of Jesus in the modern sense. Always we shall see Jesus through the memories, faith, and missionary experiences of the Gospel writers and people who furnished them their sources. This does not mean that the things we read about Jesus in Mark, Matthew, Luke, and John are untrue or fabricated.[5] It just means that they are highly colored by what Jesus had come to mean to the early Christian communities from which these writers came, after several decades of living with the proclamation of Jesus' death and resurrection, of living in a Church believed to be filled with Jesus' presence and that of the Spirit and the Father.

Last, it is useful to remember that each of the four Gospels represents emphases, convictions, and experiences of different portions of the early Christian Church. Some of these experiences and convictions of course overlap, but each Gospel writer or **redactor** (editor) has a definite point of view, a distinct theological interpretation of the sources or memories of the life, teachings, and fate of Jesus. Consider, for example, the following peculiarities of Matthew and Luke:

Matthew in chapter 18 has put together various sayings of Christ to make a "community code" aimed at the situation of a community and its problems, and passages such as Mt 7:15–23 (parallel Luke 6:43–6) and Mt 24:10–12 reflect the unsatisfactory state of such communities. The conversation between John the Baptist and Jesus which precedes the account of the baptism of Jesus in Matthew (3:13–15) clearly betrays an apologetic (defensive) purpose. It was a puzzling question for early Christian circles how Jesus, the sinless one, could come to the Baptist to receive the baptism of repentance—and by doing so subordinate himself to the Baptist. It is Matthew's intention to answer this question. The more radical reorganisation of the **parousia** (return of the Lord) speech in Lk 21:5–36 (contrast Mk 13:1–33) becomes intelligible once one takes into account the way the expectation of the imminent second coming recedes in the third gospel (Luke), and once one notes in addition that Luke clearly looks back to the destruction of Jerusalem (in 70 C.E.) as an event in the past. It is only a careful consideration of the obvious differences between the gospels and the individual tendencies they bring to light which enables us to appreciate the true character of the gospels, and also to see how the fourth gospel (John), so different not simply in literary form but also in theological content, can occupy a place beside the synoptics.[6]

With this first impression of what we mean by a Gospel in mind, let us turn specifically to Mark. As noted, it is usually considered the oldest Gospel, at least in finished form. It is also in some ways the most primitive—for instance, stylistically, and in its almost ruthless focus on Jesus' having to suffer. Originally it circulated anonymously, attributed to no particular author. In the second century, when having an impressive authorship became important, it was attributed to John Mark, one of the companions of Paul (see, e.g., Acts 12:12, 25; Colossians 4:10). The second century also developed the tradition that Mark was with Peter in Rome. Internal evidence suggests that the author had close ties to (though not good geographic knowledge of) Palestine. The circle that he represents had a strongly apocalyptic faith and was especially interested in the Gentile mission. The Gospel probably was written after 70 C.E. in Syria. Because we know that Luke and Matthew used Mark, we can conjecture that they were written about 85–90 C.E..

We may outline the gospel according to Mark as follows:

Introduction 1:1–13

    Transition 1:14–15

The Authority of Jesus 1:16–3:6

    Transition 3:7–12

Jesus as Rejected Son of God 3:13–6:6a

    Transition 6:6b

Jesus as Son of God Misunderstood 6:7–8:21

    Transition 8:22–26

Christology in Light of the Passion 8:27–10:45

    Transition 10:46–52

Before the Passion 11:1–12:44
     Transition 13:1–5a
Apocalyptic Discourse 13:5b–37
     Transition 14:1–12
Passion Narrative 14:13–16:8
Addendum 16:9–20[7]

According to this outline, Mark is highly structured. The Gospel amounts to an introduction, five major sections, an apocalyptic discourse, a Passion narrative, and a later addendum. There are transitions between all seven of the major sections. The Passion Narrative is the climax, and there are textual clues that the author orchestrates the materials that precede the Passion Narrative so that the Passion Narrative will be as effective as possible. For instance, at the end of each of the first five major sections there is a hint or anticipation of the Passion (see 3:6, 6:6, 8:21, 10:45, 12:44).

From the outline, then, it is clear that this is a version of the good news that will grapple intensely with Jesus' suffering. As much as Paul's perception that the resurrection of the one crucified meant an end to the prior covenant Law (according to which crucifixion brought down God's curse), Mark's perception of salvation pivots on Jesus' transformation of suffering and death. For Markan Christianity **discipleship** means accepting and following a suffering Lord.

Introduction (1:1–13)

Mark introduces itself as good news about Jesus Christ, the Son of God. Indeed, it alone among the Gospels describes itself as a **euangelion** or glad tidings. Some manuscripts omit the title "Son of God," and Mark's more usual self-designation for Jesus is "Son of Man." Both of these titles carry a lot of freight in the Bible, and it will profit us to make a first estimate of them right now. In the New Testament "Son of God" has an extensive range of meanings: "a being with supernatural power, possessing God's special favor, the messiah and even a divine begetting in the strict sense."[8] "Son of Man" is a term with heavy overtones from the book of Daniel and Ezekiel (see for instance Daniel 7:13 and Ezekiel 2:1). The synoptic Gospels make at least five different uses of the term: (1) in contexts where Jesus speaks of his human condition (e.g., Matthew 8:20); (2) in contexts where superhuman powers are credited to Jesus (e.g., Mark 2:10); (3) in contexts of Jesus' messianic mission (e.g., Matthew 13:37); (4) in numerous contexts where Jesus' Passion and death are discussed (e.g., Mark 8:31, 9:12); and (5) in numerous contexts of the Day of the Lord or *parousia* (e.g., Mark 9:9, 14:2).[9]

While Mark wants the reader to understand that "Son of God" is the most appropriate title for Jesus, he feels obliged to challenge the reader's assumptions that either the Jewish or the Hellenistic understanding of this term is adequate in Jesus' case. Because of the suffering Jesus underwent, "Son of God" must be redefined before it can fit Jesus' messiahship. So too must the title "Son of Man," which is the characteristic way Jesus refers to himself in Mark's Gospel.[10]

Mark immediately associates Jesus with Israelite prophecy and John the Baptist. Citing Isaiah and Malachi, it depicts John the Baptist as the forerunner of Jesus, the one announcing him and preparing his path. Mark can assume that his readers have heard of John the Baptist, but he underscores John's call for repentance. The people would flock to John at the river Jordan to be washed in token of their repenting of their sins. We know from the **Dead Sea Scrolls** that communities such as that at Qumran were also stressing penance and purification at this time.[11] Mark casts John somewhat like the prophet Elijah, the one who traditionally would purify Israel before the Day of the Lord. However, the author also places the Baptist on the threshold of the age of Jesus and the Holy Spirit.

Jesus came to John from Nazareth of Galilee and was baptized in the Jordan. At the least this meant that he felt involved with the mood of repentance that John was arousing. The scene where the heavens are ripped apart, the Spirit descends like a dove, and a voice calls Jesus a beloved, pleasing Son is Mark's early assurance that Jesus was someone very special. The implication is that at that moment the heavens, closed since the demise of prophecy, reopened. In the background are texts such as Psalms 2:7 ("He said to me, 'You are my son, today I have begotten you'") and Isaiah 42:1 ("Behold my servant, whom I uphold, my chosen, in whom my soul delights; I have put my Spirit upon him, he will bring forth justice to the nations"). The first text probably speaks of a kingly figure, the second of Israel as God's servant. The overtones are that Jesus is focusing and fulfilling promises and hopes long held by Israel (although his fulfillment will differ from the popular expectations). However, in Mark only Jesus experiences this vision, not the crowd. So Jesus' identity is secret, something known only to himself (and the author and reader). This secret identity of Jesus, or unexpected quality of Jesus' Messiahship, will be a strong theme in Mark. The people who encountered Jesus in his earthly life largely did not realize what they were dealing with. Their Messianic hopes were cast in the form of a warrior king such as David. Jesus came not as a military or political savior but like the suffering servant of Isaiah (see Isaiah 42:1–4, 49:1–6, 50:4–11, 52:13–53:12).

The Spirit forces Jesus out into the wilderness, a traditional place of trial. Jesus undergoes a sort of initiation, having to come to grips with Satan and the manifold possibilities for evil. The wild beasts may symbolize the dawn of the messianic age taken as the time for reestablishing the harmonies of creation lost through sin. In some of the Qumran texts an army of angels fights alongside God against the evil spirits.

In his first transition, Mark notes John's arrest and the beginning of Jesus' ministry. We have stepped across the threshold into the critical moment, the **kairos** or time of opportunity and trial. Mark 1:15 is a famous summary of Jesus' whole message: "The time is fulfilled and the Kingdom of God is at hand; repent and believe in the gospel." The "Kingdom of God" is perhaps the most central notion in the synoptics' presentation of Jesus' message. The best reading of it stresses God's reigning (God's active guidance, care, and control) rather than a spatial realm or domain. The connotations are of the time and condition when human affairs will become right, as they ought to be, not disordered and unjust, as we presently experience them. Jesus is saying that human health and prosperity (in their social dimensions even more than their individual dimensions) are at hand, that God is poised to become the people's powerfully benevolent ruler. The Kingdom of God, in fact, probably had the power of an intense symbol or rich myth, able to summarize most of what Jesus' contemporaries were longing to have happen.[12]

The Authority of Jesus (1:16–3:6)

Mark starts to detail the good news of Jesus by showing him at his ministerial work, giving the reader a sense of Jesus' style. So Jesus calls Simon (Peter) and Andrew, James and John, taking them from their trade as fishermen to make them his fellow laborers, "fishers of men" (1:17). No doubt this little story draws on Church traditions about how the most veteran disciples began their association with Jesus. It is significant that Mark has them become Jesus' followers: people who make a commitment to Jesus himself and start to tread his path.

Jesus then goes into the synagogue in Capernaum (a town of Galilee) and teaches on the Sabbath. He rivets the crowd because he speaks authoritatively, from his own personal convictions. A man with an unclean spirit proclaims Jesus to be the Holy One of God (the demons would know their mortal enemy), but Jesus rebukes the unclean spirit and bids him be silent (Mark would not have the bystanders realize Jesus' true identity). Casting the unclean spirit out of the man, Jesus amazes the crowd, who exclaim over his new, authoritative teaching and his power to command unclean spirits. The crowd then starts to spread his fame throughout Galilee, Jesus' home district in the northern part of the country.

This is but the first of several cures that manifest Jesus' power. He heals Simon's mother-in-law of a fever. The people bring to him at sundown their sick and possessed and he cures them (though, again, he will not permit the demons to disclose his identity). Early the next morning he goes off to a lonely place to pray. The people are now aroused and interested in him. But Jesus wants to move on to the other towns. He must proclaim his gospel to them too. So he moves throughout Galilee, preaching and exorcizing. A leper comes to him, expressing faith in his power, and Jesus is moved with pity to cure him. He bids the leper (like the demons) to keep quiet about this, but the leper speaks freely and the news travels. The command of Jesus that the leper (one generally excluded from the religious community by the Mosaic Law) show himself to the priest and make the offering that Moses commanded is Mark's effort to present Jesus as respectful of Torah.

The overall impact of these first cures is powerful, on both the crowd and the reader. The crowd is set abuzz: Something is up here, a holy man has come with special gifts. The reader is encouraged to think that Jesus was from the beginning doing the deeds of the Messiah (not necessarily the things expected of the Messiah according to the Hebrew Bible, but things that, from the later Christian perspective of the resurrection, make sense and seem early manifestations of God's power).

Chapter 2 finds Jesus back home in Galilee, around Capernaum. When news of his presence spreads crowds flock to him, some people bringing a paralytic. Moved by their faith (their openness to God's power to heal), Jesus says to the paralytic, "My son, your sins are forgiven." Some scribes (official interpreters of Scripture) take offense at this declaration of forgiveness: "Who can forgive sins but God alone?" Mark is probably being ironic: they do not know that Jesus is uniquely empowered by God alone. Jesus senses the scribes' upset (as though he can read their hearts). Rather than causing him to draw back, however, this makes him up the ante. He cures the paralytic, to show that the Son of Man (Jesus himself, in the complexity and symbolic richness that we have seen this title to carry) has authority on earth to forgive sins. The crowd has never seen the like of this authority (or power) of Jesus.

Not only does Jesus claim the power to forgive sins but he goes out of his way to associate with "sinners" (the outcasts of his religious society). That is the point to the call of Levi, a tax collector. Tax collectors, prostitutes, and other sinners were welcome in Jesus' company and could sign up for Jesus' new movement. The religious establishment (represented by the scribes and Pharisees) found this offensive, but Jesus describes himself as a physician come to heal those who are sick. The righteous don't need him as much as those considered cut off from good religion, disreputable.

Jesus also offended the religious establishment (and puzzled some ordinary onlookers) by his lack of asceticism. He and his disciples did not do some of the "religious" things expected of a holy man; they did not fast like the disciples of the Baptist and the Pharisees. Jesus' strange explanation of this ("Can the wedding guests fast while the bridegroom is with them?") calls to mind the Israelite covenant symbol of a wedding between the people and God. (Recall also the symbolism in Ephesians 5: the marriage between Christ and the Church.) Mark's point seems to be that in Jesus the eschaton or time of fulfillment has arrived. It is a special, festive time. One should rejoice in it, enjoy the presence of God's striking envoy. There will be time enough to be grim (after Jesus' death). The figures of a new garment and new wineskins amplify this sense of the eschaton, the age of renovation and fulfillment.

The leaders of the religious establishment begin to snipe at Jesus, accusing him of trespassing on the religious laws. Jesus disputes with them in rabbinical fashion, pointing out that even their own Sabbath law admits of exceptions. In the radical statement of 2:27 ("The sabbath was made for man, and not man for the sabbath"), Mark probably is addressing a Gentile audience. Jewish audiences would have found this view (and the accompanying claim that the Son of Man is lord even of the Sabbath) at the least highly challenging, and probably quite offensive. Hallowing the Sabbath was a central part of the Torah. Mark 3:1–6 screws this conflict up another turn. Those suspiciously watching Jesus think that he should not heal on the Sabbath (there is time enough for healing on the other six days of the week). Jesus implies that their hearts have hardened so that they miss the meaning of the Sabbath. What kind of a God (object of the Sabbath hallowing) would forbid healing and doing good on his special day? So Jesus cures the man with the withered hand, convincing those suspicious of him (Mark makes the Pharisees the leading representatives of this group) that he is dangerous. (The Pharisees did not come into predominant religious power in Judaism until after the destruction of the Temple in 70 C.E. The Herodians probably were supporters of the royal family—Herod was the local ruler—who would have seen any **charismatic** figure as a potential threat. Mark also may be reading in the politics of his own day.) The transition section 3:7–12 gives substance to these fears. The crowds follow after Jesus because of his healing powers. The unclean spirits cry out that he is the Son of God. The implication is: What sort of religious establishment would oppose the Son of God, the strong man who can subdue the unclean spirits?

Jesus as Rejected Son of God (3:13–6:6a)

In this section Mark shows the increasing rejection of Jesus' message. Mark 3:13–19 portrays the choice of the twelve special disciples. Jesus' going up the mountain likens him to Moses. The number twelve seems symbolic of the twelve tribes of Israel: Jesus is founding a new version of the people of God for the new eschatological age. The disciples share Jesus' preaching ministry and authority to cast out demons. Jesus goes home, the crowds continue to pursue him, and his own family becomes upset with him. They listen to the charge of the Jerusalem scribes, authoritative types who have come from the capital and who are trying to discredit Jesus by calling him possessed by Satan. Jesus answers quite pointedly and pragmatically: Look at the things I am doing. Are they helping Satan or hindering him? And what does my power against Satan imply? For Mark it implies Jesus' status as the one come to overthrow the reign of Satan and establish the Kingdom of God. Not to see the proper outlines of the power struggle (between Jesus and Satan) going on in their midst marks the scribes and Jesus' family as allies of Satan. No sin is more serious than their twisting of all truthfulness by deliberately confusing good with evil. Jesus' true family consists of those who do God's will, who see the difference between goodness (godliness) and evil (diabolical forces) and act upon it.

Chapter 4 shifts the stress from Jesus' healing power to his teaching. Both exemplify his mysterious status as God's bringer of salvation, the one who inaugurates the kingdom. The distinctive note of Jesus' preaching is his use of parables: teasing, provocative stories. Instinctively and skillfully, Jesus uses indirection, **hyperbole**, drama, and other rhetorical devices to shake up his hearers, get their attention, and force them to face the newness and power of what he is doing in their midst. The parable of the sower and the seed brings home the crucial importance of the dispositions one brings to the Word of God. Parabolic teaching lays special stress on what is in people's hearts. Those not well motivated, not open to the divine mystery, will not catch a prophet's drift. The **allegorical** explanation of the parable of the sower in 4:14–20 probably expresses the early Christian community's puzzlement over the great diversity of the receptions that people gave its message. The original parable is more dense and pregnant: "He who has ears to hear, let him hear (4:9)." As well, the prodigious yields suggest the bounty of God's kingdom.

The enigmatic sayings in 4:21–25 about the lamp and the measure skate on the edge of this important matter of an audience's inner dispositions. Mark wants to associate Jesus' message with the light of a good conscience—with the powerful fact that openness to the light brings increasing illumination. This is a key fact for any religious teacher, a crucial part of the religious teacher-student equation. Yet in Mark Jesus' parables often are close to riddles, as if to stress the challenge and strangeness of this teacher.[13] Thus the two brief parables describing how the kingdom grows both stress its mysteriousness. Its yield exceeds human calculus and comes almost inevitably, inexorably, because it is mainly the work of God. The great shrub or tree with large branches is an echo of Daniel 4:21–22, the great kingdom of Nebuchadnezzar. When the Gentiles have come into Jesus' kingdom, the small beginnings of his ministry will seem like a tiny but potent seed.

The picture of Jesus sleeping during the storm suggests his confidence in God and at-homeness in God's world. By contrast, the disciples don't really believe that God takes care of them. For Jesus to calm the wind and the sea is but another manifestation of his mysteriousness. Not just the demons but the forces of nature obey him. (The "miracle" here, as is common in the New Testament's descriptions of Jesus' marvelous cures or works, is meant not to dazzle the curious but to rouse faith.) When the Church had come to be symbolized as the bark (ship) of Peter (on whose reminiscences the story may be based), preachers used the scene to build confidence that Christ would care for his Church.

The strange story in chapter 5 of the Gerasene **demoniac** and Jesus' casting the unclean spirits into swine (which then hurl themselves down to the sea) has baffled commentators. One possibility is that this story symbolizes the destruction of the evil powers that had held the Gentiles captive. As Lamar Williamson has noted: "This healing is in Gentile country. The story is set in the territory of one of the Hellenistic towns of the Decapolis ("ten towns") (v. 20) on the southeastern shore of Lake Tiberias (the Sea of Galilee). . . . Nothing about it is kosher; everything is unclean: the spirit(s), the tomb, the pigs, the territory. In this alien place, Jesus' authority and healing power is just as great as in a synagogue and even more amazing."[14] Once again the demons know the identity of their enemy, and this time Jesus bids the man to tell his friends what God has done for him.

The two cures that follow next, of the daughter of Jairus and the woman with a flow of blood, are more evidences of Jesus' power. It is significant that Jairus is a leader of the local synagogue (showing that not all the leading Jews rejected Jesus) and that the woman's affliction made her ritually impure. Both petitioners get help because of their faith. When Jairus' daughter seems to have died, the demand for faith becomes even greater. That the bystanders laugh at Jesus' suggestion that the girl is merely sleeping betrays their uneasiness with a demand for real faith (or their uneasiness in the presence of divine power: note in 5:17 that those who had witnessed the miracle with the swine asked Jesus to leave their neighborhood). The verb used for the girl's rising is the same as that used for Christ's resurrection (*anistēmi*). Ironically, the ecstatic amazement of the crowd is etymologically the same as the (demonic) possession attributed to Jesus in 3:22. This suggests that faith is more than amazement. Since these miracles are reported by all three synoptics (see Matthew 9:18–26, Luke 8:40–56), they furnish good materials for a case study of the different approach that each synoptic **evangelist** takes.[15] Back among Jews, Jesus charges those who have observed these two cures not to make them known.

Returning again to his own native area, Jesus teaches in the synagogue on the Sabbath, amazing many with his wisdom. Some take offense, however, thinking that because they know his humble origins ("Is this not the carpenter, the son of Mary and brother of James and Moses and Judas and Simon, and are not his sisters here with us?"[6:3]) they can take his measure. Jesus responds with a saying that has become famous about a prophet not being without honor except in his own country and among his own kin. It is the reverse of what he has been able to do among believing strangers: He can do little curing at home because of the unbelief he finds. This unbelief, like the plot to destroy Jesus that ended the first section of Mark's materials, bodes ill for the future and sets on the horizon the storm clouds of the Passion and death. The transition in 6:6b is minimal: Jesus continued with his teaching, despite the trying opposition.

Jesus as Son of God Misunderstood (6:7–8:21)

In this section we see Jesus devoting himself more to his disciples, instructing them more intensely in his message and preparing them for their part in his work. First, he calls the twelve and sends them out two by two for a sort of practicum. They travel light and beg their hospitality (exercising faith in God's providence). They preach repentance, cast out demons, and heal many sick people by anointing them. Where the parallel mission in Matthew 10:5–15 is to Jews, the version in Mark probably reflects the Church's work among the Gentiles. The anointing with oil may have been a basis for the later Christian sacramental rite of anointing the sick ("extreme unction"). The twelve are a big success.

Interposed between the disciples' mission and Jesus' further instruction of them (self-revelation to them) is the gruesome story of Herod's beheading of John the Baptist. Herod was fascinated by John yet fearful of him and he transfers this ambiguity to Jesus. In the background is the banquet (Esther 1:9) and general story of the book of Esther. In the foreground, anticipated, is the sacrificial death of Jesus, his martyrdom which will parallel the Baptist's. (The laying of John's body in the tomb parallels the laying of Jesus' body in the tomb prior to his resurrection.) Recent archeological excavations suggest that the physical arrangements implied for the banquet (e.g., the separate rooms for men and women) may be historically accurate.[16]

After their mission, the apostles go away with Jesus to rest. But the people get wind of where they are going and follow them. Filled with compassion, Jesus teaches this multitude. It becomes late and the crowd has no food. Jesus takes what they have, five loaves of bread and two fishes,

The Beheading of St. John the Baptist. Hendrick Terbrugghen. This grisly depiction of John's martyrdom is in keeping with Mark's stress on the warfare between the powers of evil and good. *(Nelson Gallery–Atkins Museum, Kansas City, Mo. [Nelson Fund])*

blesses, breaks, and distributes it. All five thousand eat to their content and the remnants fill twelve baskets. Many details in the story reflect the Christian eucharist (especially the blessing and breaking). Other details, and the general largess, suggest the banquet that was a prominent symbol for the messianic age. Once again Jesus is shown caring for peoples' bodies as well as their spirits. Salvation and the kingdom are holistic; they bring medicinal and economic benefits as well as attitudinal ones.

Following the multiplication of the loaves and fishes, Jesus sends the disciples off by boat and himself goes up the mountain to pray. The boat makes only slow headway against the wind, so between 3:00 and 6:00 A.M. Jesus comes to them walking on the water. He seems inclined to pass by (reminiscent of Job 9:11: "Lo, he passes by me, and I see him not; he moves on, but I do not perceive him"). They are terrified, but he calms them and the wind ceases.[17] Mark links their astonishment to their not having grasped the point of the multiplication of the loaves and fishes. In saying that their hearts were hardened, Mark accuses the disciples of a willful ignorance like that of the Jews who rejected Jesus. When they land, people again flock to Jesus for healing. Those that so much as touch the fringe of his garment are cured (his power is almost impersonal, almost an unconscious magnetism).

Mark 7:1–23 presents more of Jesus' teachings. Some Pharisees and scribes challenge Jesus for letting his disciples eat with their hands unwashed, a violation of strict religious interpretation. (Mark's explanation of Jewish customs is evidence that his expected readership was non-Jewish.) Jesus takes the conflict to another level, saying that these are just human conventions, much less important than God's call for worship from the heart. Because the stinging quotation from Isaiah 29:13 is more pertinent in the Greek (**Septuagint**) version (which Mark's church probably would have used) than in the Hebrew version (which Jesus would have used), some scholars infer that this rebuke was never uttered by Jesus himself but came from the editor after Jewish-Christian relations had thoroughly soured. Jesus is presented as going on to criticize the Pharisees for their practice of **Corban**, a legal fiction by which one could dedicate wealth to sacred uses (while keeping control of it), even when this meant being unable to use such wealth for supposedly profane practices like supporting one's parents. Thus one would be legally pure while disobeying a basic Mosaic precept. In 1955 an inscription found on a first century C.E. ossuary (vault for bones of the dead) in Jerusalem used "Corban" in precisely this sense.

Jesus then calls the people to him and goes to the religious heart of these legalities. It is the interior of a person (the heart or conscience or motivation) that makes for purity or defilement, not externals. The disciples fail to grasp this point (it may have been quite an original teaching, for there seem no parallels in the contemporary rabbinic literature), and Jesus somewhat disgustedly gives them a further tutoring. In 7:19 the evangelist, in what seems an editorial comment, draws the implication that Jesus' teaching about externals meant his rejection of the assumption of the kosher laws that some foods are unclean. This would have been a serious break with prevailing Jewish opinion. More significant for Jesus was the great question of how murder, theft, wickedness and the like lodge in the human heart. Unless people are converted away from such perversions, they will be defiled to the core. (This makes Jesus sound quite like Paul, riveted onto the core moral question of openness or closure to God from the heart.)

In 7:24–37 Mark returns to Jesus' cures. A Gentile woman asks Jesus to free her daughter of an unclean spirit. The story is somewhat reminiscent of the cure worked for the Phoenician widow by the prophet Elijah (1 Kings 17:9 ff.). The woman bests Jesus in a little battle of wits. Jesus seems to limit his benefits to Jews, calling Gentiles such as the woman "dogs" (actually "pups"), as Jews sometimes derogatorily did. She says she is willing to accept help on any basis, and implies that Gentiles such as she have the right to what Jews are rejecting. Jesus takes this boldness as an expression of faith and grants her petition. Mark makes it serve his important theme of the spread of the gospel to the Gentiles.

In curing the man who was deaf and mute Jesus acts somewhat like the Gentile faith healers of his day, using exclamatory words and touches.

But his looking to heaven and sighing suggest his special status or familiarity with God. The wording of the cure may show an influence of Isaiah 48:8 ("You have never heard, you have never known, from of old your ear has not been opened"). The people are even more astonished than usual, and they will not obey Jesus' charge to keep the incident secret. The phrase about Jesus' doing all things well calls to mind Genesis 1:31 ("And God saw everything that he had made, and behold it was very good") and so implies a new creation. In Isaiah 35:5–6 cures such as these were to accompany the messianic age ("Then the eyes of the blind shall be opened, and the ears of the deaf unstopped; then shall the lame man leap like a hart, and the tongue of the dumb sing for joy"). Mark's point is plain: The eschatological or messianic time has come in the person of Jesus.

In chapter 8 we have another version of the multiplication of the loaves and fishes. This one reflects a Gentile source and places more stress on the physical hunger and distress of the people. There are again allusions to the Christian eucharist (e.g., 8:6 has the disciples distributing the food after receiving it from Jesus, as **deacons** would distribute the eucharist after having received it from the presiding liturgical officer). The number of people (four thousand) is different from that in the first account, as are the number of loaves and baskets of fragments, but probably these details are not significant. However, the number twelve that figures in the first feeding may suggest the twelve Tribes of Israel and so the mission to the Jews, while the number seven that figures in the second feeding may suggest fullness or completion and so the Gentile mission that makes Jesus' significance universal.

Next the Pharisees come back for another round of confrontations, and Jesus seems weary of them. They ask for a sign from heaven (a miracle), which in the literary context of Jesus' having just performed so many signs makes them appear either obtuse or cynical. Jesus simply refuses. He will have no truck with their hardness of heart. (By their own traditions, the Pharisees may have been justified in asking any would-be Messiah to show apocalyptic signs.) The "this generation" of 8:12 is quite pejorative. Echoing Deuteronomy 32:5b ("They are a perverse and crooked generation") and Psalms 95:10 ("For forty years I loathed that generation and said, 'They are a people who err in heart, and they do not regard my ways'"), Mark uses the term to summarize all the contemporaries (of both Jesus and the early Church) who rejected the messianic dawning.

Mark 8:14–21 summarizes the meaning of what has gone before. The disciples are presented as dull, lacking in understanding, unable to realize the implications of Jesus' signs. They take things on a literal, worldly level, while Jesus constantly refers things to the presence of God that has drawn near. He warns them against the leaven (yeast) of the Pharisees, their concern with externals and closure to real (mysterious) meanings. In the lines, "Why do you discuss the fact that you have no bread? Do you not yet perceive or understand? Are your eyes hardened? Having eyes do you not see, and having ears do you not hear?" (that is, do you not remember how I miraculously supplied the bread?), Mark suggests to the reader that the disciples were little better than the rest of the crowds, little better even than the Pharisees. They may have had better intentions, but they were as stupid as the rest. (The "leaven" of the Pharisees may also have been a nationalistic or political view of the messiahship, to which the disciples probably were equally prone.)

The transition story in 8:22–26 suggests that Jesus himself is the only cure for blindness like that of the disciples. He can only keep doing the deeds of divine power until the light dawns (ultimately, through his death and resurrection). The cure again is described as worked somewhat the way Gentile faith healers did their healings.

Christology in Light of the Passion (8:27–10:45)

With this section the light does start to dawn and the disciples do begin to entertain the idea that Jesus is the Christ. So the cure of the blind man is like a hinge or symbolic pointing. When Jesus asks what people are

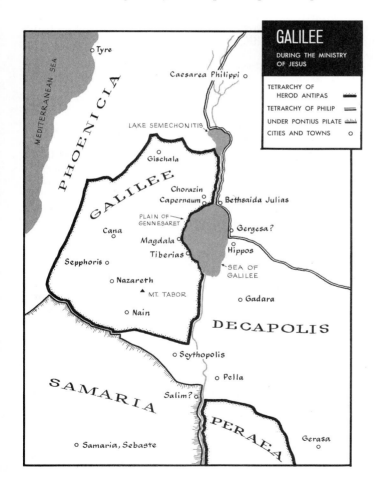

GALILEE

DURING THE MINISTRY OF JESUS

TETRARCHY OF HEROD ANTIPAS

TETRARCHY OF PHILIP

UNDER PONTIUS PILATE

CITIES AND TOWNS o

saying about him, the disciples come up with various provocative answers: John the Baptist, Elijah, one of the prophets. When he asks who they think he is, Peter answers, "You are the Christ" (8:29). Jesus again charges them not to reveal this to outsiders. There follows the first prediction of the Passion, which Peter (who has now become the spokesman for the disciples) will not hear. (He may have confessed that Jesus is the Christ, but he hasn't understood what this means.)

Edward Mally has summarized the critical questions that one must answer about this passage as follows:

> This passage must be related to 9:31 and 10:33–34. Its importance in Mark cannot be overstated for its main burden is to correct any possible false notions of the messiahship involved in the confession just made. It is impossible to deny that the formulation of this and the other two predictions (9:31, 10:33–34) has been colored by the events themselves. However, to conclude from this that the whole is a literary device and merely *vaticinium ex eventu* (prophecy after the fact) would be illegitimate and exceeding the evidence, such as it is. The major affirmation of these sections is, after all, that Jesus did try to give the disciples some inkling of what lay before him. Undoubtedly it was only after the event itself that the full import of his hints and the formulation of the story and predictions themselves took shape.[18]

The harshness of Jesus' repudiation of Peter's misunderstanding is striking: "Get behind me, Satan! For you are not on the side of God, but of men" (8:33). It would be hard for Mark to say more clearly that Jesus' suffering was God's chosen way of redemption.

The rest of the chapter draws some conclusions for Christian discipleship. If the Messiah was a suffering servant, his followers will have to suffer similarly. They must not be ashamed of the way God has chosen to redeem sinful humanity. They must see very clearly the self-denial that Christian faith entails. If they do not stand up for Christ as he was, they will find themselves disowned by Christ when he returns. Yet there is also the implication that what one sacrifices by giving up worldly views and advantages for Christian faith is not much. Real life is not to be found in worldly things but only in faith and the Gospel. The use of the cross as a symbol of penance was a Jewish practice (based on Roman understandings of the cross) that preceded Christ's crucifixion.[19] In 9:1 Jesus seems to be predicting the early coming of the parousia, giving evidence of his own conviction that God would soon establish the kingdom (and of Mark's conviction that with the destruction of the Temple in 70 C.E. Jesus' return [as Son of Man] was imminent).[20]

The scene known as the Transfiguration follows, as though Mark now makes a major effort to drive home the real identity of this Messiah who must suffer. Peter, James, and John, the leading disciples, accompany Jesus up a high mountain (a place with holy connotations). Jesus is transfigured, so that his glorious heavenly identity shines through. The scene is reminiscent of the manifestation of God to Moses and the Israelites on Mount Sinai (see Exodus 24:15–18, 34:29–30, 40:34–38). There are also parallels with Mark's earlier story of Jesus' baptism and later story of Jesus' agony in the

Garden of Gethsemane. Elijah and Moses probably stand for the prophets and the Law, suggesting that Jesus is the fulfillment of the covenant promises. (They also remind the sophisticated reader of prior religious wonder workers whose marvelous deeds did not always win faith-filled response.) When Peter offers to make three booths many of Mark's readers would call to mind the Jewish custom of erecting booths for the feast of Tabernacles. Mark may be saying that Peter and the disciples thought that the eschaton had come and Hosea 12:9 ("I will again make you dwell in tents") now applied. (See also Zechariah 14.) Whatever the historical incident that gave rise to this literary scene, the meaning is clear enough: Even during his earthly life, while he had to set his face toward suffering, Jesus carried hidden within him the glory and power of God.

After the Transfiguration Jesus tells the disciples not to reveal what happened until the Son of Man has risen from the dead. They puzzle over what this possibly could mean. The question and answer about the coming of Elijah, who according to Jewish expectation would precede the Day of the Lord, leads to Jesus' interpreting John the Baptist as his Elijah (who was not welcomed but treated with contempt and put to death, as Jesus will be). Jesus' cure of the epileptic boy is occasioned by the disciples' being unable to heal him. Jesus may not have uttered the words about a faithless generation on the original occasion. They seem likely to be Mark's editorial effort again to emphasize the importance of faith. Jesus wrings from the boy's father an honest expression of all the faith that he can muster. The phrase "I believe; help my unbelief!" has long been a Christian prayer.

In 9:31 Mark has Jesus repeat his prediction of the Passion, death, and resurrection. Once again the disciples do not understand, and now they are afraid to ask. To underscore their distance from Jesus' vision of the kingdom, 9:33–37 has Jesus repudiate the disciples' concern with status. Leadership in the messianic community will be a matter of service. The best way to serve Jesus will be to care for vulnerable people (children, for instance) in his name. The next verses, 38–50, repeat this message. It is what one does for others that is significant. People who cure others in the name of Christ have to be Christ's disciples. People who support Christ's disciples will receive their fair reward. On the other hand, people who corrupt the vulnerable will answer for it dearly. One should go to great extremes to avoid such sin. The Kingdom of God is worth sacrificing everything to obtain. The description of hell is based on Isaiah 66:24: "And they shall go forth and look on the dead bodies of the men that have rebelled against me; for their worm shall not die, their fire shall not be quenched, and they shall be an abhorrence to all flesh." The salt of Christians is the Holy Spirit, to whom the disciples should cling. They should stop their bickering about status and make sure they stay true to their calling, so that they will have something distinctive to offer the world.

Chapter 10 presents the Pharisees back on the attack, testing Jesus. They ask him about divorce, and he interprets the Mosaic permission as an indulgence conceded because of the hardness of human beings' hearts. Ideally, there would be no divorce. Husband and wife become one flesh. Divorce therefore is a kind of adultery. In taking this radical view, Jesus is again teaching with a breathtaking authority. The assumption that a wife could institute divorce proceedings suggests a Gentile context, for that probably was not true among Jews.[21] There seems nothing in the Hebrew Bible, contemporary rabbinical literature, or Qumran literature that takes so absolute a stand as Jesus'. The best analogy from Jewish materials consists of the rules concerning the marriage of priests (e.g., Leviticus 21:7: "They shall not marry a harlot or a woman who has been defiled; neither shall they marry a woman divorced from her husband; for the priest is holy to his God"; see also Ezekiel 44:22). Those suggest that Jesus is thinking of how marriage should be when God is reigning as God ought to reign.

The people bring children to Jesus for his blessing, and when the disciples try to prevent this Jesus is angered: of all human beings, children are most like the citizenry of the kingdom (probably because they are the most vulnerable). A man comes up to ask Jesus about gaining eternal life. Jesus deflects his honorific address ("Good Teacher"): Only God is good. Then Jesus answers by laying out the basic commandments. The man says that he has kept the commandments since his youth, and this draws Jesus' love. Jesus tells him that he lacks only one thing: to sell his possessions, give to the poor, make heaven his treasure, and follow Jesus. But this is too much for him, since he has many possessions. Jesus makes him an example of how riches can impede discipleship: "Children, how hard it is to enter the kingdom of God! It is easier for a camel to go through the eye of a needle than for a rich man to enter the kingdom of God" (10:24–25). The disciples are amazed, but Jesus assures them that all things are possible with God. They may expect a rich reward for the sacrifices they make in following Jesus. This story, along with the teaching about divorce, seems to emphasize that discipleship requires a radical shift in values, the end of business as usual, a wholehearted commitment to God. In the wake of what Jesus has suffered, having to sacrifice material possessions seems paltry.

The disciples now are afraid, probably because they glimpse what following Jesus may require.[22] Jesus again predicts his Passion, death, and resurrection, and in this, as in the other two predictions, Mark's tendency is to blame the Jewish leaders for Christ's death (contrary to the fact that it was the Roman authorities who actually killed him). Even after this prediction, however, the disciples continue to seek status. Here, though, Jesus implies that they will share in his sufferings. What sort of glory they will have is up to God. The figures of the cup and baptism perhaps indicate the early Church's sacramental rites, through which believers participated in Jesus' Passion, death, and resurrection. True greatness, this Christological section concludes by saying, is being a servant. The Son of Man came to serve and give his life as a ransom for many—the Messiah is not the military figure that worldlings expect but one who suffers because of his love and goodness. In the transition passage 10:46–52, Jesus is identified as the Son of David (the heir of the promises of the Davidic kingdom, the messianic realm). The blind beggar Bartimaeus receives his sight because of his faith. The implication is that he was one of the few who sensed who Jesus was and that the messianic age had arrived.

Before the Passion (11:1–12:44)

The little troop comes to Jerusalem, where Jesus' predictions of the Passion will be fulfilled. Jesus' entry on a colt shows that he is now willing to receive acclaim. As well, it shows that he is no man of war but a lowly, humble sort of Messiah. He receives acclaim as the one bringing the promised kingdom of David. The spreading of leafy branches probably draws on the ritual for the feast of Tabernacles described in Psalms 118:27: "The Lord is God, and he has given us light. Bind the festal procession with branches, up to the horns of the altar." (Matthew's account [21:1–11] more explicitly draws on Zechariah 9:9–10.) Despite the lowliness of Jesus, his lack of worldly impressiveness, what is happening religiously is highly significant: The Messiah is coming to the holy city, the age of the kingdom is advancing another crucial step.

Jesus curses a fig tree for not having fruit (even though it was not the right season). Mark probably sets this incident here between two references to Jerusalem and the Temple, to imply that Jerusalem, too, was useless, not yielding the religious fruit Jesus or God wanted. Jesus cleanses the Temple of its money changers and small businessmen, apparently disgusted with the way that what should have been a holy place has become corrupted. This further expresses Jesus' authority and amazes the crowd. Therefore, it further alienates the scribes and Pharisees, who now seek a way to destroy Jesus. When Jesus and the disciples again pass by the fig tree, which is now withered by Jesus' curse, Mark puts together a lesson in faith and prayer. The lines about forgiveness in Christians' prayer reflect the ancient traditions behind the "Our Father." In another confrontation, the priests and elders ask Jesus his authority for such bold acts as cleansing the Temple. Jesus parries their thrusts by forcing them to take a stand on the mission of the Baptist. When they will not he disregards them: They are not interested in the real questions of authority; they don't want to decide who Jesus is and what John started.

Mark 12:1–12 is a stinging parable. Israel is God's vineyard (see Isaiah 51:1–7). Those sent to the tenants are the prophets. Jesus is the heir, the beloved Son, whose slaying will bring the whole history of the abuse of the prophets to a climax. The destruction that Jesus' slaying will earn may refer to the destruction of Jerusalem in 70 C.E., while giving the vineyard to others probably refers to the new covenant welcomed more by Gentiles than Jews. Mark 12:10–11 on the cornerstone quotes Psalms 118:22–23 and in almost Pauline fashion makes Jesus the paradoxical foundation of a new religious construction. The Jerusalem authorities try to arrest Jesus but fear the crowd. The pre-Passion tension is building.

Some of the Pharisees and Herodians come with a question about paying taxes to Caesar, seeking to put Jesus in a double bind. If he counsels nonpayment of taxes he will offend the Roman authorities. If he counsels payment he will offend Jewish nationalist sensibilities. Once again Jesus undercuts the proposed dilemma. By their practice (of paying) they have already made their choice. The phrase in 12:15, "knowing their hypocrisy," is withering. Mark now paints the Pharisees as unworthy of any respect. The saying, "render to Caesar the things that are Caesar's and to God the things that are God's," has been a biblical anchor for Christians' attempts to strike a balance between their heavenly and worldly allegiances. We may suspect that it reflects struggles the Markan community was having, either because of pressure from Rome or because the expectation of the parousia had lessened.

The probings of the Sadducees, a largely priestly group who considered only the five books of Moses (Genesis, Exodus, Leviticus, Numbers, and Deuteronomy) authoritative and did not believe in the resurrection, show that Jesus has by now alienated all of the Jerusalem establishment. In contrast to their concern with the dead, Jesus is interested in a living God, the vital deity of Moses and the patriarchs. Jesus' description of the afterlife in heaven suggests that heaven brings a whole new set of relations to God and other human beings, relations as free as those of the angels. The conversation with the scribe who asks about the greatest of the commandments is more fruitful. Jesus refers to the **Shema** (call) of Deuteronomy 6:5 on the love of God, and to Leviticus 19:18 (as broadened in Jewish practice to include more than just fellow Jews) on love of neighbor. The scribe wins Jesus' praise for agreeing, apparently in all sincerity, with this radical thrust to the heart of the religious matter. The saying about David draws on the tradition that the Messiah would be of David's line. Jesus implies that the Messiah is much more than just a descendent of David. The conclusion to this whole section on Jesus' arrival in the holy city is his condemnation of the scribes. By contrast with the generous faith of the poor widow who gives her mite, they have little genuine religion; rather they are concerned mainly with externals and their own glory. Thus Mark is saying, in yet another fashion, that the former religious regime has withered away and the new order of the eschatological time has come. The transition section in 13:1–5a predicts the destruction of the Temple, the symbolic center of Judaism (this probably was written after 70 C.E.). When the disciples ask about this, Jesus prefaces his apocalyptic discourse with a warning (relevant in all times, but especially in times of persecution) not to be led astray.

Apocalyptic Discourse (13:5b–37)

Mark 13 probably is a composite of various elements from the early Christian **catechesis** or religious instruction, perhaps based on Jesus' own apocalyptic teachings.[23] It first strikes a note of upheaval: wars and rumors of wars. Verses 9–13 perhaps reflect the suffering that the Markan community itself was experiencing for preaching the gospel. The desolating sacrilege probably refers back to the opening verses of the chapter: the destruction of the Temple. Some of the horrors likely to come have antecedents in earlier writings (see for instance Baruch 10:13–19; 2 Esdras 5:8, 6:21; Daniel 12:1). The coming of the Son of Man in clouds with great power and glory reflects a Christian adaptation of Daniel 7:13 (in light of Zechariah 12:10).[24] No doubt the discourse also reflects the continuance of great eschatological expectation through several generations of early

Christianity, especially when Jewish political resistance to Rome and Roman oppression had started building in Judea. The advice to watch what is happening and stay alert applies to all hours, but had greater acuteness when Christ was still vividly awaited. Under all the violent imagery, Mark makes Jesus assure the reader that history remains in God's hands. The time and way of history's consummation are uncertain, but without doubt Jesus' words and messianic accomplishment secure his followers' success.

The transition section 14:1–12 introduces the upcoming Passion that will occur during the Passover festival (which was a memorial of Israel's liberation from Egypt). The chief priests, according to Mark, were seeking to arrest Jesus by cunning and kill him. The story of how Jesus went to his death is the climax of Mark's Gospel and probably represents something close to the first Christian narratives of Jesus' saving deeds. Mark stresses Jesus' innocence and the working out of God's will. The story about the woman anointing Jesus with costly ointment occurs here explicitly to consecrate Jesus' coming suffering and death.[25] The betrayal of Judas Iscariot is the means the chief priests use to accomplish their cunning will to destroy Jesus. That Judas was one of Jesus' twelve most intimate disciples is a special horror.

Passion Narrative (14:13–16:8)

The climactic movement begins with the Jewish Passover, which furnished the early Christians some of their most central symbols for understanding Jesus' saving work.[26] For them Jesus was the new **paschal** lamb; his death and resurrection were the new exodus and entry into the promised land; the Christian eucharist redid the paschal meal. In a tone almost of inevitability, Jesus announces that one of the twelve will betray him. Mark 14:22–25 probably reflects an early Palestinian eucharistic liturgy. Mark's eucharist is both a way for Jesus to continue to be with his disciples and a symbolic version of his suffering death. The drinking of wine anew in the Kingdom of God implies the messianic banquet to come. Mark credits Jesus with foreknowledge of what is going to happen to him. Peter, in particular, will betray him. Mark 14:28 includes a prediction of the resurrection and later appearances in Galilee. The author is leaving the reader no doubt that Jesus was the Messiah and Son of God.

They move out to the Mount of Olives, to the place called Gethsemane, and Jesus becomes sorely troubled in spirit. He knows what is to come upon him, his bitter cup, and the disciples cannot even stay awake to comfort him. Even Peter, James, and John, the three who witnessed his Transfiguration, cannot bear the reality of the situation. Mark portrays Jesus as completely submissive to the will of his heavenly Father. Finally the hour comes and the teacher is betrayed by his pupil into the hands of sinners. Judas identifies Jesus with a kiss, the soldiers seize him, and the disciples flee. Mark makes this both the fulfillment of the scriptures and an absurd display of force. (Jesus heals the slave who is the first victim of this force.) The young man who runs away naked traditionally was identified as Mark himself.

Mark's presentation of the trial of Jesus before the high priests stresses its falsity.[27] The witnesses do not agree. The charge that Jesus will destroy the Temple is ridiculous on its face, ironic in its depths (where the Temple is Jesus' own body, which will be killed and raised). Jesus stays silent until the high priest asks him whether he is the Christ. The messianic secret is now abandoned: Jesus answers that he is (with overtones of the divine "I am" of Exodus 3:14 and Deuteronomy 32:39),[28] and uses imagery of the Son of Man from Daniel 7:13 to promise a day when he will be vindicated. The high priest tears his garments at this blasphemy. The judges vote for death and bystanders begin to abuse Jesus. (Meanwhile, with telling irony, Mark has Peter stay on the fringes and, when challenged by a slip of a maid, deny that he is a disciple.) Mark either does not know the niceties of Jewish law or he knows or assumes that Jesus' trial was quite irregular.

Chapter 15 brings Jesus before Pilate, the Roman authority. Pilate is interested in the political factors: Is Jesus the King of the Jews (one seeking political leadership)? Jesus answers enigmatically: "You have said so" (15:2). From Mark's perspective Jesus is the King of the Jews and very much more, so the whole exchange is ironic. Jesus will not defend himself against the charges of the chief priests, and Pilate finds this strange. Seek- · ing a way out, Pilate tries to use the custom (attested nowhere else in the New Testament) that the Roman governor might release a prisoner during the festival time. Mark makes it a grim verdict on all involved that Jesus is rejected and the choice falls on Barabbas, a common criminal. Pilate tries to get the crowd to ask for Jesus' release, but they call for his crucifixion, even though they can bring forward no evil that he has done. So Pilate, "wishing to satisfy the crowd," has Jesus scourged (lashed) and delivered to be crucified.

The soldiers who take Jesus away mock his supposed royalty, strike him, and spit upon him. (He is delivered into the horror of mindless human cruelty.) They lead him out to the place of crucifixion, Golgotha. One Simon of Cyrene carries his cross. The soldiers crucify him (nail him to the cross and raise it up) between two robbers with an inscription reading, "The King of the Jews." The crowd mocks him and challenges him to save himself. Darkness (a sign of the awesome divine presence) comes over the land. Jesus cries out, "My God, my God, why hast thou forsaken me," lines from Psalms 22 which probably are not a cry of despair but a call upon God for help.[29] Some in the crowd think Jesus is calling Elijah (to begin the eschaton).[30]

The actual death is more realistic in Mark than in the other Gospels. Jesus utters a loud cry, perhaps of pain, and breathes his last. The tearing of the (inner?) Temple curtain probably symbolizes the destruction of the Temple religion and the new access to God that has become possible through Jesus' death. (See Hebrews 6:9, 9:3.) It may also draw on Jewish traditions to the effect that the tearing of the outer curtain of the Temple would be a portent of doom for the Temple and Judaism. The centurion, a Gentile, finally speaks the acknowledgment for which we have waited throughout the whole Gospel: "Truly this man was the Son of God"

The Flagellation of Christ.
Vincenzo Danti. Sculpture.
The picture expresses well
the realism of the early faith
in Christ's full humanity and
intense sufferings. The artist
was considerably influenced
by Michelangelo. *(Nelson
Gallery–Atkins Museum, Kansas City,
Mo. [Nelson Fund])*

(15:39). (That he does this because of the cross, and not because of miracles or wonders, is another indication that Mark locates genuine faith away from prodigies and close to a suffering Messiah.) Some women disciples (who have not fled like the men) witness the end. Joseph of Arimathea obtains the body after Pilate certifies that Jesus is dead. Joseph lays him in a tomb that he closes with a stone. Mary Magdalene and Mary the mother of James see where Jesus is laid. Mark is underscoring the fact that Jesus was verifiedly dead. The precise chronology of Mark's account of the Passion, including the note that Jesus died on the day before the Sabbath, is confusing and does not completely square with the accounts of the other evangelists.

Mark 16:1–8 is Mark's account of the resurrection (more precisely of the empty tomb). Mary Magdalene, Mary the mother of James, and Salome go to the tomb and bring spices, that they may anoint the body. They find the stone rolled back from the tomb and a young man dressed in white sitting there.[31] He tells them that Jesus has risen. They are to tell the disciples and Peter that Jesus will see them in Galilee. But they are terrified and tell no one.

This brief resurrection account has received special notice in recent New Testament scholarship.[32] First, most scholars agree that Mark deliberately intended to end his Gospel at 16:8 with the words "for they were afraid" (*ephoubonto gar*). He never had any appearance stories in mind. Since Paul and the other evangelists do narrate appearances, why did Mark

The Resurrection. Attributed to Pieter Cornelisz. The artist clearly has stylized Jesus' rising and added a much different sensibility to Mark's bare account. Although the format is basically Gothic, the sarcophagus and the costumes of the guards reflect a growing Renaissance interest in adornment. *(Nelson Gallery— Atkins Museum, Kansas City, Mo. [Nelson Fund]).*

differ? Norman Perrin has put forward three reasons. First, in Mark's interpretation of the Passion we find three predictions of the resurrection (8:31, 9:31, 10:33). On analysis they suggest that Mark is interested in the resurrection as a prelude to something else. This something else is manifest in the account of the Transfiguration. According to Perrin, Mark paints the transfiguration as symbolic of the postresurrection situation. Jesus is in heaven like Moses, awaiting the parousia. Second, Mark's reference to seeing Jesus (16:7) also refers to the parousia. Third, the failure of the women to report the resurrection, along with the signal failure of the male disciples throughout the Passion, suggests that all the disciples now await a parousia that will pass judgment on their faith (sift things out definitively). Overall, then, Perrin makes Mark much more interested in the parousia (what we might call the definitive realization or spread of the resurrection) than in Jesus' rising from the tomb. Jesus' finale, like the other marvels of his life, raises as many questions as it gives answers. Mark continues to stress the need to accept a suffering, inglorious Messiah.

The empty tomb, therefore, has come in for considerable commentary. Reginald H. Fuller has recently summarized much of it:

Now of course it cannot be proven that Mary Magdalene actually discovered the empty tomb. All we can claim for it [the story] is that it belongs to the earliest recoverable tradition. As such, however, it was taken into and formed an integral part of the New Testament proclamation. At the same time, however, the empty tomb taken by itself could be dangerously misleading. For it could suggest that the raising of Jesus was the raising of his earthly body rather than an eschatological transformation. But even Mark intends to safeguard the fact of eschatological transformation by his use of the words, "He is not here," in the angelic proclamation, while the other gospels add appearance stories which adequately safeguard the eschatological transformation. This is true even of the later more materialized stories of Luke and John, in which the Resurrected One exhibits his bodily character by inviting touch and by eating in their presence. These elements doubtless spring from apologetic motives. But even in these later stories Christ appears and disappears in a different mode of existence.[33]

Partly on this basis, Fuller concludes that we should not call the resurrection a historical event. It does not fulfill the criteria for what we normally mean by "historical": No one (that we know of) actually witnessed it; the New Testament does not actually narrate its occurrence; and the attestations to it occur in kerygmatic (preaching or heralding) contexts (i.e., as expressions of faith). This does not mean that the resurrection was unreal, let alone that it is not central to Christian faith. It just means that all of our data for it, including the narrative in Mark, present it as something that falls outside what we normally mean by historical occurrences. All of our data make it and the risen Jesus extraordinary, unique, something and someone we are unable to judge by our usual standards and space-time referents. They are speaking about something eschatological and heavenly, something that occurs when divine power makes its presence felt in special ways. For Mark and the other evangelists, the resurrection shows that the Kingdom of God did come, the messianic age was begun, the realm of heaven did arrive on earth as Jesus' contemporaries were hoping it would.

Addendum (16:9–20)

The addition to what scholarly consensus takes to be the original ending of Mark at 16:8 does present some resurrection appearances. Jesus first appears to Mary Magdalene (who in parts of later Christian tradition gains apostolic status as the first herald of the resurrection). He also appears to two disciples walking in the country. Neither they nor Mary are believed when they report what has happened to them. So Jesus appears to the eleven (the twelve minus Judas) at table and upbraids them for their hardness of heart, their lack of faith. Then he sends them forth into the whole world to preach the gospel. The people who believe and are baptized will be saved. Those who do not will be condemned. The marvelous signs that will come with belief are indications of the power of God's kingdom. Mark 16:9 proclaims what Christians have come to call the ascension of Jesus: "So then the Lord Jesus, after he had spoken to them, was taken up into heaven, and sat down at the right hand of God." (See Psalms 110:1.) The disciples then go forth and preach everywhere, experiencing God's help.

WHY WAS THIS WRITTEN?

In a well-known study of Mark, Etienne Trocmé has written, "Everything inclines us to believe that the writer of Mark composed his Gospel to meet the needs of the Church of his day. It is even plain that he wishes to combat certain ideas and persons whose influence he finds harmful."[34] High among the candidates for such status are the Pharisees, but Trocmé finds Mark less critical of the Pharisees than Matthew is. Characteristically, Mark presents the Pharisees as Galilean opponents of Jesus, not as Jerusalem leaders whose decisions shape the lives of all the Jews. In fact, to consolidate power Mark's Pharisees have to ally themselves with the Herodians. Nevertheless, Mark is hardly fair to Pharisaism as a whole, and his negative picture of the Pharisees perhaps reflects the problematic relationship that developed between the Christian communities and the synagogues after the destruction of the Temple in 70 C.E.: The local synagogues and the Pharisees became more powerful while the Jerusalem priesthood waned.

Herod is another major target for Mark. Where the Pharisees show an excess of strait-laced respectability, Herod is simply corrupt, a spiritual zero. Pilate receives rather mild treatment, as do the Sadducees. The scribes, however, come in for strong censure.

> They are mentioned more often than in the other Gospels and appear in each section as the leaders of the opposition to Jesus and to his teaching. From the beginning their prestige is undermined by the innovative action of Jesus (1.22); it is with them that Jesus has his first controversy (2.6) and it is they who level against him the formidable charge of collusion with Beelzebub (3.22). It is with them that the disciples come into conflict as soon as the Master leaves them (9.14). It is they too whom Jesus ridicules in public at Jerusalem (12.35–37) before denouncing their hypocrisy (12.38–40). True, Mark is no more severe where the scribes are concerned than Luke (cf. Luke 11.45–52) and Matthew (cf. Matt. 23.1–36). But in Mark they are presented as a more organized and omnipresent group than in the other two synoptic Gospels.[35]

This probably means that Mark was denouncing the intellectualist wing of Judaism, saying that the theological leaders among Jesus' countrymen had become blind to the clear meaning of the Scriptures (which foretold Jesus, or at least would have prompted people of good heart to recognize Jesus).

Still another group whom Mark attacks are the high priests, the guardians of the Temple. They were responsible for order in the sacred precincts, and Trocmé thinks that Mark's community may have suffered particularly from their policemanship. Mark sees the Temple itself, with its sacrificial ritual, as bound for destruction, but his Gospel is less opposed to the Temple cult as such than to the high priests who regulated it. On the other hand, Mark is sufficiently critical of the whole Temple institution to place him at odds with many of the early Christians who wanted to retain much of the traditional Jewish ritual and law.

Indeed, one can also read Mark's criticisms of the Pharisees and scribes as an effort to belittle Christian legalism or moralism. Similarly, Mark's stress on Jesus' ministry probably was an effort to counteract images of the Church that were pushing Christians away from a strongly pastoral and missionary focus. By emphasizing Jesus' Passion so strongly, Mark also was counteracting any preaching of Jesus' messiahship that neglected what kind of Messiah Jesus actually was—how he was rejected, had to suffer and die, and only rose to God after dire endurance. To Mark's mind omitting Jesus' suffering, or even not making it the first thing said about Jesus, was to show oneself ashamed of the historical Lord and an unworthy disciple. Equally, fixating on Jesus' miracles, and making them a shield against the need for a disciple to develop a deep faith that could withstand persecution, was setting oneself up for a hard fall. Finally, Mark is especially hard on the leading early disciples: Peter, members of Jesus' family, James, and John.

Overall, Trocmé summarizes the conclusions to which his study of Mark's aversions has led him as follows:

> We can say now that this Gospel was born in a milieu which despised the Pharisees slightly without having lost hope of converting them; where the scribes and the leaders of the Jerusalemite priesthood were feared and hated; where the Jerusalem Temple was execrated; where certain Christians were criticized for their legalistic scruples and their naive apocalyptic beliefs, whereas the claims of a popular and emancipated Christianity were upheld against a tendency to express the new faith in intellectual and apologetic terms; where there was constant emphasis on the martyrdom of Jesus, whereas certain Christians preferred to gloss over this painful aspect of his ministry; where, lastly, it was commonly felt in spite of the great merits of James and John, the sons of Zebedee and, above all, Simon Peter, these men no longer had the monopoly of any special revelation and had not always been equal to the tasks Jesus had entrusted to them.[36]

Surely Mark was not written only from negative motives, however. Surely the author also wanted to put forward his community's positive views of the beloved Lord who had changed their lives. These positive views included Jesus' mysterious identity, his independence of popular support, and his great power to cure and heal. Mark's Christ is enigmatic, authoritative, strong minded and capable. He fights with Satan, confronts his earthly enemies head-on, knows the full implications of his actions, and accepts the price he will have to pay. In debate with the Pharisees and scribes he is sovereignly free, constantly closer to the heart of the religious matter than they. Before the chief priests and Pilate he is much more the judge than the judged, clearly the superior party. He endures his sufferings and degradations with dignity. He places his fate in the hands of a Father whose will he completely accepts. So he can be a clear and powerful example for all Christians, especially those in communities suffering persecution. As the Lord has comported himself bravely, borne up and sacrificed for the kingdom, so should any true disciple.

WHAT BACKGROUND DOES THIS TEXT PRESUPPOSE?

Mark presupposes an appreciation of the fluid state in which the early Christian memories of Jesus first circulated. We shall deal with this question more thoroughly in the next chapter, but here we need at least to allude to it. Any careful reading of Mark takes note of the way in which materials are blocked together: healings, teachings, abrupt transitions. It seems clear that the author is not composing his narrative from scratch but weaving together bits of tradition he had inherited. His authorship and artistry therefore show more in the way he has arranged his materials than in any fashioning of them from scratch. In all probability he inherited a large batch of traditions, some common to all Christians and some peculiar to his own local church, and gained canonical status by imposing on them a profound theological stamp.

Second, and relatedly, Mark presupposes the informal situation in the early Christian decades when a variety of local churches saw Jesus the Lord differently. The personality behind Mark appears rather contentious— inclined to do battle with interpretations of Jesus that the author and his community do not favor. As we have noted, interpretations that slighted Jesus' suffering especially drew his ire. He also took hard swipes at the scribes and chief priests, partly because his traditions made them Jesus' enemies and partly because they continued to vex the Church in his own day. Unless we realize that this Gospel in all likelihood was composed rather polemically, as a salvo in a war being fought on several fronts, we will be puzzled at its harshness.

Third, Mark presupposes a Gentile audience and community, with peculiarly Gentile interests in salvation and healing. Jews were interested in salvation and healing too, of course, but we noted the affinities in some of Jesus' cures to practices of contemporary Gentile healers and we should pause here to reflect more fully on the power that goes out from Mark's Jesus. This power shows most dramatically in the cures, like that of the woman with the flux of blood, that seem almost magnetic or mechanical. Jesus is full of a power from God that is like a physical force, electricity perhaps. People who open themselves to Jesus in faith can receive this power and can be jolted and changed by it. (It is Jesus, though, not the power, that is the proper focus of Markan faith.) So Mark's notion of salvation is nothing genteel or nicely restrained. It is the healing, restoring force of the mighty God, the raw force that originally formed the world and now crackles in thunder and lightning. This raw force relates to Jesus' authority. Jesus is not crude or socially gross, but he is no one with whom to trifle (unless, perhaps, you are a child). What he says comes straight from the shoulder as a direct expression of a passionate adherence to God. So by comparison with the often convoluted legal reasonings of the scribes and Pharisees his teaching is dauntingly authoritative. It both amazes and affronts people who are not willing to be similarly radical.

Fourth, granted this stress on power and authority, it is all the more striking that Mark so resolutely makes Jesus a suffering Messiah or Savior. The acceptance of his Father's will that takes Jesus to his destiny is active and energetic. Jesus is engaged in mortal combat with Satan—all the evils that oppose the reign of God, that corrupt human society. He comes to realize that the prevailing understandings of the Messiah will do nothing to change the core problems. They only will lead to more physical violence or external shuffles. What is needed is a conversion of human hearts, a tearing up of old rotten roots. So Jesus' combat becomes profoundly spiritual, a wrestling with ignorance and sin, principalities and powers. If we have no feel for these dimensions of the human heart, if we do not see their relevance to the social problems that have twisted every generation, we shall miss Mark's main point. Like Paul, Mark presents a Christ who has redone the human condition by suffering evil in love. He has broken the old law of tit for tat and stopped the cycle of returning hurt for hurt. Christians who cannot handle this, Mark implies, ought to turn in their baptismal certificates. They are not following the authentic Messiah.

Fifth, perhaps we should note the rather obvious fact that Mark tends to read his Scripture (the Old Testament) through a quite peculiar lens. Neither today's historico-critical methods (which aim at a certain objective determination of what the original author meant or the text itself can mean) nor the rabbinical methods of Mark's own day determined his readings. Rather he interpreted Scripture largely in terms of his faith that Jesus was the Christ and Son of God. So texts that have quite different meanings apart from Christian faith come to be predictions of Jesus' fate. Things that happen to Jesus bear a suspicious similarity to things that happened to Moses. Scripture is a sort of free-floating collection of divine wisdom into which Mark thinks it legitimate to dip for whatever insights apply to his task at hand.

Moreover, Mark gets some sanction for this use of Scripture from Jesus himself (assuming that some of Mark's versions of Jesus' sayings go back to Jesus himself). Jesus, too, apparently dealt with Scripture as a guide to God's present workings, a source of paradigms from the past that could illumine what was happening today. The God of Jesus is a God of the living, a Father with whom he personally communes. So he especially loves prophets such as Isaiah, because they so beautifully describe the ways of the living God, his concern for the poor and needy. Thus we have to accept the fact that Mark was bound to read Scripture differently, more existentially, than we now do. He was bound to read Scripture in the light of the most dramatic events of his faith: the ministry, death, and triumph of Jesus of Nazareth.

Sixth, Mark presupposes an understanding of apocalyptic, both the literary form that we find in such scriptural sources as Daniel and the general mentality of expecting the return of the Lord to consummate history. Howard Clark Kee, in a work that deals with Christian origins from a sociological perspective, has stressed apocalyptic and alienation (being at odds with the current times) in his characterization of the community that produced the Markan Gospel. That community was not purely eschatological. It made some provision for ethics and everyday life. Overall, however, Kee finds it rather apocalyptic and sectarian (separatist):

> What we have in Mark is the foundation document of an apocalyptic Christian sect. Although there are only bits of evidence by which to hypothesize the provenance [source] of Mark, there is a convergence of factors that point to rural and small-town southern Syria: the mode of house-building and of

farming, as well as the place names mentioned, point to this area; the document was written in crude but fluent Greek . . . yet with traces of Semitic usage behind the Greek. The refusal of the Markan community to side with either the nationalists or the assimilationists in the war with Rome also makes historical sense in that area. . . .

Unlike the Qumran community, which withdrew to the desert in order to maintain ritual purity, the Mark group was both inclusive and evangelistic. Nevertheless, its sectarian quality is evident in the claim to have secret knowledge (Mark 4:11); to have received private visions followed by private explanations (9:2–9); and to possess the clues to understanding cryptic documents (13:14). The community's hopes are to be fulfilled within the lifetime of their own generation (13:30). Their sacrifice in abandoning houses, families, and lands is soon to be compensated for "in the age to come" (10:30). One can perceive behind this gospel a community bound together by zeal, commitment, and expectation. There is no evidence of structure or chain of command. All the ordinary socio-economic structures have been abandoned in the service of the proclamation of God's rule. Founded by itinerant charismatics, these conventicles [small groups] had no basis for survival after the expectation [of Jesus' return] was disappointed, or for ongoing organization, or for cooperating with other and more sociologically stable elements of early Christianity. The chief contribution of the Markan group was the creation of a new genre, the Gospel. Since the Gospel served a specific function in the esoteric, eschatologically oriented group that produced it, there should be no surprise that the structure of the Gospel was significantly altered as it was adapted to other functions by other Christian groups with a different life world than the Markan outlook.[37]

Seventh and last, Mark presupposes a world view with an important place for what we consider parapsychological phenomena, especially demons or unclean spirits. Jesus is presented as a powerful exorcist. One of the main ways in which he wages war against Satan and Satan's realm of bondage is by casting out unclean spirits that possess and torment unfortunate souls. Some of this possession we may explain in terms of epilepsy or psychosomatic problems. Intuiting the emotional disorders that can aggravate if not cause the physical symptoms of "possession," Jesus is able to bring the sufferer to calm and peace. But another dimension involves a world of spirits, some of them malign, that we today pay little heed. We do not have to take on a first-century world view to understand the main implications of Jesus' exorcisms, but we do have to respect the inner logic and wisdoms of that world view. Many traditional peoples have explained the presence of evil or destructive powers in their lives as the workings of bad spirits. For many traditional peoples the "space" between human beings and the ultimate sacral powers, the God or the true gods, has been populated with lesser spirits that had to be appeased or accommodated. Only an excess of empiricism or concern with measurable data can lead one to draw such a world view with no sympathy.

Related to this parapsychological world is our sense of what is possible: whether people can be resuscitated, the future can be foreseen, someone actually can walk on water. We do well to be skeptical of these things, because they do not occur very often in our experience, but probably there is enough evidence for their *possibility* to suggest that we should stay a bit open, should suspend a fragment of our disbelief. This is the claim of Rosemary Haughton in her remarkable book *The Passionate God*. In asking her readers not to be cavalier in dismissing biblical claims, Haughton argues:

> We are so stiff in our categories, so laced up in corsets of eighteenth-century rationalism, that we can scarcely bend, and even normal breathing is difficult. So what follows is intended as a mental un-lacing, so that we can get a full breath of reality. It tastes odd, at first, but it is our world, and it *is* odd—much odder than we have been inclined to believe. We live, in fact, in a universe whose behaviour is stranger and less predictable (predictable, that is, according to the categories of possibility we usually admit) than our familiar models of reality allow. . . .
>
> I can only refer to a few examples, and among the weirder ones are "rains" of unlikely articles such as fish, nails or frogs, recorded at different times and places by reliable (and understandably angry or frightened) witnesses. There are cases including several contemporary ones of bodies found totally burned up, but with clothes (even stockings) or nearby furnishings unharmed and even unscorched. There are cases of people being reported seen in two different and distant places simultaneously. Possibly "poltergeist" phenomena should also come into this category, since they often involve the moving around or smashing, or arbitrary disappearance or appearance, of objects. "Levitation"—the capacity of people in certain mystical states to leave the ground and float around—is another in the same category, and also violent changes in temperature, so that some mystics have felt (and been felt to be) so hot as to be painful to touch, while sudden extreme cold often accompanies the appearance of ghosts, or is experienced by itself as a type of "haunting." Some people have given off intense light, and by no means all of these were mystics. Evidence for these and many other incidents is plentiful and accessible. This does not mean that all must be accepted, but it does mean that unless we continue to reject such evidence as *necessarily* false we have to admit that the world is a great deal odder than we normally recognize. . . . [38]

Haughton is saying that what may strike us as odd, something we have a difficult time explaining rationally or scientifically, may reflect purposes that lie outside our ken. The author of Mark probably would agree, naming these purposes the mysterious will of God. Mark invited his readers to risk opening themselves to the mysterious will of God, letting the world be amenable to more than they might initially have accredited (for example, a suffering Messiah). The Gospels continue to make the same invitation today, forcing modern readers to question whether their own limited horizons aren't a fundamental part of their problems in understanding Jesus of Nazareth.

WHAT LASTING SIGNIFICANCE DOES THIS HAVE?

The lasting significance of Mark is not its pressure to make us consider the possibility of parapsychological realities. We can get that pressure from many other places, and parapsychology is not the first or even the tenth of the things that Mark would have us contemplate. The first thing that Mark would have us contemplate is "the gospel of Jesus Christ, the Son of God" (1:1). Particularly, Mark would have us contemplate the sufferings of Jesus Christ, which are laced throughout Mark's distinctive brand of good news. The lasting significance of the Gospel according to Mark is the power with which it presents the suffering servant from Nazareth, the Messiah whom God raised because of the depth of his obedience and love. Without Mark neither Christianity nor world literature would have so striking a memory of Jesus. For enigma and challenge, Mark's Christ is the best around.

When it comes to comparing heroes, Christ and Socrates are often ranged side by side. Socrates, the exemplary wise man of Greece, went to his death serenely, after a long life rich in experience. He knew that he was dying for high principles, and he thought that life after death for such as he probably would be preferable to an earthly living that had been compromised. So Plato, who gives Socrates his literary existence, makes him the savior whom Athens rejected out of ignorance. Athens did not appreciate the redemptive power of Socrates' nescience, of his understanding that he did not understand. Athens was unwilling to face the great disorder in itself, the reams of pomp and pride, that such an appreciation would have disclosed. Jesus is only partially parallel. He does not, by Mark's lights, die young for a principle or to preserve his integrity (fine as either might have been). He dies cursed as a criminal and blasphemer (Socrates was accused of impiety) for having incarnated the Kingdom of God.

Among recent appreciations of Jesus few are more lucid than Monika Hellwig's *Jesus: The Compassion of God*. In a chapter on the dynamics of tragedy in the death of Jesus she writes:

> The movement of Jesus into this conclusion of his extraordinary life and ministry is also quite consistent in another respect with all that went before. A special character of his personality and attitudes that all had remarked upon was his simplicity in human relations which undercut all the distortions caused by abuse of authority and status and by various kinds of role playing to meet false expectations and standards of society. He had never shown any desire for status or honors himself and had associated with equal readiness with the privileged and the disreputable, careless of the aura of sin which his association with the latter cast around him in the eyes of the respectable and pious. His interest had always been in the simply human reality of the women and men and children around him, and he had presented himself to them as simply human, rejecting titles and speculations about himself as well as the attempt to confer a royal role upon him.

> In the account of his arrest, trial and execution, he follows this through consistently. Even in the arrest and trial he speaks as one free man to another, indeed as though God alone reigned in human society and there were no consequences to fear. He does not offer a defense in the trial, as though he has no need to make his case before this court, but he also suffers the consequences stripped of any claim to special protection or consideration. Jesus crucified is a naked man among the stripped and unprotected of the world who cannot clothe themselves in the privileges of power. And that is his last

word to us. He died as he lived, among the poor and disregarded and unprivileged by his own choice.[39]

Mark derives most of its lasting significance from this striking Jesus whom it and the other Gospels depict. Beyond the wisdom of the particular sayings that it records lies the deeper matter of Jesus' overall personality. Partly because of Mark, Jesus stands as one of the few figures in human history who seems truly to have been free. (The Buddha is another.) On the evidence of the Gospels, which are our main sources, Jesus also seems to have attacked the problem of human suffering at a depth that few other historical figures have even suspected. (Once again the Buddha is comparable.) Because of Jesus and the Gospels that so sharply portray him, first the West and then the world has had to question its prudent judgment that evil can never be conquered, that at best it can only be contained. While this judgment has led to some admirable laws and lofty correlations of behavior witih ideals, Jesus spoke of something different: a transforming love, a wholehearted faith, that could remake the human spirit and reset the tilted human situation.

The prophet Jeremiah had depicted some of this renovation in terms of a new covenant:

> Behold, the days are coming, says the Lord, when I will make a new covenant with the house of Israel and the house of Judah, not like the covenant which I made with their fathers when I brought them out of the land of Egypt, my covenant which they broke, though I was their husband, says the Lord. But this is the covenant which I will make with the house of Israel after those days, says the Lord: I will put my law within them, and I will write it upon their hearts; and I will be their God, and they shall be my people. And no longer shall each man teach his neighbor and each his brother, saying, 'Know the Lord,' for they shall all know me, from the least of them to the greatest, says the Lord, for I will forgive their iniquity, and I will remember their sin no more. [Jeremiah 31:31–34]

Both Jesus and Mark knew of passages such as this that spoke of new beginnings, changes at the core. Both knew of a Messiah, a Day of the Lord, a Reign of God that implied a radical re-creation. The Markan Jesus speaks out of this knowledge when he asks his hearers for faith. Without faith he is powerless. With faith he can work cures, dramatic signs that God is nigh. With strong enough faith any of his hearers could move mountains. Faith is the openness to Jesus' God that allows that God to operate. Strangely enough, Jesus' God needs permission to operate, openness and space. So the drama in Mark's portrayal of Jesus' interactions with the scribes and Pharisees is a drama of faith and unbelief. As Mark writes the scenes, those who reject Jesus do not really want the Kingdom of God, a renovated human situation. This is their tragedy. They reject the one set of possibilities that could bring them what their hearts have been made for, what their hallowed religious traditions have been moving toward. They choose not to become what they have been made to be: people taken over by a God of love, people fulfilled by the master of the universe.

Even apart from its Christian colorations, this Markan tragedy would be lastingly significant. Simply as a reading of human perverseness it would command ongoing interest and respect. The crowds who draw Jesus' compassion because they are like sheep without a shepherd repay Jesus few favors. The scribes and Pharisees get the role of the leading villains but the people as a whole show little faith. Even the disciples, on whom Jesus has lavished such care, flee when it comes to the crunch. Mark is saying that human perverseness is so widespread that we may call it universal. The ultimate claim that human beings have upon God (or one another) may be their self-destructiveness. Again and again we choose against our own best interests, miss the gold ring because we will not let go of the brass.

The crucified Savior at the climax of Mark's Gospel is a verdict on this human wretchedness. Jesus does not stand condemned by the Law so much as the Law and its supporters stand condemned as slaughterers of innocence. "The light has come into the world," Johannine Christians said (John 3:19), "and men loved darkness rather than light, because their deeds were evil." The Messiah finally arrived, Markan Christians said, and he was not to warped human beings' liking. So they killed him, because their deeds were evil. Yet human darkness and evil are not the ultimate word, in either the Johannine or the Markan universe. It is true that God needs human consent or permission (faith) to work the divine effects, yet it is also true that human denial cannot frustrate God's will. God is always greater.

For Mark the greatness of God blazes forth in the effectiveness of the crucifixion. Human beings thought that they were destroying Jesus, yet God made their very destructiveness a means of re-creation, redemption, resurrection. The religious world, too, is much odder than we normally acknowledge. Since the time of Mark and the other evangelists, people seriously pondering the turns of the human heart have had to go another level down. No wonder that Paul, Mark, and the rest of the ponderers whose writings have become scriptural, classical, in the West were amazed, electrified, forced to shout about good news. Take the worst human will in the world, they said, and it cannot defeat God.

Their thesis was no idle speculation, no academic bantering. Their thesis was an exegesis of the actual experience of Jesus of Nazareth, what had happened to the one man they knew who really had gambled everything upon God. Monika Hellwig described Jesus as speaking as though God alone reigned in human society and there were no consequences to fear. Lucas Grollenberg has described Jesus similarly.[40] The question for us now is, How transferrable is this fearlessness? How universal is the experience behind the Johannine dictum that perfect love casts out fear (1 John 4:18)? Much of Mark's lasting significance comes from his portrait of a man who does not fear, a man whose Godwardness gives him not only power but incomparable freedom. Without such portraits, it is likely that humankind would be imprisoned, would see no way around its worries and dreads. On just a human level, therefore, one may speak of writings such as Mark as redemptive, saving, powerful good news. Assuming that Jesus did live and die as Mark describes, anyone who reads the Gospel seriously has to question ordinary human fearfulness, cowardice, lack of soul. Because it is not easy or pleasant to question in this way, most people do not read the Gospel seriously. Mark might say, "Therefore they never will be free."

Does Mark's Jesus offer a realistic way to freedom? Does the resurrection stamp approval on a way of life, a sort of faith, that has hit the salvific bulls-eye? Those are questions that the evangelists would rejoice to hear their readers raising. They are also questions that some models of higher education would say have no place in a college classroom. It might be significant to let Mark make us take a stand on this matter. What sort of good news should American higher education allow us to study?

SUMMARY

In starting to determine what we have in front of us in the Gospel of Mark we first dealt with the New Testament's own concept of "gospel": the living, spoken word of Christ's saving message. Then we stressed that all the Gospels are proclamations of faith rather than detached historical reports. We pointed out that each Gospel has its own distinctive emphasis or theology and noted that Mark, the oldest Gospel, probably came from a Syrian community suffering distress shortly after 70 C.E.

In outline we divided Mark into an introduction, five main sections (most of them gathering materials on Jesus' rejection or failure to be understood because of the kind of Messiah he was), an apocalyptic discourse, a Passion narrative, and an Addendum. The key to this outline consisted of clues within Mark itself that the materials were being orchestrated toward Jesus' Passion. In commenting on the Gospel's subunits we found ourselves noting Jesus' power to cure, his call for faith, his enigmatic identity, overtones from the Hebrew Scriptures, Jesus' struggle against Satan, his parabolic preaching, his conflicts with the Jewish religious establishment, the Kingdom of God, the misunderstanding of the twelve, the emergence of the necessity of Jesus' suffering, his cutting to the heart of the religious matter, and Mark's eschatological orientation. These themes, and no doubt many others, interweave and complement one another. A great deal goes on in sixteen short chapters.

The apocalyptic discourse is a tipoff that Mark probably was written from a community under duress, and it shows this Gospel's dependence on Old Testament apocalyptic. The Passion Narrative is stark and realistic, emphasizing Jesus' aloneness, dignity, and commitment to his Father's will. The trial is something of a mockery, while the crucifixion (like so many of the discussions of Jesus' identity) is painfully ironic. Mark's final verdict comes when the centurion says, "Truly this man was the Son of God" (15:39).

The account of the empty tomb is very brief and restrained, in some scholars' opinion because Mark is more interested in the parousia. (The resurrection was probably not a historical event, but this is in part a matter of semantics.) The Addendum (16:9–20) adds accounts of Jesus' appearances after the resurrection that parallel appearances in the other Gospels.

In dealing with why Mark was written we began with the groups that Mark attacks. Primary among these were the scribes and high priests. Among Christians, Mark singles out for criticism those who wanted to cling to Jewish law, those who downplayed Christ's sufferings, and the leading original disciples. More positively, Mark is eager to present an authoritative, mysterious, suffering Messiah who can be a model for Christians forced down toward the bedrock of faith.

By way of background, Mark presupposes the fluidity and diversity of the early Church situation, with its many different local church traditions. Probably this Gospel was directed toward Gentile Christians and came from an apocalyptic, sectarian community. It also presupposes a world view with more space for demons and miraculous phenomena than that of the modern West.

The lasting significance of Mark is intimately tied up with the lasting significance of Jesus. As a strong portrait of the suffering servant whom Christians believe ripped out the heart of evil, Mark stands or falls by the wisdom, power, and relevance of its Christ. If the freedom that Mark's Jesus displays is pertinent to readers' struggles after fulfillment, readers' experiments with God and faith, Mark will never go out of style. If human beings continue to reject the light for which they have been made, because their deeds are evil, Mark will always be tragically significant, a good news with many a deep passage.

STUDY QUESTIONS

1. Why were the writings we now call "Gospels" recognized to have a value equivalent to oral preaching?
2. How does Christ's Passion dominate Mark?
3. How does Mark 1:15 summarize Jesus' message?
4. What is the significance of Jesus' teaching with authority?
5. Explain the parables of the kingdom in Mark 4.
6. Explain the probable significance of the story of the Gerasene demoniac.
7. Why are the Pharisees and scribes opposed to Jesus?
8. What does the Transfiguration seem to mean in Mark?
9. How does 12:1–12 color Jesus' messiahship?
10. How is apocalyptic an expression of faith?
11. How does Peter fare in Mark's Passion Narrative?
12. Why does Jesus die as the King of the Jews?
13. What is the significance of the empty tomb?
14. Why does Mark attack the high priests?

15. How does Mark use Scripture?
16. How open should we be to Jesus' actually having cast out demons?
17. What powers and values most make Mark's Jesus lastingly significant?

NOTES

1. Josef Schmid, "Gospel," in *Encyclopedia of Biblical Theology,* ed. J. B. Bauer (New York: Crossroad, 1981), p. 330.
2. See Eugene Boring, *The Words of the Risen Jesus* (Cambridge: University Press, 1983).
3. See C. H. Dodd, *The Apostolic Preaching and its Developments* (New York: Harper & Row, 1964).
4. See Howard C. Kee, *Jesus and History,* 2nd ed. (New York: Harcourt, Brace, Jovanovich, 1977).
5. See Nils A. Dahl, *Jesus in the Memory of the Early Church: Essays* (Minneapolis: Augsburg, 1976).
6. Schmid, "Gospel," pp. 331–32.
7. See Norman C. Perrin and Dennis C. Duling, *The New Testament,* 2nd ed. (New York: Harcourt, Brace, Jovanovich, 1982), pp. 239–40.
8. Xavier Leon-Dufour, *Dictionary of the New Testament* (San Francisco: Harper & Row, 1980), p. 379.
9. See John L. McKenzie, *Dictionary of the Bible* (Milwaukee: Bruce, 1965), p. 832.
10. See Geza Vermes, *Jesus the Jew* (London: Fontana/Collins, 1976), pp. 160–213; Norman Perrin, *A Modern Pilgrimage in New Testament Christology* (Philadelphia: Fortress, 1975).
11. See Geza Vermes, *The Dead Sea Scrolls* (Philadelphia: Fortress, 1977).
12. See Norman Perrin, *Jesus and the Language of the Kingdom* (Philadelphia: Fortress, 1976).
13. See Donald Juel, *An Introduction to New Testament Literature* (Nashville: Abingdon, 1978), pp. 91–92.
14. Lamar Williamson, Jr., *Interpretation: Mark* (Atlanta: John Knox, 1983), p. 104.
15. See H. Verweyen, "Einheit und Vielfalt der Evangelien am Beispiel der Redaktion von Wundergeschichten (insbesondere Mk 5, 25–34 parr.)," *Didaskalia* 11 (1981), pp. 3–24.
16. See F. Manns, "Marc 6, 21–29 a la lumière des dernières fouilles des Macheronte," *Studii Biblici Franciscani Liber Anmis* 31 (1981), pp. 287–90.
17. On the theophany (manifestation of divinity) implied here, see H. Fleddermann, "And He Wanted to Pass By Them (Mark 6:48c)," *Catholic Biblical Quarterly* 45 (1983), pp. 389–95.
18. Edward J. Mally, "The Gospel According to Mark," in *The Jerome Biblical Commentary,* ed. Raymond E. Brown and others (Englewood Cliffs, N.J.: Prentice-Hall, 1968), vol. 2, p. 41. See also Joachim Jeremias, *New Testament Theology: The Proclamation of Jesus* (New York: Charles Scribner's Sons, 1971), pp. 276 ff.
19. See M. P. Green, "The Meaning of Cross-Bearing," *Biblia Sacra* 140 (1983), 117–33.
20. See H. Giesen, "Mk 9, 1—ein Wort Jesu über die nahe Parusie?" *Trierer Theologische Zeitschrift* 92 (1983), 134–48.
21. See the debate between B. Brooten, "Könnten Frauen im alten Judentum die Scheidung betreiben? Überlegungen Zu Mk 10, 11–12 and 1 Kor 7, 10–11," *Evangelische Theologie* 42 (1982), 65–80, and H. Weder, "Perspektive der Frauen?" *Evangelische Theologie* 43 (1983), 175–78.
22. See M. J. Selvidge, "And Those Who Followed Feared (Mark 10:32)," *Catholic Biblical Quarterly* 45 (1983), 396–400.
23. See G. R. Beasley-Murray, "Second Thoughts on the Composition of Mark 13," *New Testament Studies* 29 (1983), 414–20.

24. See John J. Collins, *The Apocalyptic Vision of the Book of Daniel* (Missoula, Mont.: Scholars Press, 1977), pp. 123–52.

25. See F. Schnider, "Christusverkundigung und Jesuserzahlungen: Exegetische Überlegungen zu Mk 14, 3–9," *Kairos* 24 (1982), 171–80.

26. See Anthony J. Saldarini, *Jesus and Passover* (Ramsey, N.J.: Paulist, 1984).

27. See Donald Juel, *Messiah and Temple* (Missoula, Mont.: Scholars Press, 1977); John Donahue, *Are You the Christ?* (Missoula, Mont.: Scholars Press, 1973).

28. See V. Howard, *Das Ego Jesus in den Synoptischen Evangelien* (Marburg:L. G. Elwert, 1975).

29. See C. Burchard, "Markus 15:34," *Zeitschrift für die neuer-Testamentliche Wissenschaft* 74 (1983), 1–11.

30. See K. Brower, "Elijah in the Markan Passion Narrative," *Journal for the Study of the New Testament* 18 (1983), 85–101.

31. See A. K. Jenkins, "Young Man or Angel?" *Expository Times* 94 (1983), 237–40.

32. See the report in Reginald H. Fuller, "The Resurrection Narratives in Recent Study," in *Critical History and Biblical Faith: New Testament Perspectives*, ed. Thomas J. Ryan (Villanova, Penn.: The College Theology Society/Horizons, 1979), pp. 91–107, with special emphasis on Norman Perrin, *The Resurrection According to Matthew, Mark and Luke* (Philadelphia: Fortress, 1977).

33. Reginald H. Fuller, "The Resurrection Narratives in Recent Study," p. 103.

34. Etienne Trocmé, *The Formation of the Gospel According to Mark* (Philadelphia: Westminster, 1975), p. 6.

35. Ibid., p. 95.

36. Ibid., pp. 136–37.

37. Howard Clark Kee, *Christian Origins in Sociological Perspective* (Philadelphia: Westminster, 1980), pp. 138–39. See also his *Community of the New Age: Studies in Mark's Gospel* (Philadelphia: Westminster, 1977).

38. Rosemary Haughton, *The Passionate God* (Ramsey, N.J.: Paulist, 1981), pp. 27, 28, 29.

39. Monika K. Hellwig, *Jesus: The Compassion of God* (Wilmington, Del.: Michael Glazier, 1983), p. 95.

40. See Lucas Grollenberg, *Jesus* (Philadelphia: Westminster, 1978).

6

The Gospel for Matthew's Church

WHAT HAVE WE HERE?

In Matthew we have a Gospel whose Jewish overtones are strong. The author wants to locate Jesus within Jewish tradition, showing how Jesus stepped out of Jewish customs and expectations while at the same time fulfilling them. This makes Matthew a Gospel taut with a peculiar tension. The author cannot let go of Jewish traditions yet he believes Jesus has transformed those traditions. Oldness and newness dance together in an intricate duet. Specifically, Matthew tries to show that Jesus' fate conformed to the prophecies of the Jewish Scriptures. For example, Jesus' Passion and death were foreshadowed by the will of God expressed in God's dealing with the people of Israel. On the other hand, Jesus' teaching sometimes seemed to abrogate or go beyond the demands of the covenant Law. To explain this Matthew underscores Jesus' special position as the Son of God. It is because of his unique closeness to God that Jesus had the right to reinterpret God's Law.

"Son of God" is only one of several scriptural titles that Matthew uses to try to convey Jesus' significance. Others are "Son of David," "Messiah" ("Christ"), and "Wisdom." Matthew also uses "Son of Man," agreeing with Mark that Jesus used this title to refer to himself. The title "Son of God" often referred to a king (see Psalms 2 and 110, for example). In Matthew's hands it is transformed, coming to focus on Jesus' filial relation to God and giving later Christian theology one of its several reasons for concluding that Jesus himself was divine.

Just as Matthew places Jesus in a tense relation to Jewish tradition, so does he place the Church. The community that pledges allegiance to Jesus is also poised between past tradition and something radically new. Matthew never doubts that Israel is God's people. He quite accepts the story of Hebrew Scripture to the effect that the covenant brought about a special bond between the Jews and the one God. But Jesus inaugurated a new chapter in this story, bringing changes that altered or to some extent consummated the covenant. Thus the Church as the community centered around Jesus is the inheritor of much of Jewish tradition and privilege. In a word, for Matthew the Church is the new people of God. Both Jews and Gentiles may belong to this new people. Anyone who follows Jesus is eligible. But Jesus is something of a crisis or crux. Those who refuse him their allegiance have synagogues or gatherings outside the newly constituted people of God.

When we ask where Matthew got the sources for his version of the good news, we come up against what is called "The Synoptic Problem."[1] Briefly, the synoptic problem is the question of how to correlate Mark, Matthew, and Luke. They narrate many of the same things: teachings of Jesus, healings, reports of where Jesus went and what happened to him. Yet they also differ in their arrangement of many of the details. As well, there are materials common to Matthew and Luke that Mark does not present, and there are materials peculiar to both Matthew and Luke individually that are not found in any other Gospel. The form "Gospel," as we have seen, was something fashioned to deal with the remarkable career and teaching of Jesus of Nazareth. If Mark was indeed the earliest Gospel, Matthew inherited this literary form from Mark. He also inherited a good deal of Mark's actual materials. For example, what Matthew reports in chapters 3–4 and 12–28 can largely be found in Mark.

Part of the answer to the synoptic problem, then, is that Matthew and Luke probably had Mark available to them and used this earlier Gospel as one of their primary sources. They would have considered the contents of Mark common Church property, only one collection of the stories and reminiscences about Jesus that all Christians treasured. Another part of the answer to the synoptic problem is to postulate that Matthew and Luke shared a second source. The warrant for postulating this second common source is the fact that Matthew and Luke share about 200 verses not found in Mark. Because of this, New Testament scholars for some time have spoken of a second collection of materials (in addition to Mark) called "Q." The name Q traditionally has been said to derive from the German word **Quelle** ("source"), although recently this has been questioned.[2] At any rate, the current hypothesis is that Matthew and Luke independently had access to both Mark and Q. This is a reasonable, if not completely verified, explanation of the likenesses among Mark, Matthew, and Luke.[3] (It is not completely verified because no one as yet has found Q or come up with a manuscript of the postulated second source.)

The differences among Mark, Matthew, and Luke, finally, derive from two other causes. First, Matthew and Luke each seem to have had access to different, further materials that none of the other evangelists knew. In the case of Matthew this further source unique to himself sometimes is called "M." Materially, then, Matthew's Gospel was put together from Mark, Q, and M. Second, however, Mark, Matthew, and Luke all differ formally or theologically. Each evangelist put his own stamp on the materials in his Gospel, even when they were materials he shared with the other two synoptics. Sometimes this distinctive stamp is more obvious, sometimes it is less obvious, but the overall result is that even the stories or sayings that occur in other Gospels have a special resonance or set of implications in Matthew (or Mark or Luke). Each synoptic writer was creative in his own right. In each Gospel we get an original view of Jesus and the community that Jesus called forth.[4]

The current scholarly conjecture about the identity of Matthew and the circumstances in which he composed his Gospel suggests that he was not the tax collector of that name who became an apostle (9:9, 10:3). Rather it is more likely that he was a devoted Christian living in Syria or some other area of strong Jewish influence. He certainly was familiar with Jewish teaching methods and may have written his work shortly after 85 C.E. The community for which he wrote probably had more Jewish Christians than Christians of Gentile origin. Antioch is a possible center for Matthew's church. The views expressed in this Gospel had evolved over almost sixty years (since the death of Jesus around 29 C.E.), and they no doubt were greatly influenced by the fall of Jerusalem to the Romans in 70 C.E. that brought about the destruction of the Jerusalem temple (see 22:7). This event, along with the rise of a Judaism (reorganized under the Pharisees) that was more hostile to Christians, was a further stimulus for Matthew and many others to conclude that the Christian Church was the new carrier of God's promises.[5]

In outline the Gospel according to Matthew takes shape as follows:

Jesus' Genealogy and Birth 1:1–2:23

The Beginning of Jesus' Ministry 3:1–4:25

The Sermon on the Mount 5:1–7:29

Jesus' Mighty Acts 8:1–9:38

Jesus' Missionary Discourse 10:1–42

Jesus' Importance and Rejection 11:1–12:50

Parables about the Kingdom of God 13:1–53

Miracles and Controversies 13:54–16:4

The Approach to the Cross 16:5–17:27

Advice to the Church 18:1–35

Rising Opposition to Jesus 19:1–23:39

The Coming of the Kingdom 24:1–25:46

The Death and Resurrection of Jesus 26:1–28:20[6]

Among the features of this structural outline worth noting are the first two chapters, in which Matthew deals with Jesus' genealogy and birth. Mark has none of this material, so Matthew (as well as Luke) is working another lode. At the end of his Gospel Matthew adds to Markan materials the story of Jesus' appearance to the eleven disciples (28:16–20). The intermediate chapters are punctuated by five speeches that Jesus gives: the

Sermon on the Mount (5–7), the Missionary Discourse (10), the Parables about the Kingdom (13), the Advice to the Church (18), and the Eschatological Discourse about the Coming of the Kingdom (24–25). This arrangement might reflect the five books of Moses that anchor the Hebrew Bible.[7] At the least, it says that Matthew was very interested in Jesus' teaching, and that he saw him as a great new lawgiver or prophet.

Jesus' Genealogy and Birth (1:1–2:23)

In his well-received book *The Birth of the Messiah*, Raymond E. Brown has expanded on some suggestions of Krister Stendahl, a leading scholar of Matthew, to offer the following breakdown of the first two chapters of this Gospel. Matthew 1:1–17 deals with the *Who* of Jesus: his identity as Son of David and descendant of Abraham. Matthew 1:18–25 deals with the *How* of Jesus' appearance: his begetting by the Holy Spirit of Mary. Matthew 2:1–12 deals with the *Where* of Jesus' birth: at Bethlehem. Matthew 2:13–28 deals with the *Whence* of Jesus' destiny: The hostile forces of Herod and the Jewish authorities cause Jesus to imitate the experiences of Moses and the Israelites in Egypt and the Exodus; Jesus finally arrives in Nazareth of Galilee, a fitting home town for the Messiah.[8]

The purpose of the genealogy with which Matthew begins is to establish that Jesus had the lineage expected of the Messiah. Principally, this involves showing that Jesus was in fact a descendant of David. David's line was the line of royalty. The Judaism of Jesus' time thought of the Messiah as the kingly personage who would bring God's purposes for Israel to completion. In fact Matthew's layout of Jesus' genealogy is quite artificial. Jews of Matthew's day had no birth records or files as detailed as he would have needed. If we place Abraham, Isaac, and Jacob in the period 2000–1700 B.C.E. (the common conjecture), we see that Matthew is purporting to summarize at least 1700 years of Jesus' family line. He gets part of his table from the first three chapters of 1 Chronicles. Where he gets the other names is not clear. Nor is Matthew's counting faultless. His listing varies from that of Luke and he omits three names from the Chronicler's list to get his second group of fourteen. For his third group of fourteen, Matthew must either include Jeconiah twice or add in the Virgin Mary.

Why Matthew's concern with the number fourteen?

It is clear that he attaches great significance to the number fourteen, and the most probable explanation for this is that he sees in it a mystical meaning. Fourteen is the sum of the numerical values of the three letters that make up the name of David in Hebrew (*daleth, waw, daleth* = 4 + 6 + 4). In his mind, this number reflects the thought that in Jesus the promises of God to Israel are brought to fulfillment, and that the appointed channel of fulfillment is the Davidic monarchy in the person of the "son of David" who will be acknowledged also to be the Son of God. This kind of number symbolism [technically known as *gematria*] has no longer any appeal to us, but it is not unusual in the world in which Matthew lived. . . . It is unlikely that Jesus himself ever claimed to be the Messiah, or thought of his mission in anything like the traditional Messianic categories; but the title was certainly attributed to him

Madonna and Child with the Infant St. John. Lorenzo di Credi. About 1485–90. The Virgin, Child, and Infant John have carefully modeled, round bodies reflecting the naturalistic bent of the era. Notice that John is kneeling, in deference to the higher status of Jesus. *(Nelson Gallery–Atkins Museum, Kansas City, Mo. [Nelson Fund])*

by his disciples as soon as they were convinced that he had risen from the dead. To Matthew, it is of cardinal importance; the demonstration that Jesus is indeed the Messiah, though his own people repudiated him, is one of the main themes of his entire Gospel.

As "Son of David" then, Jesus fulfills all the promises that God had made through the ancient prophets for the restoration and blessing of Israel under the rule of a future descendant of David, the legitimate heir of the divinely ordained monarchy. As "Son of Abraham," Jesus fulfills the promise made to the founder of the holy community that he would be "the father of a multitude of nations," and that in him "all the families of the earth" would be blessed (Gen. 17:6; 12:3; cf. Gal. 3:8, 15–18, 29).

The genealogy as a whole stresses the continuity between the mission of Jesus and the history of Israel, and paves the way for the doctrine that the church which Jesus will found (Mt. 16:18) is the true Israel of God and the heir of all the promises.[9]

The story of Jesus' conception and birth continues the thrust of the genealogy. Matthew makes more of Joseph than Luke does, because Matthew's intent is to give Jesus a Davidic lineage through Joseph. Thus Joseph is called "son of David" (1:20) and marries Mary to legitimate her child. Matthew's account attributes Jesus' conception to the Holy Spirit, as does

Luke's, and it plays on two names for the child. "Jesus" probably meant "Yahweh is salvation," while Emmanuel, as the text says, meant "God with us." Joseph, being a righteous man (a strict observer of Jewish Law), had a serious problem with Mary's pregnancy. According to Deuteronomy 22:23–27, he could not marry her. So he planned to divorce her (betrothal was already a strong commitment) quietly. The story also explains Jesus' special holiness, although Matthew's main intent perhaps was not to teach a doctrine of virgin birth ("virgin" could simply mean "young girl").

The account of why Jesus was born in Bethlehem (2:1–12) also established his royal character. (Bethlehem was the birthplace of David, the ideal king and prototype of the Messiah.) The homage of the Magi was worthy of a kingly Messiah. The prophecy about the birth of the Messiah in Bethlehem was not as clear as Matthew makes out. Neither the Masoretic text (Hebrew) nor the Septuagint translation (Greek) have the prophecy in Matthew's form. Herod is portrayed as devious and fearful that he will lose his own power if a kingly Messiah should be born. The gifts of gold, frankincense, and myrrh echo Isaiah 60:6 (and Psalms 72:10). The Isaiahan text says, " . . . all those from Sheba shall come. They shall bring gold and frankincense, and shall proclaim the praise of the Lord."

The rest of 2:13–28 continues the motif of miracles. As Joseph had been told in a dream to marry Mary, and the Magi were warned in a dream not to return to Herod, so the flight of the Holy Family into Egypt, as it has come to be called, is at the insistence of an angel who speaks to Joseph in a dream. (The parallels between the Joseph of the New Testament and the Joseph of the Old Testament [Genesis 39–50], who were both dreamers, may be meant to suggest a parallel between Jesus and Moses, the two greater figures whom they preceded.)[10] Matthew is relying on the belief, widespread in his time and culture, that God could communicate revelatory matters in dreams. This is a common biblical occurrence (e.g., Genesis 15:12, 28:12–15), perhaps related to the experience many people have of waking up with a problem solved (an answer apparently surfacing after a night's tussle at the subconscious level). The sojourn in Egypt connects Jesus with both Moses and the key moment in Israelite history, the Exodus of the Hebrew slaves out of Pharoah's grasp. For Matthew Jesus is a new, greater liberator, taking a new Israel out of slavery to sin.

The slaughter of the innocents is not confirmed by any other contemporary documents. It fits the character of Herod, but Matthew may well have been creating a symbol of the opposition to Jesus' messiahship that eventually would lead to Jesus' death. In the background is Pharaoh's slaughter of the Israelite children (Exodus 1:15–22). The quotation from Jeremiah 31:15 adds weight to Matthew's theme that Jesus' life was played out in accordance with the divine will, that it was an extension of the purposes displayed in the Jewish Scriptures. An angel again directs Joseph, after Herod's death, to bring the child back to Israel, and the family ends up in Nazareth. Matthew's reference to a prophecy that makes Nazareth the home of the Messiah is obscure. Judges 13:5 and Isaiah 11:1 are outside possibilities. The word "branch" in Isaiah 11:1 sounds, in Hebrew, something like Nazareth. Judges 13:5 speaks of the Nazirite vow involved in Samson's somewhat extraordinary birth.

The Beginning of Jesus' Ministry (3:1–4:25)

Matthew begins the public life of Jesus just where Mark does, with the preaching of John the Baptist, and throughout this section Matthew's dependence on Mark is clear. An interesting original point is that Matthew has the preaching of John and Jesus strike exactly the same note. Thus John says (3:2), "Repent, for the kingdom of heaven is at hand," while the first words of the Matthean Jesus' preaching are, "Repent, for the kingdom of heaven is at hand" (4:17). At the least, then, Matthew is linking the work of John with the work of Jesus. Both preached the same message: Repent, turn around, make the radical changes that the new age of the dawning kingdom demands. It is characteristic of Matthew to call the kingdom "the kingdom of heaven," rather than the Markan "the kingdom of God," because Matthew follows the pious Jewish practice of not using the divine name, out of respect for God's holiness. However, Matthew's phrase does not mean that the Kingdom or Reign is otherworldly. As much as Mark he

Virgin and Child. French. About 1475. This sculpture comes from the private chapel of the castle of Gisors, near Rouen. It reflects the last phase of a Gothic style (school of Troyes) that soon was replaced by the Renaissance. *(Nelson Gallery– Atkins Museum, Kansas City, Mo. [Nelson Fund])*

looks forward to a renovation of all of human life, bodily and temporal things, as much as spiritual ones.

In both Matthew and Mark, the appearance of John the Baptist reminds the informed reader of Elijah. In 2 Kings 1:8 Elijah is described as follows: "He wore a garment of haircloth, with a girdle of leather about his loins." It is probably significant that John castigates the Pharisees and Sadducees, the two groups who will be Jesus' bitter enemies. (Luke, for instance, has John simply attack the "multitudes" [3:7].) They are foolish to rely on Abraham. Jesus, more a son of Abraham than they, offers a new belonging to God that is far deeper than ethnicity. The imagery of winnowing was a traditional way of depicting God's judgment. Matthew is careful to subordinate John to Jesus, making John the forerunner of the Messiah rather than a serious competitor.

Jesus receives baptism from John because this is part of the divine plan. Only Matthew gives John the insight to realize the paradox involved: "John would have prevented him, saying, 'I need to be baptized by you, and do you come to me?'" (3:14). The opening of the heavens, descent of the Spirit of God like a dove, and heavenly voice expressing pleasure are all drawn from Jewish Scripture (see Ezekiel 1:1, Isaiah 64:1, Genesis 1:2, Genesis 22:2, Psalms 2:7, Isaiah 42:1). The climax of this theophany is the designation of Jesus as the divine Son, which harkens back to the infancy narrative and the angel's message to Joseph.

The account of Jesus' temptation in the wilderness is more developed in Matthew and Luke than in Mark. The devil fixes the contest of wills on Jesus' divine Sonship: "If you are the Son of God . . ." Jesus answers Satan's various challenges with quotations from Deuteronomy (8:3, 6:16, 6:13). The progression in the temptations is from material food to displays of religious power to idolatry for the sake of worldly kingdoms. In rejecting them all Jesus shows that he is a Son of God unconcerned about worldly things, totally obedient to the will of God expressed in the Jewish Scriptures, which (as befits God's new spokesman) he knows intimately and applies incisively.

Jesus begins his public ministry in Galilee, and Matthew, true to his tendency to fit Jesus' life to Old Testament prophecies, justifies this with a quotation from Isaiah 9:1–2. The quotation implies that the light and power of the kingdom have begun to shine, the dank captivity of those who are either physically or spiritually wretched is about to end. Jesus preaches repentance, because the Kingdom of Heaven, the Reign that is the spread of God's righteousness, is at hand. Matthew's account of the call of the first disciples largely agrees with Mark's. The "immediately" in 4:20 and 4:22 exemplifies the generous response that the Gospel deserves. Although they did not know Jesus, his bearing and word were enough to make Simon Peter and Andrew, James and John, leave their nets and become lifelong disciples. Jesus toured all of Galilee, preaching in the synagogues and healing many different kinds of diseases. This made him famous throughout the entire region. The gospel of the kingdom, demonstrated in Jesus' power to cure, was initially a great success.

Study for the "Baptism of Christ." Perugino (Pietro Vannucci). The artist has captured well the humanity of Christ as a vigorous and serious young man about to embark on a testing vocation. *(Nelson Gallery–Atkins Museum, Kansas City, Mo. [Nelson Fund])*

The Sermon on the Mount (5:1–7:29)

The Sermon on the Mount is probably the most famous summary of Jesus' preaching. If we consider the first four chapters of Matthew as preparation for it, it stands as the preaching of the royal Messiah, the superior of John the Baptist, the Son of God who (as the authoritative interpreter of God's will) has bested Satan. Although the Beatitudes (5:3–11) are better known, the central theme of the sermon echoes in 5:20: "For I tell you, unless your righteousness exceeds that of the scribes and Pharisees, you will never enter the kingdom of heaven." Matthew is portraying Jesus as the spiritual or religious superior of the scribes and Pharisees. What he teaches is as far above their teaching as the Kingdom of Heaven is above present, disordered conditions.

Daniel Harrington divides the Sermon into four sections:

The introductory section (5:1–20) describes those who are blessed (5:3–12), the role of the disciples (5:13–16), and the role of Jesus (5:17–19). The second major section (5:21–48) contrasts the holiness or righteousness of the experts in the interpretation of the Old Testament law ("the scribes") and the better holiness or righteousness taught by Jesus. The third section (6:1–18) warns against the purely external holiness cultivated by groups like the Pharisees, and the fourth section (6:19–7:29) furnishes more advice for Christians in their pursuit of holiness.[11]

Jesus preaches the Sermon like a new Moses, come with a revelation to surpass that of Mount Sinai. The formula "Blessed are . . ." comes from the Psalms and wisdom literature of the Old Testament. Matthew's Beatitudes, by contrast with Luke's, deal more with the spirit or underlying condition of the groups that Jesus is blessing. (This may well reflect a different sociological setting in a new wealthy community. Matthew, for a further instance, suggests that disciples might have gold and silver, as well as copper coins [10:9], whereas Mark 6:8 mentions only copper coins.)[12] It is those brought low by their poverty, those saddened by their sufferings, those without the power or status to be aggressive, and those who with all their being want things to be as they ought who will find the coming of the kingdom a blessing. It is the merciful, those quick to forgive others and give alms, who shall find God merciful to them. Those who are pure in their hearts, not just externally, shall become close to God. Reconcilers will be considered the children of God. The persecuted will possess the kingdom. If these promises are startling today, they were perhaps even more startling in Jesus' own time:

> It is difficult for us to appreciate the paradoxical character of the Beatitudes. They institute a moral revolution that has not yet reached its fulness. They are opposed to all the conventional values of the Jewish and the Hellenistic-Roman world and pronounce blessings on those who do not share these values. Not only the external values of wealth and status are repudiated but also the goods of the person that are achieved and defended by self-assertion and strife.[13]

Scholars debate the source of the Beatitudes, some arguing that Q is the main source, used independently by Matthew and Luke, and others saying that Luke gets his version through Matthew.[14] What is not debated is the impact of these sayings on the history of Christian faith. They stand as strong evidence that Jesus had a vision bound to contradict most hearers' or readers' notions of happiness. Verses 11 and 12 add to this evidence. By the touchstone of the prophets, whom he could assume were the heroes of Israelite faith, the Matthean Jesus says that those who suffer for his sake are both blessed and sure to be rewarded in heaven. That was the fate of the prophets: both suffering and high favor with God.

Matthew 5:13–16 exhorts the disciples of Jesus to be effective. Unless they are strong and distinctive, they will be like salt that has lost its tang, like a lamp that has been shielded. They must see to it that people are moved by their lives to praise God, to find that what they do and are is reason to say that God is good. In 5:17–20 Matthew makes Jesus the fulfillment of the Jewish Law. Jesus is not a source of laxity or lessening of religious effort. Rather he penetrates to the heart of Torah and calls for a righteousness greater than that of the scribes and Pharisees. Part of Matthew's motivation in this section may have been a desire to appease Christians of Jewish background who still had a profound reverence for Torah. Another part may have been a desire to oppose the growing power of the Pharisees as the interpreters of Torah in a Judaism increasingly hostile to Christianity.

Matthew 5:21–48 spells out in some detail what the loftier righteousness of Jesus ought to mean. It is not enough that people refrain from murder. We ought also to avoid the anger that usually is the source of murder and violence. Unless we are reconciled to one another and bring ourselves back from anger and alienation to good relations, our acts of worship will not please God. Similarly, Jesus proposes stricter or deeper standards regarding adultery, divorce, and swearing. In light of the Reign of God we must get to the heart of our sins, our relationships going sour, our idle and irreverent speech. What God offers us in the kingdom shows that we can be better than we tend to be, that we should be challenged to cleanse our hearts.

Matthew 5:38–48 drives this theme of a greater perfection home with stunning force. No longer can "justice" be an eye for an eye, tit for tat. Such a level of justice, required by Jewish Scripture (e.g., Exodus 21:23–24, Leviticus 24:19–20, Deuteronomy 19:21), will not solve the problem of human divisions. Jesus' followers must stop the flood of violence and counterviolence, hurt and counterhurt, by refusing to retaliate. They must try to return good even to those who do them evil. In striving for this very demanding ideal, which reaches the extreme of loving their enemies and praying for those who persecute them, Jesus' followers will be imitating God, behaving like their heavenly Father, "for he makes his sun rise on the evil and on the good, and sends rain on the just and on the unjust" (5:45). There is a universal benevolence in God, a stable disposition always to do good, that Jesus would have his followers try to match. It is natural to love our friends, benefactors, or fellow countrymen. To love our enemies, those who are ruining our lives, is something so extraordinary that it points to the perfection of God.[15]

Matthew 6:1–18 sounds a theme of sincerity. The piety of Jesus' followers must be more than an external performance, let alone something for show. It must be directed toward God in secret, with no thought of human applause. (In saying this does the Matthean Jesus forget his earlier demand that his disciples let their light shine before others?) Almsgiving, prayer, and the rest must be humble, simple, and sincere. Otherwise they will not please God.

To be still more concrete, Jesus demonstrates the sincere piety he has in mind by teaching the "Our Father." Much of the content of this ("the Lord's") prayer has close parallels in Jewish prayers of Jesus' day. Its main themes are begging the coming of God's kingdom, the doing of God's will, satisfaction of our material needs, and forgiveness for our sins. Disciples should forgive those who have offended them. They should ask protection against temptation and evil. Forgiveness from Jesus' God requires willingness to forgive other people. Fasting, almsgiving, and the rest must avoid all hypocrisy. Matthew gives Jesus such a keen aversion to hypocrisy that he implies hypocrisy was rife in the established religion of Jesus' day.

Matthew 6:19–7:29 gathers together more spiritual advice, more indications of how Jesus thought life should be in the coming kingdom. It should not, for instance, be overly concerned about the material things which so easily can be destroyed and so easily can distract us from more important things (such as social justice and deep obedience to God). The treasure of a truly religious, truly human life is a right relation to God, a deep intimacy with the holy mystery at the center of things. Disciples should stress a good conscience and not be beholden to mammon, the riches and power of worldlings. They should trust that God will provide what they need for a simple, good life, as God so beautifully provides for the birds of the air and the lilies of the field. If they burn with a passion to know and love God, they will meet their material needs rather easily. Sufficient for each day is its own troubles. Excess worry can mean a lack of faith.

Life in Jesus' kingdom also requires one to become less judgmental than most people are. Disciples should be more concerned about remedying their own gross defects than about pointing out other people's minor failings. Proper faith appreciates what it has and does not waste its treasures. Jesus' followers should expect that God will answer their prayers the way a good friend or a kindly parent answers a sincere request for help. The golden rule in human relations is treating others the way we long to be treated ourselves.

The middle sayings of chapter 7 are rather severe. In the background is the Old Testament teaching that there are two "ways," death and life, and that we must choose which way we shall walk (see Deuteronomy 30:15–20). So Jesus counsels his followers to enter the narrow gate[16] and walk the hard road, because a life without discipline leads to perdition. Similarly, his followers should not be credulous or uncritical about those who come to them preaching this or that. False prophets are ever about. The stable test is the fruits of the person's or doctrine's life. If people produce good fruits—faith, hope, love of God, and love of neighbor—they must themselves be good. If a doctrine leads to wisdom, prudence, and justice, it must be sound. The Matthean Jesus is a high-minded pragmatist. The touchstone for him is what people do, how they act. Words are easy, promises come and go. "Not every one who says to me 'Lord, Lord,' shall enter the kingdom of heaven, but he who does the will of my Father who is in heaven" (7:21). God's will is justice, truth, and love. Without these even exorcisms and predictions about the future are what Paul called tinkling brass and clanging cymbal (1 Corinthians 13:1).

The Sermon on the Mount concludes soberly but with considerable hope. Those who hear Jesus' words and obey them will build their lives on solid ground, even rock. Those who do not obey Jesus' words will have their lives washed away when storms of passion or rains of adversity put them to the test. The people found Jesus' sermon astonishing, Matthew says. Like Mark, he underscores the authority with which Jesus taught, his direct interpretation of God's will. Matthew is scoring points in his ongoing debate with the Jews who did not accept Jesus' messiahship or teaching (especially the Pharisees, who came to power after 70 C.E.). To his mind this authority is a major reason for preferring the Church of Jesus to the synagogues of the scribes.

Although the Sermon on the Mount is not a complete code of Christian ethics, it represents the principles (and some of the main illustrations) that Matthew's church (a church with Jewish orientations) had distilled from perhaps sixty years' experience of trying to follow Jesus. The major principle is love, and this ultimately is God's gift. But the Matthean Jesus also stresses doing, praxis, getting one's life in gear. He assumes that people have a say in what they become, that they are free agents. They had best realize that he forces a basic decision, a central for or against.

Jesus' Mighty Acts (8:1–9:38)

As if to present further credentials for Jesus' teaching, the next section describes ten of his cures and miracles (which may suggest the ten wonders performed by Moses at the Exodus. See also Micah 7:15).[17] Jesus performs most of these on behalf of people marginal in his society: lepers, Gentiles, women, servants, people possessed. So Jesus rewards the faith of a leper by making him clean. He rewards the wholehearted trust of a centurion by curing his servant. (Matthew makes Jesus' response to this Gentile a forecast of the way salvation will pass to non-Jews.) Jesus cures Peter's mother-in-law, people possessed by demons, and all who are sick. Fitting this to his theme of fulfillment, Matthew recalls the verse of the prophet Isaiah (Isaiah 53:5): "He took our infirmities and bore our diseases." Since the Isaiahan prophecy relates to the suffering servant, its use here intimates Jesus' coming Passion.

The section 8:18–22 is a pause, between describing Jesus' cures, for some teaching. To the scribe who says that he will follow Jesus wherever Jesus goes, the Master replies that he has no place to lay his head (he must wander as the service of God and proclamation of the kingdom dictate). To the disciple who wants to tarry for his father's funeral, the Master replies almost brutally: "Follow me and leave the dead to bury their own dead." When it comes to matters of bedrock allegiance, Jesus and the kingdom clearly have to come first.

Jesus then rebukes the winds and calms the sea, a scene that we witnessed in Mark 4:36–41. He moves on to the country of the Gadarenes, where he casts demons into swine that rush over a steep bank, plunge into the sea, and drown (compare with Mark 5:1–20; Matthew's upping the number of demoniacs to two is a good example of his general tendency to give more play to the miraculous). The people fear this demonstration of unearthly power and ask Jesus to leave their neighborhood. Matthew's main point emerges in the dialogue between Jesus and the demons. They respond to him as their master, one they are bound to fear and obey.

Chapter 9 opens with the cure of a paralytic—another reward for faith. But, as in Mark, some of the scribes in attendance make the judgment that Jesus blasphemes when he assures the paralytic that his sins (which in Jewish thought could have been the cause of his paralysis) are forgiven.

Christ and the Centurion. Veronese (Paolo Cagliari). The artist's tendency to portray biblical scenes in elegant terms got him in trouble with the Inquisition in 1573. The bearded, balding soldier at the extreme right is thought to be the artist's self-portrait—a dramatic way of making the scenes of Christ's life contemporary.
(Nelson Gallery—Atkins Museum, Kansas City, Mo. [Nelson Fund])

The cure therefore takes on an added dimension. It is proof that the Son of Man has authority on earth to forgive sins—a divine prerogative. Matthew 9:9–13 recalls the sort of people with whom Jesus consorted: tax collectors (despised for doing Rome's dirty work) and sinners. Matthew's Jesus repeats the Markan saying that it is not the healthy who need a doctor but the sick. He adds, however, the powerful saying (Hosea 6:6), "I desire mercy and not sacrifice." Jesus tells the Pharisees, who were affronted by his consorting with sinners, "Go and learn what this means." That is like slapping them with the back of his hand, telling them they haven't mastered the kindergarten reading book. For Matthew Jesus' controversy with the Pharisees boiled down to which would prevail, mercy (meeting people's needs) or sacrifice (external obedience to Torah). Jesus is wholly on the side of mercy.

Matthew 9:14–17 further defends the people with whom Jesus consorts and whom he accepts as disciples. When followers of John the Baptist ask why Jesus' people do not fast, as they and the Pharisees do, Jesus replies with the figure of a bridegroom we have seen in Mark 2:18–22. The kingdom is something joyous, a gift of God. The best way to honor the reality of the kingdom and the significance of the one who brings it is to accept God's gift gratefully and enjoy God's largess. There is a time for celebrating and a time for mourning. One must fit old habits, past modes of thought, to new realities, making sure that they match. When resistance to Jesus and the kingdom have led evil people to lash out destructively, there will be plenty about which to fast and mourn. As long as the bridegroom is present people should celebrate his wedding, entering into God's widespread embrace.

Matthew 9:18–26 reports the resuscitation of the daughter of a ruler (Mark made him a ruler of the synagogue named Jairus; see Mark 5:21–43) and the cure of a woman with a twelve-year hemorrhage. Jesus rewards the faith of both with healings. In 27–31 two blind men beg mercy. Ascertaining their belief that he can give them sight, Jesus touches their eyes and they see. (Matthew again increases the marvel—compare Mark 8:22–26.) A bit of Markan secrecy remains in Matthew's account: "And Jesus sternly charged them, 'See that no one knows it.' But they went away and spread his fame through all that district." Matthew 9:32–34 describes the cure of a dumb demoniac. The crowd is thoroughly impressed, but the Pharisees say that Jesus casts out demons by using the prince of demons. To Matthew's mind the Pharisees are now closed. No demonstration of God, not even a resurrection from the dead, could turn them around.

Matthew 9:35–38, the conclusion to this section on Jesus' mighty acts, is a miniature account or summary of Jesus' ministry. He went all about the district of Galilee, to all the towns and synagogues, preaching the gospel of the kingdom and curing the infirm. The crowds moved him to pity and compassion, because they were like sheep without a shepherd. Seeing all the good that might be worked, he bade his disciples pray that God would send laborers to bring in the potentially rich harvest.

Jesus' Missionary Discourse (10:1–42)

The mention of harvest and recruiting new laborers bridges Matthew's way to a summary of Jesus' sayings about Christian mission. (No doubt the early Church's experiences in trying to spread the gospel also shaped this section.) Jesus calls the twelve, his closest disciples, and gives them authority to cast out unclean spirits and heal diseases. (How he communicated this authority is not said.) Matthew lists the twelve as Simon Peter, Andrew, James, John, Philip, Bartholomew, Thomas, Matthew (the tax collector), another James, Thaddeus, another Simon, and "Judas Iscariot, who betrayed him." The charge given the twelve is to preach only to Jews, ignoring Gentiles and Samaritans (whose faith was deviant in the eyes of the orthodox). We can assume, then, that Jesus thought of himself and his little group in quite infra-Jewish categories.

What the twelve are to preach is the arrival of the Kingdom of Heaven. They are to heal the sick, raise the dead, cleanse lepers, and cast out demons—the things that Jesus himself has been doing to demonstrate the power of the kingdom. They are to take no pay. They are to travel light. They should bless those who receive them well. When others do not receive them well they should shake the dust from their feet (a sign of dissociation). On Judgment Day God will render a harsh verdict on the towns that have missed this golden opportunity. Sodom and Gomorrah, symbols of wickedness, will have it better on Judgment Day than such places.

The missionaries should not expect an easy time. They are like sheep compared to the wolves who prowl the world. So they must be as wise as serpents and innocent as doves. Reflecting what actually happened to some of the early Christian missionaries, the Matthean Jesus warns the disciples that they will be delivered up to councils, flogged in synagogues, and dragged before rulers. (Mark places this warning later [13:9–13] and makes it eschatological—a sign of the end. Matthew stresses that hostility arose during Jesus' own ministry.) They should trust that the Spirit of God will show them what to say.

The gospel will be a cause of family division. Many will hate the disciples because they represent Jesus, who asks so much. But they need only hang on, persevere, to assure their salvation. In 10:23 the disciples' mission takes an eschatological turn: "When they persecute you in one town, flee to the next; for truly, I say to you, you will not have gone through all the towns of Israel, before the Son of Man comes." Obviously the Son of Man had not returned at the time of Matthew's writing, so Matthew's including this problematic saying may speak for its authenticity. Unlike Luke (Luke 9:1–10), Matthew does not have the twelve return from this mission, and the "great commission" (Matthew 28:19–20) at the end of the Gospel may imply that, after the resurrection, the mission has been recast in more universalist terms—to all nations, rather than just the towns of Israel.[18]

Chapter 10:24–25 reminds the disciples that they are likely to suffer their Master's fate. Discipleship, one might say, is walking the way one's Master has trod. But Jesus assures the twelve that nothing escapes God. They may proclaim openly what Jesus has told them. Their real enemies are not the people who can slay them bodily. Bodily death is far from the worst evil. Their real enemies are the people who can destroy both the body and the soul in hell—the people who can corrupt them, make them unworthy of God. If God takes care of the birds of the air, the disciples may be sure God will take care of them. The Father numbers the very hairs of their heads. They need only keep faith with Jesus and he will acknowledge them before the Father. (Early Christian belief pictured the ascended Jesus at the Father's right hand, able to intercede for his followers.) If they do not keep faith with Jesus, if they recant their allegiance, Jesus will deny them. Once again, the choice is plain.

Matthew 10:34–39 continues Jesus' warning not to underestimate the costs of discipleship. The gospel can be a sword, cutting previously intimate people off from one another. Jesus demands a choice for God that makes natural blood ties secondary. A disciple is one willing to carry the cross that serving the kingdom is likely to bring. Only those willing to lose earthly "life" (money, status, acclaim) will find truly human, heavenly life. Jesus is a transvaluator of values, a challenge to set one's life on a quite new, more profound basis.

For their comfort, Jesus tells the disciples that those who accept them accept him, and that accepting him is accepting the God who sent him.

Indeed, people of goodwill who take the gospel to heart will be rewarded like those who spend themselves preaching the gospel. Even little acts of kindness and support will be rewarded. (Once again, the missionary experiences of the early Church shine through. Matthew is trying to encourage both missionaries and those missionized, doing his level best to make the cause of the Church identical with the cause of Christ and God.)

Jesus' Importance and Rejection (11:1–12:50)

Having completed his missionary discourse, his preparation of the twelve, the Matthean Jesus sets out on his way again, resuming his own preaching of the gospel. John the Baptist, imprisoned by Herod, hears about Jesus' doings and sends his disciples to ask Jesus whether Jesus is the Messiah, "He who is to come" (Psalms 118:26, Malachai 3:1). Jesus' answer is oblique: The things he has been doing fulfill the expectations set forth in such texts as Isaiah 35:5–6 and 61:1. The conclusion of Jesus' answer, though, is ominous: "And blessed is he who takes no offense at me." Such "offense" is at the core of our word *scandal*. Jesus will suffer and die like a common criminal. Continuing to cling to him even through this disgrace will require unusual faith.

Just as he had been firm, even harsh with the disciples in the missionary discourse, training them like experienced recruits for demanding service, Jesus becomes more demanding with the crowds. Perhaps the superficiality of their response has begun to bother him more, to make him wonder about the value of their enthusiasm. So he challenges their prior interest in John: "What did you go out into the wilderness to behold? A reed shaken by the wind? Why then did you go out? To see a man clothed in soft raiment? Behold, those who wear soft raiment are in king's houses. Why then did you go out? To see a prophet? Yes, I tell you, and more than a prophet" (11:7–9). John was not a symbol of luxury. He was a desert creature, heir to Israel's tradition of purification and bedrock faith. Indeed, he was an Elijahan figure, a precursor of the messianic age. In the judgment of Matthew's Jesus John was the greatest of the prophets, the preachers of the old dispensation. Still, the new inbreak of the kingdom is more important even than John and his holy call for penance. John himself, in prison, epitomizes the violence swirling about the kingdom, the present and coming contests for allegiance. Jesus will lose his life to this violence. The crowds had best sit up and take notice.

They also should sift out their motives and become more responsible. "This generation," of which they are a part, is perverse in its changing expectations, infantile in its shifts of desire. Jesus, ever on the verge of poetry, pins their irresponsibility to the board with a brilliant simile: "It is like children sitting in the marketplace and calling to their playmates, 'We piped to you, and you did not dance; we wailed, and you did not mourn'" (11:16–17).

John was ascetic and for his pains the crowd called him possessed. Jesus was not ascetic, was companionable, and the same crowds called him a glutton and drunkard, a friend of tax collectors and sinners. The reader senses across 1900 years the irritation and frustration in Matthew, indeed the even older frustration of Jesus himself. It is unjust, this unwillingness of the people at large to be pleased. Worse, it is perverse, a sign of a radical hardness of heart. What is one to do with people who insist on being negative, judgmental, untouchable? How can one save their souls? Jesus' simile implies that one cannot save their souls. Until they turn around and accept offers like the kingdom (which spells the end of their egocentricity), they are beyond the pale. Anyone who has suffered perversity like this will sympathize with Jesus' anger.

The ending line (11:19), "Yet wisdom is justified by her deeds," is both obscure and tantalizing. The commentators tend either to note that it is reminiscent of Old Testament proverbial literature, which was rather pragmatic (concerning itself with people's performances), or to connect it with the early Church view that Jesus himself incarnated the divine wisdom. Perhaps it is better taken as deeply ironic: Let the wise guys have their way. See the shabby ends to which their closure brings them, how they help crucify the wisdom of God.

Continuing his lament, Jesus upbraids the places where he did so much to demonstrate the arrival of the kingdom. Had he gone to pagan towns such as Tyre and Sidon he would have gotten a better reception. Sodom itself will not be so harshly judged as Chorazin, Bethsaida, Capernaum, and the Jewish rest. (Matthew may be injecting some of the early Church's bitterness at the rejection of its message.) Matthew 11:25–30 links the wisdom of Jesus not with the wise guys dominating this generation but with the childlike, the people who are open. By placing this teaching in the midst of Jesus' conversation with his heavenly Father, Matthew interjects a Johannine tone. Such an address of the Father and conception of himself as the Son is very strong in the fourth Gospel's portrait of Jesus. Especially Johannine are the lines, "All things have been delivered to me by my Father; and no one knows the Son except the Father, and no one knows the Father except the Son and any one to whom the Son chooses to reveal him" (11:27; see John 3:35, 7:29, 10:14–15, 17:1–3). We may infer that either Matthew was familiar with some Johannine materials, or Johannine authors knew parts of a basic synoptic source.[19] Matthew 11:28–30 offers rest to those who labor and are burdened. Discipleship has its compensations. The discipline of the gospel may seem hard but once accepted it is easy and light.

Chapter 12 begins with controversies about the Sabbath, which marks a return to the Markan outline of events and confirms the impression we got from Mark that the Sabbath was a great bone of contention between Jesus and the Pharisees.[20] Jesus has to defend his disciples' plucking grain on the Sabbath when they were hungry. In so doing he again criticizes the Pharisees as not knowing the basics of religion: "And if you had known what this means, 'I desire mercy, and not sacrifice,' you would not have condemned the guiltless." If Old Testament heroes such as David had the right to interpret the Sabbath, how much more does the Son of Man, the bringer of the kingdom. Similarly, when Jesus is asked whether it is lawful to heal on the Sabbath, his anger flares: Which of the interrogators would not save one of his sheep on the Sabbath? So Jesus heals the withered hand of the man who had occasioned this questioning, further alienating the Pharisees (who now begin to plot how to destroy him). Prudently, Jesus withdraws from the area. (Matthew underlines the rising price of his messiahship by quoting Isaiah 42:1–4, another description of the suffering servant of God.)

The cures continue and the opposition of the Pharisees hardens (see Mark 3:19–21). When Jesus heals a blind and dumb demoniac the crowd wonders whether he isn't the Son of David or Messiah they have been awaiting. But the Pharisees attribute the cure to Jesus' being possessed by the prince of demons. Hearing this, Jesus makes a simple but telling rebuttal. Casting out demons obviously hurts Satan's cause. Why would the prince of demons hurt his own cause by supporting or empowering Jesus? The argument is another call to common sense. If Jesus' deeds demonstrate a godly power and goodness why not accept him? (To hide behind a legalistic view of the Sabbath is bad faith.) The famous figure of Jesus as a strong man binding Satan up summarizes the early Church's view of the ultimate struggle going on in Jesus' ministry. It was a warfare between basic evil and basic good. His followers were utterly convinced that Jesus had bested Satan and had made it clear once and for all that God's grace is stronger than sin. The evidence of Jesus' life, they were saying, cannot be avoided. It demands a ground-level choice. To warp the evidence, calling evil what obviously was good, is to close oneself to the Holy Spirit and snuff out one's light of conscience. That is the unforgivable sin.

Continuing in this vein, Matthew's Jesus heightens the contrast between good and evil fruits. Using a figure employed earlier by John the Baptist (3:7), Jesus assails his lying enemies: "You brood of vipers! how can you speak good, when you are evil?" Jesus may be meek and humble of heart (11:29), but he can be incensed by evil, reaching out to grab it by the throat. What people say manifests their hearts. Destructive speech like that of the Pharisees reveals evil hearts that will be their condemnation before God.

When certain scribes and Pharisees ask him for a sign of his authority, Jesus gives them the sign of the prophet Jonah. An evil and adulterous generation, they will only get the sign of Jesus' death and resurrection. What happens to Jesus, someone far greater than Jonah, will testify eloquently to the corruption, the evil, of Jesus' enemies. They are people who had a chance to cleanse their souls but completely surrendered to evil. Their last state will be worse than their first. (The destruction of the Temple in 70 c.e. may be in Matthew's mind.) The only people worthy to be Jesus' disciples are those who do his Father's will, repent, and embrace the kingdom. They are his true family, his real brothers, sisters, and mother. (This text suggests that Jesus' blood family did not fully understand or agree with his ministry.)

Parables about the Kingdom of God (13:1–53)

Chapter 13 has some of Jesus' most famous parables (compare with Mark 4). In describing the kingdom Jesus would strike off wonderful little stories. So there is the story about the sower and the seed, to illustrate the various responses that the preaching of the kingdom receives. And there is the story of the man who sowed good seed but found that his field, tampered with by an enemy, produced weeds as well as wheat. At harvest time, after both weeds and wheat have grown, he (God) will make a great separation. The kingdom is also like a grain of mustard seed, which starts small but becomes the biggest of shrubs.[21] It is like the leaven a woman takes to make her bread rise. In all these stories, Jesus stresses the vital, growing character of the kingdom. It goes ahead, makes progress, even when we are not aware. The implication is that God reigns despite human opposition or inadvertence.

The people, even the disciples, did not fully understand Jesus' parables, and Matthew has Jesus quote Isaiah (6:9–10) to explain this fact. (See also Psalms 78. Where Mark makes the parables provocative—the key to realizing how far people are from understanding Jesus[22]—Matthew views them more benignly, as concessions of Jesus.) Understanding is in good part a function of basic preparedness or dispositions. If one is blind to the values of the kingdom one will not see it though it is plain as the nose on one's face. The allegorical explanations of the parables that the disciples draw from Jesus probably reflect the early Church's efforts to understand the varying reactions its missionary efforts drew. There is a mystery about human response, human freedom to say yes or no. Matthew is greatly preoccupied with this mystery, greatly puzzled by the rejections of Jesus and the Church.

Further parables liken the kingdom to a treasure hidden in a field that one should buy at all cost, to a pearl of great value, to a net catching all sorts of fish. The kingdom is precious, yet it works through daily life, common society, which is a mixture of good and bad. Only on Judgment Day will the full dimensions of the kingdom come clear. (Insofar as he awaited Jesus' return Matthew may have been expecting an early judgment.) After the disciples claim they have understood the nature of the kingdom, Jesus says that such understanding makes one like a householder able to bring from his treasury new things and old (as the occasion requires). To grasp the nature of the kingdom is to see how Jesus fulfills the old covenant, and also to see how his gospel is new. (Matthew himself is like an archivist or treasurer, finding precedents for Jesus in Jewish tradition and guarding Jesus' parables like sacred prophecies.)[23]

Miracles and Controversies (13:54–16:4)

In this section the opposition to Jesus, the blindness to his light, continues. Herod kills John the Baptist, in a stupid manner completely in keeping with Herod's bent character. Jesus, hearing about this, withdraws to a lonely place, as if he needs to ponder it. But the crowds follow him, and at nightfall, after he has healed their sick, there is a problem: where to get food for so many. In Matthew's account of the multiplication of the loaves and fishes (see Mark 6:30–44), Jesus prods the disciples to provide for the crowd. He blesses the little food they have (in a quite eucharistic fashion), and five thousand men, plus women and children, eat their fill and have food left over.

After dismissing the crowd Jesus goes up the mountain alone to pray. He comes to the disciples, who are out on the lake rowing, by walking on the water. They are terrified and think he is a ghost. When Jesus calms them Peter bids Jesus ask him to walk on the water. Jesus does so and Peter repeats the miracle, until his faith fails. He starts to sink and Jesus saves him. The disciples worship Jesus and call him the Son of God. With the boat symbolizing the Church, the story teaches the need for faith in Christ's word, power, or divinity. Peter now has a position of leadership among the twelve. The quality of his faith is especially important. When the boat lands the people bring their sick and Jesus heals all who touch him.

The Pharisees and scribes reappear on the scene, bringing forward more niggling objections. Why do Jesus' disciples break with tradition and not wash their hands before eating? Jesus answers with a heavier question: Why do the scribes and Pharisees break (by the practice of Corban we discussed in connection with Mark 7:11) the weightier command to honor father and mother? Jesus' mood is contemptuous: "So, for the sake of your tradition, you have made void the word of God. You hypocrites!" (15:6–7). Isaiah might have had the Pharisees and scribes in mind when he castigated Jews of old for their lack of heartfelt faith (Isaiah 29:13).

Expanding on his own position, Jesus teaches the people that purity is not a matter of food or what goes into the mouth. It is a matter of what comes out of the mouth (as an expression of what is in the heart). When some of the disciples, apparently worried, report that this attack on ritual purity has offended the Pharisees, Jesus is resigned: "Every plant which my heavenly Father has not planted will be rooted up. Let them alone; they are blind guides" (15:13–14). Anyone who follows them will end up in a pit (perhaps hell). Peter, not very quick, asks for an explanation of this imagery. Jesus expands on it, teaching that the heart is where good and bad behavior, purifying or polluting actions, originate. External things like washing are of little account.

The story of the Canaanite woman, who wins her daughter's exorcism because of her great faith, implies that the kingdom can extend outside of Israel and include the Gentiles.[24] Jesus moves on, around the Sea of Galilee, curing many of various infirmities. Matthew's description of this is reminiscent of Isaiah 35:5–6 and 29:18–19, and amounts to another argument that Jesus has fulfilled the messianic prophecies: " . . . the throng wondered, when they saw the dumb speaking, the maimed whole, the lame walking, and the blind seeing; and they glorified the God of Israel" (15:31). There follows another version of the multiplication of the loaves and fishes, this time with different numbers fed. The entire portrait of Jesus stresses his care for the people, in all the dimensions of their misery or need.

The Pharisees return, this time accompanied by some Sadducees. They are becoming a counterpoint to Jesus' manifestations of messianic power. The more Jesus does to demonstrate the arrival of the kingdom, the more these leaders of the people generate difficulties. Once again they ask him for a sign. He points out that they know how to read signs such as the weather. If they wanted to, they could interpret correctly what he has been doing. But, an evil and adulterous generation, they have lost the capacity to see what is obvious. So the only sign they will get is the sign of Jonah. (After

Jesus' death and resurrection, the Church saw Jonah, stuck in the belly of the whale, as a type or prefigurement of Jesus passing through death to heavenly life.)

The Approach to the Cross (16:5–17:27)

The disciples, as in Mark's account (Mark 8:14–21), misunderstand when Jesus relates their concern about bread to the leaven of the Pharisees and Sadducees. Jesus is still musing about the spiritual disorder of his enemies and the disciples are worrying about food. He has just multiplied the loaves and fishes and they are again anxious. One can hear him sigh, see him roll his eyes at the poor material from which he must fashion an elite corps for the kingdom.

The section 16:13–20 is important for Peter's confession that Jesus is the Christ. This confirms Peter's leadership among the twelve. The notion that Peter will be the "rock" is a play on his name (*Petros* is cognate to *petra*, "rock" or "stone").[25] The keys symbolize authority, while binding and loosing are rabbinic terms for forbidding and permitting. Matthew repeats Mark's report that, his confession of Jesus notwithstanding, Peter misunderstood the nature of Jesus' messiahship. Because Peter was opposed to Jesus' suffering servanthood, Jesus had to rebuke him. Discipleship means following a suffering leader, carrying one's cross. The end of chapter 16 is eschatological: At this point Jesus (or Matthew) is still expecting an early parousia.

Chapter 17 opens with Matthew's version of the Transfiguration (see Mark 9:2–8). The link to what has preceded may be that Matthew sees the Transfiguration as an anticipation or preview of the parousia. Moses and Elijah probably represent the old Law and prophets. The cloud is a strong symbol of the divine presence. The scene adds nuance and depth to the suffering servanthood emphasized in chapter 16. Jesus is both the suffering Messiah and the glorious Son of God. The mystery of his identity covers both sets of attributes and begs their correlation. When the disciples question Jesus about how the Transfiguration fits into the sequence of the Messiah's coming, which they understand will be preceded by the return of Elijah, Jesus answers that Elijah has already come, in the person of John the Baptist. Just as John suffered and was put to death, so will the Messiah whom John preceded.

Matthew 17:14–21 reports another cure, this time with a new slant on faith. A man brings his epileptic son to Jesus' disciples and they cannot cure him. Jesus cures the boy, and then explains to the disciples that they failed because their faith was too little. Strong faith can move mountains (Mark 9:14–27 gives an account of this incident that stresses prayer more than faith.) As if to confront the disciples with the depth their faith must soon reach, Jesus announces clearly that the Son of Man will be delivered up and killed. Even though he promises that he will also be raised on the third day, the disciples are very upset. Things are now becoming stark. Matthew 17:24–27 seems designed to show Jesus' (and later the early Christians') freedom from the religious Law. As a Son of God, Jesus does not have to pay the tax for God's Temple. The miraculous method of getting the coin is another indication of Jesus' faith and God's provision.

Advice to the Church (18:1–35)

This chapter gives us the fourth of the Matthean Jesus' five major discourses (5–7, 10, 13, 18, 24–25). It deals with problems within the Christian community. First, there is the problem of status or greatness. Jesus gives primacy to those who are humble and unaffected, like little children.[26] Scandalizing such people is a terrible sin. The severe verses 7–9 depend on a memory of a Jesus implacably opposed to sin (moral evil and hurtfulness): "And if your hand or foot causes you to sin, cut it off and throw it away."

Second, there is the related question of how to regard sinners. Interestingly, the same Jesus who is so harsh about sin is utterly devoted to reclaiming sinners. God's will is that not one of his little ones be lost. Disciples therefore should do their best to heal divisions and convert brothers and sisters back from sin. They should make the whole local church party to this effort. If the sinner still refuses to change, they should treat him or her like a Gentile or a tax collector. (The initial interpretation of this would be, "like an alien or person unclean." On reflection, however, Jesus' own example of consorting with tax collectors and Gentiles may soften it.) Verses 18–20 probably represent Matthew's efforts to convince his readers that Jesus stands behind what his community does, ratifying the Church's judgments. Balancing any rigorism, however, Jesus says in 18:22 that one should forgive a brother (or sister) seventy times seven (a Semitic way of saying "infinitely").

Third, Jesus proposes a parable about forgiveness in the kingdom. A king settling accounts with his servants finds that one servant cannot pay his debts. The servant should be thrown into prison, but he begs mercy and the king grants his plea. This same servant, however, refuses to forgive another servant who owes him a much lesser debt. Indeed, he has the fellow servant thrown into prison. Alerted to this by the other servants, the king is furious. Summoning the wicked servant he reads him the riot act and throws him into prison. The lesson is made plain in 18:35: "So also my heavenly Father will do to every one of you, if you do not forgive your brother from your heart." Membership in the kingdom demands imitating the goodness and mercy of God. Otherwise one will forfeit membership and feel God's wrath.

Rising Opposition to Jesus (19:1–23:29)

In this section we see more of the teachings for which Jesus earned the enmity that caused his death. In 19:3–12 Jesus gives a strict teaching about divorce, demanding a higher standard than the prevailing interpretation of the Mosaic law (which allowed men to divorce their wives quite easily). Jesus thinks that marriage makes man and woman one indissoluble flesh. The only grounds for divorce (19:19) is "unchastity" (perhaps incest).[27] The disciples are overwhelmed: Who can live up to such a standard? Jesus places the ideal of indissoluble marriage, like the ideal of celibacy for the sake of the kingdom, in the context of God's gifts. Those given the gifts to fulfill the lofty standards or ideals of the kingdom should do so.[28]

Once again Jesus shows his love of children, who best exemplify the kingdom, and then he offers a young man who asks about eternal life a way of perfection: "If you would be perfect, go, sell what you possess and give to the poor, and you will have treasure in heaven; and come, follow me" (19:21). The young man, who is wealthy, is not equal to this ideal. That causes Jesus to reflect on the impediment that riches can be. It is easier for a camel to pass through the eye of a needle than for the wealthy to enter the kingdom. The disciples again are astonished, and Jesus again says that all things are possible with God, even living free of material possessions. The disciples themselves will receive a great reward for the sacrifices they make in serving the kingdom. (Matthew may be interpreting Jesus' teachings to help buoy up Church recruits.)

Chapter 20 opens with a famous and important parable.[29] A man who owns a vineyard hires workers at different hours of the day, promising each a fair wage. When it comes time to pay them for their work, he gives those who have worked all day the wage he had promised them. However, he gives the same wage to those who have worked only a short time, the butt-end of the day. Those who worked longer grumble, but the man points out that he has given them what he pledged. It is not justice but a lack of generosity that stirs them to complain. The application to the kingdom is plain. God is the vineyard owner, free to be generous to latecomers (e.g., Gentiles) if he wishes. All may be sure that God will honor his commitments, give them a fair shake. If God further chooses to be generous to sinners, the unclean, Gentiles, or any other classes, that is God's business. A true child of God would rejoice at God's large-heartedness, take pleasure in others' good fortune. Grumbling shows the smallness of soul that legalistic living can create.

Matthew 20:17–19 is another clear prediction of Jesus' Passion, death, and resurrection, laid out in such specific details (mocking, scourging, crucifixion) that it must reflect Matthew's post-factum knowledge. Matthew 20:20–28 offers another lesson in greatness in the kingdom. Both passages follow Mark 10:32–45. The mother of the sons of Zebedee (James and John) asks a special place for them. Jesus wryly inquires whether they are able to share his suffering, probably doubting that they are. (Like Mark, Matthew was impressed by the flight of the disciples when Jesus was arrested.) Regardless, it is not up to Jesus to make such awards but to his Father. Primacy in the community of Jesus' followers depends upon service: "Whoever would be great among you must be your servant, and whoever would be first among you must be your slave, even as the Son of man came not to be served but to serve, and to give his life as a ransom for many" (26–28). The chapter concludes with another cure. The Son of David, moved by pity, gives sight to two blind men (double Mark's number—see Mark 10:46) who believe in him enough to ask his help.

Chapter 21 begins with Jesus' entry (reported in all four Gospels) into Jerusalem, the holy city in which his fulfillment of God's plan will come to completion. His entry on an ass (or a colt) is for Matthew the fulfillment of Zechariah 9:9. The crowd greets him enthusiastically as the Son of David who comes in the name of God. All the city is stirred up. Jesus goes to the Temple and cleanses it of its money changers and pigeon sellers (pigeons were the usual sacrifice of the poor).[30] This is a direct attack on the Temple authorities, a direct assertion of Jesus' claims to be a higher authority. He heals the blind and the lame. The overall effect is to outrage the chief priests and scribes. How can Jesus accept the acclamation of the crowds? (Who does he think he is?) Matthew has Jesus quote Psalms 8:2 to show that such acclamation was predicted. Jesus curses a fig tree for not being ready when he needed it (as Jerusalem is not ready), and he makes its withering another example of what strong faith can do. His confidence in God shines through the promise of 21:22: "And whatever you ask in prayer, you will receive, if you have faith." (A theologian might say that this makes sense because prayer inspired by deep faith wants only God's will.)

As in Mark, the chief priests and the elders (the capital establishment) ask Jesus by what authority he does these things. He is willing to answer them if they will say how they regard John the Baptist, whether John's baptism was from God or simply a human matter. They will not answer (will not come clean and be honest), so Jesus refuses to answer their questions about his authority. The parable that follows, about the man who had two sons, is interesting. Jesus is making the point that outward shows of obedience are not the key. It is actually doing God's will that matters. By this criterion, the chief priests and scribes are in bad shape: "Truly I say to you, the tax collectors and the harlots go into the Kingdom of God before you. For John came to you in the way of righteousness, and you did not believe him, but the tax collectors and the harlots believed him; and even when you saw it, you did not afterward repent and believe him" (22:28–32). It is no mystery that the Matthean Jesus deeply offended the Jerusalem establishment. He touched the sorest points of their bad consciences and made them look like hypocrites.

The parable in 21:33–41 is deadly serious, marking the movement of the kingdom to the Gentiles. God is the householder who plants the vineyard of Israel. The prophets are the servants he sends who are killed. Jesus is the son whose death is the final outrage. The destruction of the Temple in 70 C.E. colors the punishment predicted. Now the vineyard is more the property of the Gentiles than of Israel. Matthew 21:42–45 draws the final lessons from the parable. Quoting Psalms 118:22–23, the Matthean Jesus makes himself the rejected stone that has become the basis for God's new building. The kingdom will be taken from the Jews because of their rejection of Jesus. The chief priests and Pharisees would like to arrest Jesus for this frontal assault on them, but they fear his popularity with the multitudes. The bitter parable and bitter interpretation reflect the disintegration of relations between Christians and Jews by Matthew's time. Matthew sees the Jews as passed over by God because of their refusal to accept Jesus.

Chapter 22 does not soften the situation. The parable about the king who gives a marriage feast has the same point as the parable about the vineyard owner. God is the king and the marriage feast is the consummation of the covenant in Jesus' kingdom. The Jews are the people who reject the king's invitation. Sinners and Gentiles are the lowlife brought in to fill the hall. The man without a wedding garment who gets thrown into outer darkness (perdition) is probably a reminder that being of wretched estate (speechless) also is no guarantee of acceptance by God. One must welcome the kingdom and be converted to its values of honesty, mercy, and love.[31]

The Pharisees put their heads together and try to trip Jesus up. Most Jews resent paying tribute to Rome, so they ask Jesus whether this tribute is lawful (see Mark 12:13–17). Jesus calls them hypocrites. Their only motives for posing the question are bad. The very money they use shows that they accept their situation as subject to Rome. They should be more concerned about rendering to God the things that are God's. In a similarly misguided venture, some Sadducees ask Jesus about the resurrection (in which they themselves do not believe). Their convoluted question about the wife with seven husbands depends on the practice of levirate marriage (Deuteronomy 25:5–10), according to which a man had the obligation to marry the wife of his dead brother. Jesus undercuts their entire argument by denying their assumptions about the resurrection. (In passing he says scornfully, "You know neither the scriptures nor the power of God.") The true God is a God of the living. Resurrection is a state so different from earthly life that all earthly institutions, including marriage, will be cast in a new light. The Pharisees then take up the attack again, asking Jesus which is the greatest commandment. Jesus says total love of God, and love of neighbor as oneself. These two are the basis of all the Law and the prophets.

Then Jesus turns things around and asks the Pharisees a question. Whose son is the Christ? They give the accustomed answer: David's. Jesus quotes Scripture (Psalms 110:1) to show that it is not so simple. In some ways the Messiah is greater than David; he is David's Lord. This silences the Pharisees and takes away their appetite for argument. In Matthew's eyes Jesus was a far sharper rabbi than the people who tried to trap him.

Chapter 23 opens a scathing attack on the scribes and Pharisees. They have authority from Moses (the giver of the Law that they interpret). Therefore, their teachings are to be respected. But their practice is not to be imitated, for they don't practice what they preach (another charge of hypocrisy). They are insensitive to the human effect of the religious requirement they stress. They are vain and concerned about how they appear. No follower of Jesus should imitate them and let himself be called rabbi. Jesus is the disciples' only Teacher, as their only Father is in heaven. Only the Christ is Christians' Master. Among themselves Christians should act as servants.

Then, in 23:13–36, Matthew, writing at a time when Christian relations with a Judaism led by the Pharisees have broken down, has Jesus lace his preaching with acid. Seven times he prefaces withering descriptions of the establishment with the words, "Woe to you, scribes and Pharisees, hypocrites!" Why are these leaders of the Judaism contemporary with Jesus hypocrites? Because they keep people from entering the kingdom (for example, by opposing Jesus). Because they warp converts to their own bad image. Because they miss the point about such things as swearing, confusing what is secondary with what is primary. Because they tithe tiny things and neglect great things like justice and mercy. Because inside they are full of extortion and rapacity. Because inside they are full of hypocrisy and iniquity. Because they profess to venerate the prophets murdered in the past while being murderous themselves (first toward Jesus, later toward the Christian missionaries). Seven is the number of fullness. The Matthean Jesus completely condemns the leaders of the Jewish religion of his day. The time for reconciliation is past. Matthew's Jesus feels he has nothing to lose by naming his enemies in all their inner hatred and disorder. (As noted, this may reflect Matthew's time more than what the historical Jesus himself actually felt.) The chapter ends with Jesus' lament over Jerusalem. The city will become desolate (as it did in 70 C.E.) and will not see Jesus again until his return, when the kingdom has fully come.[32]

The Coming of the Kingdom (24:1–25:46)

Chapters 24 and 25 are Matthew's eschatological discourse (much of it borrowed from Mark 13). Jesus foretells the destruction of the Temple, the coming of many false prophets, wars and rumors of wars, famines and earthquakes. Disciples will be persecuted and divided against one another. Wickedness will multiply and love grow cold. The "desolating sacrilege" spoken of by Daniel is obscure. Perhaps Matthew's Jesus expects some new desecration on the order of the profanation of the Temple by Antiochus IV Epiphanes in 167 B.C.E.

Jesus paints the end as a scene of wild confusion and suffering: people fleeing, women pregnant or nursing deserving great pity. The disciples are to disregard rumors of Christ's coming. The true coming will be unmistakable: like lightning from the east. The imagery throughout is drawn from Old Testament apocalyptic or prophetic literature. It should be read symbolically rather than literally. The fig tree from which Jesus would have people learn how to read the signs of the time was one of the few annuals in Palestine that allowed an observer to calculate where the year presently stood. The main charge laid on the disciples is to stand ready. No one knows the day or the hour of God's judgment. The truly faithful are ever alert.

That is also the message of the parable in 25:1–13. The wise are prepared for the coming of God. The parable in 25:14–30 is to the same effect. God will require at the judgment a strict accounting of what he has given to his people. The judgment scene in 25:31–46 is probably the strongest linkage in Jesus' teaching between love of God and love of neighbor. It is by what they have done or not done for their neighbors that people will be judged. Works of justice and mercy are the marrow of the kingdom. Even if one does them unawares, not thinking of any further dimension, they can make one blessed.

The Death and Resurrection of Jesus (26:1–28:20)

Chapter 26 opens with Jesus' announcement that the climax is near. In two days Passover is coming and with it his crucifixion. Matthew pictures the chief priests and elders of the people (the highest leaders) as gathering in the palace of the high priest Caiaphas and plotting Jesus' death. The anointing of Jesus with expensive ointment is a nearly sacramental act, a preparation for his burial. The indignation of the disciples is another instance of their missing the point. For all his absoluteness, Jesus is no Puritan. At the proper time he favors celebration and prodigality. Recent feminist theologians have made the anonymous woman (in John's Gospel she is named Mary) a heroic representative of all the nameless women who played irreplaceable roles in Jesus' life.[33]

Judas Iscariot decides to betray Jesus and makes a deal with the chief priests. He will do it for thirty pieces of silver. This was the price set in Exodus 21:32 for the life of a slave gored by an ox (see also Zechariah 11:12). The disciples, at Jesus' direction, make preparations to celebrate Passover, the commemoration of the Exodus. At the Passover meal Jesus announces that one of the twelve, his closest disciples, will betray him. Indirectly Matthew's Jesus names Judas as his betrayer (a sign that he is fully aware of what is happening). Matthew 26:26–29 records the institution of the eucharist. Through bread and wine Jesus gives himself to his friends. The blood that he will shed is a sacrifice for the forgiveness of sins.

The Last Supper. Dutch. About 1440–1504. This print by an engraver of the fifteenth century Dutch school seems quite medieval in crowding in so many blocky, contorted figures. The disciples are everymen, a rather unimpressive lot, whose bearing foreshadows Jesus' coming defeat in worldly terms. *(Nelson Gallery–Atkins Museum, Kansas City, Mo. [Nelson Fund])*

He will not sup with the disciples again until they are all together in the Father's kingdom.

They exit to the Mount of Olives, which is not far from Gethsemane, the place where Jesus will be arrested. Jesus predicts the defection of the twelve, and also that he will be resurrected and go before them into Galilee. Peter explains that he will never betray his Master. Jesus assures him that he will. Going off by himself to pray, Jesus becomes desolate and asks his Father to release him from this trial. Finally, after three long bouts of struggle, he finds peace in resigning himself to the Father's will. (This is Matthew's distinctive note.) The inability of the disciples even to stay awake and comfort him is a perfect summary of their weakness. Matthew's message for the later Church is that the earliest leaders were no heroes; they owed all that they became to the power of Jesus' Spirit.

A crowd advances into Gethsemane, led by Judas, who identifies Jesus by kissing him. Jesus' question to Judas, "Friend, why are you here?" is the last chance for Judas to stop his betrayal. The crowd seizes Jesus and Jesus' followers fight with them. Jesus heals a slave of the high priest whose ear was cut off, admonishing his followers that his way does not countenance violence. What is happening is in accordance with God's will as laid out in the Scriptures. Were it otherwise God's angels would see to Jesus' defense. To the crowd he puts the question, "Have you come out as against a robber, with swords and clubs to capture me?" (26:55). Like most crowds they are beyond the reach of reason.

His captors take Jesus to Caiaphas and the scribes and the elders (contrast with John 18:13). Peter follows at a distance to see what unfolds. Witnesses come forward to accuse Jesus but their charges make little sense.

Christ in the Garden of Gethsemane. This fifteenth century Flemish tapestry shows three apostles sleeping while Jesus prays. In the background Christ appears in a later scene, being led off by the soldiers. The armor, picket fence, gateway with pitched roof, and the like reflect the artist's efforts to render the scene contemporary. Note the chalice that Christ figuratively says he is willing to drink. *(Nelson Gallery–Atkins Museum, Kansas City, Mo. [Nelson Fund])*

Present-day Garden of Gethsemane.   *(Photo by J.T. Carmody)*

Finally two witnesses agree that Jesus said he was able to destroy the Temple of God and build it up again in three days. To Matthew's mind the charge is ironic, a prediction by Jesus that he will die and be resurrected. Jesus keeps silent and does not defend himself. The high priest then charges him most solemnly, by the living God, to say whether he is the Messiah, the Son of God. Jesus accepts this designation (he is more forthright in Mark), adding that hereafter the priest will see the Son of Man seated at the right hand of power, confirming the prophecy of Daniel 7:13. The high priest cannot admit the possibility that Jesus is the Messiah or Son of Man that Daniel described. Whether in honest or contrived revulsion, the high priest proclaims Jesus' answer a blasphemy and tears his robes. Those in attendance agree: Jesus deserves to die. So they abuse him and mock him, asking him to prophesy.

Peter, sitting outside, has a chance to own up to being a disciple of Jesus, but he denies he even knows the man. When the cock crows, Peter remembers Jesus' prediction of his betrayal and weeps bitterly.

Chapter 27 continues the trial and condemnation of Jesus. The Jewish authorities, who have no secular power to carry out the death penalty, lead Jesus off to Pilate, the Roman governor. Judas repents of his betrayal and wants to halt the whole proceedings. When the chief priests and elders reject Judas' confession of guilt and efforts to halt their proceedings against Jesus, Judas goes out and hangs himself (contrast with Acts 1:16–20). The chief priests (hypocritically, in Matthew's view) ponder what to do with the thirty pieces of silver that Judas has returned. It is blood money. That they buy a field for a public burial ground (an unclean place) fulfills

Matthew's sense of prophecy. (The reference to Jeremiah 18:1–3 is obscure.)[34]

Standing before Pilate, Jesus continues to be reserved. He accepts Pilate's title for him, "King of the Jews," but otherwise he stays silent. Pilate senses something extraordinary in all this and tries to get the crowd to call for Jesus' release. Matthew has Pilate's wife warn him that through a troubling dream she has become sure of Jesus' innocence. The crowd prefers that Pilate release Barabbas, a notorious criminal. Stirred by the chief priests and elders, the people cry for Jesus' death. Pilate will not buck this popular will. He washes his hands of the affair. Matthew 27:25 is a fateful text. The people supposedly accept responsibility for Jesus' blood: "And all the people answered, 'His blood be on us and on our children.'" (See Acts 5:28.) In periods of Christian anti-Semitism Jews' supposed responsibility for Jesus' death was a major pretext for abusing them. Pilate releases Barabbas and has Jesus scourged and led out to be crucified.

The soldiers strip Jesus, dress him like a king, and mock him. Matthew, like the other evangelists, is preserving this memory of the twistedness of human hearts, and the irony that so many people missed what could have been their salvation. A man named Simon of Cyrene is made to carry Jesus' cross. Jesus refuses the wine that might have dulled his pain. He is nailed to the cross and set upright. That the soldiers cast lots for his clothes fulfills Psalms 22:18. The title "King of the Jews" is put over Jesus' head as the charge for which he is being punished. (This suggests that the immediate reason for Jesus' death was political: He threatened Roman rule.) The people, led by the chief priests, scribes, and elders, mock Jesus and dare him to get God to deliver him.

Darkness, a sign of the divine presence (and of the mourning of nature), covers the land for three hours. At the end of this time Jesus, quoting Psalms 22:1, cries out, "My God, my God, why hast thou forsaken me?" (The psalm, as a whole, is an outcry not of despair but of faith and hope.) The crowd thinks that Jesus is calling for Elijah. Jesus finally cries out in a loud voice and dies. As in Mark's account, the curtain of the Temple is torn in two, marking the end of the religion centered there. In contrast to Mark, Matthew also has the earth quake, rocks split open, and many holy dead people resurrected from their tombs. A centurion again utters the definitive interpretation: "Truly this man was the Son of God," although this time he has company. Matthew notes that many of the women who had followed Jesus throughout his ministry stayed faithful to the end and watched Jesus die. Joseph of Arimathea obtains the body from Pilate and has it buried in his own new tomb. Mary Magdalene and Mary the mother of James and Joseph sit watching at the tomb.

The next day (the Sabbath) the chief priests and Pharisees, remembering Jesus' prediction that he would be resurrected, try to get Pilate to set a guard around the tomb. Pilate forces them to use their own guard. They seal the stone at the mouth of the tomb and leave a watch. After the Sabbath, on the first day of the week, the two Marys go back to the tomb. There is a great earthquake. An angel of the Lord comes from heaven, rolls away the stone, and sits on it. "His appearance was like lightning, and

Crucifixion. Philippe de
Champaigne. The artist was
influenced by the ascetic
doctrines of the Jansenists
and presents a stark Christ
and crucifixion scene.
*(Nelson Gallery–Atkins Museum, Kansas
City, Mo. [Nelson Fund])*

his raiment like snow" (28:3). The guards tremble and are terrified. (Typically, Matthew's account heightens the miraculous element.) No one actually sees the resurrection of Jesus, but the angel tells the women that Jesus has risen, and invites them to see the place where he lay. The women are to tell his disciples of his resurrection and that they will see him in Galilee.

The women leave quickly, in a mixture of fear and joy. On their way they meet Jesus, whose feet they grab in worship. (This suggests that Jesus was no ghost or apparition.) The guards tell the chief priests what has happened and the chief priests bribe them to give out the report that Jesus' disciples came and stole the body. Only Matthew has this story. Probably it is an effort to counter a Jewish interpretation of the empty tomb that circulated in opposition to Christian accounts of the resurrection.

The disciples meet Jesus in Galilee at the mountain he had indicated. (Mountains are holy places for Matthew, probably in reflection of Mount Sinai, where the Jewish Torah was given.) Although the disciples worship him, some doubt (right to the end the disciples' faith is imperfect). Jesus gives them a great commission[35] to make disciples of all nations, baptizing converts in the name of the Father, and of the Son, and of the Holy Spirit. The disciples are to teach all that Jesus has commanded, confident that he will be with them until the parousia. There is no account of the ascension. The final word is that Jesus lives in the midst of his missionary church. This final scene brings together many of Matthew's main motifs, finally showing Jesus' community receiving Abraham's promise that the nations will be his inheritance.

WHY WAS THIS WRITTEN?

Matthew was written for several reasons. First, the author wanted to show his (largely Jewish Christian) community that they were the heirs of the promises of the Jewish Bible. Second, he wanted his church to look at the Gentiles as a fertile field for evangelization. Third, he wanted to make a persuasive argument that Jesus was the Messiah, mainly by showing that Jesus fulfilled what Jewish Scripture should have led Jesus' contemporaries to expect of the Messiah. Fourth, Matthew wanted to discredit Jesus' enemies (both those of Jesus' own day and those opposing the Church in Matthew's day) by showing that their rejection of Jesus came from blindness and bad will. Fifth, Matthew wanted to compose a more vivid picture of Jesus the Teacher than was available in Mark or the other contemporary sources. The artificial arrangement of Matthew's materials into discourses, and the many efforts to show Jesus as the perfector of Jewish Law, argue for this intent.

Behind these intentions we may picture a community that was hungry for a clear conception of its Master as the supreme rabbi and prophet, especially in a context of opposition to Pharisaic Judaism. Such a church, largely Jewish in background, delighted in memories of Jesus that showed how his teaching and fate were the consummation of the traditions founded in Abraham and Moses, how his kingdom was the messianic era for which Israel had long hungered. According to one influential interpretation, Matthew probably belonged to a rabbinic-like school for church teachers and leaders. His literary product may, in fact, have been a sort of manual for Jewish-Christian church leaders:

> No one would say that Matthew is merely a handbook as is the Didache [early Christian] or the Manual of the Qumran Sect [Jewish]. Of course, Matthew is a gospel, and from the point of view of literary form the gospel is an unparalleled feature, an *ad hoc* creation of a church which claimed a more absolute doctrine of incarnation than is found in other accounts of religious heroes; on the other hand, this incarnation is more closely related to very recent historical facts than is the case in other mythological systems. Yet when we consider what is most typically Matthean in Matthew's treatment of the gospel material, we get the impression that the pattern which guided him in systematizing his material was that of a handbook.[36]

Not all students of Matthew now follow this opinion, but the Matthean effort to bring forth a vivid, prophetic portrait of Jesus continues to be highly regarded.[37]

As the Gospels became Christian Scripture, they were used in liturgical settings. At baptisms or eucharistic ceremonies Gospel passages would be read to recall what Jesus the Master had said or done. Even before they gained scriptural status however, the materials they brought together must have served the nurture of the early churches' faith. Matthew's intent in casting these materials into his five books (reminiscent of the five books of Torah) would not, therefore, have been academic. The goal was the better living of Christian faith, the better flourishing of the Christian community. He was combatting any reluctance to consider Jesus the true fulfillment of Jewish religion. He was attacking any defense of the chief priests, scribes, and Pharisees who had failed to discern Jesus' messiahship. Matthew was not attempting a detached account of Jesus' life and battles with the religious establishment. His Gospel meant to convey to believers the superiority of the good news that Jesus brought, Jesus' preaching and effecting of the kingdom.

WHAT BACKGROUND DOES THIS TEXT PRESUPPOSE?

Matthew presupposes, first, some knowledge of Jewish law and scriptural prophecy. Again and again he links what Jesus has said or done with Old Testament passages, seeing these as forecasts or predictions. Second, and relatedly, Matthew presupposes a background in Christian faith. If Jewish prophecy is an important matter, much more important is the teaching, death, and resurrection of Jesus that fulfill that prophecy. Third, behind both these assumptions is the expectation of a background in biblical monotheism. Matthew would have little claim upon a reader with no grounding in the God of the Bible. True enough, Matthew's materials can be of simply humanistic interest, as we shall see. But in terms of the text's own presuppositions, life apart from the biblical God and covenant gets little heed. As much as Paul, Matthew is thoroughly Jewish in outlook. The reality of God is as obvious to him as the reality of Roman rule or Palestinian weather.

Fourth, there are more precise assumptions that Matthew makes. For example, his presentation of Jesus' trial goes contrary to what Jewish law of the time required. The most likely explanation for this is Matthew's conviction that Jesus was not treated fairly (justly, legally) by the powerholders of his time. Matthew assumed that his readers would recognize the discrepancies between what he was reporting as happening to Jesus and what should have happened. (Even readers not skilled in the law, however, were to have no doubt that justice was never served.)

Other specific presuppositions come from the Christian side of Matthew's background. His account of the multiplication of the loaves, for example, has overtones of the most ancient formulas for the Christian eucharist. Similarly, his account of the Last Supper assumes the Christian understanding of Jesus' death as a sacrifice for the forgiveness of sins and a perfecting of the Jewish Passover. Jesus was the new victim making the people pleasing to God. Jesus' exit from earthly life (whose imperfection showed clearly in the Pharisees and other corrupt leaders) to heavenly union with God was a new, more perfect exodus. The baptism with which converts were welcomed into the Church moved beyond cleansing rites like those of John the Baptist, being considered not just a preparation for the kingdom but an actual entry into the kingdom's life.

Fifth, Matthew's manner of quoting Scripture, which stresses the fulfillment of prophecies by Jesus, has been compared to the **pesher** (commentary) manner that flourished at Qumran; whether or not he assumes some familiarity with Qumran, he certainly assumes the acceptability of the pesher style. This style contrasts with the emphases that ruled in most of the rabbinic schools of both Matthew's day and later Jewish history. The leading emphases among the rabbis were **halakic** (focused on the legal aspects of a text, its significance for Torah understood as the rules for living out a holy life) and **haggadic** (more legendary, inspirational, concerned with warming the heart). The fulfillment of prophecy was not prominent.

The result in Matthew is a sense that past events only gain their true significance in the light of the Christ-event. So, for instance, the slight references to a potter's field (burial ground) and thirty pieces of silver that Matthew can find in Jewish Scripture become solid and significant in view of the story of Judas' betrayal. It does not matter that the original texts could not (by today's literary canons) have had Judas in mind. The original texts were the Word of God; what happened later could be considered their deepest or truest import. This means a rather dynamic (if manipulative) view of history and Scripture. Jesus did not come out of a vacuum. To Matthew's mind he came as the meaning that had been latent and growing through all the prior centuries, as the end or *telos* (perfecting goal) that would reveal what all the struggle had been for.

Sixth, Matthew, like the other Gospel writers, presupposes a God who can break into "ordinary" human life and do the miraculous, often to alleviate human suffering and give human beings new reasons for hope. Gerd Theissen, an influential contemporary New Testament scholar, has cautioned against the tendency to write off the miracle stories because they do not fit the modern world. We should rather let them be, in all their strangeness, and should try to fathom what they meant in their own circumstances, on their own soil. We should, in fact, try to love their distinctiveness and strangeness:

> The miracle stories are alien visitors in our world. Should we not therefore pay them great attention? Should we not try to love them as they are, in all their distinctiveness and strangeness? The point of the miracle stories is the revelation of the sacred in miracles, in tangible, material, saving miracles. Respect for the men and women of primitive Christianity, who told them and were attached to them, obliges us to make this admission and not all the modern perplexities about these texts can justify modifying it.[38]

As he sketches his summary understanding of the miracle stories, Theissen takes the line that they are symbolic actions that show the sacred dimension of life overcoming the negativities of human existence. The stories say that there exists more than is humanly possible. Jesus possessed a power that made him the "Holy One of God" and this power allowed him (and others) to cast out demons, multiply bread, walk on water, raise the dead, and the like. It is too simple to write the miracle stories off as wish projections, things human beings would like to feel could happen. Their slant rather is the transformation of human wishing itself, through faith. What is hopeless by "normal" criteria is put into brackets. "Normal" is not more powerful than God, something to which the Lord of the Universe necessarily has to bow.

As a consequence, the negativities of human life—blindness, death, demonic possession, disease, racking poverty, and so much more—are not absolute. The human spirit that wants to rebel against them gets support from the stories of Jesus' rebellion against them, Jesus' superiority to their (not so) ironclad embrace. The result is a revelation of a transcendent (beyond-going) dimension in human life that well accords with the deepest, most defining characteristics of the human spirit.

Theissen characterizes the revelation of this transcendent or sacred dimension of reality under five headings:

1. It is pregnant, in the sense that Jesus is special, extraordinary, full of something that arouses wonder and interest. No one ever spoke (or acted) like he had.

2. It is competitive. Jesus' miracles are part of a warfare between himself and Satan, himself and other (to Matthew's mind less authoritative) interpreters of God's Law.

3. The revelation of the holy through Jesus' miracles shows his dominance over nature, disease, demons, and all sorts of human distress. He is Lord of the world he inhabits, Master of the situations into which he comes. (This only heightens his free acceptance of abuse and suffering in the Passion, only deepens the Matthean sense that he was following a divine plan and living out a profound obedience to the holy mystery.)

4. The miracles make the divine transparent. Their purpose is more than to settle the human crisis at hand. They are acts that make present and somewhat visible, somewhat palpable, the creative and restorative power of God. Thereby, they are acts that make the divine itself somewhat palpable. The faith for which Jesus calls is not a credulity that would accredit any bizarre happening. It is an openness to the power of the true God, a receptivity to the manifestation of the really Holy.

5. The miracles are ambivalent. Those who do not have faith, will not be open, can attribute them to a demonic force.[39] In Matthew's Gospel we see the faithlessness of the Pharisees, scribes, and high priests harden. The more miraculous things Jesus does, the more they close their minds, blocking out the possibility that Jesus may be revealing God. By

the time Jesus turns on them so scathingly in chapter 23, he has taken the measure of their hardness, has come to see them as object lessons in closure, blockage, inauthenticity. Though they have eyes they will not see.

WHAT LASTING SIGNIFICANCE DOES THIS HAVE?

Like Mark, Matthew derives most of its lasting significance from its portrait of Jesus. Just as it is the stories of the Old Testament (especially the account of Genesis and Exodus) that had the greatest impact on the Western imagination, so it is with the stories of the New Testament. Jesus the healer, the teacher, the crucified, is the marrow of Christian spirituality. Through Christian spirituality, both Greek and Latin, Western culture derived a great deal of its sense of human perfection. That sense came under heavy attack during the eighteenth-century European Enlightenment, and in modern times it has become somewhat countercultural, opposed to a general rush after material prosperity and power. But for almost seventeen hundred years it was the most powerful humanism of the West. The divinity portrayed in Jesus was also humanity at its most significant, profound, and beautiful. What does the Matthean Jesus say that humanity ought to be?

It ought to be, first, religious—riveted onto the holy mystery of the Beginning and the Beyond, open to the love that moves the stars and might cure diseased human hearts. Jesus is not pious, religious in an affected sense. He makes no distinction between religion and human life generally. One Lord is the crux and treasure of everything that human beings do. Alone or together, contemplating political things or things of nature, followers of the Matthean Jesus should be searching for the will and power of the Father, looking for the signs of the kingdom. Whether Jesus prays or preaches, heals or castigates, Matthew presents him as following the Father's plan and exemplifying the new Law of the Father's reign. Jesus is very much a son of the Israel that summarized its faith in the passionate Shema. He learned very well from the best rabbis of his time that love of neighbor as self is the social key.

Second, humanity as exemplified by the Matthean Jesus is docile, in the root sense of "teachable." In the past God gave the people of Israel prophets (above all the several prophets behind the book of Isaiah) to teach them the meaning of the Law given on Sinai. Prior to these writing prophets, of course, was the great lawgiver himself, Moses. The whole conception of life on which Jesus drew centralized Torah, the divine instruction. Jesus never for a moment called into question the propriety of divine instruction, the necessity of Torah. But Matthew, looking back from the vantage point of Jesus' resurrection, sees Jesus as a second Moses. Jesus is the lawgiver for a new and perfecting phase of divine instruction, the prophet whose word and person actually brought the messianic time. Where prophecy had been reduced to barely glowing embers (after the return from Babylon), Jesus brought it back to full flame.

This prophecy was not so much a matter of prediction as a matter of fulfillment. The Word of God that Jesus uttered broke apart and clarified present times even more than the future. Matthew sees the great Israelite prophets as writing under divine inspiration and serving a scenario that Jesus would complete. In that sense much of their work was predictive and Jesus fulfilled the forecasts they created. But the Matthean Jesus himself (apart from the apocalyptic discourse and some anticipations of his death and resurrection) is concerned with here and now, a kingdom knocking at the door. With him divine instruction leaps from the scrolls and becomes peripatetic—he walks around to instruct and heal on the spot. Torah had long had the sense of a living instruction, a guide for all the minutiae of daily life. In the hands of the best rabbis it was not an arid code but a help in sanctifying God's name, preparing a people fit for covenant closeness with the Holy One.

The Matthean Jesus wants the people to be docile to the spirit of the kingdom. Other writers (especially Paul and John) tend to capitalize this notion: Jesus wants the people to let themselves be taught by the Spirit of the kingdom, the divine breath that gives flesh and life to dry bones. This spirit and Spirit both stress interiority, dispositions, purification of heart. External matters are secondary, derivative. In today's terms the gospel calls for authenticity, honesty, being what one seems, meaning what one says. True devotion, religion, love, and the rest are shown by deeds. Anyone can say, "Lord, Lord." Professions of faith are a dime a dozen. What matters is what one does, what one is. By these criteria the Matthean Jesus finds the tax collectors and whores more docile, real, and savable than the heads of the religious establishment. Perhaps because of their misery, the despised are alert to the kingdom's gift of new beginnings, readjustments, renovations of heart.

Third, a humanistic reading of the religious Jesus who urges humanity to become docile perhaps most profitably circles around the notion of instruction or character formation itself. What sort of people did Jesus try to raise? What sort of people are we trying to raise through our parenting, educating, advertising, preaching in church, pressuring in offices and factories? And how are our efforts, whether deliberate or unconscious, actually affecting the great problems of human coexistence, our race's several-sided inability to maintain progress, to come closer to justice and peace? The both damnable and blessed fact about the human species is that we must face these questions afresh each generation. Very little is secured once and for all. The progress that homo sapiens has made over the millennia is indeed impressive, but we still struggle with most basic questions of evil and good. Nuclear energy, for example, is but a contemporary focus of an age-old puzzle. How shall we use the might our amazing brains have generated? Will it be (clean) atoms for peace or dirty mushroom clouds?

The central paradox that all humanistic inquiry comes upon is the puzzle of the human heart. Brains are not enough. Intellectual progress alone will not suffice. Nazism sprang from a culture—artistic, literary, scientific—with few historical peers. The Crusades and European religious wars lived cheek by jowl with the holiest aspirations. So the mind is not enough and the heart needs constant guidance. The evil that we would not we do and the good that we would we do not. It is unintelligible, absurd, impenetrable, this self-twisting and self-destruction. We get ourselves so cabined into darkness, so blinkered, that injustice, waste, and mayhem become business as usual. Jesus and the other great religious seers denounce this sick normalcy. "The kingly virtues of money and status, pride and arrogance, have no moral clothes," they say and say again. And the greatest among the religious seers, the people who have seen human nature most deep and entire, do more than diagnose. They also prescribe medicinal regimes that bring down our feverish pursuit of trash, actually purify our blood of stupid vanities and desires. "Here is health," they say, "near as a **metanoia**, a change of mind and heart."

The change the Matthean Jesus wants, the character reformation, is summarized in the twofold commandment. When Jesus boils down the Law and the prophets, it is love of God and love of neighbor that remain. For all their familiarity they are still a rich, productive distillate, good measure packed down and overflowing. The love Jesus preaches and demonstrates is no saccharine gloss on a greeting card, no relative of sleazy television. It is the core emotion, the inmost passion, of being human: to know and unite with things as they really are, to lose oneself in the world's beauty. Jesus' love is humanity making and doing what is beautiful, profound, true. Children gather his special affection because children are wide-eyed with this potential and still may grow large-hearted and wise. The world has a special glow because Jesus senses that this love is the nature of the God who makes the flowers of the fields, the birds that are the first musicians.

So too with Jesus' love as directed socially, to make the way to a human community worthy of our best hopes. The body of Jesus' neighborly love is justice: doing to others what is right. The soul is compassion: feeling others' pains, shouldering others' burdens. We all are simply people and our lives are short. None of us has ever seen God or mastered the central mystery. So we all ought to go gently, speak kindly, try to be of help. The goods of the earth are for all the earth's people. The Source of all we have makes her rain to fall, her sun to shine, on just and unjust alike. A radical equality before the divine love makes our divisions by money or sex or color or culture secondary. In any healthy human community no one has the right to luxuries so long as anyone lacks necessities.

Dicta such as these, born out of meditation on the synoptic Jesus, show the utopian implications of the Sermon on the Mount. If the Beatitudes alone do not make it plain that the kingdom is no place we ourselves inhabit, the ruminations developed in later Christian tradition must. And yet Jesus' utopia, his "no-place" where the Father truly reigns, is the (often unrecognized) powerhouse of every noble reform that has ever kept humanity from falling back into the muck of our gene pool. What Theissen and others see going on in the miracle stories is present in all of Jesus' preaching: a promise that things can change, that people might help one another, that if we wished there could be bread broken and joy shared, hunger appeased and justice done.

That our developed Northern cultures, which are now powering the world, piping the economic tunes, and engineering the ecological disasters, do not accept Jesus' (or any other great seer's) utopian sense of reality is directly relevant to the lasting significance of Matthew. Without Matthew and his like we might come to think that there were no grounds for hope, that human greed and stupidity had done us in. The end of the world could seem as inevitable as acid rain, as reliable as governmental lying. It is impossible, therefore, to overestimate the significance of Matthew (and his like in other cultures). The symbols of Easter and resurrection, like the symbols of Passover and Exodus, are what keep us from terminal despair. These symbols did not come from perfervid brains, people only made ill by the stresses of violence and destruction. They came from positive experiences of going down and rising up, being trapped and finding outlet. In the specific case of Jesus, they came from disciples who found his words revelatory, his actions turning their hopelessness mute. What happened in front of their eyes was not too strange to be believed but too good. The blind were seeing, the lepers were being cleansed, the lame were walking, the dumb were crying out in praise. It could happen because it was happening. Humanity was possible because at last someone fully human had appeared.

In the wake of Matthew, death and resurrection take on a many-leveled significance. The dying and rising of Jesus, the defeat and victory, are as much psychological as historical, as much matters of character reform and the healing of imagination as matters of Caiaphas, Pilate, and the Marys who came to joy by the tomb. The power of the Matthean Jesus lies in this fusion of history and psychology, fact and inner movement. Read with any degree of attention and sympathy, his Gospel still forces us to ask what is possible among human beings, whether our horizons haven't grown almost comically restricted, our heart almost terminally clogged. These are the questions of eternal life, the self-criticisms crucial to any true humanism. As long as the cross is recognizable and gripping, Matthew will be significant.

SUMMARY

In dealing with what Matthew places before the reader, we first stressed that his presentation of Jesus' person and preaching shows a sharply Jewish character. The best orientation we could summon was a suggestion that Matthew presents Jesus as the consummation of Jewish Scripture, the Son of God and Messiah who brings the covenant to completion. And as Jesus is the heir of Moses and the prophets, the Christian community is the heir of Israel. Drawing on Mark, Q, and sources peculiar to himself, Matthew fashioned a distinctive, almost rabbinic interpretation of Jesus. Written shortly after 85 C.E., his Gospel tried to help the Church accept its commission to perfect the covenantal relation with God and open the kingdom to the Gentiles. In outline, we broke Matthew down into thirteen different units, noting that five speeches (5–7, 10, 13, 18, 24–25) compact much of

Jesus' teaching material (and perhaps symbolize a new five books of Torah).

The opening chapters, dealing with Jesus' genealogy and birth, have the manifest intent of showing that Jesus' who, how, where, and whence prove him to be the Messiah. The beginnings of Jesus' ministry link his work to that of John the Baptist, who plays Elijah to Jesus' Messiah. Jesus calls for conversion, just as John did, and belief in the Kingdom of Heaven. In besting Satan he makes it plain that his messiahship and kingdom are quite otherworldly, devoted only to the biblical God. The Sermon on the Mount is the most famous summary of Jesus' teaching. For Matthew Jesus is the new Moses enunciating the fulfillment of the covenant Law. The Beatitudes, especially, present a kingdom radically different from the kingdom that human sensuality and ambition would desire. Jesus' God is more concerned with marginal people than with power brokers. His religion of whole mind and heart has very different values than those most ages have loved. By the fruits of justice and wisdom one can judge any person or group's claims and compare them with those of Jesus.

Jesus' mighty acts, his cures and miracles, are warrants for taking his claims most seriously. When he finds faith he can move mountains of disease and despair. As his missionary discourse to his disciples shows, his faithful must travel light and not be afraid to affront the world. God will provide for those who serve God faithfully. As opposition mounts among the established religious leaders, Jesus toughens the discipline of the kingdom. The wisdom to see God's hand is not prevalent among the mighty, who mainly want to protect their own advantages. It is not prevalent among the crowds, who mainly want a diversion. The intimation grows that Jesus will have to die for his provocative preaching and healing. Nonetheless, the parables of the kingdom suggest that it was bound to be that way. Until judgment time the wheat and the tares must grow up together. If the people cannot embrace the great treasure offered them in the miracles and parables, they will be the heavy losers. If they want grudging, legalistic views of the Sabbath and dietary laws, they will have souls like the Pharisees, too narrow for the living God. Jesus is bound to be at war with Satan and all religious hypocrites. Transfigured on the Mountain, he is both the servant suffering from this warfare and the victorious, risen Lord. Without mercy (rather than sacrifice) people cannot understand this duality. Without mercy, they cannot grasp a God as generous as the vineyard owner of chapter 20.

As opposition against Jesus hardens into a resolve to bring about his death, Jesus enters Jerusalem and prepares for the final battle. His cleansing of the Temple, like his previous bestings of the scribes, shows his great authority. More parables suggest that the kingdom will be taken from the people who have not welcomed this latest of God's envoys. By chapter 23 Jesus has fully rounded on his enemies and lashed them witheringly. They are hypocrites, enemies not just of him but of truth itself, of God. The apocalyptic discourse predicts the final paroxysms that will come from the tension between the kingdom and the powers resisting it. The drama of Jesus' betrayal by Judas, Last Supper, agony in the garden, trial, crucifixion, death, and resurrection are the final revelations of the nature of the Matthean Son of Man. This wholly human, completely **passible** figure truly was the Son of God. His death was blood poured out for the forgiveness of sins. His resurrection was the definitive arrival of the kingdom, God's taking human flesh once and for all into the divine embrace.

In dealing with why Matthew was written, we stressed the author's desire to represent his church as the heirs of the biblical promises, encourage evangelization of the Gentiles, prove Jesus' messiahhood, discredit Jesus' enemies, and compose a more vivid picture of Jesus the teacher. Matthew may well have been a member of a Christian rabbinic school who saw his literary task as the production of a Christian manual or handbook strong on materials showing Jesus fulfilling scriptural prophecy. The author presupposes some background in Jewish law and prophecy, as well as a strong Christian faith. He also assumes biblical monotheism, a knowledge of Jewish legal procedures, and a knowledge of Christian rituals. Matthew's pesher manner of using Scripture suggests some familiarity with Qumran practices, while his presentation of Jesus' miracles presupposes a faith that the divine can do much more than humans usually consider possible.

For lasting significance we nominated Matthew's portrait of Jesus as a healer, teacher, and suffering servant. This was a powerful force in the formation of the Western religious imagination. Powerful too was the conception of humanity that Jesus' modeling encouraged. If they looked to Matthew's Jesus people would see human nature as religious and docile to the Spirit of God. This raises interesting questions about the docility and instruction most pertinent today, when the modern mentality has largely broken with Matthew's religious assumptions. The Matthean Jesus still says provocative things about the flaws in the human heart from which most of the world's troubles derive. The twofold love that Jesus commands still is a worthy candidate for the best education in survival and prosperity. So the final significance of the Gospel according to Matthew probably is the hope its counterculturalism holds out. If things are as the death and resurrection of the Son of Man indicate, not even our aberrant nuclear technology need have the final word.

STUDY QUESTIONS

1. How was Jesus a crisis in the history of biblical salvation?
2. What is the synoptic problem?
3. What is the intent of the genealogy of chapter 1?
4. Who do the birth stories make Jesus out to be?
5. What does the Matthean Jesus mean by the Kingdom of Heaven?
6. What are the features common to the people blessed in the Beatitudes?
7. How is Jesus' righteousness superior to that of the scribes and Pharisees?

8. How do Jesus' cures show that God desires mercy rather than sacrifice?

9. Why should God be harsher with the towns that reject Jesus' disciples than with Sodom and Gomorrah?

10. What sort of suffering is inseparable from genuine discipleship?

11. What was the scandal in Jesus' death?

12. How does Jesus describe the motivation of the crowds or people at large?

13. Why should the Sabbath have been such a bone of contention between Jesus and the Pharisees?

14. What sort of leadership does Peter represent?

15. How does forgiveness figure in Jesus' scheme of things?

16. Explain Jesus' views of marriage and celibacy.

17. Explain the parable of 21:33–41 in light of the probable situation of Matthew's church around 85 C.E.

18. How does Jesus describe the resurrection (chapter 22)?

19. What do the apocalyptic symbols of chapters 24 and 25 predict?

20. How is Judas a shadow figure or image of negativity?

21. In what ways does Matthew show Jesus' innocence of the charges brought against him at his trials?

22. What effect does Matthew achieve in his depiction of the crucifixion?

23. Explain the function of the angel at the empty tomb.

NOTES

1. See Raymond F. Collins, *Introduction to the New Testament* (Garden City, N.Y.: Doubleday, 1983), pp. 50 ff.

2. See Jack Dean Kingsbury, *Jesus Christ in Matthew, Mark, and Luke* (Philadelphia: Fortress, 1981), p. 2.

3. See William R. Farmer, *The Synoptic Problem* (Philadelphia: Fortress, 1982).

4. See Norman Perrin, *What Is Redaction Criticism?* (Philadelphia: Fortress, 1969).

5. See W. D. Davies, *The Setting of the Sermon on the Mount* (Cambridge: University Press, 1963), pp. 256–315.

6. See Daniel J. Harrington, *The Gospel According to Matthew* (Collegeville, Minn.: Liturgical Press, 1983), p. 9.

7. See Jack Dean Kingsbury, *Matthew: Structure, Christology, Kingdom* (Philadelphia: Fortress, 1975).

8. See Raymond E. Brown, *The Birth of the Messiah* (Garden City, N.Y.: Doubleday, 1977), pp. 53–54. See also R. Laurentin, *Les Evangiles de L'Enfance du Christ* (Paris: Desclee, 1982).

9. Francis Wright Beare, *The Gospel According to Matthew* (San Francisco: Harper & Row, 1981), pp. 63, 65.

10. See George M. Soares Prabhu, *The Formula Quotations in the Infancy Narrative of Matthew* (Rome: Biblical Institute Press, 1976).

11. Harrington, *The Gospel According to Matthew*, p. 26.

12. See Kingsbury, *Jesus Christ in Matthew, Mark, and Luke*, pp. 97–98.

13. John L. McKenzie, "The Gospel According to Matthew," *The Jerome Biblical Commentary*, ed. R. Brown and others (Englewood Cliffs, N.J.: Prentice-Hall, 1968), vol. 2, p. 70.

14. See C. M. Tuckett, "The Beatitudes: A Source-Critical Study," *Novum Testamentum* 25 (1983), 193–207.

15. See D. A. Losardo, "La Paz y el amor a los enemigos," *Revista Biblica* 45 (1983), 1–15.

16. See J. M. Derrett, "The Merits of the Narrow Gate," *Journal for the Study of the New Testament* 15 (1982), 20–29.

17. See Davies, *The Setting of the Sermon on the Mount*, pp. 86–93.

18. See Norman Perrin, *Rediscovering the Teaching of Jesus* (New York: Harper & Row, 1976), p. 202; David Aune, *Prophecy in Early Christianity and the Ancient Mediterranean World* (Grand Rapids, Mich.: Eerdmans, 1983), p. 184.

19. See D. Moody Smith, "John and the Synoptics," *New Testament Studies* 26 (1980–81), 424–44.

20. See D. A. Carson, "The Jewish Leaders in Matthew's Gospel: A Reappraisal," *Journal of the Evangelical Theological Society* 2 (1982), 161–74.

21. See G. Granata, "Some More Information about Mustard and the Gospel," *Bibliotheca Orientalis* 25 (1983), 105–106.

22. See James S. Ackerman, *Teaching the Old Testament in English Classes* (Bloomington: Indiana University Press, 1973), pp. 270–71.

23. See O. Lamar Cope, *Matthew: A Scribe Trained for the Kingdom of Heaven* (Washington: Catholic Biblical Association, 1976), p. 31.

24. See A. Dermience, "La Péricope de la Cananeene (Mt 15, 21–28). Rédaction et Théologie," *Ephemerides Theologicae Lovanienses* 58 (1982), 25–49.

25. See M. A. Chevallier, "Tu es Pierre, tu es le nouvel Abraham (Mt 16/18)," *Etudes Théologiquer et Religieuses* 57 (1982), 375–87.

26. See F. Carrillo-Guelbert, "Si vous ne devenez commes les enfants . . . ," *Bulletin du Centre Protestant d'Etudes* 34 (1982), 5–24.

27. See James R. Mueller, "The Temple Scroll and the Gospel Divorce Texts," *Révue de Qumran* 38 (1980), 247–56.

28. See J. Thomas, "Tout est grace: lecture de Matthieu 19, 1–12," *Christus* 29 (1982), 338–44.

29. See C. Dietzfelbinger, "Das Gleichnis von den Arbeitern im Weinberg als Jesuswort," *Evangelische Theologie* 43 (1983), 126–37; David C. Steinmetz, "The Superiority of Precritical Exegesis," *Theology Today* 37 (1980), 27–38.

30. See W. W. Walty, "Jesus and the Temple—Cleansing or Cursing?" *Expository Times* 93 (1982), 235–39.

31. See W. Radl, "Zur Struktur der eschatologischen Gleichnisse Jesu," *Trierer Theologische Zeitschrift* 92 (1983), 122–33.

32. See D. C. Allison, "Matt. 23:39 = Luke 13:35b as a Conditional Prophecy," *Journal for the Study of the New Testament* 18 (1983), 75–84.

33. See Elisabeth Schüssler-Fiorenza, *In Memory of Her* (New York: Crossroad, 1983).

34. See J. A. Upton, "The Potter's Field and the Death of Judas," *Concordia Journal* 8 (1982), 213–19.

35. See G. Friedrich, "Die Formale Struktur von Mt 28, 18–20," *Zeitschrift für Theologie und Kirche* 80 (1983), 137–83.

36. Krister Stendahl, *The School of St. Matthew* (Philadelphia: Fortress, 1968), p. 24.

37. See Robert Gundry, *The Use of the Old Testament in St. Matthew's Gospel* (Leiden: E. J. Brill, 1967); William G. Thompson, *Matthew's Advice to a Divided Community* (Rome: Biblical Institute Press, 1970).

38. Gerd Theissen, *The Miracle Stories of the Early Christian Tradition* (Philadelphia: Fortress, 1983), p. 300.

39. Ibid., pp. 301–2.

7

The Gospel for Luke's Church

WHAT HAVE WE HERE?

Luke is the third of the synoptic Gospels and the first part of a two-part (Luke-Acts) interpretation of Christian history from the time of Jesus to the arrival of Paul in Rome around 60 C.E. The author therefore is a very important contributor to the New Testament—Luke-Acts is the largest block of material from one source. Present-day scholarly opinion is that Luke originated about the same time as Matthew (roughly 85 C.E. or perhaps a bit later) but from a Gentile church.[1] Antioch in Syria or some place in Asia Minor (current Turkey) are considered the likeliest places of origin.

Literarily, Luke is the most accomplished of the Gospel writers. His Greek is the most polished and his narrative art the most impressive. Often it is the Lukan form of a story (for example, the stories of the infancy narratives) that most capture the readers' imagination. In addition, Luke is the only source for such memorable stories as the prodigal son (15:11–32) and the widow of Nain (7:11–17).

The traditional indentification of the author has come from Colossians 4:14 (see also 2 Timothy 4:10–11; Philemon 24), where the Pauline author refers to a Luke who is "the beloved physician." Modern scholarship finds some problems with this designation, many of them deriving from the differences between the theology of Acts and the theology of Paul:

> In his christology the author of Acts is pre-Pauline; in his natural theology, idea of the law, and eschatology, he is post-Pauline. He has presented no specifically Pauline ideas. He has rather depicted Paul in his zeal for the worldwide evangelization of the Gentiles. He [Vielhauer] considers the theological distance between Luke and Paul to be such as to raise the question whether there was not also temporal distance between them, i.e., whether one may really consider Luke, the physician and travel companion of Paul, as the author of Acts.[2]

Whatever his actual name and occupation, the author of Luke-Acts seems (on internal evidence) to have been a Greek-speaking Christian concerned to make the message and story of Jesus intelligible to a Greek-speaking, Gentile church (perhaps many of whom previously had been "God-fearers"—people well disposed toward Jewish faith). He draws on Mark and Q, as Matthew did, plus sources peculiar to himself (sometimes called "L"). His use of geographical information suggests that he was writing for people unfamiliar with Palestine. His readers may well have wanted to know about the Hebrew origins of Jesus and their faith, so he explains some of Jesus' Jewish background. He is more favorable to Roman occupation than Matthew and depicts both Jesus and Christian life as compatible with good citizenship in the Roman empire. The sweep of his vision comes from his overriding conviction that salvation has become a universal offer. No longer is salvation a peculiarly Jewish affair. With Jesus' resurrection, the work of Paul, and the general growth of the Church the biblical God now addresses all nations.

Concerning more specific themes, the following stand out as peculiar to Luke and worth watching develop:

1. The concern of the Lukan Jesus with the poor, the sinful, the marginal people of society: Luke's Jesus is especially gentle and merciful.
2. Joy: Salvation is the fulfillment for which human nature and history alike have long been hungering.
3. Universalism: The Gospel is now being preached throughout the world; in principle the Church is open to all humankind.
4. The role of the Holy Spirit: It is the Spirit who guides both Jesus and the Church.
5. Current Christian living: Luke is concerned to show how middle-class Christians can live out their faith in the world. He is neither a separatist nor an apocalyptic visionary. Although he makes a large place for poverty he does not require a withdrawal from ordinary life.
6. An interest in Jesus' journeying, his being on the move: The most prominent literary hinge of his Gospel is the journey from Galilee to Jerusalem (9:51–19:27), which builds toward the final drama of Jesus' life.

Lesser themes are an interest in Jesus' ascension, which Luke sees as the consummation of the resurrection and the prelude to the sending of the Holy Spirit, and the fulfillment of Jewish prophecy. This fulfillment is not as strong a theme as in Matthew but Luke, too, has the notion that what happened to Jesus was foreordained and necessary (see, for instance, 18:31–33 and 24:26).

In outline Luke breaks down as follows:

The Prologue 1:1–4
The Infancy Narrative 1:5–2:52

The Preparation for the Public Ministry 3:1–4:13
The Galilean Ministry 4:14–9:50
The Journey to Jerusalem 9:51–19:27
The Ministry in Jerusalem 19:28–21:38
The Passion Narrative 22:1–23:56a
The Resurrection Narrative 23:56b–24:53[3]

The Prologue (1:1–4)

Luke begins with an address to one Theophilus, who we may presume was a prominent Christian convert. Theophilus is also addressed at the beginning of Acts, at which point mention is made of a first book, undoubtedly this Gospel. Luke's prologue to his Gospel admits that his narrative will not be the first. Many others have attempted to tell the story of "the things which have been accomplished among us" (the story of the salvation and glad tidings that have come with Christ and the spread of the Church). Luke and the other narrators have depended on materials delivered to them ("tradition") by those who preceded them in faith. Some of these sources were eyewitnesses of Jesus (whose career is the main subject of the word or story that they have narrated).

> While introducing his book and giving his reasons for writing, Luke also tells us a fair amount about himself and the readers he is trying to reach. He admits that he is not one of the original eyewitnesses of the deeds and words of Jesus; he is a "second-generation" Christian like his readers. The classical Greek style of his preface may indicate that he is an educated convert writing for others like himself scattered throughout the Roman Empire. [It may also indicate that he was familiar with Jewish apologetic writings, which sometimes had similar prefaces.] The gospel story has already had wide circulation through traveling preachers and through the teaching of established Christian communities; it has even been circulated in written form by this time. Only one product from these "many" earlier gospel-writers, however, has come down to us in complete form—the Gospel of Mark, which Luke uses as a source. [Luke has about 350 of Mark's 661 verses.][4]

The name "Theophilus" means "Lover of God," so perhaps Luke uses it symbolically. The last verses of the Prologue suggest that Luke is writing this account to Theophilus in part because the accounts presently circulating do not fully meet either his own needs or those of his church. His account will be orderly, something that may make better or more cogent sense to people like Theophilus (Gentiles). Luke 1:4 implies a certain critical-mindedness on Luke's part, as though he has sifted his sources carefully and feels confident that what he tells Theophilus is the solid truth about Jesus and the Christian faith.[5]

The Infancy Narrative (1:5–2:52)

Raymond E. Brown, whose work on the infancy narratives we used in our study of Matthew, thinks that (contrary to Matthew) Luke did not start out his Gospel with his materials about Jesus' birth in hand or in mind but added them later to a narrative already essentially complete.[6] One major argument for this position is the solemn nature of the beginning of Luke's account of the preparation for the public ministry (3:1–2). Stylistically, this solemnity speaks for an original beginning of Luke that, like Mark (but with a historical orientation that Mark lacks), plunged right into a description of Jesus' forerunner, John the Baptist. Indeed, the statement in Acts 1:22 that John the Baptist was the *beginning* of Jesus' "going in and out" among his disciples also suggests that the Lukan infancy narratives were added to the Gospel after the writing of Acts. The fact that Luke places Jesus' genealogy in his third chapter, after the opening of the public ministry, is another indication that his infancy narratives were a late addition.

Nonetheless, the first two chapters of the Gospel play a useful role, as do the first two chapters of Acts. In the case of Acts the first two chapters provide a transition from the story of Jesus to the story of the Church. In the case of Luke's Gospel the first two chapters bridge the way from the story of Israel to the story of Jesus. Zechariah and Elizabeth, for instance, stand within the story of Israel. With Simeon and Anna, they represent the piety of faithful Jews of the generation that preceded Jesus. Even Mary's hymn ("The Magnificat") may be seen as a summary of Old Testament faith. (The parallel "summary" in Acts 1–2 is the ascension of Jesus and Pentecost [the coming of the Holy Spirit to guide the life of the Church that continues Jesus' presence and work].)

The infancy narratives themselves begin with the story of the priest Zechariah and his wife Elizabeth, righteous Jews living in the time of Herod, king of Judea. Although they kept the Law blamelessly, God had not blessed them with children (a sore trial, especially for Elizabeth). While Zechariah is serving in the Jerusalem Temple (a most holy place), the angel Gabriel announces to him that their prayers have been answered: Elizabeth will bear a son and they should call him John (the Baptist). The similarity of this birth announcement to that of important Old Testament heroes (for instance, Isaac in Genesis 17 and Samson in Judges 13) argues that Luke drew from Jewish sources at this point.

Luke 1:5–56 sometimes is called "The Dyptich [two-panel painting] of the Annunciation," because following the announcement of the conception of John comes a parallel announcement of the conception of Jesus. For instance, Gabriel also comes to Mary, telling her not to be afraid, that she has found favor with God and will conceive a son (1:30–31, paralleling 1:13). Indeed, the whole pattern of 1:5–25, concerned with John, parallels the pattern of 1:26–38, concerned with Jesus. There is a notice of the parents, an appearance of the angel, anxiety on the part of the person addressed, a comforting "Do not fear," an announcement of the coming birth, a question about how this can be, the angel's answer, the giving of a sign, a response, and the angel's departure. Mary's visit to Elizabeth (1:39–56) brings the two parallel stories together, fusing them in the connection between Jesus and John. (In the background of the annunciation also are allusions, to 1 Samuel 1 and 2 on the conception of Samuel by Hannah.)

Moreover, the births of John and Jesus compose a second, similar dyptich. Luke 1:57–80 parallels 2:1–20 in that both narratives speak of joy at the birth, a canticle (song of praise), the baby's circumcision, the first manifestation of his future role, another canticle, and the baby's growth. Once again there is a further episode at the end of the second panel of the dyptich (the finding of Jesus in the Temple), but this time the link between Jesus and John is not clear.[7]

Looking at the first dyptich in more detail, we note that the angel's predictions about John (1:14–17) fit the picture of John we have seen in Mark and Matthew. He was a man led by the divine Spirit to call the people of Israel to repentance. He brought to mind the prophet Elijah. The reference to his drinking no wine suggests his asceticism (and the Nazirite vow of Numbers 6:1–21). Zechariah is reminiscent of Abraham, wondering how this conception can come about when he and his wife are so elderly.[8] He is punished for his lack of faith by being struck dumb until the day of John's birth. Elizabeth looks upon her pregnancy as taking away the reproach that her barrenness has been (see Genesis 16:2 for the parallel with Sarah, the wife of Abraham).

Elizabeth is six months pregnant when the angel Gabriel makes a second visit, to the virgin Mary, the betrothed of Joseph. Luke notes that Joseph was of the house of David (the Messiah's line). The angel calls Mary "favored one," saying that the Lord is with her. Calming her upset, he again notes her favor before God and says that she will conceive a son to be called Jesus. The prediction about Jesus says that he will be called "The Son of the Most High," will inherit the throne of David, and will reign over the house of Jacob forever. This is a most amazing prediction: Mary, who has no husband yet (and has not had sexual relations), will bear the (final?) king of Israel. The angel says that God's Spirit will be the source of this wonder. He points to Elizabeth as a sign that all things are possible with God. Mary, in contrast to Zechariah, submits in complete faith: Whatever God wants is her will.

Mary's visit to Elizabeth connects the two announcement stories. Luke portrays the baby John as recognizing from the womb the mother of the One whom he will precede. Elizabeth blesses Mary and calls her "the mother of my Lord." Mary's faith draws Elizabeth's further blessing. The prayer that Mary utters in praise of God comes largely from the prayer of Hannah in 1 Samuel 2:1–10. Its main themes are God's exalting of the lowly, mercy toward those who fear him, dethroning of the mighty, feeding of the hungry, and remembrance of Israel according to the promises made to Abraham and the patriarchs. It fits well Luke's themes of the Spirit's inspirations and God's special concern for the poor (the sort of people the Matthean Jesus beatified).

The second dyptich begins with the birth of John. At his naming his parents have to fight to fulfill the angel's instructions, for the family wants him named after Zechariah. Zechariah's muteness falls away and the people wonder at the strangeness of this birth. The hand of the Lord seems to be upon this child. Zechariah utters a song of praise that has come, from its first Latin word, to be called the "Benedictus": "Blessed be the Lord God of Israel . . ." The prayer praises God for redeeming his people Israel and rings with phrases that stir up faith in the covenant struck long ago with the patriarchs. The child John will be a prophet, going before the Lord to prepare the Lord's ways. In the background may be the predictions of Malachai 4:2, 5 about the day of the Lord and coming of Elijah, but Luke has turned them from wrathfulness to blessing. Luke 1:79 recalls Isaiah 9:2, a text that we have seen (Matthew 4:16) used to depict Jesus' ushering in the messianic time: "The people who walked in darkness have seen a great light; those who dwelt in a land of deep darkness, on them has light shined." The birth story concludes with a description of John's growth to adulthood "strong in spirit" and then alludes to his time in the wilderness.

The parallel birth of Jesus begins with the decree of Caesar Augustus that a census should be taken. (This, to square with Matthew, would have occurred about 5 B.C.E., but several confusions in Luke's report suggest that his main purpose in beginning this way is symbolic. Luke wants to correlate Jesus' appearance with the period of peace that the reign of Augustus brought. He also wants to bring the Holy Family to Bethlehem, the predicted place of the Messiah's birth.) The birth of the child Jesus in a manger indicates the lowliness of his earthly origins. Luke has humble shepherds, rather than Matthew's lordly Magi, witness the birth. (David, however, was a shepherd-king.) The angel and heavenly host interpret the joyous significance of this event: "For to you is born this day in the city of David a Savior, who is Christ the Lord" (2:11). Mary "keeps" all these things, pondering them in her heart. For Luke Mary is the first Christian believer, a prime exemplar of faith. (By contrast, Mark portrays Jesus' whole family as having serious misgivings about him. See Mark 3:21.) In 2:51 Luke repeats this notion of Mary keeping all these things (here the finding of the child Jesus in the Temple) in her heart. The obvious inference is that, despite her great docility and faith, she had to develop in herself an understanding of what Jesus meant. At his circumcision Jesus receives the name designated by the angel Gabriel (a name that suggests his saviorhood).

The purification of Mary after the child's birth was a matter of Jewish law. The real point to the arrival in the Temple, however, is the homecoming of God's Son (this is God's house). The fulfillment of the promise to Simeon links the old covenant with the new. Characteristically, Luke gives the Holy Spirit a key role. The "Nunc Dimittis," as Simeon's song of blessing sometimes is called (from the Latin of its first words), has a universal tone: This child will be salvation for the Gentiles, as well as glory for Israel. Luke has Simeon predict the division that Jesus will cause in Israel and the pain that Mary will suffer. (He is saying that all that happened to Jesus was foreordained.) The prophetess Anna stands as another representative of righteous Israel. For such as she and Simeon, Elizabeth and Zechariah, the coming of the messianic age with John and Jesus is the fitting climax to a long life of faith. The second panel of the second dyptich concludes with Jesus' growth (parallel to John's). He became strong, was filled with wisdom, and enjoyed God's favor (**charis**, or grace).

The Presentation in the Temple.
Jacopo del Casentino. This
fourteenth century work
from the Florentine school
has a rather solemn tone,
befitting Mary's sense that
her child is destined to
suffer and Simeon's sense
that he is receiving the
deliverer of Israel.   *(Nelson
Gallery–Atkins Museum, Kansas City,
Mo. [Nelson Fund])*

The restrained story of the boy Jesus in the Temple contrasts instruc-
tively with the farfetched, heroic accounts of Jesus' childhood one finds in
some of the **apocryphal** gospels. The point to Luke's story is the fittingness
of Jesus' learning and teaching in his Father's house. Jesus is just before the
age of his **bar mitzvah**, on the verge of adulthood. Luke underscores the
mystery of Jesus' personality. Even his parents wonder about him. Yet he is
obedient to them and grows up handsomely. Because Jerusalem is so
important in Luke's sense of Jesus' journeyings, we may suspect that the
scene in the Temple is another deliberate effort to tie Jesus' identity to the
holy city.

Before leaving the Lukan infancy narratives we should note two further characteristics. First, the contrast between Matthew and Luke is
strong. While they cover roughly the same part of Jesus' life, Luke has
many more incidents than Matthew. For example, Matthew does not report
the promise of John the Baptist's birth, the annunciation of Jesus' birth to
Mary, Mary's visit to Elizabeth, the birth of John the Baptist, Jesus' circumcision, the presentation in the Temple, or the finding of the boy Jesus in
the Temple when he was twelve. On the other hand, peculiar to the Matthean infancy narrative is the genealogy of Jesus (Luke has his equivalent
later, in chapter 3), Joseph's deliberation whether to divorce Mary, the
several revelations in dreams, the coming of the Magi at Jesus' birth, the
flight into Egypt, and the slaughter of the innocents. The obvious inference
is that the two evangelists used different source materials and had different
purposes. Luke's is a gentler account, greatly concerned to link the Chris-

tian dispensation with a past Jewish dispensation that deserves great respect. For him the spread of salvation from Israel to the Gentile world is rather harmonious, intended by God from the beginning. Matthew is bitter over Jesus' rejection by his own people, concerned from the beginning to show that this man whom his people would misunderstand and reject was the royal Son of God and Messiah. That the Jews would misunderstand and reject such a figure shows their tragic sinfulness.

Second, certain features of the Lukan infancy narratives suggest the influence of Johannine Christianity. Perhaps the most prominent of these is the appearance in Luke 1-2 of a number symbolism dear to the Gospel of John and Revelation. For example, the number twelve (Luke 2:42) regularly was used in Johannine circles to stand for the twelve tribes or fullness of Israel. The number three (Luke 2:46) frequently epitomized the time between Jesus' death and resurrection (the crucial passover when salvation history shifted dramatically). The time from the angel's announcement to Zechariah to the presentation of the baby Jesus in the Temple is seventy weeks. In Johannine circles seven was a number of completeness. Luke's seventy times seven (490 days) may symbolize completeness squared and raised to the second power. Additionally, the schematization of the scenes in the first chapters of Luke reminds some commentators of the plan of Revelation, behind which stand Daniel 9:24 and Jeremiah 25:12.

The Preparation for the Public Ministry (3:1–4:13)

The main subunits in this section are a description of the Baptist, Jesus' forerunner; the preaching of John and baptism of Jesus; the genealogy of Jesus (who is both Son of Man and Son of God); and the temptation in the wilderness.

As he located the birth of Jesus with reference to secular (Gentile) history, so Luke locates John's prophetic arrival on the public scene: in the fifteenth year of the reign of Tiberius Caesar (about 29–30 C.E.). John is impelled to start preaching because, in classically prophetic fashion, the Word of God comes to him (see, for instance, Jeremiah 1:2). He comes from the wilderness (a place of trial and purification) and may have been a disciple at Qumran, a community of Jews around the Dead Sea who wanted to purify themselves for the coming of the Messiah.[9] John's prophetic word focuses on repentance for the forgiveness of sins. The quotation from Isaiah 40:3–5 is longer than in Matthew and Mark, and the extra verse extends the universal implications of the time that is dawning. John is harsh with the crowds, telling them not to presume that their lineage from Abraham will be enough. A time of judgment or crisis is at hand. They will be judged by their fruits, not their bloodline.

When the multitudes ask John what they should do, he gives a rather mild response. (It is significant that he specifically addresses tax collectors and soldiers, two groups disparaged by rigorous Jews.) Basic generosity and sympathy are important: sharing one's surplus with those who are hard pressed. One can stay in one's job, even though it is potentially compromising, as long as one is honest and peaceable.

To the growing question of the crowds about his identity and whether he might not be the Christ, John answers negatively. His baptism is with water, something preparatory. The One coming, who is mightier than he, will baptize with the Holy Spirit and fire (a more profound cleansing and renewal). This mightier figure will execute the judgment that John has been announcing, separating wheat from weeds like a ruthless harvester. John's announcement of the coming of this mightier figure was good news, a gospel. Because of it and John's earlier rebuke of Herod's semi-incest, Herod has John put in prison. Luke's account of Jesus' baptism places more stress on the Spirit then does Mark's. It also notes the opening of the heavens (the renewal of prophecy) and God's approbation of his Son.

Who is this Jesus whom God has anointed (through the descent of the Spirit) for the crucial ministry of the kingdom? Luke's genealogy of Jesus in 3:23–38 is designed to answer this question. The list of Jesus' antecedents differs significantly from Matthew's list, although both evangelists trace Jesus through Joseph, to bring out his Davidic blood. Luke has seventy-seven names compared to Matthew's forty-one; where Luke begins with Jesus and works backward, Matthew begins with Abraham and works forward. The tipoff to Luke's intent is his extension of Jesus' orgins beyond Abraham (the point at which Matthew begins). Jesus derives directly from Adam, the first human being, the son who was fashioned by God himself. Luke, then, is interested in showing Jesus' generically human significance. If Matthew wants to portray Jesus as the full ripening of what began with Abraham, Luke wants to portray Jesus as the full ripening of what began with Adam.

Chapter 4 opens with Luke's version of Jesus' temptation by Satan in the wilderness. After his baptism by John in the Jordan River Jesus was "full of the Holy Spirit." The forty days that Luke mentions call to mind the forty years that Israel wandered in the desert before it entered the promised land. Since popular imagination pictured wilderness areas as populated by demons, it was logical to depict Jesus meeting Satan in the desert. That Jesus was led to this encounter by the Spirit shows that it completely served God's purposes.

Like Matthew, Luke elaborates on Mark's simple, two-verse account (Mark 1:12–14), describing a testing in three stages. Probably, then, the threefold temptation was part of the Q tradition. Satan addresses Jesus as one who may be the Son of God and tries to get Jesus to violate filial obedience to God. That Satan claims all the authority and glory of the world shows that Satan is a liar to the core. Jesus answers Satan's challenges with the quotations from Deuteronomy that we saw in Matthew. What for Matthew is the second temptation is for Luke the third. Most likely this is a deliberate change on Luke's part in order to make the Jerusalem Temple the scene of climax. Artfully, Luke is having Jesus complete his initiatory trial at a place that will figure prominently in the final drama. Luke 4:13 is a pregnant and ominous line, suggesting both that there were further temptations and that Satan will return when the time is ripe and Jesus is vulnerable.

The Galilean Ministry (4:14–9:50)

Fresh from his triumph over Satan, Jesus begins his public work in his native area of Galilee. From the outset a pulsation of acclaim and suspicion starts beating. Jesus moves in the power of the Spirit, teaches in the Galilean synagogues, and is glorified by all. In his home town of Nazareth he announces the fulfillment of the prophecy of Isaiah (Isaiah 61:1–2; 58:6) that looked forward to an anointed prophet or messianic king. This hero would overturn the people's misery and bring a universal jubilee year (see Leviticus 25:8–55) when all debts would be wiped out. (This reading from Isaiah is the only direct indication we have that Jesus was literate.)

The initial reaction of most onlookers is wonder and pleasure: Jesus has spoken most graciously. Some, however, refuse to accept prophecy from a source they feel they know well: "Is not this Joseph's son?" (4:22). This line certainly is ironic, since Jesus is only Joseph's son in name. Luke presents Jesus as discerning the resistance of his townspeople and (perhaps sorrowfully) remarking that no prophet is acceptable in his own country. His further reference, to the works of the prophets Elijah and Elisha on behalf of Gentiles, is Luke's foreshadowing of the movement of salvation out beyond a strictly Jewish constituency. The wrath of the Nazarean Jews at Jesus' suggestion that their resistance will be the Gentiles' gain, and their murderous attempt to throw Jesus over a cliff, are quite similar to the reactions that greet the preaching of Stephen (Acts 7:58) and Paul (Acts 13:50). But Jesus escapes, probably because no one finally dared to destroy him. This incident may be a pale analogy for Jesus' eventual death, at which time his enemies will seem to destroy him but actually will completely fail.

Following Mark's account (with editing to suit his own purposes), Luke presents Jesus at work at Capernaum, an important town on the northwest shore of the Lake of Galilee. Jesus teaches on the Sabbath and his authority astonishes his hearers. He exorcises a demon who has named him as the Holy One of God, causing further amazement. (Much of the *power* of the Markan Jesus remains in Luke's account.) Jesus cures Simon Peter's mother-in-law, although he has yet to meet Simon and call him to discipleship. The people bring various sick and possessed people and Jesus heals them all. (Like Mark, Luke has Jesus forbid the demons to declare his identity.) When Jesus prepares to move on to other areas, the Galileans try to restrain him. He explains that he has been sent to preach the Kingdom of God all over the land, not just where he has been working.

Chapter 5 begins with the call of the first disciples. From the outset Simon is the spokesman or main character. The story of the great catch of fish is peculiar to Luke. Part of the rationale is to reward Simon for his faith: "Master, we toiled all night and took nothing! But at your word I will let down the nets." Another part probably is to suggest that future ministerial effectiveness will come from deep faith. Simon (now called Peter) is astonished at the catch and falls to his knees: He feels unworthy to be in the presence of such holy power. His address of Jesus as "Lord" (5:8) is Luke's first use of this important Christological title. The generous response of the first disciples in leaving everything to follow Jesus is important because Luke considers poverty or detachment essential to lively Christian faith.[10]

The Jesus whom the first disciples so generously follow is a spectacular healer. When a man full of leprosy professes faith in Jesus' ability to help him, Jesus makes him clean (and bids him fulfill the rules for purification given in Leviticus 13:13). Jesus also cures a paralytic, drawing the wrath of the Pharisees by claiming to forgive the man's sins as well. We have seen this account before (Mark 2:1–12, Matthew 9:1–8) and Luke adds nothing new. (In Luke's church, too, Jesus was remembered as a holistic healer, one able to cure both the body and the spirit.)

Perhaps it is the theme of forgiving sins that links the cure of the paralytic to the call of Levi the tax collector and the discussion of Jesus' familiarity with sinners. Jesus describes himself as a physician, come to help the sickly. The righteous have less need of him than sinners. Still, Jesus is not merely a healer or a prophet. He is also the bridegroom whose presence alone is cause for rejoicing. With Jesus the Kingdom of God has appeared. Fasting and penance, therefore, are not the only fitting motifs. Equally important is a sense of at-homeness in a world made palpably good by the inrush of the kingdom, a sense of joy and appreciation for what God is doing. The figures of a new garment and a new wineskin stress the originality of the kingdom, the discontinuity (as well as continuity) between Jesus and the old Torah.[11]

Chapter 6 exemplifies this discontinuity or newness with reference to the Sabbath. When the Pharisees chastise Jesus' disciples for breaking some minor Sabbath laws, Jesus proclaims a new view of the Sabbath: It is subject to his interpretation, not something greater than he but something less. Thus Jesus feels quite free to heal on the Sabbath (technically, healing might be considered work, and would be forbidden on the Sabbath). The man with the withered hand is exactly the sort of unfortunate person whom the grace and kingdom of God would heal. The grace and kingdom of God give the Sabbath its context, not vice versa. This overturning of their assumptions infuriates the scribes and Pharisees. To their perverse credit, they see that Jesus threatens the entire legal edifice they have erected.

In 6:12–13 Luke depicts Jesus at prayer (an activity more prominent in Luke than in the other synoptics). Come from an entire night on the mountain communing with God, Jesus chooses his twelve closest disciples. Like Matthew (but unlike Mark), Luke notes that these were called "**apostles**" (people "sent" out on a mission). In his Gospel and Acts apostles are crucially important because they were the prime witnesses to Jesus' ministry and resurrection. Standing on a level plain (instead of Matthew's mountain), Jesus preaches and cures before a great crowd assembled from a wide variety of places. Then he lifts his eyes to his disciples and proclaims (especially to them?) the blessings of the kingdom.

Luke's account of the Beatitudes differs significantly from Matthew's. First, it has only four blessings instead of Matthew's nine; Luke's four approximate Matthew's first, fourth, second, and eighth blessings. Where Matthew is extreme, perhaps proposing the ultimate ideal for which Jesus' disciples ought to strive, Luke is rather moderate, more palatable to the middle class. That is not to say that Luke has taken all the punch out of Jesus' sayings. Indeed, he actually spiritualizes the Beatitudes less than Matthew. They still ring as a forceful opponent of worldly values. Poverty, hunger, weeping, and being hated are never likely to captivate the society pages. But Luke may be read as assuring people that these negativities, which may come into any life, will be more than offset by the rewards of living in the kingdom.

Third, the four woes that Luke puts in counterpoint to his four Beatitudes are not found in Matthew, and they make the Lukan Jesus sterner than he otherwise would appear. Skillfully, Luke is laying down some of the reasons why Jesus was rejected, showing that from early on Jesus' preaching was more than the impure could bear. So after blessing those currently downtrodden the Lukan Jesus says, "But woe to you that are rich, for you have received your consolation. Woe to you that are full now, for you shall hunger. Woe to you that laugh now, for you shall mourn and weep. Woe to you, when all men speak well of you, for so their fathers did to the false prophets" (6:24–27).

The acceptance of Jesus brings a reversal of what people spontaneously judge to be success, an overturning. Both riches and poverty, for example, become potentially paradoxical. Those who flourish materially, rich in money and goods, may be spiritually impoverished. Possessions and idolatry often go hand in hand. Those who have little in material terms, who might even be hurting financially or culturally, may be wise, deep, or holy. Luke is not canonizing poverty or failure. There is no inevitable connection between deprivation and holiness. Even more strikingly, however, there is no inevitable connection between riches and true human success, between riding high and being pleasing to God.[12]

Luke 6:27–36 is perhaps the high point of the Lukan Sermon on the Mount/Plain. Here Jesus shows beyond doubt the distance of his vision from what people spontaneously feel and judge. How can he urge his disciples to love their enemies, do good to those who hate them, and the rest? By making his measure of goodness nothing finite, flawed, or partial. Jesus' measure of goodness is the infinite God, his and all people's consistently loving Father. That is the measure to which all who would enter deeply into the kingdom must stretch. In some ways, it is an inhuman measure, more than ordinary humanity can bear. The implication, in fact, is that the kingdom transforms "ordinary" human nature and brings out capacities seldom hinted at on the nightly news. (The Pauline and Johannine theologies root these capacities in the divinization that God's favor produces.)

Thus Jesus' disciples are not to judge others harshly; they are not to condemn or refuse to forgive. They are to give generously. In this way they themselves will reap nonjudgment, forgiveness, generosity: "Good measure, pressed down, shaken together, running over will be put into your lap" (6:36). The disciples also are to cling to a teacher who is not blind, be more concerned with their own great defects than with other people's small defects, and make sure they judge themselves and others by the fruits they bear. It is only those who take Jesus' words to heart and make them the foundation of their lives who will build their houses solidly. Others will not stand up in time of trial and their ruin will be great.

Chapter 7 opens with Jesus' cure of the slave of the Gentile centurion (Matthew 8:5–13), a God-fearer or person well disposed toward Jewish faith, whose complete faith in Jesus becomes a model for all disciples. Pointedly Luke, the evangelist most interested in the Gentile church, has Jesus say: "I tell you, not even in Israel have I found such faith" (7:9). And where for Matthew this is a bitter saying, the prelude to throwing the "sons of the Kingdom" out into outer darkness, for Luke it is a simple fact: The kingdom has passed outside of Israel, as God always planned that it would. Luke's, then, is the more radical view of Jesus' relation to the Gentiles. For him it had to be that the kingdom would come to embrace all peoples of good faith.

Perhaps to soften the harshness or demanding nature that he had written into Jesus' character in chapter 6, Luke attributes the raising of the dead son of the widow of Nain to Jesus' compassion. The lot of a childless widow was extremely difficult and Jesus was moved by the whole misery that the son's death might entail. It is also typical of the Lukan Jesus to sympathize with women, who were rather marginal in the patriarchal Judaism of his time.

The spectacular cure of raising a dead person provokes fear in the crowd and adds to Jesus' rapidly spreading reputation as a great prophet. (Deuteronomy 18:18, predicting that God will raise up a great prophet like Moses, often seems to be in Luke's mind.) When report of Jesus' wonders reaches John the Baptist (Luke, unlike Matthew, does not specify that John is in prison), John sends two of his disciples to ask Jesus whether Jesus is the Messiah. As if in answer, Jesus cures more people and works more wonders. Pointing to these, he tells John's disciples to return to their master and report what they have seen. John will have to make up his own mind, based on the evidence of Jesus' deeds. Jesus' praise of John might be taken as a vote of confidence: Surely this great prophet will be able to read Jesus' signs. Luke emphasizes that the common people and tax collectors praised God for Jesus' words, as they had eagerly accepted John's baptism. It was the Pharisees and lawyers or scribes who remained closed to the purpose of God, just as they had refused John's baptism.

There follows the simile between the "men of this generation" and the children in the marketplace who find that neither their happy songs nor their wails win acceptance. John was ascetic and forbidding and Jesus is not, yet the religious establishment rejects them both, because they both call for a profound religious reform. The enigmatic line we saw in Matthew (11:19) punctuates Luke's simile: "Yet wisdom is justified by all her children" (Matthew has: "by all her deeds"). The implication is that Jesus is true wisdom while the shrewdness of the present generation is sophistry or ignorance.

A Pharisee invites Jesus to eat with him and Jesus accepts. (Jesus is not an ideologue and has not written the Pharisees off as a class.) A woman who is a sinner enters and, weeping, cleanses Jesus' feet with her tears, hair, and

The Penitent Magdalene. El Greco. About 1580–85. El Greco frequently painted Magdalene. Catholic Reformation art favored ecstatic portraits of the saints. The skull symbolizes Magdalene's repentance to a serious religious life, while the vase suggests the tradition that she was the woman who anointed Christ's feet. *(Nelson Gallery–Atkins Museum, Kansas City, Mo. [Nelson Fund])*

some ointment she has brought. The Pharisee, knowing that the woman has a public reputation as a sinner, thinks that if Jesus were all the crowds crack him up to be (a great prophet) he would know the woman's reputation and, presumably, keep himself apart from her polluting influence. Jesus senses these feelings of his host and tells him a story. The story, found only in Luke, has the point that human beings stand to God much like debtors to the one who has loaned them money. The greater a person's sin the greater his or her reason for gratitude to God. When a person breaks out of closure to God (lovelessness, the core sin) and weeps with remorse and love, as the woman has, she evidences an inner disposition likely to move God to forgive all her trespasses. So Jesus tells the woman that her sins are forgiven. This disturbs the onlookers, making them ask what sort of man Jesus is. Unperturbed, Jesus tells the woman that her faith has saved her. The parallel incident in Matthew 26:6–7 does not have this story elaborating Jesus' reaction. There Simon (Luke's host Pharisee) is called Simon the leper. One may conjecture that the woman was a prostitute and that Jesus sympathized with the wretchedness she felt at having been brought (or pushed by cruel social circumstances) to such a condition.[13] By moving the story earlier in Jesus' life Luke has severed the connection the other evangelists make between the woman's action and Jesus' coming death (she is as it were anointing Jesus for burial). On the other hand, Luke more effectively brings out Jesus' deep forgiveness.

In chapter 8 Jesus resumes his itinerary through the towns and villages of Galilee, preaching and curing so as to make plain the good news of the kingdom. The twelve accompany him, as do some women whom he has cured or exorcized. Luke names these women, who seem to have become part of Jesus' permanent entourage, and notes that they and still other women provided for the traveling group out of their financial resources. Jesus' teaching for the disciples included stories such as the parable about the sower, which is a figure for the different receptions people give the gospel. Luke 8:16–18 has some enigmatic verses that point to a tension between secrecy (especially prominent during Jesus' earthly life) and openness (now called for in light of the resurrection). As one recent commentator has put it:

> . . . there is a contrast between the secrecy and the humility which characterized the ministry of Jesus, culminating in the cross, and the open declaration that Jesus was Lord and Christ made in the light of the resurrection. If, then, for the moment Jesus teaches the crowds in parables, one day he will be openly declared to them through the resurrection and proclamation of the disciples.[14]

Like all the evangelists, Luke must depict Jesus' historical ministry knowing that it led to Jesus' death and resurrection, which retrospectively give the historical ministry much of its significance.

Luke repeats the tradition (Mark 3:31–35, Matthew 12:46–50) that Jesus to some degree set aside his earthly family and gave greater praise to those who hear the word of God and do it. He then has Jesus walk upon the water and calm the sea (but not bid Peter also walk on the water). Jesus cures the Gerasene demoniac and allows the exorcized demon-swine to rush over the bank into the water. The man who had been possessed wants to travel with Jesus but Jesus sends him home to proclaim what Jesus has done for him. The cures of the daughter of the synagogue ruler Jairus and the woman with a flux of blood follow, largely as we have seen them in Mark and Matthew.

Chapter 9 reports Jesus' commission of the twelve, stressing how lightly they are to travel. Herod, who has beheaded John, wonders at the reports he is getting about Jesus and is curious. Upon the return of the apostles Jesus multiplies the loaves and fishes to feed a great multitude. (At this point Luke omits a large block of Markan material, 6:45–8:26. Insofar as Mark's events reflects a move away from Galilee and no progress toward Jerusalem, they do not fit Luke's purposes.) After this, while Jesus is praying alone with the disciples, he asks them who they think he is. Peter answers, "The Christ of God," but in rather Markan fashion Luke has Jesus command secrecy about this identification. Jesus goes on to say that the Son of Man will have to suffer and die, but Luke does not report Peter's objection to such suffering and Jesus' consequent rebuke of him.

The motif of suffering passes into Luke's characterization of discipleship. Although his stress is neither as aggressive as Mark's nor as connected with the Servant of God that Matthew spotlights from Israelite prophecy, Luke faithfully records Jesus' words about the necessity of disciples' carrying their crosses. The eschatological motif (at the parousia disciples will be judged by whether or not they have been ashamed of their suffering Lord) links the passage with Luke's account of the Transfiguration. Once again it is as though Jesus were giving his disciples a foretaste of his glory, to sustain them through the dark times that are to come. Luke 9:31 has Elijah and Moses speaking to Jesus about his coming departure or exodus, which he is going to accomplish in Jerusalem. Only Luke adds the note that the original motive for going to the mountain was to pray.

After Jesus cures the son of a man who appeals to him (a cure that the disciples could not work, it seems for lack of faith), he again tells the disciples that the Son of Man will be "delivered into the hands of men." They cannot understand this saying (Luke adds: "It was concealed from them," as though by divine design) and are afraid to ask Jesus about it. Luke is not as harsh on the disciples as Mark, perhaps because he finds their witness to the traditions about what Jesus said and did more crucial. Hard on the heels of the disciples' failure to understand about suffering comes their dispute over which of them is greatest. Once again Jesus uses a child to symbolize his message that greatness in the kingdom derives from simplicity and openness of heart. Luke's disciples are no quicker on the uptake than they are in the other synoptics.

Jesus interprets the exorcisms of an unknown imitator benignly ("He that is not against you is for you"), and the ministry in Galilee concludes. It has been Luke's framework for presenting Jesus among his own people and showing the mixed reception that Jesus' gospel received. The leaders of the religious establishment have grown opposed to Jesus (though not as murderously as in Matthew), but the crowds have been amazed by his power to heal and his compassion. Luke has established that Jesus is especially sensitive to the needs of women and the poor. He has shown Jesus' glory and predicted Jesus' suffering. So the stage is set for Jesus' climactic journey to Jerusalem.

The Journey to Jerusalem (9:51–19:27)

This large, central portion of Luke's Gospel comes mainly from Q and sources peculiar to himself. In keeping with the anticipatory note struck during the Transfiguration (9:31), the journey is cast as Jesus' exodus from Galilee to Jerusalem, his pilgrimage toward the preordained place for his passage from life to death, from death to resurrection. Luke increases the suggestions that this march proceeds according to God's will, under the guidance of the Holy Spirit. The opening verse (9:51) marries God's plan to Jesus' free resolve: "When the days drew near for him to be received up [ultimately, on the cross], he set his face to go to Jerusalem."

Jesus would enter a Samaritan village, but the people do not want him, "because his face was set for Jerusalem." This strange phrase, echoing the opening verse of the journey-story, may mean that it was God's will that Jesus not tarry with the Samaritans. (In Acts they will come in for consideration in a second phase of the Gospel's outreach.) It may also refer to the argument between Jews and Samaritans concerning the proper place for worship. Where orthodox Jews considered Jerusalem and its Temple the privileged place for worship, Samaritans preferred Mount Gerizim near Shechem in north-central Palestine. In rebuking the hot-headed disciples James and John, Jesus refuses to get involved in the bitterness between Samaritans and Jews. Just as he is willing to consort with tax collectors and sinners, so he has no prejudice against Samaritans.

Luke 9:57–62 reports sayings of Jesus that we have largely seen in Matthew. Here their significance seems to be that early in his decisive journey Jesus warns any would-be followers that they must be decisive and wholehearted. Jesus has no resting place, no sympathy for any cause that would conflict with the kingdom: "No one who puts his hand to the plow and looks back is fit for the Kingdom of God" (9:62).

Chapter 10 has another missionary commission. The number of disciples now has grown to seventy (or seventy-two, according to other readings). (According to then-contemporary Jewish readings of Genesis, this was the total number of Gentile nations.) A bountiful harvest awaits them. They are to travel light, living off those who accept their ministry. They are to accept the provisions offered them, heal the sick, and announce the arrival of the kingdom. If the people of a town reject them they are to shake the dust of that town from their feet, reassert the arrival of the kingdom, and warn the townspeople that Sodom will have it easier on Judgment Day. Several touches in this account, as in the sayings about the cost of discipleship, suggest that Luke is writing from considerable Church experience of the difficulties of discipleship and ministry. Enthusiasm is not enough. One must have a sober, realistic view of how hard the work will be.

Jesus next casts woes upon Chorazin and Bethsaida (as we saw in Matthew 11:21–23). He assures the disciples that they have a solid charge to represent him and his message. They return from their mission exulting with success. Jesus says that he has seen Satan falling like lightning from heaven. This phrase, suggestive of Revelation 12:7–12, may be a touch of Johannine influence. It implies that the eschatological battle between good and evil has begun. Luke 10:19 seems to be a symbolic way of asserting Jesus' power against all that opposes the kingdom. (No doubt the postresurrectional viewpoint is strong at this point.) The best cause for joy, however, is not overt ministerial success but God's favor in heaven.

Jesus communes with the Spirit, rejoicing, and prays thanks to the Father for having turned simple instruments like the disciples to such good use. Luke 10:22, like the parallel Matthew 11:27, is Johannine in both conception and phrasing. The blessing given the disciples is another expression of Jesus' joy and satisfaction. Their eyes are seeing the consummation that great prophets and kings longed to see and did not.

Next a lawyer, trying to test Jesus, asks him about the path to eternal life. Jesus refers him to the Law and approves the answer that the lawyer brings forth (the twofold commandment of love of God and love of neighbor). When the lawyer presses for a clarification of "neighbor," as if to show that subtlety or superior intellect was behind his question (he was looking for something more than just the surface of the twofold commandment), Jesus answers with the famous parable of the good Samaritan. This parable, unique to Luke, is a fine example of the art that has made Luke's Gospel so memorable. The priest and Levite are formally religious figures, but they fail to help the suffering victim (who might have polluted them). A Samaritan, who might have avoided the Jewish victim as a natural enemy, has compassion and takes care of him. This is love of neighbor: nothing convoluted or esoteric; rather straightforward helpfulness and compassion. With one concrete story Jesus makes "love of neighbor" more vivid than a dozen legal treatises could.[15]

The story about Martha and Mary, which in Christian tradition became a typology for the active and contemplative lives, again shows Jesus friendly with women, as the typical rabbi would not have been, since women were a religious danger. Jesus praises Mary's absorption in his teaching. Just as the disciples should not be overly ascetic, but should rejoice while the bridegroom is with them, so they should not be overly practical. Without retracting anything from the praise he has given the practical good Samaritan, Jesus provides a large place for a direct focus on himself and the kingdom. There will always be dozens of practical affairs begging attention. The disciples must make sure that busyness does not crowd out the religious center: absorption in the divine mystery.

The Good Samaritan. Jusèpe Ribera. This seventeenth century Spanish painting shows the Samaritan dressing the victim's wounds. *(Nelson Gallery–Atkins Museum, Kansas City, Mo. [Nelson Fund])*

From this praise of contemplation we move, in chapter 11, to Jesus' teaching about prayer. As Luke presents the sequence, the disciples observe Jesus at prayer (for Luke this was a regular occurrence), and ask him to teach them what he is doing, as the Baptist taught his disciples. Jesus answers with the Our Father. In its simplicity and depth, it has become the foremost Christian prayer. Then, expanding on the attitudes proper to faithful prayer, Jesus proposes several teaching stories. The person who goes to a friend at night and asks for bread and the son who asks his father for a fish are symbols of the needy human being moved to pray. If they can expect a fair amount of goodwill from imperfect fellow humans, how much more ought believers to expect Gods' goodwill and so pray confidently: "If you, then, who are evil, know how to give good gifts to your children, how much more will the heavenly Father give the Holy Spirit [the supreme gift, with which come all other gifts] to those who ask him!" (11:13).

Jesus then performs an exorcism and suffers the charge that he is casting out demons by Beelzebub, the prince of demons (see Mark 3:22–27, Matthew 12:22–30). He answers as we have already seen: This charge makes no sense, for it would pit Satan against himself. Rather, Jesus is like a strong man who comes and disarms the previous owner of a castle. If Jesus is casting out demons he has Satan on the run. People must decide which side they will support. Those who are not on Jesus' side are against him. Those who do not gather (or help him harvest) scatter. If people are cleansed and then lapse back into the power of Satan, their last state will be worse than their first. (When a woman praises Jesus' mother for having borne so amazing a son, Jesus praises rather those who hear the Word of God and keep it.)

The crowds increase and Jesus becomes suspicious of their motives. They will get no sign but the sign of Jonah. For their lack of repentance they will go down as an evil generation, condemned more harshly than Nineveh (which repented at Jonah's preaching). Their problem is a lack of sincerity, an inner eye that has grown dark. There is little one can do for such people. By contrast, the person of good conscience is like a shining light. Jesus then applies this general religious psychology to a foolish Pharisee who equates external cleanliness with real purity. To his disciples Jesus proposes a far deeper vision: "But give for alms those things which are within; and behold everything is clean for you" (11:41). The generosity that God most wants is interior, a whole gift of self. In God's world nothing is defiled of itself. Bad human motivation is the great defiler. The Pharisees are hypocritical because they preoccupy themselves with external and secondary things like tithes while neglecting internal and primary things like justice and the love of God: "Woe to you! for you are like graves which are not seen, and men walk over them without knowing it" (11:44). How devastating Jesus' critiques can be.

The scribes rightly realize that Jesus' critique of the Pharisees applies to them as well. Jesus does nothing to lessen the affront: "Woe to you! for you build the tombs of the prophets whom your fathers killed" (11:47). The theme of killing the prophets is heavy with dark portent. Jesus, the fulfillment of the prophets, is on his way to die in the holy city from the sickness of the scribes and Pharisees. They have now become his enemies, the main obstacle to the people's welfare. Luke almost pictures them as snarling and surrounding Jesus, trying to pressure him into making a mistake that they can exploit. The mood is ugly, as only distorted religious zeal can be.

Chapter 12 has Jesus starting to prepare his disciples for the onslaught of the Pharisees. Their leaven is hypocrisy, against which the best defense is honesty: full revelation and disclosure. The disciples must not fear them. The Pharisees have no power over anyone's soul. The most they can do is afflict the body. In God's perspective that is far from ultimate. In addition, the disciples must trust to God's care. Every one of their hairs is numbered. The real challenge is to keep faith with Jesus, especially when under persecution.[16] (Obviously this would be apt advice for people trapped in the crossfire between Jews and Christians around 85 C.E.)

With an eye to infra-Christian affairs, Luke has Jesus reject a request to judge an inheritance dispute between a man and his brother. Such problems arise from bad motives and will only be settled when the parties' values have changed. Covetousness, for instance, is the root of many antagonisms. The parable about the rich man who contentedly contemplates a long and fat future is the classic warning against settling down into worldly perspectives: "Fool! This night your soul is required of you; and the things you have prepared, whose will they be? (12:20). To Jesus wisdom is being rich before God, ready to pass God's judgment at any hour. The language in 12:22–31 (whether ultimately from Jesus or Q) turns wonderfully poetic (see Matthew 6:19–34). Life is more than food, the body more than clothing. If God clothes the grass of the field, how much more will God clothe human beings? Luke is showing Jesus as a great counselor to peace. The person deeply in love with God loses most of the anxieties that steal away the worldling's peace. Many things in life are out of our hands. If we see the world as come from an always loving parent the world will seem much less threatening, and each day will be a gift. Consider the lilies of the field, how beautifully they grow. Are they not a pledge of God's care?

The great thing, then, is to have one's treasure in heaven. Only there will it be imperishable: "Sell your possessions, and give alms; provide yourselves with purses that do not grow old, with a treasure in the heavens that does not fail, where no thief approaches and no moth destroys. For where your treasure is, there will your heart be also" (12:33–34). Leaving behind him language such as that, the Lukan Jesus had to become unforgettable, indelibly inscribed into Western consciousness.

Luke 12:35–40 turns eschatological. Disciples must be ever ready, for the Son of Man is coming unexpectedly. Jesus then elaborates for Peter and the disciples. The stress on good stewardship suggests applications for Church leaders. (Applications to ecological resources remain to be made.) Jesus is a crisis, an urgent cause demanding a choice. The end of chapter 12 is part of Luke's version of Jesus' apocalyptic discourse (see also chapters 17 and 21). Here the stress is on reading the signs of the times, realizing that Jesus is demanding a basic choice. The implication is that anyone with eyes to see and an honest mind could have assessed the situation: "And why do you not judge for yourselves what is right?" (12:57). Judging wrongly, or refusing to face the signs of the time, will bring complete disaster.

Chapter 13 begins with sayings about suffering and punishment. Jesus denies that sin is the direct cause of persecution or natural disasters. Natural disasters and persecutions, however, alert the wise to the deeper punishments that evil inevitably will reap (before God). The parable in 13:6–9 clearly is a warning to Jesus' contemporaries that they have one last chance before God punishes them for their fruitlessness. When Jesus cures an infirm woman on the Sabbath this fruitlessness surfaces. The leader of the synagogue is indignant that Jesus would do such work. Jesus makes plain the man's hypocrisy. He who would care for an animal on the Sabbath is blackening human healing because it suits his warped conscience.

There follow Lukan parables about the kingdom. It is like a mustard seed or a woman's leaven, growing almost effortlessly, because it is encoded in the nature of things by God. Still, human freedom is a factor in the growth of the kingdom and the way into the kingdom in not easy. Jesus' description of who will enter is calculated to upset those who assume that official piety is enough for salvation. Only a strict, good life is enough.

Some Pharisees come to Jesus (apparently in friendship but perhaps serving their own purposes) to warn him that Herod is seeking his life. Jesus is not impressed and tells them to tell Herod that this prophet will do what he has to do, that he will walk to his appointed destiny in Jerusalem. Jesus' lament over Jerusalem is heart-wrung. He would have given it tender, motherly love and it clung to its murderousness. For that reason it is forsaken by God (as Christians interpreted the destruction of 70 C.E.).[17]

In chapter 14 Jesus dines on the Sabbath with a Pharisee and feels the eyes of his enemies, watching for their chance. When a man with dropsy comes before him he challenges the Pharisees to clarify their postion about Sabbath cures. Probably because Jesus' humanity has won the crowds, the Pharisees will not speak out about their reservations. Jesus works the cure and embarrasses them. Probably in reference to the Pharisees' pretentiousness, he then tells a story about a wedding feast (a symbol for the kingdom), with the point that one should not take a place of honor (exalt oneself as the Pharisees do) but wait to be honored by the host (God). Similarly, one should target for one's charities not the prosperous but the needy.

The parable of the great banquet (14:15–24) is instructive for the differences between Luke and Matthew. Where Matthew 22:1–10 makes the story a grim forecast of God's rejection of the Jews, Luke emphasizes the good fortune of those (symbolic of the Gentiles) who get invited because the original guests can't come. Pheme Perkins has spelled out this difference more fully:

> Matthew takes it [the parable] as a tragic warning about divine judgment. Luke's version brings to the fore the good fortune of those included by the disgruntled host. Even the final judgment saying ["For, I tell you, none of those men who were invited shall taste my banquet"] does not preclude further relationships between the man and his friends. (Contrast Matthew's irre-

trievable break). The man speaks out of a temporary but understandable anger or disappointment. You doubtless noted that Matthew makes the refusal to come an affront. The guests ignore a king's invitation, and worse yet mistreat the servants. Luke/GTH's [Gospel of Thomas, an apocryphal source with the same parable] guests offer acceptable or at least probable excuses in polite form. They do not insult the host. In short, the original scale of the story presents a social disappointment or setback as an occasion of good fortune for others.[18]

Great multitudes are now following Jesus and he speaks sternly, lest they misjudge the demands of discipleship. Followers must "hate" their family, bear their crosses, and come after Jesus. They must calculate before they build their tower, realizing what it is they are pledging. (By Luke's time the delay of the parousia had meant the growing appreciation that faith was a commitment for the long haul.) If they are not equal to this project they must strike a compromise, like a king who knows that he is not ready for war and sues for peace. Renunciation of worldly goods and ambitions is a precondition of discipleship. Otherwise, the salt of the gospel would go flat.

Chapter 15 reminds us that Jesus continually upset the scribes and Pharisees by dealing with tax collectors and sinners. The contrast between Jesus' concern with religious essentials and their formality has become a great divide. To explain the logic of his own position Jesus tells a story about a shepherd searching out a single lost sheep. So does Jesus' Father in heaven search out one lost sinner and rejoice when that sinner repents. The story about the woman sweeping her house for a single coin is to the same end. "Just so, I tell you, there is joy before the angels of God over one sinner who repents" (15:10). The stories originally probably stressed God's gracious initiative in salvation. Luke may want to help early recipients of God's grace (e.g., Jewish Christians) be generous to Gentile latecomers.

Luke 15:11–32 is probably the most beloved of Jesus' parables. Once again it is unique to Luke and unthinkable apart from the beautiful way that he has written it. The good father's two sons are both complex, true-to-life characters. The younger one is a sinner, like the people Jesus has been seeking out. He treats his father (who stands for God) thoughtlessly, even cruelly. But in his misery he "comes to himself," turns around, and is adult for the first time. He confesses his sins but his father brushes them away. Indeed, long before he has come up to the house the father has spied him out and rushed forth to embrace him. Killing the fatted calf and making merry is the father's version of the joy of the angels in heaven. The first point of the parable, then, is the prodigal love of God the Father. He cares so much more for the well-being of his children than for his own honor that the mere repentance of a sinner gives him great joy.

The second point of the parable concerns the older, dutiful son, who has always been helpful and obedient. To his mind this feasting at the return of the wanton younger son is unjust. He has never gotten such a party, and he has always been virtuous. Like Matthew's parable about the workmen hired at different hours (Matthew 20:1–16), Luke's story spot-

The Prodigal Son. Giuseppe Bazzani. The prodigal is tearfully welcomed home by his parents but the man at the left (presumably his elder brother) is less than joyous at his return. *(Nelson Gallery–Atkins Museum, Kansas City, Mo. [Gift of Samuel H. Kress Foundation])*

lights the inability of human beings to raise themselves to the level of God's generosity. Consistently we interpose a false concern for what we take to be "justice." The father in Luke's parable has never treated the older son unjustly. Indeed, he has paid him the great compliment of relying on his obedience, assuming that their interests completely coincide. But the older son begrudges the younger son his welcome home, just as the scribes and Pharisees begrudge the tax collectors and sinners Jesus' attention. The father's final line is the tipoff to how Jesus thinks God feels about the return of any child: "It was fitting to make merry and be glad, for this your brother was dead, and is alive; he was lost, and is found" (15:32).

Chapter 16 opens with a story about prudence.[19] The unjust steward is not commended for his wastefulness or dishonesty but for his wit in doing something about his hard situation. So should Jesus' hearers do something about their hard situations, releasing themselves from their wretchedness by striking a deal to get in on the kingdom. Luke 16:10–13 links the story to some general sayings about fidelity. The important contrast is between service of God and service of mammon. One must choose which will be the master. In answer to the scoffing of the Pharisees, whom

Luke accuses of being great lovers of money, Jesus turns paradoxical: What human beings exalt can be an abomination to God.

The sayings in 16:16–18 are somewhat random, but they all point to the stern demands of the kingdom. The parable in 16:19–31 may betray Jesus' lowered expectations, as well as Luke's predilection for the poor. Lazarus, on earth a wretched beggar, is happy in heaven. The rich man who failed to help him is tormented in hell. Abraham refuses the rich man's request to send someone to warn his five brothers. Moses and the prophets have made it plain that helping the wretched is a strict obligation. The final line is utterly ironic: "If they do not hear Moses and the prophets, neither will they be convinced if some one should rise from the dead" (16:31). Whatever disillusionment Jesus felt at the failure of his signs to win the religious leaders was felt by the missionary Christians even more. They had an unprecedented sign in Jesus' resurrection and still the leaders would not hear.

Chapter 17 presents snippets from Jesus' regular preaching. It is a terrible sin to give scandal to the innocent. There can be no limit to one's willingness to forgive others' sins. Faith is the condition of all great religious achievements. Solid disciples consider themselves but unworthy servants doing their humble duty. The story about the ten lepers makes the point that gratitude for God's gifts runs shallow in the majority. It is not accidental that the one leper who returns is a Samaritan. One should not think of the kingdom as something exotic, coming with dazzling portents. Since the coming of Jesus the kingdom is in the people's midst. For Luke, then, the kingdom is a present, as well as a future, reality.

Speaking apocalyptically, Jesus assures the disciples that a time will come when they will long for portents of Daniel's Son of Man coming in glory. But before this Jesus must suffer and be rejected (another of Luke's hints that Jesus is following God's inevitable plan). The coming of Daniel's Son of Man will be like the days of Noah and Lot, when most people were caught unprepared. Still, the signs will be clear enough. So people should not live distractedly or with foolish concern about such portents but in daily readiness.

Chapter 18 has two well-known parables on prayer and hope. The widow who wears down the unjust judge shows the determination that believers should have at prayer. Their prayer is the way they will endure the trials between the present and the consummation of the kingdom. The contrast between the Pharisee and the tax collector is not new, but it goes to the core of what Jesus thinks God wants: repentance, humility, and trust. Those who exalt themselves usurp the judgment of God. Only God can declare a person just or righteous. The people who have the best chance of pleasing God are those who sense the exhaustive claims that God's holiness might make and so see their own sinfulness or distance from the divine perfection.

The crowd brings infants for Jesus to bless and when the disciples would forbid this Jesus rebukes them, repeating the conviction that we have seen: Children are perhaps the best symbols of the citizenry of the kingdom. There follows the story about the rich man who would gain eternal life. Luke does not stress his youth but rather the fact that he is a ruler. He has kept all the commandments (which lead to eternal life) from his youth. He is lacking only a thorough detachment from mammon and a thorough commitment to God. That he cannot accept Jesus' counsel to poverty and radical discipleship occasions Jesus' famous saying about the camel and the eye of a needle (Mark 10:25, Matthew 19:24). This hyperbole points up the great need for God's grace. To accomplish the deeds of the kingdom one must be transformed, so that one's powers and viewpoints partake of God's own holiness. Jesus assures Peter and the other disciples that their sacrifices for the kingdom will be handsomely rewarded, both in this life and with heaven.

Jesus then takes the twelve apart and tells them that the climax is near: It is time to go up to Jerusalem and fulfill the destiny of the Son of Man, which will be deadly. The disciples do not understand; the saying is hid from them, perhaps by a mercy of God. (Once again, Luke is softening any overly harsh portrait of Jesus' prime witnesses.) Near Jericho a blind man begs Jesus for mercy and will not be prevented from crying out. (He refers to Jesus as "Son of David," a royal title.) Jesus gives him his sight, as though rewarding the inner vision (of Jesus' true identity) that his faith had generated.

Chapter 19 opens with the almost humorous story of Zaccheus, the wealthy tax collector who is too short to see Jesus through the crowd and so climbs up a tree. Jesus notices him and infers his serious interest. As a reward Jesus chooses to stay at his house. Predictably, this angers the legalistic among the onlookers, who consider Zaccheus a sinner. Zaccheus explains that he is most scrupulous in his dealings and extremely generous to the poor. (Although a sinner by extrinsic norms he is saintly in fact—a good warning against judging people by classes, apart from their individuality.) This manifestation of a good conscience moves Jesus to proclaim that this day salvation has come to Zaccheus' house. Even though he is lost in the shafts of a disreputable occupation, Zaccheus is a true son of Abraham (the father of faith). It is such as he that Jesus has come to seek and save.

The parable in 19:11–27 that concludes the ministry of the journey to Jerusalem is another teaching about God's judgment and the coming of the kingdom.[20] The nobleman in this case is Christ. The citizens who will not receive him as their ruler are the Jews who reject Jesus' messiahship. Nonetheless, he takes his kingdom (at the ascension) and asks his servants for an accounting of the monies he left with them. Those who used his capital wisely to generate further riches are warmly commended. Those who feared to act and brought the master no return are condemned. The likely background of the parable is the early Christian Church, so the implication is that Jesus expects his disciples to use the powers he has given them, the investment he has made. Those who do nothing with his gifts will earn his wrath (at the parousia). Those who rejected his rule may expect wrath. The message combines a warning about prudence (as in Matthew 25:14–30) with a prediction of punishment for rejecting God's Messiah.

The Ministry in Jerusalem (19:28–21:38)

Finally Jesus has arrived at his appointed place. For Luke his whole ministry has been a movement toward this denouement. Jesus sends two

disciples to obtain the colt on which he will enter Jerusalem (rather mysteriously assuring them that the owners will understand the code words "The
Lord has need of it"). Jesus enters the city riding on the colt and the crowd
acclaims him as a king coming in the name of the Lord. When the Pharisees, affronted by this acclamation, ask Jesus to have it stopped, Jesus
replies: "I tell you, if these were silent, the very stones would cry out." It has
now become massively clear, part of the unmovable order of things, that
Jesus is presenting Jerusalem an unavoidable challenge. His sayings and
works have receded before his being. For him even to be close to Jerusalem
is throwing down the gauntlet.

Still, Jesus finds this situation terribly sad. Weeping over Jerusalem,
he wishes that even now it could know the things that would bring it peace.
Luke's implication is that if Jerusalem had accepted Jesus it would not have
come to grief in 70 C.E. Jesus enters the Temple and drives out the sellers.
The Temple was made for prayer and they have made it a den of robbery.
He teaches daily in the Temple and the religious leaders seek to destroy
him. Despite themselves, however, they can do nothing, because he so
entrances the people. At the outset of chapter 20 they try to trip him up,
asking by what authority he does these things (such as cleansing the Temple). He says he will tell them if they are willing to take a stand on the
baptism of John. They will not declare themselves so Jesus refuses to say by
what authority he does what he does. The public character of Jesus' ministry in Jerusalem is remarkable.

The vineyard parable in 20:9–18 (see Mark 12:1–12, Matthew 21:33–
46) loses little of its bitterness in Luke. Jesus is the son whose slaying by the
vineyard tenants is but the climax of their long history of abusing the
owner's servants (the prophets). The people understand that the punch
line ("He will come and destroy those tenants, and give the vineyard to
others") predicts God's taking away their election, letting Israel be the
divine vineyard no more. It is time for a showdown. Luke's Jesus, looking
them straight in the eye, says that he is the rejected stone that will be the
foundation of a completely new edifice (in Luke's view, the Church). This
stone will be scandalous and will cause many their utter ruin.[21]

The scribes and chief priests take Jesus' parable to heart and want to
lay hands on him. Only their fear of the people prevents them. They send
spies to get something on Jesus that will warrant delivering him to the
Roman governor. These spies ask Jesus whether it is lawful to pay tribute to
Caesar. Jesus finds the question child's play: the very coinage they use bears
Caesar's inscription and so shouts their willingness to pay tribute. (Luke is
stressing that Jesus was not a political revolutionary.) It is similar with the
question of the Sadducees, who ask Jesus about marriage in the resurrection. Jesus undercuts their assumptions by stressing that God's blazing life
transforms all relations. Resurrection, Jesus implies, is just living "to" (in,
with) this God. This profundity silences the scribes, so Jesus puts to them a
question about the relation between the Christ and David. The quotation
suggests that the Christ, though David's son, is greater than David. The
end of chapter 20 warns the disciples to beware of the scribes. They are

vain, in love with honors, and do great religious damage. Their condemnation by God will be great.

Chapter 21 opens with Jesus near the Temple. His eye for detail notes the little alms of a poor widow. Her mite is a greater contribution than the big gifts that the wealthy give without hurt. A disciple admires the noble adornments of the Temple and so occasions Jesus' eschatological discourse. The stones of the Temple will tumble down. Rumors and false alerts will arise. There will be international conflicts, famines, pestilences. Prior to this, however, the disciples will suffer persecution and hatred. They must believe that God will save every hair on their heads. Luke 21:9 makes the Lukan eschatology distinctive. The parousia will delay until wars and tumults have taken place.

The rest of the apocalyptic discourse deals in the Old Testament symbolism that we have previously seen. One peculiarity of Luke's version is its focus on the destruction of Jerusalem. Luke 21:31–33 suggests that the Christian community still had a lively expectation of Jesus' return. Nonetheless, the perennial value of the discourse is clear in 21:34–36: Disciples should live ready to meet the Lord on any day. As the chapter concludes, Luke pictures Jesus teaching in the Temple by day and lodging on Mount Olive at night (probably to pray). Jesus has come to the center of Judaism and is making a public, dramatic (nonrevolutionary or seditious) impact. What good things might not have happened had he met with a generous faith?

The Passion Narrative (22:1–23:56a)

Passover draws near and the chief priests and scribes receive the break they have been seeking. Judas Iscariot succumbs to Satan and goes to the chief priests, offering to betray Jesus (although for Luke, all lay in God's hands). "And they were glad, and engaged to give him money. So he agreed, and sought an opportunity to betray him to them in the absence of the multitude" (22:5–6).

Jesus sends Peter and John to prepare the Passover meal, again (as in the case of the colt) giving rather mysterious directions. (This fits Luke's thesis that God was directing the entire drama of Jesus' ministry and death.) At the table Jesus speaks of his earnest desire to eat this Passover with his disciples, as if glad that finally the crucial hour has come. Luke records the institution of the eucharist, noting the overtones that link it with Jesus' sacrificial death. The reference to Jesus' betrayer is rather veiled, and we get another indication that everything that happened was providential: "For the Son of man goes as it has been determined" (22:22).

The disciples, obtuse to the end, dispute about who is the greatest among them, and Jesus asserts that the only greatness in his community comes from service. Indeed, he himself is among them as one who serves. For Matthew (Matthew 20:25–28) this saying is not part of the Last Supper. By placing it in a eucharistic setting Luke heightens the irony or pathos of the disciples' resistance to Jesus' moral revolution. Still, Jesus promises the disciples that they will eat and drink at the messianic banquet and will sit on thrones judging the twelve tribes of Israel. One suspects that either there was some ambiguity in Jesus' original sayings about servanthood and glory or that the early Church could not decide whether discipleship was mainly a service or a prelude to heavenly rule.

Jesus almost grieves over Simon Peter, for whose faith and community leadership he has prayed. Satan has tried to sift Peter like wheat. (Luke is more sympathetic to Peter than Mark is. In Mark we are not so sure that Peter will be restored to good standing.) The return of Satan—his entering into Judas and testing of Peter—fulfills the promise that Luke dangled at the end of the temptation in the wilderness (4:13). Peter protests that he is ready to die with Jesus but Jesus predicts his threefold denial. The atmosphere has changed since the days when Jesus sent the disciples out on missions. Then they could be almost careless and trusting. Now (in the days of the early Church's testing, as well as the literary time of Jesus' final conflict) the disciples must be prepared for battle.

Jesus goes out to the Mount of Olives to make his customary prayer. The disciples accompany him and he urges them to pray that they not enter into temptation. He asks the Father to remove the cup of his coming sufferings, if that be the Father's will. The scene is less protracted than in Mark and Matthew, where there are three such requests, and Luke has Jesus accept the Father's will easily, almost automatically. The disciples, however, fail just as dramatically as in the other synoptics, not even being able to stay awake. Judas arrives with a crowd and would betray Jesus with a kiss, but Jesus prevents this hypocrisy. There is a skirmish,[22] which Jesus quickly halts, and then the climactic lines, "When I was with you day after day in the temple, you did not lay hands on me. But this is your hour, and the power of darkness" (22:53). What the chief priests and Satan could not accomplish by day they achieve at night, when the people cannot witness. Jesus, who was no secret plotter, is dealt with in secret.

They take Jesus away to the house of the high priest and Peter trails at a distance. Three times he denies Jesus, all too fully verifying Jesus' prediction. The guards mock Jesus and beat him. Before the assembly of Jewish elders Jesus despairs of getting an honest hearing: If he tells them that he is the Christ they will not believe him. He predicts that soon he will be at the right hand of the power of God. When they ask him whether he is the Son of God he accepts this designation. They call this blasphemy and sufficient charge. No further testimony is needed. Luke's account of Jesus' appearance before the Jewish leaders therefore differs significantly from those of Mark and Matthew. Jesus does not keep silent and is the only witness. (The charge of planning to destroy the Temple is transferred to Acts 6:14 and the prosecution of Stephen.) As in the other accounts, however, Jesus is rejected for claiming to be the Son of God.

Before Pilate Jesus' Jewish accusers charge him with "perverting our nation, and forbidding us to give tribute to Caesar, and saying that he himself is Christ a king" (23:2). The charge of perversion is ironic, since Luke and all the Gospel writers see the scribes, Pharisees, and chief priests as the perverters of Israel. The charge of forbidding tribute to Caesar is, on the basis of what Luke has reported about Jesus' teaching, an out-and-out lie. The charge of making himself the Messiah, a king, is playing fast and loose with Jesus' teachings about the kingdom, so as to make it seem that he is a political threat to Rome. Jesus lets Pilate's repetition of the title "King of the Jews" stand, but even so Pilate finds no crime in him. The elders are insistent, however, that Jesus is a dangerous agitator. Pilate seeks to shift responsibility to Herod, since Jesus is a Galilean and comes under Herod's jurisdiction.

Herod is happy to see Jesus, about whom he has long been curious. Luke (who alone tells us of this interrogation) implies that this interest includes an unhealthy fascination with miracles. However, Jesus refuses to answer Herod. The chief priests accuse Jesus vehemently while Herod and his soldiers treat him with contempt and mockery. So Jesus returns to Pilate dressed in a royal robe, an intended humiliation but in Luke's eyes an ironically fitting garb. Pilate wants to chastise Jesus and release him, since neither Herod nor he has found any substance in the charge that Jesus has been perverting the people. But the chief priests, rulers, and people cry out that they want Barabbas released to them and Jesus done away with. Pilate wants to release Jesus but the crowd calls for Jesus' blood. Yet a third time Pilate tries to set Jesus free, but the crowd shouts for crucifixion and Pilate will not stand against their feverish will: "He released the man who had been thrown into prison for insurrection and murder, whom they asked for; but Jesus he delivered up to their will" (23:25). By now the irony of the situation has become bitter. With human justice grown so absent or perverted, Luke has to take comfort in a divine plan, a providential necessity.

Simon of Cyrene carries Jesus' cross and Jesus comforts some women who lament the way things have turned out. The prediction of hard times soon to come for the women's children probably refers to the destruction of 70 C.E. Jesus is crucified between two criminals and asks the Father to forgive his persecutors: They know not what they do. The soldiers cast lots for his clothing and the Jewish rulers mock him to the end. Their steadfastness in hatred is striking. They are so unmoved by justice, religious signs, and now human suffering that they must be partisans of Satan, Jesus' fierce enemy. The soldiers also mock Jesus and his claim to be King of the Jews (as the inscription over his cross reads). One of the two criminals crucified with Jesus rails at him and asks for help. The other defends Jesus as innocent and begs admission to Jesus' kingdom. Jesus promises that this day he will enjoy paradise.

The sky darkens and the curtain of the Temple tears in two. Crying out with a loud voice "Father, into thy hands I commend my spirit!" Jesus dies. The centurion standing by does not, as in Mark and Matthew, proclaim Jesus the Son of God but he does proclaim Jesus' innocence. The crowd seems to have a change of heart and returns home wailing. Jesus' acquaintances and women friends have watched his death from a distance. Joseph of Arimathea goes to Pilate and obtains permission to bury Jesus. He takes the body down from the cross, wraps it in a linen shroud, and lays it in a new rock-hewn tomb. Because the Sabbath is coming on there is little more that can be done. The women see the tomb and how Jesus' body is laid in it. They return home to prepare spices and ointments for anointing Jesus' body after the Sabbath.

Luke has paced us through Jesus' Passion rather quickly. Without departing radically from the narratives of Mark and Matthew, his account is less gruesome and more matter-of-fact. The bitter quality of Matthew's tale, which is so troubled by the Jews' rejection of Jesus, is softened by Luke's sense that all this is serving God's ends. Moreover, special touches, such as the story of the two criminals talking with Jesus, humanize Luke's account. It still reports a dreadful miscarriage of justice, but Jesus' sufferings seem less exceptional, especially since it was a society and time that routinely could be brutal.

The Resurrection Narrative (23:56b–24:53)

The women have witnessed Jesus' death and his burial in Joseph of Arimathea's new tomb. Early in the morning on the day after the Sabbath they come to the tomb with their spices to anoint the body. The stone is rolled away and inside they find no body. Two men in dazzling clothes suddenly appear. They so frighten the women that the women bow low to the ground. The men ask why they seek the living among the dead. Had

The Mourning Virgin. Hans Tilman Riemenschneider. This early sixteenth century German sculpture originally was part of an altar scene of the crucifixion. A few simple touches (downcast eyes, joined hands) suggest Mary's profound grief. *(Nelson Gallery–Atkins Museum, Kansas City, Mo. [Nelson Fund])*

Jesus not told them that he was to be delivered up, crucified, and then raised from the dead? The women recall Jesus' saying this and return to tell the eleven and the other disciples what they have witnessed. Their group includes Mary Magdalene, Joanna, and Mary the mother of James. However, the apostles do not believe their story.

Only Luke has the incident of the two disciples on the road to Emmaus. It is another tale beautifully and vividly told. Jesus appears to the two but they do not recognize him. They give him news of what has happened to Jesus of Nazareth, a prophet mighty in deed and word, whom they had hoped would prove to be the Messiah. Jesus' death has saddened the two greatly, and apparently they credit neither the story of the women about the empty tomb nor its confirmation by other disciples. Jesus upbraids them for their folly and slowness to believe the prophecies about the Messiah. (Luke's predestinarian convictions come through triumphantly in 24:26: "Was it not necessary that the Christ should suffer these things and enter into his glory?") Then Jesus explains to them all the Scriptures concerning the Christ. (This may hearken back to 9:44 and 18:34.) Still not recognizing him, they ask Jesus to stay the evening. At supper, when he blesses and breaks the bread (a clear symbolism for the eucharist), their eyes open and they finally know who he is. He vanishes from their sight and they recall how their hearts burned within them while he opened the meaning of the Scriptures. They return to Jerusalem to report their experience to the eleven and find that Jesus (now called the Lord) has also appeared to Simon Peter.

While the disciples are assembled and the joyous reality of the resurrection is sinking in, Jesus appears in their midst. They are startled and suppose him to be a spirit. He invites them to handle his body and assure themselves that he is no ghost. While they still disbelieve for joy he asks for something to eat. Then he explains that what has happened is the fulfillment of the Law of Moses, the prophets, and the psalms (all the portions of **Tanak** or the Hebrew Bible). The next chapter of the story is implied in 24:47: ". . . repentance and forgiveness of sins should be preached in his [the risen Christ's] name to all nations, beginning from Jerusalem." This is the theme of Acts. The disciples get their high station from having witnessed these decisive events of salvation history. Verse 49 alludes to the Holy Spirit as the promise of the Father that Jesus will send upon the disciples (at Pentecost). The Spirit will be power from on high that will fit them like new clothing.

They all go out to Bethany. Jesus blesses the disciples and departs, being carried (ascending) up to heaven. The disciples return to Jerusalem in great joy (the hallmark of believers in the resurrection) and go to the Temple each day to bless God. The implication is that initially they thought of the resurrection as the fulfillment of messianic prophecy, something still completely Jewish. Acts tells the story of how and why following Jesus took the disciples out of the community of Israel. Luke's final episode resumes such prior themes as the fulfillment of Scripture, offering forgiveness of sins, universality (all nations), Jerusalem (the holy center), witnesses, the Spirit, and continuity with praise to God in the Temple.

WHY WAS THIS WRITTEN?

From its literary character we can say that Luke was written to place before Christians (especially those of Gentile origin, many most likely God-fearers) an interpretation of Jesus not at variance with Mark and other Jewish Christian interpretations but complementary to them. Luke's church had sayings, traditions, instincts about Jesus and Christian life that Mark and other Jewish Christian accounts did not adequately represent. High among these treasures of Luke's church stands a memory of Jesus as gentle and sensitive. Throughout Christian history, in fact, Luke's parables have conveyed to the West a portrait of a Jesus exquisitely human. Thus Dante Alighieri, the great Italian poet, called Luke the scribe of Christ's gentleness.

Luke's portrait of Jesus, of course, connects closely with his notion of the ideal Christian. The sensitive, gentle Christ is a model for all his followers. And behind the goodness of this so-human Christ is the incalculable goodness of his God.

So, one of Luke's first ambitions or goals seems to have been to place before cultured people a Christ who would seem exquisitely human. Another clear ambition was to establish the historial significance of the Christ-event. In both his Gospel and Acts Luke is aware of the full sweep of the Roman empire. He has no temptation to interpret Jesus in purely Jewish terms. Rather he sees Jesus as bringing a message, accomplishing a mission, of universal significance. Thus he has Paul declare before King Agrippa (Acts 26:26): ". . . the king knows about these things, and to him I speak freely; for I am persuaded that none of these things has escaped his notice, for this was not done in a corner." Where some people might be inclined to think of Jerusalem as a provincial corner, and of Jesus as a purely provincial phenomenon, Luke was convinced (in good part because of the rapid spread of the early Church among the Gentiles) that the phenomenon of Jesus was the center of world history. The "these things" of Paul's speech, like the "these things" of the disciple Cleophas explaining recent history to the unknown Jesus, are the things crucial for all people's salvation. The death and resurrection of Jesus of Nazareth are the hinge on which the doors of God's treasury have swung open to make grace available to the whole world. Luke's "narrative" or report of "the things that have been accomplished among us" (1:1) is meant to furnish all people of goodwill like Theophilus a firm basis for believing that Jesus began a completely new era. As Joseph Fitzmyer has noted, Luke carefully relates Jesus to contemporary Roman, Palestinian, and Church history, making sure that no reader can miss Jesus' absolutely crucial significance.[23]

Related to this sense of Jesus' historical import is Luke's notion of the historicity of salvation. To his mind we should picture God's work to heal humanity as unfolding in three main stages. Hans Conzelmann is the scholar who has done the most to clarify this schematization.[24] In his interpretation Luke thinks of the first epoch of salvation history as extending from creation to the imprisonment of John the Baptist. This is the time when Israel is the center or carrier of God's purposes. The second epoch is the life of Jesus—more precisely, the short period from Jesus' baptism to his ascension. The third epoch is the period of the Church. In Luke's understanding the period of the Church is not the millennia of what we now know as Church history but the relatively short, troubled time from the ascension of Jesus until Jesus' return.

Textual evidences for these three epochs include Luke 16:16, which sets a border at John the Baptist. Before John was the era of the Law and the prophets. With John's coming the kingdom of God was preached. Thus John was the threshold to something new, a phenomenon partly continuous and partly discontinuous with the Law and the prophets. One could call this phenomenon the kingdom of God or the arrival and work of the one who preached the kingdom most fully, Jesus of Nazareth.

Luke 4:21 is another text suggesting this demarcation. Jesus, standing in the synagogue in Nazareth, interprets Isaiah 61:1–2 as being fulfilled "today." With his preaching has come a new era, the arrival of what the prophets had foretold and longed to see. From the viewpoint of Luke's church (slightly after 85 C.E.), the time of Jesus' ministry was *the* period of salvation. Short though the stretch from Jesus' baptism to ascension was, it accomplished the full arrival of the kingdom, most dramatically in Jesus' resurrection. The later age of the Church, for all its stresses, could be a period full of confidence. Because Jesus' time had secured the great triumph, the Church had only to hang on (and spread word of the victory) until its hero returned.

Luke 22:35–37, where Jesus at the Last Supper instructs the disciples in the changed missionary tactics that the new circumstances dictate, suggests a Church thinking of itself as under assault or pressured to be more calculating than when the Lord was physically present. One might see Jesus' eschatological discourse similarly. From Jesus' ascension to the parousia the Church will be hard pressed, suffering the final throes of a battle between evil and good, Satan and Jesus. Although the battle is basically won, painful skirmishes continue. Jesus has broken the spine of his enemy but the beast continues to thrash. Certainly the Church enjoys the power of the Spirit, but one of the Spirit's main tasks is to keep the Church mindful of the things Jesus did to recenter history, to give human time its once and for all victory. In this context, Luke tries to explain why the parousia has delayed. He also provides a framework for understanding the hostility of the synagogue to Christians after 70 C.E. Finally, his peaceful theology of history encourages Christians to develop the public, nonseditious profile of their founder.

Two other themes that have surfaced in the recent scholarly debates about Luke-Acts will have to suffice for our interpretation of the vision that impelled Luke to write. The first concerns Luke's alleged shift of focus from Jesus' sufferings to his glory. By contrast with Mark and Paul, one finds in Luke a more positive and less accusatory view of Jesus' relations with his Jewish countrymen, Jesus' death on the cross, the efficacy of Jesus' preaching, the spread of the Church, and so on. This is not to say that Luke ignores the conflicts that Jesus aroused. As early as 2:34, for example, he has the child Jesus marked for the fall and rise of many in Israel. But

Luke's Gentile background, combined with his profound faith that God's plan led Jesus every step of the way, tends to mute the violence, tragedy, and scandal that rivet the accounts of Mark (and the theology of Paul) onto Jesus' cross.

Second, Luke for some time has been described as a locus of "early Catholicism," a shorthand phrase for Church structures or institutionalism. To some biblical commentators this phrase has a sad ring, connoting a fall from a pristine simplicity and charismatic freedom to a complication and hardening toward bureaucracy. The main evidence for early Catholicism in Lukan theology comes from Acts, where the twelve play an important role and there is a concern for "overseers" (*episkopoi*) to guard the flock against perverse doctrines (22:28–30). Other evidences, however, suggest a summary of Lukan ecclesiology as showing a Church guided by the Spirit to develop an elementary organizational structure and the beginnings of a sacramental system. Only a rather prejudicial understanding of "Catholicism" need make this a bad thing, a basis for criticizing Luke as having warped the good news.

WHAT BACKGROUND DOES THIS TEXT PRESUPPOSE?

In keeping with our characterization of Luke as a Gospel most likely written for Gentile Christians (living in a Gentile milieu), we probably should look first at the sorts of assumptions such a church book would make. In the background were more than fifty years of Church experience, the most dramatic happening of which had been the opening of the Church to those outside Israel. This event receives considerable prominence in Acts and we have seen how it shaded Luke's presentation of the materials he had received from Mark and Q. Perhaps because he wanted to buttress the respectability of the Gentile churches, Luke sometimes depicted the now-open Church as triumphant, if not invincible in the Spirit.

For it is the Spirit who presides over the unfolding of Luke's three stages of salvation history. Indeed, some commentators, such as Raymond Brown, speak of the Spirit as the central actor in Luke's two-book drama:

> I have mentioned that for Luke the Spirit plays a connective role between the prophecy of Israel and the prophetic activity surrounding the birth of Jesus and the birth of the church. Indeed, the distinguishing feature of Lucan ecclesiology is the overshadowing presence of *the Spirit*. The 70 times that **pneuma**, "spirit," occurs in Acts constitute almost one-fifth of the total NT usages of that word. Some have suggested that the second Lucan book could have been more appropriately named the Acts of the Spirit rather than the Acts of the Apostles. . . . The Spirit is the main actor.[25]

Luke assumes, then, that his readers know about Jesus' career under the guidance of the Spirit and about the Spirit's inspiration of the Church in the third stage of salvation history, from Jesus' ascension to the parousia. He assumes as well that his readers know something about the spread of faith and consider it their own story. He may also have assumed the powerful action of the Spirit in local Gentile churches, on the model of the charismatic outpourings that we have seen in the Pauline churches. So whatever the presence of early Catholic features, the main Lukan emphasis is pneumatic.

Mention of Paul raises again the question of the relation between the apostle to the Gentiles and the evangelist who most had the Gentiles in view. Even if Luke was not an actual companion of Paul (our opinion at the outset of this chapter) he felt Paul's heavy influence. For it was Paul who had spearheaded the outreach of the originally Jewish Christian Church, making known to Gentiles such as Luke the good news that salvation was now offered not only to Israel but to the whole world. In fact, Paul was the main human actor in what had thus far transpired of the third phase of salvation history. We have seen that the Spirit was important for Paul, and perhaps Pauline sources encouraged Luke to spotlight the role of the Spirit in Acts. On the other hand, the Lukan ecclesiology is not as mystical as the Pauline ecclesiology that we find in Colossians and Ephesians. For Luke the accent falls not so much on the mystery of the universal Church, the whole organic Body of Christ, as on the local communities where Christian life may be worked out with considerable diversity.

Despite this stress on local churches, Luke both assumes and forwards the notion that the Christian community has four marks that have become classical: oneness, holiness, catholicity, and apostolicity. Naturally he suggests these marks more clearly in Acts than in the Gospel, since the Gospel is more concerned with the second phase of salvation history, where Jesus is more important than the Church. Still, one can see even in the Gospel an assumption that the community which Jesus initiated has its center in this one Lord and his Spirit; that the community's doctrines and sacraments nurture the holy life of the kingdom or grace; that the community is open to all people willing to accept its message and in fact is spreading rapidly throughout the world; and that the community derives from the twelve, the original witnesses of Jesus, who participated in the second period of salvation, when the most crucial things happened.

There are liabilities with assuming such an ecclesiology, especially when it becomes **triumphalistic**: certain that the Church is the unfailing carrier of God's message and life. When hard times come and the Church's virtue or missionary efforts fail, triumphalists easily become perplexed, even disillusioned. The upbeat tone of Acts might lead the incautious reader to expect the quick conversion of the whole world, which of course did not happen. On the other hand, if we recall the note of being under pressure or in the midst of an eschatological battle that Luke's Gospel struck when characterizing the third phase of salvation history, we will have to say that Luke was no simplistic triumphalist. His joy at Christ's resurrection and the outpouring of the Spirit may have led him to downplay the human deficiencies of the Church or the size of the battles that lay on the road to the parousia but it did not blind him to the need for fidelity and ongoing struggle.

Indeed, perhaps Luke assumed that sources such as Mark and Q had dealt sufficiently with Jesus' suffering, the inadequacies of the disciples, the wickedness of Jesus' enemies, and the rest and that his Church required a gospel that made the march of salvation less agonized, the message of salvation more consonant with the light and warmth that Gentiles of good-will were seeking. Similarly, Luke may have been able to assume as well known the **kenotic** Jesus of Philippians, the Son who emptied himself and took the form of a slave. Certainly Luke retains Jesus' own stress on service, poverty, and obedience to God's will. His Gospel is not triumphalistic in the sense of leading Christians to think they should be lording it over other people.

Finally, Luke may have sensed among his fellow Gentiles the need for a Jesus more humane, positive, and hopeful than the Jesus the sometimes convoluted theologies of Paul and Mark (and Matthew) provided. That would offer a partial explanation for the lovely parables peculiar to Luke, so many of which bring out Jesus' sympathy for human suffering and profound trust in the sheer goodness of God. Certainly Luke assumed that a Jesus interested in the mite of the widow, a Jesus in love with the uncondi-tional love of the prodigal father, would touch a deep chord in his readers. Like Jesus' appreciation of the birds of the air and the flowers of the field, these are qualities that might convey his message in elemental terms, basic human virtues below which one could not go. If something like that stands behind the poetry and large-heartedness of Luke's very human Christ, Luke anticipated some of the later Christian theology which spoke of grace as fulfilling human nature, healing and elevating a part of creation bruised but still very good.

WHAT LASTING SIGNIFICANCE DOES THIS TEXT HAVE?

Certainly Luke's humane portrait of Jesus qualifies his Gospel for lasting significance, but we have worked this theme sufficiently. Therefore, let us develop two other Lukan motifs whose significance would seem to extend to all times and places: predestination and prayer.

Luke does not speak much of predestination in the modern Christian theological sense, where the focus has been on trying to clarify the Pauline idea (e.g., Romans 8:29–30) that God has predestined some people to heaven and salvation and other people to damnation in hell. (See, however, Acts 13:48.) Most of Luke's allusions to God's control of history take the form of references to God's plan, or to the necessity that things unfold the way they do (especially the things that led to Jesus' Passion, death, and resurrection). Thus Hans Conzelmann notes Luke's references to God's *boule* (plan):

> A number of passages speak of God's *boule*. On two occasions the word is used to signify that Jesus' death was according to plan, and in one instance it serves to sum up the whole message. . . . the idea of the plan of God by itself is of course an old one, but now it is taken up by Christians for the purpose of argument on the point which is most pressing in the dispute with the Jews: it

can be used to explain the fate of Jesus. From this original purpose the sayings then extend to cover past and future. This can be seen in the fact, not that on the basis of this idea the broad course of future history can be constructed, but that the sayings concentrate on the one point in the future which is directly implied in the original Christological reference—the coming of the Judge. In Acts i, 7 the thought of pretermination is used specifically to prevent apocalyptic speculation. Because God alone ordains, the course of events is hidden from us, but on the other hand for the very same reason we can be certain that the plan will be carried through. We receive, not knowledge, but assurance, through the sending of the Spirit (v. 8) and through fulfilling one's calling as a witness.[26]

Whatever may be the connection between this sort of assurance and human responsibility or freedom, the fact that it is foundational to Luke's theology suggests some reflections on its general utility. One thinks, for example, of the conviction of Islam that God's will is prevailing. In a less personalist and theistic context, one thinks of the **karma** that plays such an important role in Indian thought, both Hindu and Buddhist. Each of these doctrines, in its different way, gives the believer a reason for thinking that history is not casual, that sufferings and joys subserve a bigger scheme.

Modern Western thought has tended to treat this conviction negatively, either attacking it as superstition and fatalism or simply ignoring it. But then modern Western thought, by and large, has had a hard time furnishing human beings transcendent (ultimate) reasons for living. It has tended to say that what we become is up to ourselves and there isn't much out "there" (in evolution or history) to make people of sense think that any particular use of their freedom will promote a holy cause. That, in turn, has contributed to a vacuum of ultimate significance, and one can hardly fail to note how many people, with quite varied agendas, rush in to fill this vacuum with a "cause" for living. For instance, from this comes a significant idolatry of money and the good life, an equally significant idolatry of the Bible (taken as a literal answer book), and many souls being sold to work, sports, politics, war, and other finite, unworthy divinities. Many of our contemporaries will fixate on just about anything that will let them avoid facing the crushing yet also strangely invigorating mystery that holds the meaning of both their sufferings and their joys. By laying out Jesus' fate as something planned by God, and assuring his readers that every hair of their heads, too, is numbered, Luke brings before any generation an all too relevant question: What is the pattern of the whole? Who is running the world?

A similar universalism attaches to Luke's stress on prayer, which at first blush may seem to contradict or badly fit his predeterminism. After all, if God has a plan by which things go, why should we pray to God for this or that, ask God to make this or that happen? Luke, in fact, sharpens the point of this question by making many of Jesus' instructions on prayer (see, for instance, 11:2–13; 18:1–14) bear on what Christian tradition has called "prayer of petition": asking God for specific help. Contemplative prayer, in which one simply attends to the divine mystery in love, is somewhat easier to relate to predestination than petitionary prayer. Thus the attention of a

Mary (10:39–42) to Jesus' teaching and person seems less opposed to a sense of, and surrender to, the divine plan than do specific prayers for specific happenings. The Lukan "Our Father" (11:2–4) sidesteps the hardest part of this puzzle, since its requests are rather general (and are all implicitly subject to the hallowing of God's name: whatever will serve God's purposes). In Jesus' own petitionary prayer in the garden of Gethsemane (22:42), Luke enters something on both sides of the equation: a petition for a specific favor and a surrender to God's will. The fact that the favor is not granted (Jesus has to drink the bitter cup of suffering) makes the surrender to God's will the more impressive.

One might hypothesize, then, that much of what Luke means to imply through his many references to Jesus being at prayer is an attunement to the divine will. His Jesus may well have been asking the Father to keep him on the track and to increase his docility to the Spirit. This is not to say that Jesus could not have been praising God, communing in quiet love, begging specific help, or doing any of the several other things that "prayer" rightly can denote. But we may guess that Luke's strong sense of the divine plan may well have made him think of Jesus' prayer, and the prayer of Jesus' disciples, as centrally concerned with making them better servants of God's will, more submissive ministers and worshipers. When the Lukan community remembered the story of Jesus and enacted its sacraments of initiation or the Lord's Supper, it would then in large part have been reminding itself of the frame into which believers lives had been set, asking the Spirit to guide them along ways that would bring them to the parousia safely and fruitfully.

A broader question about prayer that Luke can stimulate separates from specifically Christian forms and asks about any human being's relationship to the mystery of life, the pregnant darkness at the Beginning and Beyond of both one's own lifetime and the time of the species or the universe as a whole. Does the contemplation of this mystery have a valid, useful place in any person's life? Can one be fully human without studying the starry heavens above, the moral law within, and the rich darkness into which such study invites us? Further, is there an inclination in this natural contemplation toward acceptance, agreement, surrender? Do the ordinary people who sit by the ocean gazing at an endless horizon or contemplate a spread of vast land from a hilltop feel a movement to merge themselves with the greater whole laid before them? And, if so, how are we to evaluate this kind of surrender, to correlate it with the more historical surrender (to God's plan) that Luke and others have taught? Is there a "Que será, será" that is fulfilling rather than diminishing, adult rather than infantile? Is it a telltale sign that, despite our recent secularization, the early morning spirit still hungers to pray and commend itself into Fatherly or Motherly hands?

SUMMARY

Luke places before us a third synoptic account of Jesus' life and teachings. His most apparent sources are Mark and Q, and his most apparent goal is writing a version of the Jesus-story that will appeal to Gentile Christian churches. Antioch is a possible place of origin for this gospel and 85 C.E. is a rough date. Luke is the most skillful writer among the evangelists, and his portrait of Jesus (especially the Jesus of the parables unique to Luke, such as the good Samaritan and prodigal son) is probably the most memorable. The Gospel of Luke is the first book in a two-book project, so the full sweep of Lukan theology only emerges when one studies the doublet Luke-Acts. The most prominent structural feature of the Gospel is the journey of Jesus to Jerusalem (9:51–19:27), and a prominent theme is that what happened to Jesus was but the enactment of a providential divine plan.

The outline of Luke that we followed breaks the Gospel into eight parts: the Prologue, the Infancy Narrative, the Preparation for the Public Ministry, the Galilean Ministry, the Journey to Jerusalem, the Ministry in Jerusalem, the Passion Narrative, and the Resurrection Narrative.

The Prologue tells Theophilus, Luke's addressee, that Luke intends an orderly account of the things that have been accomplished by Jesus for salvation. The Infancy Narrative locates Jesus in the midst of Palestinian and Roman history, in keeping with Luke's nonparochial, universalist interests. Most likely the stories of the Infancy Narrative were added to the body of Luke's Gospel after the body was completed. Structurally, the Infancy Narrative provides Luke a transition from Jewish history to the time of Jesus. The main characters who appear in the first two chapters are pious Jews representing Old Testament faith at its best. Probably the most illuminating way to read the Infancy Narrative is to analyze the double dyptich of the announcement and birth stories of John and Jesus.

The Preparation for the Public Ministry first describes the work of John, Jesus' forerunner, who is the threshold between stages one and two of Lukan salvation history. At the baptism of Jesus, when the heavens open, stage two begins. The Lukan genealogy of Jesus stresses that he is the Savior of all humankind by taking his origins back to Adam. Luke arranges the three incidents of Jesus' temptation in the wilderness so as to have Jesus' victory over Satan climax on the pinnacle of the Temple. Jesus verifies that he is the Son of God by being wholly obedient to his Father, and Satan departs until their next meeting in Jerusalem at the last battle.

The Galilean Ministry shows Jesus winning both early acceptance and early suspicion. When Jesus proclaims the fulfillment of the Isaiahan vision of a golden time the reader senses that the second stage of salvation history is in full swing. Jesus' cures and authoritative teachings win much admiration, but his suggestion that the lack of faith among his countrymen will cause their privileges to pass over to the Gentiles raises great wrath. Luke's version of the conflict between Jesus and the Pharisees (important in all the Gospels) begins to heat up. The crux is Jesus' sense that the Sabbath and dietary laws are not absolute ends but relative means to a wholehearted love of God and a practical helpfulness toward one's neighbors. The Lukan woes that balance the Lukan Beatitudes put a stringent or sober shading on an otherwise gentle portrayal of Jesus. Overall, Jesus preaches a God much better than people can easily believe.

The journey to Jerusalem is dominated by Luke's conviction that Jesus was guided by the Spirit to die and rise in the holy city. On the string of this journey Luke hangs Q sayings of Jesus that we have already seen in

Matthew and striking stories from sources peculiar to himself. The disciples come in for considerable (and more positive) attention, as Jesus prepares them to spread the message of the kingdom and be prime witnesses of salvation. Jesus is often seen at prayer and stresses that the disciples should pray with great confidence.

In contrast to the Pharisees and scribes Jesus wants a thoroughly interiorized religion. His disciples are not to lose their peace of soul by worrying about worldly things. He begins to predict that the Son of Man will suffer and die, but the disciples do not understand. The parable of the great banquet conveys Luke's overriding sense that the Gentiles have come into the kingdom partly because of God's generosity and partly because the guests first invited did not generously respond. The parable of the prodigal son is perhaps Luke's highest artistic achievement. The stories of the unjust steward and the beggar Lazarus suggest the wonderful teaching flair that Jesus must have had. Zaccheus is a good symbol of Jesus' constant concern for tax collectors and other sinners, while the story of the woman who washes Jesus' feet epitomizes the sensitivity to women that Luke's Jesus often displays. The parable that concludes the journey summarizes the situation of both Jews and Christians in light of God's sending of the Christ.

The ministry in Jerusalem shows the climax of the struggle between the teachings of Jesus and the teachings of the religious establishment. Jesus is frequently at the Temple, the navel-point of his religious nation, and the religious leaders' hatred makes them resolve to do away with this new teaching authority. The Passion Narrative begins as Passover approaches, symbolizing a new exodus from Israel to the Church. At Passover Jesus eats a final meal with his disciples and inaugurates the prime Christian sacrament. The betrayal of Judas and coming denial of Peter and the rest is predicted. Jesus prays to do the Father's will and surrenders to the forces of night. The religious leaders cannot find any honest charge against Jesus, so they take his acceptance of the title Son of God as blasphemy. Pilate, representing the secular powers, finds nothing to the charge that Jesus is seditious, but he will not go against the will of the people, who want to do away with Jesus. The charge for which Jesus is killed, that he proclaimed himself King of the Jews, is both dishonest and ironic. The crowd's preference for Barabbas rather then Jesus shows the depth of their corruption. Luke's version of the Passion proper is rather brief and subdued. The dialogue between Jesus and the two thieves crucified with him is another Lukan touch of humanity. Jesus dies commending his spirit into his Father's hands. The women witness Jesus' burial in the tomb of Joseph of Arimathea.

The Resurrection Narrative makes these women the prime heralds of the resurrection, the core of the good news. Jesus appears to the two disciples on the road to Emmaus to explain the necessity of his suffering and death. The appearances to the disciples conclude with a mission to preach to all nations and Jesus ascends to the Father. The third stage of Lukan salvation history, displayed in Acts, will proceed under the guidance of the Spirit whom the heavenly Jesus has sent.

In dealing with why Luke wrote this Gospel, we stressed motives that radiate from its Gentile character. Thus it seemed likely that he wanted to present a more refined Jesus, a greater sense of Jesus' place in overall world history, and an unfolding of salvation history in three stages, the last of which made a large provision for the Gentile mission. We admitted some validity in descriptions that characterize Luke's Gospel as shifting from a Pauline or Markan theology of the cross to a theology of glory, and also as showing signs of early Catholicism. On the other hand, we found countervailing or balancing emphases within Luke-Acts itself. Among the major background assumptions that Luke makes we listed faith in the large role of the Spirit and a partially triumphalistic view of the Church. In Luke's defense we theorized that he was able to assume that Jesus' sufferings and the weaknesses of the disciples were well known, and that this may have allowed him to develop emphases he felt Gentile Christians would find more helpful. The lasting significance of Luke certainly stems from his artistic portrait of Jesus, but we also dealt with Lukan predestination and prayer. Both raise the question of how the creature relates to the creative mystery, a question seldom likely to be irrelevant.

STUDY QUESTIONS

1. What do we know about the identity of the author of Luke?
2. What are the main features of Luke's Jesus?
3. What are the main reasons for thinking that the Infancy Narratives were a later addition to Luke's Gospel?
4. What is the significance of the parallels between the infancies of John and Jesus?
5. How does Luke portray the birth of Jesus?
6. What are the implications of Jesus' claim that Isaiah 61:1–2 is fulfilled?
7. Why is Jesus the bridegroom justifying a nonascetic discipleship?
8. What is the perennial value of the Lukan woes?
9. What does Jesus' interpretation of the faith of the woman who anoints him say about the relation between sin and love?
10. Why does Luke structure so much of his Gospel in terms of Jesus' journey to Jerusalem?
11. How does the parable of the good Samaritan fit in with Luke's theme of universalism?
12. What is the basis for the Lukan Jesus' counsel to pray and never lose heart?
13. Give some indications that Luke conceives of Jesus' overall ministry as a struggle against Satan.
14. What does Jesus infer from the lilies of the field?
15. Why does Jesus tell would-be disciples that they should calculate before building their tower?
16. What is the main failing of the elder brother of the prodigal son?

17. Explain the parable that concludes the journey to Jerusalem.
18. Why does the Son of Man go through the Passion as it has been determined?
19. How does Luke's account of Jesus' trials differ from the accounts of Mark and Matthew?
20. What place do the faithful women play in Luke's version of Jesus' death and resurrection?
21. Why does Luke have the two disciples recognize Jesus in the breaking of the bread?
22. What is Luke's schematization of salvation history?
23. What does Luke assume that his readers believe about the Church?
24. What do you find to be the lasting significance of Luke's Gospel?

NOTES

1. See, however, the arguments for a Jewish-Christian Lukan church in Jacob Jervell, *Luke and the People of God* (Minneapolis: Augsburg, 1972).
2. Joseph A. Fitzmyer, *The Gospel According to Luke, Luke I–IX* (Garden City, N.Y.: Doubleday Anchor, 1981), p. 50, summarizing P. Vielhauer, "On the 'Paulinism' of Acts," in *Studies in Luke-Acts*, ed. L. Keck and J. Martyn (Nashville: Abingdon, 1966), pp. 33–50.
3. Ibid., p. 134.
4. Jerome Kodell, *The Gospel According to Luke* (Collegeville, Minn.: Liturgical Press, 1983), p. 12.
5. See R. J. Dillion, "Previewing Luke's Project from His Prologue (Luke 1:1–4)," *Catholic Biblical Quarterly* 43 (1981), 205–27.
6. See Raymond E. Brown, *The Birth of the Messiah* (Garden City, N.Y.: Doubleday, 1977), pp. 239–43.
7. See Carroll Stuhlmueller, "The Gospel According to Luke," in *The Jerome Biblical Commentary*, ed. R. Brown and others (Englewood Cliffs, N.J.: Prentice-Hall, 1968), vol. 2, p. 120.
8. Ibid.
9. See Howard C. Kee, *Jesus in History*, 2nd ed. (New York: Harcourt, Brace, Jovanovich, 1977), p. 65; Geza Vermes, *The Dead Sea Scrolls* (Philadelphia: Fortress, 1977), p. 219.
10. See Luke T. Johnson, *The Literary Function of Possessions in Luke-Acts* (Missoula, Mont.: Scholars Press, 1977).
11. See, however, R. S. Good, "Jesus, Protagonist of the Old, in Lk. 5:33–39," *Novum Testamentum* 25 (1983), 19–36.
12. See David Peter Seccombe, *Possessions and the Poor in Luke-Acts* (Leuven: Peeters, 1982).
13. See J. Dupont, "Jésus et la pécheresse (Luc 7, 36–50)," *Communautés et Liturgies* 65 (1983), 11–17.
14. L. Howard Marshall, *The Gospel of Luke* (Grand Rapids, Mich.: Eerdmans, 1978), p. 328.
15. See Norman Perrin, *Jesus and the Language of the Kingdom* (Philadelphia: Fortress, 1976), pp. 89–193.
16. See R. J. Dillon, "Early Christian Experience in the Gospel Sayings," *The Bible Today* 21 (1983), 83–88.
17. See Jerome Neyrey, "Jesus' Address to the Women of Jerusalem," *New Testament Studies* 29 (1983), 74–86.
18. Pheme Perkins, *Hearing the Parables of Jesus* (New York: Paulist, 1981), p. 96.

19. See B. B. Scott, "A Master's Praise: Luke 16, 1–8a," *Biblica* 64 (1983), 173–88.

20. See L. T. Johnson, "The Lukan Kingship Parable (Lk. 19:11–27)," *Novum Testamentum* 24 (1982), 39–59.

21. See R. Doran, "Luke 20:18: A Warrior's Boast?" *Catholic Biblical Quarterly* 45 (1983), 61–67.

22. See J. Gillman, "A Temptation to Violence: The Two Swords in Lk. 22:35–38," *Louvain Studies* 9 (1982), 142–53.

23. See Fitzmyer, *The Gospel According to Luke*, pp. 172 ff.

24. See Hans Conzelmann, *The Theology of Saint Luke* (New York: Harper & Row, 1960).

25. Raymond E. Brown, *The Churches the Apostles Left Behind* (New York: Paulist, 1984), pp. 65–66.

26. Conzelmann, *The Theology of Saint Luke*, pp. 151, 152.

8

Acts: A History
of Early Christianity

WHAT HAVE WE HERE?

Acts is the second volume of Luke's two-volume interpretation of Jesus and the Christian Church. In his Gospel Luke stressed the movement of salvation from Israel to Jesus. Where prior to Jesus the cutting edge of God's will to heal and fulfill humanity lay with such pious Jews as Zechariah and Elizabeth, with the coming of John the Baptist Jesus became the sharp focal point. Acts interprets the third era of salvation history, from the ascension of Jesus to the outreach of Jesus' community. And just as Luke's Gospel was not a detached biographical report about Jesus, so Acts is not a detached historical report about the first decades after Jesus' death. To Luke's mind the life of the Church was unfolding under the guidance of the Holy Spirit, according to God's sure plan.

New Testament scholars tend to think that Acts was written about the same time as Luke (about 90 C.E.), by the same person (an educated Gentile Christian), from the same Gentile church (perhaps in Antioch). Although Acts reports Paul's missionary journeys, the author seems unfamiliar with Paul's letters and theology, so he probably was not a close co-worker of Paul. Acts is most valuable for its general picture of the missionary life of the early Church, a picture probably more faithful to the spirit of the early missionizing than to the exact historical details.[1]

For the author of Acts clearly has been selective in composing his narrative. He has themes he wants to illustrate, theses to prove. Many of these we have already seen in his Gospel. He thinks it of paramount importance, for example, to show that the spread of the Gospel to the Gentiles was providential. The fulfillment of Israelite prophecy begun in Jesus continued in the outreach of Jesus' community. Perhaps the major question that the first generation of Jesus' followers had to answer was how they stood with regard to Judaism. Both the Gospel of Luke and Acts were a Gentile response to this question.

William Kurz has explained the situation at the origins of Luke-Acts through an interesting analogy:

> Confusion began when this subgroup of Jews, the Christians, started to admit non-Jews as fully equal Christians, without making them first become Jews. Imagine the confusion today if a Catholic parish began a prayer group for its parishoners, and soon admitted so many non-Catholics into the group that the parishoners were outnumbered. Would the group still belong to the Catholic parish? And imagine the trauma if either the parish expelled the prayer group or the group left the parish to begin its own "nondenominational church." Bitterness on both sides would most likely be deep. Certainly people would question how this new nondenominational church could claim to be a continuation of the Catholic parish from which it began. These kinds of questions were also asked about the relationship of the new subgroup from its parent Judaism, especially after it became an independent group. Luke's Gospel and Acts tried to answer some of these questions. He showed how what happened to Jesus and the early church was according to God's plan in the Old Testament. God willed both the restoration of Israel and the blessing of all nations through Christ. Acts 1–6 demonstrate especially the restoration of Israel, through the thousands of Jews who accepted the good news about Jesus and became Christians. The later parts of Acts show how the good news blessed the Gentiles.[2]

Stylistically, Acts has several peculiarities worth noting. First, the author uses a great many speeches. It was a convention of Luke's Hellenistic culture that an author rewrite source materials to make the narrative smooth and uniform. Thus what Luke puts in the mouth of Stephen, Peter, Paul, and the rest probably is a reworking of records or memories that the early Church possessed, rather than a literal rendition. In addition, some of the speeches fall into recognizable types. For instance, there are missionary speeches to potential Jewish or Gentile converts and defense speeches that Paul makes before various accusers. Besides suggesting how the early missionaries and Paul expressed themselves, these speeches allow Luke to relate his information and theological convictions to early heroes of faith.

Second, there are notable repetitions in the narrative of Acts. For example, Luke describes the conversion of Paul three times (chapters 9, 22, 26). He also repeats the story of the conversion of Cornelius and the decree of the council in Jerusalem. The obvious suggestion is that he considered these very important events—keys to the significance of the first Christian generations. Third, Luke arranges the materials in Acts to bring out parallels between the work of Jesus and the work of the apostles Peter and Paul. As the Master preached, suffered, healed the sick, and raised the dead, so did his leading apostles. This parallelism seems a rather unconcealed effort to convince the reader that the work of the apostles fits the pattern that God laid out in Jesus and so merits an admiring acceptance.

Among the main themes that Luke unfolds in Acts are the continuity between the time of Jesus and the time of the Church, the continuing fulfillment of God's plan, the triumph of Christianity despite serious obstacles, the emergence of the apostles as the new leaders of God's people, the power of the Holy Spirit, the healing that Christianity brings to body as well as spirit, and the legitimacy of the apostolate of Paul. Overall, Acts portrays Christianity as "the Way" that God has laid out through Christ and the Church, a way that runs straight from Israel to salvation for all nations.

In outline Acts breaks down as follows:

Introduction 1:1–11
The Church in Jerusalem 1:12–8:3
The Mission in Judea and Samaria 8:4–9:31
The Status of the Gentiles 9:32–15:35
Paul's Mission to the Gentiles 15:36–18:23
Paul's Third Journey 18:24–21:14
Paul in Prison 21:15–26:32
Paul in Rome 27:1–28:31[3]

Introduction (1:1–11)

The opening lines of Acts link the work with Luke's Gospel. Once again Theophilus is the addressee. Verses 1–8 summarize the narrative of the Gospel, attending especially to the days between the resurrection and

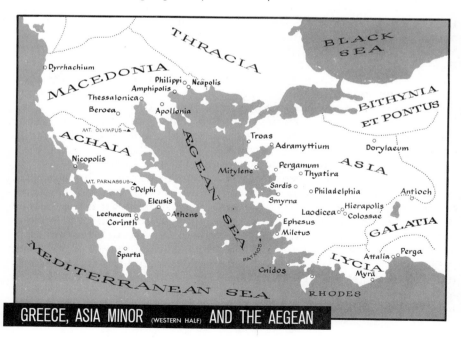

GREECE, ASIA MINOR (WESTERN HALF) AND THE AEGEAN

the ascension. Luke emphasizes that Jesus gave directions to his apostles through the Holy Spirit, appeared to them frequently during the forty days after his resurrection, and told them to wait in Jerusalem for the promise of the Father: the Holy Spirit who would baptize them into the fullness of Christian life. When the apostles ask whether the time of Israel's restoration has come, Jesus tells them that they shouldn't concern themselves with this question. The Holy Spirit will give them plenty to do witnessing to Jesus in Jerusalem, Judea, and Samaria, and to the ends of the earth.

Acts 1:9–11 fills out the brief description of the ascension given at the end of the Gospel (24:50–52). Jesus is lifted up out of the disciples' sight and enters into a cloud (a symbol of the divine presence). Two men in white robes (reminiscent of the angels at the tomb [Luke 24:4]) tell the disciples that Jesus will return from heaven (at the parousia) in a similar way. The implication is that the narrative that follows is the first chapter in the story from the ascension to the parousia.

The Church in Jerusalem (1:12–8:3)

The disciples obey Jesus' instructions and return from Mount Olivet, the site of the ascension, to Jerusalem. Their center is a place called "the upper room" and their number includes the eleven, the female disciples, Jesus' mother, and some of Jesus' relatives. Altogether they number about 120, which is the minimum number for a small sanhedrin, or Jewish council, according to the **Mishnah** or first collection of rabbinic law. Peter is the accepted spokesman and the first order of business is securing a replacement for Judas, so that the symbolic twelve will again be whole. Peter interprets Judas' betrayal of Jesus and death as the fulfillment of a prophecy inspired by the Spirit (see Psalms 69:26, 109:8; also Matthew 27:3–10). Of two candidates who have been eyewitnesses of Jesus' ministry (from his baptism by John to the ascension), Matthias is chosen by lot to take Judas' place.

Chapter 2 is famous for its description of Pentecost, the time (fifty days after Passover) when the Spirit came to Jesus' followers in full power (compare with John 20:19, 23). The experience of this coming felt like a mighty wind and tongues of fire. People felt filled with the Spirit and began to speak in tongues (**glossolalia**, although this was a more public phenomenon than Paul describes in 1 Corinthians 14). Some of this imagery appears to be derived from the Old Testament (see, for instance, Isaiah 66:15). Pentecost originally was a Jewish agricultural feast, and after the New Testament period it also called to mind Moses' reception of the Law on Mount Sinai. The ability of Jews from many different lands (the diaspora symbolizes Judaism in its most universal form) to understand the tongues may suggest a reversal of the Tower of Babel incident in Genesis 11:1–9, the ancient Jewish symbol for humanity's painful division into different language groups.

Peter, who has already made a speech to the disciples gathered in the upper room, makes another speech, defending the disciples to outsiders who were mockingly saying that all the hubbub came from drunkenness. Once again Peter interprets the event in question as a fulfillment of Old Testament prophecy, this time the verses of Joel 2:28–32, famous as a description of the messianic age when the Spirit would be given prodigally. Luke may also have in mind Jesus' first appearance in the synagogue of Nazareth (Luke 4:16–22).

Peter then preaches what some commentators have seen as a summary of Jesus' significance close to the earliest Christian kerygma or proclamation.[4] He stresses Jesus' mighty words and mighty works, death according to God's plan, and resurrection. The whole summary bears quoting for its prophetic and almost accusatory style (Peter certainly is not diplomatic in accusing his Jewish hearers of Jesus' death):

> Men of Israel, hear these words: Jesus of Nazareth, a man attested to you by God with mighty works and wonders and signs which God did through him in your midst, as you yourselves know—this Jesus, delivered up according to the definite plan and foreknowledge of God, you crucified and killed by the hands of lawless men. But God raised him up, having loosed the pangs of death, because it was not possible for him to be held by it. [2:22–24][5]

St. Peter. Bartolo da Fredi Battilori. The leader of the apostles is shown with the keys that symbolize his authority. *(Nelson Gallery–Atkins Museum, Kansas City, Mo. [Nelson Fund])*

The basic charge in the speech is that Jesus had offered more than enough reasons for believing in his message, so rejection of him had to be a sinful act. Even in his death, however, God triumphed, working the greatest sign of all: Jesus' resurrection. Peter sees the resurrection foretold in Psalms 16:8–11. The source of the Spirit that Peter's audience has just witnessed is none other than the resurrected one. The coming of the Spirit in this fashion is therefore a climactic moment in the arrival of the messianic age. Acts 2:36 is the punchline, Peter's condensation of what the whole panoply of Jesus and the Spirit means: "Let all the house of Israel therefore know assuredly that God has made him both Lord and Christ, this Jesus whom you crucified." In calling Jesus "Lord and Christ," Luke implies that Jesus is the messianic king now enthroned in heaven. (Whether at this stage of Christian reflection these titles connoted divinity is debated. Most likely a full conviction of Jesus' divinity took some time to develop.) Peter's speech may be designed as much for Christian as for Jewish consumption—to bolster the conviction of those Christians whose faith had deep roots in Israelite tradition.

The response that Peter asks of those to whom he addresses this interpretation of Jesus is repentance and baptism in Jesus' name. That can mediate a forgiveness of sins and reception of the Holy Spirit. Acts 2:39 links Jesus' achievement with prophetic hopes recorded in Isaiah 57:19 and Joel 2:32. The crowd accepts Peter's words and swells the rolls of the Christian community by some three thousand.[6] They take instruction from the apostles and celebrate with them the fellowship meal. A mood of awe prevails, as the apostles do great signs and wonders. The group practices a simple communism of goods and prays regularly.

Chapter 3 opens with a healing quite parallel to those that Jesus used to work. The cure of the lame man that Peter and John work at the Temple is "in the name of Jesus of Nazareth." Peter preaches to the crowd that gathers as word of the healing spreads. His speech is similar to his sermon in chapter 2, stressing that the cure testifies to the great significance of what happened in Jesus' death and resurrection. It is faith in Jesus' name that worked this cure. Acts 3:17 is more diplomatic than Peter was previously: "I know that you acted in ignorance, as did also your rulers. But what God foretold by the mouth of all the prophets, that his Christ should suffer, he thus fulfilled." One senses that just as Paul was greatly concerned to explain the scandal of the Messiah dying like a criminal on the cross, so were Peter and Luke. The response that Peter asks is repentance, which will eventually bring the return of Jesus at the parousia.

The raising up of an Old Testament prophet is likened to the resurrection of Jesus. Because the Jews are the children of the prophets and heirs of the covenant, they are the ones who first receive the news of the fulfillment of the messianic prophecies. (The implication is that the Gentiles will be addressed later.)

The priests, captain of the Temple, and Sadducees come on the scene in chapter 4, like a rerun of the confrontations that Jesus used to have with them in the Temple. They are annoyed that the apostles are teaching the people and proclaiming the resurrection of the dead (in the *de facto* rising of Jesus—the Sadducees did not believe in the resurrection of the dead). So they arrest Peter and John, but about five thousand people believe their message. The next day the rulers, elders, and scribes examine the apostles, asking them how they worked the cure of the lame man. Peter, "filled with the Holy Spirit," as Jesus had promised the disciples would be on such occasions (see Luke 12:11–12, 21:14–15), explains that the cure is due to Jesus, whom these leaders crucified but God raised from the dead. Peter then draws on the imagery of Psalms 118 (see Luke 20:17–18) concerning the rejected stone that has become the main element of a new construction. Acts 4:12 has been important in Christian history, helping **orthodox** believers to think that all salvation depends somehow on Jesus: "And there is salvation in no one else, for there is no other name under heaven given among men by which we must be saved."

This speech astounds the leaders hearing the case, because Peter and John are uneducated (they have not had rabbinical training). But the healed man standing there is proof that will not go away. The leaders take counsel to minimize the damage that the apostles are doing by their preaching, but Peter and John will not accept the injunction not to preach the name of Jesus. They cannot but speak of what they have experienced. There was no overt violation of the law in what the apostles had done, so the leaders have to let them go. The contrast between the faith and rectitude of the apostles and the unbelief of the leaders continues the contrast struck by all the synoptics between Jesus (and the common people who accepted him) and the scribes and Pharisees.

When the apostles return to their Christian community they interpret what has just happened to them in terms of Psalms 2. The attack was in line with the solidarity of both the Gentile and Jewish leaders against Jesus during his lifetime. So the disciples pray for the boldness and signs (healings and wonders) necessary to testify to Jesus faithfully. As if in answer to their prayer the room is shaken and they feel the inrush of the Spirit, who empowers them to speak the gospel boldly. Luke paints an idyllic portrait of the Church at this stage. It is brimming with the influence of the Spirit and all the members share a deep sense of unanimity. They possess all things in common, spend their time testifying to the resurrection of Jesus, and live in great grace. Out of the common treasury the poor receive all the care they need.

Chapter 5, perhaps by way of counterbalance, tells the troubling story of Annanias and Sapphira, who hold back from the general communism of the Christian group. Peter reads their hearts and criticizes their duplicity. They were not compelled to sell their property, but having sold it and offered it to the community they should not have held back a portion for themselves or lied about what they were doing. Both Annanias and Sapphira cannot bear this accusation and are struck dead. This rather grim tale may reflect a perfectionism owed to Qumran influence,[7] but the main point is the need for absolute honesty in a situation where the holiness of God (the outpoured Spirit) is so clear and dominant.

This sign is but one of the many wonders that the apostles work in evidence of the rightness of their gospel. Converts come in large numbers and the common people think that even the cast of Peter's shadow will cure their sick. All this traffic of the sick and those with unclean spirits to Jesus' disciples arouses the jealousy of the high priest and the Sadducees. (The stronger part played by the resurrection in Acts seems to make the Sadducees more prominent than they were in Luke's Gospel.) These leaders again arrest the apostles, but this time an angel of the Lord releases them from prison and charges them to stand in the Temple and preach the words of "this Life" (5:20) flowing from Jesus Christ. (Luke 4:18 promised release to captives.)

The high priest and his colleagues call a council to examine the apostles and are chagrined to find that the apostles have escaped in the night. They are even more chagrined to find the apostles back in the Temple preaching, and they have the guards haul the apostles away. When the high priest charges the apostles with disobedience and protests their intent to make him and the other Jewish leaders guilty of Jesus' blood, Peter responds more than boldly: "We must obey God rather than men. The God of our fathers raised Jesus whom you killed by hanging him on a tree. God exalted him at his right hand as Leader and Savior, to give repentance to Israel and forgiveness of sins. And we are witnesses to these things, and so is the Holy Spirit whom God has given to those who obey him" (5:29–32).

This speech boils with implications. First, Luke's early Christians disavow the authority of the Jewish leaders and claim direct allegiance to God. Second, Peter and the others still think of themselves as heirs of Israel, believers in the God of Abraham, Isaac, and Jacob. Third, the apostles hold the chief priest and leaders of the people responsible for Jesus' disgraceful death on the cross. Fourth, God has ratified Jesus' message and person by the resurrection, and Jesus now lives at God's right hand as the guide and healer who can give Israel the turnaround it needs to find the path to God's forgiveness. Fifth, the authority of the apostles lies in their being eyewitnesses of the dramatic events of Jesus' messiahship, especially of his death and resurrection. Sixth, the Spirit offers an inner corroboration of the apostles' witness to all who obey him (by being open and docile).

The Jewish leaders are deeply affronted by Peter's speech and want to kill the apostles. Only the wise counsel of the respected Pharisee Gamaliel keeps them from murder. Gamaliel is a man open to the Spirit, willing to judge people and movements by their fruits. (The movements that Luke has him cite, however, were almost forty years apart.) If the high priest and leaders do not use this criterion they may find themselves opposing God. This is ironic, since in Luke's eyes they have long been opposing God, but it allows him to suggest that honest Jews found the apostles intriguing and deserving of a prudent hearing. The apostles get a beating (as the innocent Jesus was scourged) and are charged not to speak in the name of Jesus, a charge they quickly disobey. They rejoice that they have been found worthy to suffer dishonor for Jesus' name (to be treated like the suffering Christ).

Chapter 6 starts to broaden the perspective from a Jewish Christian Church to a Church turning toward the diaspora.[8] Indeed, the concord of the idyllic early Church breaks on a dispute between Jewish Christians who speak Aramaic and Jewish Christians from the diaspora whose language is Greek. The dispute concerns the care of Greek-speaking widows. Dealing with its resolution allows Luke to depict how Church authority started to take shape. The twelve think that their commission is to preach the word of God. They should not be distracted by practical matters. So they pick a corps of helpers (later called "deacons") to distribute alms and oversee the practical affairs of the community. Prominent among this corps is Stephen, who works great wonders and signs. (In fact, Stephen and the others perform the same sort of tasks among the Hellenistic Christians that the twelve perform among the Jewish. Acts clearly is trying to stitch together a period when the different factions of the Church were not sure how to cooperate.) Stephen is powerful in dispute with diaspora Jews and earns their wrath. They have him brought before the Jewish council on charges much like those that confronted Jesus.

The speech Stephen makes before the council is a lengthy interpretation of Jewish history, from Abraham to Jesus. Its two main points are that Moses fulfilled the promises to Abraham and Jesus fulfilled the expectations of Moses. Indeed, Moses was to some extent rejected like Jesus and Jesus was in many ways a prophet like Moses. Stephen also challenges the very notion of the Jerusalem Temple, noting the conviction of Isaiah (Isaiah 66:1–2) that God does not dwell in a house. (This fits the anti-Temple sentiments of the Hellenists and may explain why the anti-Temple charges made against Jesus in Mark 13:56–60 do not appear in Luke's Gospel. Luke makes all this blame fall on Stephen.) The climax of Stephen's speech suggests the bitterness that broken relations between Jews and Christians had by then generated: "You stiff-necked people, uncircumcised in heart and ears, you always resist the Holy Spirit. As your fathers did, so do you. Which of the prophets did not your fathers persecute? And they killed those who announced beforehand the coming of the Righteous One, whom you have now betrayed and murdered, you who received the law as delivered by angels and did not keep it" (7:51–53).

This climax enrages the council and when Stephen claims to see the Son of Man (the resurrected Jesus) standing in heaven they stone him for blasphemy.[9] His prayer to Jesus ("receive my spirit") is like Jesus' prayer to the Father on the cross, as is his prayer for God's forgiveness of his murderers. Luke notes that a man named Saul is witnessing all this and agreeing to it. Stephen's martyrdom signals the beginning of a great persecution of the Church in Jerusalem. The disciples stay in the holy city but others scatter throughout Judea and Samaria. Saul rages in persecution of the Church, dragging believers off to prison. So the earliest period of Church history ends in trouble, as Jesus continues to be a cause of great division in Israel.

The Mission in Judea and Samaria (8:4–9:31)

When the disciples scatter from Jerusalem Philip, one of the administrative helpers chosen along with Stephen, begins a successful evangelization in Samaria—a mission to the Gentiles prior to that of Peter and Paul. His cures of the possessed and signs bring great joy to the Samaritans, many of whom Philip baptizes. He even converts a magician named Simon, who prior to Philip's coming had been influential. Peter and John follow up on Philip's mission and help the Samaritans receive the Holy Spirit. (The distinction between the Samaritans' baptism and later reception of the Spirit is one of the bases for the distinction between the Christian sacraments of baptism and confirmation. It may also suggest that not all Church leaders can mediate the Spirit.) Simon offers the apostles money, that he too might receive the Spirit, but Peter rebukes him for this evil action (from which we get the word "simony": trying to buy a spiritual gift). The cause of Simon's wrong is his being "in the gall of bitterness and in the bond of iniquity."

The apostles return to Jerusalem and Philip, instructed by an angel, heads out for another missionary adventure. On the road to Gaza he meets an Ethiopian eunuch reading the prophet Isaiah.[10] Philip explains how Isaiah 53:7–8 (part of a suffering servant song) was fulfilled in the fate of Jesus. The eunuch believes and asks to be baptized. As they finish the baptism the Spirit whisks Philip away for more preaching.

The focus now shifts to Saul, who is still persecuting the young Church. On the road to Damascus, supposedly with authority to drag any adherents of the Way (as Luke calls Christian faith) back to Jerusalem and prison (this possibility has recently been disputed),[11] Saul is thrown to the ground by a lightning bolt. A voice says to him, "Saul, Saul, why do you persecute me?" Saul asks the identity of the voice, receives the answer that it is Jesus who is speaking to him, and rises from the ground blinded. (This identification of the risen Jesus with the Church is important for the [deutero-] Pauline understanding of the organic union between the head and members of Christ's Body—see Ephesians 5.) Saul's companions, who have heard the voice but seen no one, take him to Damascus, where a Christian named Ananias receives a call from God to restore Saul's sight and mediate the Holy Spirit to him. Ananias' dialogue with the Lord lets Luke show the providential nature of Saul's conversion and the great vocation that God has in store for him. Indeed, since Luke also describes this conversion (with some variations) in Acts 22:1–16 and 26:9–18, he leaves no doubt about its significance. (Compare Paul's own references in Galatians 1:11–16.) Saul's conversion and subsequent preaching of Jesus amaze all who know of his previous persecution of the Church. Thus his conversion counts as another sign of Jesus' great power.

The Jews attempt to kill Saul, but he escapes. The Christians cannot believe that he is a genuine believer in their Way. Only the intercession of Barnabas, who must have been well regarded, wins Saul acceptance before the apostles. Saul preaches boldly in Jerusalem and his life continues to be in danger. The summary that Luke offers (Acts 9:31) shows how he regards the overall results of the dispersion from Jerusalem to a wider missionary area: "So the church throughout all Judea and Galilee and Samaria had peace and was built up; and walking in the fear of the Lord and in the comfort of the Holy Spirit it was multiplied."

The Status of the Gentiles (9:32–15:35)

Peter also travels outside Jerusalem and works cures and resuscitations. At Caesarea a man named Cornelius, a pious Gentile, has a vision instructing him to bring Peter to Caesarea. Peter himself, lodging in Joppa, has a vision in which God seems to declare all foods clean. The Spirit instructs Peter to go with Cornelius' men and Peter associates with Cornelius and other Gentiles in Caesarea. (Both Peter's vision and his going to Cornelius imply serious breaks with the Jewish laws of cleanliness.) The key line in this episode is 10:28: "But God has shown me that I should not call any man common or unclean." In principle, then, all people are fit subjects of salvation. Peter's speech in 10:34–43 interprets Jesus for the Gentiles. The outpouring of the Holy Spirit that results confirms God's approval of such an outreach beyond Israel. It is clear to Peter that if God has given the Spirit to Gentiles such as the household of Cornelius they are worthy of baptism. (The fact that the Spirit may precede baptism is significant for the later Christian theology of grace and the sacraments: God is always the prime mover.)

In chapter 11 we hear of a "circumcision party" (a group thinking that Gentile converts ought to be circumcised) within the Jerusalem church who question the wisdom of Peter's association with Gentiles. Peter explains the visions that directed him. (This allows Luke to repeat the entire proceeding and so emphasize the divine quality of the move to open the gospel to the Gentiles.) In explaining his actions Peter recalls the words of Jesus about a coming baptism with the Spirit and applies them to the Gentiles: "If then God gave the same gift to them as he gave to us when we believed in the Lord Jesus Christ, who was I that I could withstand God?" (11:17). The circumcision party cannot refute this argument and so the Jerusalem church accepts the startling notion that God has also granted the Gentiles "repentance unto life."

Whereas the first missionizing had been only to Jews, Luke now reports successful missions to Greeks. Barnabas goes out to verify these missions and brings Saul to Antioch to help him organize a Gentile church. Luke notes that the Antiochene community was the first where disciples were called "Christians." At the prophecy of Agabus about a coming famine the Antiochene Christians gather alms for the Jerusalem disciples—a first instance of the Pauline project to integrate the Gentile Christians with the Jewish Christians through the Gentiles' generous gifts of alms.

The Jerusalem church comes under the persecution of the Jewish king Herod Agrippa, the grandson of Herod the Great, who ruled at the time of Jesus' birth. (Herod Agrippa is not to be confused with Herod Antipas, the Jewish ruler to whom Pilate sent Jesus for trial.) At Passover Herod Agrippa kills James the son of Zebedee and arrests Peter, both of which actions please the Jews. Peter again is delivered from prison by an angel. He reports this wonder to the Jerusalem disciples and then goes into hiding. (Some of the symbolism attached to Peter is reminiscent of John the Baptist, suggesting that in Acts, Peter is something of a forerunner of Paul.) Herod is enraged and has the men who were supposed to be guarding Peter killed. This is typical of his evil. When people of Tyre and Sidon come before him to beg for food and make the idolatrous acclamation, "The voice of a god, and not of a man!" God smites Herod dead. This contributes to Luke's summary assessment, "But the word of God grew and multiplied" (12:24).

The church at Antioch,[12] under the inspiration of the Spirit, lays hands (a solemn act of consecration) on two leading figures, Barnabas and Saul, and sends them off for missionary work. Thus begins the first of Paul's three missionary journeys. (Interestingly, Paul never mentions in his letters any of the churches Acts reports him to have visited on the first journey.) Barnabas and Saul start by proclaiming the word of God in the Jewish synagogues of Salamis, a city of Cyprus. In 13:9 Saul is called by his Roman name Paul for the first time (sometimes a change of name signifies a change of status) and starts to take charge of the mission. His first powerful deed is to blind an evil magician named Elymas who has been obstructing the missionary work. The result is the conversion of the Roman proconsul Sergius Paulus. Paul preaches powerfully in the synagogue of Antioch of Psidia (different from Antioch of Syria). His first sermon (13:16–41) is an impressive interpretation of Jewish history as having been fulfilled in the death and resurrection of Jesus. The key lines, in view of what we know from other sources about Pauline theology, come in 13:38–39: "Let it be known to you therefore, brethren, that through this man forgiveness of sins is proclaimed to you, and by him everyone that believes is freed from everything from which you could not be freed by the law of Moses." (The picture of Paul's ministry that we get in Acts perhaps is rather idealized, in part to portray Paul and his companions as traveling philosophers. Paul's own letters suggest a greater concentration on the Gentiles and humbler circumstances.)[13]

The success of Paul and Barnabas at Antioch stirs envy and opposition among the Jews. The missionaries' response conveys Luke's convictions about the origins of Gentile Christianity: "It was necessary that the word of God should be spoken first to you [Jews]. Since you thrust it from you, and judge yourselves unworthy of eternal life, behold, we turn to the Gentiles" (13:46). Luke's interpretation of Isaiah 49:6 ("a light for the Gentiles") buttresses the Church's move to greener pastures. Luke understands the handsome harvest among the Gentiles as providential, "as many as were ordained to eternal life believed." Jewish opposition drives Paul and Barnabas from the city. They shake the dust from their feet (see Luke 10:11) and move on to nearby Iconium. There the missionaries' preaching wins over a great many listeners, both Jews and Gentiles, but once again Jews who resist the message stir up trouble. When things reach the point where Paul and Barnabas are in danger of being stoned, they flee to Lystra and Derbe, two nearby towns.

At Lystra Paul's dramatic cure of a cripple moves the Gentile crowds to liken the missionaries to the Greek gods Zeus and Hermes. The missionaries repudiate this paganism but identify the true God with the benevolent force that provides for all nations.[14] Jews from Antioch come on the scene and stone Paul. Undaunted, he and Barnabas continue their work in Derbe and then return to the towns where they have made converts. They exhort these converts to hold true to the faith, explaining that suffering for one's beliefs is the order of the day. Luke notes that the missionaries would appoint elders in every church to provide a governing structure. After working in several other towns they return to Antioch in Syria, their starting place, to report the success of their mission and God's opening of the faith to the Gentiles.

Chapter 15 shows, however, that within the Christian community as a whole the status of the Gentiles was far from clear. Representatives from the parent church near Jerusalem come to Antioch teaching that Gentile converts have to be circumcised. Paul and Barnabas dispute this and it is decided to take the question to the apostles and elders in Jerusalem. On the way to Jerusalem Paul and Barnabas gladden the churches of Phoenicia and Samaria with reports of their successes among the Gentiles.

The elders at Jerusalem welcome the missionaries and the debate over the Gentiles begins. The circumcision party wants to impose this Jewish rite of entry upon Gentile converts and make them keep the Mosaic Law. Peter finally speaks up for the equality of Gentiles with Jews in the Church, referring to his experience that God had equally given the Spirit to Gentiles. His words at the end of 15:10–11 sound very Pauline: "Now therefore why do you make trial of God by putting a yoke upon the neck of the disciples which neither our fathers nor we have been able to bear? But we believe that we shall be saved through the grace of the Lord Jesus, just as they will."

James, the brother of the Lord, who with Peter is the main authority figure of the Jerusalem church, supports Peter's views, interpreting the Gentile mission as foretold by the prophets in Amos 9:11–12, Jeremiah 12:15, and Isaiah 45:21. He would have the Gentiles admitted without requiring them to accept circumcision or the full Mosaic Law. The only requirements laid upon them would be "to abstain from the pollutions of idols and from unchastity and from what is strangled and from blood" (15:20). (This would allow table fellowship between Gentile Christians and Jewish Christians still sensitive to Mosaic kosher laws.) 1 Corinthians 8–10 suggests that Paul knew nothing of this legislation.

The Jerusalem community sends Paul and Barnabas back to Antioch with two leading Jerusalem Christians, Judas Barsabbas and Silas. They carry a letter explaining the decision of the council about the requirements for Gentile converts. The Antiochene community receives all this gladly. Judas and Silas return to Jerusalem, after strengthening the Antiochenes, and Paul and Barnabas continue to work in Antioch.

Paul's Mission to the Gentiles (15:36–18:23)

After a little while Paul becomes restless and wants to revisit the churches formed during the first missionary journey. Paul and Barnabas disagree over whether to take John Mark, a helper who had left them during the first journey. So they go off in separate directions, Paul heading to Syria and Cilicia with Silas (who either did not go back to Jerusalem or had returned to Antioch). At Derbe Paul picks up a new helper, Timothy. Because Timothy's father was Greek he has not been circumcised. Paul arranges for Timothy's circumcision, a rather strange decision in view of Paul's strong advocacy of the Gentiles' freedom. (This may be a tactical move, to block Jewish objections to Timothy, and it fits Luke's view that Paul thought of himself as sent first to the Jews of a given locale and only second to the Gentiles, after the Jews had rejected the gospel.) Paul and Timothy make a point of informing the church groups they visit of the decisions of the Jerusalem council about the requirements for Gentiles.

They go to Asia and in Troas Paul has a vision of a Macedonian beseeching him to go to Macedonia. (Throughout Luke portrays Paul's missionary decisions as flowing from the direction of the Spirit.) At 16:10 Luke starts to use "we." Traditionally this has been taken to mean that from this point Luke is reporting as an eyewitness and companion of Paul. (This plural also was a Hellenistic literary device for making travel narratives more vivid.) At Philippi in Macedonia Paul converts a woman named Lydia, a seller of purple dyed goods, who opens her house to the missionaries. When Paul casts a spirit of divination (the ability to read fortunes) out of a slave girl, the girl's masters take offense (because their livelihood is threatened), drag the missionaries before the magistrates, and accuse them of being Jews advocating practices unlawful for Romans. (The usual interpretation is that conversion to Judaism ran counter to some Roman statutes.) The missionaries are beaten and thrown into prison. While they are praying at midnight an earthquake opens the prison. The jailer, who is about to kill himself for having lost his prisoners, is so moved by the kindness of Paul and Silas that he converts, is baptized, and takes the missionaries into his own household. The next day the magistrates want to let them go but Paul wants a public apology (which, as Roman citizens, the missionaries deserved). They get the apology, visit Lydia, and depart.

At Thessalonica Paul begins in the synagogue, debating the Scriptures with the Jews and arguing that Jesus fulfilled them. Acts 17:2–4 is a familiar Lukan argument: " . . . he argued with them from the scriptures, explaining and proving that it was necessary for the Christ to suffer and to rise from the dead, and saying, 'This Jesus, whom I proclaim to you, is the Christ.'" Some Jews take this message to heart, as do some Gentiles and some leading women of the community. Other Jews are jealous and create an uproar. The charge they bring is reminiscent of the trial of Jesus: " . . . they are all acting against the decrees of Caesar, saying that there is another king, Jesus" (17:7). Paul and Silas depart for nearby Beroea, where they find a kindlier reception at the synagogue. Many Jews accept the missionaries' scriptural interpretations and believe, along with some Greeks (both upper-class women and men). However, Jewish enemies from Thessalonica arrive to make trouble, so Paul goes by sea to Athens. While awaiting Timothy and Silas he debates with both Jews and Greek philosophers. The Greeks are especially intrigued by his preaching about Jesus' resurrection.

Paul's speech at the Areopagus, a revered hillside dedicated to Ares and the site of the high Athenian religious tribunal, suggests an early

Christian interpretation of the gospel in non-Jewish terms.[15] (The reference to the unknown God is rich, for it could apply in any cultural area, Hindu as well as Greek.) The crowd follows with interest until Paul reaches the resurrection. This is too much for most of them to bear (their lack of seriousness has been hinted at in 17:21: "Now all the Athenians and the foreigners who lived there spent their time in nothing except telling or hearing something new"). However, Paul wins some converts, including a man named Dionysius the Areopagite (whom later Christian history mistakenly made the author of some influential mystical treatises). Some commentators on Pauline theology think the speech on the Aeropagus a significant failure: Because Paul was unable to achieve much by interpreting the Christian message in neutral or nonbiblical terms, he resolved thenceforth to preach nothing but Christ crucified (see 1 Corinthians 2:2). (Clearly, however, this meant no abatement of vigorous intellectual work, as Romans eloquently testifies.)

Chapter 18 finds Paul in Corinth, working as a tentmaker and enjoying the company of Aquila and Priscilla, "Jews" (most likely, Jewish Christians) forced to leave Rome because of their bloodline. The edict of Claudius suggests that we should date this stay of Paul in Corinth shortly after 49 C.E. Silas and Timothy arrive to find Paul at his usual post, preaching Christ to the Corinthian Jews in their synagogue. When these Jews reject his gospel he gives up on them and heads for the Gentiles. Paul then has a vision strengthening him in his resolve to keep preaching that Jesus is the Christ. He stays eighteen months in Corinth, until the local Jews drag him before the civil authorities. The charge is not clear. They may be repeating the accusation raised in Philippi (16:21) that Paul is trying to convert Roman citizens away from Roman gods. The stronger likelihood, however, is that they want the civil authorities to stop Paul from enticing Jews to Christianity. The magistrate Gallio dismisses the matter as an intra-Jewish affair. Paul departs with Priscilla and Aquila for Syria, cuts his hair in connection with a vow (content unknown), and works for a while in Ephesus. Finally he goes back to Antioch, completing the circle of the second missionary journey.

Paul's Third Journey (18:24–21:14)

The third journey begins from Antioch in Syria and first takes Paul through Galatia. A Jewish convert named Apollos is helped by Priscilla and Aquila in Ephesus and turns his powerful talents to the Christian cause. Paul comes to Ephesus and finds disciples who, like Apollos, had known only the baptism of John. Paul has them baptized in the name of Jesus and lays hands on them, and they receive the Holy Spirit. In Ephesus Paul works in the synagogue but after three months of frustration gives up. In a hall apart from the synagogue he preaches to both Jews and Gentiles. God works extraordinary miracles through Paul: healings and exorcisms. Indeed, even unbelieving exorcists come to use the name of Jesus (see Luke 9:49–50), although not without being harmed by the evil spirits. This testimony to Jesus' power helps purify the region of magicians and pagan practitioners. As Luke says in another of his many summary lines, "So the word of the Lord grew and prevailed mightily" (Acts 19:20).

Paul next feels inspired to head for Jerusalem, with the hope of going on to Rome. Before that the Ephesian community of the Way suffers more turmoil. The local silversmiths, disturbed that the Christian teachings against idols are ruining their business, drum up a patriotic fervor against the Ephesian Christians and for the goddess Artemis. (The leading silversmith, Demetrius, specializes in statues of Artemis.) The town clerk finally quiets the uproar, telling the pagan Ephesians to take their grievances to the regular town meeting.

Paul departs for Macedonia and Luke reports that they "sailed away from Philippi after the days of Unleavened Bread" (20:6). In Troas Paul meets with the local Christians for the Sunday eucharist and preaches a long sermon. A young man named Eutychus falls asleep and tumbles out of the window of the third-floor assembly room. Paul raises him from apparent death. Paul's band sails from Troas and arrives at Miletus. Since Paul wants to press on for Jerusalem he determines to bypass Ephesus. Yet he also wants to encourage the Ephesian Christians, so he calls to himself some elders of the Ephesian church. His speech in 20:18–35 is an apologetic or self-defense, justifying his missionary ways.

A note of premonition runs through the speech, as though Paul suspects that something bad will happen to him in Jerusalem and is driven to reflect on his missionary career to date. Especially striking is his solemn testimony that he has fulfilled his responsibilities to the Ephesians: "Therefore I testify to you this day that I am innocent of the blood of all of you, for I did not shrink from declaring to you the whole counsel of God" (20:26–27). Paul warns against fierce wolves (perhaps Gnostics) coming to ravage their flock (see Mark 13:22, Matthew 7:15). He notes pointedly that he alway supported himself by his own manual labor. Acts 20:35 is interesting for both its own sentiments and (the Lukan) Paul's quotation of Jesus (a rare occurrence): "In all things I have shown you that by so toiling one must help the weak, remembering the words of the Lord Jesus, how he said, 'It is more blessed to give than to receive.'" (This saying is not recorded in the Gospels.) The Ephesians weep at Paul's prediction that they will never see him again. (The Lukan theme of predestination exerts itself once more).

Paul's troop departs by sea and after several stops reaches Caesaria. There they stay with Philip, the evangelist we met in chapter 8. The prophet Agabus (see 11:28) predicts that the Jews at Jerusalem will deliver Paul into the hands of the Gentiles (as Jesus was delivered up). Paul refuses to be deterred from going to Jerusalem, and Luke concludes the third missionary circuit with the words, "And when he would not be persuaded, we ceased and said, 'The will of the Lord be done'" (21:14).

Paul in Prison (21:15–26:32)

Paul's group proceeds to Jerusalem and is received by James and the elders of the Jerusalem church. Paul reports how the mission to the Gentiles has gone. The Jerusalem Christians hear this report gladly but mention that many Jews, too, have become Christians, and that these converts remain zealous for the Mosaic Law. To allay the fears of such Jewish converts (they have been told that Paul tells diaspora Jewish converts not to circumcise their sons or obey the Mosaic Law), the elders suggest a Jewish purification rite. This would demonstrate that Paul still observes the Law. The elders then reaffirm their previous position and letter (see 15:23–29) concerning Gentile converts, emphasizing the abstinences that would make the Gentiles fit table fellows for observant Jewish Christians. We are told that Paul takes their advice and performs the purification rite, although that seems uncharacteristically docile for one with such strong convictions about the freedom Gentiles should have. (See Galatians 1–2.)

Despite this, Jews who see Paul in the Temple (recall Jesus' public ministry in Luke 20–21) clamor about his nefarious teachings and falsely accuse him of bringing Gentiles into the Temple (a capital offense). The ensuing riot gets the Roman militia involved. They rescue Paul from the Jewish mob, which is beating him up. Paul is arrested by the Romans, while the mob cries for his blood (see Luke 23:28 for the parallel with Jesus). At the barracks Paul wins permission of the tribune to speak to the people. His speech is another apologia, this time to his Jewish brethren. The autobiographical highlights include his training under Gamaliel (which some scholars now question),[16] his persecution of the Way, and his dramatic experience on the road to Damascus.

Acts 22:14–15 gives Luke's exegesis of Paul's vocation: "The God of our fathers appointed you to know his will, to see the Just One [Jesus] and to hear a voice from his mouth; for you will be a witness for him to all men of what you have seen and heard.'" Acts 22:17–21 gives us new information about Paul's inspiration by God to go to the Gentiles. The Jewish crowd cannot bear the notion that their God has welcomed the Gentiles and again call for Paul to be done away with. As the soldiers are about to scourge Paul he informs them that he is by birth a Roman citizen, so they fear to do him harm.

Turned over to the chief priests and Sanhedrin, Paul, like Jesus, Peter, and Stephen before him, makes a strong impression. Luke stresses Paul's clean conscience and the council's violation of its own laws. (The innocence of the Christians brought before the council, and the council's own illegalities, is a regular early Christian theme.) Paul foments a dissension between the Pharisees and the Sadducees and once again has to be protected from the Jews by Roman soldiers. (Luke puts into the mouth of some Pharisaic scribes, "We find nothing wrong in this man. What if a spirit or an angel spoke to him?" [23:9]. The parallel with the declarations of Jesus' innocence in Luke 23 is clear.) In the barracks Paul receives an encouragement from God and a prediction that he shall also bear witness in Rome.

Luke reports a conspiracy among the Jerusalem Jews to secure Paul's death. Paul learns of this plot through his nephew and has the nephew inform the Romans. The Roman tribune arranges safe passage for Paul to the governor Felix in Caesaria. The covering letter stresses Paul's innocence of any offenses against Roman law.[17] (Paul's Roman citizenship is the reason for all this careful treatment.) The accusations that the Jerusalem Jews bring against Paul before Felix emphasize the agitation he has aroused among Jews and call him a ringleader of the sect called Nazarenes (followers of Jesus of Nazareth). The Jewish tactic, then, is the same as it was with Jesus: trying to prove menace to the public peace.

Paul denies that he has been causing trouble in Jerusalem but fully admits being a follower of Jesus, emphasizing that this Way entails worshiping "the God of our fathers, believing everything laid down by the law or written in the prophets . . ." (24:14). Felix postpones a decision and keeps Paul in loose custody. Somewhat like Herod Antipas with Jesus, Felix is both intrigued by Paul and troubled (in his bad conscience) by Paul's gospel. He also hopes for a bribe. His successor, Festus, detains Paul as a favor to the Jews. Another trial takes place at Caesaria, and once again the Jews cannot prove their accusations against Paul. (In all these trials, Paul is made parallel to Jesus.) Festus wants to turn Paul over to a Jewish tribunal in Jerusalem, but Paul insists on a Roman hearing. Festus sees this as a way out and decides to ship Paul to the emperor in Rome.

Marcus Julius Agrippa, king of Judea, comes to visit Festus and Festus discusses Paul's case. Festus' interpretation is that Paul has done nothing contrary to Roman law but rather is the focus of an intra-Jewish dispute ("about one Jesus, who was dead, but whom Paul asserted to be alive" [25:19]). Agrippa asks to hear Paul himself. The rationale is that this will help Festus describe the case to the Roman emperor. So yet once more Paul must defend himself. Stressing his Pharisaic upbringing, he interprets his plight as the result of his taking seriously God's promises to the Jews. A note of impatience or frustration breaks out in 26:8: "Why is it thought incredible by any of you that God raises the dead?" Paul reviews his previous persecution of the Christians and his conversion experience on the road to Damascus. (Luke inserts a new element in 26:14: "I heard a voice saying to me in the Hebrew language, Saul, Saul . . . It hurts you to kick against the goad.'" Since Jesus would have been speaking Aramaic, and Paul's first language was Greek, the story seems somewhat contrived.) Luke also expands upon his previous descriptions of Paul's vocation to the Gentiles: "I send you to open their eyes, that they may turn from darkness to light and from the power of Satan to God, that they may receive forgiveness of sins and a place among those who are sanctified by faith in me" (26:17–18). Paul explains his gospel as proclaiming the fulfillment of the prophets and Moses: the Christ must suffer, rise from the dead, and proclaim light to both Jews and Gentiles.

Festus is impressed by Paul's learning but finds his talk of visions and the resurrection mad. In reply Paul claims that he is speaking sober truths that King Agrippa surely knows about, "for I am persuaded that none of these things has escaped his notice, for this was not done in a corner" (26:26). (As we noted in discussing Luke's Gospel, the author goes out of his way to stress the universal historical implications of the Christ-event.) Agrippa puts off Paul's speech with the slightly smiling, slightly disdainful note that Paul must not expect to make him a Christian in one preaching.

When Agrippa and Festus consult, Agrippa gives the opinion that had Paul not appealed to Caesar they could have set him free. He has done nothing deserving of death or imprisonment (note the parallel with Luke 23:15).

Paul in Rome (27:1–28:31)

The conclusion of the Acts of the Apostles takes Paul to Rome, which for Luke is the center of the world. The final scenes show the apostle to the Gentiles bringing the gospel to the heart of the Gentile empire. The narrative voice for the final voyage is again Luke's "we." At Sidon the centurion Julius, who is in charge of the prisoners, allows Paul to meet with some friends. At Myria the centurion finds an Alexandrian ship bound for Italy and puts them on board. Their progress is slow, the season turns unfavorable, and Paul predicts a disaster if they continue. Against Paul's advice they forge ahead, and near Crete they suffer a serious storm. Paul has another premonition and predicts the loss of the ship but no loss of life. He is convinced that he will make it to Rome to stand before Caesar. The sailors are sufficiently afraid of the hazards to want to abandon ship but the soldiers prevent them by cutting the lifeboats adrift.

Paul urges the ship's company to break their fast (undertaken because of the rough conditions?) and promises that they will lose not a hair of their heads. His own eating in 27:35 has overtones of a eucharistic ritual. The vessel runs aground and the soldiers plan to kill the prisoners, lest they swim to freedom. But the centurion saves Paul. They get ashore to the island of Malta where the natives give them a kindly welcome. Gathering sticks for a fire, Paul is bitten by a poisonous snake. The natives interpret this bad luck as a sign that Paul is a serious criminal. However, when Paul suffers no harm they change their minds and consider him a god. Paul heals the father of the island chief, and then many other island sick who are brought to him. When they set sail again the Maltese load them with provisions and gifts.

On the last part of the voyage to Rome they stop in Puteoli and converse with some fellow Christians. In the capital the Roman brethren meet Paul at the Forum of Appius. The officials allow Paul to stay by himself with only a single guard. These relaxed conditions allow Paul to resume his regular missionary procedure.[18] He calls together local Jewish leaders and explains how he happens to be in Rome. His summary explanation in 28:20 is eloquent: "For this reason therefore I have asked to see you and speak with you, since it is because of the hope of Israel that I am bound with this chain." The Jewish leaders reply that they have heard nothing about the particulars of Paul's case, and they seem fair-minded, wanting to hear from Paul about the Christian sect that has been making such a stir. When they return to hear Paul preach he speaks about the kingdom of God and tries to convince them that Jesus is the fulfillment of Moses and the prophets. Some accept what Paul has to say but others disbelieve—a rather typical result.

Paul's parting shot to the Roman Jews seems almost nasty and may serve Luke's summarizing purposes more than historical accuracy. The

Holy Spirit is credited with having predicted the Jews' rejection of the Christian gospel through the prophet Isaiah (Isaiah 6:9–10). A certain mystery plays through the text: How can people have eyes and not see, have ears and not hear? To Luke it is both the mystery of divine providence and the mystery of conscience, the strange warfare of sin and grace. Acts 28:28 is the sort of Lukan summary we have come to expect: "Let it be known to you then that this salvation of God has been sent to the Gentiles; they will listen." Luke's final picture shows Paul continuing his preaching ministry in Rome. That he could teach about the Lord Jesus Christ "quite openly and unhindered" says that the center of the world showed itself cordial to the gospel and accepting of the Holy Spirit's intentions. On this high note Luke is content to end.

WHY WAS THIS WRITTEN?

The purpose of Acts cannot be separated from the audience that the author had in mind. Unfortunately, scholarly opinion is divided on this question. Advancing the opinion that Luke wrote for Gentile Christians in both the Gospel and Acts is Joseph A. Fitzmyer, author of the impressive Anchor Bible commentary on Luke.[19] Arguing for an audience of Jewish Christians is Donald Juel, who draws on recent scholarship that places considerable emphasis on the war with Rome that climaxed with the destruction of the Jerusalem Temple and slaughter of many Jews in 70 C.E.:

> When read in the context of this history, Luke-Acts, like Matthew and John, seems to make most sense as a pastoral word addressed to Jewish Christians. For such people, cut adrift from their heritage, the two-volume history would have offered a renewed sense of their identity as God's people. In such a setting, the case Luke set out to argue would not have been the legitimacy of a sense of newness and discontinuity with the past, but rather the appropriateness of the claim of messianists [people calling Jesus the Christ] to represent the true Israel. Of course life for Jews who believed in Jesus had changed drastically from the early days by the time Luke wrote. Jerusalem was no longer the center of the earth; Gentiles were flooding into the church; relations with Jews were troubled. In the face of all contrary evidence, however, Luke-Acts argued that the history of Jesus and his followers belonged within the history of God's people, Israel. From beginning to end, the story is about divine promises fulfilled—about what has been "accomplished among us" (Luke 1:1). Luke's history is about continuity. As he viewed it, human events were the arena not of blind and capricious forces but of God's providence. "Necessity" was a category basic to his view of history. What had occurred, he insisted, had been ordained by a God whose primary attribute was faithfulness to promises.[20]

What are we to make of this situation (by no means unique in current New Testament studies) in which two competent scholars read the same data quite differently? Probably the safest approach is to study whether the differences are irreconcilable and to note the main data each argument stresses.

Among the principal factors inclining Fitzmyer to judge that Luke-Acts was written for a predominantly Gentile Christian audience are Luke's concern to connect his two-volume work with a Greco-Roman literary tradition (especially in the Gospel Prologue), his dedication of the work to a person bearing a Greek name, and his interest in relating to non-Jews the salvation promised in the Old Testament. Further factors include Luke's filtering from his sources (Mark and Q) predominantly Jewish preoccupations (e.g., questions of ritual purity lessen). Similarly, Luke's redaction of Jesus' sayings seems better suited to a Hellenistic setting than to a Jewish Palestinian one. Luke often substitutes Greek names or titles for Hebrew ones. He traces Jesus' genealogy back to Adam. Most of his Old Testament quotations use the Greek (Septuagint) translation, and he tends to refer to Palestine as Judea, which suggests that he had a non-Palestinian audience in mind.

What then about Juel's case for a Jewish Christian audience? Certainly it makes sense to reason that all people of Jewish background, those retaining a traditional religious loyalty to Israel and those modifying their loyalty in light of Jesus, would have sought shoring up after the Roman war. In light of what we have seen Luke do with the speeches of Paul and Peter, it also makes sense to claim that he was much concerned to show how Jesus was the fulfillment of messianic prophecy. Finally, it seems indisputable that Luke interpreted history (the ancient history of Israel, the history of Jesus, and the then-current times after Jesus) as proceeding according to the divine will, with a certain necessity. The nub of the controversy therefore becomes whether Luke's main stress is as Juel suggests in the key sentence: "In such a setting, the case Luke set out to argue would not have been the legitimacy of a sense of newness and discontinuity with the past, but rather the appropriateness of the claim of messianists to represent the true Israel."

Several things may be said about this sentence. First, the conditional verb "would" depends on the prior "in such a setting," and "in such a setting" is somewhat extrinsic to the internal evidence of Luke-Acts itself. Almost all Christians were affected by the Roman-Jewish war, but probably Jewish Christians more than Gentile Christians. If Luke wrote for Jewish Christians, the lines that show both the divine necessity of what happened to Jesus and the early church and the fulfillment of Old Testament prophecy would have been a consolation. Whether these themes alone suffice to designate a Jewish Christian audience, however, is debatable. In view of internal evidence (such as Fitzmyer's) that favors a Gentile Christian audience, their sufficiency becomes quite questionable.

Second, there is the related question of just where Luke comes down (especially in Acts) in his interpretations of Jewish prophecy. Certainly a large theme is that Jewish unbelief was the reason for passing on to the Gentiles. Consider again 28:28, the very last summary. The quotation from Isaiah underlines the hardness of Jewish hearts—a theme of discontinuity. The sentence, "Let it be known to you then that this salvation of God has been sent to the Gentiles; they will listen," is another loud vote for discontinuity. Paul has passed from Jerusalem to Rome, trading the center of Jewish history for the center of Gentile history. At both his beginning (the Gospel prologue) and his end, therefore, Luke seems more concerned with bolstering Gentile Christians than Jewish ones.

Third, there is a compromise that may accommodate much of Juel's instinct. This compromise supposes that Luke wanted to support all Christians willing to consider the events of salvation history providential, but especially the God-fearers who needed explanations in terms of the Jewish traditions they had come to revere. To Jewish Christians who spoke Hebrew (or Aramaic) and lived in a Palestinian cultural setting, Luke would offer the somewhat bitter but nonetheless salutary news that the opening of the Church to the Gentiles was the fulfillment of Israel's mission to be a light. Further, he would make Paul regularly go first to the Jews and would show that the Jerusalem church, led by Peter and James, was the most honored center. That church permitted Jewish converts to retain much of their Mosaic loyalty, and it asked that Gentile converts keep a minimum of the Law so as not to be polluting to scrupulous Jewish Christians.

To Jewish converts of the diaspora, whose main language was Greek and whose cultural setting was Hellenistic, Luke would offer a somewhat broader set of comforts. First, he would imply that they were natural mediators between Palestinian Jewish Christians and Gentile Christians. On the one hand, they had grown up as Jews and knew Israelite religion from the inside. The prophecies that Jesus fulfilled were their own. On the other hand, they knew the Hellenistic world at first hand and could appreciate what the gospel could mean to people of goodwill outside the house of Israel. Second, Greek-speaking Jews probably would have been glad to have it suggested that the transition from a Jerusalem-centered Church to a multiethnic Church with important centers at Antioch in Syria, Corinth, Ephesus, and even the imperial capital of Rome was providential. The Spirit that Luke so stresses had shown itself active in the formation of these extra-Palestinian centers. The Pentecostal scene of a polyglot gathering of Israelite children united under the Spirit could show Greek-speaking, diaspora Jewish Christians a mirror image of themselves.

To Gentile Christians, however, Luke would still offer the richest consolations. For certainly their entry into the Church is the most dramatic lesson being read out in Acts. True enough, Acts interprets this opening of salvation to the Gentiles as the fulfillment of the Hebrew Scriptures. The story is by no means one of complete discontinuity. But the story definitely has discontinuous elements, breaks that signify a new chapter or part. In terms of the historical scheme we took from Conzelmann for Luke-Acts, the Gentile Christians could see themselves as the leading actors in the third and current phase. They would be the successors to both Israel and Jesus' contemporaries, as directly connected to God as what had happened of old with Abraham or recently with Jesus himself.

Moreover, it is likely that the implication would be that the most decisive action of salvation had passed to them. For Luke to end with Paul in Rome is to stress the new Gentile fields ripe for the harvest. To be sure, we know that the Church that actually developed in Rome probably was more Jewish, and perhaps more Petrine, than Gentile and Pauline. But here we are speaking about Luke's literary intentions. Overall, these come down on the side of Gentile Christianity. Certainly he shows the Gentiles how much they owe to Israel, but he also shows them how the Spirit inspired the Church to reach out to the nations beyond Israel—partly because of God's own good pleasure and partly because of Israel's rejection of the gospel. Luke's Gospel showed Jesus predicting that God's help would turn to the Gentiles (see 4:25–28, for instance); Acts shows the fulfillment of that prediction.

Finally, where does this leave Juel's stress on the devastating effects of the Roman war? As a factor to be taken seriously and probed, but not as the factor that should dominate one's whole interpretation of Luke-Acts. If we knew from independent sources that Luke himself was a Jewish Christian who had lived through the war and its aftermath, or whose church had lain directly in the line of fire, we might cast Luke-Acts as a support for similar Christians and see whether such a casting brought the work a greater coherence or integrity. But the strongest suggestions in Acts itself are that Luke considered Antioch in Syria his center (note that all three of Paul's journeys originate in Antioch). The Christian church at Antioch certainly felt shock waves from the Roman war, but it could not have been as directly affected as the Palestinian churches. Its population in all likelihood was much more Gentile than that of the Palestinian churches, and its need for an interpretation of the disastrous recent events as continuous with Old Testament prophecy considerably less pressing.

So, the likelihood is that Luke rather deliberately balanced a theme of continuity with discontinuity, to show all his readers (but especially the Gentile majority) that what had happened recently had taken the story of Israel through Jesus to a new phase. In this new phase the Law merits some respect but is by no means as pressing as it was in the Israelite phase, or as it would be if Luke's church had a Jewish Christian majority. The future that Luke anticipates for the Church has a Gentile cutting edge, so dropping circumcision and declaring all people eligible for salvation were the (relatively discontinuous) decisions of most moment.

WHAT BACKGROUND DOES THIS TEXT PRESUPPOSE?

In probing Luke's motivation we have suggested much of the background necessary for grasping the nuances of Acts. Whether or not one agrees with the emphases we have placed, it is clear that Luke presupposed a new Church situation in which one had to explain the increasing importance of Gentile converts. So, for instance, the second half of Acts concentrates on the work of Paul, the apostle most responsible for the Church's accommodation to the Gentiles. The depiction of Peter in the first half of Acts runs in the same direction: Peter himself believed that the Spirit had been given to Gentiles of goodwill and so realized that the Church could hardly refuse such Gentiles baptism. The decision of the Jerusalem council was a compromise, a vote to honor both Jewish and Gentile rights, but the constant theme of Acts that many Jews would not accept the apostles' preaching of Jesus' messiahship leaves little doubt where Luke thought the Church's future lay. The basic background presupposed, then, is the somewhat complex overall situation of the Church around 90–95 C.E. Luke expected his readers to know about both Peter and Paul, both Jerusalem and Rome, both the rights of the Spirit to breathe where it would and the rights of Jewish Christians to have their heritage respected.

Richard J. Cassidy has recently argued for a diverse audience and set of background presuppositions like those we have proposed. In addition, he has stressed the political dimension of Luke's enterprise. For Cassidy, Luke's Jesus was a serious threat to the socioeconomic arrangements of his day. If so, Luke presupposed in his readers both a memory of Jesus' radicalism and a deep sense that the social arrangements of the Jewish and Hellenistic establishments ought to change. Consider, for example, Luke's description of Jesus as a social critic:

> In his teaching and ministry, Jesus in Luke espouses a concern for persons and groups from all social levels and backgrounds, but especially for the poor and the sick, for women and Gentiles. In some instances Jesus expressed this concern in ways not particularly disruptive of existing social patterns, and not particularly challenging to those who benefited from them; but more often than not he taught and acted in such a way as to explicitly or implicitly call for radical modifications in these patterns. This is especially evident with respect to the use of material possessions. Luke includes many passages that pertain to this theme of Jesus' ministry; considered together, they form a truly striking picture. As we have seen, Luke indicates that Jesus adopted an extremely strong position against surplus possessions. Jesus himself lived simply and sparingly and he praised others like Zaccheus when they took steps to do likewise. However, even more important (in terms of its disruptive effect) Jesus stringently criticized the rich for accumulating possessions that they did not need instead of sharing their goods with the poor and the hungry.[21]

On the other hand, Luke's editorial changes of traditional materials suggest that in his community there were well-to-do people joining the Church—perhaps again the God-fearers, who generally were of good social status.[22]

To this teaching of Jesus we may add some of Luke's emphases in Acts. We have seen that Luke paints the earliest Christian community gathered in the upper room as an egalitarian group (under the leadership of Peter and the twelve) who shared material possessions. Before long the community took steps to care for its less fortunate members, such as widows, by developing the ministerial responsibilities (diaconate) of Stephen, Philip, and the other five. The mortal punishment visited on Ananias and Sapphira, whatever the actual historical occurrence, functions for Luke as a dire symbol of what happens to the greedy and vow breaking. In the second half of Acts, where we follow the missionary adventures of Paul, the stress is on mobility, being stripped and free to go wherever the Spirit sends one. The Paul of Acts, like the Paul of the Epistles, emphasizes his self-support by manual labor. He is content to be in prison, if the service of God requires it, and shows no sign of considering food, clothing, or material possessions of much account.

Another theme of Acts along this line is almsgiving. We noted the response of the Antiochene Christians to the prophecy of Agabus that a great famine was coming: "And the disciples determined, every one according to his ability, to send relief to the brethren who lived in Judea; and they did so, sending it to the elders by the hand of Barnabas and Saul" (11:29–30). Walter Pilgrim has sketched the Old Testament background that Luke could presuppose in presenting such a response, and then goes on to suggest how this incident carries the seeds of a solution to the problem of inequalities in the global distribution of goods:

> Another economic crisis occurs during a time of worldwide famine. According to Luke's account, Christian prophets came from Jerusalem to Antioch, and one of them, Agabus, who reappears in Chapter 20, predicted a coming famine throughout the world. Luke adds parenthetically that this famine occurred during the reign of the Emperor Claudius (A.D. 41–54), a fact verified by other sources. Palestine was especially vulnerable and hard hit, so that it must have suffered much. Therefore, recognizing the great need of the community in Judea, the church in Antioch of Syria made provisions to share its greater abundance with its suffering neighbors. Thus the first "world-relief" program in the church's history was begun. The program itself is briefly described in vv. 29–30. Two principles emerge from this description. The first is that of giving relief according to their ability. That is, the aid was given in proportion to the wealth of the giver. Thus Luke recognizes differences between both the wealth of the members and their ability to give. Without becoming legalistic, one could say that the earlier principle of "sharing according to need" in Acts 2 and 4 has a parallel principle of "giving according to ability." . . . The second principle found in this text is that of Christian solidarity in need. The whole church stands together in a solidarity of Christian love for one another. One community of believers in one nation should come to the aid of believers in other lands.[23]

A central part of the picture of Jesus and early Christianity that Luke presupposed therefore was great freedom regarding material goods. One could not serve God and mammon. Material things, money and possessions, were only means to love of God and love of neighbor. This could be a radical, potentially explosive doctrine in the first century, and it certainly has proven explosive in subsequent centuries. Whatever one thinks of the "socialist phenomenon" analyzed critically by Igor Shafarevich, Aleksandr Solzhenitsyn, and others who have suffered from Marxist-Leninism,[24] the historical fact is that the communism of the primitive Christian community was a powerful influence down the ages.

On the question of Jesus' political threat to Roman authorities and Luke's overall positioning of the Church in respect to Rome, the scholarly authorities divide. Cassidy thinks that Jesus was at least a potential threat because he refused deference to and cooperation with the political authorities responsible for maintaining the (unjust) status quo.[25] Paul Walaskay thinks that Luke-Acts constitutes a sizable apology for the empire:

> Where he found anti-Roman innuendos in his sources he has done his best to neutralize such material and to emphasize the positive aspects of Roman involvement in the history of the church. . . . But Luke did more than meet anti-Roman sentiment, anxiety over a delayed parousia, misrepresentation of Christian loyalties, and a potential conflict over the notion of power and authority. Luke was a theologian who, like his contemporaries, could not divorce theology from history. If God was truly at work in the world, then he did his work not only through the church but through the secular realm as well. God has called both church and state into his service. The state may be ignorant of his dual ordination, but the church must not be. Therefore, Luke makes certain that the church is fully cognizant of the divine calling given to both institutions. The empire which has exonerated Jesus and saved Paul can continue to sustain the work of the church through its public administration and services, legal apparatus and protection.[26]

What are we to make of these different scholarly interpretations? Once again, if we take them back to their data bases and refresh our sense of Luke's whole, they turn out amenable to compromise. The program of Jesus, for example, is radical but not **antinomian**. In the background of Luke's evangel is a Christ who brought a new kingdom, centered in love and justice from the heart, but a kingdom meant for people of flesh, blood, and sociability. Jesus did not throw out the notion of Torah or secular guidance. He merely strove to make both Torah and secular guidance serve the heart of the religious and human matter: love of God and love of neighbor. He did not object to having a Sabbath to worship God or a tax to support public works. He thoroughly objected to misusing these institutions and letting them become crushing burdens rather than aids. If they stood in the way of healing or worship in truth and justice, they were ripe for overthrow. For that reason, Jesus was potentially a revolutionary. But good government, whether religious or secular, presented Jesus no great problem. Nothing about him suggests he was so romantic that he expected people to live together without conventions or rules. The general impression left in the Gospels is that Jesus moved through all conventions and rules lightly, keeping all in the order of means. Only when they claimed to be ends in themselves did he oppose them.

The last bit of background we shall be able to consider is Luke's presuppositions about the parousia. Writing later than Paul, his theology is less eschatological, not as tense with the expectation of Jesus' return. It is more historical, in the sense of being more reconciled to the open-ended flow of time, more patient with God's perhaps slowly paced plans. In the existential interpretations of the past generation of New Testament scholars who followed Rudolf Bultmann, this historical-mindedness set Luke against Paul. Paul was the pure preacher of a personal decision for or against Jesus and the Christian gospel. Luke was the herald of early Catholicism who helped take the bite from the gospel's call for decision. Luke's generation had ceased to place salvation in the return of Jesus the Lord. Rather it believed that salvation had already arrived in Jesus' historical person.

Ulrich Wilckens has elaborated this view of Luke and made a less damaging contrast with Paul. The foundation of Wilckens' reading of Luke is Luke's having received a well-developed tradition of the sayings and interpretations of Jesus:

> This late stage was the essential basis upon which he thought through the various traditions and traditional tendencies which he found in such a way as to make the story of Jesus "the center of time" (Conzelmann). This fact explains why Luke, while reinterpreting the expectation of the imminent end, never found the delayed parousia to be in any way a disturbing problem. To overstate the matter for emphasis: an essential fact about the Jesus-tradition which Luke received was that it had already basically solved the problem of the delayed parousia by concentrating salvation in Jesus himself and by affirming that his followers participate in salvation now. Only when we recognize that the Lucan theology of redemptive history fits into the history of the Jesus-tradition in this manner can we properly evaluate Luke's personal theological achievement and its significance in the light of his contemporary situation.[27]

Wilckens goes on to argue that, with respect to the history of the Jesus traditions, Luke and Paul stand on different ground. Paul did not have available to him the reflections about Jesus that had accumulated by the time Luke was writing. So, for example, Paul makes little use of Mark and Q materials (virtually no direct literary use; whether he knew early forms is uncertain).[28] Therefore Paul did not have Luke's option of making the history of Jesus the center of his theology. In a sense he had to make do with the bare kerygma of the crucified and risen Lord. Wilckens also assumes that Luke knew neither Judaism nor Gnosticism from personal experience, while Paul had received a strict Jewish upbringing and the Pauline school was forced to contend seriously with Gnosticism (see Colossians and Ephesians).

Still, the most important factor that pushed Luke's theology in a direction different from Paul's, and that shaped his own distinctive interpretation of Paul's career, is Luke's living in a time when Christianity seemed to be expanding into a worldwide religion. So, for instance, the speech that Luke's Paul gives on the Areopagus has a **natural theology** that makes Christianity the final stage of all genuine religion. The effort Luke makes to present Christians as good citizens of the Roman empire fits his strong interest in the secular realm and in the developments of contemporary history. Relatedly, Luke is interested in the Church's development of institutional structures to guide it through what may be a lengthy future. He presupposes that his readers are at least second-generation Christians who think of salvation as having been accomplished in the past rather than as arriving in the near future.

WHAT LASTING SIGNIFICANCE DOES THIS HAVE?

The lasting significance of Acts derives principally from its being our fullest and most authoritative picture of the early Church. Despite the fact that Acts is not an objective history in our contemporary sense, but rather a theological interpretation, it provides vignettes of early Christian life that have pride of place in our slender album.[29] Where we must conjecture the Markan, Matthean, and Johannine communities from the theologies of those Gospels, the Lukan community seems closer. Acts has described how the early Christians came to think of themselves as a missionary community, what they had to decide, and how they had to suffer. Our pictures of Pentecost, Peter, and Paul depend crucially upon Acts. Imprecise as the fit between the Paul of Acts and the Paul of the Epistles is, our sense of the Gentile mission would be much poorer if Acts did not complement the Pauline writings.

The Christianity depicted in Acts is, by the consensus of scholars such as Wilckens and Walaskay, relatively comfortable with history.[30] One might conjecture, in fact, that Acts was an important station on the road to an incarnational faith. By an incarnational faith we mean one that views human flesh as a sacrament of God. The prime stimulus to such a faith in the Christian case was Jesus, but for Jesus to become the sacramental Christ Christianity had to become comfortable with time, and to accept the world and the flesh as trustworthy presences of the divine holiness. True enough, the divine holiness would only fully be revealed at the parousia or in heaven (the state of resurrection). But as the incarnationalist instinct perceived, divine holiness has a solid, reliable presence here and now in Jesus and Jesus' community. Acts mediated incarnationalism by legitimizing the opening to the Gentiles. For the Gentiles to enter God's household, the delay of the parousia was necessary and therefore providential. Since it was providential, human affairs drew near to sacramentality. (One must ask, therefore, whether Lukan theology sees history as sufficiently tragic or marred by evil.)

But what about this more historical, sacramental, or incarnational interpretation of Jesus' significance? How insightful is it twenty centuries after the birth of its main warrant? We can only begin to answer that question, because the Johannine literature bears directly on the sources we ought to canvas, but even a beginning may be significant. We could not, for example, have modern or postmodern consciousness without the historicity that is linked to Christian incarnationalism. We could not have the personalism that arose in the West. Both this historicity and this personalism began earlier than Christianity, of course, with Israel and Greece. But Jesus and Christology took Israelite revelation and Greek wisdom another turn of the helix. In the flesh of Jesus' actual history the West found a conjunction of opposites, a fusion of time and eternity.

As a result, the West developed the doctrine of the image of God, the capacity of all *homines sapientes* to reflect the ultimate mystery, to the point where being human was an incarnate, temporal participation in the eternal knowing and loving that ran the cosmos. When people of deep faith and good heart probed this inference, they glimpsed a dignity nearly impossible to exaggerate. God had entered time, taken flesh, blessed the efforts of the human race to evolve. Therefore all human beings were precious, sacred, inviolable. To injure any of God's developing images wantonly or cruelly (as many supposedly Christian regimes unfortunately did) was to blaspheme and mimic the crucifixion. The crucifixion showed the nadir of human evil, the lowest ebb. On the cross human beings tried to destroy the blessed flesh God ached to give them. On the cross God took incarnationalism so seriously that God nearly let human evil triumph.

Pauline theology laid a foundation for an incarnational view of the human person by associating the human person with the risen Lord. Because it was capable of receiving the risen Lord and his Spirit, the human person was incalculably precious. Johannine theology contemplated the wonder of the Word's having become flesh. Where Paul was preoccupied with Jesus' passover from death to resurrection, John could not take his gaze from the new abode of the divine presence that came with Jesus' birth. Between them, Lukan theology worked out the historicity of the Lord and community that were the heirs of Israelite revelation. In the predestined history of Jesus God had brought Israelite prophecy to fulfillment. In the predestined missionary spread of the Church, the Spirit was making the Gentiles the beneficiaries of both Israel and Jesus.

The emphasis that Lukan theology placed on poverty and concern for society's marginal people was a check on any excessive appreciation of time and current human achievements. The history of Jesus and the first decades of the Christian Church could lead no sane observer to conclude that the present eon was God's full kingdom. On the other hand, the Lukan stress on predestination and the value of the Roman political rule gave Christians a rationale for working out ways to be good citizens and consecrate history to God's purposes. Without the Lukan portions of the New Testament, the Church might have remained an apocalyptic sect too concerned with the parousia to take on the responsibilities of redeeming human history.

Luke-Acts therefore is a strong contributor to the balanced, somewhat sophisticated view of history that has characterized Christianity at its healthiest. This view has avoided a choice between either time or eternity. It has rather insisted that both temporal and eternal instincts have their place and are necessary if a society is to be healthy. Against those who would say that life is merely a vale of tears, that nothing matters presently but getting one's soul to heaven, the balanced view of such primary sources as Luke-Acts has argued that God made human beings historical, with wants that are compatible with the divine twofold commandment of Love. Thus Gnostics, **Manicheans**, and others who have despised human flesh and secular life in the name of a heavenly perfectionism have been branded heretics. The Incarnation of Jesus, the spread of the early Church, the sacramental life of the Christian community, and the original intention of the Creator God as outlined at the beginning of Genesis have all risen up to debunk such a masochistic, self-hating view. Loving one's neighbor as oneself has meant loving the self that God created and Christ redeemed. Loving the self that God created and Christ redeemed has meant accepting human historicity and human work, including human efforts to make politics, economics, art, science, and the rest.

Against those who would say that time is the only arena of human activity and that heaven and redemption are chimeras, Luke-Acts and the other primary Christian sources have answered with an equally firm "no." The resurrection of Jesus and Christians' experience of Jesus' Spirit have led the main Christian authorities to make both God and human destiny larger than what time and space can contain. This instinct has analogues in other religious cultures. Israel, Greece, and India, to name only three cultural basins, all thought that human experience contains a transcendence of time, a spiritual dimension free of matter's constraints. In relatively rare but nonetheless real times of imaginary, intellectual, and emotional transport, the mystics of most religious traditions have become absolutely sure there is an unseen, immaterial world without which we cannot define human nature adequately.

This world has beckoned poets, artists, philosophers, and radical seers like Plato, the Buddha, and Zoroaster. It has also depended on such visionaries for its continued vitality in human culture. Unless people honor contemplation, taking the time and discipline to maintain a liturgical and reflective life, they flatten into semihumanity and forget why making money and waging war so easily become destructive idols. The Lukan stress on the Spirit, like the Buddhist stress on emptiness or the Muslim stress on the sovereignty of Allah, expresses the perennial defense we have against idolatry, the inbuilt resources we only need to activate to again see reality whole. Not to see reality whole, not to realize that life is much more than banking and wielding power, is to become sick, insane in the root sense of mentally unhealthy. It is to spend time on worthless trinkets and not know the things necessary for one's peace and joy. When Jesus wept over Jerusalem, because it did not know the things necessary for its peace, he symbolized the constant human tragedy. Despite the rich legacy of poets and sages, most generations have only learned the wisdom of a more than worldly perspective through suffering war, famine, and suicidal depression over the emptiness of a purely material life.

The perennial relevance of an incarnational balance also shows in the equivalents to Christian sacramentality that have developed in non-Western cultures.[31] The cultures of nonliterate peoples such as the American Indians, Eskimos, traditional Africans, and Australian aborigines, for instance, have all been visionary to the core. While they have generated admirable arts and crafts and ingenious ways of adapting to their local ecologies, they have placed the substance of human fulfillment in vision quests, shamanic singing, dances that vitalized the tribe's myths, or immersions in the dream time when the ancestors created the world. This basically shamanic cultural pattern dominated all areas of the globe until about three thousand years ago, and it still is very influential in South America, Africa, Australia, and Asia.

Indian culture pursued an incarnational, sacramental balance by blending yoga, which seeks a repose the world cannot give, with intricate, often beautiful rituals and myths. Yoga gives the spirit access to an unconditioned, matter-free state. The myths, rituals, many deities, and shrewd political experience of India's constituent peoples, Aryan invaders and Dravidian natives, became a body that yogic peace tried to fill. In East Asia, where Confucianism supplied the essential ethics or social philosophy and Buddhism or Taoism was the meditative core, sacramentalism came in the form of aesthetics. Grace, harmony, and beauty lured East Asians to find peace in nature, to make a hierarchical whole of family life and social relations. Confucian ritual permeated politics, education, and business life. Buddhist funerary rites reminded people that craving this-worldly success is a dead end. Only when one broke the cycle of rebirths could one be fully satisfied and know the being, bliss, and awareness of nirvana.

Christianity is by no means alone, then, in its struggles after an incarnational balance. It is distinctive, however, in drawing so much of its incarnationalism from the experience and significance of one historical figure, Jesus of Nazareth, raised by God to become Lord of time, what Eastern Christianity has called the Pantokrator (cosmic ruler). Today the question is how to translate the perennial wisdoms of incarnationalism to show a way through our crushing global problems of nuclear arms, overpopulation, ecological ruin, and gross economic injustice. In most cases the haves presently are too materialistic, so stunted spiritually that they cannot see the folly of worshiping money and power. The have-nots are insufficiently historical, unable to handle recent technology and political science. So we all could use a latter-day Luke, a historian most impressed by providence and the Spirit.

SUMMARY

Acts is the second volume of Luke's two-volume work, interpreting the third period of Lukan history, from the time of Jesus' ascension to the missionary outreach of Jesus' community to the Gentiles. Acts probably originated at Antioch around 95 C.E. Among its stylistic peculiarities are the author's use of speeches and summaries and his way of drawing parallels between the work of Peter and Paul and the work of Jesus. Thematically, Acts stresses the continuity between the age of Church expansion and the time of Jesus, the legitimacy of the mission of Paul, and the guidance of the Holy Spirit. In outline Acts falls into eight subunits: 1:1–11, 1:12–8:3, 8:4–9:31, 9:32–15:35, 15:36–18:23, 18:24–21:14, 21:15–26:32, and 27:1–28:31.

The Introduction (1:1–11) ties Acts to Luke's Gospel, again introduces Theophilus, and stresses Jesus' command that the disciples wait for the Holy Spirit. It concludes with Jesus' ascension and the prediction of two angels that Jesus will return from heaven at the parousia.

The portrait of the Church in Jerusalem (1:12–8:3) emphasizes the election of Judas' successor, the events of Pentecost, and the first of several speeches that argue the case for Jesus' fulfillment of Jewish prophecy. Peter is the community leader and the first object of missionary activity will be the Jews in the holy city. The community lives in idyllic harmony, as all share their resources. Peter is a great healer. Before the Jewish religious authorities Peter defends Jesus and accuses the Jewish leaders of responsibility for Jesus' death. The Spirit inspires all the disciples to boldness in proclaiming Jesus. The apostles feel they must obey God's inspirations rather than the commands of the chief priests to stop preaching. Gamaliel speaks for Luke in urging the Sanhedrin to let the new movement bear whatever fruit God wishes. The speech of Stephen in chapter 6 is a full example of early Christian scriptural interpretation and suggests the vision of the first Christian martyr. After Stephen's death the Jerusalem church suffers serious persecution.

The Mission in Judea and Samaria (8:4–9:31) shows the first outreach of the Church. Philip the deacon is a leading missionary. The conversion of Saul is a key incident, for Saul had been a leading persecutor of the Way. The status of the Gentiles (9:32–15:35) is Luke's next major concern. Peter's experiences convince him that the Spirit has come to Gentiles. That tells Peter he cannot forbid the Gentiles' baptism. Barnabas and Saul work at Antioch, one of the most successful early Gentile churches. In Jerusalem Peter and the others feel the wrath of King Herod Agrippa. The Antiochene Christians consecrate Barnabas and Saul for a ministry to the Gentiles and so begins the first of three Pauline journeys that Luke narrates. Paul's regular tactic is to go first to Jewish synagogues and then, when the Jews have rejected their chance, to preach to the Gentiles. Chapter 15 is important for the story of the council in Jerusalem and the compromise decision about the requirements to be asked of Gentile converts.

Paul's mission to the Gentiles (15:36–18:23) takes over Luke's narrative. With Timothy and Silas, Paul sets out on his second journey. At 16:10 begin the "we" references that may indicate Luke's eyewitness status. We see some of Paul's activities in famous churches such as Philippi and Thessalonica. Chapter 17 recounts Paul's important speech on the Areopagus in Athens. Chapter 18 shows Paul at work at Corinth where, typically, he runs into trouble from Jews who resent his preaching. Luke shows that the secular authorities considered these clashes intra-Jewish affairs.

Paul's third journey (18:24–21:14) again begins from Antioch in Syria. He works in the synagogue in Ephesus but once more is harassed by angry Jews. Paul defends his apostolate to the Ephesians. The journey ends with Paul's determination to go to Jerusalem. Luke's portrait of Paul in prison (21:15–26:32) attributes Paul's troubles to the contentiousness of the Jerusalem Jews. Only Paul's Roman citizenship protects him against great abuse. Throughout this section Luke stresses Paul's innocence. Paul has violated neither Jewish nor Roman law. Before Festus and Marcus Agrippa Paul defends himself skillfully. He could have been released, both authorities judge, had he not appealed to Caesar in Rome.

Acts ends with a narrative of Paul's progress toward Rome (27:1–28:31). The clear symbolism is that the apostle to the Gentiles is providentially being carried to the capital of the Gentile world. The many mishaps on the way underscore God's care for Paul. On this last trip, as on the previous three, Paul moves many listeners to conversion. Acts 28:28 is close to a summary of its overall message: "Let it be known to you [Jews] then that this salvation of God has been sent to the Gentiles; they will listen."

In investigating why Acts was written we wrestled with the currently debated question of Luke's intended audience. We noted the arguments for a Jewish Christian audience, which tie into the emphasis scholars recently have been placing on the Roman war that came to disastrous climax for the Jews in 70 C.E. However, we tended to favor a primary audience of Gentile Christians, many of them perhaps former God-fearers. We also suggested how Luke may have thought Acts could comfort Christians of any stripe.

Primary among the background presuppositions of Acts is the increasing importance of Gentile Christianity. The prominence given Paul and the various justifications of the Gentile mission seem crucial to Luke's literary intent. In addition, Luke assumes a socioeconomic situation in which Christian poverty was significant. Jesus emerges as something of a social critic in Luke's Gospel and Acts portrays a countercultural community sharing its goods evenhandedly. Almsgiving is an important virtue. Concerning Luke's political assumptions, the recent scholarship divides. Some authors think Luke's Jesus and early Christianity took Roman rule so lightly as to be a threat to imperial authority. Others point to Lukan efforts to legitimize Roman rule and show it as God-given. Our own position makes Luke a moderate, praising laws and social conventions that know their place as a way to help humans flourish. Relatedly, we found Luke balanced about the parousia and history. Writing with a quite well-developed tradition about Jesus, Luke could be more patient of history than Paul and the earliest evangelical sources, better able to make the lifetime of Jesus the accomplishment of basic salvation.

Our ruminations about the lasting significance of Acts followed through on this characterization of Luke's historical-mindedness. By trying for a balanced view of time, an incarnational faith that joined time and eternity in Christ, Luke exemplified the perennial wisdom many religious traditions offer. For Luke God directs history and human beings have to love the world. They also have to realize that resurrection takes them beyond the world. We noted critics of this balanced view from both right and left and then indicated incarnational parallels with other religious traditions.

STUDY QUESTIONS

1. What sort of history of early Christianity is Acts?
2. What stylistic devices give us clues to Luke's intentions in Acts?
3. How does Luke show the continuity between the age of the apostles and the time of Jesus?
4. What does the ascension of Jesus symbolize?

5. Explain the significance of 2:22–24 as typical of the earliest Christian kerygma.

6. What is the guiding principle in the early Christians' interpretation of Jewish prophecy?

7. What is the significance of early Christian communism?

8. Explain the wisdom of Gamaliel.

9. Why is Stephen stoned?

10. How does Saul's conversion identify the Church with Jesus?

11. What is the significance of Peter's encounter with Cornelius?

12. How is the missionary success of Paul and Barnabas interpreted as a judgment on the Jews?

13. Explain the decision of the Jerusalem council (chapter 15).

14. What do the miracles that happen on Paul's journey signify?

15. Summarize Paul's speech on the Areopagus.

16. Why did Paul have to defend himself to the Ephesians?

17. Why did Paul appeal to Caesar?

18. What is the symbolism of Paul preaching in prison in Rome?

19. What was Luke's primary audience for Acts?

20. How countercultural was the early Church that Acts portrays?

21. Why can Luke be more patient with history than Paul?

22. How does Lukan theology display an incarnational balance?

23. Explain the parallels to Christian incarnationalism that one may find in other religions.

NOTES

1. See Martin Hengel, *Acts and the History of Earliest Christianity* (Philadelphia: Fortress, 1979); Robert Wilken, *The Myth of Christian Beginnings* (Notre Dame: University of Notre Dame Press, 1980).

2. William S. Kurz, *The Acts of the Apostles* (Collegeville, Minn.: Liturgical Press, 1983), p. 10.

3. Ibid., p. 13.

4. See C. H. Dodd, *The Apostolic Preaching and Its Developments* (New York: Harper & Row, 1964).

5. See Nils A. Dahl, *Jesus in the Memory of the Early Church* (Minneapolis: Augsburg, 1976), p. 89.

6. See Gerd Theissen, *Sociology of Early Palestinian Christianity* (Philadelphia: Fortress, 1977), p. 112.

7. See Richard J. Dillon and Joseph A. Fitzmyer, "Acts of the Apostles," *The Jerome Biblical Commentary*, ed. R. Brown and others (Englewood Cliffs, N.J.: Prentice-Hall, 1968), vol. 2, p. 180.

8. See N. Walter, "Apostelgeschichte 6.1 und die Anfange der Urgemiende in Jerusalem," *New Testament Studies* 29 (1983), 370–93.

9. See T. L. Boudie, "The Accusing and Stoning of Naboth (1 Kgs 21:8–13) as One Component of the Stephen Text (Acts 6:9–14, 7:58a), " *Catholic Biblical Quarterly* 45 (1983), 417–32.

10. See R. F. O'Toole, "Philip and the Ethiopian Eunuch (Acts VIII 25–40)," *Journal for the Study of the New Testament* 17 (1983), 25–34.

11. See Steven T. Katz, "Issues in the Separation of Judaism and Christianity after 70 C.E.," *Journal of Biblical Literature* 203 (1984), 44–48.

12. See S. E. Johnson, "Antioch, the Base of Operations," *Lexington Theological Quarterly* 18 (1983), 64–73.

13. See Wayne Meeks, *The First Urban Christians* (New Haven: Yale University Press, 1983), pp. 28–29.

14. See F. G. Downing, "Common Ground with Paganism in Luke and in Josephus," *New Testament Studies* 28 (1982), 546–59.

15. See R. F. O'Toole, "Paul at Athens and Luke's Notion of Worship," *Révue Biblique* 89 (1982), 185–97.

16. See Abraham J. Malherbe, *Social Aspects of Early Christianity*, 2nd ed. (Philadelphia: Fortress, 1983).

17. See Mark Black, "Paul and Roman Law in Acts," *Restoration Quarterly* 24 (1981), 209–18.

18. See P. Davies, "The Ending of Acts," *Expository Times* 94 (1983), 334–35.

19. See Joseph A. Fitzmyer, *The Gospel According to Luke I–IX* (Garden City, N.Y.: Doubleday Anchor, 1981), pp. 57–59.

20. Donald Juel, *Luke-Acts: The Promise of History* (Atlanta: John Knox, 1983), p. 117.

21. Richard J. Cassidy, *Jesus, Politics, and Society: A Study of Luke's Gospel* (Maryknoll, N.Y.: Orbis, 1978), pp. 77–78.

22. See Theissen, *Sociology of Early Palestinian Christianity*, pp. 7–23.

23. Walter E. Pilgrim, *Good News to the Poor* (Minneapolis: Augsburg, 1981), pp. 155–56.

24. See Igor Shafarevich, *The Socialist Phenomenon* (New York: Harper & Row, 1980).

25. See Richard J. Cassidy, *Jesus, Politics, and Society*, pp. 78–79.

26. Paul Walaskay, *And So We Came to Rome* (New York: Cambridge University Press, 1983), pp. 64, 66.

27. Ulrich Wilckens, "Interpreting Luke-Acts in a Period of Existentialist Theology," in *Studies in Luke-Acts*, ed. L. Keck and J. L. Martyn (Nashville: Abingdon, 1966), p. 67.

28. See Dale C. Allison, Jr., "The Pauline Epistles and the Synoptic Gospels," *New Testament Studies* 28 (1982), 1–28.

29. See Wilken, *The Myth of Christian Beginnings*.

30. For a contrary view, see Eric Franklin, *Christ the Lord* (Philadelphia: Westminster, 1975).

31. See Denise Lardner Carmody and John Tully Carmody, *Shamans, Prophets and Sages* (Belmont, Calif.: Wadsworth, 1985).

The Gospel for John's Church

WHAT HAVE WE HERE?

The Gospel of John is quite different from the synoptics. **Tradition** attributed it to the apostle John, one of Jesus' first disciples. Current scholarly opinion about its origin and composition is divided, but many believe it stems from a follower of the "beloved disciple" (see John 13:23) and was worked over by several hands. Perhaps 90 C.E. is a fair estimate of the original date. Ephesus is the most popular suggested site.

From the outset we must stress the intricacy of both the Gospel and the debates over how best to interpret it. Pheme Perkins, for instance, has found that even a "minimal hypothesis" must provide for four stages in the Gospel's composition.[1] First, the author must have had access to sayings and traditions about Jesus like those arranged by the synoptics and he assumes that his community knows much of what the synoptics present. This does not necessarily mean that the Johannine church had Mark and Q, let alone Matthew and Luke, actually in hand. It does mean that the Johannine church had access to the fund of memories about Jesus that the synoptics used. Second, the Gospel incorporated materials already quite polished for preaching. The scholarly conjecture, therefore, is that some parts of John directly reflect sermons or instructional materials used in the Johannine church.

Third, in composing the Gospel the original author set these two stages of materials into a new organizational framework. His scheme extends Jesus' public life into a three-year period, in contrast to the single year presented by the synoptics. As a result, some materials (for instance, chapters 5–8) appear to have been wrenched from a different earlier setting and refitted none too neatly into the author's new framework. Fourth, after the death of the main writer another editor added final materials and last touches. For example, he inserted 21:23 as an explanation of the death of the beloved disciple, and he probably added on such sections as 3:31–36, 12:44–50, and 21:1–18. Indeed, some whole chapters (8, 15–17) may be late additions.

Perkins concludes her minimal hypothesis about the composition of the Gospel with a comment on authorship representative of mainstream Johannine scholarship:

> Since the gospel was written sometime around A.D. 90, the gospel cannot reasonably be attributed to John son of Zebedee as is sometimes done. Besides that, John was martyred (Mk 10:38 f.) while we know that the author of the fourth gospel was not (21:21 f.). Chapter 21 suggests that the beloved disciple of Jesus was the founder of the Johannine community and the source of its traditions [not necessarily the author or redactor of those traditions in their present written form]. They looked back to him as on par with the apostle Peter to whom Jesus had entrusted the Church.[2]

But if the beloved disciple was not John the son of Zebedee (Jesus' early disciple, who with Peter and James stood out among the twelve and witnessed such crucial events as Jesus' transfiguration [see Mark 9:2–28, Matthew 17:1–8, Luke 9:28–36]), who was he? Xavier Leon-Dufour has summarized the almost embarrasing silence with which scholars must greet this question.

> The "beloved disciple" is a personality proper to the Fourth Gospel, whom we cannot designate further, other than to indicate that he belonged to the Twelve [many other New Testament scholars would dispute this]; he is sometimes designated as "the other disciple" [John 18:15f.; 20:3f.], at other times as "the disciple whom Jesus loved" [John 13:23–26; 19:25–27; 20:2; 21:7, 20–23, 24]. The one and the other are the same person [John 20:2], a historical person whose symbolic significance is undeniable, but difficult to define precisely. Explicitly set over against Peter by John [the Gospel], this disciple always takes the better part by his intelligent presence and by the fact of his "being loved" in a special way. He might symbolize the function of the disciple who is able to perceive, understand and speak, because he knows that he is loved by Jesus.[3]

Among the central theological themes of John are revelation, mission, and the **Paraclete**. For the author Jesus is the best expression of God:

> John's central theological teaching concerns revelation: God's revelation of himself in his completely unique Son, Jesus of Nazareth, one with the Father, the living and incarnate Word, who in himself bespeaks, proclaims, identifies, immediately the Father. To know Jesus is to know God. And so, too, John gives us the Book of Glory [chapters 13–20], which climaxes in the ultimate revelation of the Son as self-sacrificing love. It is on the cross that Jesus glorifies/manifests the Father. God the Father, therefore, is love. This will be the final, simple, concise definition of I John 4:16, "God is love, and he who abides in love abides in God, and God in him."[4]

Jesus' mission, consequently, is to reveal the Father. This is the work he has been sent to accomplish. Jesus' disciples inherit this mission. The

St. John the Evangelist.
Bernardo Daddi. This
fourteenth-century Italian
painting, probably originally
part of a tryptich, portrays
the evangelist twice: at work,
and then with a completed
scroll.   *(Nelson Gallery–Atkins
Museum, Kansas City, Mo. [Nelson
Fund])*

Christian community's main work is to reveal the Father (and the Son who
made the Father known). The best way to accomplish this work is to show
the world self-sacrificing love. If the world sees a community outstanding
for genuine helpfulness, warmth, light, and service offered at cost, the
world will believe in Jesus' mission. The Paraclete functions as a source of
enlightenment and strength for the community. Where the synoptics speak
of the Spirit, John sometimes speaks of the helper or advocate Jesus left.
The Johannine Spirit comes when Jesus dies on the cross (19:30). The
resurrected Jesus breathes on the disciples and gives them the Spirit
(20:22). We shall note other special interests of John as we proceed
through the text. From the outset, though, we should point out the strong
feelings the Gospel displays against "the Jews"—those who reject Jesus'
messiahship. Taken uncritically throughout the ages, these sentiments
have fueled much anti-Semitism.

In outline the Gospel divides as follows:

Introduction 1:1–51

The Book of Signs 2:1–12:50

   New Beginnings 2:1–4:42

Jesus' Life-Giving Word 4:43–5:47
Jesus the Bread of Life 6:1–71
Identity Crisis 7:1–8:59
Jesus the Light of the World 9:1–10:42
Life Conquering Death 11:1–54
Life Coming through Death 11:55–12:50
The Book of Glory 13:1–20:31
    The Farewell Discourses 13:1–17:26
    The Passion Narrative 18:1–19:42
    The Resurrection 20:1–31
Epilogue: Christ's Appearances in Galilee 21:1–25[5]

Introduction (1:1–51)

The Gospel of John begins with a famous prologue (1:1–18) that may well have been an early Christian hymn. It is at least as memorable as such other early hymns as Philippians 2:5–11 and Colossians 1:15–20. The Prologue suggests a semicircular movement from heaven to earth and back to heaven. Many of the verses run in parallel (1–2 = 18, 3 = 17, 4–5 = 16, 6–8 = 15, 9–11 = 14; 12–13 are the hinge or bottom of the semicircle where the two parallel columns of verses connect). The first line ("In the beginning was the Word, and the Word was with God, and the Word was God") conjures up the opening lines of Genesis. The implication is that John is reworking the creation account, suggesting a new interpretation of the old story of how God fashioned the universe. The Word of God, active in the prophets, medium of the divine will (in the Genesis account), is made coexistent with God at the origin of time. Indeed, John makes it codivine with the Creator. All things came into being through the Word. The Word possessed life, a vitality that brought light to all creatures with intelligence. (For the Hellenistic thought contemporary with John, the word or **logos** was the main means through which divinity expressed itself.) This lively divine light shone in the darkness of chaos (the disorder that preceded the Genesis creation account, and the disorder of human sinfulness) and has always been greater than the darkness.

John the Baptist was sent by God to prepare people to accept this light. With Jesus the light came into the world in a new, absolutely concrete fashion. Ironically, the world did not recognize the light through which it had been made. So the world (by which John usually means sinful humanity) rejected Jesus. As Raymond Brown puts it,

> The presence of the Word in the world is rejected, for the world does not recognize the Word (10c). In like manner the presence of Jesus in the world meets rejection (iii 19), for men do not recognize who Jesus is (xiv 7, xvi 3; I John iii 1). The particularly poignant rejection of the Word by his own people (11b) is also matched in the ministry of Jesus as he is rejected in Galilee (iv 44) and by the Jewish people in general (xii 37) . . . vss. 11 and 12 are really short summaries of the two parts of the Gospel: the Book of Signs and the Book of

Glory. The opening line of the Book of Glory (xiii 2) announces: "Having loved *his own* who were in the world, he now showed his love for them to the very end." In other words, in place of the Jewish people who had been his own (i 11), he has now formed around himself a new "his own," the Christian believers (1 12).[6]

The children of God created by faith in the glorious Jesus were born by God's doing. Their life is something supernatural, the product of grace. The source of this heavenly life, paradoxically enough, is the human flesh of Jesus. John 1:14 expresses John's utterly incarnational faith (perhaps against Gnostics who denied a literal incarnation). The divine, creative Word became flesh. He was perceptible to human beings, full of grace and truth. Indeed, his glory (splendor) was such that he must have been the Father's only Son. The author sees a prophetic anticipation of this in the Baptist's self-depreciation.

By contrast with earlier Israelite prophecy such as that of Isaiah 40:6–8, however, the Incarnation of the Word is astounding. For Isaiah all human nature is grass, unable to withstand the breath of the Lord: "All flesh is grass, and its beauty is like the flower of the field. The grass withers, the flower fades, when the breath of the Lord blows upon it; surely the people is grass." Small wonder, then, that many Jews could not accept an Incarnation of God's Word. To the author of John's Gospel, however, the experience of Jesus, what beholders had seen and felt, quickly led to the conclusion that he was God's most intimate self-expression come in human form. His fullness was the source of all grace or favor with God. It far exceeded what the Mosaic Law could accomplish. The climax of John's prologue (1:1–18) is the revelation trumpeted in 1:18: "No one has ever seen God; the only Son, who is in the bosom of the Father, he has made him known."[7]

John 1:19–34 summarizes the testimony of the Baptist. Like the synoptics, the author of John remembers the Baptist as subordinating himself to Jesus. John 1:26 is distinctively Johannine in making the Baptist stress that Jesus' people did not know him. The Lamb of God imagery of 1:29 comes from Exodus 12 and Isaiah 53. In both passages the emphasis is on sacrificial victimhood. John 1:31 makes the Baptist the revealer of the revealer, and it suggests that God inspired John to recognize Jesus by the descent of the Spirit at Jesus' baptism. The Baptist bears witness that Jesus, the Lamb of God, the one especially anointed by the Spirit, is the Son of God. (Here "Son of God" most likely is a messianic title. In 1:18 the term suggests heavenly generation by the Father.) Insofar as some commentators see the Johannine community as battling with disciples of John the Baptist, this clear subordination seems significant.

John 1:35–51 gives the testimony of Jesus' first disciples. As with the testimony of the Baptist, the author is preparing the reader to recognize the nature or status of the man whose drama he will narrate. The structure of these two sets of testimonials suggests the seven-day creation account. The Baptist describes his relation to Jesus on day one, calls Jesus the Lamb of God on day two, and inspires two disciples to follow Jesus on day three.

St. John the Baptist. Michelangelo Merisi da Caravaggio. The young Baptist wears the scanty garb of a biblical ascetic and seems to be brooding about the difficulty of his mission. *(Nelson Gallery–Atkins Museum, Kansas City, Mo. [Nelson Fund])*

On day four Andrew goes to Simon Peter. Jesus goes to Galilee and finds Philip on day five. On day six Nathaniel goes to Jesus. The climax comes on day seven with the miracle at Cana in Galilee. Obviously interpreters must scramble to fit these happenings into a seven-day creation cycle, explaining such awkward texts as 2:1 ("On the third day [the resurrectional day] there was a marriage at Cana of Galilee"). Still, the importance of symbolism in Johannine theology justifies their hypotheses. The Baptist, the proclamation of Jesus as Savior, the two disciples, Peter, Philip, Nathaniel, and the Cana miracle are a seven too pregnant to overlook. There are seven major episodes in the Book of Signs. The Book of Revelation (often considered closely related to John) is full of sevens (thirty-three occurrences). Seven is the Johannine number of fullness. The argument, then, is that 1:19–51 is a complete testimony to Jesus' crucial significance.

Other Johannine introductory motifs we should note include the reference to Jesus as rabbi (teacher) in 1:38, Jesus' asking the two disciples the portentous question, "What do you seek?" (1:38), and the fact that it is because they go, see, and remain with Jesus that the first disciples find the Messiah (1:41). From the first (1:42) the Johannine Jesus calls Simon the rock. He tells Philip to follow him. By following, Philip, too, finds the One predicted by Moses and the prophets. Jesus is from Nazareth and is the son of Joseph. Nathaniel is convinced by Jesus because Nathaniel is an Israelite in whom there is no guile. Jesus claims a vision of Nathaniel that moves Nathaniel to proclaim Jesus the Son of God and King of Israel. Jesus says

Nathaniel will see the fulfillment of Jacob's vision (Genesis 28:12). The Johannine Son of Man is a heavenly messenger, come to reveal God, and he is also the world's judge (see 3:13, 5:27).

Clearly the first chapter of John's Gospel is busy with symbolism. If the synoptics are peculiar historians, arranging the details of Jesus' life to fit their interpretations of Jesus' meaning, John is much more so. The entire Gospel has the form of a mature contemplation of Jesus' meaning. Looking back from the perspective of perhaps sixty years after the resurrection, the author packs into the being and career of Jesus a many-sided revelation of divinity. From the outset his hero is strangely attractive, mysterious, a lure to true Israelites. From the outset he is the Son of God and Messiah whose every word and gesture is a sacrament, a symbol of divinity in human terms. (Contrast this with the hidden quality of the Markan Jesus.) The author discreetly suggests that he himself is the second of the two disciples of the Baptist who moved over to Jesus. Andrew is named and the unnamed second disciple may be telling the story. Philip is one of the twelve. Nathaniel may well have been Bartholomew, another of the twelve. For John the early disciples owe their dignity to their early recognition of Jesus. They were called and followed Jesus from the beginning.

The Book of Signs (2:1–12:50)[8]

New Beginnings (2:1–4:42)

The first of Jesus' seven signs (the structure John uses to anchor Jesus' public ministry) occurs at Cana in Galilee. It introduces a theme of new beginnings that dominates chapters 2–4. Jesus attends a wedding feast and, at the prompting of his mother, changes water into wine. The human details of the story make the scene memorable: the wine giving out, the dialogue between Jesus and Mary, the strange remark ("My hour has not yet come"—for John Jesus' supreme hour was his time on the cross), and the precisely described miracle itself. The author notes that Jesus' wine is better than the original wine. The climactic line is 2:11: "This, the first of his signs, Jesus did at Cana in Galilee, and manifested his glory; and the disciples believed in him." Jesus' signs (**semeia**) are not raw prodigies but expressions of his splendid reality, the divinity shining through his flesh.[9] Jesus works them to solicit faith, a full acceptance of his revelation of the Father.

At Passover Jesus goes up to Jerusalem (much sooner, for instance, than in Luke). He cleanses the Temple (see Mark 11:15–19, Matthew 21:12–17, Luke 19:45–48; only John mentions the whip of cords). John emphasizes the profanation of the house of Jesus' Father. The disciples recall the zeal spoken of in Psalms 69, the psalm most frequently used in the New Testament. The Jews (John's antagonists)[10] ask for a sign (Johannine irony) and Jesus speaks enigmatically about the destruction and rebuilding of "this temple." They think he is referring to the physical Temple. Jesus is saying he will raise his body up in three days. Jesus gives more signs during the Passover period, and many believe in him, but he does not trust this "because he knew all men and needed no one to bear

The Marriage at Cana. Sabastiano Ricci. The artist makes the marriage a rather grand occasion and has several of the guests concentrating on the impending difficulty about the diminishing supply of wine.   *(Nelson Gallery–Atkins Museum, Kansas City, Mo. [Nelson Fund])*

witness of man; for he himself knew what was in man" (2:25). To the Word and Light, human favor is a thin reed. John has told us, then, that Jesus is the new temple and that Jesus' signs are the new pointers to life. Whereas in the past people found God in the Jerusalem Temple, now that has needed to be cleansed and has been replaced by Jesus himself, the new site for encountering God. "The Jews" who reject Jesus are shadow people, counterplayers to Jesus' drama. Jesus' witness depends on no human acknowledgment. He is his own authentication.

In chapter 3 Nicodemus, a leading Pharisee, comes to Jesus by night (lacking full faith). He knows that Jesus is a teacher come from God because of Jesus' signs. Jesus shifts the focus to a loftier plane. The Kingdom of God demands a rebirth (baptism would have flashed in the minds of John's readers). In another ironic misunderstanding, Nicodemus takes Jesus' assertion literally: How can one reenter the womb? Jesus speaks spiritually: Rebirth by water and the Spirit is the way to the kingdom.[11] The Spirit moves like the wind, where it wishes. Nicodemus confesses his perplexity. He has stumbled among the puns and several-sided figures of speech that Jesus has strewn. Jesus wonders at the paltry religion of this leading Jew.

Leaving Nicodemus behind, Jesus begins a monologue (like the author of Acts, John frequently employs speeches) concerning the new knowledge that makes the views of Jews like Nicodemus passé. John stresses the immediacy of Jesus' knowledge: "We speak of what we know, and bear witness to what we have seen" (3:11). The Jews, however, do not accept the Christian testimony. The only one who has ascended into heaven (either by Spirit-given insight or after the resurrection) is the one who descended from heaven (the Son of Man and Word Incarnate). The Son of Man must be raised on the cross, like the serpent of Moses (Numbers 21:4–9) that in wisdom literature (Wisdom 16:6) became a symbol of salvation. The lifting up of the Son of Man (on the cross, to heaven) makes it possible for believers to have eternal life.

John 3:16–21 is dense Johannine theology. God gave the Son (made the Word Incarnate and allowed Jesus to die) so that believers should not perish (be victims of Satan, people self-ruined) but instead should have eternal life (be children of God). The purpose of Jesus' coming was positive: salvation, not condemnation. The crux, from the human side, is faith. To believe is to escape condemnation. Not to believe in the name of God's only Son is already to be condemned. There is nothing contrived in this judgment of people. The light came into the world (people had their chance), but people by and large loved darkness (crucified Jesus) rather than the light, because their deeds were evil (belief would have meant conversion and repentance). Thus the Johannine exegesis of the human heart, which was read out of the fate of Jesus: "For every one who does evil hates the light, and does not come to the light, lest his deeds should be exposed. But he who does what is true comes to the light, that it may be clearly seen that his deeds have been wrought in God" (3:20–21). Their response to Jesus shows what is in people. Thus for John, as we shall see more fully later, eschatology—including judgment—is largely something that takes place in the present, in terms of how people respond to Jesus.

Jesus goes in motion again and his disciples start baptizing in Judea. This leads to comparisons with John the Baptist. When John's disciples complain that Jesus is drawing greater crowds, John repeats his earlier submission to Jesus. He is but the friend of the bridegroom, rejoicing in the bridegroom's joy. He is not the Christ, merely the forerunner. From 3:31 the author leaves John behind (perhaps suggesting that the passage has fallen out of its original place) and starts another train of thought, like the one Jesus entered when he left Nicodemus behind. The first note of this thought, reminiscent of Jesus' contrast with Nicodemus, is that heaven and earth are distinct, dualistic planes. The implication is that Jesus, the Messiah and Son, moves on a different level from that of John or Judaism and so is hard to grasp. To receive Jesus is to say that God is true. God has sent Jesus to utter divine words and give the Spirit without measure. Jesus is full of the Father's love and has all responsibility from the Father. To believe in the Son is to have eternal life. Not to believe in the Son is to miss life and earn God's wrath. Jesus, then, is a new crisis, a revelation making the Law and the Baptist's work old news.

John 4:1 calls Jesus the Lord and suggests the opposition of the Pharisees to Jesus' growing success. Jesus heads for Galilee, passing through Samaria. He sits at Jacob's well and makes contact with a Samaritan woman (a person doubly unclean). When he asks her for a drink of water another ironic, several-leveled exchange begins. Typically, the Johannine Jesus takes a physical or "earthly" object (water) and reveals its spiritual or "heavenly" potential (living, baptismal power). Jesus' living water can quench a human being's deepest thirst. It will well up into eternal life. The woman wants this water, because she thinks it will lessen her work at the well. Jesus then reads the woman's situation (long-standing man trouble) like a prophet. The woman veers off into the controversy between Samaritans and Jews, but Jesus puts aside that old quarrel. Salvation is from the Jews, but in the future, which has begun with Jesus, worship will reach out to the Father in spirit and truth, making both Mount Gerizim and Jerusalem incidental. The woman professes her faith in the coming of a Messiah. The Johannine Jesus, in heavy contrast to the Markan Jesus, declares that he is the Messiah: "I who speak to you am he"(4:26).

The disciples, who have been off getting food, return and are amazed to find Jesus speaking with a Samaritan woman. The woman calls out her whole village to see a man who has read her heart and may be the Messiah. The disciples want Jesus to eat but he can think only of heavenly food: "My food is to do the will of him who sent me, and to accomplish his work" (4:34). Jesus' likening Christian mission to harvesting is reminiscent of Matthew 9:35–10:1 and Luke 10:2. The Johannine version of the saying, however, is more paradoxical and mysterious, implying providential relations between sower and reaper, prior workers and present ones. Probably it represents missionary reflections of the Johannine church. The Samaritans of the woman's village believe, in contrast to many Jews. She is, in effect, one of Jesus' best heralds.[12] The first portion of the Book of Signs concludes with the Samaritans' ringing proclamation: "We know that this is indeed the Savior of the world" (4:42). In his first episode, then, John has made Jesus a new thing in Israel, a presence of heaven on an earthly soil that cannot comprehend him. John's Jesus consistently gives ordinary things—water, wine, food, birth—a third dimension. The Incarnation, we might say, leads directly to a sacramental view of the world.

Jesus' Life-Giving Word (4:43–5:47)

The second great sign also occurs in Galilee. At Cana an official, probably a Gentile, whose son is ill at Capernaum begs Jesus to heal the boy. Jesus almost bitterly mutters that unless people see signs and wonders they will not believe. The man is only concerned that his son live. When Jesus gives him a verbal cure (he has been seeking Jesus' physical presence in Capernaum), the man believes and heads for home. On the way his servants meet him with news that his boy lives. The official verifies that the boy began to improve at the very time Jesus gave his word. So the man and his whole household become followers of Jesus. The implication is that Jesus has power over human flesh as well as over such natural matters as wine and water. The sign reaps its intended effect because the recipient of the favor takes Jesus to heart. John is saying, then, that the man's faith played a part in the efficacy of the sign. Had he only been curious, interested in the superficial level of Jesus' wonder-working, it is doubtful Jesus would (or perhaps could) have cured the boy.

In chapter 5 Jesus is again back in Jerusalem, and the narrative of his signs starts to fold into John's interpretation of the major Jewish festivals.

The third sign, the cure he works at the pool called Bethesda, is unique to John's Gospel, as are signs one and seven. Jesus takes pity on a bedridden man who had been hoping for a cure for thirty-eight years and gives him back his mobility. Because the cure occurs on the Sabbath, however, the man runs into trouble (for carrying his pallet, which could be considered work). When Jesus finds the man later he warns him to sin no more. The man tells the Jews it was Jesus who cured him, so they begin to persecute Jesus for violations of the Sabbath law. In contrast to the synoptics, who make the Sabbath something subject to the Son of Man for the sake of human welfare, John locates Jesus' freedom in his divine nature. In working on the Sabbath Jesus is simply imitating his Father, who works always. (By Jesus' day the rabbis had realized that for God literally to rest on the seventh day would have meant the cessation of the world.) The Jews (rightly enough, from John's point of view) interpret this to mean that Jesus is claiming equality with God. To John's mind, however, their shock at the supposed blasphemy of this claim is blind and badly motivated. If they had allowed themselves to see the works Jesus was doing, and had let Jesus' signs make the proper impact, the Jews would have accepted Jesus' union with God joyously, appreciating it for the splendid revelation it was.

Jesus then begins another monologue. The Son only does what he sees the Father doing. Because he loves the Son, the Father shows him everything the Father himself does—greater things, surely, than Jesus has demonstrated thus far. For instance, as the Father raises the dead to life, so will the Son. (The life being discussed is not just the resurrection but also the divine life begun with grace.) The Son has power of judgment from the Father so as to reap the equal honor he deserves. One cannot honor the Father and refuse to honor the Son whom the Father sends. Jesus' word (the agency of his cure of both the crippled man by the pool and the official's son), when taken to heart, brings eternal life, escape from condemnatory judgment and death.

John 5:25 makes Jesus' very presence the beginning of the end-time when the dead will be resurrected. C. H. Dodd, whose division of the Gospel into a Book of Signs and a Book of Glory has dominated recent Johannine studies, has called the Johannine stress on the present "**realized eschatology**." With Jesus' appearance the substance of the fulfillment expected at the parousia has arrived. As Dodd himself explains:

> In the Fourth Gospel the language of "futurist eschatology" is little used. The sense of realization has extended itself over almost the whole field, and expectation has shrunk correspondingly. It is not entirely gone, for the Lord is represented as forecasting for His Church a universality which the evangelist can hardly have supposed to be realized in his time, and as speaking of a day when the generations of the dead will be raised up. We need not regard such expectations as merely vestigial remains of the eschatology of the primitive Church. They are part of the evangelist's own faith. But it is nevertheless true that they no longer have the full significance which belongs to the hope of the second advent in some other New Testament writings. The all-important fact for this evangelist is that the universality of the Christian religion is already given in the moment when Christ being "lifted up" begins to draw all

men to Himself; and that the eternal life to which the dead will be raised is already the possession of living men in union with Him.[13]

The Father, then, already has given resurrecting life to the Son, who in turn has the power of judgment (discretion over who shall be granted this life) because he is the Son of Man, Daniel's heavenly figure. Soon the dead will stream from their tombs to undergo the final judgment. None of these things does the Son speak or do on his own. In everything he seeks only the will of the Father, depends only on the Father's witness to his truth. John the Baptist was on the right track. He sensed Jesus' true identity. But the works Jesus does, in virtue of the Father's power in him, are Jesus' main witnesses. The Jews have never heard the Father's voice or seen his form. They think they have God's Word in their Scriptures, but their closure to Jesus makes it plain that God's Word is not alive in their hearts. The Scriptures testify to Jesus. Because they don't have the love of God in them, the Jews cannot move from the Scriptures to the Christ who brings the eternal life the Scriptures promise. Ironically, the Jews are more inclined to accept purely human characters, false messiahs who promote only themselves, rather than the genuine emissary of the Father who cares only for the Father's glory. The Jews' whole bearing is impure. On Judgment Day Moses will be their accuser. If they truly believed in Moses and lived the spirit of the covenent Law, they would recognize Jesus and believe his words of life. They are, then, hoist on their own petard. Their niggling about the Sabbath law and blindness to the meaning of Jesus' Sabbath cures show in a nutshell their lack of faith.

Jesus the Bread of Life (6:1–71)[14]

The fourth Johannine sign testifying to Jesus' power and identity is the multiplication of the loaves and fishes. (This is the only miracle recorded by all four Gospels.)[15] The parallels with Mark's account suggest that John was familiar with Mark. John makes it plain that Passover is near. The eucharistic overtones are strong (giving thanks and gathering the fragments have close linguistic ties to the formulas of the primitive Christian liturgy). The twelve baskets suggest the presence of the twelve apostles, or the full measure represented by the twelve tribes of Israel. (John is making Jesus the fulfiller of Passover, Sabbath, and all the other major Jewish institutions.)

The people interpret the sign as the arrival of the Moses-like prophet who was to bring the messianic time.[16] However, Jesus rejects the political conclusions the people draw and will not let them make him king. There follows the episode of Jesus walking on the water (Mark 6:45–51; Matthew 14:22–27). In John's staging it is the fifth of Jesus' signs. When the people catch up with Jesus the following day, he contrives to set their understanding straight. They have not come to him again because they seek real signs of the kingdom but because he filled their bellies. They must raise their sights and seek the food that gives eternal life. He, the Son of Man, will give them this food if they believe. Belief in God's revealer, in fact, is *the* work that God requires.

The people then ask for a sign, supposedly to warrant their faith. The multiplication of the loaves reminds them of Moses and the manna in the wilderness (see, for instance, Exodus 16:4, 15. Some messianic scenarios had the Christ duplicating this miracle). Jesus reinterprets the giving of manna in the wilderness as a mercy not of Moses but of God (the source of all good gifts). It is Jesus' Father who gives the true bread from heaven (for Johannine Christianity: the eucharist of Jesus' flesh). In speaking of the bread of God as that which comes down from heaven and gives life to the world (6:33), the Johannine Jesus suggests the incarnation of the Word. When the people ask for this spiritual bread, Jesus speaks plainly: "I am the bread of life; he who comes to me shall not hunger and he who believes in me shall never thirst" (6:35).[17] Chapter 6, which acts as an account of the institution of the eucharist (lacking in John) is thoroughly sacramental.

Although the people have seen Jesus in action they do not believe. Faith is somewhat mysterious, something that recedes into the Father's predetermining will. Jesus will accept any whom the Father sends him. He lives only to do the Father's will, and the Father's will is that he should raise the whole contingent of believers up on the last day. God wants the people to appreciate the revelation given in Jesus and so have eternal life and be raised up on the last day. However, the Jews take offense at Jesus' claim to be the bread of life come down from heaven. Who is he to say he has come down from heaven? As with the protests of Jesus' fellow Galileans recorded in Mark 6:3, the voice here is ironic. The Jews think they know Jesus because they know his human lineage. For John the whole point is that Jesus is the Son of the eternal Father.

Jesus rebukes their murmuring (which is reminiscent of the complaints against Moses in the desert). Much of this business is out of his hands, a matter of the Father's grace. The prophetic anticipation (Isaiah 54:13) of docility to the Spirit in the golden age applies right now. Those docile to Jesus' Father come to Jesus in faith. Only Jesus, the one come from God, from heaven, has seen the Father. To believe this is to gain access to eternal life. In contrast to the manna of Moses, the living bread of Jesus can give eternal life. John could hardly make the connections among Jesus, the eucharist, and eternal life stronger than he does in 6:51: "I am the living bread which came down from heaven; if any one eats of this bread he will live for ever; and the bread which I shall give for the life of the world is my flesh." (Any attempt to reduce the New Testament vision to a this-worldly activism founders on such a text. Johannine incarnationalism or sacramentality makes heaven and grace the immanent *and* transcendent fulfillment of this-worldly life.)

The Jews again protest (the Johannine literary dynamics make that inevitable; they are in good part foils).[18] John implies that they have understood Jesus' sacramental literalism very well. Lest there be any doubt, however, he has Jesus drive the point home in 6:53–56. Only by eating the flesh of the Son of Man and drinking his blood can people have eternal life. Such eating and drinking establish a symbiosis, a living of the believer in Jesus and of Jesus in the believer. The model for this symbiosis is the mutual life of the Father and Jesus. Eating the living, eucharistic bread which came down from heaven will bring eternal life (an ongoing abiding in God). Even the disciples, however, find this a hard saying. Jesus shakes his head: If they cannot accept this, how will they accept his ascension to the Father, which will take him completely out of their sensible range? They must become spiritual, advancing beyond the limitations of fleshly thought. They must have more faith. (Here John refers to Judas, the prototype of the faithless disciple. John's Jesus knows from the beginning who will betray him.)

This is all part of God's order of grace. No one can come to Jesus in faith unless the Father chooses. The disciples divide over this saying, some staying and some walking away. Peter speaks for the twelve and others who stay: "Lord, to whom shall we go? You have the words of eternal life" (6:68). (This is the closest John comes to the "confession of Peter" [e.g., Mark 8:27–33] that the synoptics associate with Peter's leadership of the apostles.) The implication is that anyone drawn by the Father and possessed of faith, anyone really wanting to hear the words of eternal life, will come to know that Jesus is the Holy One of God (see Mark 1:24). Jesus seems to confirm the twelve as having been chosen for such faith. Yet, one of the twelve is a devil: Judas Iscariot. Although a member of the inner circle, he will turn betrayer for lack of faith.

Identity Crisis (7:1–8:59)

Jesus now feels he must stay in Galilee, because in Judea the Jews seek to kill him. His "brothers," however, want him to make a splash before the Jews and convince them. John interprets this as a lack of faith, either within Jesus' own family or among the disciples. Jesus responds caustically: His time (of final revelation, on the cross) has not yet come, but the time of worldlings is always ripe. The world cannot hate unbelieving disciples because the world loves its own. It hates Jesus, however, because Jesus bears witness to its evil. So he will not go up to Jerusalem for the feast of Tabernacles (a Fall festival commemorating the wandering in the wilderness). Let them go.

Jesus does go, however, not for public display but privately. The Jews are on the lookout for him and the people are muttering: He is a *cause célèbre*. Jesus goes into the Temple and teaches. (John repeats the tradition [e.g., Mark 1:22] that Jesus astounded the people by teaching with authority while not having received rabbinic training.) Jesus avows that he only expresses the teaching of his Father, the one who has commissioned him. People of goodwill will know that he teaches on the Father's authority. The crux is whose glory a teacher seeks, his own or God's. Moses gave the Jews God's Law. Yet they do not keep God's Law (so much for authoritative teaching). Why do they seek to kill Jesus, who also only gives them God's teaching? The Jews protest: Jesus is possessed! No one seeks to kill him. Jesus is unrelenting: They do seek to kill him, because he cured the bedridden man on the Sabbath and called God his Father (5:18–19). Yet their hypocrisy or stupidity is plain from Moses' own Law: They circumcise (do a good work) on the Sabbath. To protest making a man whole on the Sabbath is to miss the obvious intent of the Mosaic Law: healing, consecration in wholeness and holiness. The Johannine challenge to Judaism rings loudly in 7:24: "Do not judge by appearances, but judge with right judgment." In John's view no one of goodwill could have witnessed the person, teaching, and deeds of Jesus and not believed in him.

People in the crowd confirm Jesus' instinct that the Jews are out to kill him, and so make the Jews' protests to the contrary lies. (Here we sense the deep bitterness that the author of John feels for those who to his mind rejected God's light.) How can it be that Jesus is speaking openly? Have the authorities accepted his messiahship? Yet these people, too, are superficial, thinking they know where Jesus comes from and that therefore he cannot be the Christ. Jesus asks from the Temple: "You know me and you know where I come from?" If the situation were not so serious one could paint him smiling ironically at their fatuousness. They do not know him because they do not know the God who sent him; they have no genuine faith. Jesus, however, does know God, because he comes from God. The Jews take this as blasphemy and seek to arrest Jesus. They cannot, because Jesus' hour has not yet come (a bit of Johannine predetermination). Many believe, however, because Jesus' signs seem more than enough to qualify him as the Messiah.

Upset by the crowd's favorable impression of Jesus, the chief priests and Pharisees send officers to arrest Jesus. Jesus predicts that his time among the people will be short: Soon he will return to the Father. The Jews typically misunderstand: What does he mean by saying they cannot come where he is going? The reference to the diaspora and the Gentiles is ironic: That is precisely where Jesus' Church did go. On the last day of the feast Jesus takes up the symbolism of water important in the liturgy of Tabernacles: "If any one thirst, let him come to me and drink" (7:37). John interprets the line about rivers of living water flowing out of the believer's heart as referring to the Spirit, who only came after Jesus had been glorified on the cross and through the ascension.

Many are so struck by Jesus' words that they acclaim him as a prophet like Moses or as the Messiah. Others hold back because of an ironic textual quibble: The Messiah is supposed to come from Bethlehem, not Nazareth. (Whether or not John knows the tradition that Jesus was born in Bethlehem, he considers the Messiah's more significant origin to be from "above.") The soldiers sent to arrest Jesus are so impressed that they cannot carry out their assignment. The lines (7:47–49) in which the Pharisees deprecate Jesus and the crowd because the Jewish "authorities" have not accepted Jesus as the Christ are ironic to the point of black humor. Nicodemus stands up for Jesus and fair play, only to be rebuked on the trivial grounds that the eschatological prophet was not expected to come from Galilee. (The prophet Jonah had been a Galilean [2 Kings 14:25] and possibly the prophet Hosea.)

Chapter 8 opens with the incident of the woman taken in adultery (omitted in many of the most reliable ancient manuscripts). It is John's version of the trick questions we have seen the Pharisees put to Jesus in the synoptics. They think they have Jesus caught in a dilemma: Either he will appear careless of the Law of Moses or he will seem inhumanly cruel. Jesus first disregards their game. When they persist he cuts them off at the knees: "Let him who is without sin among you be the first one to throw a stone at her" (8:7). In a single sentence John has captured the insistence of the Matthean Jesus (Matthew 9:13, 12:7) that God wants mercy rather than sacrifice. He has also captured the quickwittedness that must have driven Jesus' legalistic foes to distraction. Humiliated, the scribes and Pharisees slink away. The final scene between Jesus and the woman is beautiful: "Neither do I condemn you; go, and do not sin again" (8:11).

Jesus has another dialogue with the Pharisees (who clearly have the literary function of being Jesus' and John's foils), this time centered on light and witness. It begins with Jesus describing himself as the light of the world (at Tabernacles great lamps lighted the Temple court). To follow Jesus is to avoid darkness and death, to gain the straight path of light and life. The Pharisees object that Jesus is promoting his own cause (as though they would be open to disinterested testimony). Jesus moves below the legal question of interested or disinterested testimony to the question of truth. What Jesus says is true because he belongs to heaven (whence he has come and whither he is going). Their judgments are fleshly, unable to grasp spiritual or heavenly things. Jesus isn't interested in condemning anyone. Should he judge, however, his judgment is true, because the Father judges with him. If one counts Jesus' own testimony and that of the Father (perhaps this means the depth of Jesus' words and the power of his works), Jesus has more than enough testimony. When the Jews ask where Jesus' earthly father is (a rather stupid question), Jesus insists that if they knew him they would know the Father (if they were honest and intelligent they would grasp his oneness with God). Despite these bold rebukes to the Pharisees Jesus avoids arrest, because his hour has not yet come.

Resuming the dialogue or controversy, John has Jesus again refer to his going away (his departure, through death on the cross, for heaven). The Jews will seek him (to find his true meaning? to put him to death?) and will die in their sin (the cause of their unbelief). They miss the point and conjecture that when Jesus says he is going away he is contemplating suicide. Jesus clarifies: They cannot go where he is going because he is from above (heaven, where he is returning) and they are from below (of this world). They will die in their sins unless they believe that "I am he." This difficult phrase may be taken as one of the "I am" pronouncements in John that reflect the self-naming of God in Exodus 3:14.[19] Jesus would then be saying that he is identified with the divinity. One might also take the phrase as referring to the Messiah.

What Jesus told the Jews from the beginning (8:25) is also rather obscure.[20] At the least it recalls that Jesus consistently has claimed to be sent by God, to be so closely identified with God that to reject him is to reject God. Jesus repeats that he has been declaring what he has heard from the One who sent him. The Jews do not understand but John clarifies that Jesus meant the Father. When Jesus is lifted up, the Jews will know "that I am he." Once again the "I am" has divine overtones. (The whole chorus of such sayings—"I am the good shepherd," "I am the bread of life," "I am the light of the world"—makes it plain that John is identifying

Jesus with the Old Testament God. The Son is so intimate with the Father that he may use the divine speech.) Jesus' authority derives from the Father. He speaks as the Father taught him. The Father is always with him, for Jesus always does what is pleasing to the Father.

To the Jews who believe and accept him, Jesus promises knowledge of the truth and thereby freedom. They consider themselves already free, because they are children of Abraham. Jesus refers rather to the bondage of sin. If the Son of God frees them from sin (basic alienation from God), they will be free indeed. Although they are physical descendents of Abraham, they are sinful, as their murderous designs toward Jesus show. The contrast is plain: Jesus speaks of what he has seen with his divine Father; they would murder, like their father Satan. Were they truly children of Abraham, people who lived in Abraham's spirit, they would be believers, not legalistic murderers. That they are not children of God, either, is shown by their not loving Jesus, who proceeds and comes forth from God (terms influential in later Christian reflection about the Trinity). They don't believe because they cannot bear the truth. This shows their descent from Satan, a murderer and the father of lies.[21] Although none of the Jews can convict Jesus of sin, they won't believe (they prefer the irrationality of sin). If they were children of God they would hear in Jesus' words the resonances of God. They do not and so manifestly are not of God.

The Jews charge that Jesus is a Samaritan (heretic?) and possessed. Jesus replies that he is not possessed, but merely a person who honors God. The Jews dishonor Jesus, but Jesus' Father will take care of Jesus' honor and glory. Yet were they to honor Jesus by accepting his words, the Jews would never see (spiritual) death. They again misunderstand: Abraham, the paragon of faith, certainly died. Is Jesus claiming to be greater than Abraham? Jesus repeats that he cares nothing about claims of glory. His Father, the One the Jews call their God, will care for his glory. Jesus knows God but the Jews do not. Abraham looked forward to Jesus (the blessing of all nations; see Genesis 12:3, 18:18). The Jews mock Jesus for speaking as though he had been with Abraham. John 8:58 is perhaps the most powerful of the "I am" sayings: "Truly, truly, I say to you, before Abraham was, I am."[22] The Jews cannot miss this use of the divine self-naming and take up stones to kill Jesus for blasphemy. He (rather mysteriously) hides himself and goes out of the Temple.

Jesus the Light of the World (9:1–10:42)

Chapter 9 deepens the theme that Jesus is the light of the world and shows Johannine irony at its most biting. Jesus notices a man blind from birth.[23] When the disciples ask whose sin caused this defect, Jesus dismisses the notion that sin and physical infirmity have a one-to-one causal relationship. Then, as though echoing Lukan predeterminism, John sets the happening (Jesus' notice of the man) in the context of the divine plan. This man will occasion the sixth of Jesus' great signs that testify to his oneness with God. John 9:4 associates Jesus, God, and Jesus' miracles with daylight. By contrast, night symbolizes the time when Satan and evil hold sway. John 9:5 repeats 8:12: "I am the light of the world." The cure that Jesus works in

9:6–7 has strong baptismal overtones. The neighbors of the man ask him how he was cured, and his reply shows that matter-of-factly (but with considerable faith) he did what Jesus had told him to do. The Pharisees object because this sign was worked on the Sabbath. Jesus' works have them in a bind: How can he do these things and not be from God? When they ask the man born blind what he thinks, the reply is again laconic: "He is a prophet." Clearly John is presenting this man as the sort of witness Jesus ought to have found everywhere: an honest person of common sense.

The Jews cannot let the matter go. By badgering the man's parents they only confirm that he had been blind from birth. John 9:22 shows the closedness of the Jews. (Probably this is written in light of the Jewish hardening against Christianity that occurred after 85 C.E.) They simply will not hear testimony that Jesus is the Christ. When they again interrogate the man himself, he sticks to what he knows: He used to be blind and now he sees. Finally their stupid, badly motivated questioning gets to him. John 9:27 drips with sarcasm: "Do you too want to become his disciples?" They revile him but he blasts them out of the water: "Never since the world began has it been heard that any one opened the eyes of a man born blind. If this man were not from God, he could do nothing"(9:32–33). (John is also symbolizing spiritual blindness, of course. Never since the world began has anyone come with divine light capable of bringing people to eternal life.) They have no answer but abuse. (For the second time [see 9:22] John charges that confessing Jesus meant excommunication from the synagogue.) Jesus finds the man and completes his faith, informing him that he has been cured by the Son of Man. John 9:39 is the Johannine version of the Isaiahan paradox (Isaiah 6:9–10; see Mark 8:18 and Matthew 13:13–16). The coming of Jesus makes worldly sight into spiritual blindness and cures worldly blindness with spiritual vision. The Pharisees compound their guilt by their pride. If they would confess their need Jesus could do something for them.

Chapter 10 continues the contrast between Jesus and the false leaders or shepherds of Israel. Jesus is the true shepherd and gate to life. The symbolism suggests the classic messianic text of Ezekiel 34: "'Son of man, prophesy against the shepherds of Israel, prophesy, and say to them, even to the shepherds, Thus says the Lord God: Ho, shepherds of Israel, who have been feeding yourselves! Should not shepherds feed the sheep?'" (34:2–3). Jesus works and teaches with no guile. His own people (genuine Israelites) know his voice (because they are attuned to God). The way to light and life passes through Jesus. (The festival context, heavy with messianic overtones, gives this Johannine conviction further resonance.) For John Jesus mediates all salvation. Jesus even lays down his life for his people (the greatest sign of love; see 15:13). Jesus' knowledge of his own people is like the knowledge of the Father and the Son: symbiotic, **connatural**. It is more intimate than concepts, an immediate effect of shared being and singleness of life.

John 10:16 suggests that Jesus envisions his shepherding as (one day) extending beyond Israel to the Gentiles. Eventually the division between Jews and Gentiles should cease, since they both have the same shepherd.

The Father loves Jesus' complete dedication (to the point of sacrificing his life). John 10:18 is John's plain belief that Jesus died according to the divine will. Human forces were only means to God's purpose of exalting Jesus through the cross and resurrection. Jesus' deep, challenging words again divide the people. Those on Jesus' side rebut the charge of demonic possession by pointing to Jesus' holy sayings and healing works.

Time passes and it is the feast of the Dedication, celebrated about three months after Tabernacles (to commemorate the rededication of the Temple in 165 B.C.E. during the Maccabean wars). Like Tabernacles the feast of the Dedication had a strong theme of light (the light of liberty) and clear messianic overtones. The Jews approach Jesus and want a clear declaration: Is he the Christ? Jesus says he has told them (through his work) and they will not believe. They will not believe because they are not part of his flock; they don't belong to the people to whom he will give eternal life. No one can take Jesus' people (those the Father has predestined) from him.

John 10:30 is a more than messianic claim: "I and the Father are one." This verse not only repeats Jesus' claim (as Word and divine Son) to intimacy with the Father. It also suggests a plural form of the divine "I am" and recalls the oneness (the prime attribute) of the Israelite God (Deuteronomy 6:4). The Jews understand the blasphemous implications and grab their stones (only in a new framework, justified by Jesus' signs, would Jesus' claims not be blasphemous). Jesus asks what he has done wrong. They accuse him of a blasphemy that John implies is superficial, on the level merely of language. Jesus shows that on that level of language Scripture itself (Psalms 82:6) can seem blasphemous. Jesus forces the matter to another level. He has not claimed divine sonship lightly. His works are eloquent proof of what he claims. John advances a very pragmatic, hardheaded set of criteria (as with the man born blind): "If I am not doing the works of my Father, then do not believe me; but if I do them, even though you do not believe me, believe the works" (10:37–38).

Jesus' works show his union with the Father, the force of the Father in him. But the Jews continue to block their ears and Jesus must again escape. The end of chapter 10 places Jesus across the Jordan River and recalls the Baptist's testimony, which Jesus has been fulfilling. The Book of Signs throughout has subordinated John the Baptist to Jesus, and chapter 10 shows signs of being its first ending. (Chapters 11 and 12 may be taken as a second, more climactic ending.) By now, as well, the bitter view John has of the people who rejected Jesus is plain. Although historically the Johannine polemic against "the Jews" has stimulated much anti-Semitism, in itself it is more a protest that God's light was rejected.

Life Conquering Death (11:1–54)

The seventh and greatest of Jesus' signs is the raising of Lazarus (which prefigures Jesus' own resurrection). John 11:2 identifies Mary, Lazarus' sister, with the woman who wiped Jesus' feet at the table (12:1–3). When Jesus hears of Lazarus' illness, he hints that it is another happening that will serve God's revelatory will (the manifestation of God's glory through powerful signs) and delays for two more days. John goes out of his way to stress the love Jesus bore this family. The disciples would prevent Jesus from returning to Judea, where the Jews seek to stone him, but Jesus says this is still a period of light (his enemies have not yet come into their dark hour). The disciples misunderstand Jesus' reference to Lazarus' sleeping. John implies that Jesus intuits that Lazarus has died. The remark of Thomas in 11:16 is ironic, in view of the disciples' scattering at Jesus' Passion.

When Jesus arrives Lazarus has been four days in the tomb. His sister Martha implicitly asks Jesus to raise him. The Johannine Jesus is the resurrection and the life, the source of immortality. Martha accepts this and makes a full protestation of faith: "I believe that you are the Christ, the Son of God, he who is coming into the world" (11:27). (In view of John's Gospel having no confession of the Christ by Peter, this is extraordinary.) Mary goes out to Jesus and repeats Martha's conviction: If Jesus had been there Lazarus would not have died. Jesus is deeply moved by the sisters' grief. At the tomb Jesus prays to his Father, who always hears him, and John sets up another chance for Jesus to manifest the Father's having sent him. At Jesus' loud cry Lazarus comes forth.

Many of the onlookers believe in Jesus, because of this powerful sign. Others, however, report Jesus to the chief priests and Pharisees. Not even Jesus' having raised a dead man to life can crack these leaders' hardness. They are only concerned that Jesus will draw away the crowds and so endanger the Jews' standing with Rome. The Johannine irony is plain: Precisely what the Jewish leaders fear happened in 70 C.E. (because they did not believe in Jesus?). The high priest Caiaphas utters the logical conclusion of their closedness (the definitive choice for death rather than life): "You know nothing at all; you do not understand that it is expedient for you that one man should die for the people, and that the whole nation should not perish" (11:50). For John this saying was an official and prophetic anticipation of Jesus' death on the cross for the salvation of the whole people, Jews and Gentiles alike. So the Jewish authorities take counsel to put Jesus to death. Jesus therefore departs to the wilderness town of Ephraim, about fifteen miles from Jerusalem.

Life Coming through Death (11:55–12:50)

Before Passover Jesus returns to Bethany to visit with Lazarus, Mary, and Martha. Mary anoints Jesus' feet with costly ointment and wipes his feet with her hair. Judas Iscariot protests: The money spent on this ointment should have been given to the poor. John accuses Judas (who kept the community purse) of being a thief (wanting the money for himself). Jesus defends Mary and interprets her action as a preparation (a kingly anointing?) for his death (time of triumph). The crowd that gathers to see Jesus and Lazarus so troubles the chief priests that they contemplate putting Lazarus to death also.

The next day (the beginning of what for John is the final week of a new creation), Jesus goes to Jerusalem, entering the city on a young ass. The people greet him with branches of palm (a detail that only John has; see Mark 11:1–10, Matthew 21:1–9, Luke 19:28–40) as the Messiah (see

Zechariah 9:9). If Jesus is a king, he is not a warrior king but a ruler of peace. Only after Jesus' death did his disciples understand the symbolism of this entry into the holy city. The people are Jesus' for the asking because he raised Lazarus. The Pharisees seem resigned: The whole world is going after Jesus (12:19). In Jerusalem some Gentiles ask to see Jesus. (John is contrasting their openness with the closedness of the Jewish authorities, who have not responded well even to Jesus' appearance at the festivals that should have helped them grasp his identity.) In terms of John's literary dynamics, this triggers Jesus' announcement that his hour has come. Soon he will be glorified. His death will be like the burial of seed in the ground: a phase necesary for fruitfulness. John 12:25 repeats a saying familiar from the synoptics (Mark 8:35, Matthew 10:39, Luke 9:24): "He who loves his life loses it, and he who hates his life in this world will keep it for eternal life." Serving Jesus means following Jesus even to death. This will bring the disciple honor from Jesus' Father.

Jesus' soul is troubled (the equivalent of the upset the synoptics place on the Mount of Olives just prior to Jesus' arrest). John's Jesus does not ask release from his fate ("hour"), however. It is necessary for the Father's glory. A voice from heaven (a sign of approbation) ratifies Jesus' stance. (The Johannine references to Jesus' baptism omit this voice, and the synoptics do not mention it when recounting Jesus' agony. Perhaps John is baptizing Jesus for his death. As well, this voice may echo the synoptics' account of the Transfiguration. See, for instance, Mark 9:1–13.) Jesus says the voice was for the sake of the crowd. They should know that the hour of judgment has drawn near. Soon the ruler of this world (Satan) will be cast out and Jesus, from the cross, will draw all people to himself. In other words, Jesus' death will be paradoxical: a seeming defeat and abasement but really a great victory and glorification. The people wonder at the notion of a Messiah who must die on the cross. (Psalms 89 and 110, for instance, make the rule of the messianic king everlasting.) Jesus warns that the light will only be with them a short while. This is their last chance to become children of the light. Those who walk in Satan's darkness do not know where they are going.

Jesus departs and hides himself. His signs have not been enough. In keeping with Isaiah 6:9–10, the people could not believe because their eyes were blinded and their hearts hardened. It is as though they were fated (for the sake of a later greater good?) to miss the meaning of Jesus. Still, Jesus had his successes. Many people did believe in him, even though often they were not courageous enough to profess their faith openly. John 12:43 is a terse bit of Johannine religious psychology. Often people did not embrace Jesus because "they loved the praise of men more than the praise of God." Faith in Jesus demands a decision and a willingness to part with worldly praise.

The last lines of the Book of Signs (12:44–50) summarize Jesus' preaching and meaning. To believe in Jesus is to believe in the Father who sent Jesus. Jesus comes as light, to rescue people from darkness. He is not a judge but a savior. The words that Jesus has spoken will stand before people on Judgment Day and take their measure. Everything Jesus has said and done has been on the authority of the Father, by the Father's inspiration. What the Father has commanded Jesus to say is eternal life (it is about eternal life and gives eternal life). So the Book of Signs concludes: "What I say, therefore, I say as the Father has bidden me" (12:50). Jesus' public life has had but a single goal: witness to or revelation of the Father.

The Book of Glory (13:1–20:31)

The Farewell Discourses (13:1–17:26)

The second major portion of John's Gospel is distinguished from the first by several notable differences. Thus Raymond E. Brown, beginning his commentary on the Book of Glory, remarks:

> There are notable differences between the Books. First, during the public ministry, as described in the Book of Signs, Jesus' words and deeds were addressed to a wide audience, provoking a crisis of faith—some believed and some refused to believe. The Book of Glory, however, is addressed to the restricted audience of those who believed. Second, the signs of the first Book anticipated what Jesus would do for men once he was glorified. The second Book describes the glorification, i.e., "the hour" of passion, crucifixion, resurrection, and ascension wherein Jesus is lifted up to the Father to enjoy again the glory that he had with the Father before the world existed (xvii 5).[24]

These differences appear with the very first verse of the Book of Glory. John 13:1 places Jesus before Passover and says, "When Jesus knew that his hour had come to depart out of this world to the Father, having loved his own who were in the world, he loved them to the end." Jesus is leaving the scene of the Book of Signs. The Book of Glory will focus on what his love for his own (believers of whatever background) implied, necessitated, and accomplished.

At supper (which is not a Passover meal; John places that on Friday evening), knowing that Judas will betray him and that he is going back to God, Jesus plays servant to the disciples and washes their feet.[25] (The synoptic accounts of the Last Supper do not have this scene. It is probably John's equivalent of their suffering servant motif.) The dialogue between Peter and Jesus both shows Peter's passionate character and suggests baptismal cleansing. John inserts a bit of the synoptic Jesus' stress on inner cleansing. Judas will betray Jesus because inside Judas is unclean. Jesus then asks the disciples if they understand what he has done. He has given them an example of service. As he, the Teacher and Lord, has waited on them, so should they wait on one another.

Judas' coming betrayal weighs heavily on the heart of the Johannine Jesus. John attempts to reconcile Jesus' foreknowledge with Judas' betrayal by making it scripturally necessary (Psalms 41:9). That Jesus predicts this betrayal to the disciples should help convince them that "I am he." John 13:20 parallels Mark 9:37 and Matthew 10:40. It probably is included here to add to the unity between Master and disciple expressed in 13:16.

Jesus expresses his heartsickness about Judas. The disciples become uneasy and look at one another. John 13:23 refers to the beloved disciple (for the first time) lying close to Jesus' breast. At the urging of Peter he asks Jesus who the betrayer is. Jesus dips a morsel of food (an act of courtesy or honor) and gives it to Judas (again in keeping with 13:18 and Psalms 41:9). When Judas rejects the grace offered him with the morsel, John's literary eye sees Satan enter into him. Then Jesus tells Judas to do what he is going to do quickly. Judas goes out and it is night, the hour of Satan's dominance.

More truly, however, it is the beginning of Jesus' hour of glorification. The process of crucifixion, resurrection, and ascension that will trumpet God's love has commenced. The disciples will not be able to go with Jesus. Like a parting gift, Jesus gives them a new commandment: "A new commandment I give to you, that you love one another; even as I have loved you, that you also love one another" (13:34). This love and imitation of Jesus are to be the hallmark of Jesus' disciples. Peter asks Jesus where he is going and Jesus promises that later Peter will follow after him (experience a similar martyrdom?). Peter generously promises to lay down his life for Jesus, but Jesus knows better. Peter will deny him three times before the night is over. (Luke 22:31–34 also places Jesus' prediction of Peter's denial at the Last Supper; Mark 14:27–31 and Matthew 26:31–35 place it later, on the way to Gethsemane.)

Chapter 14 is mainly a long speech, the beginning of Jesus' so-called "high priestly prayer," in which he often leaves the disciples behind and gazes upward toward the Father. His first words are of comfort: "Let not your hearts be troubled" (14:1). He is going to the Father to prepare a heavenly place for the disciples. He will return to take them to himself, so that Master and disciples may be together always. They know the way (faith). Thomas protests that they know neither where Jesus is going nor the way. Jesus' reply is for John an epitome of Jesus' meaning: "I am the way, and the truth, and the life; no one comes to the Father, but by me" (14:6). To know Jesus, as we have frequently heard, is to know the Father. The disciples' knowledge of Jesus henceforth will bring them to know God.

Philip, like Thomas a literary foil, asks Jesus to show them the Father. Jesus is saddened by this obtuseness: Whoever has seen Jesus has seen the Father. Jesus is in the Father and the Father is in Jesus. (Later Christian trinitarianism was virtually predetermined by John 14–17.) The Father speaks and works through Jesus. If the disciples cannot believe the identity between the being of Jesus and the Father, let them (like the Jews) believe the works the Father has done through Jesus. Those who believe in Jesus will do similar, even greater works. They will take Jesus' (revelatory) place, because Jesus goes to the Father. Let the disciples only ask in Jesus' name and Jesus will grant their requests, that the Father may be glorified (showing the plan of salvation to be sound and splendid).

To love Jesus is to keep his commandments. This will lead him to pray to the Father and will lead the Father to send the Counselor (Paraclete). For John the Counselor is both an ongoing presence of Jesus and the Holy Spirit. The Counselor (advocate or helper) will be with the disciples forever, as the Spirit of unworldly truth. The disciples will know the Spirit because he will dwell with them and be in them. (This is a cardinal feature of Johannine faith. The inner guidance of the Spirit is a major source of enlightenment and certitude.)[26] Jesus will not leave them desolate. He will soon return (at the resurrection, along with the Spirit, and at the parousia). John is foreshadowing the Christian doctrine of grace, the indwelling of the divine trinity in believers' hearts. By keeping the commandments the disciples will show their love and enjoy intimate communion with the Father and the Son. The crux is love. Jesus manifests himself to those who love him. The Father and Son make their home in those who love them. Those unwilling to love, to keep Jesus' word, reject the word (and presence) of the Father.

The Counselor will bring all these sayings of Jesus back to the disciples' minds. Sent by the Father in Jesus' name, he will teach the disciples all things. Jesus leaves the disciples peace, his own unique tranquillity. This should prevent them from being troubled and fearful. His going is cause for rejoicing more than sorrowing. He goes to the Father, who is greater than he (the Father is his source). Jesus is telling the disciples about his resurrection and return to the Father before it happens to help them believe when it occurs. The ruler of the world (Satan) is coming. Jesus' time is short. But all this serves the Father's plan and occurs to show the world Jesus' love for the Father.

Chapter 15 (the start of a section—chapters 15 to 17—showing many signs of being a later addition) begins with the most famous Johannine figure for the relation between Jesus and the disciples.[27] He is the vine, and they are the branches. The Father cares for their organic life, pruning the branches that they may bear more fruit. Jesus' word has cleansed the disciples. If they abide in him and let him abide in them, they will bear much fruit. Apart from the vine the branches can do nothing. Abiding in Jesus, the disciples may ask anything. The fruitfulness of the branches (the Church) glorifies the Father. It is the proof of genuine discipleship. Jesus has loved the disciples the way the Father has loved him. They are to abide in his love. By keeping his commandments they will abide in the divine love. Jesus tells them these things to give them joy, his own rich plenitude.

Once again Jesus commands the disciples to love one another as he has loved them. The greatest love is to lay down life for one's friends. If they keep his commandments (abide in his love) they are his friends. No longer does he call them servants, because he has told them everything he has heard from the Father (he has unburdened his heart to them, as friend does to friend). Their discipleship is not ultimately a matter of their own choosing. Jesus has chosen them to go and bear fruit. They will have abiding fruit, and access to the Father, if they love one another, keeping Jesus' central and summarizing command.

Should the world hate the disciples, they must remember that the world hated Jesus before them. Because Jesus chose them out of the world, the world finds them hateful. They must remember what happened to Jesus and not expect a different fate. Mistreating the disciples, like mistreating Jesus, reveals an ignorance of the Father who sent Jesus (a practical atheism). Jesus' revelation of the Father leaves the sinful world with no excuse. To hate Jesus is to hate the Father. Their cause is one. Jesus did unique works among "them" (the Jews or the world) which convict them of sin. Only willful blindness, John believes, let the Jews reject Jesus' works. Such a rejection displays a hatred of both Jesus and the Father. The Jews have hated Jesus without cause (Psalms 35:19). The Counselor will make all these things clear to the disciples, showing them the truth and bearing witness to Jesus. He will make them witnesses to Jesus, for they have been with Jesus from the beginning (the mark of the most authoritative apostles).

Chapter 16 begins with a brief Johannine eschatological prediction (compare with Mark 13). The disciples will be excommunicated from the synagogues and enemies will seek their lives. Behind this persecution will lie the Jews' ignorance of Jesus and the Father. Then Jesus returns to his theme of departure. He is telling the disciples these things now because he must withdraw from their midst. This makes them sad, but in fact Jesus' going is to their advantage. For his going is the condition of the coming of the Comforter, who will convict the world of sin (and vindicate the disciples' cause). The sin of the world is not believing in Jesus. Jesus is proclaimed righteous by his resurrection and return to the Father. By Jesus' triumph, Satan stands judged and overthrown. The Spirit will tell the disciples all that he has heard (much as Jesus did) and will guide them into all truth. He will show the Church all that is to come. He will glorify Jesus and make over Jesus' patrimony to the disciples. Father, Jesus, and Spirit share a common fund of truth.

Highly conscious that his time is short, the Johannine Jesus speaks of the "little while" before his death and the further "little while" before his return. His Passion will be sorrowful for the disciples, for the world will seem to triumph. (Looking back, John is remembering the tumult of the disciples' emotions during Jesus' Passion.) Soon, however, the disciples' sorrow will turn to joy, like a woman who forgets her labor pains once her child has been born. At the resurrection the disciples will receive a joy that no one will take from them. They will sense the completeness of Jesus' work and feel they can ask the Father for all their needs in Jesus' name. The Father loves them because they have loved Jesus and believed in his mission. John 16:28 show the great circuit the Johannine Jesus travels: "I came from the Father and have come into the world; again, I am leaving the world and going to the Father."

The disciples think this makes everything plain and makes their faith easy. Jesus knows they will soon scatter and leave him alone. Yet he is never alone because the Father is always with him. Jesus is telling the disciples all this for their peace. The world will trouble them, "but be of good cheer, I have overcome the world" (16:33).

Chapter 17 shifts Jesus' focus from the disciples to the Father. The hour has come for the Father to glorify the Son (support him through the Passion), that the Son may glorify the Father. The Father has given the Son charge of all humanity, to give all people eternal life. Eternal life is knowing the Father, the only true God, and his missionary Jesus Christ. Jesus has done his work on earth. It is time for the Father to glorify him with the glory he had in the Father's presence before creation.

Jesus has made the Father's name known to the disciples whom the Father gave him. The disciples now know that Jesus derives all he has from the Father. The disciples have received Jesus' words and have believed that the Father sent him. Jesus is praying for his believers, the good fruit of his mission. He is not praying for unbelievers, the sinful humanity that has opposed his message. His believers belong to him. As such, they belong to the Father, for with Father and Son "mine" is "thine." The disciples represent Jesus' glory, the splendid work he has achieved. Because Jesus is leaving the world for the Father, and the disciples must continue in the world, Jesus prays for the disciples. May the Father keep the disciples in his name. May the Father preserve the disciples he has given Jesus. Let them be one, a community of love, as Father and Son are one. While Jesus was with the disciples physically, he kept them safe in the Father's name. He guarded all whom the Father had given him, losing only Judas, the son of perdition (whose loss fulfilled the Scriptures). But now Jesus is coming to the Father, so he speaks these words about providence and protection for the disciples' joy.

The disciples have Jesus' word, which is the word of the Father (John cannot repeat this theme too much). The world hates the disciples because they do not belong to the world (they rebuke the world by their very being). Jesus does not ask the Father to take the disciples out of the world (a strong Johannine rebuttal to any Gnosticism that would make faith wholly unworldly). He prays that the Father will keep the disciples from the evil one, Satan. The disciples do not belong to the world, any more than Jesus does. May the Father sanctify the disciples in truth. The Father's word is truth (it alone can sanctify them). Jesus is sending the disciples into the world the way the Father sent him into the world. The missions are parallel. Jesus consecrates himself (by his coming Passion), so that the disciples may be hallowed in divine truth.

The last verses of the high priestly prayer have become especially poignant among Christians working for ecumenical reunion.[28] Jesus prays not just for the disciples standing before him but for all their successors, all the believers who shall come from their missionary efforts. His prayer is for the unity of his followers: that they may be one. Indeed, may their unity be as absolute as the unity of Father and Son. May they be united in Father and Son, that the world may believe Jesus' mission from the Father. (The implication is that disunion among the disciples calls Jesus' work into question.) Jesus has given his glory to the disciples to make them one as he is one with the Father, who gave him his glory. The unity the disciples have in Jesus, who himself is filled with the Father, will show the world that the Father has both sent Jesus and loved the disciples, as he has loved Jesus.

Jesus then prays that his disciples may come to be where he is (in heaven, with the Father), to behold his glory, the splendor he has as the uncreated Son. The world has not known the righteous Father (as its persecution of Jesus so horribly shows). But Jesus has known the Father and the disciples have known that the Father sent Jesus. (That may be enough.) Jesus has made the Father's name known to the disciples, and he will make it known again (on the cross and in the resurrection). This will publish the love of the Father for Jesus and make it present in the disciples just as Jesus will be present. So the highly priestly prayer closes on a sublime note of unity.

The Passion Narrative (18:1–19:42)[29]

Despite the differences between the first part of the Johannine Book of Glory and what we find in the synoptics, the Johannine Passion Narrative is quite consistent with the synoptic accounts. When the Johannine Jesus ends his Last Supper discourse, he goes directly to the garden of Gethsemane to be arrested. Thus John omits the stories of Jesus' agony, Jesus' prayer, the comfort of the angel, and the like found in Mark 14:26 and 32–52 and its synoptic parallels. Judas knows the garden of Gethsemane well, since Jesus often met there with the disciples. Judas gathers a band of soldiers, officers of the chief priests, and Pharisees. They converge on Gethsemane with lights and weapons. John 18:4 displays John's conviction that Jesus is in full control of the situation: "Then Jesus, knowing all that was to befall him, came forward and said to them, 'Whom do you seek?'" When the crowd says that it seeks Jesus of Nazareth, Jesus does not hide his identity but speaks out boldly, "I am he" (another "I am" saying). The power of Jesus' "I am he" makes some of the crowd stagger and fall to the ground.

Once again Jesus asks them whom they seek. When they again say Jesus of Nazareth and he again affirms that he is he, John leaves no doubt that Jesus is meeting his fate freely. In addition, Jesus is trying to protect his disciples: "If you seek me, let these men go" (18:8). To John's mind this request of Jesus stems from his charge to keep all those whom the Father had given him. Only John gives the details that it was Peter who struck the slave of the high priest with a sword and cut off his right ear, and that the slave's name was Malchus (see, for instance, Mark 14:47). Jesus disapproves of Peter's action (but does not, as in Luke 22:51, heal the man's ear). The Father's will demands that Jesus suffer this abuse.

The Johannine version of the scene before Annas, the father-in-law of the high priest, does not square with the synoptic accounts in all details. John seems to be going his own way (perhaps drawing on other witnesses). Moreover, John's exalted theology of Jesus has no place for a serious interrogation of Jesus by the Jews at this point. Jesus has given all the self-explanation necessary. The motif that John emphasizes is the counsel of the high priest Caiaphas that it was expedient for one man to die for the people. In that perspective, Jesus' fate is foregone.

John 18:15 mentions that not just Peter but also another disciple followed Jesus from the fringes. Traditional conjecture has made this other disciple the one whom Jesus loved (the source of the special Johannine tradition). Both this disciple and Peter gain entrance to the court of the high priest (to whom Jesus has been brought). Peter denies that he is a disciple of Jesus but lingers near his master, warming himself by the fire.

When the high priest questions Jesus, Jesus answers that he has always taught openly. His teaching is well known and the priest might easily ask any people who heard him. (The openness of Jesus, which makes it absurd that he was trying to mount a revolution, contrasts markedly with the deceits and lies of his enemies, who are pawns of the Father of Darkness.) For this reply Jesus is struck by one of the officers of the high priest. The Johannine irony is almost crude: Truth is abused for answering honestly a representative of falsehood. Jesus asks that this abuse be justified by his abusers pointing out any wrong in his speech. None is forthcoming and Annas sends him bound to Caiaphas.

Once again Peter is asked whether he is a disciple of Jesus and once again he denies that he is. Still a third time this happens, and the cock crows. The leader of Jesus' band has already forsaken him. Not entering the Roman praetorium, so that they will not become ritually unclean (let us forget the murder on their minds), the representatives of the Jews meet with Pilate, the representative of Rome. They want Pilate to accept their judgment that Jesus is an evildoer. Pilate says that their judgment is to be the crux: They should deal with Jesus themselves. The Jews protest that they don't have the power to execute capital punishments. This shows that they want Jesus' death. (To John it also explains how Jesus came to die on a cross, by a Roman method of execution.)

Seeing that this is serious business, Pilate goes to interrogate Jesus himself. The charge obviously is political mischief. When Pilate asks Jesus whether he is King of the Jews, Jesus asks where Pilate got this information. (Has he had independent information to the effect that Jesus was building a political power base?) Pilate scoffs and misunderstands: Such Jewish things hardly concern him. Jesus' own people have handed him over to the Roman arm. What has he done? Jesus proceeds to define his kingship (and thereby show how little he is a political threat). The distance between Jesus' rule and a Jewish messiahship conceived in terms of a golden this-worldly rule is remarkable. The principles of Jesus' rule forbid his contesting on the level of might and worldly power. Otherwise, Jesus' disciples would band together to keep him from being handed over to the Jews. Jesus' kingship is far different from revolutionary politics (for John it is something heavenly, an aspect of the divine Sonship).

Still, Pilate senses that Jesus does claim to be royalty. Jesus accepts this: He was born for this (kingship, glorification through suffering, witness to the truth). His kingship is inseparable from his witness to the truth. Everyone (including Pilate, if he wishes) who belongs to the truth, craves the truth, will listen to Jesus' voice. Pilate breaks the spell with an outburst of cynicism: "What is truth?" (18:38). When people do not know what truth is, or do not care, Johannine theology can do nothing for them. They are free to choose the darkness and their own destruction. Still, Pilate has enough regard for the truth to tell the Jews that he finds no crime in Jesus. He tries to win Jesus' release through the custom the New Testament reports of a Passover amnesty. They, however, will not have Jesus, the King of the Jews, but insist on the thief Barabbas.

Chapter 19 is the fairly terse Johannine version of Jesus' Passion and death. Pilate has Jesus scourged. The soldiers plait Jesus a crown of thorns, array him in purple robes, and mock and strike him. Then Pilate brings Jesus out to the crowd, announcing that he has found no crime in him (and perhaps hoping that this humiliation will be enough). When Jesus appears in mock-kingly garb, Pilate utters his famous "Ecce homo." Probably Pilate meant this "Behold the man" as a dramatic effort to bring home to the crowd the pathos in Jesus' humiliation. In the Johannine context it has overtones of the "Son of Man" and of the representative of the people (see 11:50–52) whose death would bring salvation.

According to John the chief priests and officers take the lead in crying for Jesus' death by crucifixion. Pilate tries to get them to crucify Jesus themselves but they remind him that they have no capital power. Still, they want Jesus to die as a blasphemer. According to their law one who made himself Son of God ought to die. This frightens Pilate even more than the discussion of kingship. (John is at pains to show the power Jesus had over Pilate, their ironic reversal of roles.) However, Jesus will not answer Pilate's question about his origin. When Pilate tries to bully him, Jesus reminds Pilate that all power is from God (a last appeal to Pilate's conscience). The one who delivered Jesus to Pilate (the high priest) has the greatest responsibility for this travesty.

This again moves Pilate to try to release Jesus, but the Jews know Pilate's weakness. To release Jesus might be to encourage sedition, which would directly undermine Pilate's own responsibility in Judea. If Jesus is a king he is a threat to Caesar. Pilate is not strong enough to decide that Jesus is a purely spiritual king and no physical threat to Caesar at all. So Pilate takes his formal judgment seat and announces to the Jews, "Behold your King!" Doubtless this is double-edged for John, as is the notice of the time: about the sixth hour of the preparation day before Passover. This time conflicts with Mark 15:25, which places the crucifixion about 9:00 A.M. a day later (Passover itself). Probably the Johannine symbolism is meant to suggest the paschal lamb, which was slaughtered about noon on preparation day. The Jews call for Jesus' crucifixion and the chief priests say they have no king but Caesar.

Jesus goes out to Golgotha, the place of crucifixion, bearing his own cross. He is crucified between two other criminals. Pilate writes on Jesus' cross the title, "Jesus of Nazareth, the King of the Jews." He will not yield to the requests of the chief priests that this be changed to, "This man said, 'I am King of the Jews.'" John is having Pilate defend far more than he knows. The soldiers take Jesus' garments and cast lots for his tunic, to fulfill Scripture (Psalms 22:18). By the cross stand Jesus' mother, Mary the wife of Cleophas, and Mary Magdalene. Seeing with his mother the disciple whom he loved, Jesus commends them to one another. Let her consider the disciple her son and let him consider her his mother. Henceforth she will live in the disciple's home.

Jesus now knows that everything is finished. To fulfill the Scriptures (Psalms 69:21) he says, "I thirst." Johannine theology would read this as a statement of his desire to finish his Father's mission. After taking some vinegar (the hyssop recalls the sprinkling of the blood of the paschal lamb on the doorpost in Exodus 12:12), Jesus bows his head and dies (gives up his spirit: hands over the Spirit). The Jews ask that the death process be hastened, so as not to pollute this special ("high") Sabbath (another Johan-

The Procession to Calvary. Flemish. About 1510. The passion of Christ was a favorite theme of Gothic tapestries. Christ bears a wooden cross with the help of Simon the Cyrenean. He is followed by the Virgin and St. John. He pauses to quiet the women of Jerusalem. The woman holding the cloth is probably Veronica, who legend said received an impression of Christ's face. The sumptuous clothing and detailed flora are characteristic of late Gothic art. *(Nelson Gallery—Atkins Museum, Kansas City, Mo. [Nelson Fund])*

nine irony). The soldiers find Jesus already dead and so do not break his legs. They do, however, pierce his side. For later tradition, the blood and water that come out symbolize the Christian eucharist and baptism. Here John is emphasizing Jesus' real death.

At this point the author insists on the eyewitness character of his testimony. He has seen these things and is telling the truth for the sake of his readers' faith. What happened was destined by God and fulfilled the Scriptures—for instance, Exodus 12:46, which forbade the breaking of a bone of the paschal lamb, and Zechariah 12:10. After Jesus' death Joseph of Arimathea, a secret disciple, obtains the body from Pilate. With Nicodemus, who had brought myrrh and aloes to anoint the body, he binds Jesus in linen cloths, and lays him in a new tomb in a garden of the place where Jesus had been crucified. Both the mention of Nicodemus and the note that the burial place was close to Golgotha are unique to John. It is preparation day, so the disciples do no more.

The Resurrection (20:1–31)[30]

John notes that the resurrection occurred on the first day of the week, a fitting day for a new start. Mary Magdalene comes to the tomb while it is still dark and sees that the stone has been rolled away. She runs to tell Peter and the beloved disciple. Peter and the beloved disciple run to the tomb and see for themselves. They see the linen cloths and the napkin that had been on Jesus' head. John seems to intend this physical evidence as an anchor for their perception of the empty tomb. (By contrast with Lazarus—11:44—Jesus does not need to be unwrapped.) Since the disciples do not anticipate a resurrection, they don't know what to make of the empty tomb.

Mary Magdalene stays at the tomb weeping. Looking in, she sees two angels in white. They ask why she is weeping. Her reply summarizes her love and her loss: "Because they have taken away my Lord, and I do not know where they have laid him" (20:13). At this moment the loss of Jesus' body seems the final blow. Turning around she sees Jesus but does not know it is he. Like the angels, he asks why she is weeping, who it is she seeks. Taking him for the gardener, she asks where they have laid Jesus. She will go there and take him away. Jesus speaks her name and immediately she recognizes him (his own know his voice). He is her teacher. John 20:17 seems to be a hinge. Mary is not to cling to Jesus because he no longer exists in his earthly condition. He is on the way to ascending to the Father, his God and hers. She (not Peter) is to announce the resurrection to the disciples (she is to be the apostle to the apostles). She goes and tells them, "I have seen the Lord" (now Jesus is much more than a teacher).

That evening Jesus comes to the disciples, who are behind closed doors for fear of the Jews. His words are pregnant: "Peace be with you" (see 14:27). They see his hands and his side (the wounds of his crucifixion) and are glad. Again Jesus wishes them peace. As the Father has sent him, so does he send them (the Johannine parallelism of missions). Jesus breathes on the disciples and gives them the Holy Spirit (a sort of Pentecost). If they forgive sins, such sins will be forgiven. If they retain sins, such sins will be retained (see Matthew 16:19, 18:19). (Perhaps John wants to provide a historical foundation for the Christian practice of forgiving sins. The omission of Peter seems significant.)

Thomas, one of the twelve, is absent from this appearance of Jesus and doubts that it happened. His skeptical words seem designed to reinforce the physical realism of Jesus' death and resurrection: "Unless I see in his hands the print of the nails, and place my finger in the mark of the nails, and place my hand in his side, I will not believe" (20:25). So did "doubting Thomas" assure himself immortality as the symbol for lack of faith. Eight days later Jesus again appears and this time he convinces even Thomas. After wishing the disciples peace, he has Thomas feel his wounds and admit his reality. Thomas bursts out, "My Lord and my God!" (20:28), the fullest affirmation of Jesus' exalted status by any Gospel character. It translates the *kyrios theos* used by the Greek version of the Hebrew Bible for the name of God (*Yahweh Elohim*). The Johannine Jesus then preaches on faith: "Have you believed because you have seen me? Blessed are those who have not seen and yet believe" (20:29). The disciples who follow after the original eyewitnesses may have stronger faith.

John 20:30–31 seems clearly to have been the original ending of John's Gospel. These verses affirm the wealth of signs Jesus gave, far more than are narrated in this book, and give the purpose of John's narration: "that you may believe that Jesus is the Christ, the Son of God, and that believing you may have life in his name." Both the Book of Signs and the Book of Glory are cries from faith to faith. Both stem from the ardent convictions of the Johannine Christians and invite readers to enter the riches of Christian life. For John's church Jesus is the Messiah, come in fulfillment of the Scriptures. Even more he is the Son of God, the only begotten offspring of the eternal Father, come into the world in flesh-and-blood terms. Belief in him brings eternal life (light, love). The name or reality of Jesus is the way of life.

Epilogue: Christ's Appearances in Galilee (21:1–25)[31]

Despite their appended character, the appearances narrated in John 21 are quite famous. Probably they stem from disciples who worked over the text after the death of the original author or editor.[32] By the time John's Gospel had begun to circulate through the entire Church, John 21 was an accepted part.

The appearances take place by the Sea of Tiberias, the hub of Jesus' Galilean ministry. The Gospel speaks of them as further revelations. Peter, Thomas, and some of the other disciples are together and Peter proposes that they go fishing (usually a symbol of mission or ministry). They go out in the boat but catch nothing that night. At daybreak they see Jesus standing on the beach (though they are not sure it is Jesus). He asks them about their catch. Finding they have caught nothing, he tells them to cast their net on the right side of the boat. They do and are not able to drag in the tremendous haul (see Luke 5:1–11). The beloved disciple discerns the hand of Jesus in this sign. When Peter hears it is the Lord he puts on his clothes and plunges into the sea headed for shore. The other disciples follow, dragging the net. It is a vivid scene, suggesting an eyewitness.

On land they find a charcoal fire laid with fish and some bread (eucharistic symbols). Jesus tells them to bring some of the fish they have caught. Simon Peter hauls the net and the count is 153 fish. Commentators dispute what this number might symbolize. Perhaps it anticipates the haul of the kingdom. Jesus gives them breakfast, but none of them dare ask him who he is. They know he is the Lord. (He seems rather mysterious, as would befit one resurrected into a new state.) The author makes this the third revelation to the disciples after Jesus' resurrection. (The first was without Thomas, the second with Thomas, and this is the third.)

After breakfast Jesus elicits from Peter a threefold profession of love, probably in deliberate parallel to Peter's threefold denial. It is interesting that the Johannine school (at some points quite critical of Peter) should use the formula, "Do you love me more than these?" If he loves Jesus, Peter must feed Jesus' lambs or sheep. As we have seen, brotherly and sisterly love is the great virtue in the Johannine church. Here Jesus' instruction to the head of the twelve makes it plain that Church leadership is a primacy in the obligation to serve the community. At the third questioning of his love Peter is grieved. He can only call on Jesus' own certainty: "Lord, you know everything; you know that I love you" (21:17).

John 21:18–19 traces the fate Peter will follow. Like his Lord, he will die by crucifixion. In this will his discipleship, his following of Jesus, climax. Before ending, however, the author apparently cannot resist a last sketch of Peter's impetuous character. When Peter sees the beloved disciple following close by, he asks Jesus about this man's fate. (The lines about the beloved disciple may reflect his recent death in the Johannine community and be an effort to correct the impression that he was supposed to live until Jesus' return.) The picture of Jesus telling Peter to mind his own business and not meddle in what does not concern him squares well with other parts of the Gospel. Jesus' Father deals with people differently, individually. The final verses of the appendix come from the last editors. They imprint a concluding seal: The things in this book come from the beloved disciple and are fully trustworthy. Still, these things are but a fraction of Jesus' sayings and doings. The world could not contain all the books necessary to do Jesus' mystery full justice.

WHY WAS THIS WRITTEN?

In addition to the common reasons behind the New Testament writings (the desire to communicate and preserve the traditions about Jesus, the wish to shore up the faith of a particular community, the need to combat false teachings or trends, and the like), the Johannine writings seem to take special aim at trends later developed in **Docetism**, the heresy that denied Jesus' full humanity. Certainly they transmit a form of Christian wisdom, but at the core of this wisdom is the Incarnation—the insistence that in Jesus God's Word took flesh. So strong, in fact, is the author's focus on Jesus' revelatory flesh that one suspects a felt need to buttress this portion of Christian faith. We know that Docetic Christians soon came to depreciate Jesus' flesh, denying that he really was a God-man. Thus, it seems likely that John was written at least in part to attack such trends. Indeed, Johannine Christianity is undoubtedly the most sacramental school and the one most insistent on the sign character of matter and the human body. For the Gospel of John everything about Jesus was revelatory. To see Jesus was to see the Father. Minimally, therefore, the authors thought this message bore repeating. Had there been no difficulty about the Incarnation, had there been a full acceptance of sacramentality, the Gospel probably would not have been written. One doesn't labor to gift the world with a redundancy.

A second likely motivation behind the Johannine writings is a desire to complement the synoptic traditions. Whether because the Johannine Christians had another generation's worth of religious experience, because their traditions had matured somewhat in isolation from the other churches, or because the authors of John were trying to legitimate their church's high Christology in the face of strong opposition, the Jesus who appears in John is more mysterious, symbolic, and divine than the Jesus of the synoptics. From the outset John makes it plain that Jesus is the eternal Word become flesh. Thus everything Jesus says and does in this Gospel has a third dimension, a heavenly resonance. The formal signs of the first half of the Gospel are only the clearest examples. Everywhere John sees scriptural allusions, the certain plan of God, and multiple levels of significance. Throughout, the narrative voice is ironic, an intelligence keenly aware of how differently things look when one has faith. This irony reaches several climaxes in the dialogues between the Johannine Jesus and "the Jews," his antagonists. The literary structure is quite formally and deliberately dramatic. No doubt the authors of John bore their former Jewish compatriots much resentment for the death of Jesus and the troubles of the struggling early Church. Nonetheless, the Jews also function as literary foils, stupid everymen representing the blindness of the world, the inability of the faithless and those in thrall to Satan to grasp God's Word.

Nowadays it is common to note that the Johannine presentation of the Jews probably does violence to the historical reality of their interactions with Jesus and certainly has been a source of Christian anti-semitism. In the wake of the Holocaust, one can hardly make this point too often.[33] Literarily, however, the Jews are necessary to John's dramatic proclamation of Jesus. After all, John is presenting a hero who died for telling the truth, who was rejected for being the pure Son of God. The light Jesus cast forced people to choose for or against him, a choice that also was for or against God. To mount such a tension, to depict such a time of critical decision (*kairos*), John had to pummel Jesus' enemies. He was not writing a serene, objective account of Jesus' fate but a thoroughly partisan view. When Jesus was raised on the cross, the utter paradox of history stood naked and high. The Holy One of God was being killed, murdered, because of human evil. Yet God so outloved human evil, so outwitted human stupidity, that the hour of Satan's triumph was the hour of Satan's demise. Like all the Gospel writers, the authors of John find Jesus' death-resurrection a complete overturning of human values and possibilities. If the Johannine "revolution" seems harsher, stronger, more sharply edged, it is because the Johannine Jesus is a deeper wisdom of God, a more sensitive and vulnerable humanity.

Third, these tonalities may well have originated with the beloved disciple, a follower and friend especially close to Jesus. Deep love gives the most creative vision. In the case of John's Gospel deep love is the likeliest source for the unique penetration of Jesus' consciousness that we find in chapters 14–17.

Insofar as it ratified this interpretation of Jesus' consciousness by taking John 14–17 into the canon, the early Church said that Jesus did indeed live as though he and the Father were one, and could indeed have spoken the thoughts about love that center the Johannine reminiscence. The keen eye of John sees to the depths where love begets union and life, where basic reality is not atomic but metaphoric and communal. The being of Jesus is a being-with the Father (and the Spirit). The Father is not a splendid monarch dwelling apart in isolation but a generative source, an engaged parent and commissioner. From his experience of the love of Jesus and the love needs of Jesus' community, the fourth evangelist pored over the elemental terms of the spiritual life. Light, for instance, was basic, an experience below which one could not go. To be open in conscience to the light was to be open to God. God is light, truth, the Word that makes spirits free. To be closed to God's light was to be spiritually dead, blind about the only thing that finally counts. The point is not learning or virtue in the sense of doing what one has been told is right. The point is central goodness, openness or closure of the heart.

The synoptics do not teach a different message, of course, but neither do they insist on these interior matters so cogently. John is the contemplative Gospel, the good news spawned by long rumination on what had appeared in Jesus and how that masterful icon of God could have been rejected. For John the rejection of Jesus was at once a lack of faith, a lack of love, a lack of goodness, and a lack of honesty. All four virtues or spiritual qualities were but facets of a central diamond, faces of the comprehensive "yes" one must say to God. John could not conceive of an honest person meeting Jesus and saying "no." That formula did not compute. In his experience Jesus had been wholly good, completely without sin. To meet Jesus with faith was to be healed, loved, made a recipient of God's self-disclosure. At the same time, to meet Jesus was to be instructed in one's sinfulness, one's distance from God, one's need of healing and reform.

"The Jews" stand for the unregenerate humanity that could not bear the light that shone in the darkness, that would not admit the shabbiness of the moral bargains the people had struck, the religious compromises. In John the tone of this accusation is not legal so much as ontological. Jesus does not so much supersede the Law as make the Law peripheral to the central calculus. If one would be free one must love God's revealer, cling to God's Word made flesh. The beloved disciple had felt this burning love, developed this ultimate ambition. It made his memories of Jesus configure quite distinctly from the configurations of the synoptics.

In Pauline Christianity, the key moment is Jesus' passage from death to resurrection. In Johannine Christianity, the key moment is the Word's taking flesh. To be sure, John also underscores the hour of Jesus' glorification, the time when the cross becomes a regal throne. But the first verses of the Gospel make it plain that the Johannine reflection is most comfortable locating Jesus in the divine eternity. The beginning of the Johannine good news is the beginning of the eternal Word's action on human beings' behalf, the heavenly resolve to take flesh. Like a new ark of the covenant, a new glory of God, the flesh of Jesus makes present in the world the love that can heal it. No one has ever seen God—except the Son who has never left God. John's Gospel was written to make this faith plainer than it had been previously. It was written because love of Jesus made a talented disciple a mystical poet.

WHAT BACKGROUND DOES THIS TEXT PRESUPPOSE?

We have discussed most of the key tenets of Johannine Christianity. In the background of our discussion has been a certain dualism.[34] Light and darkness, truth and falsehood, love and hatred demarcate in John two warring realms: what is above and what is below, the sphere of God and the sphere of the world. To be sure, Johannine realized eschatology and sacramentality overcome some of this dualism. By Jesus' becoming flesh, grace has permeated the realm of space and time. But the fourth Gospel still exudes an air of sharp contrasts.

Some of this contrast may have come from the Qumran community near the Dead Sea, whose thought was quite dualistic.[35] One also finds strong indications of it in the world views of the Gnostics. But John's reflections on the fate of Jesus and the sufferings of the Christian community are the more likely source of his own blend. From meditating on Jesus, he knows that God must be light, in whom there is no darkness at all. God must be life, the enemy of all that would destroy human prospects. And God must be love, the sole force stronger than hatred and murder in all their many gradations.

When John reflected on the career of Jesus, he saw Satan dog Jesus' progress to the cross. Satan, the father of lies, a murderer from the beginning, knew Jesus was his enemy. If Jesus were to triumph, Satan's realm of death would have to fall. The glory that comes into the world with the Johannine Incarnation is already Satan's death blow, but John is impressed by the resistance Jesus' glory encountered. If even the disciples did not understand Jesus and seldom penetrated the deeper levels of his multileveled discourse, John will not underestimate the distance between the world and God.

We see this as early as Nicodemus, a good man but completely over his head. Although his heart is in the right place and he has religious learning, Nicodemus does not grasp the primer of Jesus' catechesis. The foundation of Jesus' teaching is the sovereignty of the Spirit, and on this teaching Nicodemus draws a complete blank. If Isaiah said God's ways are as high above human beings' ways as the heavens are above the earth, the author of John probably would say "higher."

The most glaring contrast, however, the most jarring dualism, came when the two ways met on Jesus' cross. What the crowd and human justice did to Jesus shows the enormity of human evil, while what Jesus did shows the infinity of God's goodness. Johannine theology has no greater love than Jesus' laying down his life for his "friends" (all human beings, even those who hated him to the death). God gave humanity the best heaven had to offer, and humanity abused this gift as viciously as it could. When John marches Jesus through his trial and crucifixion, he is writing the historical equivalent of the synoptics' parable of the wicked vineyard renters. Worse, he is showing humanity trying to slay the "I am" to whom it owes all that it has or is.

The climax of Johannine dualism therefore is deicide. When the above of God and the below of sinful humanity meet on the cross, the below tries to slay the above. It cannot do this, of course. After the event, in the light of full faith, the resurrection (in some form) appears inevitable. But in the Johannine Jesus God so perfectly identified with the human cause that the world seemed to have its evil way. For a while darkness could think it had overcome. When Jesus speaks peace to the disciples after the resurrection, giving them the Spirit, he breathes into their souls the divine deathlessness. In the midst of their mortality the Spirit will always keep the divine light and love alive. The dualistic antagonism between truth and lying will continue, because human beings will remain free to reject their God. But the resurrection of Jesus says the end-time has begun, the battle in principle is decided. Unless one grasps this background, Johannine dualism will seem world hating. It is not world hating, because on the cross Jesus took the world's evil up into his stronger love.

A second background assumption of John is the notion of judgment that had developed in the Hebrew Bible. In the early writings of what the Christians came to consider their Old Testament, the judge was primarily the one to whom a person could appeal for the defense of his or her rights. Judgment therefore was a vindication of one's appeal, a sentence that one's cause was valid. This could also be applied to God. To invoke the judgment of Yahweh was to ask his assistance in righting one's sorry situation, in gaining one's proper justice or relief. For the nation in its political troubles, the "Day of Yahweh" was the time when the enemies of Israel would receive their comeuppance.

By the time of Amos, however, the idea of judgment had deepened. For this prophet the day of God's judgment could well turn against the people, calling the people themselves to account: "Woe to you who desire the day of the Lord! Why would you have the day of the Lord? It is darkness, and not light; as if a man fled from a lion, and a bear met him; or went into the house and leaned with his hand against the wall, and a serpent bit him. Is not the day of the Lord darkness, and not light, and gloom with no brightness in it?" (Amos 5:18–20).

In the fall of Jerusalem (587 B.C.E.), the contemporary prophets Jeremiah and Ezekiel saw a fit punishment for the people's sins. Through the Chaldeans God was passing judgment on a nation that had been deeply unfaithful. Still, even in this painful punishment the people would find the voice of God and be healed, if they would listen. For Second Isaiah the judgment of God would pass on to become redemption, the rescue of a people that had suffered enough. Finally, we may read the apocalyptic literature that arose toward the end of the Old Testament period as an extension of judgment to the entire world. In Daniel, parts of Isaiah, and Joel, for instance, we find late or early forms of the conviction that the world itself must be purged of its sinfulness by catastrophe.

The author of John takes this background and joins it with a Christian interpretation of Jesus as the eschatological prophet who brought the hour of God's judgment. In John's hands the Day of Judgment becomes the hour of Jesus' glorification. At that time God applied to humanity's account the glory the Son had had from the beginning in heaven. Insofar as this glory came into the world with the Incarnation, the judgment of the world began with the birth of Jesus. It is a benign judgment, in keeping with God's loving will to save humanity. Nonetheless, it is also the separation of good and evil, light and darkness. Thus to reject Jesus is to reject the Father who sent Jesus and condemn oneself to ruin. The faithless Jews who will not open themselves to Jesus' words, and who refuse to believe in Jesus' signs, have snuffed out the light of conscience. The hour of Jesus' glorification becomes the hour of their darkness. Jesus would have brought them into the day, to walk in the light, but they chose to be creatures of the night.

Johannine judgment therefore appears as more existential than synoptic judgment. For John much of God's judgment is occurring right now, as people open or close themselves to the light. John does not deny the notion of a final, eschatological judgment. His stress, however, falls on the judgment that is the reverse side of salvation. If Jesus comes to save the world, to take into the divine life all who accept his word in faith and obey his command of love, he inevitably also comes to effect judgment. Salvation, we might say, is positive judgment: setting oneself before God and being healed. Condemnation is negative judgment: keeping away from God's light and love. The Day of the Lord can be any day one is challenged by the light, any time one is asked to love and believe.

Last, we must repeat that John's Gospel is a quite original redoing of the traditions about Jesus, with its own symbolic logic, special vocabulary, and peculiar intents. John has taken wisdom interests, and perhaps theological accents peculiar to Samaritan concerns with the prophet greater than Moses (or a Mosaic messiah), to focus on Jesus as the one in whom one can see God (the Father). For Edward Schillebeeckx, John 12:44–50 summarizes this central Johannine theme:

> John 12.44–50 forms a literary unit, but this is simply one ingredient which is integrated into the final pattern of the Fourth Gospel. Within this gospel it has the purpose of expressing the essence of Johannine christology. And this Johannine gospel—the message of the Johannine Jesus—is: anyone who believes in Jesus, really believes in the Father who has sent him. Whoever sees Jesus, sees the Father. "I have come as light into the world, that whoever believes in me may not remain in darkness" (12.46, see the prologue). Jesus has not come to judge, but to save the world (12.47). He speaks only words of salvation, life-giving words. To reject him is to reject the Father who sent him. This is the summary.

The Johannine terminology of light, life, and love circles around such revelation. In Jesus John sees divine love, life, and light compacted. Against the backdrop of the Jewish festivals that ought to frame his signal identity, Jesus stands forth as the light of the world, the love of God that brings salvation, the divine life that makes all who believe children of God. These themes are not foreign to the synoptics, but they are much more richly expressed.

WHAT LASTING SIGNIFICANCE DOES THIS HAVE?

One could easily show the personal significance of the Gospel of John. The author's meditations on the person and teaching of Jesus are a high point in Western religious reflection. They probe some of the deepest matters of conscience so they challenge anyone intersted in light, life, and love. The social significance of Johannine theology may be less apparent, however, so perhaps that is the challenge we should take up. Does the fourth Gospel say anything relevant to a Western history that has spent almost two thousand years failing to achieve peace and justice? Has the vision of the beloved disciple any direction for a global culture now confronting the ultimate issues of survival?

José Miranda is a student of Johannine thought with a strong conviction that the vision of the beloved disciple offers precisely the sources of strength and hope humanity has most needed. Miranda is a Mexican liberation theologian, well versed in both biblical and political theory. In his interpretation the Johannine stress on realized eschatology, on present judgment and salvation, offers the basis for a strong commitment to change the world, to bring society's present injustices before the transforming power of God and make justice roll down like a mighty stream. Western society and Western scholarship have colluded to keep the radical implications of Johannine faith at bay. Where John says the kingdom of God has arrived in the person of Jesus and that the power to change the world is now in our midst, Western society holds back out of bad will:

> Western civilization's overwhelming rejection of the historical Jesus might persuade us that the West lacks a historical sense. But the West is not *unable* to understand that the hour of the kingdom has already arrived; it is *unwilling* to understand it, because to understand it would oblige us to change. To circumvent this obligation we have invented and for centuries believed in a celestial Christ and an "eternal life." And this total distortion of the gospel has been accomplished with the tacit consent—indeed, the connivance and cooperation—of ecclesiastical authorities. The fate of our world depends on our believing Jesus Christ when he says that the hour of the kingdom has come (Mark 1:14–15), but the masters of our world lose their power if we believe it.[36]

Now, Miranda employs Marxist rhetoric, and many biblical scholars would not accept his completely this-worldly interpretation of Johannine "eternal life." On the other hand, Miranda certainly makes a point worth pursuing. The historical Jesus wanted to be an agent of social change. He did not address himself only to people's minds or inner spirits. He cured people's bodies and was interested in almsgiving and social justice. True, he did not accept a political interpretation of his mission or messiahship. On the other hand, it would be false to make him a wholly spiritual teacher, a rabbi or holy man interested only in a heaven to come, and not concerned about the problems and pains of present history.

For John the eternal Word of God became flesh for the sake of needy humanity. Miranda is completely right, therefore, to see in Johannine eschatology a conviction that people can change the world if they wish. Were people to take the love commandment of the Johannine Jesus to heart, they could revolutionize social relations. The reason they (we) will not do this is the same reason John found for the murder of Jesus: People love darkness more than light, because their deeds are evil. When John speaks of the Spirit given by Jesus, the Counselor who can keep believers in Jesus' truth, he points to a sanity that Miranda and other social reformers have become convinced the world is aware of but does not want to acknowledge. When John records Jesus' promise that whatever believers ask the Father in his name they will receive, he points to a power of creation and renewal that might undercut any age's political impasses.

The lasting political significance of John therefore is inseparable from its faith in the revelatory character of Jesus' flesh. If Jesus was as John presents him, the light is always stronger than the darkness. At any moment God may raise Lazarus from the dead. The apparent end of the grave is merely penultimate, only a first moment in the process of resurrection. Were people to live in this faith, they might find the freedom to reconsider their present value judgments. In a horizon of eternal life (what Miranda could call "the primordial creativity of God"), they might see how money and power are but idols. It would become clear, in the grasp of the Johannine Spirit, that the ways of most people are foolishness. The Spirit blows where it will, trying to make children of God. Most people don't know enough to follow. They might have freedom but they enslave themselves to mammon or unwashed dictators. They might see signs and enjoy sacraments, but they thin reality to village atheism. So might Johannine disciples denounce their times for stupidity.

On the other hand, we might ask these disciples why it should be so difficult for the Johannine message to get through. What torpor or basic flaw keeps humanity deaf to Jesus' message? A potential problem with the Johannine writings is their sectarian character. They are quite ready to divide the world into "us and them," and they can be surprisingly harsh or hostile (especially for a tradition that lays so much stress on love). Like the other evangelists, then, John finally forces us to question the realism of the gospel. Where has the gospel triumphed long enough, thoroughly enough, to show us a Christian society? But even this question is not the end of John's significance. Beyond it lies the question of what counts as "significant," what achievements make a person or writing a landmark. Does Jesus' having left a vision of resurrected life mean more than Jesus' earthly defeat? Do the still stunning signs of the Johannine Christ mean more than the rarity of Johannine love? To answer such questions one must choose, lay out one's own priorities. If the capital thing is adjusting people to a world of constant strife, a human condition shot through with injustice, John probably is not the reading to recommend. If the capital thing is suggesting how people can find a great deal of heaven on earth, can live now in the presence of the eschaton, John is more than relevant.

We don't pretend to settle this debate about priorities, though undoubtedly our sympathies have shone through. The point is not our sympathies but the sympathies of the Gospel of John. If the Gospel of John says that faith and love can bring divine life, and if divine life manifests itself in the peace and joy that are the marrow of human fulfillment, the Gospel of John makes a powerful claim. Since God is not likely to change, and human nature remains much as it was in John's day, this claim might often preoccupy us.

John says that the light shone in the darkness. He claims that the words of Jesus are eternal life. To eat the flesh of Jesus and drink his blood is to share in the divine deathlessness. Whether one interprets this literally, symbolically, or as a sacramental in-between, it is an astounding claim. An education overlooking it or ruling it outside the scope of humanistic learning would be laughable to serious students. With the world in manifest disarray and death threatening from a dozen sources, ignoring the Johannine program for reform (or any other truly venerable program) might well be criminally irresponsible. Certainly the beloved disciple would insist that today is a time of judgment.

SUMMARY

Our first look at the Gospel of John suggested that it is quite different from the synoptics, and much more symbolic. A product of "the beloved disciple" and several redactors, perhaps dating from 90 C.E., and arising from a Palestinian community relocated in Ephesus, the fourth Gospel is intricate and hard to interpret. Behind it appears to lie a complicated process of composition. At its intellectual center stand such rich themes as revelation, mission, and the Paraclete. The Gospel divides into the Book of Signs (chapters 2–12) and the Book of Glory (chapters 13–21). In full outline we distinguished an Introduction, seven subdivisions of the Book of Signs, three subdivisions of the Book of Glory, and an Epilogue.

The Introduction includes the famous Johannine prologue (1:1–18), a hymn to the career of the Incarnate Word. Here John redoes the creation account and makes the flesh of Jesus the fullest revelation of the God who made the world. Verses 19–34 summarize the testimony of John the Baptist, Jesus' precursor. Verses 35–51 are a first witness from Jesus' earliest disciples. By the end of his first, introductory chapter, John has placed Jesus before us as the spectacular Word and Lamb of God who made the human condition sacramental.

The seven signs in the first of John's books summarize Jesus' ministry. At Cana in Galilee Jesus turns the water into wine, the first manifestation of his glory. The dialogues with Nicodemus and the Samaritan woman suggest the ironic and multileveled character of Jesus' interactions with various seekers. Chapter 4 shows us Jesus' second sign, the curing of the son of a Gentile official. Where he finds faith, Jesus can shield life from death. The third sign, the cure by the pool of Bethesda, has a baptismal motif. As well, it brings Jesus into conflict with the Jews about the Sabbath and shows his claim to equality with God. The fourth sign is the multiplication of the loaves and fishes, a eucharistic miracle to the theme of eternal life. The fifth sign is Jesus' walking on the water, meant to confirm the disciples' faith.

These signs only partially accomplish Jesus' goal. They draw some people to faith but others only grow more blind. Before long the opposition to Jesus becomes murderous. Jesus is the good shepherd, the Son of the Father, the one in whom God can be found, but many in the crowd will not accept him. He is the light of the world but many insist on the dark. John builds a fierce tension between Jesus and those who will not believe ("the Jews"). The sixth sign, Jesus' cure of the man born blind, is a bitter metaphor for spiritual blindness. In his seventh and summary cure, the raising of Lazarus, Jesus asserts his power over death and prefigures his resurrection. By the end of the Book of Signs, John has built a full case that Jesus is the revelation of the Father.

The Book of Glory opens with the famous farewell discourses of chapters 13–17. Although hard to place in logical sequence, their insights into Jesus' relations with the Father, the Spirit, and the disciples make them a high point of New Testament reflection. By their end John has convinced us that it is better for the disciples that Jesus go. The Johannine Passion Narrative is succinct and almost bitterly ironic. Jesus is the Holy King who could not find worthy subjects. He dies innocent and free, a tribute to human malice. The Johannine resurrection account stresses the roles of Mary Magdalene and Peter. Jesus is a mysterious figure, both like and unlike the Master the disciples used to know. Mary's deep love of Jesus wins her a special appearance. Doubting Thomas provides the occasion for focusing on Jesus' wounds. His profession of faith gives Jesus the most solemn titles: Lord and God. The Gospel probably first ended with 20:30–31, which cites the author's motive for writing (to incite faith) and makes it plain that Jesus' revelation of the Father was far richer than this book could record.

The Epilogue we now have in chapter 21 is precious for several concrete features. The scene of the miraculous haul of fish and lakeside breakfast is richly eucharistic. Peter's triple attestation of love shows the depth of the leading apostle's character. Jesus leaves his disciples a strong mandate to community service. The stories of the beloved disciple pay a last tribute to his high status in the Johannine community.

Among the reasons why John was written we stressed an anti-Docetic intent. By its strong emphasis on Jesus' flesh, the Gospel gave the lie to any interpretations wanting to dilute the Incarnation. Jesus was uniquely revelatory precisely because his humanity shone with the light and life of the Father. A second motivation may have been to complement the synoptic traditions. The Johannine Christ is deeper, more mystical, quite likely the fruit of a longer contemplation. John's ironic narrative voice is sharper than the synoptics'. The sacramentality of his Jesus' person, deeds, and speech is richer. For all its theological dangers, John's presentation of the conflict between Jesus and "the Jews" makes his work a powerful drama.

Perhaps the beloved disciple's special insights into Jesus' relation with the Father provided a third motivation for his contribution to the Johannine writings. Elaborating his warm love of Jesus, the author may have sensed he'd been granted a special appreciation of the interrelations among God's love, light, and life. Finally, the Johannine faith is most comfortable locating the inmost reality of Jesus in eternity. It therefore offers the whole Church a gospel rich in the motifs of Christ's divinity, stronger in its insistence on Christ's "I am," than previously existed.

In discussing the background the fourth Gospel presupposes, we considered its peculiar dualism. Playing with a dichotomous view of light and darkness, above and below, the author sets sharp contrasts between the ways of God and sinful humanity. Johannine realized eschatology and sacramentality qualify this dualism, yet it still shapes the author's mind. The Old Testament notion of judgment is a second background assumption worth noting. Against the Israelite anticipation of the Day of the Lord, John makes Jesus' crucifixion the hour when the divine glory passes judgment. Overall, Johannine thought has existentialized the divine judgment. Without denying a last eschatological sentence, John prefers to make present choices (for or against the light) the substance of salvation or condemnation.

The lasting significance of the Gospel depends on one's assessment of its realized eschatology. For political theologians such as José Miranda, John unveils a faith that could energize social justice. Thereby, the Gospel reveals the bad will of those who cling to an oppressive status quo. Beyond this political question lie the theological questions of why people choose darkness rather than light and how the Johannine Jesus could be rejected. If these are profitable questions, John is very significant. Last, we considered as a final question what qualifies a text or person as significant. By many criteria, the fourth Gospel could not be studied too thoroughly.

STUDY QUESTIONS

1. What is Perkins' minimal hypothesis necessary to account for the textual composition of John?
2. Who was the beloved disciple?
3. How does revelation function as a central Johannine motif?
4. What is the dominant characteristic of the Book of Signs?
5. How does the Johannine Introduction rework the Genesis account of creation?
6. What are Jesus' seven signs?
7. How does John use Nicodemus?
8. How does the dialogue with the Samaritan woman exemplify Johannine irony?
9. If the author of John has made up Jesus' monologues, what is their value?
10. Explain the concept of "realized eschatology."
11. How does Jesus function as the bread of life?

12. What is the crux of the controversy between the Johannine Jesus and the Jews?
13. What is the force of the "I am" passages?
14. Explain the bitter humor of the incident where Jesus heals the man born blind.
15. To whom is Jesus the good shepherd contrasted and why?
16. Why does Jesus raise Lazarus?
17. What does John mean by eternal life?
18. What is the glory that dominates John's second book?
19. What is the foremost example of Jesus' new commandment?
20. How does John 14–17 correlate the Father, the Spirit, and Jesus?
21. Why is it good for the disciples that Jesus go to the Father?
22. In what sense is the world Jesus' enemy?
23. How does John equate unbelief and sin?
24. Why does the Johannine Jesus lay such stress on unity?
25. How does John show Jesus' control of his Passion?
26. What is the paradox in the interplay between Jesus and Pilate?
27. In what sense is Jesus the King of the Jews?
28. How does Jesus die like a paschal lamb?
29. How does Mary Magdalene recognize Jesus?
30. Why is Jesus Thomas's Lord and God?
31. How is Peter to show his triply strong love?
32. How is the fourth Gospel anti-Docetic?
33. What insights may we attribute to the beloved disciple's special love?
34. Describe the Johannine dualism.
35. How does Johannine judgment dovetail with realized eschatology?
36. Explain the political significance of realized eschatology.
37. Why do people flee Jesus' light?

NOTES

1. See Pheme Perkins, *Reading the New Testament* (New York: Paulist, 1978), pp. 241–43.
2. Ibid., p. 243.
3. Xavier Leon-Dufour, *Dictionary of the New Testament* (San Francisco: Harper & Row, 1980), p. 166.
4. Neal M. Flanagan, *The Gospel According to John and the Johannine Epistles* (Collegeville, Minn.: Liturgical Press, 1983), p. 101.
5. See Ibid., p. 3.
6. Raymond E. Brown, *The Gospel According to John I–XII* (Garden City, N.Y.: Doubleday Anchor, 1966), p. 29.

7. See M. Girard, "Analyse Structurelle de Jn 1, 1–18," *Science et Esprit* 35 (1983), 5–31.

8. See D. K. Clark, "Signs in Wisdom and John," *Catholic Biblical Quarterly* 45 (1983), 201–9; Robert Fortna, *The Gospel of Signs* (Cambridge: University Press, 1970).

9. See M. Pamment, "The Meaning of *doxa* in the Fourth Gospel," *Zeitschrift für die Neutestamentliche Wissenschaft* 74 (1983), 12–16.

10. See Edward Schillebeeckx, *Christ* (New York: Seabury, 1980), pp. 331–40.

11. See M. Pamment, "John 3:5 'Unless one is born of water and the spirit, he cannot enter the Kingdom of God," *Novum Testamentum* 25 (1983), 189–90.

12. See Raymond E. Brown, *The Community of the Beloved Disciple* (New York: Paulist, 1970), pp.187–89.

13. C. H. Dodd, *The Interpretation of the Fourth Gospel* (Cambridge: University Press, 1968), p. 7.

14. See M. Girard, "L'Unité de composition de Jean 6, au regard de L'Analyse Structurelle," *Eglise et Théologie* 13 (1982), 79–110.

15. See D. Moody Smith, "John and the Synoptics," *New Testament Studies* 26 (1980–81), 425–44.

16. See Wayne A Meeks, *The Prophet King* (Leiden: E. J. Brill, 1967).

17. See M. Roberge, "Le discours sur le pain de vie (Jean 6, 22–59). Problèmes d'interprétation," *Laval Théologique et Philosophique* 38 (1983), 265–99.

18. See R. Alan Culpepper, *Anatomy of the Fourth Gospel* (Philadelphia: Fortress, 1983).

19. See P. Harner, *The "I Am" of the Fourth Gospel* (Philadelphia: Fortress, 1970).

20. See E. L. Miller, "The Christology of John 8:25," *Theologische Zeitschrift* 36 (1980), 257–65.

21. See Nils Dahl, "Der Erstgegorene Satans und der Vater des Teufels," *Apophoreta* (Berlin: Topel-Mann, 1964), pp. 70–84.

22. See E. D. Freed, "Who or What Was Before Abraham in John 8:58?" *Journal for the Study of the New Testament* 17 (1983), 52–59.

23. See M. Gourges, "L'aveugle-né (*Jn* 9)," *Nouvelle Révue Théologique* 104 (1982), 381–95.

24. Raymond E. Brown, *The Gospel According to John XIII–XXI* (Garden City, N.Y.: Doubleday Anchor, 1970), p. 541.

25. See A. J. Hultgren, "The Johannine Footwashing (13.1–11) as Symbol of Eschatological Hospitality," *New Testament Studies* 28 (1982), 539–46.

26. See F. Porsch, "Der 'andere Paraklet.' Das Wirken der Geistes nach der Johanneischen Abschiedsreden," *Bibel und Kirche* 37 (1982), 133–38.

27. See F. F. Segouia, "The Theology and Provenance of John 15:1–17," *Journal of Biblical Literature* 101 (1982), 115–28.

28. See P. Bonnard, "La Prière de Jésus pour une église divisé (Jean 17)," *Tantur Yearbook* (1979–80), 15–25.

29. See C. L'Eplattenier, "La Passion dans L'évangile de Jean," *Foi et Vie* 81 (1982), 25–30.

30. See F. J. Moloney, "John 20: A Journey Completed," *Australian Catholic Record* 59 (1982), 417–32.

31. See P. S. Minear, "The Original Functions of John 21," *Journal of Biblical Literature* 102 (1983), 85–98.

32. See Alan Culpepper, *The Johannine School* (Missoula, Mont.: Scholars Press, 1975).

33. See J. E. Leibig, "John and 'the Jews.' Theological Anti-Semitism in the Fourth Gospel," *Journal of Ecumenical Studies* 20 (1983), 209–34; also Samuel Sandmel, *Anti-Semitism in the New Testament* (Phildelphia: Fortress, 1978); Charlotte Klein, *Anti-Judaism in Christian Theology* (Phildelphia: Fortress, 1978).

34. See Bruce Vawter, "Johannine Theology," *Jerome Biblical Commentary*, ed. R. Brown and others (Englewood Cliffs, N.J.: Prentice-Hall, 1968), vol. 2, pp. 830–31.

35. See James H. Charlesworth, ed., *John and Qumran* (London: Chapman, 1972).

36. José Miranda, *Being and the Messiah* (Maryknoll, N.Y.: Orbis, 1977), p. 199.

10

The Book of Revelation:
New Testament Apocalypse

WHAT HAVE WE HERE?

Scripture scholars place the Book of Revelation in the literary genre called "apocalyptic," from the Greek word for "revelation" or "disclosure." Generally, this genre is concerned with supposed disclosures of heavenly truths, usually through visions.[1] The Book of Revelation presents twentieth-century readers formidable problems, because it "is full of images that have a long history, stretching from ancient Near Eastern myth through the Old Testament prophets to Jewish apocalypses like the book of Daniel. These images were being used and reused in Jewish writings from New Testament times."[2] Characteristically, apocalypses were written in times of persecution. At the time of Daniel (about 165 B.C.E.), for instance, the Syrian ruler of Palestine was trying to force the Jews to renounce their faith. Those who refused to recant risked death. Thus the Jewish community had to ponder martyrdom and find solid reasons for dying for its beliefs. About the same time that Christians were composing Revelation (perhaps 95 C.E.), Jews were writing such apocalypses as 4 Ezra and 2 Baruch, trying to find the meaning of the destruction of Jerusalem and burning of the Temple in 70 C.E.[3]

The situation of the Christians who wrote or received Revelation is inseparable from the question of when the book was written.

> The strongest external evidence for the date of Revelation is the testimony of Irenaeus. He says that the Apocalypse was seen at the end of the reign of [the Roman Emperor] Domitian. This comment refers to a date of 95 or 96 C.E. It is not clear whether Irenaeus believed that the text was written down at the same time or somewhat later. Since there is no positive evidence for a later date, it seems best to consider Irenaeus' remark to support a date of about 95 or 96 C.E. The clearest internal evidence in Revelation is the use of the name

Babylon for Rome. In Jewish literature this name is explicitly associated with Rome as the second destroyer of Jerusalem. The symbolic name Babylon for Rome was probably taken over by the author of Revelation from Jewish tradition. Its use thus indicates a date after 70 C.E.[4]

While many commentators on Revelation have argued that the spur to its writing was the persecution of Christians under Domitian, Adela Yarbro Collins recently has disputed this view. In her opinion a more likely cause is a social crisis composed of such elements as conflicts with Jews, antipathy toward neighboring Gentiles, and disputes over wealth. Since there is little strong evidence that Domitian singled out the Christians for special persecution, and recent sociological analyses of millennial movements suggest that they arise more from frustration than persecution, Collins favors a psychosocial prod. In the social environment from which Revelation sprang the new expectations raised by faith in Jesus' messiahship and kingdom were not being realized. We may read Revelation as a protest against the forces thought to be keeping Christians from living their faith successfully and prospering in their environment.[5]

In outline the Book of Revelation breaks down as follows:

Prologue 1:1–8

The Seven Letters 1:9–3:22

The Seven Seals 4:1–8:1

The Seven Trumpets 8:2–11:19

The Seven Unnumbered Visions 12:1–15:4

The Seven Bowls 15:5–16:21

Interlude on Babylon 17:1–19:10

Seven More Unnumbered Visions 19:11–21:8

Interlude on Jerusalem 21:9–22:5

Epilogue 22:6–21[6]

Prologue (1:1–8)

Revelation begins with a solemn announcement: This (vision) is what God disclosed to Jesus Christ to show his servants what must soon take place. The recipient of this vision was a prophet named John. (In contrast to most contemporary apocalyptic literature, which was pseudepigraphal, John seems to use his own name.) It came to him through an angel. John is merely testifying to what he saw, and he blesses those who read, hear, and keep his prophecy.

The seven churches of Asia to which John writes probably symbolize the fullness of the Christian community in Asia Minor. The imagery of 1:4 is striking: "Grace to you and peace from him who is and who was and who is to come, and from the seven spirits who are before his throne, and from Jesus Christ the faithful witness, the first-born of the dead, and the ruler of kings on earth." Most likely this speaks of the Trinity: The Father fills all time. The Spirit is a fullness before the Father's throne. Jesus is the primary witness to God, the resurrected one, and the ruler of all earthly forces. John wishes glory and dominion to Jesus, "who loves us and has freed us from our sins by his blood and made us a kingdom, priests to his God and Father" (1:5–6). This wealth of poetic images is characteristic of Revelation. Much of the author's power comes from piling figure upon figure (often in triads)[7] to suggest the splendor of the divine reality, the wonders of the economy of salvation, and his own authority (against the false, mocking authority of evil). In promising that Jesus is coming with the clouds (1:7), John implies that Jesus is the Son of Man. His coming will be the day of judgment when the wicked will wail. He is the alpha and omega ruling all reality.

The Seven Letters (1:9–3:22)

Next John turns to the circumstances of his vision. He was on the island of Patmos (off the coast of Asia Minor, opposite Miletus), probably in exile for his faith and missionary work. He was communing with God on Sunday. Behind him a loud voice like a trumpet (see Exodus 19:16, 19) told him to write his vision and send it to the seven churches. (Roughly, they make a semicircle with Patmos in Asia Minor.) Turning, John saw seven lampstands (the fullness of the Church) and in their midst the exalted Christ. The portrait of Christ suggests his blazing state of resurrection into full godly power. Much of the symbolism comes from Daniel (Daniel 7:9, 13, 10:5). It makes Jesus a high priest and the "Ancient of Days," with attributes unmistakably divine. The seven stars may stand for the fullness of creation, as well as the seven angels of the churches. The two-edged sword is a common image for the divine Word (see Isaiah 11:4, Wisdom 18:15) and also for the Emperor. Jesus, like the Father, is alpha and omega. He is alive for evermore and has power over Death and Hades.

The seven letters each begin with a description of Christ the sender. The first description, in the letter to the church of Ephesus, stresses that Christ holds the angels of the churches and walks among the churches. First, he approves the Ephesians' endurance and purity of faith. However, they have lost their early love. They must repent and return to their previous ardor. Otherwise their church will be extinguished. The Nicolaitans probably were Christians who accommodated the state cult. The Ephesians' reward for renewed faith will be to eat of the tree of paradise (to gain heaven or resurrection).

To the church of Smyrna Christ appears as the first and last, the one who died and came to life. He knows their difficulties: material poverty, slander from Jews, danger of prison. They must not fear but stand firm. If they do they will receive the crown of (eternal) life and will not be hurt by the second death (damnation).

The Christ speaking to Pergamum has the sharp two-edged sword of God's Word. In that locale Satan is strong, yet they have held fast to the point of martyrdom. Still, some of them have succumbed to loose teaching about idolatrous feasting. Others have fallen prey to the Nicolaitans. If

St. John the Evangelist on Patmos. Erhard Altdorfer. The tradition long thought that the author of the Gospel of John also wrote Revelation. John is portrayed as the (young) disciple whom Jesus loved. He gazes as in a vision, writing with two pens as though automatically. His symbol traditionally was the eagle, and the Lord had committed Mary to his care. *(Nelson Gallery–Atkins Museum, Kansas City, Mo. [Nelson Fund])*

they do not repent, the Word of God will press upon them like a sword. If they triumph they will receive hidden manna and a new name (see Psalms 78:24, Isaiah 62:2), tokens of God's favor. In the first three letters, like a firm bass rhythm, occurs the phrase, "He who has an ear to hear, let him hear what the Spirit is saying to the churches." This will continue in the last four letters, linking all seven in a round of seriousness. John's vision and Jesus' admonitions are utterly urgent, direct inspirations of the Holy Spirit that frequently lay out the conditions for Christians' religious prospering.

To Thyatira Jesus appears as the Son of God with eyes like a flame of fire, feet like burnished bronze. The vision seems designed to buttress Christian readers' convictions of Jesus' lordship. Elisabeth Schüssler-Fiorenza has conjectured why readers of Revelation might have needed such support:

> The Christians experienced again and again that their situation in no way supported their theological conviction that they already participated in Christ's kingship and power. This tension between theological conviction and

experienced reality must have provoked difficult theological problems: Why do the Christians have to suffer if Christ is the true Lord and King of the world? Why are the Christians persecuted if the living God is on their side and the gods of the other religions are powerless idols?[8]

Christ knows the Thyatirans' works, love, faith, service, and patient endurance. Indeed, their recent works outstrip their earlier ones. But a woman derisively called Jezebel (see 2 Kings 9:22), a false prophetess, has been beguiling some of them to act immorally and eat food sacrificed to idols. (The author of Revelation seems a rigorist on this question of food sacrificed to idols, seeing it as a fatal accommodation to paganism. Recall how this also troubled Paul.) Those who soil their faith by following her will suffer. "And all the churches shall know that I am he who searches mind and heart, and I will give to each of you as your works deserve" (2:23). Revelation uses both the carrot and the stick, not hesitating to threaten God's chastisements for a breach of faith. In contrast with certain Pauline passages (for example, Romans 3:28), it lays great stress on works—doing the deeds of faith. Still, Jesus goes gently with the Thyatirans who have not fallen to Jezebel. They need only hold fast until the parousia (which may be soon). If they do they will have power over the nations (a phrase suggesting that John's audience was mainly Jewish Christians), whom they will rule with a rod of iron. As a symbol of victory they will receive the morning star, the lovely sign of a fresh dawning (resurrection).

Chapter 3 opens with the letter to the church in Sardis. This comes from the One who has the seven spirits of God (the Holy Spirit) and the seven stars (the whole assembly of the angels of the churches, or the full Church membership). Here Christ's knowledge of the church's works brings stern judgment: It seems alive but is dead. The church of Sardis must revive itself. Otherwise it will find its judge coming like a thief in the night (see Matthew 24:42–43). Yet some have kept faith and will walk in the white robes of victors. Their names will be written in the book of life and Jesus will confess them before the Father. Such a prospect must have been quite consoling.

The church of Philadelphia hears words of Christ the holy, the true, the holder of the key (rule) of David and the power to admit or reject from the kingdom. He sets before it an open door and is pleased with its efforts. He will chastise the synagogue of Satan, Jews who are harassing Philadelphia. He will keep the Philadelphian Christians from the trial soon to come upon the whole world. He is coming soon. Let them guard their crowns (their precious faith). If they conquer they will become pillars in the temple of God and bear the name of the heavenly Jerusalem.

The last letter, to Laodicea, brings the words of the Amen (God's sealing Word), the faithful and true witness, and the beginning of creation (the first-born from the dead). The Laodiceans' problem is tepidity. They think they are much and in reality they are little. They had best obtain from Christ a renewed faith. His chastisement is a sign of his love. Revelation 3:20 sounds like an invitation to the eschatological banquet (see Matthew 26:29): "Behold, I stand at the door and knock; if any one hears my voice and opens the door, I will come in to him and eat with him, and he with me." It is remarkable that, in the midst of much stern advice to repent, the Jesus of Revelation can become the good shepherd, going out of his way to bring people salvation. Those who persevere will sit on his throne (he is the Messiah-King), as he sits on his Father's throne. "He who has an ear, let him hear what the Spirit says to the churches" (let him not be deaf, as Isaiah portrayed those destined for perdition).[9]

The Seven Seals (4:1–8:1)

The seven letters symbolize a full message to the full Church. The seven seals symbolize a full disclosure of what has been hidden but is soon to be visited upon the earth. The disclosure begins when a door opens in heaven. A voice like a trumpet calls John to ascend to heaven and see what must soon take place. Transported in the Spirit, he sees a throne in heaven and on it a dazzling (divine) king. The king is splendid with blazing jewels and around him are twenty-four elders (probably the twelve Old Testament patriarchs and the twelve New Testament apostles). The sea of glass suggests the distance between heaven and earth. The magnificent four living creatures stem from Ezekiel 1:10. Christian tradition made them symbols of the four evangelists. As in the vision of Isaiah 6:3, they praise the holy God ceaselessly. The twenty-four elders join this praise. The lofty suggestion is that the main business of heaven is pure worship, constant appreciation of God's goodness and beauty. As Creator, God deserves credit for everything good.[10]

The scene with the scroll reflects Ezekiel 2:9–10. Only Jesus holds the key to the future. He is the lion of Judah and root of David—the inheritor of all the Old Testament promises. Shifting images, John makes Jesus the paschal Lamb, slain for salvation yet full of power (seven horns, seven eyes). The new hymn of the twenty-four elders harmonizes with the previous hymn. That hymn praised God (the Father) for creation; this one praises the Son for redemption. The prayers of the saints (all the holy believers) rise like incense before the Lamb. The heavenly people is drawn from all tribes and nations (a significant universalism). All who enter heaven rejoice to praise the Lamb and the Creator.

Chapter 6 begins the unsealing of the seven secrets. There come a white horse and rider, a red horse and rider, a black horse and rider, and a pale horse whose rider is death. Commissioned by heaven, they will ride forth to visit judgment, testing, and vengeance upon the sinful earth. In terms of contemporary history, the author may have been recalling the scourge of the Parthian king Vologesus, who terrorized Rome in 62 C.E. The fifth seal reveals the claims of the martyrs to justice from God. The sixth seal reveals a great earthquake, as in the eschatological discourses of the Gospels. In Old Testament terms the imagery conjures the Day of the Lord (see Isaiah 34:4, Joel 2:30–31, Amos 8:9).

Revelation 7:1–17 is an interlude between seals six and seven. Four angels of God standing at the four ends of the earth (it was not then thought round) hold back the four winds. God offers a respite: "Do not harm the earth or the sea or the trees, till we have sealed the servants of God upon their foreheads" (7:3). Some modern commentators have suggested this as a prime ecological text. Originally the dominant motif was predestination: The elect are sealed (see Ezekiel 9:4–6) on their foreheads to keep them from the powers of destruction.

The number of the sealed (144,000) is a multiple of the twelve tribes of Israel. (Here it seems to signify the predetermined number of Jews who will enter the Kingdom of God. In chapter 14 the predetermined elect seem to be Christians.) Beyond this horde is a greater number of people, drawn from all nations, who praise the Lamb for their salvation. Once again the scene is pure worship and thanksgiving. The elect or saved, splendid in their white robes, have been washed clean in the blood of the Lamb. They have found fulfillment, the richest pasturage of the good shepherd. Revelation 7:17 summarizes the Christian doctrine of salvation and heaven: "God will wipe away every tear from their eyes." The opening of the seventh seal brings silence in heaven for half an hour. This reflects the notion of the prophetic tradition (Isaiah 41:1, Habakkuk 2:20, Zephaniah 1:7, Zechariah 2:17) that stillness precedes the startling coming of God.

The Seven Trumpets (8:2–11:19)

The next cycle of revelations hangs on seven angels blowing seven trumpets. The context is incenseful worship rising to God and rebounding to earth full of justice or vengeance. The trumpeting of the first angel brings hail and fire mixed with blood. It burns up a third of the earth. The second, third, and fourth trumpets bring similar devastations. The eagle of 8:13 warns from midheaven: "Woe, woe, woe to those who dwell on the earth . . ." The last three woes will afflict humankind directly. So the fifth trumpet brings smoke from the bottomless pit and locusts with power like scorpions to torture those not having God's protective seal. The fantastic appearance of the locusts develops the warnings in Joel 1:4 and 2:4. The horrors of the depths of sheol (hell) have been unleashed. The sixth trumpet brings the release of four angels who will kill a third of humankind. Plagues will ride cavalry in destruction. Still, this will not bring the idolatrous to repent.

In chapter 10 the second of the three woes to afflict humanity continues. A mighty angel wrapped in a rainbow with a face like the sun comes with a little scroll. He roars like a lion and seven thunders sound. Although John is forbidden to write down the message of the seven thunders, the angel solemnly promises that after the seventh trumpet the mystery (plan) of God will be fulfilled with no more delay. John is instructed to take the little scroll and eat it (see Ezekiel 2:8, 3:1–3). As God's Word it is sweet to the taste, but it proves bitter in the stomach (terrible judgment).

In chapter 11 John receives the task of measuring the Temple of God. The nations will trample the outer precincts of the Temple for three and a half years while two witnesses (Moses and Elijah?) prophesy repentance for three and a half years. The two olive trees and two lampstands (11:4) likely stand for Zerubbabel and Joshua (see Zechariah 4:1–14). Their prophecy is more destruction, suitable for a humanity as wicked as Sodom and Egypt. Still, after three and a half days many will be revived and taken to heaven. The second woe will conclude with a great earthquake that will glorify God.

The seventh trumpet blows and the third human woe begins. It turns out to be more a praise of God and conquest of earth than a vision of destruction. Against the world-hating of the first six trumpeted destructions, John announces an incarnational faith: "The kingdom of the world has become the kingdom of our Lord and of his Christ, and he shall reign for ever and ever" (11:15). The twenty-four elders worship God for coming in righteous wrath to bring judgment on the nations. Judgment will be the destruction of the destroyers of the earth (11:18) and so will be wholly positive. The heavenly Temple opens and the ark of the covenant is seen. The entire panoply of the trumpeted revelations is filled with the rich symbolism of the Hebrew Bible, suggesting that Revelation shows us Jewish Christians reworking the apocalyptic tradition to make their Messiah the focus of a new judgment and heaven.

The Seven Unnumbered Visions (12:1–15:4)

The next portion of Revelation presents seven visions, although the author does not enumerate them as such. First the vision of the woman clothed with the sun portrays the conflict between Christ's Church and Satan.[11] In the eschatological age that has come with the birth of the Messiah, the warfare between God and Satan has intensified. The Church (or Mother of the Messiah) is pursued by diabolical evil, which senses that its conquerer has come. Revelation 12:7–9 draws on the myth of an angelic warfare in heaven, when Michael and the good angels defeated the evil angels led by Satan. The devil is thrown down to earth. Heaven rejoices in the victory of the Lamb, who saves earthlings from Satan's power. Since the Messiah is safe in heaven, the Evil One takes out his wrath on the Church, which flees to the wilderness and is protected by an eagle (see Exodus 19:4, Deuteronomy 32:11, Isaiah 40:31). Revelation 12:15–16 reads like an ancient **cosmogony** depicting the primal opposition between the earth and the sea. The offspring of the Church, the followers of Jesus, become the dragon's (Satan's) special targets.

Chapter 13 depicts the beastly Roman empire, agent of so much evil and threat to God's people. Much of the imagery comes from Daniel 7. The dragon Satan as it were commissions the beast Rome. In the imperial cult, where the head of Rome was worshiped as divine, the early Christians saw a peak of idolatry and evil. The beast blasphemes against God and the saints in heaven for half a time (half of seven years). The great need of the saints on earth is endurance. Whatever the particulars of his people's political and religious circumstances, the author of Revelation clearly was horrified at the destructive power of the Roman empire.

The second beast (perhaps the pagan priesthood) reinforces the imperial cult. Like the first beast, it is an ugly parody of the Lamb. (The imperial cult is a sick form of the genuine need people have to worship an exalted power.) Revelation 13:14 may refer to the emperor Nero, who wounded himself mortally in 68 C.E. but quickly was replaced as an oppressor by Domitian. Revelation 13:15 suggests the ventriloquism employed in the imperial cult to give the idols voice. Revelation 13:17 may draw on a Christian feeling that faith in Christ meant being excluded from Roman social life. The most widely accepted solution to the problem of the number 666 is that it stands for Neron Caesar (50, 200, 6, 50, 100, 60, 200 in Hebrew numerology). This sort of number symbolism (called *gematria*) was common at the time, and apocalyptic writers regularly used it as a form of code. For early Christians Nero was the embodiment of pagan evil.

After these visions of evil John receives a countering vision of the Lamb and his vast following. They bring a new song known only to the redeemed and the chaste. Then an angel flies to midheaven and proclaims an eternal good news: "Fear God and give him glory, for the hour of his judgment has come; and worship him who made heaven and earth, the sea and the fountains of water" (14:7). After the previous riot of images this plain gospel seems blessed. Other angels announce the fall of Babylon (Rome) and the punishments due those who worship the beast and its image. They shall reap eternal torment. (This is one of several places where Revelation's vengefulness takes it some distance from the synoptic Christ.) Once again the message for the saints is to hold fast to their faith and endure their persecutions. The dead who have kept faith will find full rest. Revelation 14:14–16 projects the Son of Man coming in judgment to harvest the earth. Assisted by the angels, God will bring a terrible judgment, his wrath so lashing the wicked that blood will flow high as a horse's bridle.

The last of the seven unnumbered visions shows seven angels with seven plagues. This will complete the divine wrath. The sea of glass again suggests the distance between heaven and earth. The song of those who have conquered the beast and its image seems addressed to the Creator or Father God and is woven from Old Testament images:

> Although their song is called the song of Moses, it is not one of triumph such as is found in Exod. 15; it is more like Deut. 32, also called Song of Moses. The hymn is not christological. It is addressed only to God and is woven out of OT reminiscences. The first line, "Great and marvelous are Your works," recalls Pss. 92:5, 111:2, 139:14. It is also reminiscent of the ceremony of entry into the covenant at Qumran when the priests recount the "deeds of God in his mighty works." . . . Line 3, "just and true are Your ways," recalls Deut. 32:4, Ps. 145:17. Vs. 4 is influenced by Jer. 10:6–7, Ps. 86:9, Mal. 1:6. One notes the element of fear, rather than love, of God.[12]

The Seven Bowls (15:5–16:21)

The next set of visions begins with the opening of the tent of witness in heaven (see Exodus 25). The seven angels with seven plagues come forth robed in bright linen and girdled in gold. One of the four living creatures gives them seven golden bowls filled with God's wrath (best understood as the negative side of God's judgment). The Temple fills with the glory of

God, which is like fire giving off smoke. Until God's wrath is executed no one may enter the Temple (to intercede for earth).

In chapter 16 the seven bowls of wrath are poured out upon the earth. The first angel pours out a bowl of sores to afflict those who worship the beast. The second angel's bowl makes the sea a cauldron of death. The contents of the third angel's bowl turn the rivers to blood. This is justified as a fitting recompense for the blood the martyrs have shed. The contents of the fourth bowl, poured upon the sun, scorch human beings with heat. Instead of repenting and giving God glory, they only curse God. The bowl of the fifth angel throws the throne of the beast into darkness. Once again people only rage at God for their pains, instead of being converted.

The outpouring of the sixth bowl, which dries up the Euphrates, recalls the miracles at the Red Sea (Exodus 14:21) and the Jordan (Joshua 3:17). The foul, demonic spirits like frogs are reminiscent of the second plague against Pharaoh (Exodus 7:26). John is now linking Satan, Rome, and the false prophets that threatened the faith of early Christianity. Their combined work portends the great Day of the Lord. True believers must be vigilant. The garments mentioned in 16:15 probably are baptismal robes. Armageddon may be a Greek translation of Mount Megiddo, the site of several famous Old Testament battles (see Judges 5:19, 2 King 9:27). The seventh angel pours his bowl in the air, completing the punishments. Lightning flashes and a great earthquake occurs. Rome splits into three parts, the nations fall, and God makes the pagan empire drink his wrath to the dregs. The islands flee, the mountains vanish, hail falls like hundredweights, and people curse God for his plague.

In his fine book on apocalyptic in early Christianity, Christopher Rowland has elucidated some of this symbolism as follows:

> The point of the sequence of seals, trumpets, and bowls is a way of stressing that the disasters which must afflict the earth are not a sign of divine absence from the world, but paradoxically God's involvement in human history. Such events are a necessary prelude to the new age in Jewish eschatology. All the action connected with the seals, trumpets, and bowls has its origin in heaven. In all cases, where certain events take place on earth immediately after the opening of a seal or the trumpet-blast, the point is being made that the new dispensation, inaugurated by the exaltation of the Lamb, has direct consequences for mankind. Thus the close bond which unites God with human history is emphasized throughout the vicissitudes of the events which are described on earth.[13]

Interlude on Babylon (17:1–19:10)

One of the angels comes to instruct John further about the great harlot Babylon. She is the antithesis of the chaste Bride of Christ. Rome has seduced all earth with its false glamour. The blasphemous names of the scarlet beast probably are the emperors, worshiped as divine. Rome is tawdry with worldly baubles and drunk with the blood of the saints. John marvels at her stature but the angel deprecates both Rome and the emperors. They are but passing ("was and is not and is to come"—a parody of the title given God in 1:4). The seven mountains are the seven hills of Rome. The seven kings may be the fullness of the emperorship, but many exegetes identify them with recent historical figures. For instance, the five fallen emperors might be Augustus, Tiberius, Caligula, Claudius, and Nero. Frequently such exegetes make things work out so that John is writing under Domitian (81–96 C.E.). The ten horns might be the satraps or lesser Parthian rulers who were thought to be coming to destroy Rome under Nero. All these powers agree in opposing the Lamb, yet the Lamb will defeat them, for he is Lord of Lords (Deuteronomy 10:17, Psalms 136:3). Revelation 17:15–17 depicts the conflicts among the pagans. By God's will they will afflict one another. John is reminding his readers that all the ups and downs of pagan history serve God's purposes.

In chapter 18 another angel prophesies Rome's fall. So corrupt has Rome become that destruction is its only possible future in God's sight. Another voice calls believers out of Rome (away from any thoughts of allegiance). The literary form here is a dirge or lament. The queenly Rome, unaware of her dismal fate, thinks nothing of God's judgment. Her fall will bring the kings of the earth to weep over great grandeur lost. Merchants will mourn the end of their markets. Tradesmen and sailors will cry at the death of an age. But the saints, apostles, and prophets of heaven will rejoice, for they will recognize in Rome's fall the just judgment of God. She shall go down like a great millstone into the sea, and with her all her minions and casts of supporters. Why? Because "in her was found the blood of prophets and of saints, and of all who have been slain on earth" (18:24). A critical reading of Revelation might give the opinion that prosperity such as Rome's usually is purchased at the price of great cruelty, bloodletting, and flaunting of justice.

In chapter 19 John hears the song of a multitude in heaven celebrating God's judgments on Rome. They rejoice that the blood of saints has been avenged, that the great corrupter of the nations is going up in smoke. The twenty-four elders and four living creatures ratify this praise, making it a song of worship. Revelation 19:5 expresses John's perhaps dangerous imperative to worship: "Praise our God, all you his servants, you who fear him, small and great." If God has willed the massive destruction of pagan entities such as Rome, the saints must agree wholeheartedly. John never seems to reflect on the Christian community's own stake in this, never seems to see its liability to find the visions of the future that would best revenge it on its enemies.

Revelation 19:6 begins a nuptial song. The Church, Christ's Bride, is the antithesis of the harlot Babylon. Her dress is the good deeds of the saints. To be invited to the wedding of the Lamb (a major business of heaven) is a great blessing indeed. Revelation 19:10 sits awkwardly in this context and may be a later insertion (an isolated piece of advice about not worshiping angels, only worshiping God, and holding only to the prophecy of Jesus).

Seven More Unnumbered Visions (19:11–21:8)

Heaven again opens and more visions come to John. The first shows Christ (Faithful and True) ready to make war on God's enemies. The name that no one knows probably is Christ's incomprehensible greatness. His robe dipped in blood suggests not redemption but judgment: The blood belongs to his enemies. The name by which he goes forth is the Word of God. His army is spotless: purified, virtuous. His apparatus connotes revelation, rule, and judgment. He is the greatest of rulers, the Lord most worthy of allegiance.

The next vision shows an angel calling the birds of midheaven to come like vultures and feast on Christ's enemies. The beast and the kings of the earth form ranks against Christ. The beast is captured and with him the false prophet (see 13:11–15). They are thrown into the fire of Gehenna, the Jewish hell that first-century apocalyptic often imagined (see also Luke 16:19–31). The rest are slain by the Word of God. Taken symbolically, the scene depicts the complete victory of divine revelation against pagan wisdom.

The next vision shows an angel coming down from heaven with a key to the bottomless pit. He seizes Satan, binds him, and throws him into the pit for a millennium. This notion (quite startling, on the basis of what has preceded it in Revelation) exerted considerable influence throughout Christian history. In many ages people apparently thought that Christ's golden thousand-year reign was right around the corner. After the millennium Satan will run loose for a short while.

There follows a vision of thrones and judges. John sees the souls of the martyrs who were beheaded for their testimony to Jesus. They come back to life and reign with Christ for the thousand years. Other dead do not revive until the end of the millennium. John calls this revival of the martyrs the first resurrection. Those who enjoy it need not fear hell and they reign with Christ as priests through the thousand years. At Satan's release things will change. Gog and Magog (see Ezekiel 38–39) represent peoples hostile to Israel or the Church. These hostile forces will gather for battle, surrounding the camp of the saints. But fire will come down from heaven to consume them (see 2 Kings 1:10–12). John sees the devil thrown into a lake of fire, definitively defeated. With him will suffer eternally the beast and the false prophet. The whole vivid symbolism is a dramatic way of expressing John's faith in God's coming triumph (whose literal form, of course, faith can never know).

The scene shifts to another panorama of judgment.[14] John sees a great white throne symbolizing God's absolute dominion. From the holy divine presence everything on earth and in heaven must flee. The dead stand before the throne. Books open which contain the deeds of the dead and so determine their fate. The sea, death, and hell all give up their dead for this general judgment. All people in them are judged by their deeds. (Again, John's stress is not justification by faith, although certainly deeds meriting heaven would be deeds of faith.) Then death and hell themselves are thrown to destruction. John calls this destruction the second death, the definitive ruin (missing out on resurrection) that has come into being as the counterpart or negative image of resurrection. Resurrection (as a permanent, heavenly state) is the destruction of death. If one is not found in the book of resurrected life (this has strong overtones of predestination), one misses heaven and suffers permanent ruin.

Chapter 21 opens with a famous vision of a new heaven and a new earth. In many ways it is linked with imagery of the promises to the churches made in chapters 2 and 3. John is now dealing with the ultimate matters (final judgment, the state of things after the full establishment of God's justice and Christ's victory). The old earth and sea are no more (thus they have always been provisional). The new Jerusalem, God's holy city, comes down from heaven bedecked like a bride. The message of 21:3 is striking: "Behold, the dwelling of God is with men. He will dwell with them, and they shall be his people, and God himself will be with them; he will wipe away every tear from their eyes, and death shall be no more, neither shall there be mourning nor crying nor pain any more, for the former things have passed away." The passage is both humanistic (divinity is to be found in human affairs) and visionary (there will be a state of complete fulfillment). Revelation 21:5 is the only passage of Revelation in which God himself speaks. The theme is that Christ has made a new creation. The victory is consummated. God is alpha and omega. The thirsty will receive the water of life (see John 4:13). Those who conquer (a return to the refrain of the early letters) will be children of God. The many varieties of great sinners will languish in hell, the second death.

Interlude on Jerusalem (21:9–22:5)

One of the seven angels who had the seven bowls full of plagues comes to John and promises to show him the Bride of the Lamb. They go in the Spirit to a high mountain from which they can see the holy city of Jerusalem, coming down from heaven with the glory of God. The description of the city draws especially on Ezekiel 40–48. The contrast with Babylon is deliberate. The various twelves call to mind the twelve tribes and twelve apostles. Revelation 21:22 is an important verse: "And I saw no temple in the city, for its temple is the Lord God the Almighty and the Lamb." Ezekiel had to have a Temple in his ideal Jerusalem, and John's own previous descriptions of heaven have included a Temple. But the final order of Christ does not place the divine presence within Temple boundaries (see John 2:19–22; 4:21, 24; 2 Corinthians 6:16). The light of the heavenly Jerusalem is the glory of God and the splendor of the Lamb. Anything good from any of the nations will be welcome in it, but nothing unclean. The only ones fit to enter will be those whose names are in the Lamb's book of life.

John sees one last aspect of the heavenly Jerusalem. The river of life (see Genesis 2:10) flows through the middle of it, coming from the throne of God and the Lamb. On each side of the river of life spring up trees of life. It is a paradise redone. Revelation 22:3 proclaims a complete amnesty or general salvation: "There shall no more be anything accursed." Heaven will rather be centered on the rule of God and the Lamb. Its main activity will rather be their worship. Revelation 22:4 promises the vision of God's face, something that sinful humanity could never have (see Exodus 33:20, John 1:18). There will be no more night (evil, death). The Lord God will be the whole light. And the saints of heaven "shall reign for ever and ever" (22:5).

Epilogue (22:6–21)

The basic revelation to John of Patmos is complete. Revelation 22:6 is a solemn assurance from the angel that what John has seen is true and will soon take place. Revelation 22:7 supports the vision with Christ's eschatological promise: "And behold I am coming soon." To keep the words of John's prophecy is to find oneself blessed. John swoons before the wonder of what he has seen, but the angel warns him off from worshiping a fellow creature and servant of God. John is to keep open these words of the prophecy—not seal them up for the future but make them relevant to the present. Revelation 22:11 seems to mean that the time before Christ's return is too short even to worry about changing evil people to good. Christ's coming will be everyone's just recompense. He is alpha and omega, the fullness of truth. Those cleansed from sin (by Christ's blood) will have the right to the tree of life and the heavenly city. Others will be left outside.

Revelation 22:16 has Jesus affirm that he has sent this message by his angel for the sake of the churches. He is the root and offspring of David, the bright morning star—powerful and beautiful images, summarizing both Christ's lineage and his newness as the resurrected Lord. The "Come" of 22:17 was an early Christian prayer (**maranatha**). Both the Spirit and the Church yearn for the parousia, as do all people desirous of God's holy rule. Revelation 22:18–19 warns against changing the prophecy (see Deuteronomy 4:2, 12:32).[15] Adding to what John has seen will bring the plagues previously described. Detracting from John's vision will mean the loss of heaven. Whatever the level of literalness he intended for his message, the author was utterly serious about its importance. Jesus again testifies that he is coming soon. Revelation ends like a Pauline salutation, wishing the grace of the Lord Jesus to the saints.

WHY WAS THIS WRITTEN?

The historical details of John's writing of Revelation seem irretrievably lost. The most we can say is that the author, who stands out for using his own name, wanted to comfort and strengthen his people against persecutions or upsets that finally emanated from Rome. Perhaps we do best, therefore, to follow the suggestions of commentators such as C. B. Caird, who stress the pastoral goals John probably had in view. Caird is impressed by John's depth of faith and realism:

He was a realist in his appraisal of the churches with their little strength and their variegated weakness, so realistic that we can still recognize in them the churches to which we ourselves belong; yet he never doubted God's ability to clothe the church in the robe of purity and perfection which would make her a fit bride for the Lamb (xix 7–8). He was a realist in his grasp of the power and splendour of imperial Rome and of her ability to crush the church, in his analysis of the real nature of the forces that were devastating the earth, so realistic indeed that his world, once we understand it, is very little different from our own; yet he never doubted that in the battle between the monster and the Lamb the ultimate victory would go to the Lamb.[16]

Perhaps the key to John's realism and profound understanding of how evil parodies good is his conviction that faith in Christ shows God's predestining purposes for the future. Whatever the value of the incidental predictions he may have been suggesting, the overall import of his revelation was that Christ's resurrection assured the victory of God's plan and genuine goodness over all this-worldly opposition. If John felt that persecution was imminent, that martyrdom would soon confront many believers, he reached deep into his faith to draw forth splendid symbols of hope, powerful reasons for suffering confidently. The eternity of God (1:4), the resurrection of Christ (1:5), and the priestly dignity of the Church (1:6) comprise a trinity of reasons for facing the future bravely. From the outset, John makes it plain that all this-worldly powers are relative pikers.

This is not to say that John doesn't also have to wrestle with the problem of evil, trying to explain to his readers how a good God could allow them to suffer. The sovereignty of God, which so much of the symbolism of Revelation serves to enforce, has mysteriously made itself dependent on human agents. Christ, the Lamb and Word of God, is the foremost of these agents, and his victory through death and resurrection has assured the ultimate success of God's plan. But by risking human freedom, sending his Word to people who can reject it, God has committed himself to all the imperfections of history. The struggle would not be real if loss and evil were not real possibilities.

Using Christ as his key, John probes the Old Testament and the Jewish apocalyptic tradition (which he wants to defend) to line up symbolic precedents for his vision of a cosmic battle. In the light of the Lamb, God's interventions on behalf of Israel become anticipatory or promissory pledges. And just as for the Hebrew Bible the great source of disorder was idolatry, so for John the great source of disorder is the idolatry of emperor worship. Babylon and the beast would be nothing if people were not seduced to give them ultimate allegiance (or at least a destructive accommodation that weakens biblical faith). All of their power comes from their ability to win life-and-death commitments. Through its political and economic might, John thought, the Roman empire had made itself the central enemy of God (see, however, Romans 13). That it will go down in decay, and that it is ultimately as fragile as human loyalty, is but an irony alleviating its wrongdoing. The great sufferings it has caused leave John no sympathy for the sufferings it will itself undergo.

To buoy his people up in the face of Roman evils and disorders, John both emphasizes the riches of heaven and shows the emptiness of the riches of this world, which merely parody true goods. Along with the punishments that God will visit on his enemies, the riches of heaven constitute John's main arguments for hanging on. To gain the heavenly Jerusalem, one might easily count loss of life a good bargain. Life as we now know it is a mixed blessing, a compound of suffering and pleasure. Heaven will be an unmixed blessing, the complete enjoyment of the glory of God. To John's credit, the fulfillment he depicts in heaven is not basely sensual or in any way ignoble. He has seen that the human spirit's greatest wish is to confront something wholly good, something absolutely beautiful and true, to which it can give itself in pure worship. Thus the main activity of John's heaven is the solemn liturgy in which all the angels and elect ceaselessly praise God and the Lamb. Thereby the people of heaven, the Bride and the New Jerusalem, participate in the blinding purity of the divine glory. Everything around them and in them is perfect. To gain this perfection beleaguered Christians need only hold on and cling fast to their faith.

Another, perhaps more modern way of expressing the purpose of the author of Revelation is to say that he wrote to ease the tensions of his people, who were hard-pressed by Rome, and in so doing produced the equivalent of a psychotherapy. John Gager recently has expressed this point of view, focusing his analysis of Revelation on its techniques for suppressing time (drawing the fangs of a current history that seems unbearable):

> Both Levi-Strauss and Mircea Eliade have suggested that psychoanalysis represents a secular counterpart of the same phenomenon [suppressing time]. And it is at the point of this analogy between ancient myth and ritual on the one hand and modern psychoanalysis on the other that the structure of the Book of Revelation enters the picture. For I intend to argue that the writing is a form of therapy, much like the technique of psychoanalysis, whose ultimate goal is to transcend the time between a real present and a mythical future. . . . One basic function of myth is to overcome unwelcome contradictions between hope and reality, between what ought to be and what is, between an ideal past or future and a flawed present. Clearly, the hearers (Rev. 1:3) of the book were caught in such a predicament. The occasion was persecution at the hands of the church's enemies, but the real crisis lay in the unbearable and irreconcilable tensions created by persecution. On the one hand was the belief that, as Christians, they were the chosen people of God, protected by him and assured of eternal life in his kingdom. On the other hand was the overwhelming experience of suffering, deprivation, and death at the hands of those whom they most despised.[17]

Gager goes on to emphasize the liturgical character of John's religious psychotherapy. Revelation 1:3 suggests that it was written to be read aloud to assembled communities: "Blessed is he who reads aloud the words of the prophecy, and blessed are those who hear, and who keep what is written therein; for the time is near." In addition, the language of Revelation is replete with snatches of hymns, prayers, and benedictions. If readings from Revelation were coupled with the eucharist, one could conjecture that the eschatological aspects of the eucharist were thereby emphasized. The eucharist would become the meal that anticipated the heavenly or messianic banquet. It would also become the memorial of Christ's sacrifice that riveted the community to the source of its hope. As Christ had been the first and greatest Christian martyr, gaining his glory by professing his faith in God to the end, so Christ could be the great exemplar who would see the community through its present sufferings. Since John wrote precisely to see the community through its present sufferings, focusing the liturgy on endurance and witness to the end would have served his purposes admirably.

WHAT BACKGROUND DOES THIS TEXT PRESUPPOSE?

In a recent popular study of the Book of Revelation, the noted scholar of Gnosticism Gilles Quispel has stressed three background movements as helpful to understanding John's work.[18] First, there is the phenomenon of the apocalyptic itself, which we have already briefly mentioned. Quispel grounds the Jewish apocalyptic movement in the prophecy of Ezekiel (about 593 B.C.E.), in that Ezekiel became a great model for later writers of "revelations," Christian as well as Jewish. Among the Jewish apocalypses Daniel and 1 Enoch exerted the most influence.

At the end of a solid recent study of Daniel, John J. Collins concluded:

> The book of Daniel is a literary structure in which traditional motifs and patterns are remoulded to form a new vision of life and reality. This vision is firmly rooted in a particular historical situation, the persecution of Antiochus Epiphanes [175–164 B.C.E.]. However, its use of mythic language ensures that its relevance is not confined to that situation. The persecution is presented as one crystallization of the perennial conflict of cosmos and chaos, or of human revolt against the kingdom of God. Two features of the vision of Daniel seem especially distinctive. The first is polarization—the sharp antithesis of heaven and earth, the end-time and the present, the kingdom of the "Son of Man" and that of the beasts. The second is the emphasis on wisdom—the elect are defined as "wise teachers"—which entails a measure of incipient mysticism. The visionary not only hopes for a future salvation but transcends the limitations of the present by his wisdom and his heavenly visions.[19]

One can see how John of Patmos might have been oriented by Daniel. Quispel situates 1 Enoch in the context of the Dead Sea literature. The Essene community near the Dead Sea was a breeding ground for apocalypses like Enoch in the first century B.C.E. Enoch speaks of a Son of Man who reveals all the treasures of what is hidden (1 Enoch 46:3). Quispel explains the function of this Son of Man and then goes on to show how later passages in 1 Enoch approached a hope for an incarnation of divinity into human flesh:

This particular Man is the eschatological judge of the world. He pronounces the Last Judgment upon mankind. He reveals all the esoteric mysteries. He fights for the just and rules over them as their Messiah. There is another passage in 1 Enoch [70:1, 71:14] that merits special attention. There is a description here of how Enoch, having been lifted up into the world of God, is actually identified with the Son of Man. . . . It is even possible that this particular text from the first century B.C. once formed the conclusion of the whole book. We catch here a fleeting glimpse of the Essenes in their monastery on the shores of the Dead Sea, and the extent to which they used to dream of a complete identification between God's revelation of himself and a man of flesh and blood. The god-Man had already been foreseen at the very heart of Judaism.[20]

The Book of Revelation therefore had a strong line of apocalyptic predecessors upon which John could draw. The second movement Quispel finds in its background gathered together strong astrological influences. This should not surprise us, since astrology was part and parcel of the Hellenistic world in which John lived. Thus 6:15–16 has parallels in Greek astrological texts that speak of people hiding themselves in animal burrows and longing to die. As well, the weird locusts of chapter 9 seem quite like certain representations of the Archer (Sagittarius) found on Babylonian boundary stones. Finally, the lady of chapter 12 bears similarities with the sign of Virgo, often identified by ancient astrologers with the Egyptian goddess Isis. None of these identifications is absolutely certain, but each reminds us that the general culture of John's day was full of heavenly signs and symbols.

Third, the prominence of angels in the Jewish mysticism of the centuries preceding Revelation suggests that in the background of John's angelology lay Jewish mystical thought. We have mentioned John's use of the four creatures of Ezekiel's chariot or throne vision (Ezekiel 1:4–28). The Essenes also had stories about heavenly creatures around the divine throne. The main activity of such heavenly beings was singing the praises of God. Revelation carries forward this thought in such passages as 14:3, with the addition that the song of heaven was new and could only be understood by the 144,000 who had been redeemed from the earth. John receives his vision through an angel, and various scenarios within his general vision are mediated by angels or feature them. An "angel," generally, was a messenger or functionary of God. John drew on the conviction of contemporary Jewish thought that God has many messengers busy about the divine will. (This conviction was a staple of Old Testament thought, and we have seen it in other parts of the New Testament, where angels bring visions or prompt dreams.) The upshot was a sense of reality quite different from our modern, secular outlook. Both God and angels acted more frequently and directly in human affairs than we tend to expect today. Thus it was not extraordinary for a prophet such as John to feel himself visited by a messenger of God, nor was he straining contemporary credibility in picturing angels as carrying out God's plans for the future rescue of his people.

A last background suggestion comes from Austin Farrer's studies of the influence of the Jewish liturgical calendar on the structure of Revelation. "St. John does not see the scriptures in what seems to us to be their own pattern, he sees them artificially arranged in the Jewish sacred calendar, with its feasts and lessons; and he imposes further elaborations of pattern upon the calendar itself, quite alien from the spirit of the Old Testament, and still more alien from the common sense of the modern world."[21] Farrer works out John's liturgical rhythms in terms of a diagram that ultimately owes a great deal to Platonic and Gnostic thought. The key notion is that of the pleroma or fullness. Apparently the various feasts and symbols expressed the fullness of the divine reality and power: "St. John, being no gnostic heretic but an orthodox and apostolic man, accepts nature as the direct creature of the divine goodness and the Old Testament as the expression of divine Revelation, and fills the places of his scheme with the tribal names and astral signs, symbols which God himself has appointed and ranged in order."[22] The entire Book, in Farrer's view, is the working out of the diagram of the pleroma, a certain inevitability leading John on from stage to stage of his vision.

Like the comments of Quispel, Farrer's views suggest the rather sophisticated appreciation of contemporary Jewish thought that the author of Revelation may have had. For all that his writing derived from his Christian faith and was geared to supplying his people comfort for a time of adversity, his imagery drew from a rich field of speculation (itself in heavy debt to Old Testament prophetic and apocalyptic thought) about the composition of the heavens, God's guidance of history through angels, and the like. This speculation may finally prove the background most helpful to appreciating John's full range of resonances.

WHAT LASTING SIGNIFICANCE DOES THIS HAVE?

The Book of Revelation has had an adventurous career in Christian history. During the early centuries, when persecution was quite frequent, Revelation served as a mainstay of faith. Such prominent Church fathers as Irenaeus, Tertullian, Lactantius, and the young Augustine used it to comfort believers and predict a reign of Christ (millennium) that soon would overthrow the hostile powers of the world. In the *City of God*, however, Augustine introduced a more sober exegesis of Revelation. He transferred the millennium to the Church and the tension between heaven and earth slackened.

Throughout the Middle Ages, Revelation functioned as a rallying point for those opposed to Christendom. Reformers such as the twelfth-century abbot Joachim of Fiore drew on its symbolism to forecast a new age of the Spirit. Joachim interpreted such contemporary events as the rise of Islam by reference to passages from Revelation (for instance, the beast of chapter 13). The sixteenth-century Protestant reformer Martin Luther also used Revelation in his battles, stigmatizing the Roman church as the whore of Babylon.

Overall, recent interpretations of Revelation have swung between a literalist pole, at which John is assumed to have written in a code which, if broken, would yield an exact set of predictions about actual historical occurrences, and a symbolic pole, where psychological or theological truths of a permanent or universal nature have predominated. For modern critical readers the latter approach probably has the more attraction. The only caveat is the reminder that John himself wrote out of a particular historical time, with its own needs and cultural assumptions. To understand Revelation in any scholarly sense, therefore, one must penetrate both John's background and the literary structure of his text. For personal profit, however, the psychological play of John's apocalyptic symbols may be the most fruitful angle.

Consider, for example, the symbolism John develops for Christ. Even though he takes much of this symbolism from the Old Testament and it has analogues in other parts of the New Testament, the fact remains that John is the one who has written the most blazing, iconic description of Christ the Son of Man: "His head and his hair were white as white wool, white as snow; his eyes were like a flame of fire, his feet were like burnished bronze, refined as in a furnace, and his voice was like the sound of many waters" (1:14–15). The communication attempted in this passage is much more than historical information or doctrinal persuasion. The imagery is a call to worship. For John of Patmos Jesus is alive, blazing with divine life, worthy of full wonder and praise. He is more powerful, more elemental, than any this-worldly ruler ever could be. The same message streams forth from John's depictions of the Lamb in heaven and the Bride.

Psychologically, John is manipulating his readers' deepest hopes for a time and place of utter holiness. They want the victory of what is right and true and, since they are Christians, they interpret what is right and true in terms of the death and resurrection of Jesus. John says that Jesus now rules in the realm of God or heaven, a realm more ultimate than the worldly realm of space and time. Gager is correct to interpret such communication as an effort to ease the conflicts or frustrations that Christians in John's orbit apparently were feeling. John's visionary pictures do suppress the worst threats of a present worldly time felt to be completely at odds with a faith in Christ's victory. But they do more than that, offer more than a merely psychotherapeutic relief. Like the utopian symbols of judgment in Platonic or Egyptian lore, or the Buddhist symbols of the Western paradise, the symbols of Revelation reassert the basic convictions the human spirit must possess if it is to live by reason, with confidence in either itself or God.

Such convictions are not merely therapeutic, if by therapy one means an accommodation or doctoring that brackets the question of ultimate reality, objective actuality. The health we are discussing at this point is inseparable from ultimate realism or the most profound mental balance. Against the pressures of terrible circumstances (for example, life in a depraved prison) to warp the human spirit so that it comes to call evil normal, think lying to be ordinary human discourse, the struggles of the strongest human spirits, of artists and visionaries such as John, find or fashion bedrock assurances that the mind is made for truth and that the heart has an inalienable right to most love what is most good. This is the drama one can see in the writings of an Aleksandr Solzhenitsyn. Whatever one thinks of his specific political proposals, his struggles to expose first the corrupt system of the Soviet Gulags, and then the entire diseased language and politics of the Soviet state, express a primordial conviction that such falsehood is inimical to humanity itself, and that if it is uncontested it will soon kill what makes homo sapiens at all admirable. One can find parallel struggles in the literature recording heroic opposition to Nazism. The writings of Elie Wiesel, for instance, circle around this theme. Now and again the pressures of extraordinary times, or the perceptions of extraordinary human beings, focus the human spirit on its simplest and most crucial need—to muster the conviction to say "no" to lying that has become standard, perversion that has become customary. Isaac Singer's recent book *The Penitent* makes a powerful argument for traditional Judaism in these terms.[23]

It is from this rather simple standpoint that we feel most comfortable in proposing Revelation as a book for all seasons. The great significance of Revelation is not its particular imagery or theological convictions, forceful, relevant, or beautiful as these may be. Certainly it is not its biting desire for vengeance and bloody cosmic warfare. It is Revelation's radical assertion of light against darkness, its radical conviction of the victory of goodness over evil in the total scale of things. Human beings need all the defenses of light and all the arguments for the greater power of goodness that they can muster. They need precise, logical, historical, restrained sorts of arguments. They also need wild, passionate, symbolic, extravagant sorts of arguments. When darkness and evil seem solidly entrenched, they need reminders of their better selves that can make them revolt against such masters. John of Patmos suggests that our better selves can never be satisfied with grayness or cost-free niceness, with way stations between darkness-evil and light-goodness. The conviction we shall see in the Johannine Epistles (1 John 1:5) that God is light in whom there is no darkness at all says that the bedrock of the human psyche demands a true God. John of Patmos has answered this demand with brilliant symbolism of a heaven where no more shall anything be accursed (22:3). For that alone any generation might read him gratefully.

To be sure, not all psychologists will agree with this Johannine assertion that the human psyche needs symbolic assurances of an absolute light or goodness. Many are more comfortable with systems of both-and, the coincidence of opposites that places a dark side even in ultimate reality. On their side are aspects of the symbols of Eastern religions, which sometimes suggest that destruction is as equally primal as creation. (For example, in Hindu theology Shiva is as primal as Brahma or Vishnu.) Nonetheless, orthodox Christian theology, both biblical and later, has insisted on the complete goodness of God, the absolute assurance that sin stops when one reaches divinity and the Christ. For times of dire distress (such as the time which John of Patmos probably felt himself facing), nothing less radical seems equal to the best significance the human spirit has sensed it could claim.

SUMMARY

We began our study of Revelation by noting the special difficulties this book presents the modern reader. Unless one can enter into the world of Old Testament and apocalyptic symbols on which Revelation draws, its message is likely to remain quite foreign. Apocalyptic, the basic literary genre into which Revelation falls, derives from times of persecution. Generally speaking, the famous apocalypses in whose train Revelation stands (Daniel, Enoch) were written to comfort believers suffering some species of persecution. The current scholarly consensus is that Revelation probably was written by a Christian prophet (perhaps located on Patmos, as the text claims) around 95 C.E., when the Roman emperor Domitian was pressuring Christian believers. Some authorities place more stress on actual threats of martyrdom, others (using recent studies of millennial movements) think the pressure John was trying to alleviate was a broad frustration based on a dissonance between Christian faith and the social world in which Christians found themselves. In the latter case John was trying to explain why faith in a victorious Christ was not leading to worldly peace (if not prosperity).

In outline we broke Revelation down into a prologue, a section on the seven letters, a section on the seven seals, a section on the seven trumpets, a section on seven unnumbered visions, a section on the seven bowls, an interlude on Babylon (Rome), a section on seven more unnumbered visions, an interlude on Jerusalem (the Church), and an epilogue. Obviously, Revelation is carefully constructed. The dominant symbolism of sevens stands for a series of fullnesses (of advice to the churches, visions to be disclosed, plagues to come, and so on).

The Prologue is a solemn introduction to John of Patmos and his convictions about the importance of his message. The seven letters to the churches of Asia Minor open with a stunning vision of the risen, dazzlingly divine Christ. He is the Son of Man, the Ancient of Days from Daniel, the Resurrected Victor, the Word of God. The seven letters each follow the same rhythm: a description of Christ the sender, an assessment of the church's spiritual situation, and the promise of rewards for faithful endurance and punishment for defectors. Punctuating the whole string of seven letters is the tag line, "He who has an ear to hear, let him hear what the Spirit is saying to the churches." The net effect of the letters is to display Jesus' many scriptural titles to authority, reinforce the conviction that present trials are but a short gateway to heaven (if one perseveres), and chastise those who have fallen into idolatry or licentiousness.

The seven seals represent John's symbolic promise that God will soon visit justice upon the earth. The scene is set in heaven, showing the very throne of God surrounded by the four living creatures of Ezekiel and the twenty-four elders who summarize the Old and New Testaments. The

Lamb (Jesus as paschal victim and victor) dominates this scene. The horses and riders who appear as the seals are opened are agents of God's vindication of the martyrs. Those who die for God will have every tear wiped from their eyes, while those who persecute the just will suffer dire punishments. The seven trumpets continue this theme. While heavenly worship rises to God, the trumpeting angels announce various plagues and woes that are soon to afflict the earth. The imagery is rich in Old Testament allusions and sets the splendor of heaven against the destructions soon to come upon the earth. The seven unnumbered visions predict more of the same, but with a central focus on the beastly Roman empire, the Church's great antagonist. In the Roman cult of emperor worship John sees the epitome of pagan vice. The Lamb stands in counterpoint to the beast and clearly belonging to him is worth any suffering.

The seven bowls full of God's wrath continue the promise of the punishments that will come upon the foul earth, the world that continues to spill the blood of the saints, does not acknowledge the Lamb, and worships the beast of Rome. The interlude on Babylon is a long prediction of how the Roman empire will fall and the peoples of the earth will lament its passing. Where the Church is the pure Bride of the Lamb, Rome is the great whore, the center of all foulness. The songs of heaven amount to rejoicing that the foul cause of so much suffering to God's elect has met her proper end.

The seven further unnumbered visions focus on Christ's warfare with Satan. The Word of God will ride out to conquer Satan, with Christ's angel throwing Satan into a pit for a thousand years. This anticipated millennium of Christ's rule has been very influential throughout Christian history. In various scenes of judgment John pictures all the dead coming before God, the just to gain everlasting happiness and the evil to find everlasting hellfire. Chapter 21 has the famous vision of a new heaven and a new earth, as well as God's announcement that the victory is consummated. The interlude on Jerusalem depicts the permanent abode of the Lamb and his Bride. God's fair city will have no temple and the Lamb will be its light. All good things will be welcome in it and there shall be nothing accursed. In much of its symbolism the heavenly Jerusalem is John's version of paradise restored. The Epilogue reenforces the importance John attaches to these revelations of what is to come and gives Christ's solemn assurances that he will return very soon.

In considering why Revelation was written we stressed the pastoral realism with which the author assessed his times and tried to strengthen his people. He wrestled well with the problem of evil and communicated a powerful faith that God holds the world and all history in his predestination. Further, John offers a brilliant interpretation of Christ's victory, employing both Old Testament images and allusions to the contemporary counterpowers of Rome. In more modern terms he offers a psychotherapy that could help his people suppress some of the painful tension in their time, including that of unmasking evils that parade as parodies of goodness. Several hints that he writes for liturgical settings suggest how this psychotherapy might have interpreted the Christian eucharist.

Our forays into the background of Revelation took us to the Jewish apocalyptic tradition on which John drew, contemporary astrology, and the wide stream of Jewish mysticism. Daniel and 1 Enoch furnished worthy predecessors to Revelation (both of them were interested in the Son of Man). Astrology was part of John's cultural milieu and helped him communicate his convictions about God's heavenly forces and times. The prominence of angels suggests John's ties to Jewish mysticism, in which angelic actors played important roles. Austin Farrer's studies of the Jewish liturgical patterns in Revelation offered a last suggestion of the speculative thought-world in the background of John's writing.

Our assessment of Revelation's lasting significance first noted the historical influence the book has had, both as a comfort in times of Church affliction and as a source of powerful images for reformers wanting to purify Christendom (a Church too well adapted to the world). We then noted the poles of literalist and symbolic interpretation, giving the opinion that the latter probably has the most to offer readers today. Our final judgment of Revelation's significance underscored the resources it offers the deepest human spirit to believe in the light and fight the mortal darkness.

STUDY QUESTIONS

1. How do the revelations characteristic of apocalyptic literature relate to its tendency to arise in times of persecution?

2. What is the probable context of John's writing of Revelation?

3. Why is Revelation structured by so many sevens?

4. Explain the description of God in 1:4.

5. What was your first emotional reaction to the description of the Son of Man in 1:13 ff.?

6. What is the cumulative effect of the titles given Christ in the seven letters to the churches?

7. Summarize in a single word the advice or command that the seven letters give to Christians.

8. Summarize what John sees when he ascends to heaven.

9. What is the significance of the variously colored horses and riders?

10. Why was there silence in heaven for half an hour at the opening of the seventh seal? (How might this relate to Ingmar Bergman's film *The Seventh Seal?*)

11. Why is the little scroll sweet to taste but bitter in the stomach?

12. In what sense is 11:15 an incarnational text?

13. What is the myth of angelic warfare in heaven?

14. What is the main theme of chapter 13 featuring the beast?

15. How Christian is the vengefulness expressed in chapter 14?

16. In what sense is the song of those who have conquered the beast more fearful than love filled?

17. What is the general effect of the outpouring of the seven bowls?

18. Summarize the message of the interlude on Babylon.

19. How is the Word of God a warrior?

20. How literally ought one to take the prediction of a millennium when Satan is in the bottomless pit and Christ reigns unchallenged?

21. What is the upshot of John's depiction of judgment?

22. How central to John's enterprise is the vision of a new heaven and a new earth?

23. What is the significance of the fact that in John's heavenly Jerusalem there is no Temple?

24. In what way does the "Come" of the Epilogue epitomize John's message?

25. How do the many angels of Revelation show its ties to a Jewish thought-world?

26. Explain Revelation as a psychotherapy.

27. In what sense is Revelation more than psychotherapy?

NOTES

1. See Christopher Rowland, *The Open Heaven* (New York: Crossroad, 1982).

2. Pheme Perkins, *The Book of Revelation* (Collegeville, Minn.: Liturgical Press, 1983), p. 8.

3. See James H. Charlesworth, ed., *The Pseudepigrapha of the Old Testament* (Garden City, N.Y.: Doubleday, 1983); Jacob Neusner, *Judaism: The Evidence of the Mishnah* (Chicago: University of Chicago Press, 1981), pp. 25–44.

4. Adela Yarbro Collins, *Crisis and Catharsis: The Power of the Apocalypse* (Philadelphia: Westminster, 1984), p. 76.

5. Ibid., pp. 84–107.

6. See Perkins, *The Book of Revelation*, p. 15; Collins, *Crisis and Catharsis*, p. 112.

7. See Kenneth R. R. Gros Louis and others, *Literary Interpretations of Biblical Narratives* (Nashville: Abingdon, 1934), pp. 330–45.

8. Elisabeth Schüssler-Fiorenza, *Invitation to the Book of Revelation* (Garden City, N.Y.: Doubleday Anchor, 1981), p. 64.

9. See W. Popkes, "Die Funktion der sendschreiben in der Johannes-Apokalypse," *Zeitschrift für die Neutestamentliche Wissenschaft* 74 (1983), 90–107.

10. See R. Trevijano Etcheverria, "La oración en el Apocalipsis," *Salmanticensis* 30 (1983), 41–62.

11. See R. Bergmeier, "Altes und neuer zur 'sonnenfrau an Himmel' (Apk 12)," *Zeitschrift für die Neutestamentliche Wissenschaft* 73 (1982), 97–109.

12. J. Massyngberde Ford, *Revelation* (Garden City, N.Y.: Doubleday Anchor, 1975), p. 257.

13. Rowland, *The Open Heaven*, pp. 426–27.

14. See T. F. Glasson, "The Last Judgment—in Rev. 20 and Related Writings," *New Testament Studies* 28 (1982), 528–29.

15. See W. C. Van Unnik, "De la Régle *Mete Prostheinai Mete Aphelein* dans L'Histoire du Canon," *Vigiliae Christianae* 3 (1949), 1–36.

16. C. B. Caird, *The Revelation of St. John the Divine* (New York: Harper & Row, 1966), p. 289.

17. John G. Gager, *Kingdom and Community: The Social World of Early Christianity* (Englewood Cliffs, N.J.: Prentice-Hall, 1975), p. 51.

18. See Gilles Quispel, *The Secret Book of Revelation* (New York: McGraw-Hill, 1979), pp. 19–25; Paul D. Hanson, *The Dawn of Apocalyptic*, rev. ed. (Philadelphia: Fortress, 1979).

19. John J. Collins, *The Apocalyptic Vision of the Book of Daniel* (Missoula, Mont.: Scholars Press, 1977), p. 223.

20. Gilles Quispel, *The Secret Book of Revelation*, p. 20.

21. Austin Farrer, *A Rebirth of Images* (Gloucester, Mass.: Peter Smith, 1970), p. 8.

22. Ibid., p. 310.

23. Isaac Bashevis Singer, *The Penitent* (New York: Farrar, Straus, Giroux, 1983).

11

Later "Letters"* to the Church

1 JOHN

What Have We Here?

In the three Johannine letters we have advice and teaching intended for the same basic church community that is addressed by the Gospel of John. (Revelation also often is included in the broadest designation of the "Johannine" church, but the differences between Revelation and the Gospel of John are greater than the differences between the Johannine Epistles and the Gospel.) Raymond E. Brown, probably the leading scholar of the Johannine literature writing in English, has in his recent commentary on the Epistles taken the following positions as working hypotheses:

1. The Epistles were composed after the main body of the Gospel of John (not necessarily after the final form of the Gospel as we have it today). This suggests a date in the decade 90–100 C.E., since Brown conjectures that the main body of the Gospel of John was composed around 90 C.E.

2. It is as likely that the Epistles were composed in their current order (1, 2, 3) as in any other order.

3. The Epistles probably were all composed by the same author, although one cannot prove this irrefutably.

4. The author of the Epistles probably was a different person from the author of (at least the main body of) the Gospel.

5. The Epistles (especially 1 John) probably were occasioned by a schism in the Johannine community:

*The chronology of these later letters is considerably debated. Hence the order we follow in this chapter stresses doctrinal importance more than temporal succession.

In the decade after the main body of GJohn [Gospel of John] was written (*ca.* 90), the Johannine Community became increasingly divided over the implications and applications of Johannine thought. Before the writing of I John a schism had taken place. The resultant two groups, consisting of the epistolary author's adherents and his adversaries, both accepted the proclamation of Christianity known to us through GJohn, but they interpreted it differently. . . . the Johannine tradition enshrined in GJohn, as it came to both the author and to his adversaries, was relatively "neutral" on some points that had now come into dispute. Either it did not contain direct answers for the divisive questions, or it contained texts that each side could draw upon for support.[1]

6. The likelihood is that the author's side eventually was absorbed into the "Great Church" (the trans-Johannine Christian community), at the price of accepting a more authoritative Church structure. The adversaries, probably unwilling to accept such an authority, may have merged with Christian Gnostics. As we noted in our commentary on John's Gospel, today's scholars' preferred location for the center of the Johannine community is Ephesus.

In outline 1 John breaks down as follows:

Prologue 1:1–4

Part One: Struggles Concerning Light 1:5–3:10

Part Two: Struggles Concerning Love 3:11–5:12

Conclusion 5:13–21

The Prologue stresses the incarnational character of Christian faith: "That which was from the beginning, which we have heard, which we have seen with our eyes, which we have looked upon and touched with our hands, concerning the word of life—the life was made manifest, and we saw it, and testify to it, and proclaim to you the eternal life which was with the Father and was made manifest to us" (1:1–2). No one familiar with the Gospel of John could miss the similarities. The author is writing to bolster his readers in these incarnational convictions and complete their joy.

Part One begins with an interpretation of the good news as light (1:5–2:2). God is light in whom there is no darkness. The fellowship of Jesus amounts to a (moral) walking in the light. Such a walking or truth telling is not the denial of one's sinfulness but the confession of one's sinfulness. With such a confession Jesus can expiate one's sins. Verses 2:3–11 stress that any claims to light or intimate knowledge of God are to be tested by the claimant's behavior. Unless people keep Jesus' commandments and walk as Jesus walked, their claims to intimacy with God are specious. This is both an old criterion or command and a new one, both a familiar word and something brought to sharp relevance by current controversies. Love of one's brothers and sisters is the practical measure of one's faith.

1 John 2:12–17 moves to exhortation. The author praises various categories of believers in the community (young and old) and then warns

them not to love the world. Love of the world is opposed to love of God the Father. Where the world gravitates toward lusts of the flesh and the eyes, doing the will of the Father gives one eternal life. 1 John 2:18–27 extends the author's warnings. It is the last hour (before Christ's return?) and many antichrists (a term unique to the Johannine Epistles) are roaming about. They are former Johannine Christians whose deviance has now become plain. 1 John 2:20 shows the Johannine reliance on the inner teaching of the Spirit: "But you have been anointed by the Holy One, and you all know." The implication is that those who faithfully discern the spirits will recognize the falsity of the antichrists. The antichrists' key error is denying that Jesus is the Christ (deviating from the central doctrine of the Incarnation). To have the Father one must confess the Son. Abiding in the original faith will keep one abiding in the Father and Son, and so will give one eternal life. The anointing of the Spirit will keep believers firm in this faith.

The section 2:28–3:10 contrasts the children of God with the children of Satan. Those who abide in the Spirit's teaching will suffer no shame at Christ's return. The Father's love makes believers children of God. This distinguishes them from the world, which is lawless and sinful. Those who abide in Christ do not sin, as he is sinless. Believers should not be deceived: Those whose faith is correct do not sin. Sin comes from the devil, whom Christ came to destroy. To possess God's nature (grace) and to sin is a contradiction in terms. The crux is behavioral: not sinning, loving one's brothers and sisters.

Part Two begins by developing this gospel of love (3:11–24). John calls it the message believers have heard from the beginning. From the beginning Cain, who murdered his brother because his own deeds were evil while his brother's deeds were righteous (Genesis 4:8), showed the way of the Evil One. The world hates Christians because they have passed from death (sin, bondage to Satan) to life. Love of one's brothers and sisters shows this passover to (eternal) life. Jesus exemplified such love by laying down his life. That is the antithesis of the hatred and murderousness that Satan inspires.

Following the example of Jesus, Christians ought to open their hearts to their brothers and sisters and help any people they see in need. True love is not a matter of words but of deeds. Good deeds can reassure one's conscience, but the final basis of reassurance is God's own greatness. 1 John 3:19 is a deservedly famous line: "By this we shall know that we are of the truth and reassure our hearts before him whenever our hearts condemn us; for God is greater than our hearts, and he knows everything." A good conscience means confidence before God and having one's prayers answered (because one is pleasing to God). 1 John 3:23 summarizes the Johannine program: "And this is his commandment, that we should believe in the name of his Son Jesus Christ and love one another." If believers keep God's commandments they abide in him. Their sense of the Spirit testifies that God is in them.

Still, as 1 John 4:1–6 explains, one must test the spirits, discriminate among the "inspirations" that are claimed. The Spirit of God always confesses that Jesus has come in the flesh (Docetic dilutions of the Incarnation are heretical). The antichrist denies that the Messiah came in Jesus' flesh. Children of God are stronger than the antichrist. The world listens to the antichrists, but those who belong to God listen to sound teachers like the author.

1 John 4:7–5:4 plays out the famous Johannine way of love. Verses 4:7–8 are among the most famous New Testament lines: "Beloved, let us love one another; for love is of God, and he who loves is born of God and knows God. He who does not love does not know God, for God is love." One could not put the primacy of love more strongly, nor more strongly assert the connection between love and knowing God. (The author's lack of kindness toward his enemies raises a few questions about his own practice of this central tenet, however.) God showed the divine love by incarnating the Son. It is not that human love has the priority. God's love in sending the Son to expiate humanity's sins has all the priority. Still, God's love ought to be the model for Christians' behavior. Indeed, love like God's is the way God abides in human beings: "No man has ever seen God; if we love one another, God abides in us and his love is perfected in us" (4:14).

The love of God seems to coincide with the possession of the Spirit. The Spirit in turn prompts the perception and testimony that the Son has come from the Father as the Savior of the world. The confession of Jesus brings the indwelling of God. To abide in love is to have a mutual indwelling with God. This in turn is perfected in a confidence about the day of judgment, as believers realize their kinship with God. Perfect love casts out all fear of punishment (the mature believer is not living at the legal level of reward and punishment). The great motive in Christian life is God's prior love. The test or control is love of one's neighbor. To claim to love the invisible God and not love one's highly visible neighbor is to be a liar. The Christian command is to love both God and neighbor.

In his circular fashion, the author returns to the confession that Jesus is the Christ. This makes a person a child of God. (Clearly the "confession" in question is more than a rote recitation of an orthodox formula.) Loving the children of God, one's fellow Christians, is proven by keeping God's commandments. The love of God, we might say, is realistic. Moreover, genuine love of God does not find the divine commandments burdensome. They are a natural way of channeling the divine **agape**. Whatever comes from God overcomes the world—it does not wander in the world's lawlessness and vanity.

The last section of Part Two (5:4–12) develops this theme of faith conquering the world. To believe in God and his Son is to be the victor over Satan's domain. Belief in Jesus' divine sonship defeats the faithless world. Jesus is the one who came by water and blood (see John 19:34). The implication is that baptism and Jesus' sacrifice (commemorated in the eucharist) mediate the reality of Jesus' divine sonship. The Spirit, the baptismal water, and the sacrificial blood form a trio of witnesses to Jesus' divine sonship. God, in fact, has been the great witness to Jesus (by raising him from the dead). Those who believe in God accept this testimony. Unbelievers do not accept it and so in effect call God a liar. God's testimony is that he has given believers eternal (resurrecting) life in his Son. To have the Son (by faith) is to have eternal life. Not to have the Son is to miss eternal life.

Chapter 5:13–21 is 1 John's conclusion, where the author asserts that he has written to believers that they may know they have eternal life. Believers should be confident that God will grant whatever they ask according to his will. Indeed, deep faith in God believes that one surely obtains what one asks of God (salvation, eternal life). The believer should pray for fellow believers who are sinning by superficiality or weakness. John seems to counsel not praying for mortal sinners. His conviction is that true believers, born of God, do not sin (mortally: so that they deeply reject God and kill their faith). Jesus keeps believers from mortal sin and the Evil One does not touch them. 1 John 5:19 is a rather dualistic line: "We know that we are of God, and the whole world is in the power of the evil one." Improperly understood it could suggest a Gnostic division between the elect and the evil. John's final confession of faith is a sureness that Jesus has come to provide understanding. Jesus' followers can know God, the one who is true, and they can abide in his Son Jesus Christ, who is equally true. That is the faith that gives access to God and eternal life. Any other faith probably is idolatrous. John concludes by urging his "little children" to keep themselves from idols.

Why Was This Written?

We suggested that the Johannine Epistles reflect a schism within the Johannine community that occurred after the writing of the body of John's Gospel. In his book *The Community of the Beloved Disciple*, Raymond Brown has sketched a Johannine history in four phases:

1. From the mid-50s to the late 80s Jews near Palestine, some of them followers of John the Baptist and some believers of an anti-Temple bias, accepted Jesus as a Davidic or Mosaic Messiah. This fused group developed a high Christology (a view of Jesus that stressed the preexistent **Logos** in him) that led to disputes with non-Christian Jews or Christian Jews not inclined to a high Christology.

2. Around 90 C.E. Gentile converts entered this community and the body of the Gospel of John was composed. The community moved out of Palestine to the diaspora (Ephesus?) and focused on teaching Greeks. By so doing it came to realize the more universal potential of its views of Jesus. On the other hand, its rebuffs from the surrounding pagan culture and from antagonistic Jews gave it a somewhat paranoid view of "the world" and "the Jews."

3. Around 100 C.E. there was a split in the Johannine community. The Epistles represent the views of the group that wanted to keep the Johannine high Christology firmly linked to the flesh of Jesus. The other group (labeled by the author of the Epistles "antichrists" and "children of Satan") thought that the Word was so divine that he could not really

be human. For them knowledge (gnosis) of God's Son (the fact that he came into the world?) was all-important and sufficient for salvation.

4. In the second century the group represented by the Epistles joined with the Great Church and accepted its authority. It gave to catholic Christianity a stronger stress on high Christology and the anointing of the believer by the Spirit. It accepted from the Great Church a stronger teaching authority and a more hierarchical church structure. The group that the Epistles are opposing probably withdrew from both the Johannine church and the Great Church, taking the road toward Gnosticism or the heresy called Docetism (which said that Jesus only seemed to be human).[2] 1 John therefore was written as a salvo in an intra-Johannine war. It took aim at those who were opposing the literal Incarnation of the Word or were teaching a Christianity without solid ethics and practical love.

What Background Does This Text Presuppose?

1 John presupposes the body of the Gospel of John, with its stress on Jesus' revelatory character. The author could assume that his readers knew about the birth, teaching, death, and resurrection of Jesus. He could also assume that his readers belonged to a liturgical community that celebrated a rite of baptism and commemorated Jesus' death and resurrection. The Gospel of John could be assumed, as a summary of the characteristic theology of the Johannine community. The general drift of tendencies that later developed into a Christian Gnostic thought probably was a staple of the environment, demanding a discrimination between good and bad aspects of Gnosticism. Johannine believers could label as good their kinship with the Gnostic call to the light and an interior inspiration by the divine Spirit. Johannine Christians (at least those of the persuasion of 1 John) had to reject the Gnostic denial of Jesus' full humanity as bad. They also had to be leery of the Gnostic tendency to downplay practical love and strict morality.

If Brown is correct about the final fate of the two divisions of the Johannine community, the author of 1 John perhaps could assume a growing appreciation of the need for a clearly defined Church teaching authority. At the stage of this Epistle the author can still insist that true believers know by the inner workings of the Spirit what doctrine is true and what is false. By the time the Johannine group that insisted on Christ's full Incarnation entered the Great Church, the inadequacy of this criterion alone had become apparent. Without an authorized teaching agency that could brand some interpretations of the Christian tradition valid or healthy and others deviant, the constant warfare of groups like the Johannine antagonists was inevitable. In this context, also, the development of a canon of authorized writings (Scriptures) would have become more and more inevitable. That 1 John entered this canon and became part of the official New Testament testifies to the solid impact made by its teachings about love and incarnationalism.

What Lasting Significance Does This Have?

From 180 C.E., when Irenaeus of Lyons cited the Johannine Epistles, these writings have been officially significant. They were used during the patristic controversies with Gnostics, but even prior to that time other New Testament texts and early Christian writings used phrases highly suggestive of an (uncited) influence from the Johannine Epistles.[3] Through later Christian history its strong stress on love undoubtedly was 1 John's claim to influence. By identifying God with love and making Christian love something practical and neighbor-oriented, 1 John expressed both the heart of the Christian matter and its most concrete control or criterion.

This love also gives 1 John its relevance today. In a time when "love" is sentimentalized, the Epistle's demand that love be a matter of concrete deeds (and something consonant with strict morality, not as a legalism but as a natural expression of holiness) is a welcome antidote. Since our time also frequently brushes love aside as irrelevant to politics, academics, and even theology, 1 John also remains significant as a clear statement of the radical Christian conviction that without love we know nothing about God, the central mystery of creation.

Since the sentimentalism of cheap erotic or emotionalized love is often the reason given for writing love off as irrelevant to important human concerns, the theology of 1 John opposes both aspects of a most dangerous fallacy. Like Pascal's "reasons of the heart" (the deepest wellsprings of our most important actions), Johannine love undercuts the dichotomies we tend to make between reason and emotion, mind and heart. Indeed, it shines a laserlike beam on the very center of the human person, where openness or closure to the divine mystery (which most challengingly shines forth in other people) sets all human beings their most basic test. This openness or closure, 1 John teaches, is love or hatred of God. With love of God (as light, truth, justice, goodness, creative mystery) come the best possibilities of human time, community, friendship, forgiveness, and a meaningful life. With hatred of God come the diabolical ruins: tyranny, warfare, viciousness, meaninglessness, being physically alive while spiritually dead. By spotlighting the love of God, 1 John makes our decisive battle very plain.

2 JOHN

2 John is only fourteen verses. Most likely it came from the same author, place, and general time as 1 John. 2 John 1:1 identifies this author as "the elder" (presbyter). The "elect lady" of 1:1 is probably a Johannine church (at some distance from the author's own). The love and truth that figure in the first verses are typically Johannine interests. Verse 3 links Father and Son (note that the Spirit is not mentioned: The typical Johannine formula is not fully trinitarian). Verse 4 mentions the new-old commandment of love, implying that it is the summary of Christian faith. Verse 7 is like 1 John in identifying the antichrists as those who deny that Jesus has come in

the flesh. Verse 9 is significant for linking sound doctrine with the possession of God. Believers are to keep from their houses people of unsound doctrine. Verses 12 and 13 suggest the communication that passed among sister churches of an early Christian geographical area (or doctrinal style).

2 John seems to have been written as a short, occasional expression of pastoral concern and affection. The presbyter feels some responsibility for the "elect lady" and almost chivalrously writes a brief letter of good wishes and religious exhortation. The background of 2 John probably is similar to that of 1 John. Gnostic-like tendencies in the cultural milieu cause the author to warn against Docetic dangers. The author can presuppose the sense of possessing God (here through sound doctrinal faith) that Johannine theology generally links with the Spirit, although here the Spirit itself has little visibility. The lasting significance of the Epistle is not great. If there were no Johannine gospel or first Epistle its stress on love might make it stand out as more nakedly compelling than the Epistles of the other New Testament schools. Probably, therefore, its strongest legacy is its stress on sound doctrine (which may also suggest a more advanced stage of the schismatic tensions than we see in 1 John).

3 JOHN

3 John is about the same length as 2 John (a length perhaps dictated by the dimensions of a sheet of papyrus). It shares the general Johannine context and thought-world that we have elaborated for the Gospel and the other two Epistles. Once again the author designates himself "the elder." This time, however, he writes to a specific individual, Gaius. Verse 5 suggests that Gaius is signal in hospitality (perhaps he was once the author's host). The first three verses are a warm expression of confidence in Gaius's spiritual health. Verse 4 implies that Gaius in some way is a disciple of the writer and expresses a beautiful view of the teacher-disciple relationship: "No greater joy can I have than this, to hear that my children follow the truth." Such a stress on truth is characteristically Johannine.

The hospitality to missionaries or church workers for which Gaius is praised in verses 5 through 8 is a good example of the practical cast of Johannine love. (Compare this with The Didache, an early Church manual [11–13].) Verse 9 hints at the schismatic difficulties in this Johannine community, by describing the conflict between the author and one Diotrephes. Apparently Diotrephes also begrudges hospitality to missionaries. Verse 11 equates doing good with being of God, doing evil with not seeing God. The Demetrius mentioned in verse 12 may be the bearer of the letter. Verses 13 and 14 are close to 2 John 12. The closing lines suggest the warmth between the author's church and the recipient's.

3 John seems to have been written to commend Gaius and tactfully urge him and his church to keep up their good work, especially their hospitality. It presupposes the general Johannine theology and some awareness of the tensions between the author and Diotrephes. It is not greatly significant in itself, but it does furnish us another glimpse of the

informal ties of hospitality and affection that bound many of the early Christian churches.

HEBREWS

What Have We Here?

Hebrews is not a letter but a literary sermon. Its kinship with 1 Peter and 1 Clement (a noncanonical early Christian writing), both of which probably originated in Rome and were written for Jewish Christians, suggests a Roman provenance and a Jewish Christian audience. Its extensive use of Old Testament materials also implies an audience familiar with the Jewish Scriptures. On the other hand, many of Hebrews' ideas reflect the Hellenistic notion that the earthly world is a reflection of the heavenly world. Philo of Alexandria, for instance, a first-century C.E. Jewish philosopher who used this Hellenistic notion, could have furnished the author considerable direction.

The identity of the author of Hebrews is not known, but many New Testament scholars nominate Apollos, the illustrious Jewish convert mentioned in Acts 18:24–28 (and also in 1 Corinthians). Since Hebrews is quoted by 1 Clement (about 96 C.E.), it must have been circulating before the end of the first century. The fact that it refers to Jewish Temple worship in the present tense has led some commentators to place it before 70 C.E., when the Temple was destroyed. Other commentators note that Hebrews' interest in Jewish worship is ideal and speculative rather than historical. Therefore its not mentioning the destruction of the actual Temple does not prove it was written before 70 C.E.. The conclusion (13:22–25) indicates an effort to associate Hebrews with the Pauline tradition.

Indeed, for a long time Church tradition attributed Hebrews to the apostle Paul but, as Reginald Fuller has noted, scholars of churches such as Alexandria objected to this attribution from early on:

> Trained in the classical tradition of literary criticism, they could not believe that Hebrews was by Paul. Its style and content were too different. Hebrews contains some of the best Greek in the New Testament, equalled only by that of the author of Luke-Acts when he has a free hand, untrammeled by the use of sources. As for content, the great Pauline themes are significantly absent, e.g., justification by grace alone through faith, or the church as the body of Christ. Pauline categories such as faith are used in a very different sense. Although the kerygma of both Hebrews and Paul is centered on the cross, Paul's theology derives its imagery from the law courts and salvation history (righteousness, justification), whereas the imagery of Hebrews is drawn chiefly from the Levitical cultus, the Day of Atonement. We cannot do better than to stick by Origen's scholarly verdict, "Who wrote it, God knows."[4]

In outline Hebrews breaks down as follows:

Introduction 1:1–4

Preparation for Main Argument 1:5–5:10
Main Argument: Christ the High Priest 5:11–10:39
Exhortation 11:1–12:29
Appendix 13:1–25[5]

The Introduction makes Christ the fulfillment of Jewish prophecy
(1:1). However, he is more than the greatest prophet, for in these last days
God "has spoken to us by a Son, whom he appointed the heir of all things,
through whom also he created the world" (1:2). This Johannine motif (see
John 1:3) then takes a Pauline twist: The Son reflects the glory of God, is
the stamp of the divine nature, and upholds the universe by his powerful
word (see Colossians 1:15–17).[6] Jesus' death is interpreted as a purification
for sins (1:3), and the author delights in the picture of Christ ascended to
the Father's glory (1:3) and possessed of a name superior to any angel's.

In preparing for his main argument about Christ's high priesthood,
the author first develops this notion that Jesus is superior to the angels
(1:5–2:18). No angel has ever been called a Son as Christ has. Verses 1:5–
13 are a chain of Old Testament texts (Psalms 2:7, 2 Samuel 7:14, Deuteronomy 32:43, Psalms 104:4, Psalms 45:6–7, Psalms 102:25–27, Psalms
110:1) that the author uses to argue for the Son's superiority. This sort of
textual argument shows the author's solid grounding in the Old Testament
and his tendency to regard the Old Testament as a prefigurement of
Christ's time. The point of this textual argument is to heighten the importance of Christ's work: If the things that happened through the angels were
important, how much more important are the things that happened
through Jesus! Jesus worked salvation and his work was attested by great
signs, miracles, and gifts of the Holy Spirit. For the book as a whole, Psalms
110 is the leading Old Testament text, giving the author a springboard for
his meditation on Christ's priesthood.

Hebrews 2:6–8 quotes Psalms 8:4–6 to argue that God has subjected
everything to his Christ's control. Hebrews 2:9 interprets Jesus' death as
both the cause of his glorification and something he underwent for all
humanity. Hebrews 2:10 has the important figure of Jesus as the "pioneer"
of others' salvation who became perfect through his suffering. It also indicates his divine status, speaking of him as the one "for whom and by whom
all things exist." Jesus' work of sanctifying human beings has made them
his brothers and sisters. Indeed, his motive in taking flesh was to enable
himself to destroy the devil, who has the power of death. (This imagery
became important in later Christian theology of the redemption when
some theologians pictured Christ as paying a debt to Satan to release sinful
humanity.)

Since God is concerned more with the children of Abraham than with
angels, Jesus had to become human: "Therefore he had to be made like his
brethren in every respect, so that he might become a merciful and faithful
high priest in the service of God, to make expiation for the sins of the
people. For because he himself has suffered and been tempted, he is able to
help those who are tempted" (2:17–18). This strong stress on Jesus'

humanity suggests that the author of Hebrews, like the Johannine authors we have just studied, was facing opponents who denied Jesus' humanity or argued for a Word so exalted that he had little traffic with human flesh.[7]

Hebrews 3:1–6 moves to Jesus' superiority to Moses. As the apostle and high priest of Christians' confession, Jesus has dignity that is not only higher than that of angels but also higher than that of the chief agent of the old covenant. Moses was faithful to God as a servant; Christ was faithful as a Son. Both built up God's household, but Jesus more crucially. Hebrews 3:6 offers a somewhat distinctive way of picturing the Church and stressing how it ought to regard the future: "And we are his house if we hold fast our confidence and pride in our hope."

Verses 3:7–4:16 develop Jesus' superiority to Joshua, the Hebrews' leader into the promised land. Verses 3:7–15 are a **midrash**, or exegetical commentary, on Psalms 95:7–11. The theme is not to harden one's heart to the Holy Spirit, as the Jews did during their wanderings in the wilderness. (Is the author likening current Christian existence to the Hebrews' time of trial in the wilderness?) The motif of "today" gives the passage an existential sharpness. The Jews' rebelliousness and disobedience not only provides a cautionary or negative example for Christians. It also implies why they could have rejected Jesus, the great high priest.

Hebrews 4:1 has the attractive notion of God's "rest," a figure that makes heaven the cessation of earthly toil and implies that it is an ongoing Sabbath. The key to entering God's rest (promised land, salvation) is faith, here taken as the docile acceptance of God's message or Word. Jesus, as the one who gives believers God's once-and-for-all rest, is superior to Joshua and the Old Testament dispensation (the partial rest of the promised land). Hebrews 4:12 pictures the Word of God (which the faithful must obey) dramatically and famously: "For the Word of God is living and active, sharper than any two-edged sword, piercing to the division of soul and spirit, of joints and marrow, and discerning the thoughts and intentions of the heart." Jesus is this Word and before him all creatures are laid bare. He is a great high priest, but mercifully he is able to identify with human weakness. Hebrews 4:15 was an important text in the classical Christian discussions of Christ's humanity: "For we have not a high priest who is unable to sympathize with our weaknesses, but one who in every respect has been tempted as we are, yet without sin." This should make believers confident of God's mercy and grace.

Hebrews 5:1–10, concluding the author's preparatory argument, lays out Jesus' qualifications for high priesthood. A priest is appointed to offer sacrifices to God for human sins. Ideally he identifies with human weakness and offers for himself as well as for his people. God is the caller, as was true in the case of Aaron, the first priest of the Mosaic covenant (see Exodus 28:1). Christ was similarly called by God to the priesthood (the author joins Psalms 2:7 with Psalms 110:4). Verses 7–10 stress Christ's physical suffering, obedience, and perfection into a source of universal salvation. Thus he was designated a high priest like Melchizedek (see Genesis 14:17–20), concerning whom we shall hear more in chapter 7.

Hebrews 5:11–10:39 is the full-blown exposition of Christ's high priesthood. Verses 5:11–6:20 serve as an introductory exhortation. The author berates his readers for having grown bored with, unskilled at, the basics of faith. Nonetheless, he will press on to more advanced matters. Hebrews, 6:4–6 gives out a doctrine quite controversial in the early Church (especially in the West, where Hebrews' canonicity was not assured until the fourth century): "It is impossible to restore again to repentance those who have once been enlightened, who have tasted the heavenly gift, and have become partakers of the Holy Spirit, and have tasted the goodness of the word of God and the powers of the age to come, if they then commit apostasy, since they crucify the son of God on their own account and hold him up to contempt." George MacRae has commented on this passage: "Hebrews is often said to take a hard line on the matter of penitence and forgiveness (cf. also 10:26–31), but note that the author is careful not to say that God does not forgive, but only that personal repentance is beyond the reach of one who definitively rejects the Son of God."[8] Hebrews 6:7–8 makes a point much in keeping with the Johannine stress on practical love: God is interested in fruitfulness.

Hebrews 6:9–12 somewhat tempers the author's hard line and may indicate that the community for which he writes is relatively well off (and so is capable of significant acts of charity). He is sure that his readers possess better things that indicate their salvation. God is just and surely will reward their good services toward the saints. Still, he makes it plain that he wants no sluggishness. It is those who show faith and patience that inherit the promise of salvation. For example, God promised a blessing to Abraham and Abraham received it by patiently enduring. God's swearing a promise is a lofty surety for the hope that Christians pursue. Verse 6:19 uses imagery of the Jewish Temple: "We have this as a sure and steadfast anchor of the soul, a hope that enters the inner shrine behind the curtain, where Jesus has gone as a forerunner on our behalf." The figure is of Jesus having gone to the center of the heavenly house of God (by his sacrificial death) and serving there as a great high priest.

Hebrews 7:1–28 develops the author's conviction that Jesus' priesthood is on the order of Melchizedek's. Melchizedek is a mysterious figure who appears in Genesis 14 to bless Abram (Abraham): "And Melchizedek king of Salem brought out bread and wine; he was priest of God Most High. And he blessed him and said, 'Blessed be Abram by God Most High, maker of heaven and earth; and blessed be God Most High, who has delivered your enemies into your hand!'" (14:17–20). Melchizedek by several titles was the superior of Abram. As king of peace ("Salem") and appearing without genealogy, he resembles the Son of God and continues as a priest forever.[9] (This is a fanciful exegesis, but interesting for what it reveals of the author's conception of Jesus' eternal priesthood.) Abraham gave **tithes** to Melchizedek, showing that Melchizedek was Abraham's superior. Insofar as the Levitical priesthood (the established Jewish priesthood) descended through Abraham, it bowed to Melchizedek in Abraham's tithes. The offering of bread and wine suggests the Christian eucharist.

That Jesus has come in the outline of Melchizedek argues for the inadequacy of the Levitical priesthood (the failure of the Jewish order of sacrifice). Indeed, the whole basis of the priesthood shifted, for Jesus was not the descendent of a priestly line but was made a priest by his death and resurrection. For Hebrews Jesus' new priesthood is the fulcrum of a new covenant and Law. By God's swearing, Jesus has become the surety of a better covenant (7:22). Where the old priesthood was made up of mortal men, Jesus continues in his priesthood forever. He functions for all people, "since he always lives to make intercession for them" (7:25). This suggests a mediator eternally functioning in heaven. Jesus offered himself (he was both priest and victim) once and for all on Calvary. God made a new sacrificial order by appointing as priest his perfect Son.

Hebrews 8:1–9:28 develops an argument for the perfection of Jesus' eschatological priesthood. Jesus, the Christians' high priest, sits at the right hand of God (the author's "right hand of the throne of the Majesty in heaven" is a Jewish circumlocution) as the minister of the new holy place that replaces the holy sites of the old covenant. Priests on earth are but a copy and shadow of this heavenly sacrificial order. Jesus' covenant is perfect, whereas the first covenant manifestly needed a successor. Quoting Jeremiah 31:31–34, the author argues that this supercession was foreseen.[10] Jesus is the priest of a new, inner covenant where the Law is written on believers' hearts. Thus Hebrews is quite Pauline in making a strict distinction between an old, imperfect covenant and a new, perfect relation to God achieved by Christ.

Chapter 9 details some of the particulars of Levitical worship, to show the several ways in which it lacked the perfection that came with Christ. The old priests did not fully penetrate the sanctuary and could not "perfect the conscience of the worshipper" (9:9). Christ, however, penetrated the Holy Place once and for all. His blood can do what the blood of the sacrificial animals of the old order could not do: "purify your conscience from dead works to serve the living God" (9:14). Thus through him comes an eternal inheritance.

The author then details how the copies of the heavenly sacrificial order (the scheme of the old covenant) were purified by blood, contrasting this with the purification accomplished by Christ's blood. Once and for all Jesus has entered the heavenly sanctuary "to put away sin by the sacrifice of himself" (9:26). When he appears at the parousia it will not be to deal with sin (he has dealt with sin definitively) but to save those waiting for him.

Hebrews 10:1–18 deals with the efficacy of Christ's high priesthood. Just as Jesus reached once and for all perfection, so once and for all he achieved the ends of his priesthood. The old order of repeated sacrifices could never perfect the consciences of those who availed themselves of it. Jesus came to offer a completely efficacious sacrifice, in fulfillment of God's will. Thus he has come to sit at God's right hand and now awaits the final crushing of his enemies. His new covenant is interior, as Jeremiah predicted, but it also fulfills God's promise of forgiveness: "I will remember their sins and their misdeeds no more" (10:17, quoting Jeremiah 31:34). As a result, believers can draw near to God confident of having been wholly cleansed in conscience. (They are in a new order of grace, God's unconditional acceptance.)

Verses 10:19–39 conclude Hebrews' main argument with an exhortation to faith and hope. Believers should not sin, lest they encounter a stern judgment (10:26–27). To sin would be to profane the blood of Christ. Verses 10:30–31 are lines worthy of Revelation: "For we know him who said, Vengeance is mine, I will repay.' And again, 'The Lord will judge his people.' It is a fearful thing to fall into the hands of the living God" (see Deuteronomy 32:35–36). In earlier times the author's audience did better. Now they must endure, stir up their faith, and hang on for the return of the Lord.

Hebrews 11:1–12:29 continues the hortatory mood. Verse 11:1 is a famous description of faith: "Now faith is the assurance of things hoped for, the conviction of things unseen." Because of their faith God approved the heroes of the old covenant; because of faith believers can understand God's creation. Then the author enumerates some of the great deeds of faith recorded in the stories of the Christians' Jewish forebears. Abel's sacrifice, Enoch's rapture, Noah's escape in the ark, Abraham's inheritance, and Sarah's conception of Isaac all transpired through faith. Abraham's sacrifice of Isaac, Isaac's blessings on Jacob and Esau, Moses' protection from Pharaoh, the Exodus, and many other great episodes in Jewish history equally testify to the power of faith. The author's reading of these events orients Christians toward a fulfillment in Jesus. For instance, he says of Moses: "He considered abuse suffered for the Christ greater wealth than the treasures of Egypt, for he looked to the reward" (11:26). For the author's readers, the great reward would be salvation with the Christ in heaven. This escaped the Old Testament heroes, despite their heroic faith. Only Jesus brought the definitive sacrifice and reward.

Hebrews 12:1–13 is an exhortation to endurance. Like the "cloud of witnesses" mentioned in 12:1, Christians must run their race with perseverance. Jesus himself endured the cross "for the joy that was set before him" (12:2). If they take their trials as a discipline from God, Christians will endure well. Every good father disciplines his children for their benefit. Christians must persevere, and so enter the presence of the holy God. Jesus alone made such an entrance possible. Previously the holy God was unapproachable. Now the opening of the kingdom is unshakable. Let due reverence and worship follow.

Hebrews 13:1–25, the body of the Appendix, is a catchall of ethical instructions. Verse 13:8 has become memorable for the line, "Jesus Christ is the same yesterday and today and for ever." Jesus died outside the camp or holy city of Jerusalem, so Christians should realize they have on earth no lasting city (13:12–14). Verses 13:20–22 give an eloquent final blessing. The conclusion rings rather Pauline.

Why Was This Written?

Traditionally, Hebrews has been taken as an exhortation to Christians of Jewish origin, perhaps stimulated by a sense that some such Jewish Christians were backsliding to their former convictions. On close examination, nothing in the work necessitates this view. Hebrews does assume keen familiarity with the Old Testament, but that was easily available to those who read either Hebrew or Greek. Hebrews' typological arguments (for instance, the shadow reality of the Old Testament sacrifices compared with the full reality of the heavenly sacrifice of Christ) suggest a strong foundation in Hellenistic philosophy,[11] but that too tells us little about its specific circumstances or intent. More recently some commentators have seen parallels with Essene ideas developed in the Dead Sea Scrolls, but nothing has yet emerged to make any certain historical ties.

On internal evidence, Hebrews seems to be an effort to interpret Jesus as the high priest who fulfilled the Jewish order of sacrifice and so brought both a perfect expiation of sins and a full access to God. The author must have thought his readers needed or would profit from such an exposition, which suggests people of Jewish background. However, sacrifice was important to many religions in the Hellenistic cultural milieu, so non-Jews also might have profited from Hebrews' expositions. Interestingly, the profit the author lays before his readers (if they endure) strikes a different note than that which we find in Pauline or Johannine exhortations. Perhaps, then, the author was writing out of the Roman theology that Raymond Brown recently has described as Jewish Christian in assumption and tone. Certainly Hebrews' concern with worship and priestly matters suggests a writer with rabbinical training. Its many exhortations to faith and endurance, somewhat reminiscent of Revelation, may indicate an audience suffering considerable frustration or even persecution.

In terms of faulty doctrines that the author might be trying to correct, the following points come to mind. First, Hebrews wants to be sure that no one subordinates Christ or confuses his central role with the roles of angels or other lesser players. Second, the author wants to be sure that the efficacy of Christ's atonement is clearly held in view, and that people not be confused about the seriousness of postbaptismal sin. What Christ has accomplished is too precious to be endangered by moral laxity. Third, Hebrews wants to help its readers strengthen their hope, not give in to any loss of eschatological fervor. To this end it stresses patient endurance, based on the "assurance" ("present reality" may be a better translation) of things hoped for (11:1). This sort of knowledge, based on insight into heavenly realities, considerably transforms the Pauline understanding of faith and eschatology. For Paul the stress is not (an almost Gnostic heavenly) vision but personal commitment to Jesus the crucified and risen Lord.

What Background Does This Text Presuppose?

Hebrews obviously presupposes some familiarity with the thought-world of the Jewish priesthood. If one knew nothing about the Levitical priesthood, its origins and practices, Hebrews' arguments for the superiority of Christ's priesthood would fall flat. The sermon also presupposes a strong appreciation of Jesus' suffering, death, resurrection, and ascension. Without such an appreciation, the arguments for Jesus' sacrifice and present status at the right hand of the Father similarly would fail. Sin is an important category, since without a deep sense of sin the author's interpretation of Jesus' sufferings and death would lack their full resonance. Indeed, were one not convinced of the need to be cleansed of sin by a sacrifice more intimate and exhaustive than the sacrifices of the Levitical priesthood, the whole exposition on Jesus the high priest would have little point. Apparently, then, the author could assume considerable sympathy with the goals of the Jewish priesthood and worship.

It is difficult for the average reader today to muster a like sympathy or enter into the Jewish ceremonial mentality. Even less is the average reader today quick to correlate the minutiae of the Jewish sacrificial order with Hebrews' moralistic interest in removing sin and purifying conscience. Only considerable poring over ritualistic texts and rabbinical analyses could make one familiar with the reasoning Hebrews employs. The author in effect translates Pauline notions about the Law and grace into a new language of worship and sacrifice. Where Paul speaks of the impotence of the Law to make people righteous or justified before God, Hebrews speaks of the impotence of the old sacrifice. In both cases it is the historical suffering, death, resurrection, and ascension of Jesus Christ that reveal the inadequacy of the old order and the superiority of the new. If Jesus was what Paul and the author of Hebrews thought (the Messiah and Savior), reflection was almost bound to lead to the conclusion that prior to Jesus people had only an imperfect access to God and divine grace.

What Lasting Significance Does This Have?

The lasting significance of Hebrews derives from its delineation of Jesus' priesthood. Without this New Testament document, much of the liturgical structure and theology of historical Christianity could well have developed quite differently. Hebrews was a prime justification for the evolution of the Christian priesthood, conceived as a corps of ministers commissioned to make present the eternal sacrifice of Christ. The development of the Christian eucharist from a rather simple fellowship meal to an elaborate sacrificial mass has its primary New Testament justification in Hebrews. Historically, the different branches of Christianity divided on the question of how desirable this sacrificial view of Christian ministry, eucharist, and redemption was (Eastern Orthodox and Roman Catholics being more favorably disposed than Protestants), but it is beyond dispute that for most of Christian history Hebrews' view of Christ's priesthood has been formative for Christian worship.

Beneath its perhaps dated or offensive language, Hebrews' theology remains striking for its insistence on Jesus' full humanity, temptation, and need to be vulnerable (if he was to function for his brothers and sisters as God intended). Jesus' priesthood might, therefore, be taken as a form for his self-sacrificing love—love that Johannine theology makes the great sign of God's care for the world. Relatedly, while Hebrews' language of sacrifice may obscure the everydayness of sin, a little imagination can suggest that sin, and the need to overcome it by forgiveness, remain very much with us. If people are greatly disordered, relating rightly neither to God nor their fellow human beings, both they and their society will know little health or joy. To conceive Jesus' work as opening a way to reform sinful humanity, to reset people in health and joy, could make his priesthood and sacrifice all-important.

1 AND 2 PETER

What Have We Here?

1 and 2 Peter, along with the other writings we consider in the remainder of this chapter, are distinguished by a rather practical or ethical content. Current New Testament scholarship tends to doubt that either 1 or 2 Peter came from the hand of the apostle Simon Peter. At one time 1 Peter was thought to date from the 60s, during the persecutions of Nero, but today the 90s are the more favored date. 2 Peter incorporates much of **Jude** and refers to several of Paul's letters, which argue for an author other than the apostle Peter and a date around 100 C.E. Both letters reflect a rising need for discipline (in both morals and doctrine), and both reflect a "Roman" (Jewish rather than Gentile) slant on Christian theology.

In outline 1 Peter breaks down as follows:

Introduction 1:1–2

Homily 1:3–4:6

Conclusion 4:7–11

Additional Admonitions and Consolations 4:12–5:11

The Penitent St. Peter.
Antonio del Castillo y
Saavedra. Spanish. After
1650. The artist reflects the
traditional emphasis on
Peter's betrayal of Christ
and consequent redemption
through willingness to suffer
the burdens of church
leadership and then
martyrdom. *(Nelson Gallery–
Atkins Museum, Kansas City, Mo.
[Nelson Fund])*

The Introduction proclaims 1 Peter the work of the apostle. It is a general, "catholic" letter addressed to exiles in the diaspora (sinful world) "chosen and destined by God the Father and sanctified by the Spirit for obedience to Jesus Christ and for sprinkling with his blood." The trinitarianism of this passage is remarkable, as are the note of predestination and the reference to cleansing by Jesus' blood (a Jewish sacrificial theme).

The main body of 1 Peter has the tone of a sermon preached to Christians newly baptized (or in need of a reminder of the implications of their baptism). Verses 1:3–12 bless God for the hope the divine persons have given Christians. Verse 1:4 speaks of an imperishable inheritance kept for believers in heaven. They should view present trials as refinements of their faith. Verse 1:8 makes it clear that most of the audience are second-generation believers (or later), who have not seen Jesus themselves. Their faith in the unseen works their salvation. What these believers possess was anticipated and longed for by the prophets and angels.

1 Peter 1:13–2:10 delineates the conduct that God's work on Christians' behalf should prompt. The hopes they have, and the price of their ransom from evil, should make believers strong in enduring present trials. Verse 1:20 joins predestination with a hint of Jesus' divinity: "He was destined before the foundation of the world but was made manifest at the end of the times for your sake." The "end of the times" probably means the full moment or *kairos* when Christ came for salvation. Faith in Jesus, powered by his resurrection, brings a release from mortality, a connection to the Word of the Lord that endures forever. All that they have been given should make believers people without malice or guile. Verse 2:5 is a famous image for the Church: "Like living stones be yourselves built into a spiritual house, to be a holy priesthood, to offer spiritual sacrifices acceptable to God through Jesus Christ."[12] The foundation stone for this priestly edifice is Jesus, rejected by humans but precious in God's sight. Psalms 118:22, which speaks of the rejected stone that became the corner, was an important prophetic text in early Christianity (see Mark 12:10, Luke 20:17, Acts 4:11). 1 Peter 2:9 is an even more famous description of Christians: "But you are a chosen race, a royal priesthood, a holy nation, God's own people, that you may declare the wonderful deeds of him who called you out of darkness into his marvelous light." Each phrase of that description brims with ecclesiological implications. Verse 2:10 credits God with having made no-people into people.[13]

1 Peter 2:11–3:12 develops some ethical guidelines for exiles in the sinful world. Christians should give unbelievers no cause to criticize them. (Noteworthy is 1 Peter's call to obedient citizenship.) Servants are to be submissive to their masters. Any innocent sufferings they endure they should refer to the example of Christ, who suffered innocently. Verse 2:24 is eloquent and famous: "He himself bore our sins in his body on the tree, that we might die to sin and live to righteousness. By his wounds you have been healed." Wives are to be submissive to their husbands, chaste and modest. Husbands are to be considerate of their wives, "bestowing honor on the woman as the weaker sex" (3:7). Throughout this ethical section, 1 Peter reflects the hierarchial assumptions of Hellenistic society (master-

slave, husband-wife). However, 3:7 also makes plain the equality of man and woman: "you are joint heirs of the grace of life. . . ." Verse 3:10 quotes Psalms 34:12–16 in support of living peacefully.

1 Peter 3:13–4:6 suggests how believers should conduct themselves under suffering. Those who have a good conscience cannot really be abused or troubled. Once again the author holds out the example of Christ, the innocent sufferer. Verse 3:18 sounds like Hebrews: "For Christ also died for sins once and for all, the righteous for the unrighteous, that he might bring us to God, being put to death in the flesh but made alive in the spirit." Verse 3:21 links Christian baptism with the symbolism of Noah's flood. Verses 4:1–6 speak of believers' participation in Christ's suffering and victory. If believers live sober, moral lives, they will confound the pagans. Verses 4:7–11 are a first conclusion and doxology (praise of God). Verse 4:7 speaks of the coming end of things, and 4:8–11 makes this a stimulus to generosity toward the brothers and sisters.

1 Peter 4:12–5:11 recapitulates the foregoing points and may be a later addition. Again the theme is continuing to live honestly and morally through hard times in hope of pleasing God and imitating the suffering Christ. Verse 4:17 is a line beloved of those who want the Church always to be reforming itself: "For the time has come for judgment to begin with the household of God." Verse 5:2 is a strong exhortation to fellow pastors to tend their flocks well. Christ is the chief shepherd at whose coming they will receive their reward. Verse 5:8 offers a famous figure for the dangers of the times: "Be sober, be watchful. Your adversary the devil prowls around like a roaring lion, seeking some one to devour." Endurance will bring eternal glory. The closing verses mention Silvanus and Mark, co-workers of Paul. Verse 5:13 seems a cryptic reference to the church at Rome, which may have been the writer's home base.

2 Peter breaks down as follows:

Opening 1:1–2

Exhortation to Virtue 1:3–21

Condemnation of False Teachers 2:1–22

Delay of the Parousia 3:1–16

Conclusion 3:17–18

The Opening identifies the letter as coming from the apostle Simon Peter and going to "those who have obtained a faith of equal standing with ours in the righteousness of our God and Savior Jesus Christ."

God's power has given believers all they need for escaping the corrupt world. Verse 1:4 speaks of becoming "partakers of the divine nature." This text was one basis for the Eastern Christian doctrine of **theosis** or divinization. Because of their exalted status, believers should supplement their faith with every virtue. 2 Peter 1:16–18 implies an apostle's eyewitness knowledge of Christ's majesty. Verse 1:20 introduces the problem of false prophets by making true prophecy depend on the Holy Spirit.

Chapter 2 deals with false prophets and teachers. Some even deny Christ. Following closely Jude 4–16, the author links false words with loose living and promises a stern punishment. Old Testament precedents suggest the certainty of this punishment. By contrast, God will rescue the righteous. In 2 Peter 2:4–19 evildoers come in for a thorough castigation. Verse 2:20 suggests that the author was troubled by Christians sliding back into prebaptismal vices. This makes them worse than the unbaptized. Verse 2:22 quotes Proverbs 26:11 to bring such debasement home graphically: dogs returning to their own vomit, sows having been washed only to wallow again in the mire.

2 Peter 3:1–16 offers support while the parousia is delayed, and some explanation for evil (i.e., some **theodicy**). (Verse 3:1 suggests a knowledge of 1 Peter.) Pagans may scoff that the Lord delays, but believers should cling to God's promise, since the Word of God is creative (the source of the world). Verse 3:6 appears to argue that there is precedent in the flood for the world's passing. God's time is not like human time. If God delays in coming believers should count it a mercy, as though he were giving them more time for repentance. In that way even evil times can be turned to good account. Verse 3:10 expresses the early Christian conviction that the parousia and judgment may come suddenly, and it offers a vivid picture of the consummation of the world: "But the day of the Lord will come like a thief, and then the heavens will pass away with a loud noise, and the elements will be dissolved with fire, and the earth and the works that are upon it will be burned up." (The strong eschatology of the Petrine Epistles argues that the Johannine accommodation to Jesus' delay had not deeply penetrated the communities of the Petrine Epistles. Where John had begun to stress the presence of the life or Spirit of resurrection and judgment here and now, the authors of 1 and 2 Peter were still painting Christian existence as an endurance until the parousia and still picturing the parousia itself as somewhat cataclysmic.)

2 Peter 3:11–13 is more exhortation to wait purely, with a strong expectation of the day of God that will dissolve the heavens in fire. Verse 3:13 speaks of a new heaven and a new earth (see Isaiah 65:17, 66:22) and so is reminiscent of Revelation 21. For the author of 2 Peter, however, the emphasis is not Revelation's renewal but a quick-coming dissolution and destruction. Verse 3:15 refers to the difficult writings of Paul and suggests that the author knows of some heretical misreadings of difficult Pauline passages.

2 Peter 3:17–18 offers a short final warning and a closing doxology. Readers must be careful not to be carried away into error. Jesus is their Lord and Savior, worthy of all glory. Growth in his grace and knowledge is the best use believers can make of their time.

Why Were These Written?

Judgments about the purpose of 1 Peter tend to fit a given scholar's sense of the date and occasion of its writing. Thus Joseph Fitzmyer, who takes the work as written by the apostle Peter sometime in the early 60s, thinks it aimed at bolstering Christians suffering persecution under Nero.[14] Gerhard Krodel, who argues against Petrine authorship on both stylistic and material grounds (for example, nothing indicates that the author had eyewitness knowledge of the earthly Jesus), sees 1 Peter as a general effort to offer consolation and encouragement to a Church suffering hard times.[15] The main body of the writing, which has the tone of a sermon, certainly is general, touching on many aspects of Christian faith. However, its most winning images bring out the high status Christians have ("chosen race, royal priesthood"), as if to remind them of the riches they must protect by enduring their trials faithfully. The "house-code" ethics presented in chapters 2 and 3 reflect a rather uncritical acceptance of Hellenistic patriarchal mores. One might conjecture, therefore, that the author mainly wanted to keep his readers faithful to conduct that would neither endanger their salvation nor annoy their Gentile neighbors.

2 Peter appears to have more precise motives. The author is offended by false teachers and wants to reaffirm the Day of the Lord.[16] Thomas Leahy has conjectured that these false teachers may have been forerunners of the Christian Gnostics who finally separated themselves from the Church in the second century.[17] Defenders of the apostle Peter's authorship have seen the letter as a final testament from the head of the twelve as he saw the approach of his own death. Few today hold that view.

What Background Do These Texts Presuppose?

2 Peter clearly presupposes a Christian conviction in the parousia. How this squares with a late date (some scholars have placed it as late as 140 C.E.) is not clear. Manifestly, however, the text takes any denial of a literal return of Christ as false doctrine. Perhaps most of those the author saw denying the parousia were arguing for a worldly way of life, but one senses that more than ethics was at stake. The Day of the Lord, so strong a theme in Jewish theology, was something the author was unwilling to give up. If Jesus were not expected to return, perhaps at any moment, something crucial to Christian resurrectional faith would have been lost. This reminds us that early Christianity considered the resurrection (ascension, Pentecost) as only the first moment in the transfiguration of the entire creation. When Jesus rose, ascended into heaven, and sent the Spirit, he inaugurated a new creation free of bondage to sin, Satan, and death. The return of the Lord was therefore expected as a next, consummating moment in the realization of an earth and humanity totally to be reformed. Consequently, to deny the parousia was to dilute a central motive for Christian expectation and joy.

1 Peter presupposes considerable familiarity with the Old Testament and considerable sympathy for a priestly view of both Jesus and Christian life. It sees present Christian existence as a battleground (believers being menaced by a lionlike Satan), and it recalls Jesus' sufferings as a powerful motive for enduring hard times well. Thus many of the sympathies 1 Peter presupposes are ethical. It is behavior oriented, rather than intent on doctrine. It assumes a tolerance of the general Hellenistic mores (slavery,

patriarchal households), perhaps in part because, like 2 Peter, it thinks the time to the parousia will be rather short.

What Lasting Significance Do These Have?

1 Peter has coined some striking imagery, for which alone it could claim a place in Christian memory. It supports the theology of Christ's priesthood more fully outlined in Hebrews, and it offers strong counsel to take present sufferings as relatively insignificant (compared to the riches of heaven). This latter view obviously has its dangers, and it runs counter to the incarnationalism and realized eschatology we saw in the Johannine writings. On the other hand, some interpreters read 1 Peter as similar in spirit to Romans 13—that is, they see it stressing that faith should lead to responsible citizenship and an admirable ethical life. Either way, however, 1 Peter offers the significant advice that present sufferings gain considerable clarification when we set them beside Christ on the cross.

2 Peter is most significant for its strong assertion of the parousia. Translated from its first-century context, this assertion might take the following general form: History must have a climax or consummation, with a judgment on its evils and goods, if it is not finally to be meaningless, a moral chaos incapable of grounding the pursuit of goodness and light. 2 Peter also is precious for raising so precisely (if fleetingly) the issue of human beings' sharing in the divine nature (2 Peter 1:4). If the Christian life implies this sharing, and if the divine nature is immortal, then the Christian life implies a literal defeat of death, a (Johannine) eternal life rooted in what God is and has achieved in human beings.

1 AND 2 TIMOTHY, TITUS

What Have We Here?

These three letters are frequently grouped together as "The Pastoral Epistles." Traditionally they were attributed to Paul, but recent scholarship has raised serious objections to that attribution. If they were written by Paul, dates in the 60s seem likely. If their main purpose was to grapple with problems occasioned by the death of the apostles and the growth of false teachings, as interpreters such as Reginald Fuller claim, their dates fall in the broader frame of 65–100 C.E., if not later.

Fuller also suggests that the original order of the Pastorals' composition was 2 Timothy, Titus, 1 Timothy. The main arguments against Pauline authorship are differences in theological emphasis and literary style from the letters known to be Pauline. For example, an estimated 360 words occur in the Pastorals that are not found in the certainly Pauline corpus.[18] Those who dispute the Pauline authorship have a hard time specifying the letters' place of origin. Adherents of Pauline authorship sometimes place 1 Timothy as originating at Rome, Titus as originating at Macedonia, and 2 Timothy as also originating at Rome. In terms of literary character, the Pastorals all are rather moralistic works concerned with firming up Church order.

1 Timothy may be outlined as follows:

Introduction 1:1–2

False Teachers 1:3–20

Community Order 2:1–3:13

Polemical Section 3:14–4:16

Pastoral Care 5:1–6:2

Warning and Exhortations 6:3–19

Conclusion 6:20–21

The introduction of 1 Timothy names the apostle Paul as author and calls Timothy (see Acts 16:1) his child in the faith. Verse 1:3 places Timothy at Ephesus and mentions Paul's journey to Macedonia. The first preoccupation of the letter is certain false doctrines, the main characteristics of which are a departure from tradition and a concern with nonessentials. By contrast good teaching aims at "love that issues from a pure heart and a good conscience and a sincere faith" (1:5). The false teachers the author is berating get lost in legalisms, not realizing that Law (Torah?) mainly is concerned with disciplining the ungodly. 1 Timothy 1:12–17 makes the author himself a former sinner now grateful to God's mercy. He urges Timothy to wage the good warfare (against deviance in faith).

1 Timothy 2:1–3:13 is concerned with good church order: how Timothy's community (or any Christian community) ought to function. It should pray for all people, especially those in responsible positions. It should encourage believers to live quiet and peaceable lives. Verse 2:4 is significant for proclaiming God's desire that all people be saved and come to the knowledge of the truth (Christian faith?). Verse 2:5 makes Jesus the universal mediator whose death was a ransom for all. The lifting of hands mentioned in 2:8 conjures a Jewish posture for prayer. The advice about women (2:9–15) reflects a patriarchal sense of household order and seems more restrictive than Paul's teachings in 1 Corinthians. Verse 2:14 is remarkable for suggesting that Eve (woman) was the cause of original sin.[19]

The portrait of a bishop in 3:1–7 sketches an ideal quite influential in later Christian history. Verse 3:2 makes it plain that celibacy was not required of church leaders in the first Christian generations. The standards laid upon deacons and women are rather sober: Church leaders must first have their own lives in good order.

Verses 3:14–4:16 open with a description of the author's rationale in writing: He hopes to see Timothy soon but wants him to know without delay "how one ought to behave in the household of God. . . ." 1 Timothy 3:16 sounds like a verse from an early hymn on the mystery (fullness) of Christ.

In chapter 4 the author returns to his concern about false teachings, directing his ire against extremists who forbid marriage and are overly ascetic about food. They misunderstand the goodness of creation: "For everything created by God is good, and nothing is to be rejected if it is received with **thanksgiving**; for then it is consecrated by the word of God and prayer" (3:4–5). This is somewhat reminiscent of Paul's polemic against the **Judaizers** in 1 Corinthians 8–10 and Romans 14. Timothy is to put true doctrine before his people and train himself in goodness. He should attend to the public reading of Scripture, preaching, and teaching (4:13), and use well his prophetic gifts, received at what 4:14 suggests was an ordination to church service.

Verses 5:1–6:2 provide advice of a more specific nature: how to handle older men, young men, older women, younger women, widows, and so on. Verse 5:8 is a strong endorsement of Christians' obligations to carry out their family responsibilities. The discussion of widows in 5:9–16 suggests that the status of such women was a problem.[20] Apparently they could pledge themselves to a devout life but some pledged and then reneged. Elders, too, appear to have been potential problems.[21] The author's advice reflects both sound experience and common sense. Verses 6:1–2 present a tolerant view of slavery. In general, the author's pastoral advice is shaded on the side of keeping peace and not giving offense.

Indeed, 6:3–16 sharply rebukes those who depart from peaceable, sound doctrine. The author assumes that their objections stem from conceit and contentiousness. By contrast, the author's own preferred state of mind appears minimalist or self-abasing: "for we brought nothing into the world, and we cannot take anything out of the world; but if we have food and clothing, with these we shall be content" (6:7–8). Verses 6:9–10 provide a famous warning against the love of money. Timothy ought rather to love righteousness and keep his confession of faith sound until the appearance of Jesus Christ. Verses 6:15–16 refer to God in splendid terms: "the King of kings and Lord of lords, who alone has immortality and dwells in unapproachable light, whom no man has ever seen or can see." 1 Timothy 6:17–19 gives another warning against the dangers of riches, stressing the greater importance of good deeds. The author's concluding lines (6:20–21) provide a good summary of how he would have Timothy behave: He should guard what has been entrusted to him (solid faith) and avoid false knowledge.

2 Timothy breaks down as follows:

Introduction 1:1–2

Thanksgiving 1:3–5

Exhortations 1:6–2:13

Polemical Section 2:14–3:9

Advice to Timothy 3:10–4:5

Conclusion 4:6–22

The Introduction again names the apostle Paul as the author and his child Timothy as the recipient. The Thanksgiving underscores the author's good conscience and recalls Timothy's sincere faith and family background.

The Exhortations begin with Timothy's own need to keep his gifts of pastoral office burning and be bold in professing the faith. Verse 1:9 gives the credit for salvation not to human works but to God's purpose and grace. The statement in 1:9 that grace was given "ages ago" suggests that the author is writing some generations after Jesus' own era. Verse 1:10 immediately confuses this, however, by speaking of the Incarnation and work of Christ as something quite recent ("now"). Verses 1:11–14 have the flavor of an elder church worker sharing his faith with a younger pastor. Verse 1:14 could be read as a call to a careful conservatism: "Guard the truth which has been entrusted to you by the Holy Spirit who dwells within us." 2 Timothy 1:15–18 reflects the different receptions the author found in his travels and his great gratitude to those like Onesiphorus who helped and supported him.

Verses 2:1–7 give Timothy crisp advice about keeping his aim clear and his discipline high. Verses 2:8–9 are quite Pauline: "Remember Jesus Christ, risen from the dead, descended from David, as preached in my gospel, the gospel for which I am suffering and wearing fetters like a criminal. But the word of God is not fettered." 2 Timothy 2:11–13 is another fragment suggesting an early Christian hymn. The intriguing line is 2:13, where the parallelism breaks and Christ's superiority shines clear: "If we are faithless, he remains faithful—for he cannot deny himself."

2 Timothy 2:14–3:9 brings us once more a polemical mood. Idle chatter seems especially to irritate the author. Those who know the history of Christian contentiousness or the damage church gossip does will greatly sympathize. Verse 2:16 is a sharp image revealing a sharp mind and a sharp tongue: "their talk will eat its way like gangrene." Verse 2:18 teases us with a hint about a dispute over the resurrection. The point seems to be that some are teaching a purely spiritual resurrection (perhaps experienced in baptism) that denies a bodily resurrection after death.

The seal mentioned in 2:19 carries Old Testament overtones (see Numbers 16:5, Isaiah 26:13). God seals those who are to be saved (are predestined). The discussion of vessels in 2:20–22 both urges Christians to be the best they can be morally and calls to mind 2 Corinthians 4:7: "We have this treasure in earthen vessels." In 2:23 the author is back to berating the quarrelsome, urging forbearance and gentleness. The highly unflattering description of people in the "last days" of stress (3:1–5) recalls the withering description of Romans 1:29–31. 2 Timothy 3:6–7 perhaps stereotypically paints "weak women" with the same unflattering brush. Clearly the author was familiar with churches where human weakness was very evident.

2 Timothy 3:10–4:5 has the form of personal advice to Timothy. The author refers to his own pastoral experiences, to what has befallen him for the service of the gospel, as background for the punch line: "Indeed all who desire to live a godly life in Christ Jesus will be persecuted" (3:12). Obviously this line is susceptible to both paranoid and healthy interpretations. Verses 3:14–17 stress conserving the tradition Timothy has received,

especially the teachings of the Scriptures. Verse 3:16 has been an important text for Christian discussions of how Scripture is the Word of God: "All scripture is inspired by God and profitable for teaching, for reproof, for correction, and for training in righteousness." It is well to recall that the "scripture" the author has in mind most likely is the Old Testament, and to note the practical or spiritual horizon that he assumes. He is far from envisioning a detached, academic scriptural study. (He is also far from equating inspiration with inerrancy or infallibility.)

The close connection between pastoral office and preaching the Word of God (especially stressed in Protestant theologies of ministry) becomes evident in 4:2, a much-used text: "Preach the word, be urgent in season and out of season, convince, rebuke, and exhort, be unfailing in patience and teaching." 1 Timothy 4:3–4, speaking of the prurient (those with itchy ears), is a vintage polemic that again manifests the author's assumption that going after bad doctrine is a sign of bad character. The evangelist mentioned in 4:5 is one who preaches the good news.

By way of conclusion, the author returns to his own status. He is near the end of his life and work. He can feel good about what he has accomplished. Verse 4:7 has often been used as an ideal portrait of a faithful life of evangelical service: "I have fought the good fight, I have finished the race, I have kept the faith." Like the advice and tone of 1 and 2 Peter, its primary tenor is endurance, finishing well. The parallel continues in 4:8, where the author stresses the heavenly reward he expects and links it to the Day of the Lord.

1 Timothy 4:9–22 brims with allusions to personnel of the Pauline roster. Whether one considers these names spontaneous expressions of the apostle's feelings or skillfully contrived boosts to the letter's pseudonymous character depends on one's overall assessment of the authorship. The small, concrete details are intriguing, as are the expressions of personal warmth and pique. Verse 4:18 is a bold profession of faith in God's deliverance. The ending rescues some no doubt important early Christians from historical oblivion but tells us little about their work or personal lives. We perhaps especially would like to know more about the missionary couple Prisca and Aquila (see Acts 18:2, 18; Romans 16:3; 1 Corinthians 16:19).

We may outline Titus as follows:

Introduction 1:1–4

Concerning Presbyters 1:5–9

False Teachers 1:10–16

Various Christians' Duties 2:1–10

On Redemption 2:11–15

General Christian Duties 3:1–7

Personal Recommendations to Titus 3:8–11

Conclusion 3:12–15

The Introduction names the apostle Paul as the author and characterizes his mission as: "to further the faith of God's elect and their knowledge of the truth which accords with godliness" (1:1). The elect are the household of God or Church. The hope their faith gives them is nothing less than eternal life, which God promised in ages past and manifested in the apostle's preaching. (In a Johannine context one would have expected the manifestation to be in Jesus' flesh.) The author considers Titus his true child in faith.

According to 1:5, the author left Titus in Crete to clean up some church problems. Part of Titus's task was appointing church elders. (Throughout the Pastorals the presbyterial or "elderly" structure of at least one portion of the early Church is manifest.) The qualities required of elders (or perhaps priests) and bishops parallel those laid out in 1 Timothy 3. Noteworthy is the requirement of 1:6 that the candidate's children be believers. This makes the general need to have one's own household in order quite specific, at least by twentieth-century standards. The stress on a bishop's hospitality and firm grounding in traditional doctrine could make a winning combination.

Titus 1:10–16 takes us into the question of false teachers once more. It is a major concern of the Pastorals, and no doubt a strong reason why the author or authors come through as quite conservative about church doctrine. Titus 1:10 mentions the circumcision party, confirming the suspicion we raised (on the occasion of 2 Timothy 3:4–5) that the Judaizers familiar from Paul's letters were the culprits. Verse 1:11 has a potentially ominous ring ("They must be silenced"), especially if one calls to mind later Church inquisitions and heresy trials. The same verse also implies that the false teachers were motivated by personal financial gain and were working without proper church credentials. The latter usually was not true of Paul's enemies in such areas as Galatia. Often his enemies had more official credentials (from Jerusalem) than he. Verse 1:12 again shows the author's sharp tongue (he appears, like Paul, to know contentiousness from the inside). Verse 1:14 refers to the unsound teachings (about the need for circumcision?) as "Jewish myths." Verse 1:15 is a very quotable line, the first phrase perhaps lifted from an ancient writer: "To the pure all things are pure, but to the corrupt and unbelieving nothing is pure; their very minds and consciences are corrupted." This raises the constant and central problem of how to communicate a sound message to a diseased audience.

Verses 2:1–10 mention the duties of various members of the community and offer Titus advice on how to deal with them. In addition to teaching sound doctrine he should bid older Christians be serious and a good model to the younger, urge younger Christians to self-control, himself be to all a model of good deeds, and bid slaves be submissive to their masters. The conservative mentality that we saw in 1 and 2 Timothy continues to prevail. Neither slavery nor women's subordinate status raises an eyebrow. Verses 2:11–15 focus Titus' preaching on the redemption worked in Christ. The mood is enduring present trials and disciplines for the sake of the blessed hope of salvation shining forth from the glory of Christ.

Titus 3:1–7 offers more ethical exhortation along the lines of the Hellenistic codes. Christians should be obedient to civil authorities, good workers, kindly of speech, courteous, and so on. The religious dimension of these virtues shows in the contrast the author makes with the vices that prevail before conversion. Verses 3:5–6 imply that the washing of baptism ought to produce good character. Verses 3:8–11 would have Titus insist on good behavior, as a focus of his preaching and teaching, in order to help his flock progress before God. Conversely, he should have little to do with contentious people or those unresponsive to his admonitions.

Titus 3:12 reports the incidental information that the author has decided to spend the winter in Nicopolis, a port of Thessaly on the Adriatic. The Conclusion is in the warm style of the other Pastorals. Tychicus and Apollos appear in other Pauline contexts (Acts 20:4, Ephesians 6:21, Colossians 4:7, Acts 18:24, 1 Corinthians 1:12, 16:12). Tychicus also appears in 2 Timothy 4:12. Once again the reader must decide whether these tidbits signify genuine authorship or skillful pseudonymity.

Why Were These Written?

The Pastorals make most sense when taken as efforts to correct abuses the author or authors perceived in churches within their orbit and to urge a sober, ethically oriented pastoral style. In the course of giving Timothy and Titus (whether they are real or ideal young ministers is secondary) pastoral advice, the Epistles treat several important problems. First, there is the heresy mentioned in 1 Timothy 1:3–20 and 4:1–11, 2 Timothy 2:16–3:17, and Titus 1:10–16. Fuller characterizes it as a combination of speculative mythology and rigid legalism or asceticism.[22] The mythology suggests either Gnostic tendencies (for instance, a view of the resurrection as purely spiritual, not of the body) or a Jewish source of fables and genealogies. The asceticism involves a depreciation of marriage and a concern with pure foods. The Pastorals oppose these deviances by criticizing the deviants' character and urging a simple adherence to the traditional faith and morals.

A second obvious concern is good church order, especially the good behavior of deacons, presbyters, bishops, consecrated widows, and others who have prominent roles. They should show themselves restrained, disciplined, kindly, and traditional. They should keep their affairs in good order and be a model to all they are leading or serving. The extent of the Pastorals' concern with good order suggests the size of the problem. It also suggests some temporal distance from the first church generations— enough experience both for organizational problems to reveal themselves and for early ardor to cool somewhat.

Third, the Pastorals want to promote the conservative ethical house codes popular in the Hellenistic world. These are revised somewhat to make them modes of Christian faith, but on such matters as slavery and women's status they seem little penetrated by Christian newness. Fourth, the Pastorals want to defend the solid deposit of faith (the basic doctrine of hope in Jesus and sound morals) they trace back to the Church's beginning.

What Background Do These Texts Presuppose?

As mentioned, the Pastorals probably presuppose a context of semi-established local churches with sufficient history for second-generational problems of doctrine and organization to have raised their heads. It is possible, of course, that churches organized by Paul could, after perhaps ten or fifteen years of existence, have produced the sorts of problems the Pastorals discuss. But the greater likelihood is that a second or third generation of believers was finding baptismal truths rather tame, the expectation of Jesus' return rather faint. We find in these letters little evidence of the prophetic enthusiasm Paul had to channel at Corinth, little trace of the bold theological inquiry that stamps Romans, Colossians, or Ephesians. To be sure, this could be partly a matter of temporary mood, or something dictated by circumstances. Still, it is difficult to picture the apostle who wrote Galatians and Romans becoming so disinclined to speculate, so tamely practical and traditional in his doctrinal emphases.

The Pastorals also presuppose Christians in the midst of a pagan milieu. Such Christians need to impress upon their non-Christian fellow citizens that they are obedient subjects of the Roman and local rulers, decent people of good character and strong morals. The Pastorals are not missionary letters. The main suggestion they make for influencing non-Christians is through upright behavior and good example. Last, the problems dealt with in the Pastorals imply churches sufficiently routinized to have problems of gossip, disedifying clergy, widows who pledge themselves and then hold back. They are very human churches, as we imagine them from the glimpses we get, and surprisingly modern. One would have to change little in writing pastoral or fictional church literature for character building today.

What Lasting Significance Do These Have?

The lasting significance of the Pastorals lies in the indirect picture they give of the rise of "early Catholicism." Through their polemics, moral exhortations, and instructions about church order we catch the Church moving to a more codified, doctrinalized, hierarchalized set of forms. The charismatic is giving way to the institutionalized. The itinerant missionary is still present in the person of the author but the focus has shifted to the more stable local pastor. The mood is no longer bold speculation, such as that which stamps the certainly Pauline letters. It is also not fascination with the historical Jesus, as we find in the Gospels. The mood of the Pastorals is sober, edifying, ecclesiastical. Enemies are castigated almost as much for bad manners (contentiousness) as for bad doctrine or faulty morals. Timothy and Titus are to be good chaps, preaching and living straight and true.

We might easily despise this faith if we were not the heirs of almost nineteen hundred years of the parousia's delay. Insofar as Christianity sat down to deal with the world, and even become part of the worldly establishment, it almost guaranteed the problems and moods of the Pastorals. (One easily finds parallels in the second and third generations of other religions or movements.) If one opens a store, a regular place for mundane business, someone has to mind it: keep the accounts, sweep the floors, check the supplies, and keep the customers from robbing the owners blind and beating each other up. Of course, a town composed only of stores (yard goods, grains, a butcher shop) would be considerably less than culturally vigorous. Similarly, a Scripture composed only of the Pastorals would not greatly impress the stronger mind or deeper heart. But in a variegated New Testament, the Pastorals make a modest, significant, even dignified plea for the rights of burghers and pastors.

JAMES

This relatively brief work is more a sermon than a letter—and a quite moralistic sermon at that.[23] Traditionally it was ascribed to James, the "brother" (relative) of Jesus, who came into leadership of the Jerusalem church. If this authorship is accepted, a date before 62 C.E., the conjectured date of James's death, would be necessary. However, many objections have been raised to James's authorship: the polished Greek, the lateness and difficulty with which the work entered the canon (hardly likely if so eminent an apostle had been widely considered the source), and the lack of either very specifically Christian teaching or the ritualistic strictness that Acts 15 associates with James. On the assumption that the writing is not by James, the place of origin becomes an unknown and the date recedes toward the end of the 80s.

James is difficult to outline, but a chapter-by-chapter description suggests the following:

Introduction; On Trials, Temptations, and Doing the Word 1:1–27

Avoiding Partiality and Stressing Works 2:1–26

On Guarding the Tongue and Being Wise 3:1–18

On Strife and the Uncertainties of the Future 4:1–17

On Riches, the Coming of the Lord, Prayer, and Conversion 5:1–20

The author introduces himself as "James, a servant of God and of the Lord Jesus Christ" and addresses in Jewish Christian fashion, "the twelve tribes in the dispersion." Thus James, too, has been considered a general, catholic Epistle. He advises his hearers to count their trials joy, the testing of their faith. They should confidently ask God for wisdom and not be divided by doubts. Riches quickly pass so the wealthy should humble themselves. Enduring one's tests merits the crown of (eternal) life. James 1:13 has been significant for flatly denying that God tempts anyone. Verse 1:17 is a polished and beloved verse that Christians have often used to praise God: "Every good endowment and every perfect gift is from above, coming down from the Father of lights with whom there is no variation or shadow due to change." This God alone was responsible for creation.

Believers should be slow to anger and quick to do the word of God, making their faith practical and effective. James has often been taken as the balance to Paul (or as the New Testament writer least compatible with Paul) on the question of faith and works. Perhaps they can be harmonized but their initial emphases are different. Verse 1:27 offers a famous brief definition of religion (piety): "Religion that is pure and undefiled before God and the Father is this: to visit orphans and widows in their affliction, and to keep oneself unstained from the world."

Chapter 2 begins with an injunction not to be partial to the rich or discriminate against the poor. Most likely James had met with such classism in the Church.[24] Verse 2:5 suggests the "reversal" of the Beatitudes: The poor become blessed (the rich tend to be the oppressors). James would have the second command of Jesus prevail: love of any neighbor as oneself (2:8). James 2:10 is rather rigorist: "Whoever keeps the whole law but fails in one point has become guilty of all of it." On the other hand, 2:12–13 seems an argument for placing oneself under a new, nonlegalistic dispensation (grace?).

James 2:14–17 again plumps for works as the sign of a vigorous faith. The image of feeding one's brother or sister who is in need is quite Johannine (1 John 4:20). James 2:18–26 extends the author's argument for works as the expression and evidence of faith, concluding in 2:26: "For as the body apart from the spirit is dead, so faith apart from works is dead." For the theologians of the Protestant Reformation, reconciling James's stress on works with Paul's stress on faith was a major problem.

Chapter 3 opens with a warning not to set oneself up as a teacher. That will only bring one a sterner judgment. None of us is perfect. Even so small an organ as the tongue shows most of us to be quite imperfect (James's description of the dangers of the tongue—3:6–12—is classic). True wisdom, as contrasted with worldly counterfeits, shows itself in works. Verse 3:17 fits well with the Christian tradition of the **discernment of spirits**: "But the wisdom from above is first pure, then peaceable, gentle, open to reason, full of mercy and good fruits, without uncertainty or insincerity."

Chapter 4 suggests that the strifes among people lodge in their (unruly) passions. Verse 4:4 recalls the Gospel teaching (Matthew 6:24) that one cannot serve God and mammon: "Do you not know that friendship with the world is enmity with God?" God is "jealous" and wants the Spirit given us to prevail. Quoting Proverbs 3:34, the author adds that God opposes the proud but gives grace to the humble. Drawing near to God will bring God near us. James 4:9–10 takes a rather dour tack in urging believers to repent. Christians should not speak evil of others or judge them. None of us can be certain of tomorrow, for we all are but a bit of mist. Verse 4:17 puts forward an important thesis about conscience: "Whoever knows what is right to do and fails to do it, for him it is sin."

Chapter 5 mounts an almost savage attack on the rich. James presents them as oppressors whose comeuppance is certain and harsh. Believers should trust in the judgment of the coming of the Lord. They should recall the example of the prophets who suffered in patience (sometimes). Job, who was steadfast, is another good example.

Bending off along another path, James teaches that swearing is not becoming. James 5:12 suggests that he knows Matthew 5:34–37 and Jesus' injunction to a simple speech of "yea, yea" and "nay, nay." The best way to good cheer and peace is prayer and religious song. James 5:14 describes an anointing of the sick that may prefigure the Catholic sacrament of extreme unction. Verse 5:16 calls for the confession of sins. The end of the sermon again urges prayer, this time after the model of Elijah, and the conversion of sinners. To bring back a sinner will secure one's own salvation.

James probably was written as a sermonic summary of a number of current religious precepts. It makes little attempt to organize these precepts into a coherent argument. Its outstanding themes are the importance of works, the need for a sober life-style, and the religious dangers of riches. Apparently the author felt his audience needed to meditate on these themes. James is akin to the Pastorals in focusing on practical behavior and having a keen eye for vice. He says little about heresy, however, or the need to safeguard traditional doctrine. He is more interested in the evils of the tongue, the need to control one's passions, and the great damage done by anger.

James shows considerable familiarity with 1 Peter and so may presuppose 1 Peter as background. A Jewish concern for ethical performance and sober morals predominates, so a background of Pharisaic training is also possible. The many references to the Old Testament fill out this impression. The author is familiar with church people, but is more interested in their character than their churchiness. He seems somewhat liberated from the law but much concerned with deeds and performance. The sermon has little social theory as such (apart from the implications of its attacks on the rich). The parousia is important but not the all-determining reality.

The significance of James derives from the picture it gives of Christian moralism in the early Church. Like the Pastorals, it balances the speculations of Paul and the Gospel writers' fascination with Jesus. Generalized from its too many particulars, James paints an ideal Christian of strong character: self-controlled, generous in doing good to the downtrodden, prayerful, gentle and restrained in speech. Since that's a portrait hard to fault, James has a lasting value as one of the several mirrors Christians might profitably consult on a regular basis.

JUDE

The very short letter of Jude traditionally has been ascribed to the apostle (brother of James and Jesus) of that name. There are no overwhelming reasons for doubting this authorship today. It probably was written about 80 C.E. (As noted, it was used by 2 Peter, probably around 100 C.E.) The places of origin and destination are both unknown.

The Apostle Jude. Andrea Bregno. The apostle has the staff of authority and pilgrimage and the book that signifies his commission to preach God's word. *(Nelson Gallery–Atkins Museum, Kansas City, Mo. [Samuel H. Kress Foundation])*

The opening verses announce Jude's authorship. His main reason for writing (verses 3–4) is to oppose ungodly people who are perverting the grace of God by denying Jesus. The body of the letter (verses 5–16) is a rebuttal of these false teachers. The author refers to the Exodus, the fall of the rebellious angels, and the punishment of Sodom and Gomorrah as precedents of God's punishing the wayward. So will the current heretics who defile the flesh and reject authority be chastised. Verse 9 refers to a Jewish tradition about Michael's restraint in dealing with Satan. The point seems to be that vengeance is God's. By contrast the heretics revile others, walking in the way of Cain. The several further Old Testament allusions are to the same point: The heretics will surely perish.

Verses 12–13 denigrate Jude's opponents eloquently if bitterly. The quotation from Enoch is a call for their judgment. (By this quotation the author allies himself with traditions of intertestamental Judaism that never became canonical.)[25] Verse 17, with its prediction of scoffers, is reminiscent of 1 Peter 1:5. By contrast believers should keep themselves in the love of God, pray in the Holy Spirit, and wait for the mercy (coming?) of Jesus that will bring them eternal life. The closing verses are an eloquent doxology to Jesus Christ.

Jude clearly was written to attack false teachers the author thought were imperiling his audience. It assumes a good familiarity with the Old Testament and a full acceptance of God's judgment. It can impugn the morals as well as the doctrine of the heretics. Its lasting significance is probably the glimpse it gives us of early Christian strife, the strong influence of Jewish Scripture and exegesis, and the place of judgment in the early Christian understanding of God.

SUMMARY

This chapter has surveyed the shorter and generally later writings that circulated in the early Church under the names of the apostles. The first group, the Johannine Epistles, clearly come from the same church orbit as the Gospel of John. Their likely place of origin is Ephesus, from the period 90–100 C.E. and the pen of someone other than the author of the Gospel. Using Raymond E. Brown's hypotheses about the history of the Johannine community, we interpreted the Epistles as the products of the party that eventually melded into the Great Church. In this interpretation the "antichrists" against whom the Epistles fight are a more Docetic group who downplayed a literal Incarnation and eventually separated from the Great Church.

1 John, the most important of the Johannine trio, has a first part that deals with light and a second part that deals with love. From the outset it evidences a strongly incarnational theology. The good news should lead believers to walk in the light. The test of any claims to light or knowledge are behavioral: keeping the commandments, especially the precept of neighborly love. The world is an enemy, a sphere opposed to God. The Holy Spirit teaches sincere believers the truth and makes them competent to discern heresy.

The Epistle perhaps is most famous for its stress on love. God is love, and those who abide in love abide in God. Anyone who claims to love God but does not practically help his or her neighbors is a liar. The various witnesses to Jesus (the Spirit, baptismal water, and sacrificial blood) help believers defeat the world. 1 John is precious for its simplifying stress on love and its confidence in the work of the Holy Spirit. The community struggles it suggests show why the early Church came to formalize its doctrinal and administrative authorities. 2 and 3 John have bequeathed the Church a few further wrinkles of Johannine thought and terminology but nothing crucial.

Hebrews is an important New Testament writing, more a sermon than a letter. It probably arose in Rome prior to 96 C.E., perhaps written by the Jewish convert Apollos for a Jewish Christian audience. Its imagery and logic are highly Jewish, suggesting a training in rabbinic (priestly) thought and some influence from Hellenistic philosophy or typology. The main argument of Hebrews, advanced by a somewhat convoluted biblical exegesis, is that Jesus is the great high priest who has superseded the Old Testament priesthood, sacrifice, and cultic life. He is superior to all the prior prophets, angels, and priests, because he is the divine Son. His Incarnation was necessary so that he could fully identify with the weak and tempted brothers and sisters whom his priesthood serves.

This priesthood, because it actually accomplishes the task of bringing people into God's rest, Temple, and personal presence, is far superior to the Levitical priesthood. It is on the order of Melchizedek and befits the new covenant that Jeremiah 31 foretold. Jesus, both priest and victim, has once and for all offered to God an acceptable sacrifice that can cleanse human beings of sin. Believers should persevere, taking heart from the cloud of witnesses who have preceded them and the willingness of Christ to endure the cross "for the joy that was set before him" (12:2). The text presumably serves those who wanted a ritualistic or **sacerdotal** interpretation of Jesus' death and work. It has been highly influential in the later Christian conceptions of the priesthood, the liturgy, and Jesus' full humanity.

1 and 2 Peter probably were not written by Simon Peter but by Jewish Christian authors situated in Rome around the late 90s. Their main purpose probably was to buoy up Christians of a similarly Jewish background during times of hardship. 1 Peter opens with an interesting trinitarianism, note of predestination, and reference to cleansing by Jesus' blood. After that most of its thought is quite practical, an elaboration of the implications of baptismal faith. Trials are presented as potential refinements of faith. Believers are likened to the spiritual house of God and are gilded with such honorific titles as "a chosen race, a royal priesthood, a holy nation, God's own people" (2:9). The ethical teachings of 1 Peter are quite conservative, reflecting a Hellenistic sense of patriarchal order. The sufferings of Christ offer the exemplary context that best illumines believers' pains.

2 Peter is noteworthy for the notion that believers participate in the divine nature (1:4). It exhorts the faithful to virtuous living, condemns false teachers, and argues that the parousia is merely delayed. Its general tenor is that believers should endure bravely and stay keenly aware that the world is passing. The Lord may return at any moment like a thief in the night. The closing reference to the difficulty of certain Pauline writings (3:15) suggests some tension between the author's community and Pauline Christianity.

The Pastoral Epistles traditionally have been attributed to Paul but seldom are by today's scholars. Their general content is proper church order (doctrine, discipline, morality, authority) and their general tone is moralistic. They probably originated toward the end of the first century from sites we cannot presently determine. 1 Timothy mentions certain heretical teachings that the Pastorals as a group are attacking. Timothy should hold to sound teaching and oppose the heretics' legalisms, myths, loose morals, and depreciation of creation. 1 Timothy 2:4–5 are verses significant for later Christian reflection on the universality of salvation and the mediation of Jesus. The house codes influential in the Pastorals are rather conservative and patriarchal. 1 Timothy provides influential sketches of ideal church ministers. 2 Timothy is quite polemical, hortatory, and concerned that all Christians be soberly virtuous. It lays a noteworthy stress on Scripture and preaching. Titus offers further description of how pastors should proceed, and further polemics against false teachers (whose "Judaizing" character becomes plain). It too urges believers to be sober, moral, obedient, and full of good example. The Pastorals are most significant for their depiction of early Church movements toward greater discipline and doctrinal control. They suggest a Church on the verge of institutionalization or "early Catholicism," coming to grips with the delay of the parousia and the likelihood of a long-term existence.

James is a moralistic sermon, probably not written by the apostle of that name, that perhaps dates from the late 80s (site unknown). The work wanders from one bit of advice to another, stressing the importance of works, the dangers of riches, the evils of the tongue, and the need for Christians to develop a strong moral character. In the background stands 1 Peter and the Old Testament. The author emerges as a strict moralist, probably not very humorous, who is more interested in behavior and character than doctrine or Church organization. By contrast with Paul he seems rather legalistic or self-reliant, but one may read him as mainly wanting to assure that faith bears rich fruit in practical charity and strong self-control.

Jude is a brief polemic against false teaching. It may well have been written by the apostle of that name around 80 C.E., although the place of composition and the intended audience are both unknown. The false teachings apparently revolved around a denial of Christ (his full humanity or saving power), and Jude's main message is that God will judge the heretics severely. Believers should stay away from the heretics' poison and await the return of Christ that will give them eternal life.

STUDY QUESTIONS

1. How are the Johannine Epistles probably related to the Gospel of John?
2. Explain the incarnationalism of 1 John 1:1–4.
3. What is the Johannine test of love?
4. In what sense is God love?
5. What is the Johannine faith that conquers the world?
6. Summarize Brown's historical sketch of the Johannine community.
7. What are the main reasons for denying that Hebrews was written by Paul?
8. Why is Jesus superior to the angels?
9. What is the significance of Jesus' having been tempted?
10. How is the Word of God a two-edged sword?
11. Why is Jesus a priest according to the order of Melchizedek?

12. What does it mean to speak of the "eschatological perfection" of Jesus' priesthood?

13. Explain the faith of Hebrews 11:1.

14. What is the permanent legacy in Hebrews' doctrine of sacrifice?

15. Discuss the ethics of 1 Peter.

16. What does 2 Peter 1:16–18 suggest about the author?

17. Why does 2 Peter so strongly defend the parousia?

18. What is the heresy combatted by the Pastorals?

19. Describe the ideal pastor sketched for Timothy and Titus.

20. In what ways are the Pastorals conservative?

21. What place do the Pastorals give Scripture?

22. What are the Pastorals' main titles to respect?

23. Evaluate the attack on rich people in James.

24. What place does James give to works?

25. Why should James make so much of control of the tongue?

26. What does Jude suggest about early Christian views of God's judgment?

NOTES

1. Raymond E. Brown, *The Epistles of John* (Garden City, N.Y.: Doubleday Anchor, 1982), p. 69.

2. See Raymond E. Brown, *The Community of the Beloved Disciple* (Ramsey, N.J.: Paulist, 1979), pp. 166–67.

3. See Brown, *The Epistles of John*, pp. 6–9.

4. Reginald H. Fuller, "The Letter to the Hebrews," *Hebrews, James, 1 and 2 Peter, Jude, Revelation*, ed. Gerhard Krodel (Philadelphia: Fortress, 1977), p. 3.

5. See Ibid., pp. 5–6.

6. See R. Williamson, "The Incarnation of the Logos in Hebrews," *Expository Times* 95 (1983), 4–8.

7. See C. J. A. Hickling, "John and Hebrews: The Background of Hebrews 2:10–18," *New Testament Studies* 29 (1983), 112–16.

8. George W. MacRae, S. J., *Hebrews* (Collegeville, Minn.: Liturgical Press, 1983), p. 26.

9. See P. Ellingworth, "Like the Son of God: Form and Content in Hebrews 7, 1–10," *Biblica* 64 (1983), 255–62.

10. See J.-P. Michaud, "Le Passage de l'Ancien au Nouveau, selon l'Épitre aux Hebreux," *Science et Esprit* 35 (1983), 33–52.

11. See, however, L. D. Hurst, "How 'Platonic' Are Heb. viii.5 and ix.23 f.?" *Journal of Theological Studies* 34 (1983), 156–68.

12. See D. Hill, "'To Offer Spiritual Sacrifices,'" *Journal for the Study of the New Testament* 16 (1982), 45–63.

13. See P. S. Minear, "The House of Living Stones," *Ecumenical Review* 34 (1982), 238–48.

14. See Joseph A. Fitzmyer, "The First Epistle of Peter," *Jerome Biblical Commentary*, ed. R. Brown and others (Englewood Cliffs, N.J.: Prentice-Hall, 1968), vol. 2, pp. 362–63.

15. See Gerhard Krodel, "The First Letter of Peter," *Hebrews, James, 1 and 2 Peter, Jude, Revelation*, pp. 53–59.

16. See Ernst Käsemann, *Essays on New Testament Themes* (London: SCM Press, 1964), pp. 164–95.

17. See Thomas W. Leahy, "The Second Epistle of Peter," *Jerome Biblical Commentary*, vol. 2, p. 494.

18. See Reginald H. Fuller, "The Pastorals," *Ephesians, Colossians, 2 Thessalonians, the Pastoral Epistles*, ed. Gerhard Krodel (Philadelphia: Fortress, 1978), p. 99.

19. See Jouette Bassler, "Adam, Eve, and the Pastor," in *Intrigue in the Garden*, ed. Gregory A. Robbins (Toronto: Mellen, forthcoming).

20. See Jouette Bassler, "The Widow's Tale," *Journal of Biblical Literature* 103 (1984), 23–41.

21. See J. W. Fuller, "Of Elders and Triads in 1 Timothy 5:19–25," *New Testament Studies* 29 (1983), 258–63.

22. See Fuller, "The Pastorals," pp. 105–7.

23. See E. Bousland, "Der Jakobusbrief als Neutestamentliche Weisheitsschrift," *Studia Theologica* 36 (1982), 119–39.

24. See C. H. Felder, "Partiality and God's Law," *Journal of Religious Thought* 39 (1982–83), 51–69.

25. See James A. Charlesworth, ed., *The Pseudepigrapha of the Old Testament* (Garden City, N.Y.: Doubleday, 1983).

12

Jesus

THE LIFE OF JESUS

We have studied the various books of the New Testament. Now it is time to study their central figure.

Before the dawn of critical historical approaches to the Bible, Christianity abounded in "lives" of Jesus.[1] By and large, they were meditations on the Gospels, although sometimes authors tried to harmonize the Gospel events (especially those reported in the synoptics) into a chronological narrative of Jesus' life. A generation ago New Testament studies had reached the state where main-line studies approached the question of a life of Jesus cautiously if not dubiously:

> The question is often asked, whether it is possible, on the basis of the tradition contained in the gospels, to write a life of Jesus. The diversity—in fact, the total disagreement—of the lives of Jesus produced during the past two centuries does not encourage optimism. The chronology of Jesus' ministry has been variously estimated, all the way from a few months—a year or less—to four years, or seven, or even twelve. In some lives the forced inclusion of John, with its totally different point of view (instead of Mark's theory of the "messianic secret," shared more or less by Luke and Matthew, John represents Jesus as announcing his divine nature from the outset), and even the substitution of John's three Passovers for the one in Mark, completely distorted what remained of the Markan order.[2]

The same source goes on to add that the wide divergences in interpreters' views of Jesus' social teaching and messianic consciousness only compound the problems of harmonizing the diverse textual sources. Another, similar source summarized the state of affairs in the mid-1960s as follows:

Corpus Christi. Spanish. Second half of thirteenth century. The simple yet effective wood carving represents the medieval sense of Christ's humble humanity. *(Nelson Gallery–Atkins Museum, Kansas City, Mo. [Nelson Fund])*

The following may be listed as assured findings of scholarship: a) No doubt is cast on the historical existence of Jesus by any serious scholar. Now that the debates raised by Bauer and Drews about Christ being a myth have died away, there is wide agreement about the historical fact of Jesus. b) The old-style attempt to construct "lives of Jesus" has failed; even recent books of this kind . . . are interesting for details but are no longer in harmony with the present state of scholarship as a whole. c) This is due to the character of the sources for the life of Jesus; the NT writings, even the gospels, being kerygmatic in purpose, are not strictly historical sources but testimonies of belief.[3]

In more recent times, scholarly approaches to Jesus largely have honored the kerygmatic character of the sources but sometimes have tried to tease from them historical or characterological likelihoods about Jesus. On the whole, however, scholars have felt more comfortable dealing with precise textual issues (for instance, "Psalm 110:1 and the Origin of the Expectation that Jesus Will Come Again")[4] than with biographical or psychohistorical matters. Thus it has been left to more popular works to supply what general readers often want: a sense of Jesus' "personality," an insight into what Jesus' world was like and how he tried to change it. The best such works are those written by authors who combine a solid sense of the findings of reputable recent scholarship with a rich humanity able prudently to imagine its way into Jesus' possible character. This combination tends not to produce "lives" (in the sense of biographies purporting to present what actually happened) but rather portraits: interpretive assemblages of the data, hypothetical orderings of more obscure and peripheral matters in terms of what the author determines to be more certain and central matters.

So, for example, a recent work by Gerard S. Sloyan, a distinguished New Testamant scholar, is willing to drop the sometimes endless qualifications of **empiricist** studies and make the following simple statement about Jesus' "mysticism":

> He was irrevocably committed to Israel's God. He conceived this God not only as personal, but as deeply interested in the fate of individuals. The mystical reality that can be attributed to him is twofold: Jesus did not hold intermediaries—the Torah, learning, formal worship, religious signs—to be necessary in the search for union with God; moreover, he was constantly in a state of prayer. This mystical reality of the man from Nazareth must be understood for what it was not, as much as for what it was. Nowhere does he repudiate Jewish peoplehood. If anything, he supports it at every turn. The great signs of it never come in for criticism on his lips: covenant, circumcision, law, temple sacrifice. It is true that the popular opinion of him in official circles— something we can deduce from the gospels rather than prove—seems to have been that he never stopped making statements against the holy place and the law. Yet the statements attributed to him that we have do not clearly sustain such a charge. Neither demonstrably anti-temple nor anti-Moses, Jesus committed the major offense of not speaking about either in the familiar way. He was a traditionalist in the radical sense of the word. Like the Samaritans, he appealed to the oldest traditions. He took his case for God's demands back to God himself. The directness of his appeal seems to have been his down-fall. He admitted no authority between Israel's Father and the human conscience. This setting aside of intermediate authority in favor of ultimate authority may have been his undoing.[5]

Quite like Sloyan's stress on the immediacy of Jesus' relation to God is the effort of an equally distinguished New Testament scholar, Stephen Neill, to indicate the center of Jesus' attractiveness or power over people:

> His power over men and over situations is derived from the steady concentration of his will on a single object, the glory of God. Here he stands in marked contrast to other men who are so constantly perplexed and weakened by the division and the distraction of the will. The stories of the temptation and of the conflict in Gethsemane are evidence that this was not an automatic reflex. Jesus was a man, and like other men he had to find his way amid the perplexities of life and the many things that could deflect him from his purpose, His will was as a compass that has to be guarded against everything that could deflect it in order that it may point unerringly to the north. Jesus stands before us in the Gospels as the one in whom this unerring dedication of the will was achieved. He left on the minds of his disciples the impression of one who lived in unbroken communion with the heavenly Father. He spoke of him with perfect assurance and never in terms of derivative knowledge. He used the Old Testament, but always with penetration and originality; when occasion demanded he had no hesitation in setting aside the Old Testament in the light of his own superior knowledge.[6]

With these at least plausible suggestions about the core of Jesus' personality, the hub of his life's meaning and power, let us conclude this section by sketching a bare outline of his likely career. The sources upon which we can draw are already faith interpretations, but this minimalist outline is probably close to the historical actuality. Jesus (whose name in Hebrew—Joshua—meant something like "Yahweh is salvation") was probably born before the year 4 B.C.E., perhaps in Bethlehem of Palestine, to a young Jewish woman named Mary.[7] His country lay under Roman rule, Herod the Edomite being the local Jewish delegate of Rome. The culture of the surrounding Mediterranean world was Greco-Roman but Jesus was mainly formed by Judaism.[8] His youth and early life are obscure, although he certainly received some Jewish religious education and he may have worked as a carpenter. About 27 C.E. he came to popular notice as a wandering preacher. His main message was that the reign of God was at hand (in his own preaching and person).

The Gospels portray Jesus' ministry as meeting with increasing opposition from the Jewish officials and religious leaders, who found his independent interpretation of the Law an attack on an order they considered God himself to have established. They also feared that Jesus' galvanized crowds of followers would upset the delicate balance they had worked out with the Roman authorities. However, Jesus seems to have continued his own way, refusing to restrict his message to only a remnant or separatist messianic community (like the Essenes, who posed little political threat). Indeed, there are signs that he made his message applicable to all people, heathen as well as Jews, women as well as men, and that he began to anticipate dying for fidelity to his vision of God's reign.

At least, Howard Clark Kee includes this likelihood in his sketch of the bare historical picture of Jesus that he thinks the New Testament sources allow:

> Jesus appeared on the Palestinian scene as an itinerant teacher, probably self-taught, so that there was deep resentment of his authoritative manner among the official religious leadership of Palestine. He held his central mission to be the announcement of the imminent coming of God's Kingdom, and he regarded his extraordinary powers of healing and exorcism as evidence that the powers of the Kingdom were already breaking into the present situation. He sought to call together a band of followers who by repentance would prepare themselves for the impending event, and he therefore offered a severe critique of Israel and new criteria for acceptance within the membership of the covenant community. He interpreted the Law in a radical way that challenged the authority of its official interpreters. The impetus for the redefinition of the people of God is likely to have come as a consequence of his associations with John the Baptist, although he parted company with John, probably on the issue of Jesus' conviction that the Kingdom was open to sinners and religious outcasts who truly repented.
>
> At the same time, Jesus refused to join with the insurrectionist movements of his time, which sought to establish God's rule by their own initiative. Ironically, it was through the false charge that he was a revolutionary that he was put to death by the Romans—a charge brought by the religious leaders whose authority his pronouncements seemed to threaten. His method of teaching was characterized as to content by eschatological pronouncement, and as to form by parable and reinterpretation of the Law and of religious institutions. It is likely that he came to realize that the path he had set out on would lead to

death, though we have no way of knowing when he came to this conclusion or whether he sought to force the issue.[9]

Jesus' activity probably was confined to Palestine, especially Galilee and Judea. He impressed many hearers by the depth of his message, his manifest familiarity with God, his identification with the poor and unfortunate, and his power to heal sickness. The opposition between him and the religious establishment may have started as a conflict in styles and values, but the Gospel writers saw it as developing into a clash between the light of God and the darkness of Satan (the summarizing symbol of all the forces that resist the light of God).

Jesus is depicted as having lived very simply in the years of his missionary activity, wandering from town to town, eating and lodging as need and opportunity dictated.[10] We may interpret his vision of the reign of God as portending an ideal yet realizable time when most sufferings would be eliminated because people would conspire as brothers and sisters to love one another, share their goods and worries, and make only the parental God their absolute. The central symbol of this ideal, messianic time that Jesus was inaugurating and announcing was a joyous meal: eating and drinking for the repair and renewal of the spirit as much as the body, in thanksgiving to God as much as in obedience to one's needs as a physical and social being.

THE TEACHING OF JESUS

David Abernathy, updating lectures of the late Norman Perrin, has used such categories as "the activity of God," "response to the activity of God," and "the new relationship" to summarize Jesus' teaching.[11] In discussing the activity of God that Jesus proclaimed was occurring in his hearers' midst, Abernathy uses such subfoci as "the kingdom of God," "the forgiveness of sins," and "the fatherliness of God." Each deserves at least a brief exposition.

As noted, on the basis of the New Testament materials, we are led to conjecture that the main category or conception Jesus himself used is the kingdom or reign of God. God was doing something, offering something, making the divine a force and presence that perhaps had been promised or seen as possible previously but only now, in Jesus' own time-area-person, had come to crisis and was about to be born. For Jesus that seems to have meant the presence of the grace, the divine favor, necessary to turn around both personal and social life. It could happen: hunger could be appeased, fear allayed, justice done, the blind made to see and the lame to walk, lepers cleansed, the poor given the good news, sinners forgiven, new starts made. And not only could it happen, it would happen, eventually achieving a blessed, "anointed" (messianic), eschatological state. In Abernathy's words:

The emphasis on the final blessed state of the kingdom of God in the teaching of Jesus is similar to the emphasis in apocalyptic literature. We can see this in the beatitudes, Matthew 5:3–12 (and the parallel in Luke 6:20–23): "Blessed are the poor in spirit for theirs is the kingdom of heaven. Blessed are those who mourn for they shall be comforted. Blessed are the meek, for they shall inherit the earth," and so on. The reference here is to that final state of the redeemed to which the activity of God as king will lead. It is a final state in which the values of this world may well be reversed and the values of God will be established. In such a situation, "the poor will become rich, the mourners will be comforted, the meek will inherit the earth"—in other words, the values of God will be established.[12]

To Jesus' mind, another central aspect of God's kingly, powerful presence apparently was the forgiveness of sins. In such unforgettable parables as the prodigal son (Luke 15:11–32), the evangelists have Jesus make concrete his faith that the kingdom meant new beginnings. People could rely on God's love and acceptance of them. If they would only turn around, reorient themselves, they would find that God had long ago come out on the road to greet them. God cared more for their selves and happiness than about their mistakes, offenses, vices. These would largely go, fall away, if they would but heal their hearts, reorient their central passions, make the kingdom and its justice their great love.

It is likely that a third aspect of Jesus' preaching of the kingdom was the depiction of God as a father, an intimate "Daddy" (*Abba*).[13] Jesus himself seems to have relied upon God's parental care, assuming that in all circumstances he could go to his source and find understanding, acceptance, healing. He could describe his food, according to John, as doing the will of the Father who sent him (John 4:34). Mark 11:25, which follows on a call to have faith and be confident when one prays, portrays the Father as ready to forgive the trespasses of all who forgive their debtors: "And whenever you stand praying, forgive, if you have anything against any one; so that your Father also who is in heaven may forgive you your trespasses." Even more explicit on the confidence believers should have when coming before their Father in prayer is Luke 11:11–13: "What father among you, if his son asks for a fish, will instead of a fish give him a serpent; or if he asks for an egg, will give him a scorpion? If you then, who are evil, know how to give good gifts to your children, how much more will the heavenly Father give the Holy Spirit to those who ask him!"

These three aspects or characterizations of Jesus' preaching about God's activity amounted to a dazzling vision of what was happening in his hearers' midst. What, then, were the responses Jesus asked or expected from his hearers? How were the people privileged to be addressed by this good news expected to show their acceptance or conversion? Several Gospel texts suggest the sort of response Jesus probably asked. Matthew 6:14, for example, which follows on the Lord's Prayer, drives home the need to forgive those who have injured one: "For if you forgive men their trespasses, your heavenly Father also will forgive you; but if you do not forgive men their trespasses, neither will your Father forgive you your trespasses."

The action of God on human beings' behalf, especially the action of forgiving sins, demands a response of brotherly and sisterly forgiveness.

In the Sermon on the Mount the Matthean Jesus teaches the same new morality, the same ethics of grace and thanksgiving, with a specific focus on one's enemies: "You have heard that it was said, 'You shall love your neighbor and hate your enemy.' But I say to you, Love your enemies and pray for those who persecute you, so that you may be sons of your Father who is in heaven, for he makes his sun to rise on the evil and the good, and sends rain on the just and on the unjust" (Matthew 5:43–45). However much Matthew has organized these materials, they ring true to the general mind of Jesus that the Gospels as a whole present. This text makes only ideal, abstract sense unless one has been seized by the energies, the love, of the kingdom. Apart from the experience of having been reoriented, turned around and opened up, loving one's enemies and praying for one's persecutors will seem impossible, perhaps even immoral. Conversion to the kingdom and embrace of the gospel, however, put matters on a new footing. God has shown himself so good, so much a loving parent, that old enmities seem irrelevant.

As a last example of the new morality, the gracious response, that Jesus probably expected we may cite the parable of the good Samaritan (Luke 10:30–37). The priest and Levite who turn away from the injured man who looks dead had some legal right to do so. To touch the dead could be defiling. In that case, they would have been unable to carry out their ceremonial obligations or services toward God. Jesus, however, refused to let service of God be the whole story. No ritualistic obligation was to block out the needs and rights of one's neighbor. Love of God and love of neighbor flowed together, if one was deeply enough rooted in the energies and ways of the kingdom.

To Jesus it probably seemed obvious, elementary, that one helps an injured person as the Samaritan does. It was nearly automatic, if one had felt the Father's helpful love. Jesus realized, no doubt, that many people, probably the majority, had not felt the Father's love in this way (in all likelihood because they had not been taught or did not want to be converted). But it seems that Jesus would not let the ignorance and hardness of heart that afflict the majority constitute normalcy, or be the bottom line from which one should draw the ethical expectations proper to the kingdom. God was the overwhelming reality in Jesus' life, and with God all things were possible.

In addition to asking for neighborly love, forgiveness of their enemies, and a generous discipleship, Jesus apparently expected that his followers would derive from their sense of God's action on their behalf a new, taut attitude toward the future. Under such figures as the return of a master from a marriage feast, the synoptics have Jesus teach that a final act in God's drama will soon and suddenly arrive. The return of the Son of Man (whose main implications we have also seen under such notions as the Day of the Lord, the parousia, and the judgment of God) was a surety disciples were to use to keep their wits sharpened, their faith at the ready:

Let your loins be girded and your lamps burning, and be like men who are waiting for their master to come home from the marriage feast, so that they may open to him at once when he comes and knocks. Blessed are those servants whom the master finds awake when he comes; truly, I say to you, he will gird himself and have them sit at table, and he will come and serve them. If he comes in the second watch, or in the third, and finds them so, blessed are those servants! But know this, that if the householder had known at what hour the thief was coming, he would not have left his house to be broken into. You also must be ready; for the Son of man is coming at an unexpected hour. [Luke 12:35–40]

We have now seen something of Jesus' teachings about the action of God and something of his views of how human beings were to react to God's initiative. The third category that Abernathy uses to outline Jesus' teaching is the "new relationship" that the arrival of the kingdom established, mainly in Jesus himself. In more usual terms, this is the question of Jesus' messianic consciousness: his awareness of his role and being as the anointed leader and spokesman for God.

There are few self-assertive statements of Jesus in the Gospels that cannot be explained as expressions not of Jesus' own historical voice but of the faith of the later Church. Nonetheless, Joachim Jeremias has argued that Jesus clearly thought of himself as more than just another prophet: "In short, he designated his preaching and his actions as the eschatological saving event. An awareness of mission of this kind can no longer be kept in the prophetic sphere. Rather, all these statements mean that Jesus believed himself to be the bringer of salvation."[14]

Among the texts that Jeremias thinks demand such an understanding of Jesus' self-understanding are the emphatic "I" sayings of the Sermon on the Mount (Matthew 5:21–48). (The Johannine "I" sayings make the same point—Jesus had a unique, even divine status—but their so obvious service of the author's theological convictions about Jesus makes them less impressive historically as suggestions of how Jesus himself thought about his work and person.) In this series of six antitheses between what "was said" and what "I say to you," Jesus assumes the authority to oppose or go beyond previous interpretations of Torah. He is breaking with the view of things laid out in the Mosaic Law, which for his contemporaries was the certain will of God. Every likelihood is that, if this voice was indeed Jesus' historical own, his claim to such authority expressed a conviction that he was the equivalent of the Messiah.[15] Jeremias notes the use of a similar "I" in the stories of Jesus' healings (e.g., Mark 9:25), in Jesus' sending out of messengers (e.g., Matthew 10:16), and in the words of encouragement Jesus offered (e.g., Luke 22:32).

It is true that the materials we have even about Jesus' messianic reticence are fitted into the theological profiles of Jesus that the evangelists are presenting. It is true that one cannot argue from such theologically shaped materials to Jesus' own historical self-awareness with anything like confidence, let alone full surety. On the other hand, to deny the entire drift of the synoptic's presentation of Jesus' self-understanding (both their oblique and their more direct reports) is to take so skeptical a view of one's sources that an outsider might well ask why one bothers to read such unreliable stuff. The evangelists would have been simple, crude tools indeed if they thought they could further their movement, advance the cause of their God, by radically distorting the religious reality of Jesus. We know that they were influenced by their faith (which, of course, had been decisively shaped by both the Easter-event and some years of church experience). However, unless we assume that their interpretations of Jesus were basically honest efforts to present his full truth, meaning, or significance, we badly besmirch their characters and give ourselves no serious reason to take their work as making claims to truth.[16]

This does not mean, of course, that we have to take everything the evangelists say at face value, especially in view of all the evidence that the Gospels are well-worked-over packagings from several collections of memories and stories. It just means that if a large portion of the materials about Jesus' preaching, healing, and interpretive voice ring with a striking authority and proclaim a novel, even audacious intimacy with God, we should be willing to draw the obvious (if still hypothetical) conclusion: Jesus probably thought that he had a special relationship with God, that the unique time of the kindom (come in his person) was the equivalent of the age of fulfillment for which many of the prophets and his recent ancestors had longed. To be sure, we must not overlook data, such as the Markan theme of the hidden Messiah, that suggest a more cautious estimate of Jesus' own self-consciousness. Still, if overall Jesus makes more sense taken as a person who thought he had a unique call, and who was emboldened to think he could definitively reset people's notions about God and the Law, we should be willing to say he probably did think God had anointed him to be the bringer of eschatological salvation. That is only common sense.

The last aspect of Jesus' teaching that will concern us is his provision for a community that would continue his work. The Pauline Epistles and other non-Gospel portions of the New Testament assume the reality of such a community. They have a great deal to say about the "calling out" (**ekklesia**) of Jesus' followers and imply that this is a new congregation (*qahal*) or people of God. The synoptic Gospels, to which we naturally go for the materials that might reflect Jesus' own speech, only use the word *ekklesia* twice (Matthew 16:18, 18:17). Matthew 16:18 follows on Peter's confession that Jesus is the Christ, the Son of the living God: "And Jesus answered him, 'Blessed are you, Simon Bar-Jona! For flesh and blood has not revealed this to you, but my Father who is in heaven. And I tell you, you are Peter, and on this rock I will build my church, and the powers of death shall not prevail against it'" (Matthew 16:17–18). Matthew 18:17 occurs in the midst of a discussion about reforming a sinner in the presence of several witnesses: "If he refuses to listen to them, tell it to the church; and if he refuses to listen even to the church, let him be to you as a Gentile and a tax collector."

Many scholars think that these two texts come from a later editing of

Matthean materials and reflect Christian community problems more than Jesus' own sayings. On the other hand, scholars such as Xavier Leon-Dufour and John L. McKenzie see nothing unlikely in Jesus' having proposed a gathering of followers that would be the true Israel of God.[17] Clearly Jesus called disciples and asked them to consider their relationship to him and one another their new primal community. Indeed, the Gospels are replete with Jesus' warnings that discipleship would be costly, a cause of family divisions and alienation from society at large (see Mark 1:16 ff., 8:34 ff., Matthew 4:18 ff., 10:34 ff., Luke 5:1 ff., 12:51 ff.).

Against such a background Matthew 16:18 may be read as a memory of Jesus' provision for a group he had established for ongoing work and fellowship. The second Matthean text (Matthew 18:17) shows relatively little distinction between Jesus' followers and members of a Jewish synagogue confronted with a recalcitrant member. This would argue, however, not that Jesus did not expect his group to continue but that he had not greatly differentiated it from a local Jewish assembly.

A final matter is Jesus' attitude toward the Gentiles, shown in Matthew 10:5–6 and Mark 7:24–28 (and obliquely shown to be problematic in Matthew 18:17 as previously quoted). In the context of explaining Jesus' sense of solidarity with needy humanity, Albert Nolan recently has explained the place Jesus made for the Gentiles in the Kingdom of God:

> The ambivalence of Jesus' attitude to Gentiles was one of those insoluble problems about which the scholars had endless arguments until Joachim Jeremias published his brilliant little book *Jesus' Promise to the Nations*. He has established the fact that the Jewish hope for the future did not exclude the Gentiles. In the end, after all the appropriate punishments had been meted out, the whole world including the Gentiles would come under the powerful rule of the true God.[18]

Jesus did not conclude from this expectation, as some of his contemporaries did, that one ought to missionize the Gentiles. However, when he met with faith from Gentiles (see, for instance, Matthew 8:10, 15:28), or when he consorted with Jewish "sinners" (whom the pious regarded, in effect, as Gentiles), he was willing to work the cures or show the forgiveness asked of him. Thus he opened the door to the reflections of Peter and Paul that led the young Church to admit interested Gentiles.

THE PAULINE VIEW OF JESUS

The synoptic Gospels present a Jesus who moved through space and time much as an ordinary human being does. However much they shape Jesus' words and actions because of their faith in his resurrection and messiahship, the evangelists are concerned to present a teacher and exemplar who excited a specific generation of actual people by contacts quite natural in their human forms (if quite extraordinary in their contents and effects). The authors of the Pauline corpus pay virtually no attention to this historical Jesus. Their interest is wholly with the Christ, the messianic figure alive years after the death of the historical Jesus.

For example, it is the Christ-event, pivoting on the death and resurrection of Jesus, that absorbs Paul and shapes his Gospel. He believes that this event has reset all human relationships. In summarizing what Paul knew about Jesus' crucifixion and resurrection, Leander Keck has made the following points.[19] First, Paul gives no details of the crucifixion and shows little interest in the human agents (e.g., Pilate and Caiaphas) who brought it about. Second, his references to the resurrection are only slightly less vague. In 1 Corinthians 15:8 he includes himself among those to whom the resurrected Lord appeared. It is Acts 9, however, not Paul's own writings, that presents the dramatic meeting with the resurrected one who took Paul's persecution of the church personally, as an injury done to himself.

Third, Paul shows little detailed knowledge of Jesus' life before the Passion. For instance, his own letters never mention the virgin birth, Jesus' baptism by John, or any deeds of Jesus' ministry. Fourth, Paul tells us next to nothing about Jesus' teaching. For instance, he does not mention Jesus' parables or Jesus' preaching of the kingdom. Keck therefore concludes, from these and other aspects of Paul's minimal treatment of the historical Jesus, that Paul's great interest was what God did through the summarizing event of Jesus' death and resurrection. What Jesus had said or done in God's name mattered far less than what God had accomplished in the unprecedented, and to Paul's mind indisputably decisive, event of the Passion and rising.

The frame of this decisive event, as Paul came in his mature theology to conceive it, was a preexistence and a postexistence. Insofar as the historical Jesus was the subject of the death-resurrection that was the axis of a new era of salvation, the historical Jesus was framed by the preexistent Son of God and the postexistent risen Lord. Just as for Paul's Jewish contemporaries the Torah, though given through Moses, preexisted Moses because it had always been (was eternally) with God, so for Paul Jesus before his earthly career was with God as the divine Son. Paul understood this preexistence largely in terms of what Hellenized Jewish theology had been saying for two centuries about the Sophia or wisdom of God. In Keck's view, the early Christian incarnationalists, including Paul, did not hold that Jesus preexisted. They rather held that what preexisted was God's Son. God's Son then became Jesus.

Of the three phases of Christ's career (as an incarnational Christology leads one to schematize it: preexistence, existence, postexistence), Paul was most interested in the third. Certainly he deals with the preexistence and Incarnation of the Son on more than a few occasions (e.g., 1 Corinthians 10:1–5, Philippians 2:6–11). Certainly such passages imply an interesting and important view of how God's Son became Jesus and what that becoming suggests for the form of Christian existence. For example, Paul's use of the hymn quoted in Philippians 2 strongly implies his agreement with its theme of humiliation. 2 Corinthians 8:9 runs to a similar conclusion. But the most decisive interest in Paul' theology is the present (resurrected and so post-earthly-existence) activity of the Christ.

A first group of texts expressing this Pauline interest barely distinguishes the work of the risen Christ from the work of the Spirit. For example, Romans 8:26 has the Spirit helping Christians in their weakness, but only eight verses later it is Christ Jesus who is the prime intercessor on their behalf: "Who is to condemn? Is it Christ Jesus who died, yes, who was raised from the dead, who is at the right hand of God, who indeed intercedes for us?" In 2 Corinthians 3:17 Paul can even say, "Now the Lord is the Spirit, and where the Spirit of the Lord is, there is freedom." Theologians who try to tidy up Paul's thought usually say that he means that Christ is present through the Spirit, that Christ makes an impact in the religious or charismatic experience often attributed to the Spirit. Paul himself does not pause to distinguish their roles, however. The primacy in his thought belongs to the resurrecting power of God. Both the risen Lord and the Spirit can express or communicate this force field.

A second group of Pauline texts suggests that Paul found Christ's present status only provisional. Things would change at the parousia or when the saving action of God had achieved its full effect. Thus in 1 Corinthians 15, after making a comparison between Christ and Adam, Paul speculates on the stages of Christ's communication of life:

> For as in Adam all die, so also in Christ shall all be made alive. But each in his own order: Christ the first fruits, then at his coming those who belong to Christ. Then comes the end, when he delivers the kingdom to God the Father after destroying every rule and every authority and power. For he must reign until he has put all his enemies under his feet. The last enemy to be destroyed is death. "For God has put all things in subjection under his feet." [Psalms 8:6] But when it says, "All things are put in subjection under him," it is plain that he is excepted who put all things under him. When all things are subjected to him, then the Son himself will also be subjected to him who put all things under him, that God may be everything to everyone. [1 Corinthians 15:22–28]

The present status of Christ therefore will change at the parousia. Then God will be all in all in a way that will render Christ's present mediatorship unnecessary.

However, Paul's reflections on the coming of Christ see in that consummating event more than the final subjugation of Christ's enemies. It will also be judgment upon the world (Romans 2:16, 2 Corinthians 5:10), and the arrival of the Savior from heaven (Philippians 3:20). Insofar as his imagination stretched forward to the parousia expectantly, Paul was preoccupied with the posthistorical Christ, indeed with the Christ who would usher in the end of history. Insofar as he focused on the current spiritual center of his own life and the life of the churches, Paul also looked not to the historical or preexistent Son but to the resurrected Lord. Since these two interests—the parousia and the current power center—dominated his Christology, the other two phases of Christ's three-phase career fell into relative neglect. Paul did not deny them but the dominant concern of his Christology was the Lord who had swung into action after Jesus' death.

Summarizing his discussion of Paul's doctrine of justification, Edward Schillebeeckx links it with the apostolic faith (Acts 4:12) that salvation lies in no other person or power than Jesus Christ:

> From all that Paul says about justification (Galatians and Romans, with a short, sharp summary in II Cor. 5:18–21 and Phil. 3:8 f.), it becomes clear what he means on the one hand by faith and on the other by works of the Law. Faith is putting oneself under the guidance of Jesus Christ in grace; the works of the Law mean accepting the rule of the Torah, which Paul has shown to stand under the rule of the "law of sin." Throughout the argument Torah, Law, has almost imperceptibly become the law of sin, so that the works of the Law also belong within the historical sphere of the rule of **hamartia** [sin]. Paul's argument must sound strange to a non-Christian Jew, but Paul is writing for Jewish *Christians* who in fact experience decisive salvation in Jesus from God.
>
> First of all, he had said that God's righteousness gives a reward according to works (works of the Law) ([Romans] 2:6–10), and thus creates the right-eousness that the Law accomplishes; in the later chapters [of Romans] (pre-pared for by Paul's insertion in the quotation from the Psalms in Rom 3.20) it is said that to be **saddiq** [righteous] in accordance with the sense of the Law is in no way a manifestation of the righteousness of God (see the announcement of the theme in 1.17 and the proclamation of this event in Christ Jesus 3:21–23). This manifestation has been revealed "outside the Law" (3:21a), in fact in accordance with the basic intention of the Tanach [Law-Prophets-Writings] itself (3.21b). It is clear that Paul contrasts the Law as a principle of salvation or way of salvation with Christ as a way of salvation, and in the light of his belief in salvation in Christ denies the Law as a principle of salvation (what-ever the value of the Law may have been). It is a question of the apostolic faith: "Salvation lies in no other" (Acts 4:12): no more, but also no less.[20]

On this reading, the central Pauline doctrine of justification derives from the experience Paul and the rest of the apostolic Church had of Jesus' gracious activity. Because they felt they had found God's favor in Christ, they reasoned that by contrast no other source of salvation or justification before God was effective. In the specific case of Jewish Christians, the power of the grace of Jesus Christ meant viewing the Law's previous func-tion as now superceded. Indeed, if one were to make a black and white contrast between the zone of sin and the zone of grace, the Law and its works would fall in the zone of sin, because only the experience of the risen Christ had given Paul's Jewish Christians the righteousness they had been seeking. Pauline Christology, in this light, is an exegesis of the experience of grace. The favor or making-right that came in the Spirit of Christ led Paul to reassemble all the theological elements—works, the Law, sin, God's action, and the rest—into a new constellation. In Christ (joined to him by faith) one could find justification. Apart from Christ one would not experi-ence intimate acceptance by God.

THE HERMENEUTICAL CIRCLE

Schillebeeckx comes to his interpretation of Paul's theory of justification and Paul's Christology only after a full study of the Gospel materials. In the Gospels he finds a remarkable **hermeneutical** (interpretational) circle:

> Jesus' living and dying on earth suggested to Christians, in virtue of their experiences after Jesus' death, the idea of the resurrection or of the coming Parousia of Jesus, while on the basis of their faith in the risen or coming crucified One they relate the story of Jesus in the gospels; in other words, these gospel stories of Jesus are themselves a hermeneusis [interpretation] of Jesus' Parousia and resurrection, while belief in the Parousia or in the resurrection was engendered by things remembered of the historical Jesus. The "matter to be interpreted"—Jesus of Nazareth—came eventually to be interpreted in and through the faith-inspired affirmation of his resurrection (Parousia), while that resurrection or Parousia is in its turn the "object of interpretation" which is then interpreted through the gospel narratives as remembrances of Jesus' earthly life, as also in the light of his resurrection or coming Parousia.[21]

One sees the sophistication that Schillebeeckx demands. The Gospels are inseparably a blend of what Jesus inspired his followers to hope and dream during his earthly life and what the experience of Jesus' resurrection led his followers to make of his preresurrectional person, teaching, and actions. When they looked back at Jesus' life, after the resurrection, the authors who composed the materials that constitute the Gospels found a fittingness, a preparedness, in their memories of Jesus' sayings, attitudes, and works. It fitted that he should have been resurrected (bracketing for the moment what that experience was for either Jesus himself or the apostles who encountered the resurrected one). By the same token, after the Passion, death, and resurrection the events of Jesus' earthly life took on a new significance. From the viewpoint of the "goal" of the resurrection and coming of the pneumatic Lord into the community's midst, Jesus' consorting with the poor and outcast, healing of the sick, controlling the forces of nature, disputing with the Pharisees, and the like gained a sharper relief. Indeed, in some cases the historical doings may have been radically rethought, re-remembered, reconstituted by the resurrectional experience of faith.

That leads to the difficult question of whether certain events in Jesus' life (as the evangelists narrate it) were not in fact "created" by the community's resurrectional or post-Easter faith. Some of the miracles, for example, or the accounts of Jesus' transfiguration (see Mark 9:2–13, Matthew 17:1–8, Luke 9:28–36) may derive more from what the authors retrojected (from the resurrection) than from what actually happened in ordinary historical terms. In most cases we simply cannot say with certitude. Schillebeeckx's hermeneutical circle does us the favor of reminding us that in all of the Gospel materials "before" and "after," history (in the sense of unadorned memory) and resurrectional faith are tied together inseparably.

If we accept this situation as the simple fact of the matter regarding the New Testament portrait of Jesus, what should it do to our expectations? Nils A. Dahl has suggested that it should shift our focus to the disciples' memory of Jesus:

> . . . what is to be sought in the gospels is first of all the disciples' memory of Jesus, not the life of Jesus. The question whether or not it is possible on these foundations to reconstruct an image of the "historical Jesus," is beyond the scope of this essay. But any answer would have to realize that we are incapable of producing a biographical account of his life. Today only outsiders and novelists dare to undertake such an enterprise. We can, however, construct for ourselves an idea of his message and teaching and of the impression that he produced both on his disciples and on his adversaries. We cannot retreat from a minute examination of the sayings and stories as they are variously preserved. But it will never be possible to draw a sharp line of demarcation between pious imagination and historical tradition. We have the latter only in the framework of the former. If the recollections of Jesus have been preserved for us, it is because he was preached as crucified Messiah and resurrected Lord. What **mnemosyne** [memory] would have been able to tell about Jesus of Nazareth would have been very little indeed if Jesus had not been commemorated by those whose faith was in the Risen Lord and who broke the bread *eis anamnesin Christou* [in memory of Christ].[22]

The evangelists' interpretation of Jesus' overall work, including his death and resurrection, therefore blend their memories of his earthly activity and their faith in his risen lordship. For example, the evangelists present Jesus' suffering and death as foreseen by Jesus himself, accepted as God's will for him, interpreted as necessary for the coming of the kingdom, and understood as mediatory for salvation. This is suggested, for instance, in the evangelists' use of Isaiah's suffering servant texts to depict Jesus' progress toward his death.

Mark 10:45, for example, has Jesus say: "For the Son of man also came not to be served but to serve, and to give his life as a ransom for many." The theme of service runs on several levels. Jesus would overturn the idea of a hierarchically organized community, in which the great would lord it over the small. Mark would make Jesus' ministry and death a laying down of life for the sake of expiating others' sins. Thus the "ransom" referred to is quite inclusive. Jesus is paying the price that outcasts and marginal people (sinners, women, children) must pay to become full members of the community. He is paying the price that humanity's sins have incurred, the price of a new beginning, a time when God would fully reign. The best explanation for this rich, complicated set of allusions is the evangelists' mixture of historical memories and perspectives of faith. Their steady oscillation between the earthly Jesus and the risen Lord almost always makes the Gospels both-and.

All of the Gospels therefore exhibit a Christology that is both shaped by historical memories of Jesus of Nazareth and cast in the furnace of a decisive faith in the risen Lord. Nonetheless, each of the four Gospels has its own special tone or set of emphases. Mark, for example, makes the suffering of Jesus central. By his pain, death, obedience, and the rest Jesus expiated human beings' sins, showing himself to be a Messiah quite contrary to popular expectation but far more radically efficacious. Thus at the center of Mark's Gospel we find three predictions of the Passion and resurrection (Mark 8:31–33, 9:31–32, 10:32–34). Like a drumbeat, they establish the core rhythm of Mark's work. And, not accidentally, the regular response of the disciples to this rhythm is misunderstanding or even opposition. They do not want the sort of Messiah that Jesus discovered he had to be.

So, for example, in chapter 8 Peter, the head of the twelve, remonstrates with Jesus and has to be harshly rebuked: "And he began to teach them that the Son of man must suffer many things, and be rejected by the elders and the chief priests and the scribes, and be killed, and after three days rise again. And he said this plainly. And Peter took him, and began to rebuke him. But turning and seeing his disciples, he rebuked Peter, and said, 'Get behind me, Satan! For you are not on the side of God, but of men'" (Mark 8:31–33). For Mark Jesus must always be remembered as the Lord who won his high status most painfully, showing his love by suffering the assaults of a hatefully opposed world. Discipleship therefore is misguided when it is not costly, when it is not a challenge to the world almost certain to provoke something of the diabolic enmity that forced Jesus to the cross.

The picture of Jesus we find in Matthew is built on Mark (and Q) but has its own distinctive features. For Matthew Jesus is the new great teacher, the successor of Moses, the authoritative interpreter of God's will. The historical life and postresurrectional Lordship of Matthew's Jesus fulfill the prophesies of the Old Testament about the Messiah. They found a new people of God, based on Jesus' perfect elucidation and fulfillment of God's will. The Matthean risen Lord makes a claim on all, inviting all to discipleship and membership in the new people of God. The miracles he works bring true disciples to confess that he is the very Son of God. Thus after Jesus and Peter have walked on the water, Matthew concludes: "And when they got into the boat, the wind ceased. And those in the boat worshipped him, saying, 'Truly you are the Son of God'" (Matthew 14:32–33).

For Luke Jesus the Christ is the merciful Savior of sinners and the poor. He moves through the events of his historical life with a special grace and sensitivity. His parables are marvels of insight and kindliness. The outreach of his teaching and concern is to all humankind. The Man of Peace who taught and healed openly is ironically, tragically crucified as a revolutionary. Yet Luke, too, makes it plain that Jesus walked his way with a peculiar sovereignty. Jesus sets his face for Jerusalem because he knows that Jerusalem, the city of God (as the city of the spurned prophets), is where he is destined for his final confrontation with Satan and fulfillment of God's will. The **dei** or necessity that plays such an important role in Luke's Gospel is the finger of God leading the Savior to lordship. When the two on the road to Emmaus have the Scriptures opened and see the necessity of Jesus' Passion, the entire Lukan church reconstructs the meaning of their memories of Jesus.

Last, the Gospel of John most dramatically frames its narrative of Jesus' life in terms of its celebration of Jesus' lordship. The signs Jesus strews in the first portion of the Gospel rise from the sacramental life of the Johannine community. The overture of the Prologue makes it unmistakable that from the moment the Word took flesh salvation had come into the world, with revelation flashing forth from every word and gesture of God's man. The divine "I am" that Jesus repeatedly proclaims is a none too subtle reference to the divine voice in Exodus 3:14. The combination of this "I am" with a promise of definitive revelation on the cross show the Johannine Christology to center in the decisive manifestation of God's love that Jesus' vulnerable flesh accomplished.

For John Jesus is the one who has come from above to reveal to human beings below the Father who can save them from their sins:

> He said to them, "You are from below, I am from above; you are of this world, I am not of this world. I told you that you would die in your sins, for you will die in your sins unless you believe that I am he." They said to him, "Who are you?" Jesus said to them, "Even what I have told you from the beginning. I have much to say about you, and much to judge; but he who sent me is true, and I declare to the world that I have heard from him." They did not understand that he spoke to them of the Father. So Jesus said, "When you have lifted up the Son of man, then you will know that I am he, and that I do nothing on my own authority but speak thus as the Father taught me." [John 8:23–28]

OTHER NEW TESTAMENT CHRISTOLOGIES

We have skimmed the surface of the Pauline and evangelical Christologies.[23] Paul is most interested in the presently living Lord who is with the Church as a vital spiritual force and will soon usher in the parousia. The evangelists, with a notable variety, are fascinated by the Jesus of history that the resurrection reveals. For them the whole career of Jesus is recast, relighted, reinterpreted by the events of the passover from Calvary to the ascension and sending of the Spirit.

In Acts we find hints of the earliest interpretations of Jesus' fate, as well as a full elaboration of the growth of the Church in fidelity to the universalizing thrust of Jesus' lordship. Peter's speech in Acts 2:22–24 suggests the first Christian kerygma or preaching about Jesus' life and death. From the beginning the Christians had to explain to the Jews how the Messiah could die accursed on the cross. Their basic tactic was to make Jesus' fate a matter of divine foresight, something predicted in the Scriptures and brought to glorious consummation in the resurrection God had worked. The resurrection not only empowered the disciples to believe Jesus was alive and so to preach him to the world. It also stood as God's ratification of Jesus' preaching and work, as the final drama that showed what all the prior plays had been about:

> Men of Israel, hear these words: Jesus of Nazareth, a man attested to you by God with mighty works and wonders and signs which God did through him in

your midst, as you yourselves know—this Jesus, delivered up according to the definite plan and foreknowledge of God, you crucified and killed by the hands of lawless men. But God raised him up, having loosed the pangs of death, because it was not possible for him to be held by it. [Acts 2:22–24]

Jesus is remembered as powerful during his earthly life. The speech can assume that Peter's hearers know the tradition that Jesus was a mighty prophet, healer, and teacher. The problem is the end to which Jesus came: crucifixion on a tree, which according to Scripture made him accursed. The depth of Jesus' revolution of Jewish faith shows in what God made of this accursed fate. All along God was guiding him, drawing good out of the evil that lawless men inflicted upon him. God in fact loosed the pangs of death, an unheard of miracle, because it could not be that one so joined to God, so full of God's Word and Spirit, should die. God is living, and Jesus was, is, so joined to God that Jesus now lives after, through, beyond death. "Let all the house of Israel therefore know assuredly that God has made him both Lord and Christ, this Jesus whom you crucified" (Acts 2:36). Having such an exalted status, such a victory from God, it is no wonder that Jesus is unique, that "there is salvation in no one else, for there is no other name given among men by which we must be saved" (Acts 4:12).

In the Pastorals, Jesus has a divine status colored by titles current in the Hellenistic mystery religions. Although the Pastorals were written considerably later than the Pauline Epistles, they share with them a relative neglect of the historical Jesus in favor of the risen Lord. They especially speak of Jesus as Savior. Thus Titus first speaks of "God our Savior" and then of "Jesus Christ our Savior" who gives justification and eternal life: "But when the goodness and loving kindness of God our Savior appeared, he saved us, not because of deeds done by us in righteousness, but in virtue of his own mercy, by the washing of regeneration and renewal in the Holy Spirit, which he poured out upon us richly through Jesus Christ our Savior, so that we might be justified by his grace and become heirs in hope of eternal life" (Titus 3:5–7).

2 Timothy 1:8–10 uses similar language, suggesting that reflection on the mystery religions led the early Christian Pastoral apologists to stress the salvation that had come through Jesus, the abolition of death and the gift of immortality: "[We] share in suffering for the gospel in the power of God, who saved us and called us with a holy calling, not in virtue of our works but in virtue of his own purpose and the grace which he gave us in Christ Jesus ages ago, and now has manifested through the appearing of our savior Christ Jesus, who abolished death and brought life and immortality to light through the gospel." Jesus brought a gospel of the kingdom, but that is not 2 Timothy's main interest. The gospel this author blesses is the good news of Jesus' death and resurrection that accomplished believers' immortalization.

The Petrine epistles stress the suffering of the Christ, how he was sacrificed as an innocent victim and so became the shepherd and guardian of Christians' souls. Thus 1 Peter 1:18–19 emphasizes the price of Christians' ransom. Nothing less than the blood of Christ was paid to set them free: "You know that you were ransomed from the futile ways inherited from your fathers, not with perishable things such as silver and gold, but with the precious blood of Christ, like that of a lamb without blemish or spot." Therefore the Christ whom 1 Peter lauds is the anointed suffering servant. Discipleship in his train is logically bound to mean the patient acceptance of whatever hardships God allows or hostile forces impose.

1 Peter 2:21–25 leaves no doubt about this pattern:

> . . . Christ also suffered for you, leaving you an example, that you should follow in his steps. He committed no sin; no guile was found on his lips. When he was reviled, he did not revile in return; when he suffered, he did not threaten; but he trusted to him who judges justly. He himself bore our sins in his body on the tree, that we might die to sin and live to righteousness. By his wounds you have been healed. For you were straying like sheep, but have now returned to the Shepherd and Guardian of your souls.

For Hebrews, as our earlier study made clear, Jesus is the great high priest, superior to all other mediators because he is the divine Son. Despite this high status, Jesus took flesh so as to identify himself with those he would serve as priest. Hebrews has a touch of the kenotic or "emptying" theology of Philippians 2:5–11. Like the thought of Philippians, too, is Hebrews' notion that Jesus' abasement into suffering won him more glory from God. In the thought-world of Hebrews, however, this all has a sacrificial aura lacking in Philippians. Jesus was human and exalted to perfect the worship of God anticipated in the old covenant but impossible of realization there. Only Jesus' death and resurrection made possible a full sanctification:

> But we see Jesus, who for a little while was made lower than the angels, crowned with glory and honor because of the suffering of death, so that by the grace of God he might taste death for everyone. For it was fitting that he, for whom and by whom all things exist, in bringing many sons to glory, should make the pioneer of their salvation perfect through suffering. For he who sanctifies and those who are sanctified have all one origin. That is why he is not ashamed to call them brethren." [Hebrews 2:9–11]

Last, the Christology of Revelation fills out the early Christian views of Jesus' twofoldness (Son of Man and Son of God) by enlisting a barrage of titles and images from the Old Testament. From the outset, for example, Revelation describes Jesus as both the executor of an important earthly mission ("the faithful witness," the one who proclaimed the kingdom unto death) and the regal resurrected Lord: " . . . the faithful witness, the firstborn of the dead, and the ruler of kings on earth" (Revelation 1:5). It is this Jesus Christ, the martyr and Lord, who "loves us and has freed us from our sins by his blood and made us a kingdom, priests to his God and Father" (Revelation 1:5–6).

Revelation is impressed by the hostility that Christian faith faces, and so the author rounds out a full panoply of titles for Christ in the letters to the seven churches. Title by title, they fashion a rich mosaic of memory:

what Jesus the Christ has done for the churches, how he has fulfilled the longings of Jewish Scripture, by what rights he may threaten the churches with harsh judgment if they fall from faith, by what rights he may promise wonderful rewards for endurance. So, for instance, the letter to the church at Ephesus (Revelation 2:1–7) packs into a small space such evocative imagery as a lordship over the seven stars and seven golden lampstands, a knowledge of the Ephesians' victories and losses of faith, a threat to remove their lampstand, and a promise that they will eat of the tree of life in paradise if they but conquer.

The other views of Christ that Revelation lays before us are no less provocative. He is the Son of Man and Ancient of Days envisioned by Daniel, blazing with light, his voice rumbling like the sound of many waters (Revelation 1:12–20). He is the Word of God, both a two-edged sword and a warrior riding out to conquer Satan and God's foes. Above all he is the Lamb of God, the spotless victim by whose sacrifice heaven has filled with the 144,000, in whose name and to whose praise the celestial liturgy ascends. From Revelation we get our best sense of the worship the Christ enables. It is a pure praise of God for the goodness, mercy, and power that have engineered salvation and worked evil's defeat. Perhaps the most fitting way to conclude our sketch of the New Testament's views of Jesus the Christ would be to recall several of the apocalyptic expressions of this worship.

For instance, the Lamb himself is an object of worship: "Then I looked, and I heard around the throne and the living creatures and the elders the voice of many angels, numbering myriads of myriads and thousands of thousands, saying with a loud voice, 'Worthy is the Lamb who was slain, to receive power and wealth and wisdom and might and honor and glory and blessing'" (Revelation 5:11–12). When the Lamb comes to marry the Bride (humanity or the Church), the song shifts to praise of God (the Father): "'Hallelujah! For the Lord our God the Almighty reigns. Let us rejoice and exult and give him the glory, for the marriage of the Lamb has come, and his Bride has made herself ready; it was granted her to be clothed with fine linen, bright and pure'" (Revelation 19:6–8).

Finally, near the last verses of the present New Testament, Revelation enlists the Spirit and the Bride in an earnest petition that the Lord return to consummate the marriage and victory: "The Spirit and the Bride say, 'Come.' And let him who hears say, 'Come'" (Revelation 22:17). For Revelation Jesus the historical witness has become Christ the glorious heavenly power who will soon come and wipe every tear from our eyes.

SUMMARY

We began our retrospective view of Jesus by taking up the question of his life. Once there were many "lives" of Jesus written. Since the rise of critical biblical scholarship such a biographical project has become dubious: The sources simply don't permit us to unfold the chronology or life development of Jesus of Nazareth. All of the New Testament writings are faith-filled, kerygmatic documents written in the light of Jesus' Passion and resurrection. All as well reflect the interests and needs of the particular Christian communities from which they arose. As a result, for the past generation New Testament scholars have thrown cold water on the project of writing a life of Jesus.

The best approximations to what the average reader understandably wants from such a life probably are popular works by reputable Scripture scholars who have the humanity and imagination to bring something of Jesus' times and probable personality alive. For example, Gerard Sloyan and Stephen Neill, agreeing on Jesus' singular intimacy with his God, have organized much of the data of the New Testament so that his values and behavior become quite intelligible.

The bare outline of Jesus' career that the sources allow takes him from birth (in Bethlehem?) between 6 and 4 B.C.E. (by today's corrected calendars) to death under Pilate, sometime between 28 and 30 C.E. They stress Jesus' Jewish upbringing and thought-world, his dominant notion that the reign of God had arrived, his career as an itinerant preacher and wonder worker, his call for radical trust in God and love of neighbor, his death on a cross as a supposed rabble-rouser, and his appearance after death to his disciples in somewhat strange guise as one "resurrected."

Shifting to Jesus' preaching, about which the New Testament documents give us more satisfactory information, we began with David Abernathy's general scheme of the activity of God, the response of human beings, and the new relationship (or messianic consciousness). On these three pegs we tried to hang a coherent account of Jesus' probable preaching and teaching.

Jesus' own sense of his mission is difficult to determine but scholars such as Joachim Jeremias credit him with considerable awareness of having a special status as the bringer of salvation. From the claims that Jesus made (e.g., to forgive sins), the way he spoke authoritatively in his own name, and the intimacy with God that he claimed, they deduce a sense of anointing for a definitive task, a work of mediating a brand-new relationship with the Father. If this hypothesis about Jesus' own self-consciousness makes sense of the materials we have about him, especially the materials of the synoptic Gospels, we should not back away from it. Other issues, such as Jesus' intention to found a community or make provision for the Gentiles, may be illuminated by the core notion that Jesus thought his mission from God was to usher in the definitive era of salvation.

The most striking aspect of Paul's letters, when we probe their Christology or understanding of Jesus' mission and being, is their disinterest in the historical Jesus. It is the risen Lord and future bringer of the parousia who dominates Paul's horizon. It is Jesus' passover from death to resurrection that Paul believes has reset humanity's relationship with God and begun a new creation. To be sure, Paul accepts the preexistence of the divine Son and assumes the historical existence of Jesus of Nazareth. Still, the Lord who is a living Spirit, operative in the Christian communities, is Paul's major passion. Thus he can summarize his own life as an identification with this Christ, and he can work out his central doctrine of justification by contrasting the experiential grace of Christ with the (relative) failure of Torah to free people from sin and guilt.

The evangelists present perhaps their richest fusion of memories of the historical Jesus, and reinterpretations of his life, from the viewpoint of the resurrection. Thus Edward Schillebeeckx has spoken of a hermeneutical circle in which memories and faith inextricably shape one another. Nils Dahl has spoken similarly. The individual evangelists color this general hermeneutical circle in their own peculiar ways, due to their special sources or community needs. Thus Mark stresses Jesus' Passion, Matthew makes Jesus the ultimate interpreter of God's will, Luke portrays a redeemer of the poor (**anawim**) and an innocent martyr, throughout led by God, and John is dazzled by the appearance of divinity in human flesh. All four conjoin the historical Jesus and the Christ of faith. In none can one confidently separate memory and theological construction.

The other writers of the New Testament tend to stress the Christ of faith. Acts has close links to the historical Jesus and the earliest Christian kerygma, but the Pastorals, 1 Peter, Hebrews, and Revelation all stress the salvation Jesus worked by his suffering and sacrifice, the lordship and coming rescue Jesus is actively accomplishing as the resurrected one and heavenly Lamb.

STUDY QUESTIONS

1. Why is the project of writing a life of Jesus dubious?
2. What does it mean to call the New Testament materials "kerygmatic"?
3. What was the probable mystical center of Jesus' life?
4. Sketch a basic outline of Jesus' historical life.
5. How did Jesus teach that God was newly active in people's lives?
6. Why did the kingdom entail the forgiveness of sins?
7. How could Jesus ask people to love their enemies?
8. Did Jesus found a church?
9. How did Paul understand the preexistence of Jesus the Christ?
10. What is the hermeneutic circle structuring the evangelists' presentation of Jesus Christ?
11. How does Peter explain the Christ in Acts 2:22–24?
12. What role does worship play in the Christology of Revelation?

NOTES

1. See Nils A. Dahl, *The Crucified Messiah* (Minneapolis: Augsburg, 1974), pp. 48–49; Daniel L. Pals, *The Victorian "Lives" of Jesus* (San Antonio: Trinity University Press, 1982).
2. F. C. Grant, "Jesus Christ," *The Interpreter's Dictionary of the Bible* (Nashville: Abingdon, 1962), vol. 2, p. 876.

3. Ingrid Maisch and Anton Vögtle, "Jesus Christ," *Sacramentum Mundi* (New York: Herder and Herder, 1969), vol. 3, p. 174.

4. See T. Callan, "Psalm 110:1 and the Origin of the Expectation that Jesus Will Come Again," *Catholic Biblical Quarterly* 44 (1982), 622–36.

5. Gerard S. Sloyan, *Jesus in Focus: A Life in Its Setting* (Mystic, Conn.: Twenty-Third Publications, 1983), pp. 44–45.

6. Stephen Neill, *Jesus Through Many Eyes* (Philadelphia: Fortress 1976), pp. 176–77.

7. See Raymond E. Brown, *The Birth of the Messiah* (Garden City, N.Y.: Doubleday, 1977), pp. 513–16.

8. See Eric M. Meyers and James F. Strange, *Archeology, the Rabbis, and Early Christianity* (Nashville: Abingdon, 1981).

9. Howard C. Kee, *Jesus in History*, 2nd ed. (New York: Harcourt Brace Jovanovich, 1977), pp. 298–99.

10. See Gerd Theissen, *Sociology of Early Palestinian Christianity* (Philadelphia: Fortress, 1977), pp. 7–23.

11. David Abernathy, *Understanding the Teaching of Jesus* (New York: Seabury, 1983).

12. Ibid., pp. 150–51.

13. See Joachim Jeremias, *New Testament Theology: The Proclamation of Jesus* (New York: Charles Scribner's Sons, 1971), pp. 61–68.

14. Ibid., p. 250.

15. See W. D. Davies, *The Setting of the Sermon on the Mount* (Cambridge: University Press, 1963), pp. 109–90.

16. See Nils A. Dahl, *Jesus in the Memory of the Early Church* (Minneapolis: Augsburg, 1976), pp. 11–29.

17. See Xavier Leon-Dufour, *Dictionary of the New Testament* (San Francisco: Harper & Row, 1980), p. 135; John L. McKenzie, *Dictionary of the Bible* (Milwaukee: Bruce, 1965), p. 134.

18. Albert Nolan, *Jesus Before Christianity* (Maryknoll, N.Y.: Orbis, 1976), pp. 65–66.

19. Leander E. Keck, *Paul and His Letters* (Philadelphia: Fortress, 1979), pp. 37–48.

20. Edward Schillebeeckx, *Christ: The Experience of Jesus as Lord* (New York: Seabury, 1980), p. 158.

21. Edward Schillebeeckx, *Jesus: An Experiment in Christology* (New York: Seabury, 1979), p. 401.

22. Dahl, *Jesus in the Memory of the Early Church*, pp. 28–29.

23. See Anton Vögtle, "Jesus Christ," *Encyclopedia of Biblical Theology*, ed. J. B. Bauer (New York: Crossroad, 1981), pp. 419–36.

13

Conclusion

In this last chapter we step back to consider the whole of the New Testament. To some extent we did that in the previous chapter, focusing on the Jesus of history and the Christ of faith. Since Jesus is the dominant personage in the New Testament, to whom all the documents refer in some decisive way, studying him meant in part studying the likenesses and differences in the different documents. Nonetheless, it is also important to compare the documents from other viewpoints, so that their historical origins and literary character more fully come into play. In this chapter, then, we shall first consider the diverse backgrounds from which the New Testament writings come and the diverse intents they pursue. Following this we shall inquire into their unity, the ways in which they agree, complement one another, and combine to make a harmonious statement. Last, to summarize what we have seen in our tour of the New Testament, we shall attempt a condensation of the New Testament story, suggesting the basic narrative and layout of belief that the collection as a whole presents.

THE DIVERSITY
OF THE NEW TESTAMENT MATERIALS

In his helpful work, *Unity and Diversity in the New Testament*, James D. G. Dunn discusses four major streams that flowed into earliest Christianity: Jewish Christianity, Hellenistic Christianity, apocalyptic Christianity, and early Catholicism.[1] We have mentioned each of these streams but it will be useful here, in dealing with the diversity of the New Testament materials, to focus on them more precisely.

Jewish Christianity

The beginnings of what came to be Christianity, as we find its "constitution" in the New Testament, were thoroughly Jewish. Their belief that

Jesus was the Messiah, crucified and risen, marked the early disciples as peculiar within the general community of Israel, but otherwise both they and their opponents considered them fully Jewish. Their community was, in their own eyes, a new or eschatological Israel (see Galatians 6:6, Acts 1:21 f., Matthew 19:28), but it completely derived from Moses and the prophets. Even after Peter's experience with Cornelius (Acts 10) and the flowering of Paul's missionary career to the Gentiles, the solid majority of Jewish Christian disciples probably thought of themselves as bound to the Law and, if they were in Jerusalem, were commended for frequenting the Jerusalem Temple regularly. Even their belief in Jesus' coming parousia fitted into the general framework of contemporay Jewish eschatological hope, while any thoughts they had of welcoming the Gentiles into their community probably first came in the guise of traditional Jewish hopes that in the messianic age the nations would come to worship on Mount Zion (see Psalms 22:27, Isaiah 56:6–8).

As Dunn points out, by the end of the second century C.E. the situation had radically changed. By and large the precisely Jewish features of adherence to Jesus then marked a group as heretical rather than part of the Christian mainstream. Thus faithful adherence to Jewish Law distinguished groups such as the Nazareans and **Ebionites** as dubiously orthodox.[2] A group known in scholarly circles as the Clementines ran into a *cul de sac* because they exalted James (the strictest upholder of Jewish traditions among the apostles) and downplayed Paul. The Ebionites were leaders in a trend to downplay the status of Jesus, too, since (in good Jewish fashion) they insisted on his completely natural parentage and birth. For

Three Apostles. Sculpture, Spanish. Eleventh century. Paul, Andrew, and James are rendered so similar as to suggest a uniformity in apostolic doctrine and function. *(Nelson Gallery–Atkins Museum, Kansas City, Mo. [Nelson Fund])*

them God had adopted Jesus as his Son and Christ. The incarnationalism of Johannine Christianity and the preexistence taught by Paul and Hebrews were given less play.

Inasmuch as none of these positions (which were later considered deviant) would have branded their adherents unacceptable in Christianity's first few generations, their later unacceptability shows the considerable development that occurred throughout the New Testament period. Reflection and missionary experience, discussion and church experience, had conspired to distance Christianity from Judaism. It was not just that Christians and Jews could not settle their differences about Jesus and the Law. It was also that Christian faith developed a logic that took it to positions incompatible with traditional Judaism. Above all, Christian faith came to consider Jesus more divine than a Jewish sense of monotheism could admit.

Still, the New Testament has canonized an (orthodox) Jewish Christianity that contributed central pieces to the normative Christian mosaic formed by the end of the second century. Matthew, for instance, preserves the Law, even though he makes Jesus and his love the new interpreter of the Law. The letter of James, finally admitted into the canon as validly representing Christian faith, shows the hold works continued to have on Christian conscience even after Paul's blockbuster Epistles on the theme of justification by faith. Acts 15 and 20, Galatians 2, 1 Corinthians 8–10, 2 Corinthians 10–13, Romans 14, and Philippians 3 all offer evidence that this support for a "Jamesian" position, and a concomitant opposition to Pauline views, had a long lineage. The presence within Matthean theology, the theology of Acts, and the theology of Hebrews of views somewhat like the Ebionite adoptionist Christology is another indication that Jewish Christianity made a formative mark on what became mainstream or orthodox faith. This more acceptable adoptionism helped to anchor Jesus' humanity and preserved the sense that his messianic mission or guidance by the Spirit came through religious experiences at least analogous to what other prophets or holy people had received.

In summarizing Jewish Christianity Dunn tries to clarify the criteria that marked off the acceptable from the heretical:

> First, Matthew's insistence that the law must be interpreted by love may provide one [criterion]: Jewish Christianity was counted unacceptable when it *began to regard strict observance of the law as more important than the spontaneity of love.* More clearly, second, Jewish Christianity was counted unacceptable when it *persisted in clinging to a limited view of Jesus and his role.* It could claim support for this conservatism from some of the earliest expressions of Christian faith. But since the spread of Christianity outside Palestine and the controversies of the first few decades caused these early, more fluid and provisional formulations to be left behind as inadequate, *the Jewish Christianity of the second and third centuries represents in the end a reactionary attempt to restrict the Christian estimate of Jesus within the limitations and confines of Jewish thought and practice.*[3]

A third criterion could be the failure of Jewish Christianity to develop. In other words, this portion of the early community of Jesus became too conservative; it failed to update and extend its faith as new times and projects required. Dunn seems surprised to find himself coming to such a conclusion, but he judges that the path from documents such as Matthew to later, unacceptable documents such as those of the Ebionites requires it. If this is a valid criterion, the diversity of the New Testament does indeed emerge as a variety of streams. None of the acceptable streams was standing still. All were expected to keep forging ahead. We may account Jewish Christianity precious for showing us Jesus' deep traditional roots, but we cannot avoid the Christian community's own historical decision that the universal outreach of the gospel required an adaptation to the Gentiles.

Hellenistic Christianity

The second stream of early Christianity that we consider is that shaped by non-Palestinian forces. Some of these forces were also non-Jewish—for instance, the Greek and Roman cultural influences that predominated in the Mediterranean basin. Others were religious amalgams of Jewish, Greek, and perhaps Egyptian notions, many of which would combine with Christianity to form Gnosticism. Still a third contribution to Hellenistic Christianity came from Jews who lived outside Palestine, spoke Greek rather than Hebrew, and used the Septuagint (Greek) version of the (Old Testament) Scriptures rather than the Hebrew version.

Acts 6:1 suggests that from quite early times the Christian community in Jerusalem distinguished between Hellenists and Hebrews. Indeed, it

Jerusalem. The Western Wall (of the Second Temple), perhaps the holiest site for devout Jews, with the golden dome of the famous Dome of the Rock mosque in the background. *(Photo by J.T. Carmody)*

further suggests that there were tensions between these two groups, the Hellenists feeling that they were not being treated fairly. The first martyr, Stephen, was a Hellenist, and Acts records little support from Hebrew Christians during his trial and death. Perhaps his attacks on the Temple went farther than Hebrew Jewish Christians, reverent toward the center of Jewish faith, found comfortable. The fact that Paul of Tarsus, a Hellenistic Jew raised in the diaspora, was among the persecutors of Stephen may indicate that the first moves against the Jerusalem Christian community were part of an intra-Hellenistic struggle. That is, the persecution mentioned in Acts 8 may have been largely a matter of Greek-speaking Jews expressing their outrage at what they perceived to be the excesses of Greek-speaking Jewish Christians.

In the Hellenistic orbit we also find Gnostic tendencies influencing Christian faith and inevitably having a say in what diaspora Christian theology (e.g., that of Asia Minor) came to be. In Corinth Paul had to stake out a position vis-à-vis the pneumatics or spiritually inspired members of the community, many of whom could have been following Gnostic tendencies, and this led him to write such influential passages as 1 Corinthians 2:6–3:4, with its moving initial discussion of (Christian) wisdom. Similarly, his teaching in 1 Corinthians on marriage, freedom to eat foods consecrated to idols, and the variety of spiritual gifts suggests an effort to gain a purchase on a Christian gnosis (special knowledge) that would avoid the extremes of what later flourished into full-blown Gnosticism.

Philippians, Colossians, the Pastorals, Revelation, and even Jude offer more evidence that the Hellenistic stream of Christianity was a powerful factor in the development of a wisdom, Christology, and ethics that would be more compatible with Jewish traditions than Hellenistic religious syncretism was and yet would allow the Christian community to engage in dialogue with non-Jews interested in such syncretism. We may read the Q source in the Gospels as another contributor to this search for a uniquely balanced Christian wisdom, one that would place Jesus in the light of the Old Testament Sophia, making his unique career and person (fully human yet exalted to heavenly lordship) the new paradigm of divine saving knowledge. Paul may have taken some of his lead in opposing Jewish legalism and probing the cosmic implications of Jesus' death and resurrection from Hellenistic mystery religions and quasi-Gnostic speculative pressures.

The Gospel of John certainly goes the farthest in stressing the divinity of the one who walked the paths of Galilee, so far that some have found it perilously close to Docetism, the early heresy that claimed that the divine Son only seemed to be fully human. John itself refutes this charge, and perhaps 1 John refutes it even more clearly, making it plain that Johannine incarnationalism was quite realistic about the Word's taking flesh. But the dominance of the divine voice in the Johannine Jesus' dialogues, the stress on his coming from above, and his identification with the Father seem to reflect certain Hellenistic thought patterns.

Overall, it is Hellenistic Christianity that provided the major push to break out of traditional Jewish categories and forge a distinctively Christian theology and church life. Where Jewish Christianity strove to conserve much of Torah and Jewish forms of worship, the Hellenists wanted to employ the best of what the Hellenistic philosophies and mystery religions had to offer. Thus the more speculative portions of the New Testament (Paul, John), and the more sacramental portions (John), both appear to owe a large debt to Hellenism. What would distinguish orthodox Hellenistic Christianity from heretical Gnosticism in the second century would be the confession of Jesus. The orthodox insisted that the glorified Lord, mediator, and power to come in the parousia was the Jesus who really lived in Galilee, preached, healed, suffered, and died on the cross. The Gnostics tended to downplay the historical Jesus and make the Christ but one more pneumatic or soteriological (saving) player in their grand games of cosmic fall and redemption.[4]

Apocalyptic Christianity

Whereas Jewish and Hellenistic Christianity were both largely recognized and given their formative due from the beginning, the significance of apocalyptic Christianity has clarified only in recent times, as studies of the Jewish apocalyptic have shown the kinship of many portions of the New Testament with the eschatological and messianic imagery and themes of Jewish "revelational" literature. Today scholars can discern a clearly defined "trajectory" from the later Jewish prophets, through Jewish apocalyptic literature such as Daniel and Enoch, to John the Baptist, Jesus, the early Christian community in Palestine (Mark), the early Paul (1 Thessalonians), Revelation, and such early Christian heresies or deviances as Montanism.[5]

Contemporary view of the Dead Sea, looking across from Israel to Jordan. *(Photo by J.T. Carmody)*

We have distinguished some of the dominant characteristics of apocalyptic literature in our chapter on Revelation. Were we to search for a stronger apocalyptic influence in the Gospels than we noted when studying them (we mainly concentrated on the eschatological discourses [Mark 13, Matthew 24, Luke 21]), we might stress the influence of John the Baptist's preaching of the coming winnowing, the eschatological dimension of Jesus' teaching about the kingdom (e.g., the master's quick return from the wedding feast), and the cosmological symbolism in Jesus' visions of the end (which make them cataclysmic as apocalyptic tends to be). Much of this material comes from Q, for which Jesus was an eschatological messenger.[6]

The eschatological discourses in the synoptics do not dominate the entire synoptic theology, but they show that all of these Gospel writers (but especially Mark) were working with strong memories of Jesus' own apocalyptic convictions. Problematic as it may be for some later theologies of Jesus' divinity, which had him foreseeing everything, the synoptic evidence strongly suggests that Jesus expected the end to occur in his own lifetime, probably at his own death. Then the kingdom that had begun with his preaching would come in full power. Then the Son of Man would arrive riding on the clouds for judgment and full blessing. In the other New Testament literature, in addition to Revelation, 1 and 2 Thessalonians most strongly beat the apocalyptic drum. 1 Thessalonians shows Paul's powerful expectation of the parousia. 2 Thessalonians gets into the fascinating if obscure question of what signs will show when the end has begun.

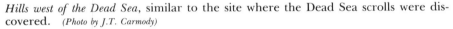

Hills west of the Dead Sea, similar to the site where the Dead Sea scrolls were discovered. *(Photo by J.T. Carmody)*

What does this apocalyptic stream bequeath the New Testament faith overall? What in the diversified unity of the whole should we attribute to early Christianity's intense expectation of the consummation? First, a specification of Jewish apocalyptic hope, which though often messianic was in general rather vague about how the golden age was to come. For the Christian apocalyptic writers the bearer of the end, the parousia, the full kingdom was not at all vague. The bearer was Christ the risen Lord, Christ the heavenly reality whom the Spirit and the Bride passionately prayed to come. True enough, the symbolism of this coming remained imprecise, probably inevitably. But the reason for an intensified hope (Jesus' resurrection), and the sense of what the end would accomplish (the promises in Jesus' preaching), were nailed down and rendered quite concrete by becoming part and parcel of mainstream Christology.

Further notes that apocalyptic introduced or strengthened include the Jewishness of Christianity (by choosing this form of enthusiasm as more acceptable than the Hellenistic tendencies that led to Gnosticism, the Church strengthened its Jewish roots); the sense that history has a purpose and goal; and a proper evaluation of present times, neither exalting them to complete importance nor denigrating the world (to which the Messiah would return, and which the eschatological age would complete and perfect).

Early Catholicism

The last stream running into the New Testament in its formative decades that we consider is early Catholicism, the development of organizational and ritualistic forms to channel charismatic Christian faith.[7] The major evidences for this phenomenon within the New Testament are the Pastorals and perhaps parts of Acts. Outside the New Testament 1 Clement, probably written about 90 C.E. and reflecting Roman theology, shows a strong move toward regularizing Church authority.

Among the causes for the rise of early Catholicism the delay of the parousia stands high. When Christians lost their tense expectation that the end might come at any moment, they gained the psychological freedom to consider how they ought to accommodate to the world and develop a coherent, unified church organization. There followed (though surely not with complete awareness and calculation) the emergence of clerical office (bishops, priests, deacons, elders), a sense of wanting to link local church authority to the apostles, a growing gap between clergy and laity, a more formal ritual structure, and an increased concern for sound (traditional) doctrine. Indeed, as we saw in the Pastorals, preserving sound doctrine and good church order is the authors' major charge to Timothy and Titus.

In Acts one also sees a cooling of eschatological fervor. For instance, the prophecy in Joel 2:28–32 about the messianic age is interpreted as already having been fulfilled at Pentecost (Acts 2:17–21). Acts 1:11 still speaks of the parousia but Acts 1:6–8 focuses on the worldwide mission implied in the Christ-event. Although Paul wrote 1 Thessalonians while in the grip of a strongly eschatological theology, the description of Paul's work in Thessalonica (Acts 17) does not reflect this mood.

The Johannine literature, although not heavy with details about growing church institutionalization, partly explains early Catholicism by providing more evidence of the cooling of eschatological fervor. The realized eschatology of the Gospel, with its clear message that the substance of salvation came with the Incarnation, suggests a reorientation of faith. The Johannine literature is saying that love, faith, and the sacramental life (baptism and the eucharist) give one access right now to the end realities, the gracious life and glory of God. The Spirit is a down payment on the full realization of God's work that will occur at the end. There will be a raising up at the last day but those who participate in Christ sacramentally, eating his flesh and drinking his blood, already share in eternal life.

Another aspect of the movement away from an ardent eschatology is the ethical accommodation prescribed in the Pastorals, Colossians, and Ephesians. The house codes, with their relative acceptance of the hierarchial social relations that obtained in patriarchal Hellenistic society, represent a shift away from a community that expected its time in society at large to be minimal. Insofar as this more hierarchical structure won out in the Great Church, determining the preeminence of clergy over laity, men over women, and (somewhat passive) good citizenship over reformism, it bespoke a solid vote for reinterpreting faith away from living in the last times, toward having to fit into society at large. Prior to this vote, many local churches probably had quite egalitarian forms of government, with liturgical and other duties rotating among different community members, female as well as male. It is likely that the basic structure of such communities was the house-church,[8] gathered around believers of such wealth or prestige that they could anchor a community on the model of a religious association of relative equals.

None of these tendencies or movements argues that early Catholicism may be found in the New Testament full-blown. The later second- and third-century heresies were probably the decisive factor in firming up doctrinal authority and church office to the point where a standardized ecclesiastical structure began to be recognizable. But the New Testament does reveal the seeds, causes, and initial tendencies of a direction toward Catholicism. If one stresses organizational matters, the Pastorals are the key documents, and one might even read such materials as the Johannine works as anti-Catholic. If one stresses realized eschatology, ethical accommodation to Hellenistic society, or sacramentalism, the Johannine and deutero-Pauline communities (Ephesians, Colossians) are in many ways already Catholic.[9]

What is clear is that the delay of the parousia forced a rethinking of major elements of the earliest faith and led to an almost commonsensical realization that, if it were going to be in for a long haul, the Church had better get its house in good order. Elaine Pagels, at the end of her study of the Gnostic Gospels, summarizes many of the virtues of early Catholicism and the debts we owe it: "Had Christianity remained multiform, it might well have disappeared from history, along with dozens of rival religious cults of antiquity. I believe that we owe the survival of Christian tradition to the organizational and theological structure that the emerging church developed. Anyone as powerfully attracted to Christianity as I am will regard that as a major achievement."[10]

Literary Diversity

The four streams of New Testament Christianity that we have described suggest something of the historical and doctrinal diversity that went into the Christian mixture from the beginning. Before turning to the unity of the New Testament materials, let us briefly consider a final diversity, the literary variety of the New Testament data (and how scholars try to handle it).

In his solid work, *Introduction to the New Testament*, Raymond Collins has described the various kinds of criticism that have become influential in recent New Testament scholarship. *Textual criticism* is the work of establishing the text of the New Testament, the best readings of the manuscripts of Matthew and Mark, John and Paul, and all the other canonical works. The scope of this task should not be underestimated:

> The Greek text of the New Testament found in the *Novum Testamentum Graece* edited by Kurt Aland et al (26th ed., 1979), the most popular handbook edition of the Greek New Testament, contains approximately 2,500 variants from the reading offered by any one of the typical ancient manuscripts. Modern editors have apparently come to the conclusion that no one of the ancient manuscripts offers a "correct" reading of the New Testament text in all its details. Accordingly it falls to the science of textual criticism to judge the ancient manuscripts and thus ascertain the "correct" reading of the text of the New Testament.[11]

Source criticism is the effort to reconstruct how the authors of the given New Testament literary entities came by their materials. For instance, the theory that Matthew and Luke arose from Mark and Q, as sources common to both of them, and from M and L, as sources unique to each respectively, is the result of probes into the provenance or sources of these works. *Literary criticism* often denotes the further effort to take these works independently of their sources and analyze their art as final products.

Redaction criticism focuses on the contribution of the final editor or redactor. It assumes that the person who put a Gospel such as Matthew or an Epistle such as Philippians into final shape collected, edited, arranged, left out, added, changed and all the rest to produce his or her own intended effects, to give flesh to his or her own particular theological inspirations. This does not deny that the final editor may have used several sources or incorporated the convictions of one or more rich church traditions (which could have their own histories). It simply takes the final document as a freely, deliberately organized whole and tries to discern the relations between its parts and its totality.

Form criticism zeroes in on the different types of expression that the biblical authors use. The assumption behind this method is that human communication employs a variety of different genres, each of which tends to have its own laws and to set up its own expectations. For example, a joke is different from an expression of condolence. A business letter has a different style and tone from that of a friendly letter home. In reading the newspaper we unreflectively distinguish ads from news stories, editorials from interviews.

Form criticism studies the different genres of the New Testament. It is interested in their oral history, semantic structure, "life-situation" (probable original context), supposed purpose, and so forth. Thus form criticism in effect follows up on the modern finding that many of the New Testament documents rather transparently borrow from collections of stories, hymns, catalogues of ethical advice, and the like. By identifying a particular independent passage or **pericope**, determining its probable history (for instance, its original context or its route to its present position within this work), its current function, and the rest a scholar can shed considerable light on both the range of meanings the pericope can admit and the redactor's probable purpose in inserting it at its present juncture. The story of the prodigal son (Luke 15:11–32), for example, begs analysis as an independent literary unit, as well as for its function in Luke's overall literary and theological endeavor. When we remind ourselves that the Gospels were written forty to sixty-five years after Jesus' death, we realize that the pericopes of the Gospels often have had quite rich and complicated histories. Form criticism has done yeoman service in elucidating these histories.

These different ways of approaching the New Testament materials are a tribute to their diversity. If we were to add other methodological approaches—**structuralism**, **decontextualism**, **semiotics**, and more—we would only multiply the richness and ambiguity that present scriptural scholarship finds in the twenty-seven books of the New Testament canon. There are sermons and sermonic units, prayers, letters, hymns, catalogues, parables, woes, Beatitudes, midrashes, metaphors, citations of the Old Testament, apocalypses, miracle stories, healing stories, and more. When blended with the different communities' histories, theologies, liturgical traditions, traditions of governance, and the rest, they make for a very diversified, complex canonical work. The more one knows about the variety of the New Testament materials, the less one is inclined to approach them flat-footedly, with a falsely simple mind or a literalistic imagination. The beginning of a mature reading of the New Testament is the confession of its complexity and **polyvalence**.

THE UNITY OF THE NEW TESTAMENT MATERIALS

Points of Agreement

In the part of his book that deals with the unity of the New Testament, James Dunn takes up nine different topics: The kerygma, the primitive confession, tradition, the use of the Old Testament, ministry, worship, sacraments, the Spirit, and Christology.[12] While admitting the many differences that the various New Testament documents reveal under these nine headings, Dunn regularly finds something commonly agreed upon, held by all, deserving to be expressed in the singular.

For example, although one must speak of the different kerygmata or proclamations of Jesus, Paul, John, Acts, and the rest, they agree that early Christianity sent out a call for faith, promised a reward for faith (salvation, the Spirit, forgiveness, life), and (with the qualified exception of Jesus' own proclamation) were spurred on by the risen, exalted Jesus. Second, the different early confessions of faith agreed that Jesus was the prime subject or matter being confessed, above all in his lordship. The most succinct and popular formula of confession, "Christ is Lord," fused the historical Jesus and the risen Lord of faith, the preresurrectional ministry and the postresurrectional power.

Third, one could say many of these same things about the early Christian sense of tradition. Through the different emphases and understandings of what had been handed on and was normative there ran the core confession about Jesus. It was his teaching, example, authority, power, and the rest, as displayed throughout his earthly life and ratified in his resurrection, that was the principal **tradition** or thing handed on. It was the significance of his life, death, and resurrection that the Spirit led the disciples to grasp more deeply and that the sacramental life of the Church articulated ever more broadly.

Fourth, the different strands of the New Testament agree in considering the Old Testament their Scripture. Again and again they try to show that there was continuity between the old covenant and the new, that prior prophecies were fulfilled in recent events, and that any breaks with Jewish tradition were for the sake of better realizing Jewish tradition's own best aims. True, Jesus became a new hermeneutic or interpretational key for the Old Testament, but the Old Testament remained a great revelation of God's will. Fifth, concerning ministry, Jesus once more supplied the point of unification. For while the egalitarian instincts of the early adherents of the Jesus movement were in many ways rejected by the later catholicizing, all church ministry or service had finally to try to justify itself on the basis of forwarding Jesus' work, expressing Jesus' Spirit, and advancing the good order and peace needed for the optimal worship, help of the poor, preaching of the gospel, and the like that Jesus demanded. So Jesus of Nazareth, now exalted as Lord and present in his powerful Spirit, was the central focus of all authority and the basic model of all pastors.

Sixth, discrepancies among the different early communities' forms and emphases in worship also radically dissolve when one moves to the level of what the communities thought their rites and prayers were accomplishing. For example, to pray to God as Father derived directly from Jesus and followed his counsel on how to address God. To remember the Lord's Supper, sacrifice, or present intercessory activity in heaven fitted the eucharist into Christ's priestly and redemptive activity. So too with baptizing as a joining with Christ, scriptural reading as a faithful search for type and fulfillment, praying over the sick in memory of Jesus' healings and confidence in God's mercy, forgiving sins as the Lord once did, expressing the prophetic insights granted by the Spirit of Jesus, and so on. Varied as the different communities' traditions of worship became, they all retained a recognizable unity as grounded in the instruction of Jesus Christ and formed by the example of Jesus Christ. Seventh, the same holds for that part of Christian worship expressed through the churches' sacramental practices. When they celebrated the admission of a new church member or the regular communal love feast, they did so in the name of Jesus, with a memory of Jesus, as an expression of their strong hope that Jesus would soon return.[13]

Dunn's eighth category for discussing unity spotlights the Spirit and religious experience. To his mind religious experience (what we have referred to as the charismatic, prophetic, or enthusiastic dimension of early Christian faith) was highly important in the New Testament era. Indeed, a similarity of exaltation in the Spirit was a major ingredient in Christians' sense of unity, their recognition of one another as members of the same community or Body of Christ. Despite the differences in tone—more abandoned in the early Palestinian groups, almost severe by the time of the Pastorals—a common factor in the churches' experiences of the Spirit was their reference of such grace to the historical Jesus. It was his resurrection that had brought this new fullness of God's outpouring. By refusing to separate what they were receiving in the Spirit from the historical Jesus handed down to them from all the churches' most central memories, the early Christian generations kept their religious exaltation manageable; they made sure it as least strove to obey the Pauline criterion of building up the community as a whole.

Dunn's ninth and last category, Christology, has already emerged as the most decisive feature from the previous eight considerations. Again and again, as we have seen, it was reference to Jesus, the Teacher and Son of Man who died and was raised to lordship, that brought the churches' different views of faith or worship together under the same umbrella and justified our calling them all Christian and their all calling themselves Christian. Concerning Christology itself, as we implied when dealing with such formative streams as the Jewish and Hellenistic ones, diversity can be the characteristic that first strikes the eye. On the other hand, none of the Christologies that became accounted orthodox and stayed in the Great Church neglected either the historical Jesus or the Christ of faith. All accepted the hermeneutical circle that placed the man from Galilee and the Easter Lord at the bull's-eye of faith. So, concluding his survey of the early unity among diversity, Dunn writes:

> In short, the identity of historical Jesus with kerygmatic Christ is the one basis and bond of unity which holds together the manifold diversity of first-century Christianity; that is, the continuity between the message of Jesus and the post-Easter proclamation, and the agreement of the different kerygmata in affirming that Jesus of Nazareth and the exalted Christ are one and the same, is the unifying core round which the diversity of NT Christianity coheres.[14]

Unity from Broader Perspectives

New Testament scholars earn their bread and render their great services largely because they are masters of detail. From their daily intercourse with detail, diversity becomes an accepted if not well-loved soulmate. It is useful, therefore, to challenge their workaday horizon from time to time, refusing to let the New Testament become only a domain of technical details, remembering as well that it has long been both the central book of a Church of nontechnicians and a classic in the annals of humanity's general gropings after wisdom. In this section we step outside the New Testament's own covers and ask about the unity it reveals when one sets it in such broader perspectives.

Those who would enjoy conducting this query on a comparative textual basis might pick up the fine anthology *Sacred Texts of the World*, edited by Ninian Smart and Richard Hecht.[15] There one finds selections from Christian Scripture set alongside Jewish, Muslim, Hindu, Buddhist, Jain, Taoist, Confucian, Shinto, Sikh, and other religions' holy texts. Moreover, the editors follow a uniform format, arranging each religion's scriptural selections in the same order: Sacred Narrative, Doctrine, Ritual, Institutional Expression, (Religious) Experience, and Ethics. In such a comparative setting, the distinctiveness of Christian faith (as well as its many similarities to the other world religions) emerges quite clearly. Placed in a broader horizon, the unity of the Christian gospel, the coherence of the confessions of all the different New Testament books, is quite impressive.

For example, there is the great criterion to which Dunn himself alluded, now freed of his slightly tainting estimate that it is an "abstraction."[16] That criterion is Jesus Christ, and no other religion or group of religious scriptures has it. Immediately the key personage who unifies the New Testament sets Christianity apart from Judaism, Islam, and all the other traditions listed above. Thus any text that derives its basic meaning, purpose, or reason to be from Jesus has much more in common with any other such text than with all non-Christian literature. Buddhist literature, for instance, despite its formidable wisdom about suffering, meditation, morality, and the like, occurs in a quite different world than that of the New Testament. Figuratively, Buddhism pushes all the New Testament texts together and collects them all in a single family bunch, because they all pivot on Jesus while Buddhist literature all pivots on something else (Buddha or nirvana or another center best left for Buddhologists to determine).

Although Jesus is the most decisive criterion for New Testament and Christian unity, and the most powerful agent of such unity, other aspects of the Christian gospel also beg consideration. For example, there is the Christian belief in a personal God. Many other religious traditions share something of this belief, but traditions enrolling hundreds of millions of people do not. Thus Christian theism, with its peculiar coloring from Jesus, places the New Testament books together (as unified) and sets them apart from much Buddhist, Hindu, Taoist, Confucian, Marxist, and secular literature. Christian theism is indeed quite like Jewish theism, but it is clearly distinguishable from much Muslim theism, where Allah is a sovereign Lord but not at all an intimate Daddy. (Neither Judaism nor Islam, of course, accepts the divinity of Jesus or thinks it compatible with monotheism. The Christian doctrine of the Trinity is also unique.)

The Christian biblical doctrine of sin is similar for our present purposes. There is nothing quite like it in the religions of India and East Asia (although of course there are discussions of ignorance, moral weakness, social disorder, and the like that deal with the same experiential area). Judaism has a teaching that is close, but Islam is significantly less concerned with culpable evil than with human weakness and creatureliness. The Christian doctrine of creation, implicit in all the New Testament, is a third conviction that separates the followers of Jesus from their Indian and Asian co-religionists, who seldom speak of a personal God making the world by a free command. Muslims and Jews, by contrast, hold views of the world quite similar to Christian creationism.[17]

A fourth central and quite distinguishing mark of Christianity is its foundational ethical teaching that the sum and substance of God's call upon our consciences is that we love one another and try to do good even to those who persecute us. There are analogies to this teaching in Judaism and Islam (limited by both traditions' legalism), and perhaps quite close similarities in Buddhist **mahakaruna** (great compassion), but overall Christian ethics stands out for its radical call to selfless love. Christians commit a colossal blunder when they confuse this ideal with the more important matter of practical performance, or when they try to argue that the history of Christian love proves Christianity's special status as God's privileged revelation.[18] But as found on the lips of the evangelical Jesus, and kept basic in all subsequent Christian tradition, the twofold commandment of utter love of God and love of neighbor as oneself gathers Christian ethical literature into a nook all its own.

The last Christian conviction, clear in the New Testament and elaborated through later Christian centuries, that we consider in our probe of Christian unity-uniqueness is the doctrine of grace. As we have seen, Jesus' own preaching centered on the reign of God. We could translate this preaching as a call to believe that God was being singularly gracious. *Charis*, the basic New Testament word for grace, means favor and acceptability. Jesus was saying that this was a special time of favor, an acceptable hour, when people could draw uniquely near to God, because God was drawing uniquely near to them. And from the drawing near of God they could expect the healing of their spirits and society, the ousting of injustice and the demonic powers.

Jesus himself manifested this favor, so much so that the Prologue to John's Gospel makes him the vehicle of (all) divine grace and truth: "For the law was given through Moses; grace and truth came through Jesus Christ. No one has ever seen God; the only Son, who is in the bosom of the Father, he has made him known" (John 1:17–18). In the rich Johannine conflation of images and concepts, grace, truth, glory, revelation, salvation, love, the Spirit, and all the rest tumble together. The "event" of Jesus, his stepping forth (from the eternal realm of God) into human history, makes available in space and time the favor of God, the divine love. This favor (light, love, life) is everything human beings crave, the totality human beings need to center themselves as they ought, to find the way for which they have been made. With the favor of God and the divine afflatus (breath, inspiration), human beings become like Jesus: sacramental, able to discern the multitude of God's signs. Without the divine afflatus they live cramped and cabined, so much less than the angels that they seem feral and flat.

As this conviction about the gracious time of the kingdom matured, it reached eschatological proportions. For both Jesus and the early theologians, the offer being made was clarified as being definitive, once and for all, never to be superseded or found essentially lacking. The parousia would reveal in full power and detail the completeness of the kingdom that Jesus was bringing, the new age of grace that had been made irrevocable in his death and resurrection. But, as several aspects of especially the Johannine and Pauline theologies make clear, with Jesus salvation was accomplished in principle. The communication of divinity to humanity that "salvation" finally connotes happened actually and finally in Jesus Christ. The Johannine realized eschatology elaborates this theme. The Pauline doctrine of grace (justification) and the Body of Christ is but another version.[19]

How does this view of grace, with its concomitant views of the divine-human relationship and the world, single Christianity out (from as early as New Testament times)? What is peculiar or characteristic about this teaching, when one places it in the spectrum of humanity's world religions and secular philosophies? It singles Christianity out as peculiarly hopeful, balanced, and concrete about the reasons that justify an adventurous view of the future.

All traditions of course are in some way hopeful. Any tradition can only gather the energy to keep handing on what it has received and tried to live by if it can point to solutions, beauties, resources for endurance, and the like that its own experience has proven viable. The theistic traditions basically rest their hopes in God. The power of God (Islam) and the saving acts of God in the past (Judaism) furnish strong warrants for hoping that God will make the future good. No matter how depraved or despicable human nature may seem to have become, the fact that God addressed it in the past (prophetic religion) suggests that it remains addressable today. If humanity were ever to use its eyes to see, its ears to hear, it could discern the way to a much better life (social, ecological, psychological, and religious combined).

By contrast with this general theism, Christianity points not only to historical times and places, to prophetic and mystical forms in which redemption became concrete. It points more audaciously to a single event in which history overturned and the future became assured of success. This event is the death and resurrection of Jesus. Right there, as Pauline theology especially stresses but all the New Testament theologies proclaim, the eschaton arrived; the fulfillment almost too good to be hoped for or believed offered itself to be loved. The death of Jesus took God's gracious availability to the point where the divine suffered human evil and swallowed it up in a greater love. That is the early Christian notion enshrined in the hymn, "Dying he destroyed our death." It is the law of the cross, the breaking of the vicious cycle of hurt for hurt by introducing a goodness, a deathless love, strictly divine and therefore capable of making rain fall on just and unjust alike, of loving the sinner back to humaneness.

The resurrection of Jesus was the definitive taking of a human being able to bear this love (in two senses: able to suffer it through and able to manifest it to others) into the divine sphere. Jesus the risen Lord passed from sinful history to accomplished salvation. With his rising came a place, an insert, a navel for the new creation about which Paul waxes eloquent. The Christian claim thenceforth is that history has been decided, the greatest questions have been answered, and nothing can separate us from the love of God in Christ Jesus our Lord (Romans 8:39).

The early Christians were wrong in thinking that this victory meant an early consummation of history in physical turmoil and universal cataclysm. But their basic instinct ran below the details of their various apocalyptic and eschatological scenarios. For their basic instinct was that Jesus was such a success, and so inseparable from the rest of nature and humanity, that in him the divine future had become present, the divine life was an "existential" or universal feature, calling all people beyond themselves, upward and onward, because any person could now share the divine nature and become a being actually divinized. Compared to this basic instinct and claim the details of physical cosmic consummation are secondary.

Neither Judaism nor Islam speaks of this definitive, eschatological grace. Judaism still awaits the messianic, eschatological era. Islam believes that Muhammad is the seal of the prophets, who has brought the final revelations, but it backs away in horror from divinizing Muhammad (let alone any other human beings). That would be idolatry, the worst of sins.

Hinduism and Buddhism offer more promising soil, interestingly enough, at least in their pantheistic strata (as a Western theist might call them). The Hindu notion that each atman or spirit-soul-self partakes of the universal Brahman, the ultimate world force and matter, can be worked to offer all people hope of *moksha*, final fulfillment in union with the unconditionedness (what the West tends to call the infinity) of Brahman. However, Hinduism seldom ties such moksha to specific historical events and has nothing so affronting as a historical crucifixion-resurrection.

Buddhism speaks persuasively of the presence of nirvana or the ultimate in the midst of *samsara* or imperfect worldly existence. There are ways, moreover, in which Buddhism ties the realization of this presence to the historical Buddha, but they are far less central, and far more contested within Buddhism, than is the centrality of the historical Jesus to the Christian doctrine of grace. Neither Hinduism nor Buddhism knows a definitive eschaton, for both keep history endlessly cyclic. Nirvana and moksha in some ways portend a heavenly fulfillment for all beings, but they don't assume bodies and a creation groaning in labor for redemption (Romans 8:22) as Christian faith expects heaven to do. Overall, then, the Christian doctrine of grace appears unique, in both its historicity and its definitive or once and for all claims.[20]

RETROSPECTIVE: THE NEW TESTAMENT STORY

What Have We Here?

In the New Testament we have the story of a man, a contest between good and evil, a God trying to save a people, a new people being born, a faith enduring hardships and hoping for relief, and much more.[21] The plotlines of the story depend on the interests of the reader almost as much as on the original actions of the main protagonists. The story begins with Jesus and at first appears to be but another chapter in the narrative of Israel. The bare bones are that Jesus came from Galilee, lived from about 6–4 B.C.E. to 28–30 C.E., grew up as a pious Jew, thought he had a mission to preach the coming of a time of special grace (a time that portended the fulfillment of messianic hopes), taught with a singular authority, healed and worked prodigies, upset the Jewish religious establishment, gathered a band of followers, was arrested and crucified as a threat to the (Roman and Jewish) peace, and was proclaimed by his followers to have been resurrected and to have appeared to them.

Jesus' person, life, teaching, death, and above all resurrection caused his followers to think they had an opportunity, indeed an imperative, to live as though he had accomplished the basic hopes of Israelite messianism and to announce his decisive character to their fellow Jews. They began their communal life in Jerusalem but soon spread out into the diaspora, becoming especially strong in Asia Minor. By two decades or so after Jesus' death, when we get our first specimens of Christian literature, his followers exist in small local bands ("churches") and have opened to the Gentiles.

This opening is a crucial moment in their reconception of their identity. Whereas for Jesus himself and the first band of disciples the framework was Judaism, by the second generation the framework had expanded to embrace the nations and become the entire inhabited world (**ecumene**).[22] What had been a Jewish sect, distinctive for proclaiming Jesus of Nazareth the Messiah and bringer of salvation, was on the way to becoming a powerful new religion, soon to outstrip Judaism in influence within the Roman empire and the Hellenistic world.

The first transition in this process was the shift from Jesus' proclamation of the kingdom to Jesus' followers' proclamation of Jesus himself as the Messiah and risen Lord. Because of the resurrection (and sending of the Spirit), Jesus' followers thought the kingdom had substantially come and salvation was available for the asking (through baptism, as the sign of faith in Jesus and conversion to his values and community). The first generation preached all this only provisionally, however, expecting the end or parousia to occur very soon.

The Pauline Epistles show the story advanced to the point where community problems and missionary questions had provoked a full reflection on the implications of Jesus' work, especially of his death and resurrection. Against the background of Jewish faith, above all of Jewish commitment to the Torah of Moses as the way to righteousness before God, Paul elaborated the notion that faith in Jesus could accomplish what the Law had proven impotent to do. By raising Jesus after the scandal of his death on the cross, God had written *finis* to the dispensation of Torah (note, however, the qualifications expressed in Romans 9–11) and had made a new beginning for human beings as radical as the first creation of Adam and Eve.

The second translation in the transformation of Christianity from a Jewish sect to an ecumenical religion was Paul's convincing the church (overall) that this new creation was open to all who would accept Jesus as the main treasure and saving force in their lives, Gentiles as well as Jews. Although (according to Acts) Paul would first preach to the Jews of a given area, his main success apparently came with Gentiles (and Hellenized Jews). He emphasized the present power of Jesus the Christ as a living Spirit, the union of all believers as the Body of Christ, the primacy of love, and the balance that ought to obtain between individual freedom and concern for the peace and edification of the whole community.

About the time that the corpus of letters from Paul's own hand was coming to completion (at least, the corpus of letters that have survived), in the 60s of the first century C.E., a new literary genre appeared called the "Gospel." The earliest specimen of this new genre that we possess is Mark, which probably represents Palestinian traditions. Whereas the Pauline letters suggest what the (Pauline) Christian communities' faith and life were like in the first decades after Jesus' death, the Gospels were announcements, proclamations, of the good news of what Jesus had been, done, and taught. Their literary peculiarity, however, was that they couched the Christian kerygma in the form of narratives of Jesus' life and person. They did not pretend to be detached biographies. Their kerygmatic character was clear to all. But they did purport to be truthful interpretations of Jesus, authoritative recollections of what he had said and valued. Thereby, they did claim authority to shape present Christians' faith and to correct current misapprehensions about either Jesus or Christian discipleship.

In content the Gospels build toward Jesus' Passion. Rather obviously they sew together materials derived from different communities' memories and traditions of Jesus' teaching stories, acts of healing, miracles, relations with his first disciples, and attitudes toward the Palestinian poor, tax collectors, sinners, women, Pharisees, scribes, Samaritans, Gentiles, and more. Each of the Gospels presents Jesus in a different light, but all agree about the key aspects of his character and message. That he preached the dawning of the kingdom, called for repentance and faith, taught in parables, blessed the poor, reinterpreted Torah, and undercut many going expectations about the Messiah therefore seem solidly likely as both historical fact and early Christian conviction. Equally solid is the likelihood that he died from a combination of fidelity to his message, antipathy he had raised among Jewish authorities, and Roman fears that he might prove an agitator (if only by causing divisions among the Jews). Clearly something influential happened after his death by crucifixion, although the nature of this happening (resurrection) is quite obscure. The Gospels, representing second- and third-generation Christianity's interpretations of Jesus, make this outline of Jesus' work apparently standard church fare.

More idiosyncratic are such particular emphases as Mark's stress on Jesus' suffering, Jesus' power and enigmatic character (the messianic secret), and the necessity for Jesus' disciples to be countercultural. Matthew's analogous stresses are Jesus' complete fulfillment of Old Testament prophecies about the Messiah, his renovation (or supersession) of Torah, and his status as God's new authoritative rabbi. Luke presents a more gentle and peaceful Jesus, who teaches and suffers in accordance with the divine plan. For Luke the Gospel deals with the central panel in a tryptich of salvation, standing between the Old Testament period of preparation and the postresurrectional age of the Church (when salvation is available to all). John's Gospel, most likely the last of the four, derives from different sources from those of the synoptics. More influenced perhaps by Samaritan and Hellenistic thought patterns, it emphasizes Jesus' divinity and the consequently sacramental (sign) quality of all his actions. John's point of view transforms the teaching of Jesus into discourses from the enfleshed heavenly Word who is the definitive revealer of God. In John's many references to baptism, the eucharist, and the Spirit we glimpse the sacramental life of Christianity in Asia Minor toward the end of the first century.

If we pause to consolidate our sketch chronologically, we find considerable overlapping. Shortly after Jesus' death and resurrection both the Pauline and the evangelical processes began. By the Pauline processes we mean the experiences, reflections, and literary efforts that came to expression in the corpus of Paul's letters: struggles between Christians and Jews, missionary efforts, foundings of Jewish Christian churches (both Aramaic-speaking and Greek-speaking), and foundings of Gentile Christian churches. Much of this activity occurred in Asia Minor and radiated out from Antioch. By the evangelical processes we mean the consolidation of traditions about Jesus' historical life, activity, teaching, death, and resurrection. The early letters of Paul appear before the earliest Gospels, but the formative processes behind both literary productions were going forward simultaneously.

By the same token, the composition of Acts, the deutero-Pauline literature, Revelation, and the miscellaneous other "letters" overlaps the composition of the later Gospels, especially Luke and John. Acts forms with Luke a two-volume work and has largely the same motivation, time and place of composition, theology, and the like. The deutero-Pauline literature suggests the work of the first generation of Paul's disciples, for whom increased contact with Hellenistic culture (including syncretistic, proto-Gnostic movements) begot both a deeper reflection on the wisdoms of the Christ and a rather new effort to adapt Christian behavior to the mores of Hellenistic society at large (in good part because of the delay of the parousia). The Pastorals, arising under Pauline influence, focus more precisely on organizational questions, displaying an early Catholicism geared to helping the Hellenistic churches fit into their civilizational milieu without being corrupted.

The Johannine Epistles, which probably arose in the last decade of the first century, show the community of the beloved disciple a little farther down the road than it appears in the body of the Gospel of John. Docetism is a major problem. The affirmation of Jesus' flesh, as well as a criterion of practical love, are the main responses. Hebrews, perhaps arising a little earlier than 1 John, offers a full-blown interpretation of Jesus' priesthood, calculatedly Jewish in its terms. Revelation, also from the last part of the first century, offers comforts to distressed Christians of Asia Minor, warns against religious accommodation and assimilation, and shows that Christian hopes for the parousia were still quite passionate. The other Epistles, also from the third or fourth Christian generation, suggest by their relative practicality and central counsel to endure that toward the end of the New Testament period the Church was preoccupied with matters of order and survival.

We have in the New Testament, then, traces of perhaps eighty years' worth (30–110) of "Christian" experience, both practical and speculative. Jesus is the central reference of all the books, at least implicitly, and both faith and morals are constantly evolving. The four Gospels, by the consensus of overall Christian history, are the center of the New Testament panorama, for they have supplied the main icons of Jesus. The Pauline Epistles have deeply influenced Christian theology and ethics, however, especially in the Protestant churches. Indeed, by supplying a rationale for Christianity's departure from the Jewish fold, they have directed the whole expansion of Christianity.

In its chronological rhythm (Pauline materials, Gospels, other materials), the pattern of the New Testament is provocative. We see believers living their faith in the risen Lord, bringing forward their memories of the historical Jesus, and trying to adapt their churches to the parousia's delay. By the time the canon had crystallized (380–90 C.E. in the West), the inner tensions of this rhythm had made the New Testament a very dynamic "book" indeed.

Why Was This Written?

The New Testament was written because of community needs.[23] The Pauline Epistles arose from pastoral motives, as a missionary sought further to instruct or correct young churches he knew. The Gospels arose from kerygmatic motives, as the churches sought to gather their memories of Jesus into a persuasive exposition of his teaching and meaning. The later New Testament materials addressed problems of order or doctrine caused by at least fifty years' experience of trying to live Christian faith in somewhat antagonistic environments.

Behind this commonsensical answer, however, lies a more philosophical response. The New Testament also came into being because the human spirit needs to objectify its beliefs, memories, problems, and convictions. This is perhaps clearest in the composition of the Gospels. While we may say that Matthew, for instance, appears to be a handbook for Jewish Christian religious teachers and thus serves a practical community need, the process of composing Matthew both sprang from and generated an outpouring of intuition about Jesus, the memory of Jesus, and conjecture as to what Jesus would have said in later circumstances.

As materials of Matthew and the other Gospels started to be used in liturgical settings, read out the way Revelation wanted to be read (Revelation 1:3), they drew more members of the community into this compositional process and made more members re-create again and again the reality of Jesus and his gospel. For example, Jesus' "Great Commission" to his disciples in Matthew 28:18–20, when read within the context of Christian worship and catechesis, is no longer a command and promise to just the eleven in the past, but a commission and word of assurance from the risen Jesus to all who would hear and give heed to his voice "today." Christians in Matthew's congregation in Antioch are made one with the disciples gathered on the Galilean mountaintop. The result was stories and symbols to live with, tales and teachings to indwell. As proclaimed, Christ became contemporary, yesterday and today the same. Correlatively, the pneumatic Christ of today and the textual Jesus of yesterday became mutually hermeneutical, interpreters of each other. Any discernment of the current Christ's operations or inspirations that flew in the face of the textual, historical Jesus became highly dubious. Any fruit of the present Christ's Spirit, any manifest wisdom and love, made the textual Jesus more pregnant with possibilities, an even richer stand-in for the physical Word become flesh.

The two answers are not separable, of course. Community needs included what we have called the philosophical response, and the philosophical response aimed at praxis, securing a better community life and faith. Somewhat knowingly and somewhat unknowingly, the authors of the New Testament worked in the most fruitful of circumstances, writing for real people with real needs that begged the deepest possible penetration of God's mystery. Thus the Pauline school finally found itself almost lost in the mystery of the divine love, the height and depth and length and breadth (Ephesians 3:18) of God's creative effort to give the divine life. Thus the Johannine school imagined its way into the recesses of the divine community, creating the speeches the Son "must" have sent the Father whose bosom he never left.

Of course, there are matters the New Testament barely takes up, such as political theory or tactics to transform business life. Even on these matters, however, the authors have left intriguing hints or implications. Moreover, in evaluating so highly the Spirit given to all believers, the Johannine school encourages us to think that Christians can generate the elaborations of faith any later time will require. In emphasizing good pastors, the Pastorals bequeath the further advice (sometimes complementary to the Johannine school, sometimes antagonistic) that church leaders, with their charism to preserve the deposit of faith from elaborations that would be destructive, are an always relevant resource. Taken generously, then, with a presumption of goodwill, the New Testament largely meets the questions it was composed to answer. In the Spirit and the community, believers usually can find sufficient light and strength to survive (and sometimes can find abundant love to flourish). For many, that is precisely what it means to call the New Testament "Scripture" or "inspired."[24]

What Background Does This Book Presuppose?

The New Testament presupposes both the world into which Jesus was born, a world that combined Jewish and Hellenistic elements, and the Hellenistic world into which the first disciples carried the Christian kerygma.[25] We have seen the concern of Judaism for Torah and Judaism's hopes for the coming of the Messiah. We have suggested the power of the mystery religions, which offered ways of salvation that many Gentiles found attractive. This does not mean, however, that the general culture into which Paul and the other early missionaries carried the gospel was ready to greet it with open arms. There were some sincere, even desperate seekers, but the culture at large was quite secular and self-satisfied: "The Hellenistic-Roman world had tried a thorough secularism, and they could have said that it works. They were not receptive to the suggestion that the world they had created lacked anything; and if it did, it was not religion, and certainly not a religion from the most obscure and backward corner of the Roman dominions; for that is what Palestine was."[26]

Against this background, the New Testament remembers Jesus as a teacher of exceptionally liberating power. More importantly, the entire New Testament assumes that his resurrection opened to both the Jewish and the Hellenistic worlds powers and possibilities they previously had only glimpsed. The main assumption of the New Testament, as a collection of documents written by people who had an intense Christian faith, and written for people of Christian faith, was that Jesus Christ, the risen Lord, was *the* treasure and key to human success (salvation, divine life).

The New Testament assumes that God has made human beings for such success, but that human beings on their own (apart from grace or the special initiatives of the kingdom) tend to miss such success. Their sin and weakness make them like blind people confronted with the light, sheep wandering without a shepherd. In the good news of Jesus the Christ, the authors and recipients of the New Testament materials found the Word of God that could convert sinners and moral weaklings into full human beings, hale children of a heavenly Father, bright pupils of a motherly Spirit. So New Testament Christianity assumed that its message was the most important thing in the world, a pearl of great price any people of sense would sell all they had to obtain.

What Lasting Significance Does This Have?

Malcolm Muggeridge, a curmudgeonly convert from skepticism to strong Christian faith, begins his very readable book *Jesus: The Man Who Lives* with an assessment of Jesus that most Christian believers would easily extend analogously to the New Testament (insofar as it bears on Jesus):

> The coming of Jesus into the world is the most stupendous event in human history. I say this as a Christian, recognizing, of course, that the coming into the world of a Mohammed or a Buddha must seem, in the eyes of a Moslem or Buddhist, of equal or even greater significance, and that had I been born in Mecca or Bangkok instead of in a south London suburb I might well have taken a different view. Similarly, for that matter, the coming into the world of a Karl Marx to a dedicated Marxist, or of a Mao Tse-tung to a dedicated Maoist. As it is, belonging to a civilization which began with the birth of Jesus some two thousand years ago, and reaching the conclusion—to me inescapable—that whatever is truly admirable in the achievements of the succeeding centuries, in art and literature, in music and architecture, in the quest for knowledge and the pursuit of justice and brotherliness in human relations, derives from that same event, I cannot but see it as towering sublimely above

all others. I have to add, too, that over and above this, the revelation Jesus provided, in his teaching, and in the drama of his life, death, and Resurrection, of the true purpose and destination of our earthly existence, seems to me, even by comparison with other such revelations, to be of unique value and everlasting validity.[27]

For people such as Muggeridge, the New Testament not only has great lasting significance, it bears to the world the most crucial message, the most decisive teacher, that human history has ever produced. People of other civilizations, as Muggeridge realizes, seldom will be prepared to agree. Case by case, the apologist for the crucial significance of the New Testament will have to show how the message of suffering love and resurrecting power applies—to African, Native American, Indian, or East Asian cultural traditions and problems. One index of the significance of the New Testament is precisely the outreach of the Christian gospel in this way today. Often the faith of the Hellenistic-European basin in which Christianity arose appears less vital today than the faith or interest of areas only recently come into contact with the New Testament message. Perhaps a major reason for this is that the profoundly human significance of the New Testament flames back into light and warmth whenever one puts off tired habituations and comes to its startling claims afresh.

So, for example, Shusaku Endo's *A Life of Jesus*, reworking the New Testament for Japanese readers, shines a new lamp on the Gospels. In its light both perennial and quite contemporary significances resurrect:

> Jesus as I depict him is a person who lived for love and still more love; and yet he was put to death, for he chose to live without violent resistance. My way of depicting Jesus is rooted in my being a Japanese novelist. I wrote this book for the benefit of Japanese readers who have no Christian tradition of their own and who know almost nothing about Jesus. . . . In brief, the Japanese tend to seek in their gods and buddhas a warm-hearted mother rather than a stern father. With this fact always in mind I tried not so much to depict God in the father-image that tends to characterize Christianity, but rather to depict the kind-hearted maternal aspect of God revealed to us in the personality of Jesus.[28]

Any book that can cross cultures and sexual stereotypes in this way, offering contemporary Asians a good news that absorbed Westerners two thousand years ago, must have overwhelming significance. Anyone hoping to prosper in the twenty-first century, when the world's cultures are only likely to interact even more, overlooks such significance at his or her spiritual peril.

SUMMARY

We began our conclusion by considering the diversity of the New Testament materials. Following James Dunn's lead, we took up successively Jewish Christianity, Hellenistic Christianity, apocalyptic Christianity, and early

Catholicism, contemplating each as an important stream that flowed into the New Testament whole.

Jewish Christianity was the matrix or home ground of Christian faith. Jesus' own thought-world was Jewish, the first disciples were Jewish, and earliest Christianity appeared, to its own adherents as well as to outsiders, a Jewish sect. From Judaism came Christian messianism, Christian mono-theism, and most of Christian ethics. Nonetheless, Christians obviously broke with Jews over the status of Jesus. After several decades of Church experience, they also moved far away from Jewish Torah. By the time that Christian reflection on Jesus had established his full divinity, through the high Christology variously displayed in John, Colossians, Hebrews, and other documents, the Jewish Christians reluctant to so glorify any man had become passé. In the Ebionite sect that arose in the middle of the second century, they became heretical.

Hellenistic Christianity was shaped by the dialogue between Christian faith and Greco-Roman thought. Often its prime developers were Jewish Christians raised in the diaspora. Hellenistic Christianity was in tension with Jewish (Hebrew) Christianity from the beginnings of Church history, as the first chapters of Acts reveal. Especially in the diaspora, the influence of tendencies that later matured into Gnosticism was quite important. Thus documents such as 1 Corinthians suggest Paul's stimulus from Gnosticism to think out Christian positions on such topics as wisdom and spiritual exaltation. The later Pauline literature advances this intellectual project, discoursing on the cosmic Christ and God's universal plan of salvation. The high Christology of John mentioned previously probably had similar stim-uli, as did the strong Johannine insistence on Jesus' full flesh. Insofar as John marks a boundary between an unacceptable Jewish restraint on Christ's privileges and an unacceptable Gnostic excess, it cuts off the major deviant vectors of the first two Christian streams.

Apocalyptic Christianity and early Catholicism further diversified the New Testament Church. Much of what Dunn calls "apocalyptic faith" might also be called eschatological: the expectation of the parousia. The Book of Revelation is the fullest New Testament specimen of this impor-tant early stream, but the eschatological discourses in the synoptics show that it was widespread and could claim a solid foundation in Jesus' own preaching. By focusing their hopes for the consummation of history on the risen Christ, early Christians specified the less precise hopes of Jewish apocalyptic. On the other hand, the reception of apocalyptic into the Chris-tian canon meant another vote to retain much Jewishness at Christianity's core.

Early Catholicism somewhat countered apocalyptic Christianity, in that much of its stimulus was the demise of eschatological expectations. By moving to stabilize Church doctrine and order, such documents as the Pastorals sought to adapt the Church to Hellenistic society. Johannine real-ized eschatology supports this adaptation (at a more theoretical level). Since the substance of the parousia has been present since the Incarnation of Christ, adaptation is quite legitimate. (However, since the world outside Christian faith is opposed to Christ's Spirit, adaptation is a problem.) Probably we should credit early Catholicism with playing a major role in Christianity's survival, although at what price this survival was purchased (what loss there was of earlier spiritual freedoms) scholars still debate.

To conclude our look at the diversity of the New Testament materials we considered their literary variety. As such disparate methods as textual criticism, source criticism, literary criticism, redaction criticism, form criticism, and even more recent approaches suggest, the New Testament documents are highly complex. Usually they have a rich history and admit several angles of interpretation. This literary variety suggests that a mature study of the New Testament begins with a confession that one has in hand no simple, obvious materials.

To suggest the unity of the New Testament materials we borrowed further from James Dunn. His survey covers nine points: the kerygma, the primitive confession, tradition, the use of the Old Testament, ministry, worship, sacraments, the Spirit, and Christology. Although the different streams and schools of the New Testament collectively bring forward a great variety of emphases under each of these headings, Dunn is able to find in each a certain unity as well. Regularly, this unity devolves from referring the disparate elements (for example, ways of preaching the gospel or confessing the core of faith) to Jesus the Christ. In the fusion of the historical Jesus with the risen Lord Dunn finds the natural center of what later became orthodoxy, an almost artless agreement on the crux of all acceptable faith. Thus the last category, Christology, emerged as the most crucial. Because they would all agree to be condensed to Jesus the Christ, the centers of the several different thought-worlds of early Christianity quite coincide.

Moving outside the New Testament to broader perspectives, we found even greater unity. Set in the spectrum of the world religions, for example, all of the New Testament materials, by their crucial reference to Jesus, immediately appear unified, siblings unmistakably related. Moreover, the consensus of even the earliest Christian documents on such matters as belief in a personal God, sin, creation, love, and grace serves to unite them over against the documents of many of their fellow human beings (who espouse quite different convictions). The death and resurrection of Christ, finally, is a decisive touchstone. To accept it as the prime hermeneutic of history is to declare oneself united to the Body of Christ. To deny it this status is to fall outside explicit Christian faith.[29] Insofar as Christianity proclaims a definitive grace radiating from the death and resurrection of Christ, it remains a scandalous religion, but one that all the New Testament authors gladly promote.

In our last retrospective, we reviewed the New Testament story. The New Testament, as a whole, places before us many themes, all of them dependent on Jesus Christ. Historically, one may speak of the time of Jesus, the first generations of disciples gathering experience and collecting memories, the Pauline literature, the evangelical literature, and the other rather miscellaneous materials. With several notable overlappings, they comprise the literary story, the way by which the text came to its current shape. The chronological rhythm of this seventy or so years' worth of exposition, memory, and practical application makes the New Testament a quite dynamic book.

Written from both community and philosophical needs, and presupposing the Jewish and Hellenistic backgrounds of Jesus and the early Church, the New Testament materials finally amount to a strong expression of what several groups of people discovered in a great teacher, martyr, and living presence almost two thousand years ago. Whether taken as the central inspiration of Western civilization, or as a new wisdom that other cultural areas are finding enriching, the materials remain full of relevance. The lasting significance of the New Testament is the light, life, and love the materials can still generate today.

STUDY QUESTIONS

1. Why did the earliest Christians think of themselves as an eschatological Israel?

2. What is the Jamesian position that keeps a strong Jewish presence in the New Testament?

3. In what sense was Jewish Christianity passed by as too conservative?

4. How did Gnostic tendencies in late antiquity influence Pauline Christianity?

5. How does the incarnational wisdom of the Gospel of John relate to Hellenism?

6. What were Jesus' eschatological convictions?

7. How does realized eschatology buttress early Catholicism?

8. How did early Catholicism help Christianity to survive?

9. What is *form criticism*?

10. How is Jesus Christ the unifying factor in the diverse early Christian conceptions of tradition?

11. How did Jesus become a new hermeneutic for the Old Testament?

12. Why should one believe that Jesus of Nazareth and the exalted Christ are one and the same?

13. How does taking a perspective outside the New Testament help to unify its materials?

14. How is the Christian conviction about a definitive grace emanating from the death and resurrection of Jesus Christ both scandalous and unifying?

15. What are the different chronological pulsations (phases, movements) in the New Testament story?

16. How did the story change with the opening of faith to the Gentiles?

17. In what sense was the New Testament written because of community needs?

18. How did Jesus' Jewish contemporaries tend to regard Gentiles?

19. Compare the statements from Muggeridge and Endo.

20. What is the central significance you find in the New Testament?

NOTES

1. See James D. G. Dunn, *Unity and Diversity in the New Testament* (Philadelphia: Westminster, 1977), pp. 235–366.

2. See Hans von Campenhausen, *The Foundation of the Christian Bible* (Philadelphia: Fortress, 1972), pp. 62–102.

3. Dunn, *Unity and Diversity in the New Testament*, pp. 265–66.

4. See Pheme Perkins, *The Gnostic Dialogue* (Ramsey, N.J.: Paulist, 1980).

5. See Dunn, *Unity and Diversity in the New Testament*, p. 309.

6. See Jack Dean Kingsbury, *Jesus Christ in Matthew, Mark, and Luke* (Philadelphia: Fortress, 1981), pp. 1–27.

7. See Victor Turner, *The Ritual Process* (Chicago: Aldine, 1969).

8. See Hans-Josef Klauck, *Hausgemeinde und Hauskirche im frühen Christentum* (Stuttgart: Katholisches Bibelwerk, 1981).

9. See Hans von Campenhausen, *Ecclesiastical Authority and Spiritual Power in the Church of the First Three Centuries* (Stanford: Stanford University Press, 1969).

10. Elaine Pagels, *The Gnostic Gospels* (New York: Random House, 1979), p. 142.

11. Raymond E. Collins, *Introduction to the New Testament* (Garden City, N.Y.: Doubleday, 1983), p. 77.

12. James Dunn, *Unity and Diversity in the New Testament*, pp. 11–231.

13. See Nils A. Dahl, *Jesus in the Memory of the Early Church* (Minneapolis: Augsburg, 1976).

14. Dunn, *Unity and Diversity in the New Testament*, p. 229.

15. Ninian Smart and Richard D. Hecht, eds., *Sacred Texts of the World: A Universal Anthology* (New York: Crossroad, 1982).

16. See James Dunn, *Unity and Diversity in the New Testament*, p. 229.

17. See F. E. Peters, *Children of Abraham* (Princeton, N.J.: Princeton University Press, 1982).

18. On the place of this argument in past Christian apologetics and its highly problematic character today, see Karl Rahner, *Concern for the Church* (New York: Crossroad, 1981), p. 17.

19. On the recent theology of grace, see Brian O. McDermott, S. J., *What Are They Saying About the Grace of Christ?* (Ramsey, N.J.: Paulist, 1984).

20. For a comparative layout of the world religions, see Denise Lardner Carmody and John Tully Carmody, *Ways to the Center*, 2nd ed. (Belmont, Calif.: Wadsworth, 1984). For an overview of Christian theology, history, and current experience that keeps grace basic, see Denise Lardner Carmody and John Tully Carmody, *Christianity: An Introduction* (Belmont, Calif.: Wadsworth, 1983).

21. See John Navone and Thomas Cooper, *Tellers of the Word* (New York: LeJacq, 1981).

22. See Eric Voegelin, *Order and History, Vol. 4: The Ecumenic Age* (Baton Rouge: Louisiana State University Press, 1974).

23. See Raymond E. Brown, *The Churches the Apostles Left Behind* (Ramsey, N.J.: Paulist, 1984).

24. See David Kelsey, *The Uses of Scripture* (Philadelphia: Fortress, 1975).

25. See John L. McKenzie, *The New Testament Without Illusions* (Chicago: Thomas More, 1980), pp. 7–18.

26. Ibid., p. 13.

27. Malcolm Muggeridge, *Jesus: The Man Who Lives* (New York: Harper & Row, 1975), p. 7.

28. Shusaku Endo, *A Life of Jesus* (Ramsey, N.J.: Paulist, 1978), p. 1.

29. See Karl Rahner, "Observations on the Problem of the 'Anonymous Christian,'" *Theological Investigations* (New York: Seabury, 1976), vol. 14, pp. 280–94.

Glossary

Acts The second of Luke's two volumes, giving a theological interpretation of the earliest Christian experiences and Paul's ministry.

Agape The sort of love that can be predicated of God—selfless, pure, willing to suffer.

Agnostic Professing not to know (whether God exists).

Allegorical Concerning the literary form that makes point-by-point correspondences between two different situations.

Anawim The poor who solicit God's special interest and concern.

Antinomian Having no regard for law or rule.

Apocalyptic The sort of literature that purports to derive from heavenly visions and usually offers a view of the future consoling to those who suffer for the faith.

Apocryphal "Hidden" writings, not admitted to the canon, that often purport to have been written by an authoritative (e.g., apostolic) author but in fact were not.

Apologetic Cast as a defense of a position or argument on its behalf.

Apologia The name of the literary form of apologetic writing.

Apostle One "sent" as an authoritative witness; sometimes restricted to the Christian disciples who had witnessed Jesus' sayings and doings from the beginning of his ministry to the resurrection.

Arianism A fourth-century heresy that denied the equality of the Logos with the Father in divinity.

Atheist One who does not believe in God.

Atman The Hindu notion of the soul or inmost substantial part.

Atonement Satisfaction, reparation.

Baptism The Christian sacrament of initiation into divine and Church life.

Bar mitzvah The Jewish ritual for (males') coming of age.

Bios theoretikos The Greek notion of the contemplative life that was the acme of human activity.

Canon A list of officially approved writings.

Canonical Officially accredited or authoritative; entered on the list of approved and directive documents.

Catechesis Instruction in faith.

Catholic Whole, universal, pertaining to all.

Charismatic Gifted, possessed of (divine) powers or talents.

Charis Grace, divine favor.

Charisms Graces, divine gifts.

Christ The anointed leader or deliverer sent by God.

Christendom The geographical realm of Christian faith and society.

Christology The study of the being and meaning of Jesus Christ.

Circumcision The Jewish rite by which males enter the covenant community.

Colossians An important letter from the Pauline school that deals with the sapiential dimensions of salvation and Christology.

Common sense Bernard Lonergan's term for the practical, shrewd, yet short-sighted kinds of intelligence that dominate the majority in any general human population.

Communion The Christian rite (eucharist, Lord's Supper) by which believers receive the body and blood of Christ.

Conciliar Concerning the general Church meetings that hammered out official doctrine in the early (especially the fourth and fifth) centuries.

Confirmation The Christian rite for passage into adulthood and receiving the Holy Spirit in order to be fit to be a mature witness to one's faith.

Connatural As though one had the same nature or character (e.g., grace is said to make the perception of the godly course of action "connatural").

Contingent Dependent for its being, begging explanation from something else.

Corban A Jewish legal practice allowing one to designate wealth for sacred uses while retaining control of it.

Corinthians Members of one of Paul's most important churches who occasioned the two of his letters that deal most strongly with disciplinary matters and best illumine the ecclesiology of the early urban Church.

Corporate personality A figure who stands for a collective, general, or even universal reality (e.g., "Adam" can stand for humanity at large, "Israel" can be depicted as a megapersonality or collective identity).

Cosmogony The birth or origin of the world (usually depicted in mythic terms).

Cosmology The study of the cosmos or full span of nature.

Covenant The solemn, almost legal bond established between God and Israel.

Covenant Law The Code or Teaching that lays out the behavioral implications of the Covenant.

Creator The maker or fashioner of the world (ultimately, from nothingness).

Critical Passing judgment or sifting evidence so as to arrive at a reasoned stance about the matter in question.

Deacons Helpers, traditionally said to have been designated for Church tasks that the apostles or later bishops and priests wished to share or relinquish.

Dead Sea Scrolls Writings found in the middle of this century near the Dead Sea in Israel that cast considerable light on the beliefs of Jewish sects such as the Essenes who flourished shortly before Jesus.

Decontextualism A current literary movement or theory that emphasizes the independence of the text from its historical origins.

Dei The Greek word for "must" or "have to" used by Gospel writers such as Luke to suggest a necessity in Jesus' sufferings and overall messianic pattern.

Demoniac One possessed or influenced by a demon.

Dialectical Having a back-and-forth, mutually influential character.

Diaspora The dispersion or existence outside Israel that characterized many Jews as exiled.

Didache An early Christian writing, supposedly presenting the teaching of the twelve apostles, that enjoyed much prestige but was not admitted into the canon.

Discernment of Spirits The determination of whether an inspiration comes from God or from unworthy (e.g., diabolical) sources.

Discipleship The following of a master or guide.

Divine liturgy The Christian eucharist or sacramental worship, especially as celebrated in the Eastern Orthodox churches.

Docetism An early Cristian heresy that denied the full reality of Jesus' humanity.

Doxology An expression of praise and giving glory.

Ebionites Early Christian heretics who overemphasized the Jewish Law and considered Jesus only an important prophet.

Ecclesial Concerning the Church.

Ecclesiology The study or theology of the Church.

Ecstatic That which takes one outside oneself.

Ecumene   The whole inhabited world.

Ecumenical   Concerning the whole inhabited world.

Ekklesia   The group that is called forth (the Church).

Empiricism   The philosophical position that gives primacy to data of experience or sensible facts.

Empiricist   A person holding or living by the primacy of data of experience or sensible facts.

Encyclical   A letter addressed to the whole Church.

Enthusiasm   The state of being filled by the divine.

Ephesians   A letter from the followers of Paul that deals with the cosmic dimensions of salvation and the Church.

Epistle to the Hebrews   An important New Testament writing (a sermon rather than a letter) that interprets Jesus as the great high priest who fulfills Jewish religion.

Eschatology   Concerning the last things or final age.

Eschaton   The consummation of history or definitive coming of God.

Essenes   A sectarian Jewish group, contemporary with Jesus, that sought a pure religious life by withdrawing to the area near the Dead Sea.

Euangelion   The good news or gospel.

Eucharist   The Christian sacrament of thanksgiving that recalls the death and resurrection of Christ and offers believers communion with him through consecrated bread and wine.

Evangelical   Concerning the gospel or taking the gospel as its primary authority.

Evangelist   One who preaches or promotes the gospel.

Evangelization   The process of preaching or promoting the gospel.

Exegesis   The interpretation of texts.

Exegete   One who interprets texts.

Existential   Concerning one's concrete, personally engaged being.

Exodus   The escape of the Hebrews from Egypt.

Exorcise   To cast out a malign spirit.

Expiation   Making amends or reparation for a wrong.

Faith   Wholehearted trust and commitment.

Fides   The Latin word for faith.

Fundamentalism   So focused upon basic things that a literalist mentality results.

Galatians   The writing of Paul that deals most critically with the Jewish Law.

Gens   The Latin word for people or race.

Gentile   Non-Jewish.

Glossolalia   The gift of tongues or speaking in a strange trancic language.

Gnosis   The Greek word for (secret or special) knowledge.

Gnosticism   A movement that claimed special knowledge or wisdom, usually regarding salvation.

Gospel   A proclamation of good news or salvation coming from Jesus Christ, or an account of Jesus' life, death, and resurrection.

Grace   Divine favor or divine life.

Haggadic   Concerning Jewish folklore or concrete, storied teaching.

Halakic   Concerning Jewish law or religious codes.

Hamartia   A Greek word for sin ("missing the mark").

Hellenistic   Pertaining to the cultural world inspired by Alexander the Great and Greek ideals.

Hermas   The reputed author of an important early Christian writing (sometimes called the Shepherd) that deals with Church penitential practices.

Hermeneutical   Concerning interpretation.

Hierarchy   The levels of Church authority.

Horizon   The mental outlook that determines much of what one can appreciate.

Hyperbole   Exaggeration.

Incarnation   The Word's taking flesh.

Inerrant   Being without error.

Infallible   Being incapable of erring.

James   The leader of the Jerusalem church; a canonical letter that stresses the importance of religious works.

John   The fourth Gospel, remarkable for its high Christology and sacramental symbolism.

Judaizers   Early Christians who wanted to retain the obligations of the Jewish Law.

Jude   One of the twelve apostles; a minor canonical letter.

Kairos   A time of special opportunity or crisis.

Karma   The Indian concept of a moral law of cause and effect.

Kenosis   The "emptying" that is hymned by Philippians 2:5–11.

Kenotic   Concerning Christ's emptying.

Kerygmatic   Pertaining to the heralding or announcement of the Christian message.

Kosher   Fitting, in keeping with Jewish law.

Liturgical   Concerning the "work of the people" or communal prayer of the Christian community.

Logos   The Word expressing the divine intelligence.

Lord's Supper The Christian sacramental commemoration of Jesus' last meal with his friends; the Christian eucharist.

Luke The synoptic Gospel that best translates the significance of Jesus for Gentiles and God-fearers.

Mahakaruna The Buddhist virtue of great compassion.

Manicheans Early Christian heretics who held to a dualism of good and evil and tended to depreciate the flesh.

Maranatha The early Christian prayer that the Lord speedily return to consummate history and relieve believers' sufferings.

Mark Probably the first synoptic Gospel and the one most concerned with Jesus' suffering messiahship.

Mass The Catholic term for the Lord's Supper or divine liturgy.

Matthew The synoptic Gospel most concerned to show Jesus as the most authoritative interpreter of God's Law and will.

Messiah The Christ or divinely sent deliverer.

Messianic Pertaining to the messiah.

Metanoia Greek term for change of mind, conversion.

Methodological Concerning the proper procedures.

Midrash A gloss, commentary, or explanation of a biblical text.

Mishnah An early collection of Jewish interpretations of the oral Torah.

Mnemosyne Greek term for memory.

Monotheists People who believe in only one God.

Mystery A surplus or excess of meaning.

Mystery religions Movements in the ancient Greco-Roman world that promised rites and teachings conducive to salvation.

Natural theology The explanations of God that one may derive from nature or reason unaided by revelation.

Orthodox Having the character of right praise and faith.

Pantokrator The Lord of All.

Parables Pointed, paradoxical, challenging teaching stories such as those used by Jesus in the Gospels.

Paraclete The helper or advocate, used in the Johannine writings mainly of the Holy Spirit but also of Jesus.

Parousia The return of the Christ in power to consummate history and render judgment.

Paschal Pertaining to Passover or Easter.

Paschal Letter A letter occasioned by Passover or Easter.

Passible Able to suffer.

Passion narratives The Gospel stories of Jesus' suffering, trial, and death.

Paul   The leading Apostle to the Gentiles and author of numerous New Testament Epistles.

Pericope   An independent textual unit.

Pesher   A Jewish form of commentary influential in the first century C.E.

Peter   The leader of the apostles; two canonical letters of middling importance attributed to the leader of the apostles.

Pharisee   A member of a lay Jewish movement contemporary with Jesus that laid great emphasis on a generous fulfillment of Torah.

Philemon   A minor canonical letter attributed to Paul and concerned with the return of a runaway slave.

Philippians   An important letter of Paul that conveys his sense of Christ's humility and generosity on human beings' behalf.

Pleroma   The fullness (of the divine mystery).

Pneuma   Greek term for Spirit.

Pneumatic   Spiritual or inspired.

Polytheism   Belief in many gods.

Polyvalence   Having many values or weights.

Prophet   A spokesperson for God or a seer whose special character is calling present times to account for their failings.

Pseudepigraphy   Writing falsely attributed to an authoritative or prestigious author (a practice relatively accepted in antiquity).

Quelle   German word for "source" (basis of "Q" according to some).

Qumran   Essene community contemporary with Jesus.

Realized eschatology   Understanding of the last things or final events that says they have substantially occurred already (e.g., the Johannine notion that with the Incarnation and death-resurrection of Christ the end-time has in principle arrived).

Redactor   An editor or final shaper of a text.

Revelation   Disclosure (usually by God).

Revelation   Last book of the New Testament canon; Christian apocalypse.

Righteousness   Rectitude, propriety, having a proper relationship.

Romans   Major letter of Paul spelling out his mature sense of sin and grace.

Sacerdotal   Priestly.

Saddiq   Jewish term for a righteous or just person.

Salvation   Process of being made whole and freed from destruction.

Sanhedrin   Jewish authoritative council of Jesus' day.

Sapiential   Concerning wisdom.

Schism   A split or fracture (of the community).

Scripture   Writing held to be sacred or authorized by God.

Sect   A party or schismatic group.

Seers   Those gifted with visions.

Semeia   Signs.

Semiotics   The study of signs and symbols.

Septuagint   Greek translation of the Hebrew Bible (supposedly by seventy scholars).

Shalom   Jewish term for peace and fulfillment.

Shekinah   The glorious divine presence.

Shema   The call that expresses Israel's belief in one God (Deuteronomy 6).

Structuralism   A method of literary analysis that focuses on underlying, often supposedly general human patterns.

Syncretism   The tendency to run several things (e.g., religious traditions) together so that they meld or form a hybrid.

Synoptic   Having the quality of being able to be taken in at a glance (applied to the first three Gospels because if one places their contents in parallel columns the majority of the similar treatments can be taken in at a glance.)

Tanak   The Law-Prophets-Writings that constitute the Hebrew Bible.

Thanksgiving   Rendering gratitude to God for benefits received.

Theodicy   The attempt to justify God in the face of evil.

Theosis   Greek term for divinization or grace as divine life.

Thessalonians   Community Christianized by Paul; two canonical letters of minor importance (except concerning eschatology).

Timothy   Supposed recipient of two Pastoral Epistles.

Tithes   Contributions of one-tenth of one's income.

Titus   Supposed recipient of a Pastoral Epistle.

Torah   Jewish term for Teaching, Divine Guidance, Law.

Tradition   What has been handed down as authoritative and helpful.

Transcendent   Going beyond (this-worldly limitations).

Trinitarian   Concerning the Christian God as Father-Son-Spirit.

Triumphalistic   Stressing the victory of Christ (usually excessively).

Yom Kippur   Jewish solemn Day of Atonement (for sins of past year).

Annotated Bibliography

ABERNATHY, DAVID. *Understanding the Teaching of Jesus.* New York: Seabury, 1983. A revision of Norman Perrin's lectures that offer a good overview, especially of "The Kingdom of God."

AUNE, DAVID. *Prophecy in Early Christianity and the Ancient Mediterranean World.* Grand Rapids, Mich.: Eerdmans, 1983. A large, rather technical but important treatment of a very significant early Christian phenomenon, set against the background of the contemporary Mediterranean world.

BARR, JAMES. *Holy Scripture: Canon, Authority, and Criticism.* Philadelphia: Westminster, 1983. Perceptive remarks about the function of the canon in the development of Christianity.

BARTH, MARKUS. *Ephesians.* Garden City, N.Y.: Doubleday, 1974. The Anchor Bible volumes, exhaustive but now somewhat dated.

BETZ, HANS DIETER. *Galations.* Philadelphia: Fortress, 1979. A massive recent study framing much of the contemporary discussion.

BORING, EUGENE. *The Words of the Risen Jesus.* Cambridge: University Press, 1983. A technical study that tries to distinguish between the words of the historical Jesus and the words of the risen Jesus as spoken through early Christian prophets.

BROWN, RAYMOND E. *The Churches the Apostles Left Behind.* New York: Paulist, 1984. Readable lectures, by a leading Catholic New Testament scholar, that bring out well the diversity of the New Testament communities.

BROWN, RAYMOND E. *The Community of the Beloved Disciple.* New York: Paulist, 1979. Probably the most creative and respected hypothesis about the complicated background of the Johannine literature.

BROWN, RAYMOND E. *The Epistles of John.* Garden City, N.Y.: Doubleday, 1982. An exhaustive study that completes the author's Anchor Bible work on the Johannine literature.

BROWN, RAYMOND E. *The Gospel According to John.* Garden City, N.Y.: Doubleday, 1966, 1970. The two-volume Anchor Bible study by the leading American scholar of John.

BROWN, RAYMOND E., and MEIER, JOHN P. *Antioch and Rome*. Ramsey, N.J.: Paulist, 1983. Interesting studies that bring out the prominence of Jewish Christianity in both of these early Christian centers.

CAMPENHAUSEN, HANS VON. *Ecclesiastical Authority and Spiritual Power in the Church of the First Three Centuries*. Stanford: Stanford University Press, 1969. A balanced, comprehensive survey of the relation between ecstatic authority and institutional demands.

CAMPENHAUSEN, HANS VON. *The Formation of the Christian Bible*. Philadelphia: Fortress, 1972. The finest treatment of the Christian canon presently available.

CASSIDY, RICHARD J. *Jesus, Politics, and Society: A Study of Luke's Gospel*. Maryknoll, N.Y.: Orbis, 1978. An analysis of Lukan theology as a theology of liberation.

CHARLESWORTH, JAMES H., ed. *John and Qumran*. London: Chapman, 1972. A series of essays dealing with Johannine portraits of Jesus against the background of Qumran—cautious, sober treatments.

CHARLESWORTH, JAMES H., ed. *The Pseudepigrapha of the Old Testament*, 2 vols. Garden City, N.Y.: Doubleday, 1983, 1984. Internationally acclaimed translations, with critical introductions and notes. Accessible to laity and scholars alike. An important work.

COLLINS, ADELA YARBRO. *Crisis and Catharsis: The Power of the Apocalypse*. Philadelphia: Westminster, 1984. A solid sociological study of the roots of the theology of the Book of Revelation.

COLLINS, JOHN J. *The Apocalyptic Vision of the Book of Daniel*. Missoula, Mont.: Scholars Press, 1977. An interpretation of Daniel that sheds light on the New Testament Book of Revelation.

COLLINS, RAYMOND F. *Introduction to the New Testament*. Garden City, N.Y.: Doubleday, 1983. A solid, somewhat technical treatment of text criticism and other staples of New Testament scholarship.

CONZELMANN, HANS. *1 Corinthians*. Philadelphia: Fortress, 1975. A solid, now somewhat dated study of a very important writing; by a leading European scholar.

CONZELMANN, HANS. *The Theology of Saint Luke*. New York: Harper & Row, 1960. Perhaps the most influential study of the past generation.

COPE, O. LAMAR. *Matthew: A Scribe Trained for the Kingdom of Heaven*. Washington, D.C.: Catholic Biblical Association, 1976. A slim but helpful monograph focusing on Matthew's use of Old Testament quotations and his tailoring of the narrative to accommodate them.

CULPEPPER, R. ALAN. *Anatomy of the Fourth Gospel*. Philadelphia: Fortress, 1983. A solid literary study that stresses the dramatic structure.

CULPEPPER, R. ALAN. *The Johannine School*. Missoula, Mont.: Scholars Press, 1975. Places the likely multiple Johannine authorship against the background of the philosophical schools and associations of the Mediterranean world.

DAHL, NILS A. *The Crucified Messiah*. Minneapolis: Augsburg, 1974. A programmatic collection of essays by a leading New Testament scholar. Reopens the question of the historical Jesus by focusing on the trial and crucifixion narratives.

DAHL, NILS A. *Jesus in the Memory of the Early Church*. Minneapolis: Augsburg, 1976. A sequel to *The Crucified Messiah* that focuses on the ways in which early Christianity preserved and transmitted its traditions about Jesus.

DAVIES, W. D. *The Setting of the Sermon on the Mount.* Cambridge: University Press, 1963. The classical study of the Sermon on the Mount. Sets the teaching of the Matthean Jesus against the background of the Pharisaic Judaism that was emerging after the destruction of the Temple in 70 C.E.

DODD, C. H. *The Apostolic Preaching and Its Developments.* New York: Harper & Row, 1964. The pioneering study of the speeches in Acts as examples of the early Christian kerygma.

DODD, C. H. *The Interpretation of the Fourth Gospel.* Cambridge: University Press, 1968. An important work by the leading Johannine scholar of the past generation.

DONAHUE, JOHN. *Are You the Christ?* Missoula, Mont.: Scholars Press, 1973. A fairly technical study of the trial of Jesus in the Gospel of Mark.

DOTY, WILLIAM G. *Letters in Primitive Christianity.* Philadelphia: Fortress, 1973. An accessible introduction to Pauline letter writing in the context of late antiquity.

DUNN, JAMES D. G. *Unity and Diversity in the New Testament.* Philadelphia: Westminster, 1977. A very thorough study that brings out most of the complexity and nuance.

ENDO, SHUSAKU. *A Life of Jesus.* Ramsey, N.J.: Paulist, 1978. An interesting study by a Japanese novelist that stresses Jesus' solidarity with the suffering and poor.

FARMER, WILLIAM R. *The Synoptic Problem.* Philadelphia: Fortress, 1982. The classic objection to the theory of the priority of Mark as the solution to the synoptic problem (Farmer argues for the priority of Matthew).

FARRER, AUSTIN. *A Rebirth of Images.* Gloucester, Mass.: Peter Smith, 1970. A somewhat idiosyncratic but still stimulating study by a well-regarded Angelican theologian.

FITZMYER, JOSEPH A. *The Gospel According to Luke I–IX.* Garden City, N.Y.: Doubleday, 1981. The first volume of a two-volume exhaustive study for the Anchor Bible; probably the most important current work.

FORD, J. MASSYNGBERDE. *Revelation.* Garden City, N.Y.: Doubleday, 1975. A large and thorough study for the Anchor Bible series.

FORTNA, ROBERT. *The Gospel of Signs.* Cambridge: University Press, 1970. An important treatment of the miracle tradition in the fourth Gospel—quite technical.

FRANCIS, FRED O., and MEEKS, WAYNE A. *Conflict at Colossae.* Missoula, Mont.: Scholars Press, 1975. A thought-provoking attempt to clarify the heresy behind the letter to the Colossians—sociologically oriented.

FREND, W. H. C. *The Rise of Christianity.* Philadelphia: Fortress, 1984. A massive (1000-page) overview of the first six centuries.

GAGER, JOHN G. *Kingdom and Community: The Social World of Early Christianity.* Englewood Cliffs, N.J.: Prentice-Hall, 1975. A slim but stimulating text on the sociology of Christian origins.

GROLLENBERG, LUCAS. *Jesus.* Philadelphia: Westminster, 1978. A lucid and beautiful interpretation of the human personality at the center of the New Testament.

GROLLENBERG, LUCAS. *Paul.* Philadelphia: Westminster, 1978. A short, readable study of the main writings of Paul and of the apostle's own personality.

HARNER, PHILIP. *The "I Am" of the Fourth Gospel.* Philadelphia: Fortress, 1970. A short but important examination, set against the backdrop of Old Testament names and titles for God—readable.

HELLWIG, MONIKA K. *Jesus: The Compassion of God.* Wilmington, Del.: Michael Glazier, 1983. A readable survey of contemporary Christology with a stress on liberation themes.

HENGEL, MARTIN. *Acts and the History of Earliest Christianity.* Philadelphia: Fortress, 1979. An attempt to reclaim Acts as a window onto the world of Paul; by a widely respected scholar.

JERVELL, JACOB. *Luke and the People of God.* Minneapolis: Augsburg, 1972. A perfect contrast to Hengel's work, showing well the Lukan shaping of Paul's ministry.

JEWETT, ROBERT. *A Chronology of Paul's Life.* Philadelphia: Fortress, 1979. A useful overview that points out most of the problems in dating and situating the Pauline materials.

JOHNSON, LUKE T. *The Literary Function of Possessions in Luke-Acts.* Missoula, Mont.: Scholars Press, 1977. An attempt to understand Luke's preoccupation with wealth and almsgiving as symbols of idolatry and genuine religion.

JUEL, DONALD. *An Introduction to New Testament Literature.* Nashville: Abingdon, 1978. An excellent introduction to the literary structure of the New Testament narratives.

JUEL, DONALD. *Luke-Acts: The Promise of History.* Atlanta: John Knox, 1983. A fresh treatment that brings out the Jewish aspects of Lukan thought.

JUEL, DONALD. *Messiah and Temple.* Missoula, Mont.: Scholars Press, 1977. A fairly technical study of Mark's account of Jesus' trial, stressing the Markan irony.

KÄSEMANN, ERNST. *Essays on New Testament Themes.* London: SCM Press, 1964. An important collection of essays by one of the great Protestant scholars of Paul.

KECK, LEANDER. *Paul and His Letters.* Philadelphia: Fortress, 1979. A good study of Pauline theology, often somewhat convoluted (as befits its subject matter).

KEE, HOWARD C. *Christian Origins in Sociological Perspective.* Philadelphia: Westminster, 1980. Stimulating studies of the likely community contexts of the various New Testament writings.

KEE, HOWARD C. *Jesus and History,* 2nd ed. New York: Harcourt Brace Jovanovich, 1977. A good introduction to the history and teaching of the Gospels.

KELSEY, DAVID. *The Uses of Scripture in Recent Theology.* Philadelphia: Fortress, 1975. A good theological treatment that gives nuance and depth to the notion of "Scripture."

KINGSBURY, JACK DEAN. *Jesus Christ in Matthew, Mark, and Luke.* Philadelphia: Fortress, 1981. A helpful introduction to the synoptics' presentation of Jesus, intended for pastors and laity. Has a good commentary on Q.

KINGSBURY, JACK DEAN. *Matthew: Structure, Christology, Kingdom.* Philadelphia: Fortress, 1975. One of the first major attempts to reorient the study of Matthew (away from a fivefold Mosaic pattern).

KLEIN, CHARLOTTE. *Anti-Judaism in Christian Theology.* Philadelphia: Fortress, 1978. An important study, focusing honestly on the theme of anti-Judaism in both the New Testament and later Christianity.

KOESTER, HELMUT. *Introduction to the New Testament.* Philadelphia: Fortress, 1984, 2 vols. Volume 1 situates Christianity within the ancient Greco-Roman religious world. Volume 2 treats canonical and extracanonical Christian literature with reference to its geographical site of origin.

KRODEL, GERHARD, ed. *Proclamation Commentaries: Ephesians, Colossians, 2 Thessalonians, The Pastoral Epistles.* Philadelphia: Fortress, 1978. Succinct commentaries on the background, main ideas, and critical problems of these letters.

LEON-DUFOUR, XAVIER. *Dictionary of the New Testament.* San Francisco: Harper & Row, 1980. A useful, sometimes conservative and fragmentary word book.

MCKENZIE, JOHN L. *The New Testament without Illusion.* Chicago: Thomas More, 1980. Clear, biting essays by a distinguished Roman Catholic Scripture scholar and Church critic.

MALHERBE, ABRAHAM J. *Social Aspects of Early Christianity,* 2nd ed. Philadelphia: Fortress, 1983. One of the first and most successful sociological approaches, focusing on the Pauline communities.

MANSON, PAUL D. *The Dawn of Apocalyptic,* rev. ed. Philadelphia: Fortress, 1979. A very technical treatment of the beginnings of Jewish apocalyptic in the religious turmoil that reigned after the Babylonian exile.

MARSHALL, L. HOWARD. *The Gospel of Luke.* Grand Rapids, Mich.: Eerdmans, 1978. A thorough study amenable to evangelical viewpoints.

MEEKS, WAYNE A. *The First Urban Christians.* New Haven: Yale University Press, 1983. An impressive sociological study of Pauline Christianity.

MEEKS, WAYNE A. *The Prophet King.* Leiden: E. J. Brill, 1967. A technical, important study of the portrait of Jesus in the fourth Gospel. Stresses the Samaritan background.

MEYERS, ERIC M., and STRANGE, JAMES F. *Archeology, the Rabbis, and Early Christianity.* Nashville: Abingdon, 1981. A pioneering study of both Judaism and early Christianity on the basis of material cultural remains.

MIRANDA, JOSÉ. *Being and the Messiah.* Maryknoll, N.Y.: Orbis, 1977. A study of Johannine realized eschatology as liberation theology.

MUGGERIDGE, MALCOLM. *Jesus: The Man Who Lives.* New York: Harper & Row, 1975. A vivid portrait by a crusty agnostic-turned-evangelical.

NEILL, STEPHEN. *Jesus through Many Eyes.* Philadelphia: Fortress, 1976. Well-written, somewhat dated presentations of the different New Testament theologies.

NEUSNER, JACOB. *Judaism: The Evidence of the Mishnah.* Chicago: University of Chicago Press, 1981. Discussion of early Rabbinic Judaism that sheds light on the contemporary Christian beginnings.

NOLAN, ALBERT. *Jesus before Christianity.* Maryknoll, N.Y.: Orbis, 1976. A spare, humanistic treatment by a South African liberation theologian.

PARRINDER, GEOFFREY. *Jesus in the Qur'an.* New York: Oxford University Press, 1977. A fine survey of how Jesus appears in Muslim revelation.

PATTE, DANIEL. *Paul's Faith and the Power of the Gospel.* Philadelphia: Fortress, 1983. A structural analysis of Paul's understanding of the Christian faith and gospel.

PERKINS, PHEME. *The Gnostic Dialogue.* New York: Paulist, 1980. A good study of the affinities of Gnosticism to early Christianity and the differences.

PERKINS, PHEME. *Hearing the Parables of Jesus.* New York: Paulist, 1981. A readable study of Jesus' parables by a well-regarded scholar and popularizer.

PERRIN, NORMAN. *Jesus and the Language of the Kingdom.* Philadelphia: Fortress, 1976. Perhaps the leading study of this central synoptic concept.

PERRIN, NORMAN. *A Modern Pilgrimage in New Testament Christology.* Philadelphia: Fortress, 1975. How the mind of a leading scholar of the synoptics evolved regarding the teaching and roles of Jesus.

PERRIN, NORMAN. *Rediscovering the Teaching of Jesus.* New York: Harper & Row, 1976. A classic example of form criticism, seeking to isolate the authentic sayings of Jesus and recapture the central importance of the Kingdom of God.

PERRIN, NORMAN. *The Resurrection according to Matthew, Mark, and Luke.* Philadelphia: Fortress, 1977. Solid, somewhat radical textual studies by a leading synoptic critic.

PERRIN, NORMAN. *What Is Redaction Criticism?* Philadelphia: Fortress, 1969. A brief but insightful essay on the fruits of this method; brilliant on Mark 8 as a particular example.

PETERS, F. E. *Children of Abraham.* Princeton, N.J.: Princeton University Press, 1982. A comparative study of Judaism, Christianity, and Islam with considerable attention to their scriptural character.

RICOEUR, PAUL. *Essays on Biblical Interpretation.* Philadelphia: Fortress, 1980. Stimulating but demanding hermeneutical studies by a leading European philosopher of language.

ROWLAND, CHRISTOPHER. *The Open Heaven.* New York: Crossroad, 1982. A recent attempt to understand apocalyptic in broader terms.

SALDARINI, ANTHONY. *Jesus and Passover.* Ramsey, N.J.: Paulist, 1984. A good popular presentation of how Passover figures in the Passion narratives of the Gospels.

SANDMEL, SAMUEL. *Anti-Semitism in the New Testament.* Philadelphia: Fortress, 1978. A thoughtful, sympathetic, but candid examination of anti-Jewish polemic in the New Testament.

SANDMEL, SAMUEL. *We Jews and Jesus.* New York: Oxford University Press, 1973. A pioneering treatment of the affinities Jews find with the New Testament Jesus and the problems.

SCHILLEBEECKX, EDWARD. *Christ.* New York: Seabury, 1980. The second of two massive volumes on Christology, focusing on the New Testament experience of grace (especially good on Hebrews and John).

SCHILLEBEECKX, EDWARD. *Jesus.* New York: Seabury, 1979. The first volume of Schillebeeckx's "Experiment," dealing very thoroughly with the synoptics and concluding that the historical Jesus is the interpretational crux.

SCHÜSSLER-FIORENZA, ELISABETH. *In Memory of Her.* New York: Crossroad, 1983. A feminist text-critical and theological reconstruction of Christian origins; finds women more prominent than has been the usual picture.

SCHÜSSLER-FIORENZA, ELISABETH. *Invitation to the Book of Revelation.* Garden City, N.Y.: Doubleday, 1981. A brief study by a leading feminist liberationist critic.

SCHWEIZER, EDWARD. *The Letter to the Colossians.* Minneapolis: Augsburg, 1982. A thorough, scholarly treatment.

SLOYAN, GERARD S. *Jesus in Focus: A Life in Its Setting*. Mystic, Conn.: Twenty-Third Publications, 1983. A wonderful short treatment, humane and well abreast of current scholarship.

STENDAHL, KRISTER. *The School of St. Matthew*. Philadelphia: Fortress, 1968. A pioneering work, no longer the state of the discussion but still stimulating.

THEISSEN, GERD. *The Miracle Stories of the Early Christian Tradition*. Philadelphia: Fortress, 1983. A thorough and sympathetic treatment of the traditions of Jesus' wonder-working and signs for faith.

THEISSEN, GERD. *The Social Setting of Pauline Christianity*. Philadelphia: Fortress, 1982. A masterful, ground-breaking collection of essays, focusing on Corinth.

THEISSEN, GERD. *Sociology of Early Palestinian Christianity*. Philadelphia: Fortress, 1977. A sociological analysis of the Jesus movement against the background of first-century Palestine—highly perceptive and quite radical.

TYSON, JOSEPH B. *The New Testament and Early Christianity*. New York: Macmillan, 1984. A text that places the New Testament literature in the context of Christian history to the end of the second century.

VERMES, GEZA. *The Dead Sea Scrolls*. Philadelphia: Fortress, 1977. The best English translation, with excellent introductions.

VERMES, GEZA. *Jesus the Jew*. London: Fontana/Collins, 1976. An influential study of the Jewish background to the Gospels and Jesus' religious profile.

WALASKAY, PAUL. *And So We Came to Rome*. New York: Cambridge University Press, 1983. A study of the political outlook of Acts that finds it relatively supportive of the Roman empire.

WILKEN, ROBERT. *The Myth of Christian Beginnings*. Notre Dame: University of Notre Dame Press, 1980. A candid and thought-provoking study of how Christianity romanticized its beginnings.

ESTIMATED APPROXIMATE MEMBERSHIP OF WORLD'S RELIGIONS (in thousands)*

Religion	North America	South America	Europe	Asia	Africa	Oceania	Total
Christianity	252,500	196,600	337,678	104,100	147,076	18,782	1,056,693
Roman Catholic	138,876	185,251	178,033	57,265	57,000	5,216	621,640
Eastern Orthodox	5,649	335	47,070	2,763	9,402	408	65,645
Protestant	107,935	10,993	112,577	44,071	80,675	13,158	369,408
Judaism	7,612	750	4,644	4,009	232	74	17,320
Islam	1,581	406	20,191	380,069	152,944	87	555,277
Zoroastrianism	2.75	2.6	14	224.4	.9	1	245.6
Shintoism	50	—	—	33,000	—	—	33,050
Taoism	33.25	12.975	13.5	20,500	.85	2.9	20,563.5
Confucianism	99.75	58.9	450.5	162,500	2.55	18.4	163,130
Buddhism	336.3	241.1	238.3	250,097	15	23.7	250,952
Hinduism	309.1	637.4	442.9	459,709	1,166	326.5	462,599
All Religions	262,483	198,709	363,672	1,414,207	301,436.5	19,315	2,559,821
Total Population	389,914	259,644	761,195	2,771,419	516,037	23,677	4,721,886

* Source: 1984 Encyclopedia Brittanica yearbook

Index

Abernathy, David, 378-79, 381, 394
Abraham, 50, 347
Action of God, 378-81
Acts, 230-63, 390-91, 400-401, 404, 416
Adam, 65, 66
Agabus, 245, 254
Agape, 339
Agreement, points of, 407-9
Aland, Kurt, 406
Almsgiving theme in Acts, 254
Ananias, 236, 239, 253
Angelology, 327
Annas, 291
Annunciation, 190-92
Antichrist, 338, 339
Antiochene Christians, 240-42, 252, 254
Anti-Semitism, 267, 298
Apocalyptic: discourses, 124-25, 213; tradition, 20-21, 73-74, 133-34, 324-25. *See also* Revelation, Book of
Apocalyptic Christianity, 402-4
Apologia, 48, 106
Apostles, choosing of, 197
Aquila, 244
Areopagus, Paul's speech at, 243-44
Arianism, 77
Ascension, 233. *See also* Resurrection
Astrology, Revelation and, 327
Athanasius, 7
Augustine, 67, 328
Authenticity, historical, 9
Authority of Jesus, 111-13, 154-55

Babylon, 18, 20, 319-20
Banquet, parable of great, 207-8
Baptism, 99, 150, 151, 195, 239, 353
Barclay, William, 84
Barnabas, 239-42
Barrett, C. K., 48
Barth, Markus, 87
Beatitudes, 152, 181, 183, 197-99
"Beloved disciple," 265, 266, 295-300
Bethesda, cure by pool of, 275
Birth of Jesus, 146-49, 189-94, 225
Bishops, 358, 362
Bread of life, Jesus as, 276-78
Bride of Christ, 90, 92, 319-20
Brown, Raymond E., 63, 146, 189, 220, 268-69, 286, 336-37, 340, 341, 350
Bultmann, Rudolf, 255

Caiaphas, 170, 171, 284, 291
Caird, C. B., 323-24
Camus, Albert, 12-13
Cana, Jesus' signs at, 271, 274
Canonicity, 7-9
Cassidy, Richard J., 253, 254-55
Catholicism, early, 220, 358, 363, 364-65, 404-6
Chadwick, H., 90

Character reformation, 180-81
Charisms of Church life, 42-43
Children, blessing of, 122, 166
Children of God, 338, 339
Christian living, 79-80, 89, 188
"Christogenesis," 78
Christologies, 119-23, 390-93, 409. *See also* Jesus; specific Gospels
Church, the: advice to, 165; as Bride of Christ, 90, 92, 319-20; doctrine, 362; early Catholicism, 220, 358, 363, 364-65, 404-6; hierarchy in early, 50; in Jerusalem, 233-38, 239; Matthew's view of, 143-44; membership, 21, 99-100; order, 358, 363; Pauline view, 95
Circumcision, 34-36, 59, 240, 242
1 Clement, 344
Clementines, 398
Collins, Adela Yarbro, 311
Collins, John J., 326
Collins, Raymond, 406
Colossians, 74-84, 102
Community, Christian, 221, 337, 340-41, 358, 359, 382-83, 417, 418
Community service, mandate to, 297
Compromise as purpose of Acts, 251
Conception of Jesus, 147-48, 190
Conciliar debates, 54
Confession, 62, 408
Confirmation, 239
Confucians, 37-38
Conscience, 41
Contemplative prayer, 223
Continuity theme in Acts, 249-52
Conzelmann, Hans, 39, 218, 222, 251, 256
Corban, 117
Corinth, Paul's mission in, 244
Corinthians, letters to, 38-49, 384, 385
Corporate personality, 65
Cosmogony, 317
Cosmology, 82
Counselor, 266, 267, 287
Covenant, 18, 348
Covenant Law, 34-37, 59, 60, 64-65, 66, 80, 94, 95-96, 246
Creation, doctrine of, 411
Criticism, types of, 406-7
Crucifixion, 34-35, 36, 126, 138, 173, 182, 215, 258, 293-95
Cultural background, 18-27
Cures, 111, 114-15, 117-18, 155-57, 161, 164-65, 196, 197, 199, 201, 202, 235, 275, 281-83

Dahl, Nils, A., 388, 395
Daniel Revelation and, 326
Day of Atonement, 76
Day of Judgment, Johannine, 302
Day of the Lord, 30, 31, 71, 73, 74, 99, 102, 109, 128, 219, 255-56, 355, 356, 404, 405-6
Deacons, 238
Dead Sea Scrolls, 110

Death, 283-86. *See also* Crucifixion; Resurrection
Dedication, feast of, 283
Deicide, Johannine dualism and, 301
Demetrius, 343
Deutero-Pauline letters, 71-104
Diaspora, 76, 237-38, 251, 353-54
Didache, 7
Diotrephes, 343
Discernment of spirits, 366
Disciples: Beatitudes and, 197-99; Jesus' appearance after resurrection to, 217, 296-97; Jesus as misunderstood by, 118-19; mission, 115, 157-59, 203. *See also* specific disciples
Discipleship, 109, 120, 122, 158, 164, 201-2, 288-89
Discontinuity theme in Acts, 250-51
Diversity of NT materials, 397-407
Divinity: Pauline vision of, 95; of Christ, notion of, 53-55
Divinization, 354
Divorce, 121-22, 165-66
Docetism, 297, 343, 401
Docility, 179-80, 277
Dodd, C. H., 275-76
Domitian, 318, 320
Dualism, Johannine, 300-301, 340
Dunn, James D. G., 397-400, 407-9, 410, 420-22
"Dyptich of the Annunciation," 190-92

Early Catholicism, 220, 358, 363, 364-65, 404-6
Early Christians: fluidity and diversity of, 131-32; history of. *See* Acts; Judaism and, 230-31; pictorial thinking of, 12; social status of, 99
Ebionites, 398-99
Ecumenic age, 25
Ecumenical reunion, 290
Education, gnosis as crux of, 82-83
Ekklesia, 382
Eliade, Mircea, 22-23
Elizabeth (wife of Zechariah), 190-92
Empiricism, 83-84
Endo, Shusaku, 420
Endurance, Hebrews' exhortation to, 349
Enoch, 326-27
Epaphras, 75
Epaphroditus, 49, 51
Ephesians, 85-94, 102
Ephesus, 244-45, 312, 337
Eschatology: defined, 31; realized, 275-76, 300, 303-4
Eschaton. *See* Day of the Lord
Essenes, 21
Ethics, 89, 91, 98-101, 353-54, 363, 405, 411
Euangelion, 109
Evangelists, 1, 381-82, 388. *See also* specific Gospels

441

Exorcisms, 134. *See also* Cures;
Miracles
Expiation, 64-65

Factionalism, 39
Faith, 37-38, 52-53, 323-24, 339-40,
349, 388
False teaching, concern over, 80-81,
358-59, 362, 368, 369
Family responsibilities, 359
Farewell discourses, 286-91
Farrer, Austin, 328
Fatherliness of God, 379
Felix, 246-47
Festus, 247-48
Fitzmyer, Joseph A., 218, 249, 250,
355-56
Flesh, Spirit vs., 35, 37
Forgiveness of sins, 379
Form criticism, 406-7
Freedom, Pauline view of, 99-101
Frend, W. H. C., 21-22
Fulfillment in Christ, 60-61
Fuller, Reginald, 128-29, 344, 357,
363

Gager, John, 325-26, 329
Gaius, 343-44
Galatai, 33
Galatians, Paul's letter to, 32-38
Galilee: Christ's appearances to
disciples in, 217, 296-97; ministry
in, 196-202, 225
Gamaliel, 237
Genealogy of Jesus, 146-49, 195
Genesis creation, 268
Gentiles, 23-24, 86-88, 132, 230-31,
238-39, 240-47, 249-53, 383
Gethsemane, garden of, 171, 172,
291
Glory, Book of, 286-96
Glossolalia, 233
Gnosis, 79, 82-84
Gnosticism, 44, 80-81, 256, 258,
300, 341, 356, 401
Gog and Magog, 321
Good Samaritan parable, 204, 380
Gospels, 21, 105-7, 176, 388, 415.
See also specific Gospels
Grace, 65-66, 86-88, 278, 288,
411-13
Great Church, 337, 405
Greco-Roman cultural climate, 22-26
Grollenberg, Lucas, 63-64, 138

Haggadic and halakic styles, 177
Harrington, Daniel, 151-52
Haughton, Rosemary, 135
Hebrews, Epistle to, 10, 26, 344-51,
392
Hecht, Richard, 410
Hellenistic Christianity, 400-402
Hellenistic religious synthesis, 24-26
Hellenistic society, 91, 353-54
Hellwig, Monika, 136-37, 138
Hermas, 7
Hermeneutical circle, 387-90
Herod Agrippa, 240-41
Herod Antipas, 115, 130, 162, 201,
215, 240
Herodians, 123, 130
Herod the Great, 146, 148, 240, 377
Hierarchy, church, 50

High priesthood of Jesus, 345-49,
351
Historical background, 18-27
Historicity, 218-19, 257
Holy Spirit. *See* Spirit
Hope, parable on, 210-11
Horizon, 11
House codes, 363, 405
Human vocation in Pauline vision,
95
Husband-wife relationship, 89-90,
100-101, 353-54. *See also*
Marriage

Identity crisis, 278-81
Identity with Christ, theme of, 53
Idols, 41-42
Imperial cult, 317-18
Incarnationalism, 257-60, 269, 297,
317, 337
Incarnation of the Word, 77-78, 269
Indian culture, 259-60
Innocents, slaughter of the, 148-49
Irenaeus of Lyons, 342
Isaiahan paradox, 282
Islam, 2, 53-54, 413
Israel, God's relation to, 61-62

James, 242; letter of, 365-67
Jeremiah, 137
Jeremias, Joachim, 383, 394
Jerusalem: Church in, 233-38, 239;
fall of (70 C.E.), 21-22; Jesus'
entry into, 123, 167, 212, 284-85;
journey to, 202-11, 225-26;
ministry in, 211-13, 226; Paul in
prison in, 245-48; Revelation
interlude on, 322-23
Jesus, 374-96; as agent of social
change, 253, 303; authority,
111-13, 154-55; baptism, 150,
151, 195; as bread of life, 276-78;
of Colossians, 84; denial by Peter,
172, 214, 287, 291, 292; diverse
understandings of, 3-5; entry into
Jerusalem, 123, 167, 212, 284-85;
genealogy and birth, 146-49,
189-94, 195, 225; Gentiles,
attitude toward, 383;
hermeneutical circle, 387-90; high
priesthood, 345-49, 351; life-
giving word, 274-76; life of,
374-78; as light of world, 280,
281-83; Luke's portrait of, 218,
221-22; mighty acts, 155-57, 161,
164-65; ministry, 149-50,
194-202, 211-13, 225, 408;
missionary discourse, 115,
157-59, 203; "mysticism," 387;
other NT Christologies, 390-93;
Pauline view of, 383-86; as peace,
87, 93; personality, Mark's
portrayal of, 137-38; power over
people, 387; preexistence, 51,
384; rejection of, 113-15, 159-61;
rising opposition to, 165-69;
salvation's dependence on, 236;
secret identity of, 110; as Son of
God misunderstood, 115-19;
teaching of, 378-83; unity in NT
and, 410. *See also* Crucifixion;
Passion, the; Resurrection; specific
Gospels

Jewett, Robert, 38
Jewish Christianity, 143-44, 249-52,
397-400
Jewish Law. *See* Covenant Law
Jews, 2; Christ's divinity and, 53-54;
cultural background, 18-22;
diaspora, 76, 237-38, 251,
353-54; Johannine presentation of,
298, 299; scorn for Gentiles,
23-24
Jezebel, 314
Joachim of Fiore, 328
Johannine community, 337, 340-41
Johannine Epistles, 336-44, 416-17
John: healing by, in Acts, 235; at
Last Supper, 213
John of Patmos, 311-23
John's church, gospel for, 194,
265-309, 341, 390, 401, 405,
411-12, 416
John the Baptist, 109-10, 115,
149-50, 159, 162, 190-92,
194-95, 199, 268, 269-70, 273,
276
Joseph (father of Jesus), 147, 148,
190
Joseph of Arimathea, 127, 215, 216,
294
Judaism, 22, 96-97, 230-31, 279,
413
Judaizers, 48, 359, 362
Judas Iscariot, 170-72, 177, 213,
214, 278, 284, 286-87
Jude, 352; letter of, 367-69
Judea, mission in, 238-39
Judgment, 301-2, 321-22. *See also*
Day of the Lord
Juel, Donald, 249-52
Justification, Paul's doctrine of, 386

Kairos, 110
Käsemann, Ernst, 66-67
Keck, Leander, 95, 384
Kee, Howard Clark, 133-34, 377-78
Kenosis, 50, 53-54, 222
Kerygmata, agreement on, 408
Kerygmatic character of gospel, 106,
415
Kierkegaard, Søren, 51
Kingdom of God, 161-62, 165, 169,
207, 211, 378-79
Krodel, Gerhard, 71, 74, 356
Kurz, William, 231

Lamb of God imagery, 269
Laodicea, letter to church of, 314-15
Last Supper, 213-14, 219, 286-91
Lazarus, 210, 283-84
Leahy, Thomas, 356
Leon-Dufour, Xavier, 266, 382-83
Letter writing, conventions of, 31-32
Levitical priesthood, 347-48, 350
Life: coming through death, 284-86;
conquering death theme, 283-84;
-giving word, Jesus', 274-76
Light: God as, in 1 John, 337; in
Revelation, significance of,
330-31; of world, Jesus as, 280,
281-83
Literary criticism, 406
Literary diversity, 406-7
Liturgical calendar, Jewish, 328
Loaves and fishes, multiplication of,
115-16, 118, 162, 276-78

Logos, 268, 340
Lohse, Eduard, 76, 81
Lord's Supper, 42
Love, 62-63, 287-88, 338-39, 342
Luke's church, Gospel for, 144, 187-229, 389, 415-16. *See also* Acts
Luther, Martin, 57, 328

Macedonia, Paul's journey to, 243
McKenzie, John L., 23, 383
MacRae, George, 347
Mally, Edward, 120
Manicheans, 258
Marcus Julius Agrippa, 247-48
Mark's church, Gospel for, 105-42, 388-89, 415
Marriage, 41, 89-90, 100-101, 121-22, 165-66, 353-54
Martha (sister of Lazarus), 284
Mary Magdalene, 127, 128-29, 293-95
Mary (mother of James), 127
Mary (mother of Jesus), 190-91, 192, 293-95
Mary (sister of Lazarus), 283, 284
Master-slave relationship, 56-57, 90, 99-101
Matthew's church, Gospel for, 143-86, 193-94, 289, 379-80, 382-83, 415
Meeks, Wayne A., 98-99
Melchizedek, 347-48
Membership, church, 21, 99-100
Memories in Gospels, 388
Messiah, Jewish expectations of, 20
Messianic consciousness in Jesus, 381-82
Midrash, 346
Ministry: Christian, 46-47; Church, 78-79; of Jesus, 149-50, 194-202, 211-13, 225, 408
Miracles, 148, 155-57, 162-64, 177-79. *See also* Cures
Miranda, José, 303-4
Missionary commission, 115, 157-59, 203
Missions: in Judea and Samaria, 238-39; of Paul, 241-45; as theme of John's Gospel, 266-67
Monotheism assumption in Matthew's Gospel, 176
Morality, Christian, 93, 366-67, 380. *See also* Ethics
Mosaic Law. *See* Covenant Law
Muggeridge, Malcolm, 419-20
Multiplication of loaves and fishes, 115-16, 118, 162, 276-78
Muslims, 2, 53-54, 413
Mystery of life, human being's relationship to, 224
Mystery religions, 26, 79, 82
Mysticism, 327, 376

Nathaniel, 270-71
Natural theology, 256
Nazarenes, 247, 398
Neill, Stephen, 376, 394
Nero, 318, 320
New Testament (NT): background presupposed by, 418-19; canonical status of, 7-9; character of literature, 9-11; guidelines for study, 11-13; lasting significance

of, 419-20; materials, diversity of, 397-407; materials, unity of, 407-13; privileged status, 1-2, 5-7; purpose of, 417-18; as scripture, 5-7; social effects of, 14-15; story of, 413-17
Nicodemus, 272, 279, 294-95, 300
Nolan, Albert, 383

Old Testament, agreement on use of, 408
Onesimus, 56-57
Order, church, 358, 363
Orthodoxy, emerging concept of, 22
"Our Father" (prayer), 224

Pagan society, dealing with, 41, 364
Pagels, Elaine, 405
Pantokrator, 86, 260
Parables, 113-14, 161-62, 165-69, 201, 207-11, 212, 226, 380
Paraclete, 266, 267, 287
Parapsychological world view, 134-35
Parousia, 30, 31, 71, 73, 74, 99, 102, 109, 128, 219, 255-56, 355, 356, 404, 405-6
Paschal Letter, 7
Passion, the, 53, 119-29, 166, 213-16, 226, 291-95
Pastoral Epistles, 357-65, 391, 405, 416
Paul: Church, view of, 95; conversion, 30-31, 34, 97; freedom, view of, 99-101; imprisonment, 49-50, 53, 245-48; influence on Luke, 221; missionary journeys in Acts, 241-45; Pastoral Epistles, 357-59, 362; in Rome, 248-49; vocation to Gentiles, 246, 247
Paul, letters to early Christians, 10, 26, 28-70, 222, 256, 383-86, 414-15
Paul's followers, letters of, 71-104
Peace, Christ as, 87, 93
Pentecost, 233
Perfection, theme of, 153, 179-82
Pergamum, letter to church of, 312-13
Perkins, Pheme, 207-8, 265-66
Perrin, Norman, 128, 378
Persecution, 71-74, 238, 239
Personal God, 92-93, 257, 410
Pervasive presence, God of Ephesians as, 92-93
Pesher style, 177
Peter: in Acts, 235, 252-53, 390-91; arrest of, 235-36, 237; authority of, 164; denial of Jesus, 172, 214, 287, 291, 292, epistles, 352-57, 391-92; Galilean ministry and, 196-97; in John's Gospel, 270, 295, 296-97; at Last Supper, 213; speech to Church in Jerusalem, 233-35; status of Gentiles and, 240-42; triple profession of love, 296-97
Petition, prayer of, 223
Pharisees: in Book of Signs, 279-80; as dominant Jewish party, 21; in Luke's Gospel, 197, 199-200,

205-10; in Mark's Gospel, 112, 117, 118-19, 121-24, 130-31; in Matthew's Gospel, 160-61, 163-64, 168-69; synagogue development, 20
Philadelphia, letter to church of, 314
Philemon, 55-57
Philip, 238-39, 270-71, 287
Philippians, 49-55, 222
Philo of Alexandria, 344
Philosophical response, NT as, 417-18
Pictorial thinking, 12
Pietas, 23
Pilate, 126, 130, 172-73, 174, 214, 292-93
Pilgrim, Walter, 254
Pleroma, 78, 88, 92
Pneumatic religion, 45
Poverty, emphasis in Acts on, 258
Prayer, 205, 210-11, 223-24
Predestination, 222-23
Preexistence of Christ, 51, 384
Priesthood: of Christ, 345-49, 351; levitical, 347-48, 350
Priscilla, 244
Prodigal son, parable of, 208-9
Prophets, theme of killing, 205-6
Protestant Reformation, 57
Prudence, parable about, 209-10
Pseudepigraphy, 74
Psychotherapy, Revelation as form of, 325-26

Q source of materials, 144, 152, 401
Quispel, Gilles, 326-27
Qumran community, 194, 300

Realism in Revelation, 323-24
Reality, transcendent dimension, 178-79
Realized eschatology, 275-76, 300, 303-4
Redaction criticism, 406
Reformation, character, 180-81
Rejection of Jesus, 113-15, 159-61
Religious establishment, authority of Jesus and, 112-13
Religious experience, agreement on, 409
Repentance in Hebrews, 347
Rest, notion of God's, 346
Resurrection, 43, 127-29, 173-75, 182, 216-17, 226, 295-97, 412-13
Revelation, Book of, 10, 194, 310-35, 392-93
Revelation theme of John's Gospel, 266
Rich, the, James' attack on, 366-67
Righteousness, 34-35, 58-62, 95
Roman Empire, 22-26, 53, 317, 319-20
Roman-Jewish war, 250, 252
Romans, Paul's letter to, 57-67
Rome, Paul in, 248-49
Rowland, Christopher, 319

Sabbath, controversy over, 160-61, 197, 207, 275, 278-79
Sacramentalism, 257-60, 297
Sacraments, agreement on, 409
Sacrifice, 19-20, 350-51

Sadduccees, 124, 130, 163, 212, 235-36, 237
Salvation, 86, 97-98, 218-19, 230, 236. *See also* Acts
Samaria, mission in, 238-39
Samaritans, 202-3, 273-74
Sampley, J. Paul, 85
Sanhedrin, 20
Sapphira, 236, 253
Sardis, letter to church of, 314
Satan, 150, 195, 321-22
Saul, 239, 241. *See also* Paul
Saving wisdom, 79, 82-84
Schillebeeckx, Edward, 302, 386, 387, 395
Schisms, Ephesians and, 93
Schüssler-Fiorenza, Elisabeth, 99-100, 313
Scripture: Mark's interpretation of, 133; NT as, 5-7
Semeia, 271-86
Sermon on the Mount, 151-55, 181, 183, 198, 380
Seven, number, in Johannine literature, 269-70
Seven bowls of Revelation, 318-19
Seven letters in Revelation, 312-15
Seven seals of Revelation, 315-16
Seven trumpets of Revelation, 316-17
Seven unnumbered visions of Revelation, 317-18, 321-22
Shafarevich, Igor, 254
Shalom, 93
Shamanic, cultural pattern, 259
Shekinah, 78
Shema, 124
Signs, Book of, 271-86
Silas, 49, 242-44
Silvanus, 28, 29
Simon (magician), 239
Simon Peter. *See* Peter
Sin: doctrine of, 410-11; forgiveness of, 379
Sincerity, theme of, 153
Singer, Isaac, 330

Slavery, Christianity and, 56-57, 90, 99-101
Sloyan, Gerard S., 376, 394
Smart, Ninian, 410
Smyrna, letter to church of, 312
Social critic, Jesus as, 253, 303
Social status of early Christians, 99
Sociological dimensions in Pauline vision, 98-101
Socrates, 136
Solzhenitsyn, Aleksandr, 254, 330
Son of God, range of meaning, 109
Source criticism, 406
Spirit: agreement on, 409; in Book of Glory, 287-88; flesh vs., 35, 37; influence on Church in Jerusalem, 236; Lukan stress in Acts on, 259; in Luke's Gospel, 188, 220-21; Paul's view in Romans of, 61, 66-67
Spirit of Christ, 1 Corinthians on, 44-45
Spirits, discernment of, 366
Stendhal, Krister, 146
Stephen, 238, 401
Symbolism, 279, 329-31. *See also* Revelation, Book of
Synagogue, 20
Syncretism, 82
Synoptic Gospels, 6, 298. *See also* specific Gospels
Synoptic problem, 144-45

Tabernacles, feast of, 278, 280
Table fellowship, 42
Taoists, 37, 38
Teaching of Jesus, 378-83. *See also* specific Gospels
Teilhard de Chardin, Pierre, 78
Temple, Jewish, 19-20, 212-13, 271-72
Temptation in wilderness, 150, 195
Textual criticism, 406
Theissen, Gerd, 177-78
Theodicy, 355
Theology: natural, 256; definition, 9

Theophilus, 189, 232
Theosis, doctrine of, 354
Thessalonians, Paul's letters to, 28-32, 71-74, 102
Thessalonica, Paul's journey to, 243
Thomas, 287, 295-96
Thyatira, letter to church of, 313-14
Timothy, 28, 29, 50, 51, 55, 243; letters to, 357, 358-61, 363, 391
Titus, 47; letter to, 361-63, 391
Torah, 18
Tradition, agreement on, 408
Transcendent dimension of reality, 178-79
Transfiguration, 120-21, 128, 164, 202
Translations, biblical, 9
Triumphalism, 221
Trocmé, Etienne, 130, 131
Tyson, Joseph, 29

Unity: of NT materials, 407-13; of the Church, 89, 290
Universalism, 25, 188

Vineyard parable, 212
Visionaries, 259
Voegelin, Eric, 25, 93-94

Walaskay, Paul, 255, 257
Water, symbolism of, 279
Weakness, human, 48-49
Weizsacker, K. H. von, 90
Wiesel, Elie, 330
Wilckens, Ulrich, 256, 257
Wisdom, 76-78, 79, 81, 82-84
Women, Jesus' relationship with, 204
Word, the, 268, 269, 346
Works, importance of, 37-38, 366
Worship, 42, 408-9
Wrath, seven bowls of, 318-19

Zaccheus, 211
Zechariah, 190-92